THE PAPERS OF

WOODROW WILSON

VOLUME 46

JANUARY 16–MARCH 12, 1918

SPONSORED BY THE WOODROW WILSON
FOUNDATION
AND PRINCETON UNIVERSITY

THE PAPERS OF

WOODROW WILSON

ARTHUR S. LINK, *EDITOR*

DAVID W. HIRST, *SENIOR ASSOCIATE EDITOR*

JOHN E. LITTLE, *ASSOCIATE EDITOR*

FREDRICK AANDAHL, *ASSOCIATE EDITOR*

MANFRED F. BOEMEKE, *ASSISTANT EDITOR*

PHYLLIS MARCHAND AND MARGARET D. LINK,
EDITORIAL ASSISTANTS

Volume 46
January 16–March 12, 1918

PRINCETON UNIVERSITY PRESS
PRINCETON, NEW JERSEY
1984

Publication of this book has been aided by a grant
from the National Historical Publications and Records
Commission.
Printed in the United States of America
by Princeton University Press
Princeton, New Jersey

INTRODUCTION

THE opening of this volume finds Wilson and his administration in the midst of the "winter crisis," set off by the Fuel Administrator's order on January 16, 1918, severely limiting the use of coal by manufacturing and business concerns. Four days later, the Democratic chairman of the Senate Committee on Military Affairs, George E. Chamberlain, declares in a public speech: "The military establishment of America has fallen down; there is no use to be optimistic about a thing that does not exist; it almost stopped functioning. Why? Because of inefficiency in every bureau and in every department of the Government of the United States." As panic spreads, the administration's critics step up their demand for passage of the Chamberlain bill to create a super war cabinet or ministry of munitions to take control of the war effort out of Wilson's hands.

Wilson strikes back with characteristic audacity. In a public statement on January 21, he labels Chamberlain's accusation as "an astonishing and absolutely unjustifiable distortion of the truth." Wilson next strongly defends his Secretary of War and then oversees the drafting of the Overman bill, which gives him absolute authority to reorganize all governmental agencies, bureaus, and departments. And, while Congress debates the Overman bill, Wilson appoints Bernard M. Baruch as head of the War Industries Board and gives him almost dictatorial authority to control the allocation and use of industrial resources. At the same time, Secretary Baker answers all but die-hard critics in a brilliant five-hour testimony before the Senate Committee on Military Affairs. A few days later, Wilson rallies his forces in the Senate to defeat the Chamberlain bill. As this volume ends, the "winter crisis" is long since past, and Wilson's leadership is more secure than ever. And Wilson and his lieutenants have effectively organized the American economy into a gigantic engine of war.

Meanwhile, discussions of peace follow in the aftermath of Wilson's Fourteen Points Address of January 8, 1918. The German Imperial Chancellor, Count von Hertling, and the Austro-Hungarian Foreign Minister, Count Czernin, reply to Wilson on January 24. Hertling is vague and evasive about the details of a peace settlement. Czernin, however, is responsive; moreover, he opens secret negotiations with American diplomatic officials in Bern looking toward a separate peace between Austria-Hungary and the United States and the Allies.

In response, Wilson goes again before a joint session of Congress on February 11 to continue his dialogue with the leaders of the Central Powers. Peace is possible, Wilson declares, but only upon the basis of four principles—that justice should govern the settlement of all issues, that "peoples and provinces are not to be bartered about . . . as if they were mere chattels," that all territorial settlements must be made for the benefit of the people involved, and that all well-defined national aspirations should be accorded satisfaction insofar as possible. The Germans reply on March 3, 1918, by imposing the harsh and punitive Treaty of Brest-Litovsk upon a prostrate Russia.

Meanwhile, Allied leaders have been pressing Wilson to consent to occupation of Siberia by Japan, ostensibly to prevent the Central Powers from drawing upon the resources of that vast area. Wilson stands firm against such a move but for a brief moment is about to yield to Allied pressure. However, as this volume ends, Wilson, on March 5, 1918, dispatches a note to Tokyo in which he stands firm in opposition to any Japanese move into Siberia. Moreover, six days later, Wilson sends a message of warm friendship to the fourth All-Russia Congress of Soviets: "The whole heart of the people of the United States is with the people of Russia in the attempt to free themselves forever from autocratic government and become the masters of their own life."

Wilson is beset by numerous other concerns during the months covered by this volume. Labor unrest and the threat of strikes persist and clearly demand the adoption of some national mediatorial machinery. The British and French governments continue to insist upon the amalgamation of American battalions with their own forces, and General Pershing continues stubbornly to reject the Allied demands. Wilson enters into personal correspondence with Emperor Charles through the King of Spain about the possibilities of a separate peace for Austria-Hungary. Indeed, as this volume ends it appears that peace between the Hapsburg Empire and the United States and the Allies is at hand.

"VERBATIM ET LITERATIM"

In earlier volumes of this series, we have said something like the following: "All documents are reproduced *verbatim et literatim*, with typographical and spelling errors corrected in square brackets only when necessary for clarity and ease of reading." The following essay explains our textual methods and review procedures.

We have never printed and do not intend to print critical, or corrected, versions of documents. We print them exactly as they are, with a few exceptions which we always note. We never use the word *sic* except to denote the repetition of words in a document; in fact, we think that a succession of *sics* defaces a page.

We usually repair words in square brackets when letters are missing. As we have said, we also repair words in square brackets for clarity and ease of reading. Our general rule is to do this when we, ourselves, cannot read the word without having to stop to puzzle out its meaning. Jumbled words and names misspelled beyond recognition of course have to be repaired. We correct the misspelling of a name in a document in the footnote identifying the person.

However, when an old man writes to Wilson saying that he is glad to hear that Wilson is "comming" to Newark, or a semiliterate farmer from Texas writes phonetically, we see no reason to correct spellings in square brackets when the words are perfectly understandable. We do not correct Wilson's misspellings unless they are unreadable, except to supply in square brackets letters missing in words. For example, he consistently spelled "belligerent" as "belligerant." Nothing would be gained by correcting "belligerant" in square brackets.

We think that it is very important for several reasons to follow the rule of *verbatim et literatim*. Most important, a document has its own integrity and power, particularly when it is not written in perfect literary form. There is something very moving in seeing a Texas dirt farmer struggling to express his feelings in words, or a semiliterate former slave doing the same thing. Second, in Wilson's case it is crucially important to reproduce his errors in letters which he typed himself, since he usually typed badly when he was in an agitated state. Third, since style is the essence of the person, we would never correct grammar or make tenses consistent, as one correspondent has urged us to do. Fourth, we think that it is very important that we print exact transcripts of Charles L. Swem's copies of Wilson's letters. Swem made many mistakes (we correct them in footnotes from a reading of his shorthand books), and Wilson let them pass. We thus have to assume that Wilson did not read his letters before signing them, and this, we think, is a significant fact. Finally, printing typed letters and documents *verbatim et literatim* tells us a great deal about the educational level of the stenographic profession in the United States during Wilson's time.

We think that our series would be worthless if we produced unreliable texts, and we go to considerable effort to make certain that the texts are authentic.

Our typists are highly skilled and proofread their transcripts carefully as soon as they have typed them. The Editor sight proofreads documents once he has assembled a volume and is setting its an-notation. The Editors who write the notes read through documents several times and are careful to check any anomalies. Then, once the manuscript volume has been completed and all notes checked, the Editor and Senior Associate Editor orally proofread the documents against the copy. They read every comma, dash, and character. They note every absence of punctuation. They study every nearly illegible word in written documents.

Once this process of "establishing the text" is completed, the manuscript volume goes to our editor at Princeton University Press, who checks the volume carefully and sends it to the printing plant. The galley proofs are read orally against copy in the proofroom at the Press. And we must say that the proofreaders there are extraordinarily skilled. Some years ago, before we found a way to ease their burden, they queried every misspelled word, absence of punctuation, or other such anomalies. Now we write "O.K." above such words or spaces on the copy.

We read the galley proofs at least three times. Our copyeditor gives them a sight reading against the manuscript copy to look for remaining typographical errors and to make sure that no line has been dropped. The Editor and Senior Associate Editor sight read them against documents and copy. We then get the page proofs, which have been corrected at the Press. We check all the changes three times. In addition, we get *revised* pages and check them twice.

This is not the end. The Editor, Senior Associate Editor, and Assistant Editor give a final reading to headings, description-location lines, and notes. Finally, our indexer of course reads the pages word by word. Before we return the pages to the Press, she comes in with a list of queries, all of which are answered by reference to the documents.

Our rule in the Wilson Papers is that our tolerance of error is zero. No system and no person can be perfect. There may be errors in our volumes. However, we believe that we have done everything humanly possible to avoid error; the chance is remote that what looks at first glance like a typographical error is indeed an error. For example, in the fourth paragraph of the extract from the House Diary on page 435 of this volume, "Spain" is first spelled correctly and then, a few lines later, is misspelled as "Sprain." Since the meaning in this case was perfectly clear, we decided not to correct the misspelling in square brackets.

We take this opportunity to thank our editor at Princeton University Press, Ms. Judith May, for continuing assistance and Professors John Milton Cooper, Jr., William H. Harbaugh, Richard W. Leopold, and Betty Miller Unterberger—all members of our Editorial Advisory Committee—for reading the manuscript of this volume and for being, as heretofore, constructively critical.

THE EDITORS

Princeton, New Jersey
July 27, 1983

CONTENTS

CONTENTS

Collateral Materials

Diaries

ILLUSTRATIONS

Following page 388

ABBREVIATIONS

AL	autograph letter
ALI	autograph letter initialed
ALS	autograph letter signed
ASB	Albert Sidney Burleson
CC	carbon copy
CCL	carbon copy of letter
CLS	Charles Lee Swem
CLSsh	Charles Lee Swem shorthand
CLST	Charles Lee Swem typed
EMH	Edward Mandell House
FKL	Franklin Knight Lane
FLP	Frank Lyon Polk
FR	*Papers Relating to the Foreign Relations of the United States*
FR 1918, Russia	*Papers Relating to the Foreign Relations of the United States, 1918, Russia*
FR-WWS 1917	*Papers Relating to the Foreign Relations of the United States, 1917, Supplement, The World War*
FR-WWS 1918	*Papers Relating to the Foreign Relations of the United States, 1918, Supplement, The World War*
Hw, hw	handwritten, handwriting
HwC	handwritten copy
JD	Josephus Daniels
JPT	Joseph Patrick Tumulty
MS, MSS	manuscript, manuscripts
NDB	Newton Diehl Baker
RG	record group
RL	Robert Lansing
T	typed
TC	typed copy
TCL	typed copy of letter
TI	typed initialed
TL	typed letter
TLI	typed letter initialed
TLS	typed letter signed
TS	typed signed
TWG	Thomas Watt Gregory
TWL	Thomas William Lamont
WBW	William Bauchop Wilson
WCR	William Cox Redfield
WGM	William Gibbs McAdoo
WHP	Walter Hines Page
WJB	William Jennings Bryan
WW	Woodrow Wilson
WWhw	Woodrow Wilson handwriting, handwritten
WWsh	Woodrow Wilson shorthand
WWT	Woodrow Wilson typed
WWTL	Woodrow Wilson typed letter
WWTLI	Woodrow Wilson typed letter initialed

WWTLS   Woodrow Wilson typed letter signed
WWTS   Woodrow Wilson typed signed

ABBREVIATIONS FOR COLLECTIONS
AND REPOSITORIES

Following the National Union Catalog
of the Library of Congress

AFL-CIO-Ar   American Federation of Labor-Congress of Industrial
                      Organizations Archives
CtY   Yale University
CtY-D   Yale University Divinity School
CU   University of California
DLC   Library of Congress
DNA   National Archives
FMD-Ar   French Ministry of Defense Archives
FO   British Foreign Office
HPL   Hoover Presidential Library
IEN   Northwestern University
IU-Ar   University of Illinois Archives
JDR   Justice Department Records
LDR   Labor Department Records
MH-BA   Harvard University Graduate School of Business
                      Administration
MH-Ar   Harvard University Archives
NcU   University of North Carolina
NjP   Princeton University
PRO   Public Record Office
RSB Coll., DLC   Ray Stannard Baker Collection of Wilsoniana, Library
                      of Congress
SDR   State Department Records
TDR   Treasury Department Records
WC, NjP   Woodrow Wilson Collection, Princeton University
WDR   War Department Records
WP, DLC   Woodrow Wilson Papers, Library of Congress

SYMBOLS

[January 23, 1918]   publication date of published writing; also date of doc-
                          ument when date is not part of text
[*January 18, 1918*]   composition date when publication date differs
[[February 19, 1918]]   delivery date of speech if publication date differs
* * * *   * * *   text deleted by author of document

THE PAPERS OF

WOODROW WILSON

VOLUME 46
JANUARY 16–MARCH 12, 1918

THE PAPERS OF
WOODROW WILSON

To Newton Diehl Baker

My dear Mr. Secretary: The White House 16 January, 1918

I have received your letter of January eleventh[1] with its enclosures, two bills with regard to legislation covering price-fixing and the conservation of food, which you send me with the approval of yourself, Mr. Hoover, Doctor Garfield, and Mr. Willard. They seem to me sound and I am trying to discover the right channel into which to launch them.

Cordially and sincerely yours, Woodrow Wilson

TLS (N. D. Baker Papers, DLC).
[1] NDB to WW, Jan. 11, 1918 (first letter of that date), Vol. 45.

To George Creel

My dear Creel: The White House 16 January, 1918

The address of James M. Beck which you send me[1] certainly shows that he can restrain himself with a certain degree of handsomeness, and I dare say he would do as well as most others for the errand suggested, but personally I strongly disapprove of the English idea of having speakers come from the United States and make anything like a systematic canvass of Great Britain. I think they have made an error in sending speakers over here, and they are making a similar error in desiring our speakers to go over there. It is the idea I am opposed to.

Faithfully yours, Woodrow Wilson

TLS (G. Creel Papers, DLC).
[1] See G. Creel to WW, Jan. 15, 1918, Vol. 45.

To William Gibbs McAdoo

My dear Mac: The White House 16 January, 1918

I take it for granted that all our Collectors of Customs are under instruction to search every outgoing vessel for possible explosives, etc., but I have just received a letter from California, the writer of which I do not know, in which this definite statement is made, that there is a carefully concerted plot on the part of all the pro-German and anti-American agencies in this country, including those disaffected elements among the Irish-Americans who are thought to be cooperating with such agencies, for a general effort to destroy American and British shipping in every port, in every ship yard, and at sea, and that the date set is the twenty-second of this month (January). His information is that where the vessel is not accessible in our harbors or in our shipyards, the purpose is to destroy it at sea on the date mentioned.[1] I think you will agree with me that no pains should be spared to take extra precautions.

Cordially and faithfully yours,   Woodrow Wilson[2]

TLS (W. G. McAdoo Papers, DLC).
[1] About this letter, see TWG to WW, Jan. 20, 1918.
[2] Wilson conveyed this warning, *mutatis mutandis*, on the same day to Gregory and Hurley: WW to TWG, Jan. 16, 1918, TLS (JDR, T. W. Gregory Papers, No. 190470, DNA), and WW to E. N. Hurley, Jan. 16, 1918, CCL (WP, DLC).

To Colville Adrian de Rune Barclay

My dear Mr. Barclay: [The White House] 16 January, 1918

Thank you for your note of January thirteenth[1] with its enclosure, which I greatly appreciate.

It has been a matter of genuine gratification to me to find my own programme of peace so entirely consistent with the programme set forth by Mr. Lloyd George, and the speech of Mr. Balfour to which Sir Cecil Spring-Rice was kind enough to call my attention has afforded me the deepest satisfaction.

Cordially and sincerely yours,   Woodrow Wilson

TLS (Letterpress Books, WP, DLC).
[1] C. A. de R. Barclay to WW, Jan. 13, 1918, Vol. 45.

To Roy Wilson Howard

My dear Howard: [The White House] 16 January, 1918

Thank you for your letter of the twelfth.[1]

I do not know what reply to make to the first question your letter propounds. Certainly I never had anything in mind in regard to cooperation among neutrals which would be particularly advantageous to the United States. My thought was only to unite the opinion of the world so far as I could in protesting against the flagrant violations of right and of international justice which had been committed. At no stage of this distressing war have I ever entertained the slightest idea of making any combination for the special benefit of the United States. My thought has been merely the establishment of international justice and humane dealing and the safeguarding of universal interests.

With regard to the question whether the war and the participation of the United States in it has served to strengthen the common bond between the democracies of the Western Hemisphere, I will say that I think that it has. I think that thoughtful men in all the democracies of that hemisphere are beginning to see the real purpose and character of the United States. She is offering in every proposal that she makes to give the most sacred pledges on her own part that she will in no case be the aggressor against either the political independence or the territorial integrity of any other state or nation, at the same time that she is proposing and insisting upon similar pledges from all the nations of the world who have its peace at heart and are willing to associate themselves for the maintenance of that peace. The very strength of her appeal in this direction comes from the fact that she is willing to bind herself and give pledges of the utmost solemnity for her own good faith and disinterestedness. If this is understood, there could be no question of fear or suspicion.

I am very much interested to learn of your proposed return to Latin-America and I wish you bon voyage with the greatest heartiness.   Cordially and sincerely yours,   Woodrow Wilson

TLS (Letterpress Books, WP, DLC).
   [1] R. W. Howard to WW, Jan. 12, 1918, Vol. 45.

To Rhoda Isabel McDonald[1]

[The White House] 16 January, 1918

May I not express my warmest sympathy and my heartfelt grief at the loss of my friend Captain McDonald? I feel his death as a personal loss.[2]   Woodrow Wilson

T telegram (Letterpress Books, WP, DLC).
   [1] Unknown to Wilson, she, McDonald's only wife known to the Editors, had died in 1906.
   [2] McDonald had died of pneumonia on January 15. This famous Texas Ranger had served as Wilson's bodyguard during the presidential campaign of 1912.

From Edward Albert Filene

Dear Mr. President: Washington, D. C. January 16, 1918.

Goodwin[1] tells me he was just on the point of officially forwarding to you a copy of the new referendum which went out to our membership last Saturday, so I take this opportunity of transmitting it to you with a personal explanation.[2]

I may say to you that I have been the prime mover in this matter, although in its final form it has received the most careful consideration first of the Boston Chamber of Commerce and then of the Board of Directors of the Chamber of Commerce of the United States. It is based on an idea which I developed in an article published in the Sunday Supplement of the New York times of September 23 which received considerable attention and comment, sufficient in my mind to justify me in carrying the matter further. I think I need not impress on you that my only desire was to aid you in your policy announced in your message on the opening of Congress and that I thought this could be done through the agency of the Chamber of Commerce of the United States in putting forth something which could not fail to impress German business men with the seriousness of the situation to them.

I am sure you will note how carefully the wording of the referendum has been drawn and how we have attempted in every way to avoid anything that could be interpreted as an action taken in a spirit of revenge or threat.

The point I wish to particularly emphasize in this letter is that this referendum has been put out to be voted on by our membership without consulting you or the Secretary of State in advance because we felt assured by your address to Congress that it was in line with your policy and because we felt that to present it to you in advance would cause you embarrassment. That you should be in a position at any time to say that neither you nor the Secretary of State had any responsibility for its issuance and that it was a matter initiated by the business men solely we thought would help your position. Well in advance of its issuance, however, I did take the step of consulting Colonel House who expressed his approval of the policy and advised us to go ahead with it without consulting you because of the embarrassment that it might cause you. I received a letter from Colonel House on the subject which is now in my files in Boston and I have taken steps to have it forwarded to me at the earliest possible moment. On its arrival I shall immediately transmit it to the Secretary of State.

I have just returned from a conference with the Secretary of State who asked Mr. Goodwin to call on him at noon today. He told us of your concern over the matter as it appeared in the papers and we took the opportunity to place in his hands several copies of the referendum and asked his consideration of the way it was worded. When a referendum is transmitted to nine hundred and fifty voting members it is impossible to maintain confidentiality, so that we invariably take the step of giving it out to the press ourselves in order to safeguard as far as possible the way it will be presented to the public. We are helpless, however, as to the way the newspapers will treat it in headlines and editorials.

The step that we have taken is, of course, merely the preliminary step of issuing these resolutions for a vote. It will take forty-five days to secure this vote. It is the resolutions as backed up by an overwhelming vote of the commercial bodies of the nation that we look to as the effective instrument to transmit to the business men of Germany and not the action which has already taken place, i.e., that of transmitting the resolutions to American chambers to be voted upon. As to the time for and the method of transmission after the vote is taken, if such transmission does not appear to you undesirable, I would be glad indeed if you would give me an opportunity to talk briefly with you.

Very sincerely yours,   Edward A. Filene

TLS (WP, DLC).

[1] That is, Elliot H. Goodwin.

[2] Chamber of Commerce of the United States of America, *Referendum No. 23: On a Proposal to Discriminate Against Germany in Trade After the War if Necessary for Self-Defense*, printed pamphlet with detachable ballot (WP, DLC). The referendum was on the following preambles and resolution:

"WHEREAS, The size of Germany's present armament and her militaristic attitude have been due to the fact that her government is a military autocracy, not responsible to the German people; and

"WHEREAS, The size of the German armament after the war will be the measure of the greatness of the armament forced on all nations; and

"WHEREAS, Careful analysis of economic conditions shows that the size of Germany's future armament will fundamentally depend on her after-war receipts of raw materials and profits from her foreign trade; and

"WHEREAS, In our opinion the American people for the purpose of preventing an excessive armament will assuredly enter an economic combination against Germany if governmental conditions in Germany make it necessary for self-defense; and

"WHEREAS, We believe the American people will not join in discrimination against German goods after the war if the danger of excessive armament has been removed by the fact that the German government has in reality become a responsible instrument controlled by the German people; therefore, be it

"RESOLVED, That the Chamber of Commerce of the United States of America earnestly calls the attention of the business men of Germany to these conditions and urge them also to study this situation and to cooperate to the end that a disastrous economic war may be averted and that a lasting peace may be made more certain."

From Robert Lansing

My dear Mr. President: Washington January 16, 1918.

I had a talk this morning with Elliot H. Goodwin, Secretary of the Chamber of Commerce of the United States, and Mr. Filene who is prominent in the organization and who was the author of the resolution which has been submitted to the various Chambers of Commerce for action.

I enclose herewith the ballot and accompanying documents which were sent out by Mr. Goodwin.[1]

I think upon reading the preamble and resolution you will agree they are not as serious as the headlines indicate or as the title on the cover indicates. Mr. Filene stated that this idea was embodied in an article which he wrote for the New York TIMES last September as a result of conversations which he had in Germany in the first months of the war with prominent German businessmen; that he sent a copy of the article to Colonel House and afterwards saw him on the advisability of submitting a resolution of this sort to the Chambers of Commerce in this country; that about the middle of October he received a letter from Colonel House which stated that the Colonel thought the plan was a good one and that it should be carried out.

I told the gentlemen that I would give the matter further consideration and after consultation with you would communicate with them again, although they both said it had gone so far it would be very difficult now to withdraw the submission and prevent the referendum.

I would be obliged if you would inform me as to your views in regard to the matter. As the vote is not counted until February 26th there is ample time to act.

Faithfully yours,   Robert Lansing.

TLS (WP, DLC).
[1] All these enclosures are missing, but see n. 2 to the preceding document.

From Newton Diehl Baker, with Enclosures

[Washington, c. Jan. 16, 1918]

For the Presidents Information

An immediate answer should be given. I am getting a general staff opinion before asking a conference with the President

AL (WP, DLC).

E N C L O S U R E   I

Received at the War Department, Washington, D. C.,
January 16, 1918.

From H A E F   To The Adjutant General, Washington.
Number 487, January 13th. Confidential, for the Chief of Staff.
Reference my 441,[1] held conference in Paris on tenth instant with General Robertson on the subject of providing additional men

for British Divisions. He presents request from British Government that American Battalions be sent over for service with British Divisions. This memorandum is practically the same as that submitted to General Bliss. General Robertson says in substance, "That he regards situation as becoming very serious on the Western Front and that Germans will undoubtedly exert every effort to win before our troops are able to play an important part in the war. Also that British will be unable to furnish many men even for draft, and that it will be necessary to reduce British Divisions from 12 to 9 battalions each. He says further that even if the German attacks can be held, as is hoped, the British Divisions will become so exhausted in the process as to be fit for little employment afterwards. And expresses the hope that serious consideration may be given to their request for help. He suggests that to bring over a given number of men completely equipped as divisions will be much greater task than to bring same number of men as battalions and to transport * * * * *Then* proposes that in order to secure these infantry reenforcements British Government is prepared to take risks as to their own supplies and provide sea transportation to these * * * without in any way interfering with present plans and arrangements for bringing our American troops. He proposes that we furnish for the above purpose 150 battalions to be distributed 3 battalions to each British division so that they can retain their present strength of 12 battalions to each division. He thinks the question of whether these battalions would be brought to France or Great Britain for training could be settled later. But of course our battalions could be trained under our own officers. Later on, after serving with British divisions, if we so desired, they could be recalled for service with our own divisions and that everything would be done to meet our wishes in this and all other respects. Although he believes it would not serve any useful purpose to put these units into British divisions for less than four or five months. He expressed himself as fully appreciating American sentiment regarding service under our own flag but it was a *question of that on* the one hand or of Germany possibly establishing herself in a winning position on the other. The necessity of temporarily breaking up some of our divisions to meet this request was also discussed.

Paragraph 2. This whole question seems to me to be one of necessity, and we must consider the probability of strong German attacks in early spring and summer. While it would not be advisable in any way to alter our own program for bringing our divisions yet the offer of the British to provide sea transportation for such extra men as we may be able to furnish for temporary service in their army would not interfere with that. In meeting this emergency by reenforcing the British, our ultimate object of building up our own forces as planned, in order to provide a strong cohesive American Army to strike a decisive blow as early as possible, should be strictly adhered to. The moral effect upon our people at home of keeping our men in our own army under our own officers is of paramount importance. And in conceding that the emergency requires this temporary supply of men for the British, it ought to be distinctly understood that these men are to be available for return to their own divisional units as soon as transports, horses, and artillery can be brought over or otherwise provided. At that time such disposition can be made of American divisions as may be determined.

Paragraph 3. Have had a full and frank discussion of this question with the French as far as any such plans relates to them. And have stated that in my opinion, generally speaking it would be a dangerous experiment on account of difference in language to put our regiments into French divisions for active work. They apparently hold the same view. Mr. Clemenceau gave his entire approval of the plan of such aiding the British as above set forth. General Petain also gave it his approval.

Paragraph 4. I would therefore recommend (1) that this request of the British Government be given serious consideration from the point of view of our National attitude regarding service in another army; (2) that it be regarded as a temporary measure to meet a probable emergency; (3) that as soon as possible the remaining troops of divisions thus temporarily broken up be brought over and the division reorganized; (4) that division, brigade and regimental commanders and their staffs be sent over with their Infantry for training with corresponding British units; (5) that the Infantry be taken from those divisions that would not otherwise be transported until after June.

Paragraph 5. The above program must be considered as entirely apart from any plans we now have in operation, including all shipments of troops now going through England and the proposed shipments through Southampton on our own ships. All of these must be held as separate projects not to be confused with General Robertson's proposition, that is only such troops as the British themselves transport in additional tonnage should be available for the service with British divisions as proposed by General Robertson. In other words those troops brought through Brest or Southampton in our own ships would come under the plans for training proposed in my 441 or be sent here to our own training areas. I consider this as very important and would not approve or accept the British proposition except as a measure for providing additional men for them that can not be provided in any other way.

Paragraph 6. In this connection it should be insisted upon that the British Government continue to provide for their army as many men from England as possible, and it would be pertinent for our government to inquire just what the British Government proposes to do to keep up its own forces. When we make this concession, the tendency is certainly going to be to relax and let the burden fall on us to the detriment of our own preparations for decisive action later.   Pershing.

[1] J. J. Pershing to H. P. McCain, No. 441, Jan. 4, 1918, T telegram (WDR, RG 407, World War I Cable Section, DNA). Pershing reported on discussions with the British concerning the use of Southampton as a port of disembarkation of American troops and their transport across the Channel. Pershing continued:

"They would allot us training area of the Amiens region. They propose to place our troops there and provide rations while training, other matters of supply to be subject of future agreement. Sole object of this on my part is to expedite arrival and training our troops. Project would include assistance of British divisional staffs of skeleton divisions for instruction if desired, also opportunity to train higher commanders and staffs by actual command of British units in the field. Command of training area would be exercised by our officers and the training of troops would be * * *. Conference leading to this contemplates no change in present plans of priority schedules which would be carried on as now through same port(s) and using all tonnage available for such ports. *But* it is thought that discharging our deep draft vessels at Southampton where they could coal quickly and return to States without delay would be advantageous. British offer to ration them would obviate aggravation of supply situation, where, through delays of supply or embarkation authorities in America, troops and supply shipments do not balance. In the discussion with British they promised also to consider the possibility of aiding us in transporting troops by using additional British tonnage not now availed by [available to] us. Question of man-power and supply so important and our shipping program so far behind that opportunity should not be lost if on further study British conclude they can handle Southampton project and especially if they can provide any additional tonnage. It is imperative however that all this be regarded as strictly supplementary to our own regular program, and not as a substitute for any part of it except such changes as may be necessary in using Southampton instead of Brest. Prompt information of feasibility of plans from your standpoint is requested."

E N C L O S U R E   I I

Received at the War Department, January 15, 1918

From H.A.E.F. To The Adjutant General, Washington.

Number 493, January 14th. Confidential. For the Chief of Staff:

Following cable sent this date to General Robertson, Chief of Staff British Army:

"Paragraph 1. With reference to our conference in Paris I have forwarded by cable to Washington the substance of your memorandum of January 10th. My cable suggested that your request for battalions of Infantry for service with British Army, three battalions for each of 50 divisions be given serious consideration, and if adopted that the following points be covered. First that the plan be regarded as a temporary measure to meet a probable emergency. Second that as soon as practicable the remaining troops of our divisions thus temporarily disorganized be brought over and the divisions be reorganized for service with our own army. Third that the divisions, brigades and regimental commanders and their staffs of such Infantry be sent over for training with corresponding British Units. Fourth that the Infantry be taken from those divisions that could not otherwise be transported until after June. Fifth that only such battalions or other units be attached to British Army as could be provided with sea transportation by the British Government. Sixth that the transportation of such battalions should in no way interfere with the present plans and means of transporting American Army to France. Seventh that above proposition be considered entirely apart and separate from any plans for sending over our own forces in our own ships through Brest, Southampton or otherwise. Eighth that these battalions loaned to British are to be returned to the American Army when called for probably when the remaining troops of the divisions to which they pertain are brought over which would likely be for at least four or five months.

"Paragraph 2. In view of the National sentiment in our country against service under an allied flag at this time, it is deemed of the utmost importance, if the above plans be considered by our Government, that the British Government declare its purpose to exert every energy to keep its own forces as strong in man-power as possible. Only with this general understanding in America would the foregoing plans meet with approval there. I have cabled the substance of this * * * to Washington and would request a full statement from you as to British resources in this regard including those at present available and to become available during this year. This information is desired in order that my Government may have all the facts before making a final decision on the important question now under advisement. Pershing."   Pershing.

TC telegrams (WP, DLC).

From the Diary of Josephus Daniels

January Wednesday 16 1918

Baker & I went with Garfield to see President about coal. G wanted to cut down 4 days soon & then ev. Sat. & Monday. I suggested 1 week in the hope of no more. WW seemed doubtful Spoke of how it would affect men who needed daily wages to live & hoped employers would pay the wage

Decided to approve Garfield for 5 days[1]

Bound diary (J. Daniels Papers, DLC).
    [1] In the late afternoon of January 16, Garfield issued an order that no manufacturing plant could burn fuel or use power derived from fuel during the five-day period beginning January 18. The order further required that, with some necessary exceptions, no busi-

ness establishment of any kind could burn fuel on Mondays through March 25. The order is summarized in detail in the *Official Bulletin*, II (Jan. 17, 1918), 1-2, and in the *New York Times* and many other newspapers published on January 17. Garfield's rationale for the order is discussed in the Enclosures printed with H. A. Garfield to WW, Jan. 18, 1918.

Garfield's order, when made public on January 17, set off an explosion of protest. Opponents of Wilson regarded it as the crowning evidence that his administration was incompetent to manage the war effort, and even many supporters of Wilson were dismayed. Newspaper condemnation of the order was almost unanimous. The impact of the order and the dismay which it aroused will be evident in several later documents and notes in this volume. For the background and effects of Garfield's *démarche*, see James P. Johnson, "The Wilsonians As War Managers: Coal and the 1917-18 Winter Crisis," *Prologue: The Journal of the National Archives*, IX (Winter 1977), 193-208.

To Newton Diehl Baker, with Enclosure

My dear Mr. Secretary: The White House 17 January, 1918

The enclosed explains itself. As I understand it, these cases have been referred to you. Our decision in the matter is evidently of critical importance and I just wanted to be sure that the division commanders could not act without a further consideration of these five cases by yourself.

Faithfully yours,   Woodrow Wilson

ENCLOSURE

From Charles Curtis and Daniel Read Anthony, Jr.

To the President: Washington, D. C. January 11, 1918.

Our attention has been called to the report that five more members of the 24th Infantry have been sentenced to be executed for participation in the recent trouble at Fort Sam Houston.[1] Recent correspondence from representative citizens indicates that the colored people of the country have been deeply stirred by the execution of thirteen members of this same organization which occurred some weeks ago.

Our understanding is that the cases of the last five men convicted have been referred to the Chief Executive for final action, and the purpose of this letter is to express the hope that an examination of these cases will lead you to the conviction that the ends of justice may be sufficiently met by commuting the death sentence pronounced upon these soldiers. We would earnestly recommend that this be done if there are any circumstances connected with these cases which you feel would warrant you in taking this action.

Respectfully submitted,   Charles Curtis
D. R. Anthony Jr.

TLS (N. D. Baker Papers, DLC).
[1] About which see, NDB to WW, Aug. 24, 1917, Vol. 44.

To Hamilton Holt

My dear Mr. Holt: [The White House] 17 January, 1918

These are certainly most generous editorials which you have sent me[1] and I know you will forgive me for enjoying them even when I know I do not deserve the praise that you bestow upon me personally. It is a great responsibility to speak for a nation like our own and I think I need not tell you what it has cost me to think things through as I believed an American ought to think them through. I thank you most sincerely.

Cordially yours,   Woodrow Wilson

TLS (Letterpress Books, WP, DLC).
[1] They are missing, but they were probably "Peace With Victory," *The Independent*, XCII (Dec. 8, 1917), 459; "For a Holy War," *ibid.*, Dec. 15, 1917, pp. 497-98; and "Woodrow Wilson," *ibid.*, XCIII (Jan. 19, 1918), 89.

To Edward Albert Filene

My dear Mr. Filene: [The White House] 17 January, 1918

I beg to assure you that it never entered my mind that you and the gentlemen associated with you had any but the very best motives in submitting the referendum about an economic boycott, but I must say to you that I am exceedingly sorry that this was done without first consulting me. No matter which way the vote turns, it will embarrass my handling of international affairs and the policy of the Government.

I dare say that it is too late now to recall the referendum, but I beg very earnestly that you will assist me in advising the directors of the Chamber of Commerce that it is my earnest hope that they will consult with me in matters of this sort before acting. I am, as you will realize, in some peculiar sense entrusted with directing the foreign relations of the nation.

Cordially and sincerely yours,   Woodrow Wilson

TLS (Letterpress Books, WP, DLC).

To Robert Lansing

My dear Mr. Secretary: [The White House] 17 January, 1918

I feel that it is too late for the United States Chamber of Commerce to recall their referendum. I have written to Mr. Filene today about it, expressing my very great regret and my hope that in the future they will not do things of this sort without consulting us.

Thank you very much for seeing the officers of the Chamber about this indiscretion.

Cordially and sincerely yours, Woodrow Wilson

TLS (Letterpress Books, WP, DLC).

To Daniel Willard

My dear Mr. Willard: [The White House] 17 January, 1918

It is with the utmost regret that I accept your resignation as Chairman of the War Industries Board.[1] I do so only because I am convinced with you that the matter of moving the coal is so critically and immediately important that it is probably your duty to give that your first attention as president of a road which does a very large part of the coal carrying.

I hope that it will be possible for you to defer the actual severance of your connection with the Board until a new chairman has been selected, but I do not wish to interfere even to that extent with the important duty to which you are turning, if you think it imperative that you should turn to it at once.

I have greatly admired the spirit of your public service and have highly valued that service in every respect. I hope you are turning away from it only for the time being.

Cordially and sincerely yours, Woodrow Wilson

TLS (Letterpress Books, WP, DLC).
[1] D. Willard to WW, Jan. 11, 1918, printed as an Enclosure with D. Willard to JPT, Jan. 15, 1918, Vol. 45.

To Claude Kitchin

My dear Mr. Kitchin: The White House 17 January, 1918

I do not know what you think of the considerations urged in the enclosed brief[1] but I am sure that I ought to send them to you and not to reply to them without your advice. I would be very much obliged for your guidance in the matter. I have no doubt that the gentlemen concerned are very serious-minded and sincere.

Cordially yours, Woodrow Wilson

TLS (C. Kitchin Papers, NcU).
[1] "Brief Submitted to President Wilson Wednesday, January 16th, on Behalf of the Conference on Democratic Financing of the War Held at the National Hotel, Washington, January 15th, under the Auspices of the Association for an Equitable Federal Income Tax, John J. Hopper, President, in Affiliation the National Party, Organized Labor, Organized Farmers and Civic Organizations," T MS (C. Kitchin Papers, NcU). This brief urged that at least one half of the cost of financing the war effort be shifted to individuals and corporations with large incomes, and it cited many facts and figures in an attempt to show that this could be done.

To Charles Curtis

My dear Senator Curtis: [The White House] 17 January, 1918

I have the letter of January eleventh signed by yourself and Mr. Anthony of the House of Representatives, and beg to assure you that the case of the five members of the 24th Infantry who have been sentenced to execution to which the letters refers is under very serious consideration by the Secretary of War and myself, and I hope sincerely that we may be led, upon the study of the case, to a right conclusion.[1]

Cordially and sincerely yours,   Woodrow Wilson

TLS (Letterpress Books, WP, DLC).
[1] The War Department on January 17 issued a general order which stated that thereafter, in cases in which the death penalty was imposed by a court-martial held within the continental United States, the sentence was to be suspended until the Judge Advocate General had examined the trial records and the President of the United States had confirmed the decision. Robert V. Haynes, *A Night of Violence: The Houston Riot of 1917* (Baton Rouge, La., 1976), pp. 278-79.

A Message from Frank Irving Cobb

(Dictated over the long-distance by Mr. Frank Cobb for the President, January 17, 1918).

Dear Mr. President:

Mr. Garfield's coal order is a terrible calamity. Hundreds and thousands of working men and women, who are absolutely dependent upon their daily wages, with the high cost of living, will be affected. They have no savings at all. They can't stand it to be out of work five days and to work only five days a week for ten weeks. Can't you modify or rescind that order. The coal situation is straightening itself out. There is no reason why they should not take what coal is necessary for these ships and let industry shift for itself. There might be a few factories that would have to close for a day or two but they can attend to that. Do not let the Government close them up. The whole of New York, both rich and poor, is seething in protest. The whole psychology of it is disastrous. It is demoralizing the whole country. It is bound in its result to smash the whole morale of business. Better a thousand times to have the few inconveniences we are now suffering than this. It is an acknowledgment at the beginning of the war of the break-down of the Government. We cannot afford to let that impression go out to the world.   (Frank Cobb)

T MS (WP, DLC).

To Frank Irving Cobb

[The White House] 17 January, 1918

You may be sure that I appreciate to the full the seriousness of the fuel order and the weight of the considerations urged in your telephone message. I beg to assure you that I approved the order only because I believed it to be necessary and the only practicable way of clearing up a situation which needed to be cleared up at once in order that we might not continue for an indefinite time to limp along imperfectly in the matter of the transportation of fuel. The working people thrown out of employment ought not to be allowed to suffer. Their employers ought to pay their wages.

Woodrow Wilson.

T telegram (Letterpress Books, WP, DLC).

Two Letters from William Gibbs McAdoo

PERSONAL.

Dear "Governor":　　　　　Washington January 17, 1918.

The papers state that Mr. Willard has resigned from the War Industries Board and that he will resume his position as President of the Baltimore & Ohio Railroad. I hope this is true as I was on the point of suggesting to you that Mr. Willard ought to return to the Baltimore & Ohio because the property is in a very bad condition and imperatively needs his directing head. If he is unable to return, then a new head ought to be chosen.

I hope sincerely you will consider Baruch for the vacancy if Mr. Willard leaves. He is by all odds the most capable man for the position.

I do not want, of course, to interfere with any of the Secretary of War's prerogatives, but the matter is so important that I have felt at liberty to submit the suggestion merely as a suggestion.

Affectionately yours,　W G McAdoo

Dear Mr. President:　　　　　Washington January 17, 1918.

I have your letter of the 16th. All vessels departing for or arriving from foreign ports are carefully searched by customs officers. While such search is not made with the special view of discovering explosives, such articles are included in the objects of the search. There are, moreover, many precautions taken, both by the customs officers and other governmental agencies to prevent the placing of explosives on board vessels with the intent to injure them. To render assurance doubly sure, I have caused special instructions to be sent, by wire, to Collectors of Customs at all seacoast and gulf ports for the institution of precautionary measures to meet any possible attempt such as that indicated in your letter, and have also brought the Secret Service into the matter.

I may add that while, up to the time of our declaration of war, there were numerous attempts to place explosives and inflamable substances on board vessels while in our harbors with the intention to destroy them, such precautions have been taken since our declaration of war that these attempts have practically ceased. The instructions issued, however, are predicated upon the theory that every possible precaution should be taken, however improbable the success of any concerted attempt along this line may appear.

As shipbuilding plants are not under the control of the Collectors of Customs, I have taken the extra precaution of bringing this matter to the attention of the Navy Department and the Shipping Board.   Faithfully yours,   W G McAdoo

TLS (WP, DLC).

From the National Association of Manufacturers

New York, January 17, 1918.

The National Association of Manufacturers composed of four thousand establishments views with gravest concern the possibilities for appalling disaster to our country and our people unless the order of the Fuel Administrator shall immediately be revoked it it [sic] is not a relief but a calamity. Our industries are now bearing burdens almost unbearable and additions to such burdens will inevitably result in a breakdown the loss of time, work and wages by our working people; will cause sickness, suffering, distress and still further strain relations which are already near the breaking point thereby causing more discontent and social unrest. The news of the Fuel Administrator's action will be welcomed by our enemies as an official admission that the United States is industrially demoralized and therefore not to be feared. For these reasons and for others we respectfully and earnestly urge the revocation of the order.   National Ass'n of Manufacturers.

T telegram (WP, DLC).

From Charles Seymour Whitman

Albany, N. Y., January 17, 1918.

In view of the overwhelming opposition to the Garfield order expressed to me by the people of this state I deem it my duty respectfully and most earnestly to protest against its enforcement. I am satisfied that the carrying out of the order will work incalculable and unnecessary hardship and injury to our industries and to our people. Of course I shall render prompt obedience to the mandates of the federal authorities; our state is willing and ready at all times to uphold the hands of the federal administration; but the well-nigh universal sentiment here is that this order is unnecessary and unwise.   Chas. S. Whitman.

T telegram (WP, DLC).

From Herbert Clark Hoover, with Enclosure

Dear Mr. President: Washington, D. C. *17 January 1918*

I enclose herewith draft of a sort of proclamation which I am anxious to have issued from you on the subject of food conservation. As I explained to you, the demands now being made upon us are much greater than we can carry unless we procure a further reduction in consumption of certain commodities and, generally, of all foodstuffs.

I have no doubt that you will be able to improve its expression and I take the liberty of asking that we may have it at as early a moment as possible.   Yours faithfully,   Herbert Hoover

TLS (WP, DLC).

ENCLOSURE E[1]

A PROCLAMATION

Many causes have ⟨cumulated⟩ *contributed* to create the necessity ⟨of⟩ *for* a more intensive effort ⟨by⟩ *on the part of* our people ⟨in the saving of⟩ *to save* food ⟨to the end⟩ *in order* that we may supply our associates in the War with the sustenance vitally necessary ⟨for their health and strength⟩ *to them in these days of privation and stress.* The reduced productivity of Europe because of the large diversion of man-power to the War, the partial failure of harvests and the elimination of the more distant markets *for food stuffs* through the destruction of shipping, places the burden of their subsistence very largely on our shoulders.

The Food Administration has formulated suggestions which, if followed, will enable us to meet this great responsibility, *without any real inconvenience on our part.*

⟨To the end⟩ *In order* that we may reduce our consumption of wheat and wheat products by thirty per cent—a reduction imperatively necessary to provide the supply for overseas—wholesalers, jobbers and retailers should purchase and re-sell to their customers only seventy per cent of the amounts used in 1917. All manufacturers of alimentary pastes, biscuits, crackers and breakfast cereals, and all bakers of bread and pastry should reduce their purchases and consumption of wheat and wheat flour to eighty per cent of their 1917 requirements. Consumers should reduce their purchases of wheat products for home preparation to at ⟨least⟩ *most* seventy per cent of those of last year, or, when buying bread, should purchase mixed cereal breads from the bakers.

To provide sufficient cereal foods, homes, public eating places, dealers and manufacturers should substitute potatoes, vegetables, corn, barley, oats and rice products, and the war bread and other products of the bakers which contain an admixture of other cereals.

In order that consumption may be restricted to this extent, Mondays and Wednesdays should be observed as Wheatless Days each week, and one meal each day should be observed as a Wheatless Meal.

In both homes and public eating places, in order to reduce the consumption of beef, pork and sheep products, Tuesday should be observed as a Meatless Day each week, one Meatless Meal should be observed in each day; while, in addition, Saturday in each week should further be observed as a day ⟨of⟩ *upon which there should be* no consumption of pork products.

A continued economy in the use of sugar will be necessary until later in the year.

It is imperative that all waste and unnecessary consumption of all *sorts of* foodstuffs should be rigidly eliminated.

The maintenance of the health and strength of our own people is vitally necessary at this time, and there should be no dangerous restriction of the food supply; ⟨However,⟩ *but* the elimination of every ⟨bit⟩ *sort* of waste and the substitution of other commodities of which we have more abundant supplies for those which we need to save, will in no way impair the strength of our people and will enable us to meet one of the most pressing obligations of the War.

I, therefore, in the national interest, ⟨call⟩ *take the liberty of calling* upon every loyal American to take fully to heart the suggestions which are being circulated by the Food Administration ⟨and to follow them implicitly⟩ *and of begging that they be followed.*

I am confident that the great body of our women who have labored so loyally in co-operation with the Food Administration for the success of food conservation⟨,⟩ will strengthen their efforts and will take it as a part of their burden in this period of national service⟨,⟩ to see that the above suggestions are observed throughout the land.

Woodrow Wilson[2]

TS MS (WP, DLC).
    [1] Words in angle brackets in the following document were deleted by Wilson; those printed in italics were added by him.
    [2] This was printed, among other publications, in the *Official Bulletin*, II (Jan. 28, 1918), 3.

From Samuel Gompers

Sir: Washington, D. C. January 17, 1918.

I had some correspondence, both by cable and mail, with Honorable George Barnes, labor member of the British Cabinet. I extended an invitation for representatives of the labor movement of England to come to this country to disseminate information in the interest of the cause of the United States and her allies in this struggle. Among the men who are coming is Mr. W. A. Appleton,[1] Secretary of the General Federation of Trades Unions. He will be accompanied by three other representative labor men. I ought to say that the invitation extended to these labor men is in full accord with the government of Great Britian [Britain].

Taking advantage of the publication of a statement by a former member of the British Cabinet, Mr. Arthur Henderson, calling for an international conference of all countries, probably at Stockholm, I sent a cablegram to Mr. Appleton under date of January 9th. Enclosed you will please find a copy of that cablegram. It seemed to me that the psychological situation demanded some such expression as I gave in my cable to Mr. Appleton.[2]

I trust you may find time to read the enclosed.

Respectfully yours,   Saml. Gompers.

TLS (WP, DLC).
    [1] William Archibald Appleton.
    [2] S. Gompers to W. A. Appleton, Jan. 9, 1918, mimeograph copy telegram (WP, DLC). Gompers stated that the American Federation of Labor and the General Federation of Trade Unions were in essential agreement on war aims. Gompers further declared that the A. F. of L. would not participate in any international conference of workers of all countries of the world until or unless either the German people had established democracy within their own country or the Allies had succeeded in crushing German militarism and autocracy. Otherwise, any international labor conference which included German representatives would be "prejudicial to a desirable and lasting peace."

From Charles William Eliot

Dear Mr. President: Cambridge, Mass., 17 January 1918.

For me the most striking thing in your address to Congress on January 8th was what you said in the two paragraphs about Russia. So far as I can judge from what I have heard and read during the last two months, your wisdom on this subject is a very rare wisdom. Till yesterday I had not discovered a single American observer who took your view. Clearly Governor Francis and his military attaché have held views very different from yours.[1]

Yesterday I talked with a connection of mine by marriage—Dr. Francis W. Peabody[2]—who has just got home from an expedition to Roumania as a member of a Red Cross Commission. He went out and returned through Russia, spent a few weeks at Petrograd, and was twice in Moscow. During his second visit to Moscow, he witnessed the worst fighting of Russians with Russians which has taken place since their Revolution. He had opportunities of talking with all kinds of Russians, and received strong impressions as to the quality of the Revolutionary leaders and of the Russian populace.

Dr. Peabody is Assistant Professor in the Harvard Medical School and an active teacher there of Clinical Medicine. He is also one of the staff of the Peter Bent Brigham Hospital, which is attached to the Harvard Medical School. He has never had private practice. All his colleagues, assistants, students, nurses, and patients are much attached to him, because he brings out all the good-will there is in the people with whom he comes in contact, and secures to a remarkable degree their willing cooperation. He is about thirty-five years of age and unmarried. He apparently had the same effect on the Russians with whom he came in contact that he has on the people— of many races—with whom he deals at home.

I have described Dr. Peabody thus at length because I think you would find his conversation about conditions in Russia and the Russian people very interesting and helpful towards the ends you have in view. He told me yesterday that he was expecting to go to Washington soon to make his report to the Red Cross authorities. Till next Sunday he can be communicated with at his father's house (Professor Francis G. Peabody,[3] the writer on Social Ethics) 13 Kirkland Street, Cambridge, Mass. He is not a striking looking man; and his conversation is informal, not to say slangy.

I am, with the highest regard, as ever,

Sincerely yours   Charles W. Eliot

TLS (WP, DLC).
[1] Many persons interpreted Wilson's remarks on Russia in his Fourteen Points Address as an indication of his approval of Bolshevik foreign policy and thought that the speech

had signaled a decision on the part of the administration to work with the Bolsheviks, at least informally. It was also widely assumed that Ambassador Francis would be recalled for his opposition to the Bolshevik regime. Herbert Bayard Swope, "Wilson's Attitude Toward Russia Big in Peace Portent," New York *World*, Jan. 12, 1918, expressed these assumptions. See also the discussion of the Fourteen Points Address and of Swope's article in George F. Kennan, *Russia Leaves the War* (Princeton, N. J., 1956), pp. 253-66.

However, it is difficult to understand how Eliot got the idea that the Military Attaché, Brig. Gen. William V. Judson, shared Francis' attitude toward the Bolshevik regime. In reality, Judson had repeatedly urged the necessity of working at least informally with that government and had made a well-publicized visit to Foreign Commissar Leon Trotsky on December 1, 1917.

[2] Francis Weld Peabody.

[3] Francis Greenwood Peabody, now retired, formerly Plummer Professor of Christian Morals and Dean of the Harvard Divinity School.

From the Diary of Colonel House

January 17, 1918.

We paid an interesting visit today to the Morgan Library on 36th Street where Mr. and Mrs. Morgan[1] showed Loulie and me the rare manuscripts and books in that wonderful collection. Morgan assured me of his desire to help the Government and Administration in every way possible. I have no doubt as to his sincerity, for patriotism is something the Morgans pride themselves on.

I tool [took] lunch at the Geographical Society with Director Bowman[2] where we have rooms for our organization in the preparation of peace data.

Last night when Garfield's coal order was given out, bedlam broke loose. Press Associations, newspaper editors etc. etc. made my life miserable. This has continued all day. There is nothing that the Administration has done that I regret so much. It may be necessary, but it certainly was not necessary to do it in such a casual and abrupt way. It is one of the things I have feared the President would sometime do. He seems to have done it. I have never heard such a storm of protest. What I am afraid of is that it will weaken confidence in his administrative ability and bring Congress about his ears. I look to see them meddling with everything from now on, and I look to see an insistent demand that some change be made in the organization responsible for the conduct of the war.

This question has disturbed me since my return from Europe. Men of every shade of political opinion condemn the organization as it now exists. The President and Secretary Baker seem to be the only ones that think the organization is as it should be. Men like Lovett, Nelson Perkins,[3] Baruch, Cyrus McCormick, Bainbridge Colby and other staunch supporters of the Administration have but one story to tell. They look to me to influence the President. I have hesitated to mention the matter to him for the reason that I tried at the beginning of the war to get him to accept what I thought to be the right sort of organization—an organization which everybody now thinks is essential. I do not like to intrude my advice upon him again. He knows quite well what I think, and he knows that I do not believe that he has an effective war organization, and I have been content to let it go at that.

The fact that he does not consult me about these matters indicates that he knows we disagree, but he has believed he could work it out along the lines which he has pursued. In foreign affairs, he does nothing without the closest possible cooperation with me, and since I am so much more interested in that than in domestic affairs, I have been willing to accept the situation as he has willed it. However, matters have gotten so bad now since this coal order of Garfield's that I have concluded, in justice to the President, that I should give a helping hand whether he asks for it or not.

I have therefore arranged for Secretary Baker to come over Sunday to be with me a large part of the day. If I can get him into a proper frame of mind and to see the necessity for a radical and thorough reorganization of affairs, I will take it up with the President. The President will not want it but, at the moment, it looks as if he will have no choice, for if he does not do it himself, Congress may force it upon him.

This storm shows how easily a situation may change from good to bad. It is literally like a storm at sea. At one moment you are sailing along through smooth seas and clear skies, and then within the hour the whole face of the water becomes turbulent and dangerous.

T MS (E. M. House Papers, CtY).
    [1] That is, J. Pierpont Morgan, Jr., and Jane Norton Grew Morgan.
    [2] Isaiah Bowman, director of the American Geographical Society and one of the leaders of The Inquiry.
    [3] Thomas Nelson Perkins, lawyer of Boston, at this time chief counsel of the War Industries Board. He had been a member of the House mission to Europe in November and December 1917.

To Charles Seymour Whitman

[The White House] 18 January, 1918

I have your telegram and appreciate the force of what it urges but beg to assure you that the order was absolutely necessary for reasons of which I am expecting presently to make a public statement. I greatly appreciate your assurance of prompt compliance on the part of the people of New York, though I had confidence in that from the first.   Woodrow Wilson.

T telegram (Letterpress Books, WP, DLC).

A Statement

18 January, 1918.

I was, of course, consulted by Mr. Garfield before the fuel order of yesterday was issued and fully agreed with him that it was necessary, much as I regretted the necessity. This war calls for many sacrifices, and sacrifices of the sort called for by this order are infinitely less than sacrifices of life which might otherwise be involved. It is absolutely necessary to get the ships away, it is absolutely necessary to relieve the congestion at the ports and upon the railways, it is absolutely necessary to move great quantities of food, and it is absolutely necessary that our people should be warmed in their homes if nowhere else, and half-way measures would not have accomplished the desired ends. If action such as this had not been taken, we should have limped along from day to day with a slowly improving condition of affairs with regard to the shipment of food and of coal, but without such immediate relief as had become absolutely necessary because of the congestions of traffic which have been piling up for the last few months.

I have every confidence that the result of action of this sort will justify it and that the people of the country will loyally and patriotically respond to necessities of this kind as they have to every other sacrifice involved in the war. We are upon a war footing and I am confident that the people of the United States are willing to observe the same sort of discipline that might be involved in the actual conflict itself.[1]

T MS (Letterpress Books, WP, DLC).
[1] This statement was published, among other places, in the *Official Bulletin*, II (Jan. 19, 1918), 2.

A News Report

[Jan. 18, 1918]

ASK FOR CONTROL OF PACKING TRADE
Union Men, Headed by Gompers, See President
to Demand Federal Operation.

Washington. Jan. 18.—President Wilson was urged this afternoon to take over all the packing plants of the country for Government operation as a war measure in the interest not only of the nation but of the packing house employes in Chicago, Omaha, Kansas City, and East St. Louis. The appeal was made to the President by a delegation of leaders of the various crafts employed in the packing plants who told him that unless conditions of which laborers in packing plants complained were not quickly remedied the men might be forced to strike.

The President gave an hour and forty minutes to the consideration of the appeal, but made no decision. He replied that he would move very carefully in the matter, and would first take it up with the Mediation Commission in the hope that some remedy might be reached short of taking over the plants.

The delegation of packing house men was headed by James[1] Fitzpatrick, President of the Chicago Federation of Labor, and Edward N. Nockels, its Secretary. The party included twelve heads of international brotherhoods identified with the packing industry. Samuel Gompers and Frank Morrison of the American Federation of Labor accompanied them to the White House. Secretary of War Baker, as Chairman of the Council of National Defense, and Secretary of Labor Wilson were present. Frank P. Walsh of Kansas City, who was formerly Chairman of the Committee on Industrial Relations, accompanied the packing house men as their counsel.

Mr. Gompers, introducing the delegation to the President, said there was so great a condition of industrial unrest in the packing houses that the labor leaders feared they would not longer be able to hold the workmen in line unless the conditions they complained of were remedied. They believed the surest remedy would be for the Federal Government to commandeer and operate all the great packing plants. The alleged objectionable conditions were brutal treatment, low pay, and long hours.

The President was told that if the Government should take over and operate the plants the labor leaders felt that full justice would be done both sides, that the conditions would be remedied, and that if this were accomplished the men would go the limit in helping to maintain a maximum output.

The President was told that the organized laborers would enlist for the period of the war in this work, and would be willing to work three eight-hour shifts daily. It was alleged that the packers had repudiated a mediation agreement to settle questions of wages and working conditions, and were discharging union men in groups, apparently with the purpose of bringing on a strike. Of the thousands employed in the plants, the union men said, 90 per cent. were foreigners without union affiliations, and of whose loyalty standards no one could judge.

As the delegation left the White House Mr. Gompers was asked whether the situation was as grave as pictured. He replied that the situation was so acute that some remedy must be found quickly. He said that the labor leaders had been doing their level best to prevent a strike but he was afraid that the packers were willing to provoke a strike and throw the blame on the workmen rather than yield in the effort to find a real remedy.

John Fitzpatrick, President of the Chicago Federation of Labor, issued this statement, following the conference:

"We have just urged the President to take all the packing plants of the country. The organized packers of the country have refused to meet us, or to co-operate with us, in any manner in this great world crisis. They have brazenly repudiated the solemn agreement entered into by the President and ourselves through his Mediation Commission on last Christmas morning.

"We made the following offer to the President, in case the plants are taken over:

"1. That we would ourselves [be] enlisted as the first members of America's industrial army.

"2. That we would guarantee to the Government full-handed equipment for every packing plant in the United States.

"3. We will furnish enough workers if need be, to operate said packing plants in continuous daily shifts so that every moment of their time may be devoted to production.

"4. We are willing to allow the pay of the workers, their hours of work, and all conditions of their labor to be determined by the President of the United States or the person to whom he may delegate this duty.

"5. We shall ask that, as long as the Government can afford to do so, these workers shall be paid a wage reasonably sufficient, considering that our country is at war, to maintain themselves, and those dependent upon them, at the minimum of comfort.

"6. We are willing to work any length of time that may be necessary for the purpose of production, only asking such limitation as will conserve health and allow a decent response to our mutual and moral necessities.

"7. The wages and conditions, respectfully submitted, so long as the Government can afford to do so, should be such that our country would have at all times a virile, contented, and enthusiastically loyal industrial army.

"8. If, however, the nation's extremity should be reached, and it should become necessary for our industrial army to work naked in the packing houses of the land with barely enough to keep strength in their bodies, we will meet the situation bravely and do that, too.

"Upon last Wednesday morning, before our departure from Chicago, Frank P. Walsh stated these purposes to the organized packers of America, assembled in the offices of the Swift Company at Room 1215, 38 West Monroe Street, Chicago. The packers present at the time were: Nelson Morris, Louis F. Swift, Gustavus Swift,

Edward A. Cudahy, John K. O'Hern, General Manager of Armour & Co., and the General Managers of Wilson & Co., Swift & Co., Morris & Co., and the Cudahy Company."

Printed in the *New York Times*, Jan. 19, 1918.
    [1] His real name was John.

To Harry Augustus Garfield, with Enclosure

My dear Garfield: The White House 18 January, 1918
    Do you think it would be wise or possible to comply with this suggestion of the theatre men? They are pretty hard hit, of course, and what they want is to take advantage of the holiday Monday crowd.   Faithfully yours,   Woodrow Wilson

TLS (H. A. Garfield Papers, DLC).

ENCLOSURE

Washington, D. C. [Jan. 17, 1917]
    Your attitude toward us today[1] touched us deeply and we ask your further indulgence and cooperation in the following suggestion. Would it not be possible to so moderate the fuel administration order as to allow the theaters to open on Monday and agree with Mr. Garfield to close another night. This would accomplish the purpose in mind and yet would give us the relief we ask. Our committee would cooperate in every way to make this arrangement effective.   George M. Cohan.

T telegram (H. A. Garfield Papers, DLC).
    [1] Wilson met with Cohan and a committee of theatrical managers at the White House at 3:45 P.M. The managers argued that the public should be allowed to attend theater, vaudeville, motion pictures, and other forms of entertainment on nonworking days when they could not go elsewhere. *New York Times*, Jan. 17 and 18, 1918.

To John Lionberger Davis[1]

My dear Mr. Davis: [The White House] 18 January, 1918
    I am heartily glad you think I was of some help to poor Morrison.[2] His death has distressed me very much indeed. I wish I could have done more for him than I did.
    Thank you for your note.[3]
    In haste   Appreciatively yours,   Woodrow Wilson

TLS (Letterpress Books, WP, DLC).
    [1] At this time, managing director of the office of the Alien Property Custodian.

[2] Harry Steele Morrison, Princeton 1905, who had died on January 14, 1918.
[3] Davis' note is missing.

To Mortimer Elwyn Cooley[1]

My dear Dean Cooley: [The White House] 18 January, 1918

I understand that there is to be a meeting of the department superintendents of the American Educational Association in Atlantic City on the twenty-fifth of next month. I would like very much to be present in person at that meeting, but since I cannot be, may I not ask you to express to the gentlemen assembled there my very great concern that none of the educational processes of the country should be interrupted any more than is absolutely unavoidable during the war.

My attention has lately been called in particular to the falling off in the number of engineering students and this has given me a good deal of concern, because it is not only immediately necessary that as many students as possible should prepare themselves for engineering duties in the Army and Navy, but it is also of the first consequence to the country that there should be an adequate supply of engineers for the period of reconstruction which must follow the war.

Not only has technical training become of enormous importance in military operations, but the role of the engineer has become more and more important in every process of our industrial life, and I hope that influences may go out from the meeting in Atlantic City which will call the attention of parents throughout the country to the importance of making any sacrifice that it is possible to make to keep their sons in the schools even during these trying times.

Cordially and sincerely yours,   Woodrow Wilson

TLS (Letterpress Books, WP, DLC).
[1] Dean of the Colleges of Engineering and Architecture of the University of Michigan.

From Waddill Catchings

New York, January 18, 1918.

Our board of directors considered at its meeting today your letter to Senator Bankhead, dated January fourteenth, regarding the coal situation [in] Alabama and voted that our position now is as we advised you in our telegram of August seventeenth.[1] We will take such action at any time as you may think best in the interest of the country. We understand that a conference with Dr. Garfield has been requested by a committee appointed by the Alabama coal operators but if in the meantime you think our company should take immediate action we are ready to do so.

Sloss Sheffield Steel & Iron Co.,

Waddill Catchings, President.

T telegram (WP, DLC).
    [1] W. Catchings to WW, Aug. 17, 1917, Vol. 43.

To Waddill Catchings

[The White House] 18 January, 1918

Thank you very much for your telegram. I think that it would be clearly in the national interest if your company would take immediate action endorsing the settlement proposed by the Fuel Administration with regard to work in the mines. Overall cooperation in the same sense throughout the country in these matters is so essential to the national safety that I am particularly pleased by the willingness of your directors to cooperate.

Woodrow Wilson.

T telegram (Letterpress Books, WP, DLC).

From Harry Augustus Garfield, with Enclosures

Dear Mr. President: Washington, D. C. January 18, 1918

Herewith, I enclose copy of a letter I am sending to the Vice-President, also, for your information, a copy of what I had intended to hand to the press over my signature. Mr. Tumulty advises me that you are contemplating issuing a statement. If so, I assume that mine should be withheld.

I venture to suggest for your consideration the advisability of calling together a few of your officers immediately affected by the order issued last night. I have in mind the Director General of Railways, the Secretary of War, the Secretary of Navy, Mr. Hoover, Mr. Hurley and myself.

The effectiveness of last night's order will be considerably enhanced, should the Director General deem it advisable to forbid the loading of material not included in my order.

Cordially and faithfully yours,   H. A. Garfield.

TLS (WP, DLC).

ENCLOSURE I

Harry Augustus Garfield to Thomas Riley Marshall

Dear Mr. Vice-President: [Washington] January 18, 1918.

Permit me to confirm the message which I sent to you yesterday afternoon by Mr. Baker,[1] the Secretary of the Senate.

It is my earnest desire that the members of the Senate should know that as an Executive officer of the Government, I would not willingly treat a request of the Senate with other than the greatest respect.[2]

The order suspending the operation of industrial plants in portions of the United States was issued only after deliberate consideration, and will, I firmly believe, aid effectively in providing coal for domestic consumers, for the prompt bunkering of ships carrying necessary war material abroad, and for the relief of the serious congestion at the docks and at many points in the section covered by the order. I still believe it should stand. To delay the application of the order would only add to the congestion. It would be but natural that industry, in the interval, would redouble its efforts to increase supplies on hand.

To permit factories with a coal supply to operate during the period of suspension, would allow many producing articles least essential to the war to continue, while some producing articles the most essential would be compelled to shut down. Moreover, continued production by those well supplied with coal would delay, if not defeat, the relief contemplated by the order.

I should add that the Resolution was presented to me at 6:35 P.M. yesterday afternoon and that the order was signed at 5:45.

With high respect, I remain,

Very truly yours   [H. A. Garfield]

TCL (H. A. Garfield Papers, DLC).

[1] James Marion Baker.

[2] Shortly after the Senate convened at noon on January 17, Hitchcock introduced a resolution (S. Res. 186) which called upon the Fuel Administrator to suspend for five days his order to close factories in order to allow the Senate time in which to make an investigation of the necessity of the order. An acrimonious debate on the resolution began at once. It was suspended at 2 P.M. to allow Garfield to testify in defense of the measure before a subcommittee of the Committee on Manufactures. Garfield defended his order for an hour and five minutes. Debate then resumed on Hitchcock's resolution, and the Senate adopted it by a vote of fifty to nineteen at 6:05 P.M. *New York Times*, Jan. 18, 1918, and *Cong. Record*, 65th Cong., 2d sess., pp. 912-22, 928-36.

ENCLOSURE II

The order suspending temporarily the operation of industrial plants in portions of the United States is drastic. Yes, war is drastic. This war is the most extensive and involves greater sacrifices than any war heretofore. The American people, led by the President, entered this war deliberately. They are staking everything for the realization of a great ideal, and the ideal is practical. We know that democracy must be made a reality at home, as well as abroad, that its benefits must be shared by all and its sacrifices borne by no single class.

Capital and labor are embarked in this war because all Americans are in it, and the American spirit cries out against the least suggestion that the burden be shifted to the backs of any one class, least of all of labor, for labor has less financial ability to meet the prolonged hardships of war than capital. We are realizing the truth now as never before that capital and labor are not two but one. Their problems present merely two aspects of the same vital question. The unselfish and patriotic impulses and the calm look ahead will lead the country to approve of the order now in force.

Industry is [in] an unbalanced condition. We lack many essentials,—food, clothing[,] fuel. We have piled up enormous stores of things not essential to life but very essential to war. We have piled them so high on our docks and in our store-houses that the ships available cannot carry them away as fast as they pile up. For lack of bunker coal, held back by traffic congestion, the number of ships in our harbors increases menacingly.

The food supply is threatened to an even greater degree than the fuel supply. This condition is in large part due to the congestion that at many points holds the loaded cars in its grip.

To single out industries not engaged to some extent in war manufacture is to select industries which in the aggregate will bring relief only if suspended indefinitely. To require all industries except a comparatively small part to cease for a few days quickly accomplishes the desired result and permanently injures none; that the order as it stands puts all industry on an equal footing favoring none and avoiding unfair competition, but this reason alone is not sufficient. This reason, plus the fact that the order will save coal, will aid in breaking up congestion of traffic and [in furnishing] an adequate supply of coal to the people who need it and to the ships which cannot sail without it.

Only those industries producing necessary war material that can be promptly delivered are permitted to operate during the suspension period. To permit industries with a coal supply on hand to operate would allow many of the least essential to continue while some of the most essential would be compelled to stop. Moreover, to allow those fortunate enough to possess a coal pile to continue would result in adding to the traffic congestion, and, unless they also are suspended at a later period, the needed saving in consumption of coal would not result. To have delayed the application of the order would only have added to the congestion. It is no condemnation of industry to say that each would have striven to the utmost to increase its supply of coal and other raw material during the days prior to the application of the order.[1]

T MS (H. A. Garfield Papers, DLC).
[1] This statement was published in slightly revised form in the *Official Bulletin*, II (Jan. 19, 1918), 2.

From Bernard Mannes Baruch

My dear Mr President,   [Washington] Friday [Jan. 18, 1918]

Under the circumstances Mr Garfield has done the only thing that could be done and I hope and know you will stand "pat." Some of the things he is doing in the direction of curtailing the less essentials will make for permanent betterments

In less than thirty days criticism will be turned to praise.

Always sincerely   Bernard M Baruch

ALS (WP, DLC).

From the Diary of Josephus Daniels

January Friday 18 1918

"There is no expression of protest when a million men are called to jeopardize their lives, but the country is aroused to a pitch of indignation if money & profits must feel the pinch of war," said WW when cabinet met. Sometimes cannot refrain from "Damn" & recalled Luther Martins defense of Judge Chase when impeached. Charged with profanity on the bench, it was shown he had used word "Damn" & Martin proved that was not profanity. 3 kinds of fool. Born fools, fools & Damn fools

A woman told her son he should not swear. Why. "Because it is wrong and worse because it is vulgar[."]

Reported the cabinet is divided. Is that true asked WW. Was it uncomfortable question? Not for any except _____

Housing proposition: Should embrace all Depts

All day telegrams asking exceptions for coal.

Conferred with Pres & Polk about Admiral Knight's cable.[1] It has been agreed that England, Japan & US should not land or keep ships in Vladivostock. Japan had one ship. Another sailed for Korea but dropped in at V_____. Consul at V_____[2] wired that Knight should come. Knight said things were quiet at V & show of force might do harm

Is Japan trying to get a foothold in Russia? Shall we send ship to V or trust Japan alone? Delicate question. No solution reached

¹ See n. 1 to Enclosure I with the next document.
² John Kenneth Caldwell.

To Frank Lyon Polk, with Enclosures

My dear Polk   [The White House, Jan. 19, 1918]
    This cable to Morris has my approval   W.W.

ALI (SDR, RG 59, 861.00/945, DNA).

E N C L O S U R E   I

From Frank Lyon Polk

My dear Mr. President: Washington January 19, 1918.
    The Secretary of the Navy told me of his conversation with you yesterday on the subject of the cables from Admiral Knight and Mr. Morris as to the presence of Japanese ships in Vladivostok.¹ We in the Department had already been discussing this very delicate situation, as it is one that presents grave possibilities.
    The attached cable has been submitted to Mr. Lansing and to Mr. Daniels, and has received the approval of both of them. It would seem necessary that our position should be tactfully made clear to the Japanese now, as it would be a serious matter if they should proceed to land an armed force in Vladivostok on the assumption that such a step met with our approval.
    You possibly recall that we expressed ourselves as being opposed to the French plan of policing Irkutsk.² As I refer to the telegram stating our position on the French proposal, I attach that³ for your information, together with the other telegrams received.⁴
    As we are expressing our views here on the subject of the Japanese having more than one ship in Vladivostok, Mr. Daniels and we agree that we can leave open for the moment the question as to whether the BROOKLYN should be sent.
    As the matter is pressing, I am taking the liberty of marking this "Rush."
    Believe me, Mr. President,
                                Yours faithfully,   Frank L Polk

TLS (SDR, RG 59, 861.00/998, DNA).
    ¹ The telegram from Morris is printed as an Enclosure with WW to RL, Jan. 20, 1918 (second letter of that date).
    ² Jusserand had given the French plan to Lansing on January 8, and Lansing had

replied on January 16. J. J. Jusserand to RL, Jan. 8, 1918, TLS, and RL to J. J. Jusserand, Jan. 16, 1918, CCL, both in SDR, RG 59, 861.00/945, DNA. Lansing's reply to Jusserand is printed in *FR 1918, Russia,* II, 28-29. The substance of Lansing's reply was transmitted to London, Tokyo, and Peking.
    [3] That is, the telegram of January 16 to Tokyo, just cited.
    [4] That is, the telegram from Morris, cited in n. 1, and perhaps others.

E N C L O S U R E   I I

AmEmbassy, Tokio: Washington, January 19 [20], 1918.

    Your January 17, five p.m. and 10 p.m.:

    You are instructed to call upon the Minister for Foreign Affairs[1] and in oral conversation remind him of the attitude of this Government towards a military mission to Siberia as set forth in Department's telegram of January sixteenth, four p.m. in which you were informed of the reply made to the French proposals, declining to cooperate in a joint military expedition to Irkutsk and expressing the conviction that a military mission to Siberia would have disastrous results. The American Government has not learned since that France has taken any action in the direction proposed. The American Government feels very strongly that the common interests of all the powers at war with Germany demand from them an attitude of sympathy with the Russian people in their present unhappy struggle and that any movement looking towards the occupation of Russian territory would at once be construed as one hostile to Russia and would be likely to unite all factions in Russia against us thus aiding the German propaganda in Russia. The American Government trusts the Imperial Japanese Government will share this conviction and hopes that no unfortunate occurrence may make necessary the occupation of Vladivostok by a foreign force. The information received by this Government indicates that the situation there is quiet and is not one to cause alarm. You will say to the Minister for Foreign Affairs that in the opinion of the American Government the presence of more than one Japanese war vessel at Vladivostok at present is likely to be misconstrued and create a feeling of mistrust as to the purposes of the Allied Governments which Japan does not desire any more than the United States.

                                        Polk Acting[2]

T telegram (SDR, RG 59, 861.00/945, DNA).
    [1] That is, Viscount Ichiro Motono.
    [2] This telegram was repeated to London, Paris, and Peking: FLP to Amembassy, London, Jan. 21, 1918; FLP to Amembassy, Paris, Jan. 21, 1918, and FLP to Amlegation, Peking, Jan. 21, 1918, all T telegrams (SDR, RG 59, 861.00/945, DNA).

To Joseph Sherman Frelinghuysen

[The White House]
My dear Senator Frelinghuysen: 19 January, 1918

I need not tell you that the subject matter of your letter of yesterday[1] has been constantly in my mind, but I believe that the fuel order was absolutely necessary in the national interest as a war measure and that it would not be wise to modify it in any particular.

I hope you understand, however, that the local fuel administrators,—I mean the state administrators,—are left a very considerable degree of discretion as to particular instances in which it might seem imperative to grant some sort of relief.

Personally, I believe that it would be very dangerous for them to exercise this discretion except in the rarest cases, because cases are very hard to discriminate one from another, but in the very nature of things this is the utmost leeway which is practicable in such circumstances. I think the public necessity for this action will be more and more perceived as the days go by.

Sincerely yours,   Woodrow Wilson

TLS (Letterpress Books, WP, DLC).
[1] J. S. Frelinghuysen to WW, Jan. 18, 1918, TLS (WP, DLC).

To Bernard Mannes Baruch

My dear Baruch: The White House 19 January, 1918

I am glad you understand and approve Garfield's order. I knew that you would. It is extraordinary how some people wince and cry out when they are a little bit hurt.

I was immensely interested the other day by my talk with Brougham and Colcord about your newspaper plans.[1] They are bully!

Cordially and faithfully yours,   Woodrow Wilson

TLS (B. M. Baruch Papers, NjP).
[1] Wilson saw Brougham and Colcord at the White House on January 16. They, together with Raymond Swing, William C. Bullitt, and Colonel House, were urging Baruch to purchase a New York newspaper which they would then make a major vehicle for Wilsonian liberalism. At this time, they were considering the purchase of the *New York Tribune*. The project came to an end when Baruch became chairman of the War Industries Board in March because Baruch did not wish to create a conflict of interest with his new position. Jordan A. Schwarz, *The Speculator: Bernard M. Baruch in Washington, 1917-1965* (Chapel Hill, N. C., 1981), p. 195.

To Samuel Gompers

My dear Mr. Gompers: The White House 19 January, 1918

May I not express my appreciation and admiration of your message to the General Federation of Trades Unions in England about a conference at Stockholm? It is splendid.

I am glad to hear of the gentlemen who are coming over, and hope I may have the pleasure of meeting them.

Cordially and sincerely yours,   Woodrow Wilson

TLS (S. Gompers Corr., AFL-CIO-Ar).

To Albert Sidney Burleson

My dear Burleson: The White House 19 January, 1918

Here are two letters on a subject which, as you know, has come up in many forms besides those referred to in these letters.[1] It occurs to me that it might serve a common purpose if you would have a talk with Mr. Kitchin about it and with Senator Martin (I assume that Mac is too busy to interview the Senators as formerly) and put this proposition up to them. Ought not the first appropriation bill passed, whether regular or supplementary, to contain a provision authorizing the Government to commandeer office space and lodgings in the City of Washington to any extent necessary, fixing and paying a rent fair all the circumstances being taken into consideration, and leaving the proprietors the ordinary recourse to the courts in case they refuse to accept the compensation decided upon?

I think that Mr. Kitchin would like also to consider the proposition contained in Mrs. Hopkins' letter about building permanent quarters which would yield the Government some return in rentals. This is becoming daily a more pressing matter and the real estate proprietors of Washington are holding the Government up in a most outrageous and piratical matter. I will cooperate with you in any way that you think best by seeing these men personally, if you prefer.   Faithfully yours,   Woodrow Wilson

TLS (A. S. Burleson Papers, DLC).
[1] L. Brownlow to WW, Jan. 17, 1918, and Charlotte E. W. Hopkins to WW, Jan. 16, 1918, both TLS (WP, DLC). Brownlow asked for an increase in the allotment for a room-registration bureau in the District of Columbia from $1,000 per month to $1,800. He also stated that he proposed to undertake a publicity campaign to locate more housing in the District but warned that the saturation point would soon be reached. After that time, "extraordinary housing arrangements" would have to be provided. Mrs. Hopkins, at this time "chairman" of the Woman's Division of the Council of National Defense in the District of Columbia, discussed the housing crisis in Washington in more detail. She revealed that the best estimates were that some 30,000 new persons would enter the District of Columbia for war emergency work during 1918, two thirds of them before July 1. To cope wih this influx, she urged that "all the furnished and unfurnished houses

within our reach" be secured to accommodate about 5,000 persons at an estimated cost of $250,000. Furthermore, she advocated the construction by the government of blocks of permanent housing called "group plan houses" on Virginia Avenue, between 21st and 24th Streets, N. W., to house some 1,000 persons a block. These would accommodate young officers called to duty in Washington and their families and could be used after the war to house clerks, officers, and naval employees.

To Albert Sidney Burleson, with Enclosure

My dear Burleson: [The White House] 19 January, 1918

Here is the letter of the Americus, Georgia, man and my reply, but you will notice that he does not ask the question which you and I understood he would ask, or, rather, that he asks an additional question, namely, whether in my opinion Mr. Harris answers the requirements of a United States Senator. I do not think, and I am sure you do not think, that I ought to be drawn into that sort of an endorsement, and yet if Mr. Mangum prints his letter with my reply, I will seem to dodge the question and, therefore, cast a doubt upon my opinion of Harris' qualifications. Can you think of any way of straightening this out? Perhaps you would be willing to forward the enclosed letter to Mr. Mangum, suggesting my quandary and perhaps suggesting a modification of his letter before it is published.   Faithfully yours,   Woodrow Wilson

TLS (Letterpress Books, WP, DLC).

E N C L O S U R E

To Franc Mangum[1]

My dear Mr. Mangum: [The White House] 19 January, 1918

May I not thank you for your letter of January twelfth with its interesting enclosure?[2] The poll of the Georgia newspapers to which you refer is certainly most interesting and is certainly a very fine tribute to the character and ability of Mr. Harris.

I am surprised and distressed to learn that any question has ever arisen as to Mr. Harris' relations with the present national administration. I am sure that no doubt has ever entered his mind, for he and I have always maintained relations of the most delightful confidence, and he has always accorded the administration the most hearty and genuine support whenever opportunity offered and in whatever way that was possible and compatible with his present official duties.   Sincerely yours,   Woodrow Wilson

TLS (Letterpress Books, WP, DLC).
  [1] Editor of the Americus *Times-Recorder*.
  [2] Both Mangum's letter and its enclosure are missing.

From Samuel Gompers

Sir: Washington, D. C. Jan. 19, 1918.

Of course I know that you are fully abreast of the conditions which prevail in Russia, and the changes which are constantly occurring. I am sure that you are aware that the constituent assembly is in session in Russia now. Information conveyed to me is that the bolshiviki is losing power and control and has only a small minority in that assembly.

You are also aware of the fact that Great Britain has sent a greeting to the assembly.

That the real, democratic, practical revolutionists of Russia, men who have made the revolution, are standing firmly for the democratization of Russia, and for the proper orderly government of that country. I am informed on good authority that the six radical daily papers of Petrograd are opposed to the bolshiviki and for democratic institutions.

I trust you will not regard a suggestion as a presumption on my part, but I am firmly persuaded that a message of greeting from you to the constituent assembly of Russia would be a wholesome influence upon the Russian people and help to bring order out of the chaos of the hour. Whatever course you may pursue with this letter or suggestion will be regarded by me as confidential and satisfying. My only purpose is to be helpful in service.

Very respectfully yours,   Saml. Gompers.

TLS (WP, DLC).

From Robert Scott Lovett

My dear Mr. President: Washington January 19, 1918.

Before sending the letter, of which a copy is enclosed, to the Chairman of the Council of National Defense,[1] I beg to have your permission. I need not reiterate the reasons. I do wish to repeat, however, that I will not retire at a time that will cause the least embarrassment.

I have no desire except to serve—and to serve wherever I can be of most service—in this great emergency; and I greatly regret that I seem to have done so little.

I beg to assure you of my unbounded admiration for the very great way in which you are carrying the world burden that has fallen upon you, and of my readiness to respond if at any time you should think I can be of greater service than in the performance of the regular duties to which I am planning to return.

Very respectfully,   R. S. Lovett

TLS (WP, DLC).
    [1] R. S. Lovett to NDB, Jan. 19, 1918, TCL (WP, DLC). Lovett asked Baker to accept his resignation as Priorities Commissioner of the Priorities Committee of the War Industries Board. He wrote that it was necessary for him to return to his duties as chairman of the executive committee of the Union Pacific Railroad since important decisions were about to be made by that committee. Moreover, Lovett added, the Priorities Committee was now so well organized that his services could be readily dispensed with.

From George Foster Peabody

New York, Jan. 19, 1918.

Now that the absurd newspaper hysteria and bombardment is subsiding may I intrude to express my appreciation of Dr. Garfield's dignity and courage through this unreasoning performance. I did not need your clear calm words to understand the necessity. I deem it absolutely essential to resist the effort at newspaper government such as is indicated in Washington despatch in today's TIMES respecting a congressional reorganization.[1] Nothing would better condition in my judgement. I reach Shoreham Hotel Sunday night for conference Monday with Reserve Board on routine bank matters. Shall be glad if I can be of any service in any way.

Geo. Foster Peabody.

T telegram (WP, DLC).
    [1] "Moves for a War Cabinet," *New York Times*, Jan. 19, 1918. This dispatch, datelined Washington, January 18, stated that Congress, especially the Senate, had been so upset by Garfield's order and revelations of inefficiency in the conduct of the war that many members, both Democratic and Republican, were now convinced that Congress had to take drastic action to improve the situation. Therefore, the Senate Committee on Military Affairs had, on January 18, reported a bill to create a director of munitions who would have complete charge of all procurement for both the army and navy. Furthermore, the same committee was at work upon a bill to create a so-called "super-Cabinet" or "War Cabinet." It would be directly responsible to the President and have powers "superseding those of the Secretary of War, the Secretary of the Navy, and other statutory officers of the Government who have to do with the conduct of the war." Some members, the dispatch continued, believed that the group should be made up of the Secretaries of War, of the Navy, and of the Treasury, together with three persons appointed from outside the government. Others strongly opposed the inclusion of Baker in the "War Cabinet" and insisted that the President "add to his aid distinguished men of proved ability."
    Moreover, according to the report, the senators who favored the measure were encouraged by "word brought to them today that President Wilson did not object to the formation of a body such as that proposed." Many senators of both parties, the dispatch went on, believed that the President should sit regularly with the proposed "War Cabinet," on the ground that he should "keep in direct touch with what was being done in the War Department, the Navy Department, and the other activities of government." Their desire for such presidential participation grew out of the belief that the Chief Executive had held himself "aloof from those with whom he should consult." The report also asserted that the Senate, through its power to advise and consent to appointments to the proposed cabinet, would reject the nomination of any man who did not measure up to "the standard of statesmanship" which the Senate had in mind. Members of Congress of both parties were being emboldened to take such drastic measures, the dispatch went on, because they had decided that the country lacked confidence in "men who have a large share in the conduct of the war." "They want bigger men . . . who should be chosen without regard to political considerations."
    The bill to create a director of munitions was a revision of one introduced by Senator Chamberlain on January 4 (S. 3311), which had provided for a Department of Munitions,

whose head would be a member of the regular cabinet during the emergency. S. 3311 is described in detail in "Bill before Senate for Munition Chief," *ibid.*, Jan. 5, 1918. Chamberlain introduced his bill to establish a "War Cabinet" (S. 3583) on January 21. The "War Cabinet" proposed in this measure did not include members of the existing cabinet. The full text of S. 3583 is printed in *Cong. Record*, 65th Cong., 2d sess., pp. 1077-78.

The Chamberlain bills were most directly the result of the continuing investigation of the administration's conduct of the war by the Senate Committee on Military Affairs, whose chairman was of course Chamberlain. The investigation had been making headlines since it began in mid-December 1917, most notably during an extended confrontation between Baker and his Senate critics from January 10 to 12 in which the Secretary of War ably defended his policies and leadership. For an extensive narrative of the investigation and the resulting legislative proposals, see Seward W. Livermore, *Politics Is Adjourned: Woodrow Wilson and the War Congress, 1916-1918* (Middletown, Conn., 1966), pp. 65-104.

From Harry Augustus Garfield

Dear Mr. President: [Washington] January 19, 1918

I think it is wise to comply with the suggestion of the theatre men. Mr. Tumulty advised me last night that a shift of the closing day to Tuesday will be satisfactory to the profession. I am issuing an order to that effect.   Faithfully yours,   H. A. Garfield

TLS (WP, DLC).

From the Diary of Josephus Daniels

1918 Saturday 19 January

Talked with Swanson about bill to create a Super War Cabinet & Minister of Munitions. We went to see Baker & agreed to see the President and fight the proposition. The President has his blood up & in a veto message would say some things. He has all the nerve any man needs. . . .

Conferred with Polk who sent suggested message to the President that Japan & England be asked each to send one ship alternately to Vladivostock & Japan to withdraw all but one now there so as to keep Russia from feeling allies were disposed to make invasion. Will Japan agree? She takes it for granted she is to have full power in the Pacific

A Statement[1]

The White House 20 January, 1918.

The President, Commander-in-chief of the Army and Navy, following the reverent example of his predecessors, desires and enjoins the orderly observance of the Sabbath by the officers and men in the military and naval service of the United States. The importance for man and beast of the prescribed weekly rest, the sacred rights of Christian soldiers and sailors, a becoming deference to the best sentiment of a Christian people, and a due regard for the Divine Will demand that Sunday labor in the army and navy be reduced to the measure of strict necessity. Such an observance of Sunday is dictated by the best traditions of our people and by the convictions of all who look to Divine Providence for guidance and protection, and, in repeating in this Order the language of President Lincoln, the President is confident that he is speaking alike to the hearts and to the consciences of those under his authority.

Woodrow Wilson

T MS (Letterpress Books, WP, DLC).
¹ This statement, published in the *Official Bulletin*, II (Jan. 22, 1918), 1, was inspired by Duncan James McMillan to JPT, Jan. 10, 1918, TLS (WP, DLC). McMillan, the General Secretary of the New York Sabbath Committee, reminded Tumulty that he had written to the President in the preceding April (the letter is missing) and had urged Wilson to follow the precedent set by Washington, Lincoln, Harrison, and McKinley by issuing "an Order or an expression or wish in regard to Sabbath Observance in the Army and Navy." McMillan's committee now wished to issue a brochure to be sent to the commanding officers of the army and navy and to Y.M.C.A. quarters in the various camps. He enclosed, "as a sort of reminder," a printed leaflet containing Lincoln's General Order of November 15, 1862, which had ordered the observance of the Sabbath by the armed services. It was this order, itself inspired by the New York Sabbath Committee, which Wilson quoted almost verbatim in his own statement, from the beginning through the words "strict necessity."

To Newton Diehl Baker, with Enclosures

My dear Mr. Secretary,   The White House. 20 January, 1918.

I have one fear about this. It is that, whatever they may promise now, the British will, when it comes to the pinch, in fact cut us off from some part of the tonnage they will promise us for our general programme in order themselves to make sure of these battalions; or will promise us less for the general programme than they would otherwise have given, had their plan for these reenforcements for their own front not been accepted. I believe, therefore, that, while we must acquiesce in this plan for battalions to recruit their own divisions, it would be wise to caution General Bliss a little more explicitly about these risks. He has the general shipping programme in his hands and will understand.

Faithfully Yours,   Woodrow Wilson

WWTLS (N. D. Baker Papers, DLC).

From Newton Diehl Baker

My dear Mr. President: Washington. January 19, 1918.

I sent you a few days ago two dispatches from General Pershing with regard to the use of additional American troops. The plan, you will recall, was worked out by General Pershing in conference with General Robertson, the British Chief of Staff, and had the approval of the French General Staff and of General Pershing. I enclose herewith a War College memorandum on the subject,[1] from which you will observe that my military advisers here approve the project.

In short, the suggestion is that 150 battalions of United States troops (50 regiments of Infantry) be transported by the British, in their own tonnage, and assigned by them 3 battalions to each of their divisions, to enable them to keep their divisions at a strength of 12 rather than 9 battalions. General Pershing's stipulation is that these troops are to be transported by the British without interfering with or lessening the tonnage aid which they are to give us to carry out our own military program as agreed upon with General Bliss.

By taking 50 regiments practically equally from the Regular Army, the National Guard, and the National Army, no discrimination would be introduced into our own service. These regiments would, of course, have to be armed by the British in order to cooperate with their forces. They would, therefore, take with them only their clothing equipment. The tonnage cargo requirements for the sustenance of these 50 regiments would be great, if we had to arm and supply them. It would therefore not be practicable for us to send these troops (about 150,000 men), in addition to our own military program of 24 divisions, until after July 1. Meanwhile, if they are sent now they will be of material assistance to the British, will be trained with the British forces, and will make a substantial contribution on our part to the military strength of the Allies on the Western front. The French General Staff has approved this project, their compensation doubtless being derived from the fact that our divisions already in France, and to go to France under our own military program, will take over a part of the line actually defended now by the French, thus relieving French divisions which can be distributed among the remaining divisions, further saturating their own defense with men.

As this project has the approval of General Pershing and of our own Staff, and is in the judgment of both the British and French General Staffs a wise course, I recommend that it be adopted. I attach hereto a cablegram which I have drafted to send to General

Bliss, feeling that as he is our Chief of Staff the arrangements for this ought to be worked out by him and the necessary stipulations put into the agreement to protect the points urged by General Pershing.

The only feeling likely to be aroused on this subject would be in our country, with regard to the distribution of American regiments under British general officers. Under normal circumstances this feeling would not probably arise, since it would be deemed a counsel of wisdom to have our battalions associated with veteran British troops under experienced division and brigade commanders; but when we select these regiments to send them abroad it will necessitate a reorganization of some of our own divisions and will leave a surplus of some division and brigade commanders, both in the Regular Army and the National Guard, who will no doubt complain at the breaking up of their commands. We will endeavor to absorb these surplus officers by assigning the best of them in the places of men found physically disqualified or otherwise relieved for lack of military efficiency.

Under all the circumstances, I think the military thing to do ought to be done, and if it meets with your approval I will send General Bliss, who arrived to-day in England, the cablegram attached hereto.   Respectfully yours,   Newton D. Baker

TLS (N. D. Baker Papers, DLC).
 ¹ Not found.

E N C L O S U R E   I I

Washington, January [19] 21, 1918.

Bliss, c/o Amembassy, London.
Number 14, January 21, Confidential.

Paragraph. General Pershing cables us the results of a conference held with General Robertson of the British General staff on the subject of providing additional men for British divisions. The proposal is that we shall supply 150 battalions to be transported by the British and to be distributed by them 3 battalions to each British division, with the understanding, first, that the battalions could be recalled for service with our own divisions should it be determined wise to do so; second, that the transportation of these troops shall not interfere with the assistance in tonnage to be provided by the British to carry out our own military program. This project has the approval of General Pershing and the French General Staff. You are authorized to make necessary arrangements with the British Government to carry the plan into execution. I infer from cablegram received from General Pershing today that he is in London. Please discuss the matter with him before acting. In order to avoid any disappointment with regard to our own program, which you are arranging, the utmost care should be taken to have an explicit understanding that these battalions and their transportation are contingent upon the supply of tonnage to us for our agreed minimum military effort. Baker.   McCain.

TC telegram (WDR, RG 407, World War I Cable Section, DNA).

To Robert Lansing, with Enclosure

My dear Mr. Secretary,   The White House. 20 January, 1918.

Here is the ever-recurring question, How shall we deal with the Bolsheviki? This particular suggestion seems to me to have something in it worth considering, and I am writing to ask what your own view is.   Faithfully Yours,   W.W.

WWTLI (WP, DLC).

ENCLOSURE

Copenhagen via London. Jan. 15, 1918.

From Copenhagen: "1823, January 14, 2 p.m.

Confidential. I venture to submit the following views with which I concur.

It is the opinion here in certain quarters—the naval attache[1] who spent some time in Russia and the informant mentioned in my telegram 1803, of January 9, 3 p.m.[2] being particularly impressed— that the first practical step towards combating German intrigue in Russia should be through the establishment by one of the Allies of relations with the Bolshevic de facto Government, the others holding aloof and confining their interests to the one chosen. Teutonic influence could thus be better counteracted, the participation in certain conferences might be realized, communication with particular parts of Russia established, courier service facilitated, etc. Should the Bolshevic Government prove more long lived than anticipated the Allies' delegate would have a voice in affairs, as soon as they fell, the others could take up the work.

At present the Allies have apparently no definite connection with the de facto Government, are cut off from the Ukraine, Finotti [Finnish] and other separatist movements while some Austro Germans have entered into direct relations with each group and consequently are enabled to pursue their plans unhindered.

Should such a course be deemed advisable is not the United States from tradition, recent entry on the scene, Latin America experience with de facto Governments and especially in the light of the President's recent message, the best suited among Germany's opponents to undertake the task. Grant Smith." Page.[3]

T telegram (WP, DLC).
[1] Lt. Col. James Carson Breckinridge, U.S.M.C.
[2] Ulysses Grant-Smith (Counselor and Chargé of the legation in Copenhagen) to RL, Jan. 9, 1918, FR 1918, Russia, I, 332-35. This dispatch consisted of a statement by "the informant," Maj. Gen. Prince Michael Cantacuzene, on political, economic, and military conditions in Russia, from which he had just fled.
[3] "In regard to this suggestion, I do not think we should be the ones to open intercourse with the Lenin crowd[.] Francis has been firm in avoiding any suggestion of recognition & I believe in supporting him in his course. If France or England wish to do this let them propose it. In view of the news today I think any step would be at present unwise as being hostile to Constituent Assembly." RL to F. L. Polk, Jan. 21, 1918, ALS (R. Lansing Papers, NjP). The "news today" was that of the dissolution of the Russian constituent assembly, or constitutional convention, on January 19 by the Bolsheviks. For a summary of this event, its background, and the American reaction, see Kennan, Russia Leaves the War, pp. 343-63.

To Robert Lansing, with Enclosure

My dear Mr. Secretary,   The White House. 20 January, 1918.

The suggestion made by the Japanese government in this despatch seems to me very significant of possible coming events, and I would be very much obliged to you if you would tell me what reply you think should be made to it.

The fact that the Japanese are sending a larger naval force to Vladivostok than they at first led us to expect makes an uncomfortable impression on me, particularly in view of this latest request.

It seems to me clear that we should show very clearly in our reply that we should look upon military action in that quarter with distinct disapproval.   Faithfully Yours,   W.W.

WWTLI (SDR, RG 59, 861.00/985½, DNA).

E N C L O S U R E

Tokio Jan. 17, 1918.

In order that Admiral Knight might have benefit first hand information he joined me yesterday in talks with my colleagues the French, the British, and The Russian Ambassadors.[1] Subsequently I had informal conversation with the Minister of Foreign Affairs; from these talks and other reliable information we agreed on the following facts: As a result of requests from the Consuls growing out of the fear that serious disorders, reported to have occurred elsewhere, might be repeated at Vladivostok the British Government and the Japanese Government despatched war vessels to that port. Neither before or since their arrival have disorders occurred and the messages received to date report everything perfectly quiet. While deeming additional ships unnecessary the Japanese Government would have no objection whatever to the presence of BROOK-LYN at Vladivostok. If, however, conditions should hereafter require occupation of Vladivostok and the lines of the Chinese Eastern and Amur Railways, Japan asks that this task be left to her alone and has definitely requested the British Government to agree to this as evidence of confidence of the Allies in her good faith, and is greatly pleased at reported refusal of our Government to a suggested plan joint occupation if conditions should require more drastic action.

Would suggest for consideration of the Department that the BROOKLYN be directed to remain at Yokohama to be in readiness to proceed to Vladivostok if conditions there become threatening. This would leave Admiral Knight in a position to act with but little delay, and would also leave the United States free from the appearance of joining in a demonstration to coerce the authorities in control at Vladivostok at a time when no necessity for such coercion is apparent.   Morris.

T telegram (SDR, RG 59, 861.00/967, DNA).
    [1] That is, Eugène Louis Georges Regnault, Sir William Conyngham Greene, and Vasilii Nikolaevich Krupenskii.

To Robert Lansing, with Enclosure

My dear Mr. Secretary,   The White House. 20 January, 1918.

I think the suggestion contained in this despatch thoroughly worth heeding, *if* we can get a corroboration of the facts stated, particularly with regard to the military supplies being available for the Polish forces referred to.

Will you not be kind enough to try to obtain corroboration, and in the mean time to sound the British, French, and Italian governments as to whether they would join us in such a declaration as to an independent Poland as the one contained in my recent address to the Congress?   Faithfully Yours,   W.W.

WWTLI (SDR, RG 59, 860C.00/C.F., DNA).

ENCLOSURE

Copenhagen. Jan. 17, 1918.

1835. Strictly confidential. Memorandum of statements relative to conditions in Poland by an American recently arrived from Russia[1]: "There is at Minsk the headquarters of the Polish army. The military authorities there have formed a committee which determines the general policy for the Polish people in so far as the Government is concerned. This committee is composed of Russian Poles. It appoints the General who shall be in command of the entire Polish army; the size of the army is in the neighborhood of sixty thousand men. It also determines policies which shall be followed in so far as they may have relation to the people of Poland. These are more or less curtailed by the Germans. It is expected Joseph Pitsudski [Pilsudski] was the head of the revolutionary movement in Poland to throw off the German yoke; he was imprisoned and is there at this date. He had organized at that time a movement for the overthrow of the Germans and German Government in Poland. The movement, however, was not stirred up and his agents still exist. The names of the agents and everything connected with them can be found in Minsk. The Polish army is now being broken up by the Bolsheviks and the Germans are offering every man who will disarm a return to Poland, but the committee in Minsk will keep track of everyone who does this and will keep his name for the future in order that the matter may be taken up again.

The committee says that there is just one thing that they require to precipitate a revolution in entire Poland against the Germans and that is the combined declaration of England, France and America that they will stand by as Allies for an independent Poland. If the Allies will do this, the committee says, (and if this information be gotten back to the committee) they will precipitate a revolution in entire Poland at any time decided on. It could be made in connection with the spring drive on the western front; they suggested that perhaps February would be the best time, but that they would leave this to the Allies. What is wanted is the guarantee of an independent Poland from the Allies.

Mr. Grant Smith: Where will the revolutionists procure their arms and ammunition?

Mr. Lewis: No definite place was given, but they said that they had them.

On the other hand the German garrison in Poland is very slim and an uprising would cause great confusion and the Germans would have to change their plans in attempting to put it down.

The Poles in Petrograd in the German pay on [in] the Bolshevik Government are as follows: Kostowski, Mandlebaum, Cedarbaum

(Letzcsuki) Jabtouski. At Minsk the editor of the Bolshevik paper is a M. Berson.[2]

The foregoing is made by James H. Lewis of the Y.M.C.A. who begs that his name and that of the society be held strictly confidential in this connection. Grant Smith.

American Legation.

T telegram (SDR, RG 59, 860C.00/C.F., DNA).
[1] James H. Lewis, identified below.
[2] "Mandlebaum" was probably Bernard Mandelbaum, a leader of the Polish Social Democratic party. "Cedarbaum" may have been Henryk Stanislaw Cederbaum, a lawyer and publicist. "Berson" may have been Stanislaw Berson, later a leader of the Polish Communist party. The other persons cannot be identified.

To George Earle Chamberlain

My dear Sir: [The White House] 20 January, 1918

You are reported in the New York World of this morning as having said at a luncheon in New York yesterday:

"The military establishment of America has fallen down; there is no use to be optimistic about a thing that does not exist; it almost stopped functioning. Why? Because of inefficiency in every bureau and in every department of the Government of the United States. I speak not as a Democrat but as an American citizen."[1]

I would be very much obliged if you would tell me whether you were correctly quoted. I do not like to comment upon the statements made before learning from you yourself whether you actually made them.   Very truly yours,   [Woodrow Wilson]

CCL (WP, DLC).
[1] Chamberlain spoke at a luncheon given in his honor and that of Representative Julius Kahn by the National Security League at the Hotel Astor on January 19. Elihu Root presided, and the other speakers were Kahn and Theodore Roosevelt. Some 1,900 persons attended the event. Actually, most of Chamberlain's speech consisted of an attack on the American tradition of opposition to a standing army. He also recalled his long-standing advocacy of universal military training. Following the paragraph quoted by Wilson in the above letter, Chamberlain urged the passage of his bills to provide for a ministry of munitions and a "War Cabinet." The full texts of all the speeches delivered on this occasion appear in the *New York Times*, Jan. 20, 1918. See also the New York *World*, Jan. 20, 1918. The *World* printed the paragraph quoted by Wilson in bold-face type at the beginning of its article. For a summary of the furor which this paragraph evoked, see Livermore, *Politics Is Adjourned*, pp. 91-93.

To Josephus Daniels

My dear Mr. Secretary,   The White House. 20 January, 1918.

This seems to me a serious case of the kind I was one day speaking to you about, this [that] is, of a naval attache assuming political and almost ambassadorial authority.

I would be very much obliged to you if you would be kind enough to get into consultation with the Secretary of State about this and would arrange for the immediate recall of this particular attache, unless there are circumstances in the case that I know nothing of.

I do not know [w]ho the Professor Cusachs spoken of is. If we have any authority over him, he ought to come back, too, and come at once.[1]

I know that you agree with me in principle about these cases and, therefore, make this very definite suggestion.

Faithfully Yours,   Woodrow Wilson

WWTLI (J. Daniels Papers, DLC).
[1] The enclosures with Wilson's letter were a number of documents written by, or relating to the activities of, Capt. Benton Clark Decker, U.S.N., Naval Attaché at the American embassy in Madrid. These materials, most notably J. E. Willard to RL, Jan. 17, 1918, TC telegram (J. Daniels Papers, DLC), suggested that Decker and his assistant, Lt. Comdr. Carlos Valérien Cusachs, U.S.N., formerly an instructor at the United States Naval Academy, not only disagreed with the policies pursued by Ambassador Willard but had made their disagreement known in conversations with both Americans and Spaniards in Madrid. In particular, Willard accused Cusachs of having intimated to a Spanish newspaper editor that the United States might be seeking a naval base in Spain and that he, Cusachs, would see that this plan was abandoned. Willard asked either that Decker be instructed to conform to the policies of the State Department and embassy or that he, Willard, be permitted to resign.

From Thomas Watt Gregory

Sir: Washington, D. C. January 20, 1918.

In reply to your note of January 16, 1918, concerning information received by you of a concerted plot to destroy American and British shipping in every port, shipyard and at sea on January 22, 1918, I have the honor to advise you that Mr. J. Edward Guelph, the man who sent this piece of information to you, has heretofore come to the attention of the Department on one or two occasions, by offering information of plots of various kinds. Some investigation of him was made in 1915 and again early in 1917, and since the receipt of your letter further inquiries have been made. I quote for your information two telegrams received from the Agent in Charge of the office of the Bureau of Investigation at Los Angeles:

"Replying to your telegram re John Edward Guelph mental condition reported normal except by Williams, probably best acquainted Guelph of persons interviewed who states heavy drinker. Guelph undoubtedly has extensive and intimate knowledge European political conditions. Guelph apparently has no following this vicinity and is not taken seriously by any persons interviewed. Unable see Van Denberg or McDonald both out of city. Dr. Allison close personal friend thinks little weight should be given this. Will make further investigation and can arrange meeting Guelph personally if desired. He called this office few days ago reported minor matters."

"Replying to your telegram Guelph just returned from his home Sierra Madre where had three hours interview he doing practically all the talking. Am satisfied he has no definite information and is suffering from dementia manifesting itself as grossly exaggerated egotist. Dr. Roads accompanied me and heard conversation and agrees my conclusions. Guelph resides cheap rundown summer hotel style frame building surrounded by dilapidated tent houses. He talked continuously to us but adduced no information, facts or conclusions unobtainable by any close student of European and Indian questions. Stated he could not reveal source information concerning destruction shipping No OK (?), but that it came from various people in divers foreign countries and not from anywhere United States. Could not give details as to how destruction was to be effected but wanted change subject this matter mentioned. He believes himself predestined fulfil old biblical prophecy and unite the two royal lines and is given to prophesying himself. I believe this warning is one of his prophecies and has no foundation outside disordered mind trying convince world how great a man he is. Do not consider any reliance whatever be placed his statements."

Despite the apparent unreliability of the man who has given the information concerning this plot, it seemed advisable to send telegraphic instructions to agents of this Department at every port to take all reasonable extra precautions to prevent the consummation of any such plot in cooperation with the Collectors of Customs and other interested officials and citizens. These instructions were sent prior to the receipt of the second telegram quoted above.

Respectfully,   T. W. Gregory

TLS (WP, DLC).

To the Duke of Devonshire

Your Excellency: [The White House] 21 January, 1918

I very much appreciate your letter of January fifteenth.[1] It was a real pleasure to Mrs. Wilson and myself to have an opportunity to see you and the Duchess of Devonshire[2] at our own table for a little while, and I hope that this pleasant meeting will be followed by others.

I welcome your suggestion very heartily that we shall write directly to each other if occasion arises to do so. You may be sure that I would be very glad to hear from you directly at any time.

I note your kind desire to have the Secretary of State visit Canada. I know that he would take great pleasure in doing so, for he has spoken to me about it, and he and I will keep your kind desire in mind in case it should be possible for him to get away from the duties which are at present so exacting here.

Mrs. Wilson joins me in the kindest regards and best wishes to yourself and the Duchess of Devonshire.

Cordially and sincerely yours,   Woodrow Wilson

TLS (Letterpress Books, WP, DLC).
[1] The Duke of Devonshire to WW, Jan. 15, 1918, Vol. 45.
[2] Evelyn Emily Mary Petty-Fitzmaurice Cavendish, Duchess of Devonshire.

To George Foster Peabody

My dear Mr. Peabody: [The White House] 21 January, 1918

Your telegram was immensely appreciated. The storm evidently has passed and the skies begin to clear, but how unnecessary this all was!   Cordially and sincerely yours,   Woodrow Wilson

TLS (Letterpress Books, WP, DLC).

To Robert Scott Lovett

My dear Judge Lovett: [The White House] 21 January, 1918

I need not tell you how it distresses me to think of your leaving Washington and the duties which you have so acceptably and efficiently performed, but I remember that you had told me when you came here that you did not think that you could in conscience stay much beyond the first of January, and I know how exceedingly important it is in furtherance of the new railway administration that we should have the benefit of your counsel and assistance in the operation and care of the Union Pacific, and therefore I do not feel at liberty, deeply as I regret the necessity, to ask you to withhold the letter which you been kind enough to submit to me indefinitely.

But I am going to take the liberty of asking you to postpone it for a few days until we can relieve the hysteria which has taken hold for the time being of the United States Senate by coming to calmer counsels and enabling everybody concerned to understand the real facts of the situation.

With warm regard and real gratitude to you for your generous support and belief in my efforts,

Cordially and sincerely yours,   Woodrow Wilson

TLS (Letterpress Books, WP, DLC).

To Samuel Gompers

My dear Mr. Gompers: The White House 21 January, 1918

I liked your suggestion about a message to the Russian Constituent Assembly, but apparently the reckless Bolsheviki have already broken it up because they did not control it. It is distressing to see things so repeatedly go to pieces there.

               Cordially and sincerely yours,   Woodrow Wilson

TLS (S. Gompers Corr., AFL-CIO-Ar).

To Charles William Eliot

My dear Doctor Eliot: The White House 21 January, 1918

Thank you for your letter of January seventeenth. You may be sure that I wrote the passages about Russia in my recent address to Congress from the heart. I wish most earnestly that it were possible to find some way to help, but as soon as we have thought out a working plan there is a new dissolution of the few crystals that had formed there.

Just at present I am in the thick of Congressional matters, but I hope that if Doctor Peabody is to come in this direction soon he will do me the favor of letting me know in order that I may have the pleasure of having an interview with him.

               Cordially and sincerely yours,   Woodrow Wilson

TLS (C. W. Eliot Papers, MH-Ar).

From George Earle Chamberlain

My dear Mr. President: [Washington] January 21, 1918.

I received last evening your favor of the 20th instant, in which you advise me that I was quoted in the New York World of same date with your letter as follows:

"The military establishment of America has fallen down; there is no use to be optimistic about a thing that does not exist; it has almost stopped functioning. Why? Because of inefficiency in every Bureau and in every Department of the Government of the United States. I speak not as a Democrat but as an American citizen."

You desire to know if I am correctly quoted, inasmuch as you do not like to comment upon the statements made before learning from me whether I actually made them.

In reply permit me to say that the words quoted are substantially those used by me. My address on the occasion referred to was extemporaneous and without notes, but the New York Times of yesterday morning purports to give a verbatim report of all the addresses made, and I believe the report made is substantially correct. In that I am quoted as saying, in part:

"Now, in conclusion, and I have only touched a few of the high spots, let me say that the military establishment of America has fallen down. There is no use to be optimistic about a thing that does not exist. It has almost stopped functioning, my friends. Why? Because of inefficiency in every Department of the Government of the United States. We are trying to work it out. I speak not as a Democrat, but as an American citizen."

You will note that there is very little difference between the two reports, and, in view of the fuller report in the Times, I am inclined to believe it correctly quotes me.

But, Mr. President, may I beg that you will do me the honor to read the whole of what I said in order that the part quoted may have its proper setting. I only had twenty minutes allotted me, and in that brief time undertook to show that since the Battle of Bunker Hill we had never had a proper military organization or policy, and that our troubles now are largely due to that fact. I was only discussing the military policy, or lack of such policy, from the earliest days of the Republic, and immediately following the language last quoted, I said:

"We are trying, my friends, and I have burned the midnight oil in an effort to do it—we have tried to centralize the power of supplying the Army in one man who can say 'No,' and has the nerve to say 'No,' when the time comes to say it. We have reported a bill, following the experience of Great Britain and France, creating a Director of Munitions for this purpose. We have gone one step further, and we have provided a bill for the creation of a Cabinet of War, whose duty it shall be to lay out what we never have had—and haven't now—a program to carry on this war to a successful conclusion. My friends, this is not an Administration measure; it is an American measure and comes from Republicans and Democrats both."

All present understood the criticism, and you will note that ex-President Roosevelt in his speech shortly following mine made substantially the same criticism of conditions during the Spanish-American War, although as he said, "It was waged by an Administration of which I was a part and in which I afterward became even more closely connected."

I have been connected with the Committee on Military Affairs of the Senate ever since I have been a member of the Senate, and have taken a very deep interest in military legislation and I believe

I know something about the deficiencies in the military establishment. Since Congress convened, the Committee have been diligently at work, endeavoring to find out actual conditions and to find some remedy for recognized or proven deficiencies in our military system. The testimony of witnesses in and out of the establishment clearly establishes the fact, Mr. President, that there are inefficiencies in the system that ought to be remedied for a proper prosecution of the war, and, further, that there are and have been inefficients connected with the administration of a disjointed and uncoordinated establishment. So feeling and so believing, I have felt it my duty to speak out, in the hope that defects in the military code may be cured, and inefficients later weeded out. I will be glad to join with other members of the Committee and go over the situation with you at any time, if you desire it, and review the testimony, which, taken in connection with an inherited deficient system, led me to the conclusion expressed in my short extemporaneous address to which you call my attention.

I have the honor to remain,
Yours very sincerely,   Geo E   Chamberlain

TLS (WP, DLC).

A Press Release

[Jan. 21, 1918]

The following statement was issued at the White House last night in reply to charges made by Senator Chamberlain in an address in New York on Saturday evening, to the effect that there "is inefficiency in every bureau and department of the Government of the United States."

When the President's attention was called to the speech made by Senator Chamberlain at a luncheon in New York on Saturday, he immediately inquired of Senator Chamberlain whether he had been correctly reported, and upon ascertaining from the Senator that he had been, the President felt it his duty to make the following statement:

Senator Chamberlain's statement as to the present inaction and ineffectiveness of the Government is an astonishing and absolutely unjustifiable distortion of the truth. As a matter of fact, the War Department has performed a task of unparalleled magnitude and difficulty with extraordinary promptness and efficiency. There have been delays and disappointments and partial miscarriages of plans, all of which have been drawn into the foreground and exaggerated by the investigations which have been in progress since the Congress assembled—investigations which drew indispensable officials of the department constantly away from their work and officers from their commands and contributed a great deal to such delay and confusion as had inevitably arisen. But, by comparison with what has been accomplished, these things, much as they were to be regretted, were insignificant, and no mistake has been made which has been repeated.

Nothing helpful or likely to speed or facilitate the war tasks of the Government has come out of such criticism and investigation. I understand that reorganizations by legislation are to be proposed— I have not been consulted about them and have learned of them only at second hand—but their proposal came after effective measures of reorganization had been thoughtfully and maturely perfected, and inasmuch as these measures have been the result of experience, they are much more likely than any others to be effective, if the Congress will but remove the few statutory obstacles of rigid departmental organization which stand in their way. The legislative proposals I have heard of would involve long additional delays and turn our experience into mere lost motion. My association and constant conference with the Secretary of War have taught me to regard him as one of the ablest public officials I have ever known. The country will soon learn whether he or his critics understand the business in hand.

To add, as Senator Chamberlain did, that there is inefficiency in every department and bureau of the Government is to show such ignorance of actual conditions as to make it impossible to attach any importance to his statement. I am bound to infer that that statement sprang out of opposition to the administration's whole policy rather than out of any serious intention to reform its practice.[1]

Printed in the *Official Bulletin*, II (Jan. 22, 1918), 1-2.
  [1] There are WWT and CLST drafts of this document in the C. L. Swem Coll., NjP.

Two Letters from Newton Diehl Baker

My dear Mr. President   Washington January 21, 1918

I have just read, with infinite gratitude, your generous public expression of confidence in the War Department and in me.

As I know the impersonal quality of your purpose I know that you will not keep me here a moment longer than is wise and I can well imagine that a time may come when you will find it possible to advance the cause and consolidate the sentiment of the country by making a change either by sending me to other service or to none. As my whole desire is to serve, not in my way but in yours,

I shall neither question nor misunderstand what you think best to have me do.

Gratefully yours,   Newton D. Baker

ALS (WP, DLC).

My dear Mr. President: Washington. January 21, 1918.

Prior to my talk with you a day or two ago about Mr. Gutzon Borglum, you will remember that I had already directed that no information be placed at his disposal which would be dangerous if indiscreetly used. Today I learn that Mr. Borglum has been seeing a large number of people, exhibiting to some of them, at least, the letter signed by you,[1] and making seemingly irresponsible statements about the Aircraft Board and the aircraft program. One of his statements is to the effect that he is endeavoring to select suitable men to replace the Aircraft Board; and another is that he is going to organize a stock company for the rapid production of aircraft, he being a stockholder in it but his stock held in some other name, and that he is to get the designs for the aircraft which the company is to manufacture by virtue of his authority to examine the records of the Signal Corps. Both of these statements were made to a friend of Vice-President Marshall who made a full report to him on the subject, which I saw.

As I understand it, Mr. Borglum intends to make a report to you, covering whatever inquiries he has made, but the strong probability is that his over-wrought state of mind will lead him to seek publicity for his report, and that, of course, would be a very serious matter, since it would be predicated upon an inquiry made by virtue of your letter to him, which would give it weight even with persons who would not otherwise be disposed to rely upon his reputation as a sculptor, and it may be that vain and impossible things might be contained in his statement.

I am extremely sorry to have to suggest that you take any trouble in the matter, but I am afraid he would regard any action taken by me as at variance with the authority he thinks he has from you, and I therefore suggest that you have Mr. Tumulty send for him at your earliest convenience, and that you impress upon him the necessity of returning your letter to him, which he has not used discreetly and ought in no event to have shown to anybody; and also that you impress upon him the seriousness of any statement he may make which has not first been worked out with your approval, as any such statement might be very prejudicial to the country and helpful to the enemy. I think you probably ought to go so far as to ask him to turn over his complete files to you, so that you could examine just what he has and form some judgment as to how dangerous he is.

Respectfully yours,   Newton D. Baker

TLS (WP, DLC).
¹ WW to G. Borglum, Jan. 2, 1918, Vol. 45.

From Robert Scott Lovett, with Enclosure

My dear Mr. President: Washington January 21, 1918

The agreement with the copper producers respecting price approved by you, September 21, 1917, was by its terms to continue in effect four months. In due time before the expiration of the period, the War Industries Board gave public notice and heard the copper men upon the question of a revision of the price and terms. Upon an intimation that the Board saw no occasion to recommend to you an increase of the price, the principal copper producers requested a re-hearing, which was granted, and thereupon they urged again an increase in the price, based upon increases in the costs of production. The Board, in the meantime, had obtained from the Federal Trade Commission data in reference to the cost of production since the price was fixed in September, and while the later data furnished by the producers showed that cost of production had increased, we believed that the increases had not been sufficient to warrant an increase in the price; and we so informed the producers when they accepted our suggestion that the existing prices and arrangements be continued in effect until June 1, 1918. That is, to say, the price to be twenty-three and one-half cents per pound f.o.b. New York, subject to revision after four months, and the conditions to continue the same; namely, first, that the producers will not reduce the wages now being paid; second, that the producers will sell to the Allies and to the public copper at the same price paid by the Government, and take the necessary measures under the direction of the War Industries Board for the distribution of the copper to prevent it from falling into the hands of speculators who would increase the price to the public; and third, that the producers pledge themselves to exert every effort necessary to keep up the production of copper to the maximum of the past, so long as the war lasts.

We have not asked for a personal conference with you concerning this recommendation because it seems to us unnecessary to take your time for that purpose, if you should be willing to approve our conclusion. Of course, we hold ourselves in readiness to respond if you should wish to see us.

We enclose form of a statement which we suggest as suitable to be issued by you in case you approve of our conclusion.

Very respectfully,   R. S. Lovett

TLS (WP, DLC).

E N C L O S U R E

The President today approved the recommendation of the War Industries Board that the maximum price for copper fixed upon its recommendation by the President, and announced September 21, 1917, be continued in effect upon the same conditions until June 1, 1918. That is, to say, the maximum price to be twenty-three and one-half cents per pound f.o.b. New York, subject to revision after June 1, 1918, upon the conditions, first, that the producers will not reduce the wages now being paid; second, that the producers will sell to the Allies and to the public copper at the same price paid by the Government, and take the necessary measures under the direction of the War Industries Board for the distribution of the copper to prevent it from falling into the hands of speculators who would increase the price to the public; and third, that the producers pledge themselves to exert every effort necessary to keep up the production of copper to the maximum of the past, so long as the war lasts.

T MS (WP, DLC).

From Josephus Daniels

Dear Mr. President: Washington. Jan. 21, 1918.

Orders have been given for the recall of Prof. Cusacks from Spain and I am going fully into the matter about which you wrote me this morning.   Sincerely,   Josephus Daniels

ALS (WP, DLC).

From Elizabeth Merrill Bass, with Enclosures

My dear Mr. President: Washington, D. C. January 21st, 1918.

Feeling sure that you would not wish me to say an unnecessary word in these overburdened days, I am only going to tell you that I am having telegrams and letters from all over the United States from women expressing their appreciation of what you did in the matter of the Federal Suffrage Amendment. In a vote so close as that, everyone who did anything feels entitled to a share in the credit, but it is willingly conceded that it could not have passed but for you.

Aside from the fundamental fact, my principal rejoicing is that we managed to outplay Republican tactics in every point. Some day perhaps you will permit me to tell you the details, which are really interesting and amusing. In connection therewith, I am enclosing printed copy of the result of the Republican caucus the night before the vote was taken. As a last stroke, Mr. Theodore Roosevelt perpetrated a colossal bluff in suggesting to Chairman Wilcox that a woman be added to the Republican National Committee from every state. He knew very well, although three-fourths of his readers would not, that the National Committees had no power to enlarge themselves,—that if women should be elected to them they would have to contest for the office in accordance with the election laws of their states. I happened to remember that the Executive Committee of the Democratic National Committee, on which I sit by courtesy, would meet last Monday, and that the Republican Committee would have no meeting until the middle of February, so I suggested a resolution to the Democratic Executive Committee, placing a woman from each state on an Advisory Democratic National Committee. This was done, and the appointments are being made, and anything legal that the Republican Committee does will have to be in a mere following of Democratic Example; so the honors are with us so far.

I am enclosing you the Senate poll. We have only to change five votes there, but they are five stubborn ones. The Republican votes against suffrage in the Senate are quite as stubborn as the southern ones. For example: Senators Lodge, Weeks and Penrose. Senator Martin, Senate Leader, while against, might be influenced by you. I thought at first that Senators Saulsbury and James might take a hint from you on the matter, but I understand they are quite likely to be immovable in their opposition. I am trying to get Senator Gerry, of Rhode Island, myself, and Senator King, of the opposed list, whose opposition was based on States Rights, I was told yesterday had agreed to vote

Respectfully yours,   Elizabeth Bass

TLS (WP, DLC).

ENCLOSURE I

The Republican Conference of the House of Representatives recommends and advises that the Republican members support the Federal Suffrage Amendment in so far as they can do so consistently with their convictions and the attitude of their constituents.

CC MS (WP, DLC).

ENCLOSURE II

Three Senators are absent, Hughes, Walsh and Broussard.[1] Two are dead:[2] 94 are voting: 61 necessary to carry the Amendment.

The latest poll shows 56 for, and 35 against. 5 votes must be changed.

OPPOSED.	MOST PROBABLE TO GET.
Senator Overman	Senator Trammel
" Trammel	" Fletcher
" Fletcher	" Beckham
" Hitchcock	" Hitchcock
" James	" Gerry
" Beckham	" King
" Williams	
" Pomerene	
" Culberson	
" King (Utah)	
" Gerry (R.I.)	
" Saulsbury	

T MS (WP, DLC).
[1] That is, William Hughes of New Jersey, Thomas J. Walsh of Montana, and Robert Foligny Broussard of Louisiana, all Democrats.
[2] That is, Paul Oscar Husting of Wisconsin, a Democrat, and James Hezekiah Brady of Idaho, a Republican.

From Daniel Willard

My dear Mr. President: Baltimore, Md. January 21, 1918.

I have received your very kind letter of the 18th instant,[1] in reply to mine of January 11th, and I am glad that you have consented to relieve me, at least temporarily, as Chairman of the War Industries Board because I feel that I can be much more useful just now with the railroad.

The railroad service has been so adversely affected by the unusually severe cold weather and by other conditions that I feel that

I ought on that account to give up the work of the War Industries Board at once. However, until my successor has been appointed, I will arrange to keep in touch with the members of the Board and should it develop that there is any particular thing that I personally can or ought to do in that connection, I will, if possible, do as I would suppose you would wish me to do under the circumstances.

I note with much satisfaction your words of appreciation concerning the work which I have tried to do in the past, and the suggestion which you also make that I may be called upon again in the future, and can only say that I should consider it not only my duty but a privilege as well to serve my country in any capacity in a time like the present if called upon to do so.

Respectfully and sincerely yours,   Daniel Willard

TLS (WP, DLC).
  [1] He meant WW to D. Willard, Jan. 17, 1918.

From Edward Albert Filene

New York, Jan. 21, 1918

Will do my utmost to meet your wishes expressed in your letter regarding trade referendum, but I should have your advice regarding the manner of handling some of the difficulties of the situation as it now is   I am coming to Washington night and will call upon Secretary Tumulty for an appointment if agreeable to you.

Edward A. Filene.

T telegram (WP, DLC).

From Henry Jones Ford

My dear President Wilson: Princeton, N. J. January 21, 1918

I feel quite sure that you will not permit the Senate to take the reins out of your hands. Cannot you turn the situation to account by stating what ought really to be done to improve our system of government, assigning Congress to its proper place as a Board of Directors to whom you have a right to go direct with public business instead of lobbying with committees and caucuses. Many indications have reached me of alert public interest in this subject, and if you will give a lead to public opinion I believe you can count upon an energetic response.

Cordially and sincerely yours   Henry J. Ford

ALS (WP, DLC).

Taylor Kennerly to Joseph Patrick Tumulty

My dear Mr. Tumulty,   New York City. Jan. 21/18.

I'm a New York Sun man and what I'm going to tell you in this letter relative to a confidential conversation with Colonel Roosevelt is something the President and his political family should know.

No doubt you and others close to Mr. Wilson have your own ideas about what Mr. Roosevelt's visit to Washington means,[1] but I do believe he will try for a time, at least, to keep his real motive in the back ground. But here's our talk—judge for yourself:

Monday night I went to the Hotel Langdon, New York, to see what the colonel had to say in reply to Senator's Stone's attack.[2] I was a little surprised and disappointed that he had nothing to say. I told him as much and added: "Colonel you do not even look as if the senator's remarks have disturbed you in the least."

He replied:

"Confidentially, and I know I can trust you, I'm not worried about such men as Stone and Hearst. I can nip them in the bud any time. My mind is on bigger game now. I'm going to Washington after the man in the White House."

Then he pulled from his pocket a copy of the President's reply to Senator Chamberlain and with true Roosevelt enthusiasm asked me if I fully realized that the "real fight was on."

The remainder of our talk was of unimportant things.

I did not violate Colonel Roosevelt's confidence and write anything about what he said. That I could or would not do, but with the position the United States is in today I feel as if I would be neglecting a patriotic duty if I failed to put this information in your hands to be delivered to President Wilson. Both Mr. Burleson and Mr. Gregory are from my home city, Austin, Texas, and friends of my father.[3] They will probably also remember me, though I was very much of a cub reporter when I last saw either of them.

If some of the Democrats playing into Mr. Roosevelt's hand knew his true purpose I can't help but feel there would be a change of front. This letter, of course, if [is] confidential. You know what it means to me as a newspaper man and my connection with The Sun. Should you care to address me kindly use home address instead of office.

                    Yours truly,   Taylor Kennerly.

Taylor Kennerly,
147 West 80th. St.
New York City.

TLS (WP, DLC).
[1] Roosevelt arrived in Washington on January 22 for a four-day visit at the home of his daughter, Alice, and his son-in-law, Representative Nicholas Longworth. "I am here,"

he said in a brief statement, "to help every man who sincerely desires to speed up and make effective our preparations in this war. I shall stand by the efficient and against the inefficient man. No man is really and intelligently loyal to this country who does not take this attitude." Roosevelt conferred with members of both the Old Guard and of the progressive wing of the Republican party and also met socially with many of them at dinners in his honor given by Longworth, Senator Lodge, and Representative Joseph Medill McCormick of Illinois. Roosevelt also conferred on at least two occasions with Senator Chamberlain. Roosevelt's only public appearance was in a speech before the National Press Club on January 24. On that occasion, he called for a speeding up of the American war effort, endorsed Chamberlain's efforts to improve the efficiency of war administration, and specifically approved the proposals for a "War Cabinet" and a minister of munitions. He also defended himself against the criticism of Senator Stone (see n. 2 below) by attacking the Senator's patriotism and alleged obstruction of the war effort. Roosevelt insisted that it was the duty of all good Americans, regardless of party, to provide constructive criticism of the war effort. His only reference to Wilson was a quotation from Wilson's *Congressional Government*: "Unless Congress have and use every means of acquainting itself with the acts and the disposition of the administrative agents of the government, the country must be helpless to learn how it is being served; and unless Congress both scrutinize these things and sift them by every form of discussion, the country must remain in embarrassing, crippling ignorance of the very affairs which it is most important that it should understand and direct. The informing function of Congress should be preferred even to its legislative function." Roosevelt left Washington on January 25. *New York Times*, Jan. 22-26, 1918.

² In a lengthy speech in the Senate on January 21, Stone bitterly attacked the leadership of the Republican party for seeking to make political capital for the campaigns of 1918 and 1920 out of the alleged mismanagement of the war effort by the Wilson administration. The Republican leaders, Stone declared, had instigated most of the congressional investigations then under way. "It is a shrewd movement," Stone continued, "to plant the mine and get some simple-hearted—I will not say simple-minded—Democrat to fire it off." Stone then referred to Roosevelt as follows: "Rising out of this cloud is the abhorrent figure of a political hag, stirring the cauldron of domestic partisanship to disturb even in this hour of national peril the sympathetic unity of the American people." Stone then quoted from Boies Penrose's newspaper interview of December 20 (about which see F. I. Cobb to EMH, Dec. 21, 1917, n. 1, Vol. 45) to support his contention that the Republicans were looking to future elections in their attacks on the conduct of the war. Stone also quoted extensively from Roosevelt's recent editorials and prefaced these quotations with the following comment: "I now introduce my star witness, Theodore Roosevelt himself, whom I characterize as the most seditious man of consequence in America. The heart of this man is aflame with ambition, and he runs amuck. On my responsibility as a Senator I charge that since our entrance into the war Roosevelt has been a menace and obstruction to the successful prosecution of the war. His chief thought has not been to help the Government solve the mighty problems they have had to solve but always his chief thought has been of Roosevelt. Almost every day this man speaks in bitter and contemptuous disparagement of the President and of the majority Members of this Congress. Every week for a long time he has been and still is publishing under contract for a money consideration—think of it, for money—villainous screeds in the Kansas City Star . . . attacking the President and the Government." Stone's speech set off a furor in the Senate. Lodge replied to it in measured and fairly temperate terms; Penrose counterattacked at length with much sarcasm and invective. For the full debate, see *Cong. Record*, 65th Cong., 2d sess., pp. 1081-99.

³ He cannot be further identified.

Robert Lansing to Frank Lyon Polk, with Enclosures

Dear Frank,   [Washington] *Monday* Jany 21/18

These papers came from the President this morning. The fact is I do not feel well enough to attend to these, and must ask you to take them up with the President, explaining that I am still in bed with bronchitis and fever and the Doctor does not encourage me to think I will be out for some days.

In case you wish to speak to me use the White House exchange phone calling my house, as it is by my bed.

Faithfully   RL.

ALI (R. Lansing Papers, NjP).

E N C L O S U R E   I

To Robert Lansing

My dear Mr. Secretary,   The White House. 20 January, 1918.

I dare say you think, as I do, that what the Secretary of the Treasury suggests in this letter is wise and necessary,—is indeed, our duty, in protection of our Treasury; but what are the other nations likely to do, if they are in a similar case, and how can the matter be best handled, do you think?

Faithfully Yours,   W.W.

WWTLI (R. Lansing Papers, NjP).

E N C L O S U R E   I I

From William Gibbs McAdoo

Dear Mr. President: Washington January 17, 1918.

I take the liberty of making a suggestion to the Secretary of State to the effect that we should make it a condition of recognition of any Government in Russia that its obligations to the United States should be respected, and so forth. I enclose copy of that letter, and earnestly hope that it may receive your approval.

You will observe that it is merely a suggestion, but it is a very important one, in my opinion, for the protection of our people.

Cordially yours,   W G McAdoo

TLS (R. Lansing Papers, NjP).

E N C L O S U R E   I I I

Williams Gibbs McAdoo to Robert Lansing

CONFIDENTIAL.

Dear Mr. Secretary: [Washington] January 17, 1918.

I need not, of course, remind you of the difficulties which have arisen in connection with the Russian revolution nor of the steps which have been taken to meet them. As to these, you have been, directly and through the Counselor of the Department of State, kept fully informed. Credits have been established to the amount of $325,000,000 against which advances, evidenced by demand obligations signed by Mr. Bakhmeteff as Ambassador of the Provisional Russian Government, have been made to the aggregate amount of $187,729,750. A further credit of $125,000,000 was established on November 1, 1917, but to it were attached conditions which, in view of the existing situation, are regarded as making it unavailable and concerning which credit, therefore, no public announcement has been made in this country.

Heavy commitments had been assumed by the Russian representatives here, as to many of which the Treasury Department had been notified, and as to some of which the Treasury Department had been in direct communication with the American contractors. In close consultation with the Department of State and the Treasury Department the Russian representatives here have made adjustments in respect to these commitments and payments to these contractors out of funds which were on deposit in the National City Bank subject to their draft before the change in the Russian situation early in November.

With reference to all of these matters, I have to suggest that if and whenever there shall be presented to you the question of recognizing any government in Russia other than the Provisional Russian Government, with which we have been dealing since the entrance of the United States into the war, the United States should make a condition of its recognition of any such government the ratification of the indebtedness incurred by the Provisional Russian Government to the United States and of all the terms and conditions thereof, and the ratification of the transactions of the representatives here of the Provisional Russian Government which have been had under the supervision or in consultation with the United States as represented by the Department of State and the Treasury Department. If and when the question of any such recognition of another government in Russia should arise, I should be glad if you would consult me in order that I may make more specific suggestions with reference to such ratification, as I shall be able to do on account of my familiarity with the details of these loans and transactions.

I am, my dear Mr. Secretary,

Cordially yours,   [W G McAdoo]

CCL (R. Lansing Papers, NjP).

From the Diary of Josephus Daniels

1918 Monday 21 January

Letter from President enclosing one from Willard criticizing Prof. Cusacks, who had talked too much in Madrid—said America would obtain a naval base in Spain. Willard virtually said his resignation could be accepted if Cusacks was allowed to dip into very delicate diplomatic situation. Creel came over & said Willard was not well & was controlled, or influenced by Wilson,[1] the counsellor of the legation. Wells[2] said Cusacks was not discreet. He was recalled by wire.[3]

Council of National Defense. Discussed the housing proposition in Washington. Decided to recommend building houses for 5,000 clerks who can now find no place to stay in Washington.

At night Billy Sunday tabernacle crowded. Patriotic program. I accepted paper signed by 9,000 employes in Washington gun factory who pledged their best & every effort to win the war. It was presented to the Presd & Secretary of the Navy

President gave out statemt that Chamberlain had made statement that was a perversion of truth

[1] Charles Stetson Wilson.
[2] Capt. Roger Welles, Director of Naval Intelligence.
[3] Decker was also recalled.

To William Jennings Bryan

My dear Mr. Bryan: The White House 22 January, 1918

I have time for only a line but I want to acknowledge your letter of the fifteenth[1] and tell you of my sincere interest in reading it. I find nothing more interesting or opening more avenues for reflection than the study of the various national problems on the other side of the water.

Cordially and sincerely yours,   Woodrow Wilson

TLS (W. J. Bryan Papers, DLC).
[1] WJB to WW, Jan. 15, 1918, Vol. 45.

To Elizabeth Merrill Bass

My dear Mrs. Bass: [The White House] 22 January, 1918

Thank you for your letter of January twenty-first. It posts me about things in which, as you know, I am deeply interested, and I am particularly interested in the way you have dished Colonel Roosevelt.   Cordially and sincerely yours,   Woodrow Wilson

TLS (Letterpress Books, WP, DLC).

To Robert Scott Lovett

My dear Judge Lovett: [The White House] 22 January, 1918

I have your letter of January twenty-first about the extension to June first of the prices agreed upon for copper and the conditions of the agreement, and take pleasure in approving the arrangement and the issuance of the statement which you were kind enough to have prepared. I will see that the statement is issued through the Committee on Public Information.[1]
Cordially and sincerely yours,   Woodrow Wilson

TLS (Letterpress Books, WP, DLC).
[1] It was printed in the *Official Bulletin*, II (Jan. 23, 1918), 4.

From William Bauchop Wilson, with Enclosure

My dear Mr. President: Washington January 22, 1918.

I am transmitting herewith the report of your Mediation Commission on the Mooney cases.

The specific recommendation contained therein is that you use your good offices to invoke action by the Governor of California and the cooperation of the prosecuting officers to secure a new trial for Mooney whereby his guilt or innocence may be determined in the light of the important change in the evidence. This result can be accomplished by postponing the execution of the sentence of Mooney and trying him upon one of the other indictments against him, allowing his guilt or innocence to be determined by the new trial.
Faithfully yours,   W B Wilson

TLS (WP, DLC).

E N C L O S U R E

REPORT ON THE MOONEY CASES BY THE PRESIDENT'S MEDIATION
COMMISSION TO THE PRESIDENT OF THE UNITED STATES

Washington, D. C., January 16, 1918.

Agreeable to your instructions, your Mediation Commission, informally and without publicity, inquired into the circumstances attending the Mooney case, and herewith begs to report the result of its investigation.

1. On July 22, 1916, while the San Francisco Preparedness Parade was in early progress, an explosion occurred on one of the city's side streets filled with paraders and the public. Without question, the explosion was murder designed on a large scale and its purpose was effectuated. Six people were killed outright and about forty were wounded, of whom three or four subsequently died. Indisputably a most heinous crime had been committed. The identification of its perpetrators alone had to be established.

2. The community was deeply stirred. Aggressive activity was at once taken by the Police Department, and the press was filled with clues and theories for the solution of the tragic mystery. No premonitory acts furnished a clue, except that a number of letters were mailed, prior to the parade, to prominent citizens and leaders in the movement for the parade, threatening destruction if the parade be undertaken. These letters undoubtedly had a common source. They all avowed pacifist purposes of threats of violence against such manifestations of "militarism" as a preparedness parade was conceived by them to be. The public authorities, however, did not deem these letters significant and the identity of their writers has never been established.

3. The police and the District Attorney[1] turned for explanation to a different quarter. Arrests were made of Thomas J. Mooney and his wife, Rena Mooney, Warren K. Billings, Israel Weinberg and Edward D. Nolan.

4. The antecedents of these five persons, particularly Thomas J. Mooney, have occasioned the war importance of the case. Mooney at the time of his arrest was a well known labor radical on the Pacific Coast. He associated with anarchists. He was a believer in "direct action" in labor controversies. He had once been indicted for attempted dynamiting of property of a San Francisco utility, but after three trials was acquitted. In the Spring of 1916, Mooney and his wife were leaders in a bitter and unsuccessful fight to organize the carmen of the United Railroads of San Francisco. Only shortly before the preparedness parade explosion it was sought to connect Mooney with the recent dynamiting of towers of the Pacific Gas and Electric Company. In a word, there can be no doubt that Mooney was regarded as a labor agitator of malevolence by the utilities of San Francisco, and that he was the special object of their opposition. Mrs. Mooney, a music teacher respected by a wide circle of pupils, was sympathetic with his general social views. Billings,

[1] Charles Marron Fickert.

a youth touched by radical propaganda, was one of Mooney's friends. He, too, was a believer in "direct action." He had been previously convicted of carrying explosives on a passenger car. Weinberg, whose son was a pupil of Mrs. Mooney, was a jitney bus driver who had occasionally driven the Mooneys. Nolan was a radical labor leader of some prominence and a friend of Mooney's. Mooney is the centre of the case; the other defendants have significance only because of relation to him.

5. The utilities against which Mooney directed his agitation or who suspected him of mischievous activity, undoubtedly sought "to get" Mooney. Their activities against him were directed by Swanson,[2] a private detective. It was Swanson who had engineered the investigation which resulted in Mooney's prosecution. It was Swanson who was active in attempts to implicate Mooney in the dynamiting of the electric towers in 1916, attempts which failed, it appears, because Billings and Weinberg refused offers of "reward" by Swanson to implicate Mooney. Shortly thereafter the preparedness parade explosion occurs. Immediately Swanson took a leading part, now acting for the District Attorney and the police, in the investigation of the crime. Within four days, under Swanson's leadership, the arrest of Mooney and the others is made.

6. Instead of an ordinary criminal case, or even a case of extraordinary interest, there thus emerge the elements of a clash of forces of wide significance. On the one hand, a community long in the grip of bitter labor struggles is outraged by peculiarly wicked murders. Accusation is made against a group whose leader has been widely associated with views which justify violence at least in industrial conflict. The public mind was therefore easily aroused to belief in the guilt of the accused. The attitude of passion was stimulated by all the arts of modern journalism. It is not surprising, then, that Billings and Mooney were tried in an impregnating atmosphere of guilt.

On the other hand, just as Mooney symbolized labor for all the bitter opponents of organized labor, so he came to symbolize labor, irrespective of his personal merits, in the minds of workers and of their sympathizers. "The Mooney case" soon resolved itself into a new aspect of an old industrial feud, instead of a subject demanding calm search for truth.

7. Billings was tried first, undoubtedly in the hope that the pressure of conviction would lead him to implicate Mooney. He was convicted. His conviction has been sustained. He has been sentenced to life imprisonment. He has not implicated Mooney and he

[2] Martin Swanson.

protests innocence. Mooney was tried early in January, 1917, and in February, 1917, convicted of murder in the first degree. Mrs. Mooney was tried and acquitted. Weinberg was recently tried and acquitted. Nolan has never been put to trial.

8. The convictions of Billings and Mooney followed trials in accordance with the established course of American procedure. It is familiar to students of jurisprudence that no system of criminal administration in the world hedges such safeguards around an accused as does an American trial. The conviction, in other words, was based on evidence narrowly confined to the specific issues. Furthermore, proof of guilt had to be established beyond a reasonable doubt and established to the unanimous satisfaction of a jury of twelve persons selected from among the people. Conviction by an American jury is guilt determined by a very democratic institution. There is no question but that the jury acted in good faith upon the evidence as it was submitted. It is because of subsequent developments that doubt is based upon the justice of the convictions. Following the trials of Billings and Mooney, there was a change in the evidence which not only resulted in the acquittal of Mrs. Mooney and Weinberg, but also cast doubt upon the prior convictions of Billings and Mooney.

Thus it is that the evidence submitted on the four trials taken together, aimed as it was at the establishment of a single issue: their joint participation in the crime, leaves the mind in the greatest uncertainty as to the complicity of the accused. While each record in itself presents evidence which would justify an appellate court in sustaining the verdict of a jury, the evidence of the four cases in their entirety must shake confidence in the justice of the convictions. This is due to the dubious character of the witnesses, the subsequent revelations concerning them, and the conflict in the testimony of the same witnesses as the need for change in the testimony developed to fit new theories of the prosecution or new evidence by the defense. But it was not deemed the province of your Commission to establish the guilt or innocence of Mooney and his associates. We conceived it to be our duty merely to determine whether a solid basis exists for a feeling that an injustice was done or may have been done in the convictions that were obtained, and that an irreparable injustice would be committed to allow such conviction to proceed to execution.

9. We find in the atmosphere surrounding the prosecution and trial of the case ground for disquietude. This feeling is reenforced by one factor of controlling importance. The most damaging testimony produced against Mooney came from a witness named Ox-

man.[3] It was Oxman who testified with convincing detail to the presence of Mooney and Billings at a place and at a time where it was essential for them to have been if proof of their participation in the crime was to be established. After Mooney's conviction there came to light letters confessedly written by Oxman prior to his having been called to testify. The plain import of these letters is an attempt by Oxman to suborn perjury in corroboration of the vital testimony which he was to give and which in fact he did give against Mooney. It is true that Oxman was tried for attempted subornation of perjury and acquitted, but this is beside the present considera- tion. The fact is that he did write letters which tend completely to discredit any testimony he might give and no testimony from Ox- man in the light of these letters would receive credence necessary to lead to conviction. In fact, after the exposure of Oxman, the District Attorney did not call him, though available, as a witness in the trial of Mrs. Mooney. When Oxman was discredited the verdict against Mooney was discredited.

10. As soon as the Oxman letters were disclosed, the Judge[4] who presided at Mooney's trial called upon the Attorney General of Cal- ifornia to take steps towards a retrial of the case. We quote from Judge Griffin's letter to Attorney General Webb:[5]

"As you will at once see, they (the Oxman letters) bear directly upon the credibility of the witness and go to the very foundation of the truth of the story told by Oxman on the witness stand. Had they been before me at the time of the hearing of the motion for new trial, I would unhesitatingly have granted it. Unfortu- nately the matter is now out of my hands jurisdictionally, and I am therefore addressing you, as the representative of the People on the appeal, to urge upon you the necessity of such action on your part as will result in returning the case to this court for re- trial. The letters of Oxman undoubtedly require explanation, and, so far as Mooney is concerned, unquestionably the explanation should be heard by a jury which passed upon the question of his guilt or innocence. I fully appreciate the unusual character of such a request coming from the trial court in any case and I know of no precedent therefor. In the circumstances of this case, I believe that all of us who were participants in the trial concur that right and justice demand that a new trial of Mooney should be had in order that no possible mistake shall be made in a case where a human life is at stake."

[3] Frank C. Oxman, a cattle dealer of Durkee, Ore.
[4] Franklin A. Griffin, judge of the Superior Court of San Francisco County.
[5] Ulysses Sigel Webb, Attorney General of the State of California.

The Attorney General asked the Supreme Court that, in view of the Oxman exposure, the case should be returned to the Trial Court for a new trial. The Supreme Court, however, under the laws of California, found itself without jurisdiction to consider matters outside the record. The case is now before that Court on appeal, to be disposed of solely on errors appearing from the record of the trial. If the Supreme Court should find error, reverse and grant a new trial, the relief the situation needs would be provided. If the Supreme Court finds that the record discloses no reversible error, and, therefore, confirms the conviction, the relief will have to be supplied through the executive action of the Governor of California and the cooperation of the prosecuting officers.

11. Such relief it is hoped will be forthcoming. It is now well known that the attention to the situation in the East was first aroused through meetings of protest against the Mooney conviction in Russia. From Russia and the Western States protest spread to the entire country until it has gathered momentum from many sources, sources whose opposition to violence is unquestioned, whose devotion to our cause in the war is unstinted. The liberal sentiment of Russia was aroused, the liberal sentiment of the United States was aroused, because the circumstances of Mooney's prosecution, in the light of his history, led to the belief that the terrible and sacred instruments of criminal justice were consciously or unconsciously made use of against labor by its enemies in an industrial conflict.

12. However strange or however unexpected it may be, the just disposition of the Mooney case thus affects influences far beyond the confines of California, and California can be depended upon to see the wider implications of the case. With the mere local aspects, with the political and journalistic conflicts which the case has occasioned, neither the Commission nor the country at large is concerned. But the feeling of disquietude aroused by the case must be heeded, for, if unchecked, it impairs the faith that our democracy protects the lowliest and even the unworthy against false accusations. War is fought with moral as well as material resources. We are in this war to vindicate the moral claims of unstained processes of law, however slow, at times, such processes may be. These claims must be tempered by the fire of our own devotion to them at home.

13. Your Commission, therefore, respectfully recommends in case the Supreme Court of California should find it necessary (confined as it is by jurisdictional limitations) to sustain the conviction of Mooney on the record of the trial, that the President use his good offices to invoke action by the Governor of California and the co-

operation of its prosecuting officers to the end that a new trial may be had for Mooney whereby guilt or innocence may be put to the test of unquestionable justice. This result can easily be accomplished by postponing the execution of the sentence of Mooney to await the outcome of a new trial, based upon prosecution under one of the untried indictments against him.

    Respectfully submitted, W B Wilson Chairman.

Felix Frankfurter	J. L. Spangler
Secretary and Counsel	E. P. Marsh
Max Lowenthal	Verner Z. Reed
Assistant Secretary.	John H. Walker

T MS (WP, DLC).

To William Dennison Stephens

[The White House]
My dear Governor Stephens: 22 January, 1918

Will you permit a suggestion from me in these troubled times which perhaps justify what I should feel hardly justifiable in other circumstances?

The suggestion is this: Would it not be possible to postpone the execution of the sentence of Mooney until he can be tried upon one of the other indictments against him, in order to give full weight and consideration to the important changes which I understand to have taken place in the evidence against him?

I urge this very respectfully indeed but very earnestly, because the case has assumed international importance and I feel free to make the suggestion because I am sure that you are as anxious as anyone can be to have no doubt or occasion of criticism of any sort attach itself to the case.

With the very best wishes for the New Year,
    Cordially and sincerely yours, Woodrow Wilson

TLS (Letterpress Books, WP, DLC).

To William Bauchop Wilson

My dear Mr. Secretary: The White House 22 January, 1918

I have taken pleasure in writing to the Governor of California in the sense suggested by your letter of January twenty-second, accompanying the report of the Mediation Commission on the Mooney cases.   Cordially and sincerely yours, Woodrow Wilson

TLS (LDR, RG 174, DNA).

To Herbert Bayard Swope

My dear Mr. Swope: The White House 22 January, 1918

Your letter of the nineteenth[1] only came to me this morning, so I read it after having seen you. Thank you for it very much and for the stand you took with your paper.

Cordially and sincerely yours,   Woodrow Wilson

TLS (received from Bruce Gimelson).
[1] It is missing.

From William Gibbs McAdoo, with Enclosure

Dear Mr. President: Washington January 22, 1918.

I hand you herewith a copy of a communication which I received recently through Sir Richard Crawford from the British Chancellor of the Exchequer,[1] setting forth certain demands upon the United States Treasury by the British Government on account of demands made upon the latter by the United States Food Administration. I am sending you this as an additional argument in support of my suggestion that the Food Administration should be represented on the Inter-Ally Council.

The essence of the demand now made upon me is that over and above all the demands, ordinary and extraordinary, now being made on Great Britain's behalf, $61,000,000 shall be advanced to Great Britain in order to buy hog products and frozen meat in advance of actual requirements for the purpose of maintaining prices. I do not, of course, undertake to pass upon the wisdom of the policy adopted by the Food Administrator taken by itself (involving, though it does, the purchase of supplies which Great Britain does not presently need in order to maintain the present high prices while the American people are being urged to deny themselves these things), but in view of the extreme difficulty which the United States Treasury is having in meeting the demands made upon it from all sides, I hope that you will agree with me that such demands as this should be discussed by the Inter-Ally Council along with demands for money, for ships and for other material supplies, and that the policies of the United States Food Administrator cannot properly be determined without reference to these other considerations.

Cordially yours,   W G McAdoo

TLS (WP, DLC).
[1] That is, Andrew Bonar Law.

ENCLOSURE

MEMORANDUM

The following is a personal message from the Chancellor of the Exchequer for Mr. McAdoo.

I sent the following urgent telegram to Mr. Crosby in Paris. As the matter is very urgent I am repeating the message to you for your information in order to save time.

Message to Mr. Crosby:

The Food Purchasing position has become critical and it necessitates my consulting with you urgently. Please refer to our interviews with Lord Rhonda[1] and Mr. Lloyd George in December regarding purchases of food in the United States other than cereals. At this interview we were compelled to agree to the purchase by Lord Rhonda on a fresh scale, even at the risk of our aggregate January requirements exceeding $235,000,000. Our applications for January, as a result, amount as you know to $275,000,000, although it is hoped that we shall get through on less than this sum as a result of postponed deliveries. Our requirements for February were anticipated to be probably approximately the same as those for January and figures calculated on this basis were laid before you in Paris. The receipt, however, of the following letter from the United States Food Administration has entirely altered the position:

"At this period of the year it has been usual that hog products accumulate in Great Britain. I recommend that in addition to its usual monthly purchases the British Government (and for other Governments which you represent) now purchase in the United States within the next two months and ship and store in Great Britain as a reserve an additional quantity of hog products (exclusive of tinned meats) equivalent to two months supply (about one hundred and fifty million pounds). This amount could be supplied now. It may become impossible to supply it any other time. Such a purchase could be made at prices based on a live stock price about 16 dollars per hundred pounds. It is not expected or intended by the United States Food Administration that the live stock price in 1918 will fall much below that figure, and it is hoped to stabilize it for the purpose of encouraging production. This recommendation, which it is believed to be in the interest of the British Government, is made because the United States Food Administration absolutely needs and desires this outlet for a portion of hog production in the United States during the period of accumulation of stocks, to aid in financing of its meat packing industry and maintaining of stable price to its swine producers. I suggest that you cable this proposal at once for consideration. If you can arrange extra shipping facilities, the United States Food Administration will give its support to such financial arrangement as may be necessary."

Ministry of Food estimate additional cost of adopting this proposal at $47,000,000. In addition to above, they desire to accept offer of thirty five thousand tons of frozen meat, cost of which would be $14,000,000, making a total of $61,000,000 in all. In regard to later proposal Mr. Hoover cables as follows: As the result of our conservation measures we have on storage full of frozen beef, and unless we can get relief we shall have to abandon our conservation. I consider this would be a disaster to the ultimate needs of the Allies as it will greatly destroy psychology of saving. It would surely be more advantageous to ship from these markets than the Argentine. Advice tendered by your Food Administration in their own interests as well as ours, coupled with growing discontent at food shortage in this country has led Lord Rhondda to advise Cabinet that it is essential that he should be authorized immediately to contract for supplies in accordance with above programme. Prime Minister and I are convinced this must be done. But the financial consequences are obviously serious. Best proposals I can make towards meeting them are as follows:

(1) If it proves practicable to carry out proposed food programme in full, our requirements for February would be about $335,000,000. As February is a short month, I think it likely that $300,000,000 would be sufficient to meet expenditure actually falling due in that month.

2. We are now negotiating with the Japanese Government for a loan of $40,000,000 in the United States and hope to secure money in course of February. We had intended to use this to meet capital liabilities, but as a temporary measure we could use it to meet current expenditure.

3. This would reduce our February requirements from the United States Treasury to $260,000,000.

I trust you will not feel we are unduly rushing you in bringing forward proposals relating to February so soon after examination of our January programme. But you will appreciate that the scale of our February commitments must necessarily be determined by the middle of January. Lord Rhondda assures me it is impossible for him to delay longer before giving instructions to his purchasing agents. Further, the United States Food Administration insist that we notify our programme for each month by the middle of the preceding month.

May I most earnestly impress on you to permit us to make our arrangements for February on the basis of a credit of $260,000,000.

In this event I would do my utmost by effecting economies in other directions, particularly munitions of war orders and remounts, to secure a reduction in subsequent months.

Unfortunately munitions orders are placed so far in advance that it would be almost impossible to effect any substantial curtailment in actual expenditure on these orders in February.

Food position here is so serious that Government would expose itself to most dangerous criticism if it were to prohibit Food Controller from purchasing essential foodstuffs which the United States Food Administration declare to be available for prompt shipment and press us to buy.

In order to save time and to facilitate your communication with Washington I am repeating this telegram to our Ambassador at Washington for information of Mr. McAdoo with intimation that we have made our application to you and hope for reply through you on your return to London.

T MS (WP, DLC).
¹ David Alfred Thomas, 1st Baron Rhondda, the British Food Controller.

From Frank Lyon Polk

Dear Mr. President: Washington January 22, 1918.

The French Ambassador tells the Department that he has received reports that item number 10 in the peace program outlined in your address to Congress on January 8th is not clearly understood abroad, especially in Italy, the impression being that we desired to see the place of Austria-Hungary among the nations "safeguarded and assured." The Ambassador interprets your statement to mean that we wish the place of the *peoples* of Austria-Hungary "safeguarded and assured," but desires our confirmation in order that he may send a cable conveying the correct interpretation. Will you kindly indicate what reply I may make to the French Ambassador?

With assurances of respect, etc., I am, my dear Mr. President,
                     Faithfully yours,   Frank L Polk

TLS (WP, DLC).

From the Diary of Josephus Daniels

                                January Tuesday 22 1918

WW said he told Senators that War Council could not be established until he was dead. Republicans conspiring to make political capital by attacks on the conduct of the war. They want, said WW, a cabinet in which representatives of privilege will have seats & be in intimate touch. They do not think as we do because they wish to act for a class.

Carnova [Cadorna], on day after Italian retreat, issued order naming as traitors the regiments that cowardly surrendered.

In cabinet discussed housing in D. C. & decided to ask legislation.

Ordered Cusacks to return from Spain because he was indiscreet.

To Herbert Clark Hoover

Confidential.

My dear Mr. Hoover: The White House 23 January, 1918

I would be very much obliged if you would give your careful consideration to the enclosed and let me have your confidential advice. The Secretary of the Treasury is, I think, right in the position he takes. The financial problems we are now handling and are facing in the immediate future are of such magnitude that I believe it is absolutely essential that we should avoid every ounce of additional weight that can be avoided. Whether the representation of the Food Administration in the Inter-Allied Council will accomplish just what the Secretary of the Treasury has in mind or not, I am not clear, but that there should be coordination of the most intimate sort in big transactions of this kind will, I am sure, be your judgment as it is mine.

Cordially and sincerely yours,   Woodrow Wilson

TLS (H. Hoover Papers, HPL).

To Joseph Patrick Tumulty, with Enclosure

Dear Tumulty: [The White House, Jan. 23, 1918]

I would not be at all willing to have the enclosed published. I think I must stand very stiffly by the rule that I am not to be quoted, and it would be quite inexcusable for me to permit the Governor General of Canada to be indirectly quoted; besides which, Mr. Taylor got a wrong impression of that part of what I said. I wish for some reasons I could consent to the publication of this interview, but I think the reasons against it are the prevailing ones.

The President.

TL (WP, DLC).

E N C L O S U R E

FROM THE PUBLICITY DEPARTMENT OF THE WOMAN'S BUREAU OF
THE DEMOCRATIC NATIONAL COMMITTEE.
FOR IMMEDIATE RELEASE.

The chairman of the Steering Committee of the House of Representatives for the Woman Suffrage Amendment, Mr. Edward T. Taylor, of Colorado, has been asked to make a statement concerning the interview which the committee had with the President late in the afternoon of January ninth, on the eve of the vote on the suffrage amendment in the House. The appointment was made for the committee by Mr. Taylor in order that there might be no doubt as to the position of the President on the passage of the amendment, each side claiming that the President favored its contention. Even the Anti-Suffrage organization had gone to the trouble and expense of getting out a handbook, made up of quotations from the President's writings, with a statement on the cover that he was "still in favor of action by the several states," but neglecting to give the date of this utterance which was made some four years ago.

"Knowing that all the members of the delegation were Democrats, the President naturally wished to make his position clear so far as the Democratic platform is concerned," said Mr. Taylor. "My memory of the occasion is quite definite, and while I am not attempting to give the exact words there is no doubt of the general substance of the President's remarks. He began by stating that only once since his incumbency of the White House had he set the party platform aside, and he attributed his success to his loyalty to that platform and the fact that Congress had upheld him in following it. The one exception was the advocacy of the repeal of the tolls upon the Panama Canal, and this was done in recognition of the binding character of a national treaty, and the obligation of the country to carry out its treaty agreements. As President he said he felt himself obligated to carry out the provisions of the treaty, even though they were in conflict with the plank dealing with that subject in the national platform of the party. Then he added with deep feeling, 'In every other official action which I have taken I have stood solidly upon the Democratic platform—I am standing there now.' He went on to say that he had been and was still of the opinion that the orderly and systematic way of adopting equal suffrage was by state action, but while he had not changed, all the conditions under which we are living have changed, and the world itself is a different place from the world of a few years ago.

"The Governor General of Canada, His Excellency, the Duke of Devonshire, had dined with the President that day and they had discussed the extension of the suffrage to women. It was the opinion of the Governor General that not only Canada and Great Britain, but all English-speaking people were going to enfranchise their womenkind, unless indeed, the United States failed to do so. The President agreed with him that no one could doubt the growth of this sentiment, and averred that it appeared to be coming as fast as possible in the United States.

"In view of all these facts and the marvelous heroism and splendid loyalty of our women, and the services they have rendered the nation, the President said he felt the time had come to extend the franchise to them, and he added that every man who had voted against this bill before because of his adherence to states' rights, and every man who now opposed it because of the national platform should not hesitate to vote for it now because the entire situation had changed since that platform was adopted. 'The party has declared for Woman Suffrage. It is a part of our pledge to the United States,' he went on. 'True, we are pledged to it in a certain manner, but we are now put in the position of either denying the right of suffrage to women, practically, and standing on the provisions of our platform, or taking this step toward carrying it out, even though it may be in a different manner. The difference in form is not sufficient reason for voting against it, and I hope every Democrat who is not conscientiously opposed to granting women this right will vote for this amendment tomorrow. You are at liberty to give this statement as much publicity as you desire.'

"I said, 'Mr. President, I wish that this statement might be reduced to writing so that no one could misunderstand or misinterpret your meaning, which you have so clearly expressed to us. Your views exactly coincide with those of the Western Democrats, and I think with those of all who favor women suffrage, and they are of such great importance, not only in substance, but that the form may not be misinterpreted or deprived of its full force, we would very much appreciate it if you will give us a statement that we might use for the press as well.' He had no objection to making a brief statement conveying the substance of his ideas, and called to one of the clerks for pencil and paper, and wrote the paragraph that appeared in the papers.[1] He sat down while writing but we remained standing, and he tore off the sheet and handed it to me. I asked if we might give it to the press, and he said he had no objection. I then said I would have copies made for the press and we agreed to refrain at that time from giving any interviews, giving simply the President's statement with a brief explanation. . . ."

Printed galley proof (WP, DLC).
[1] It is printed at Jan. 9, 1918, Vol. 45.

To Gutzon Borglum

Personal.

My dear Mr. Borglum: The White House 23 January, 1918

I am interested to learn that you are ready to report to me in the matter about which we have corresponded and about which you came to Washington. Mr. Tumulty has conveyed to me your desire to see me.

Before I see you, may I not take the liberty of making this request, that you put your report in writing for my mature consideration and that you attach to it the material upon which it is based?

I am sure it is unnecessary to say to you that this whole matter is of such a nature that it must be dealt with with the greatest care and caution, because it would be so easy to aid the enemy by any kind of information, direct or indirect, concerning the processes we are using or the details of the programme we are seeking to carry out. I must regard our relationship in this matter as entirely confidential and express the hope that you will not commit any of the matter to others, not even to stenographers. It has been necessary to deal with these matters with the utmost caution even in respect of the knowledge communicated to officers and officials of the Government itself. I beg, therefore, that you will put the whole matter as you have found it in my hands together with the evidence.

Sincerely yours,   Woodrow Wilson

TLS (G. Borglum Papers, DLC).

To Ollie Murray James

My dear Senator: [The White House] 23 January, 1918

You have been kind enough to tell me that you had heard that I had written a letter to the Chairman of the Senate Military Affairs Committee concerning the idea of a munitions minister, and you asked me whether I did write such a letter. I did and am glad to send you herewith a copy of it.[1]

The consultation referred to with Senator Chamberlain, to whom the letter is addressed, was upon the subject of the various difficulties and delays that had been encountered by the War Department, as shown by the testimony before the Senate Committee, and the Senator merely mentioned to me that he had a bill in mind to create a munitions ministry. He gave me no detail of the bill he had in mind, and it was only when I learned afterwards from others of the real character of the proposals that I felt it my duty to write to the Senator and apprise him of my attitude. I assumed from what I heard later that that particular proposal had been abandoned, and I was referring in my statement of the other day to the very surprising proposal to create a superior war cabinet of a type unknown to our practice or institutions.

I give you these details merely to reply to your kind inquiry[2] and let you know all the facts of the case as you desire.

Cordially and sincerely yours,   Woodrow Wilson

TLS (Letterpress Books, WP, DLC).
  [1] WW to G. E. Chamberlain, Jan. 11, 1918, Vol. 45.
  [2] Made orally.

To Henry Jones Ford

My dear Ford: [The White House] 23 January, 1918

Thank you for your letter of January twenty-first. I do not know whether the present heated atmosphere here is just the one in which to inject the important changes you suggest, but you may be sure that the matter is constantly in my mind.

It is always a pleasure to hear from you.

Cordially and sincerely yours,   Woodrow Wilson

TLS (Letterpress Books, WP, DLC).

To Frank Lyon Polk

My dear Mr. Counselor: The White House 23 January, 1918

I have your letter of yesterday and in reply would say that the French Ambassador has correctly interpreted my peace terms with regard to Austria-Hungary.

In haste   Faithfully yours,   Woodrow Wilson

TLS (SDR, RG 59, 763.72119/1166, DNA).

From Joseph Patrick Tumulty

The White House.

Memorandum for the President: January 23, 1918.

Senator Simmons telephoned to say that he was in receipt of a letter from a friend of his, the first line or two of which read as follows:

"I see from the papers that the President has asked Congress to give him power to fix the price of cotton."

The Senator asked if this was so. He was advised that the office knew nothing of it.

T MS (WP, DLC).

To Joseph Patrick Tumulty

Dear Tumulty: [The White House, c. Jan. 23, 1918]

I have made no such request, but I have suggested the granting of powers which would give the Government control over the prices of all articles necessary to the prosecution of the war. I did not have cotton specially in mind, but no doubt the terms of the measure proposed might include it.   The President.

TL (WP, DLC).

From Joseph Patrick Tumulty

Dear Governor: The White House. January 23, 1918

Is it your purpose to give publicity to the report in the Mooney case? J.P.T.

What does the Sec'y of Labour advise. The effect on Mooney himself must be considered. W.W.

TL (WP, DLC).

From the White House Staff

MEMORANDUM: The White House. January 23, 1918.

Secretary Wilson states that the Commission would be satisfied to have publicity given to the report. He stated that the Commission felt that the effect on Mooney was of less importance than the effect on this country and the effect on our foreign relations. The all-important thing in the mind of the Commission is the effect on the people as a whole in this country and the effect in connection with our foreign relations. The Commission thought that either the beneficial or injurious effect on the individual was of less consequence.[1]

T MS (WP, DLC).

[1] A summary of the commission's report was printed in the *New York Times*, Jan. 27, 1918, and the full text was printed in the *Official Bulletin*, II (Jan. 28, 1918), 14-15.

From Champ Clark

Dear Mr. President: Washington, D. C. January 23, 1918.

Whether of any interest or importance, I take the liberty of stating that I am dead against the Chamberlain bills & propositions and am ready, if needs be, to render any service possible against them.
Your Friend,   Champ Clark.

ALS (WP, DLC).

From Robert Scott Lovett

My dear Mr. President: Washington January 23, 1918.

I thank you very much for your generous letter of the 21st. Certainly I will withhold my letter to Secretary Baker and suspend my plans until the present disturbed state of the atmosphere about the Capitol clears, since I am as anxious to avoid everything that would embarrass as I am to do anything possible to help your Administration.   Very respectfully,   R. S. Lovett

TLS (WP, DLC).

A Memorandum by Sir William Wiseman

NOTES ON INTERVIEW WITH THE PRESIDENT

JANUARY 23rd, 1918.

On learning from Col. House that I was in Washington, the President telephoned Auchincloss at the State Department and left a message for me to call at 3.15 at the White House. I had about an hour's conversation (an unusual compliment considering how much he was occupied by the debate in the Senate), of which the following is a summary:

After saying how glad he was to see me back, the President enquired most cordially regarding Mr. Balfour. He said that he often thought of him, and should never forget his visit.

I could not help noticing that he looked tired, and that his voice was decidedly weak. He admitted that the strain was very great, and remarked that, although he had only been in the war ten months, the strain of the period of neutrality was almost as great.

The Coal and Railway situation in America was causing him additional anxiety at the moment.

He remarked that he thought the States had done fairly well considering the difficulties of organizing such a vast country; that the people were totally unused to national organization. The failures, he said, were apt to be magnified, and much of the good work could not be commented on for military reasons.

The President says that he is fully aware of the importance of the TONNAGE situation, and every effort is being made to increase and speed-up Shipbuilding; also to secure further existing tonnage (neutral and interned in neutral ports) for war purposes.

The immediate problem, he thinks, is to make the best use of the shipping now available. He does not consider the present arrangement satisfactory. The use of tonnage depends on Allied policy and military strategy. Here he referred to conflicting views among the Allies, and remarked that this made the problem of deciding priority even more difficult.

The Allies are making demands for more materials, tonnage, and money than can be supplied by the United States. The question is whether these demands are to be cut down all-round in simple mathematical proportion to meet the supplies, or, if not, how to determine which to grant and which to refuse.

I pointed out that before the States came into the war we had to make these decisions. Now the onus had fallen on him, and he must accept the position. Also that it was quite impossible to satisfy all the Allies. He must decide what was best for the cause as a whole. He said he realised this was true, and, though unwilling, he would not shrink from the responsibility of making the necessary decision. At the same time he pointed out that it was harder for him than for us because he is so far away from the Front. To my suggestion that he should delegate full authority to someone on the spot, he made no reply.

He does not consider the present arrangements for deciding priority are satisfactory, but hopes that General Bliss may be able to help the situation. I told him the purpose of READING's coming was to tell him on behalf of H.M.G. what we thought ought to be done for the common cause, and place at his disposal—in so far as one man was able—our experience in deciding these matters. He remarked that this arrangement ought to be very helpful to him. He repeated the difficulty was to decide on the questions of essentials and non-essentials and to determine the best priority.

ITALY:

The President said the Italian Ambassador called on him directly after his speech to thank him for his reference to Italian aspirations. He now hears from Rome that ORLANDO has gone to Paris and London to protest against his and Lloyd George's speeches, and demand that the Allies live up to the the full terms of their secret treaties. He would like to know what Lloyd George proposes to do about it. His judgment is not to commit himself any further. He is evidently not much in sympathy with Italian war aims, or particularly pleased with the part they have taken in the war.

FRANCE:

Referring to his last speech, he said the part about which he was most doubtful as to its reception in the Senate was the reference to ALSACE-LORRAINE. Much to his surprise it was most enthusiastically received by the Senate. It was hard to say—he observed— whether this feeling was really deep-rooted in America, or merely a romantic historic attachment. Alsace-Lorraine was, in his opinion, a wrong which had poisoned the air of Europe since 1871.

Regarding Lloyd George's speech, he was anxious to know the genesis of the speech—which he said was often as interesting as a speech itself. I told him of the discussions in London at the time of the House Mission; also of the pressure by the Labour party, which obviously interested him. He was delighted to find George's speech coincided so closely with his own views, which he earnestly believed were also the views of the American people. It was important that British and American world-policies should run on similar lines. He was glad to believe that was so at present.

Regarding George's speech—the liberal note, the policy of self-determination, and the absence of annexationist ideas would, he said, be duly appreciated in America.

He was anxious to know if British Labour was "fully satisfied" with the Prime Minister's speech. (I had no information beyond newspaper reports). The labour situation in the United States was causing some anxiety, and must be carefully handled. The American working men do not care about complicated national questions in Europe, and would be ready to take his judgment on what were fair terms of peace. Their purpose must be maintained by keeping firmly and constantly to the front certain very simple truths about the war.

ECONOMIC PEACE TERMS:

It might be true that Germany held the military advantage, but England and America held all the economic advantages. Referring to the scarcity which there will be of raw materials after the war, he said economic concessions would be cards as valuable as occupied territory. "I shall go," he said, "to the Peace Conference with these cards in my pocket, and there they will stay until the German military party give way." He had no doubt that the Senate would quickly ratify any Peace terms he submitted.

WAR AIMS:

The demand that had lately been made for a re-statement of war-aims was largely due, he believed, to the outrageous conduct of the Bolshevics in publishing the secret treaties, and the consequent fear of the people that they were being exploited for some imperial or capitalist purpose. Recent speeches he hoped and believed had put that right.

"I do hope," he said, "most earnestly that no-one in England thinks that we are in this war for any material advantage. There is, I know, a party at the Capitol who would like to see us get material advantages out of the war, but if we did we should lose our moral authority and be false to our principles. I have been opposed to that party all my life, and rather enjoy watching their efforts now that I am in the saddle."

In general, he does not approve of speakers coming to this country for propaganda, or Americans going to England. An artificial Entente would be dangerous. Anglo-American relations must rest on surer foundations.

Apropos of HOUSE's Mission to Europe, the President remarked that House has a wonderful gift for getting a detached view-point and fixing on the really important issues. His last words were: "Give my love to House, and tell him we have had a 'bully' talk."[1]

T MS (W. Wiseman Papers, CtY).

[1] Wiseman sent this memorandum in abridged form as W. Wiseman to C.S.A. (for E. Drummond), No. 41, Jan. 25, 1918, T telegram (W. Wiseman Papers, CtY). C.S.A. was Charles S. Ascherson, Drummond's private secretary.

To Robert Latham Owen

My dear Senator: [The White House] 24 January, 1918

I value your letter of the twenty-second about the Russian situation and you may be sure that what you recommend has constituted no small part of my thought in recent weeks. I shall take pleasure in consulting the Secretary of State more particularly again about the several points of your suggestion.

Cordially and sincerely yours,   Woodrow Wilson

TLS (Letterpress Books, WP, DLC).

To Robert Lansing, with Enclosure

My dear Mr. Secretary: The White House 24 January, 1918

Senator Owen is very earnest about the enclosed suggestions and I have promised him that I would discuss them with you. I would be very much obliged if you would consider them pending our next conference.

Cordially and sincerely yours,   Woodrow Wilson

From Robert Latham Owen

My dear Mr. President: [Washington] January 22, 1918.

After consulting with a number of gentlemen relative to the conditions in Russia, and the need for additional action looking to influencing favorable Russian opinion, particularly Mr. H. L. Carpenter, Mr. Raymond V. Ingersoll, and Mr. H. F. Meserve,[1] I wish to suggest to you the urgent importance—

First, of recognizing the Bolsheviki Government as *de facto*, or at least establish intercourse with them whereby they may feel that the Government of the United States has a friendly and sympathetic feeling for the present *de facto* Government in Russia. I think this suggestion is the more justified because the Constitutional Assembly, through which it was hoped a stable government might succeed, has not been able to maintain itself for lack for force.

Second, that coincident with this *quasi* recognition of the Bolsheviki Government, which I understand represents the influence of the Soviet or the delegates representing the Soldiers, Sailors and Urban workmen, there should be sent a ship-load of some of those things most urgently needed in Petrograd, permitting the *de facto* Government to indicate those things for which they are in most urgent need, so that both a compliment and a service will be coincidently rendered. I suggest that these goods shipped to Petrograd can be exchanged for food which the peasants have available for barter but not for sale, as the Russian currency system has broken down, and in this way serve a double purpose of giving them the things they need and distributing the food as a gratuity from the American Government.

Third, it is urgently suggested that to offset the German intrigue, the United States should appoint a large number of consular officers at various special centers throughout Russia and use this service as a means of contact with Russian opinion and with the Russian people. The suggestion heretofore made that the personnel giving publicity to American opinion ought to be immediately expanded and several hundred new men sent to Russia in this service. Mr. Meserve has just returned from Petrograd and he tells me that he had no serious difficulty in getting through on the Siberian Railroad. Mr. Stephens [Stevens] and several hundred men it seems are still in Japan awaiting to renew their activities in the matter of the improvement of the Russian-Siberian Railroad. If Mr. Stephens' activities can be retained by the Government I think by all means it should be done.

Fourth. The United States should establish courier service so as to keep Americans in touch with each other and so as to promote means of communication which has been so largely broken up in Russia. I am informed that the ocean way to Kola on the Arctic Ocean at a point near the borders of Finland is open and a new railway on Russian territory comes from Kola to Petrograd.

Yours respectfully,   Robt L Owen

TLS (SDR, RG 59, 861.00/1048½, DNA).
  ¹ Herbert L. Carpenter was an engineer, inventor, and businessman of New York. Raymond Vail Ingersoll was a lawyer and independent Democrat, active in politics and social work in Brooklyn. Harry Fessenden Meserve was vice-president in charge of European activities for the National City Bank of New York, which had acted as banker for the Russian government in the United States.

To Champ Clark

My dear Mr. Speaker: [The White House] 24 January, 1918
    Your letter of yesterday is mighty fine for one's spirits. It is astonishing to me what partisanship and the spirit of criticism is capable of at a time when what we need above all things else is cooperation and helpfulness. I would have expected such an assurance from you as you have sent me, but it is none the less delightful to have it thus generously volunteered.

Cordially and sincerely your friend,   Woodrow Wilson

TLS (Letterpress Books, WP, DLC).

To John Humphrey Small

My dear Mr. Small: [The White House] 24 January, 1918
    Mr. Tumulty has told me of your kind message over the telephone yesterday and I want to tell you how much I appreciate it. It is delightful to count, as I always do, upon the North Carolina delegation when anything critical arises, and I hope you will convey to them all my appreciation of your message.

Cordially and sincerely yours,   Woodrow Wilson

TLS (Letterpress Books, WP, DLC).

From Newton Diehl Baker

Dear Mr. President: Washington. January 24, 1918.

I conferred yesterday with members of the Council of National Defense with regard to the War Industries Board. Neither Secretary Lane nor Secretary Wilson was able to come.

Secretary Daniels believes that there are certain sentimental objections to the appointment of Mr. Baruch, but that his splendid loyalty to the Administration and the success which he has already achieved indicate him as the best man available for the place.

Secretary Redfield doubts Mr. Baruch's executive ability, but admits his great talents in the matter of raw material purchases with which he has been primarily engaged, and recommended the consideration of Mr. Woolley,[1] President of the American Radiator Company, who is now a member of the War Trade Board. I asked Mr. Vance McCormick about Mr. Woolley, and he says he is a man of very great ability as an organizer and executive, quiet but strong. He does not know about his political affiliations, nor have I been able to learn them.

Secretary Houston urgently believes that Mr. Baruch has not the necessary organizing and executive talents, believes in his loyalty and great ability, but thinks him spasmodic and fitful in the matter of organization and executive control.

This morning I had a talk with Mr. John D. Ryan, who came to say to me that he feared he had given me the wrong impression of his attitude toward this work in my other conversations with him. He said, tell the President that "I am ready to do anything he wants me to do and to do his way. I believe the necessary reorganizations in the War Industries Board will develop as the work progresses, and I would not like to have the President feel that I am strong-headed or obstinate in the matter. If he wanted me to undertake it, I would work it out his way." Under all the circumstances, not knowing Mr. Woolley, I believe that Mr. Ryan's appointment would be more acceptable in the eastern part of the country, and perhaps would carry the greatest assurance of strong business, executive capacity.

I think Mr. Baruch the most absolutely loyal man in sight, but I don't know enough about his executive capacity to have definite information about it.

The members of the Council present reviewed and approved the suggestion as to the form of reorganization recommended by Mr. Baruch. I think it important to have this carried out at the earliest possible moment, and if, in your judgment, Mr. Ryan's relations to mining industries throughout the west would not be prejudicial, I would recommend the selection of Mr. Ryan.

Respectfully yours,   Newton D. Baker

TLS (WP, DLC).
   [1] Clarence Mott Woolley.

From John Henry Fahey

Dear Mr. President: Boston January 24, 1918.

In view of the discussion over the Chamberlain Bill and the fact that the Chamber of Commerce of the United States has, from time to time, presented to you, Secretary Baker and Mr. Willard memoranda relative to centralizing control over the procurement of war supplies, I feel it may be worth while to call your attention to the fact that the National Chamber has not at any time advocated such a scheme as that proposed by Senator Chamberlain and I hope you have no such impression as to the Chamber's attitude. On the contrary, in considering the problem of control of purchasing, the Chamber has consistently adhered to the principle that the only safe course was to give the President full power to work out the best scheme without being hampered by detailed provisions of new or old statutes.

The thought of most of us has been that a bill should be passed, which would be very general in its terms, giving the President power to suspend provisions of existing law as to the authority of Bureaus or Departments, and to transfer the functions of any of the various Bureaus to new control as he thought necessary, so that there could be absolute freedom in making readjustments, as experience and the development of the war program indicated was necessary. To make clear this idea, so far as the members of the Chamber are concerned, the Atlantic City Convention voted:

"That Congress be requested to pass such statute as may be necessary *to give the President of the United States all power necessary to concentrate in this manner the resources and industrial energy of our country.*"

There are some of our members who have believed in a Department of Munitions, and unfortunately the idea that the Chamber was for this particular device was strengthened by certain statements in the memoranda sent you in November.[1] We found Mr. Willard received the same impression from this memoranda, but this misapprehension was corrected, I believe, in a letter sent to you by President Rhett[2] and by our personal conferences with Mr. Willard.

In your statement concerning the Chamberlain proposal, there is a suggestion that the clearing up of some problems would be accellerated if Congress would remove some of the statutory obstacles of department organization. This is quite in line with the discussions of the Chamber's Committee and it seems to me it is the only common-sense course to follow.

I am not chairman of the War Committee of the Chamber, which has been giving this organization problem attention, and I am writing only on my personal responsibility, but as a member of the Committee, and as one being rather familiar with developments since last April, it occurs to me that it may be useful to remind you of the action taken by the Convention of the Chamber concerning the legislative side of war organization.

As a member of the War Committee of the Chamber, I have been in Washington for three or four days almost every week since last May. During this period I have heard all kinds of organization plans discussed by business men and others active in the various Administrations, Council of National Defense and the War Industries Board. Through it all I have been greatly impressed with two facts:

1—That those advocating a particular scheme of organization usually considered it from but on[e] angle, based upon experience in their own environment, without study of the problem in its entirety.

2—Plans which men insisted upon six months ago they have now abandoned, because experience has proven they would not work.

All that has happened thus far has demonstrated that sound organization must develop step by step. It cannot be thrown together over night. I believe the reorganizations and readjustments have now reached the point where more effective coordination is easier of accomplishment, but even now I do not think it can be done with a rush. It is very easy for men to apply the cure-all of a particular piece of machinery when they have not really studied the situation and informed themselves as to its complications, but I am very confident that the great majority of business men must agree that proper centralization of control is not to be secured all at once and simply by adopting the British or any other formula.

The War Committee of the Chamber is meeting in Washington the first of the week and is to have a conference with Secretary Baker on Wednesday. If anything develops relating to the proposals under discussion in Congress in connection with which I can be of any service, so far as the business men are involved, I will be very glad to help in any way in my power. With this thought in mind, I will take the liberty of keeping in touch with Mr. Tumulty and will rely on his informing me if there is anything I can do.

With all good wishes,   Sincerely yours,   John H Fahey

TLS (WP, DLC).
[1] Printed as an Enclosure with R. G. Rhett to WW, Nov. 15, 1917, Vol. 45.
[2] R. G. Rhett to WW, Dec. 14, 1917, Vol. 45.

From Gutzon Borglum, with Enclosure

My dear Mr. President: Washington, D. C. Jan. 24, 1918.

My letter sent you today, & of date Jan 21st, was the preface to my report which is written and has been prepared for some days. I am ready to deliver it into your hands at an hours notice.

I agree fully with you and have painfully observed the caution you advised   Sincerely and Faithfully   Gutzon Borglum

ALS (WP, DLC).

E N C L O S U R E

From Gutzon Borglum

My dear Mr. President: Washington, D. C., January 21, 1918.

I am placing in your hands today a report upon the aeronautic situation,[1] entering as deeply as I have been able to do considering the circumstances.

The statements, grave as they appear are based upon a mass of information available to you, or to anyone you may hereafter designate to receive it, except those who have used their official position to delay, mislead and obstruct the nation's work, and my effort to get the truth and value to my inquiry.

Before I had been here twenty-four hours, I found that my presence and purpose were known, that I was watched, that officials who should have aided me had intercommunicated, attempted to mislead me and block every avenue I approached. I was in a quandary as to what was best to do, resort to the authority of your letter and demand vesture of such authority from the Secretary of War as was necessary to secure data, or to hoe my row alone. I informed the Secretary of War of my difficulties—with the result that I have made my investigation without aid.

Further than this, I have disturbed no one. My own large personal acquaintance stood me in good stead; I gained entrance and secured evidence everywhere, and fortunately have been able to connect the broken links of a chain of dishonesty and disorder that runs throughout our production department. I have seen records, received copies of reports, been the center of information volunteered from officers, members of Congress, merchants and manufacturers. I have sent agents to the factories, was refused or equally hindered by delay by General Squier, and so what I send here has been wrung from official Washington from men sworn to help, men whose whole lives would be benefitted by frank service in the work they are engaged upon for you and for the nation.

I am speaking in this way because I have only the faintest hope that what I have done will be, or can be quickly and constructively applied to our departmental government. What I suggest will require men of courage, fearless prosecution, almost immediate seizure of the manufactories engaged in the work here investigaged [investigated], without reference to the unhappy men who have crept into regular army officers' uniforms and who will get in time a regular army officer's court martial. I fear unless something of this nature is done failure in this great department and publicly investigated scandal will result, which, stepping upon the heels of preceding scandals, will accomplish little of a corrective nature—but further delays in this most important work.

I believe that you might seize this whole bankrupt program, present the situation to the Senate Military Committee, request abeyance of their investigation, complete what is here begun and then, under your own guidance, urge the Military Committee to prosecute its inquiry to the end—with your aid and direction.

This has seemed to me to be the constructive plan, to be the harmonious plan, that would result in rebuilding, would give us time to correct the present ills and with men who desire it we can still deliver some machines in Europe.

Sincerely and faithfully,   Gutzon Borglum

I am waiting to present to you in person my inquiry. GB[2]

TLS (WP, DLC).
[1] "Preliminary Report on Aeronautic Conditions," Jan. 21, 1918, T MS (G. Borglum Papers, DLC). Borglum reported that his investigation had found "a terrible state of confusion and irregularity . . . due to self-interest, and intrigue, together with predeterminism to thwart the effort of our nation and the work of able and trusted assistants." Despite the great resources assigned to produce aircraft, Borglum added, very few airplanes had actually been completed. The chief culprit, Borglum said, was Col. Edward Andrew Deeds. In Borglum's words, "Deeds dominates everything." Borglum noted that Deeds, a manufacturer of Dayton, Ohio, was not an engineer but a salesman and promoter, was of German extraction (the name was originally Dietz), and was the founder of the Delco Ignition System. Among other things, Borglum went on, Deeds had been managing vice-president of the National Cash Register Company and had

been convicted of participating in a corrupt conspiracy involving the hiring and bribing of employees of competitors. Deeds had come to Washington in 1917 as a colonel and had been appointed to the Aircraft Board and other influential posts. Borglum charged that Deeds had misused his position in several ways. In summing up, Borglum wrote that "Deed's powerful Teutonic personality" seemed to have "completely hypnotized the trusting, scientific mind of General Squier," and that Squier and Howard E. Coffin were issuing reassuring statements about aircraft production without being fully aware of what was going on.

² Tumulty attached the following note: "Dear Governor: I should like to discuss with you just how things should be handled after you have seen Borglum. J.P.T." JPT to WW, Jan. 24, 1918, TL (WP, DLC).

From Robert Lansing

My dear Mr. President: Washington January 25, 1918.

I presume you have read the telegrams from Rome indicating a measure of dissatisfaction or at least of disappointment on the part of the Italian Government and people with the statement in your address of January 8th relative to Italy and presumably the statement in regard to Austria-Hungary. The point which the Italians seem to make is that if their frontiers are to be rectified only on the basis of nationality, they will be as vulnerable to attack from Austria-Hungary as they have been in the past. That is, the Adriatic Question will remain unsettled and will compel the nation to continue its present policy of defense.

There is no doubt but that Italy's position in the Adriatic is more or less precarious and that it is one which the Italian Government seeks to make more stable in the final peace. The Italian coast is low-lying and without harbors. It offers no opportunities for naval bases from which to operate. On the other hand, the opposite coast is indented with numerous inlets and ports. As a consequence the Italian shores are difficult of defense and control of the Adriatic lies to a very considerable degree with the power possessing the eastern shores of the sea.

Manifestly an adjustment of the Italian frontiers along lines of nationality will in no way cure this situation or make Italy's position more secure than it is at present. I think that this is the ground for Italian dissatisfaction, and it is not entirely without justification.

While, as you know, I am strongly inclined to nationality as the basis for territorial limits I believe that it cannot be invariably adopted, but that in certain cases physical boundaries and strategic boundaries must be considered and modify boundaries based on nationality. These will constitute exceptions to the general rule but will be very few in number.

I mention this at the present time because I fear that if Italy gains the impression that she is not to strengthen her position in the Adriatic, the Italian people will become discouraged and feel that the war has no actual interest for them, that they will be disposed to make peace provided the Germans and Austrians retire from Italian territory, and that they will consider themselves to have been abandoned by this country and the Allies. With the present policital [political] situation in Italy and the depression following their military reverses such an impression would be most unfortunate and might be disastrous.

Do you not think that something could be done to restore Italian confidence that a satisfactory settlement of the Adriatic Question will be made at the peace conference? If anything can be done it seems to me it ought be done without delay.

Faithfully yours,   Robert Lansing.

TLS (SDR, RG 59, 763.72119/1265½A, DNA).

From Thomas Watt Gregory

My dear Mr. President: Washington, D. C. January 25th, 1918.

I have the honor to acknowledge receipt of your letter of the 8th inst.,[1] calling my attention to newspaper dispatches relating to the election of an alien enemy as mayor of Michigan City, Indiana, and asking whether there is not some way in which we could prevent his occupying the office.

After a careful investigation of the facts relating to this man Fred C. Miller, I do not believe that any action should be taken on the part of the Government. Miller took office on January 1st, having been elected for the third time as mayor. He is a middle aged man who came, as a boy, to this country with his father's family; he has claimed and now claims that he became a naturalized citizen of the United States by virtue of the naturalization during his minority, of his father. Either by reason of the destruction of the records of the court in which his father claimed to have been naturalized or some alleged clerical error, concerning which we have no accurate information, he has been unable to produce evidence of the naturalization of his father, who is now dead. Since reaching his majority he has always voted as a citizen and states that his father also voted as a citizen for many years. In the recent mayorality campaign the question of his citizenship was raised and Miller, in order to be on the safe side, applied to the United States Marshal of the district for an enemy alien permit, which was granted to him by the Marshal.

The United States Attorney for the district reports that this man could not be classed as dangerous in any respect and the United

States Marshal did not hesitate to grant him a permit in order to transact business at his office which was located within a prohibited area, surrounding a munition factory. Under your proclamation and the facts in our possession we would not be authorized to intern him as an alien enemy, even if he were such in fact, because the only evidence we have indicates that he is not dangerous.

My understanding is that some character of court proceeding was recently instituted in the Federal Courts of Indiana in order to test his right to hold the office of mayor and that the court held that there was nothing in the Law of Indiana, which prohibited an unnaturalized German from holding office,—at any rate the purpose of the suit failed.

There is at present no statute or regulation under which an alien enemy, duly elected to a municipal office can be prevented from performing the functions of such office. In my opinion however, you have the power, under the alien enemy statute, to make a regulation which would preclude an alien enemy from performing the functions of a municipal office, especially where those functions relate to police administration or have a vital relation to the conduct of the war. Apparently, with full knowledge of all the facts, the people of Michigan City, for the third time, have elected this man mayor, the issue of his loyalty and status as a citizen being one of the chief things discussed in the campaign. Taking this fact, as well as the others into consideration, I advise against any interference in this case.   Respectfully,   T. W. Gregory

TLS (WP, DLC).
  [1] WW to TWG, Jan. 8, 1918, TLS (Letterpress Books, WP, DLC).

From Philip Hiss[1]

Mr. President: New York January 25, 1918.

It is the testimony of the shipbuilders and the big gun manufacturers that skilled labor cannot be held long in temporary quarters, and that the day's output of middle-aged, skilled men is curtailed by barrack living and separation from their families. The turnover, the record of attendance and the day's record of accomplishment are ample evidence that the production of ships and munitions is directly dependent on living conditions, i.e., houses.

Plant equipment and raw material will not produce ships and guns unless enough labor can be hired and held.

Practically *every plant is operating at low efficiency because the men cannot be held*. They cannot be held *because they cannot secure homes*. In this the statement of employers and employees agree.

The problem of producing ships and guns, in so far as it is dependent on housing, is two-fold.

1. Need for temporary houses.
2. Need for permanent houses.

This is determined by:

1. Probable permanent need for labor after the war.
2. Present need for skilled men of settled years for shipbuilding and work on guns and gun carriages.
3. Present need for common labor.

The plan of the Housing Committee is:

1. To provide temporary quarters for immediate needs, and for common labor.
2. To begin at once construction of permanent quarters for skilled labor and to push the work to completion with all possible speed. It is probable that these men would consent to live in temporary quarters until the completion of the permanent houses, but they cannot stand the strain long; and the delay and expense of replacing them, even when it is possible, bids fair to defeat our war program and our commercial shipping. The promise of permanent homes will hold the best man for a time in temporary quarters.

This plan is urged:

1. Because it is absolutely essential to maximum production of ships and guns.
2. Because it will do more than any other one thing to prevent the industrial revolution which threatens our country after the war.

England has recognized this problem and is devoting untiring efforts to its solution. Are we to menace our political prestige and to lose our position in the front rank of industry and commerce by refusing to deal with the housing problem on the broad and comprehensive plans adopted by our allies?

Mr. President, by means of this housing program you have the chance to weld capital and labor together into an irresistible industrial machine. No greater opportunity has presented itself to an Administration to earn the gratitude of a great and loyal people.

I have the honor to remain,

Your obedient servant, Philip Hiss.

TLS (WP, DLC).
[1] A member of the New York architectural firm of Hiss and Weeks, Hiss was at this time chairman of the section on housing of the Advisory Commission of the Council of National Defense. He was also special assistant for housing in the Navy Department.

From Milton Andrew Romjue[1]

My dear Mr. President: Washington, D. C. Jan. 25, 1918.

It is quite evident that for political reasons and with sinister motives some effort is being made to discredit the war policy program of this Government. The main result of which is but to, in my opinion, cripple and hinder the efficiency of our Government program in the war. I am quite sure the larger number of democrats, in congress, are willing to and will stand loyally back of you.

Personally, I would be very glad to know definitely your attitude on the War Cabinet and Universal Military Training so that I may be able to render you as much help as possible. I do not desire to rely upon information which I gather from the newspapers; but prefer to have your wishes which I shall treat with confidence, so far as your correspondence is concerned. It seems to me that the War Cabinet from what I hear of it, at this time, would hinder rather than expedite our success in the war and that consideration of Universal Military Training could well be deferred for the future.

I shall be very glad to hear from you.

Most respectfully,   M A Romjue

TLS (WP, DLC).
    [1] Democratic congressman from Missouri.

To Émile Lucien Hovelaque[1]

[The White House]
My dear Professor Hovelaque: 26 January, 1918

I particularly appreciate your courtesy in sending me the souvenir of the celebration in Paris of the foundation of New Orleans. It surprised and pleased me to learn that in the midst of so many troubles and duties it was possible to turn aside for the celebration of this event so interesting to both your own country and mine. I wish I might have been present to enjoy the evidences of international friendship which made the occasion so particularly gracious.

We have greatly admired the medal, not merely because of its sentiment but also because of its truly artistic workmanship.

We retain many delightful recollections of your visit to us,[2] and Mrs. Wilson joins me in warm regard, begging with me that you will convey to all concerned in this kind remembrance of us our sincere appreciation.   Cordially yours,   Woodrow Wilson

TLS (Letterpress Books, WP, DLC).
    [1] Hovelaque, Inspector-General of Public Instruction in France, was president of the Bi-Centennial Committee of the Founding of New Orleans. At a reception for the del-

egates from Louisiana at the Hôtel de Ville in Paris on October 26, 1917, he gave to the City of Paris a commemorative medal from the committee. For his remarks and an account of the ceremonies, see "Bi-Centennial Celebration in Paris," *Louisiana Historical Quarterly,* I (Jan. 8, 1918), 18-38. Hovelaque's communication to Wilson is missing, but presumably it came with a copy of the medal.

² Hovelaque had been a member of the French mission to the United States in April and May 1917. See Wilson's conversation with Joffre, May 2, 1917, and Jusserand's telegram to the Foreign Ministry, received on May 3, 1917, both printed in Vol. 42.

To Franklin Knight Lane

Confidential.

My dear Lane: [The White House] 26 January, 1918

Your suggestion about the electrical welding is indeed very important and I shall take it up with Hurley right away.

In haste   Faithfully yours,   [Woodrow Wilson]

CCL (WP, DLC).

To Edward Nash Hurley

Confidential.

My dear Hurley: [The White House] 26 January, 1918

I think the advice contained in the enclosed letter from Lane[1] is exceedingly sound and that you ought to act on it no matter what your advisers say, at any rate up to the point of giving it an absolute testing out.

The electrical welding accomplished such wonders in the rapid repair of the extensive injuries done to the German ships which we took over that I can easily see its use might be almost indefinitely extended.

In haste
            Cordially and faithfully yours,   [Woodrow Wilson]

CCL (WP, DLC).
[1] Lane's letter is missing in the E. N. Hurley Papers, InNd.

To Ollie Murray James

My dear Senator: [The White House] 26 January, 1918

You did a great piece of work in the Senate the other day in handling Senator Chamberlain's unfair attack and I am warmly obliged to you. It was an artistic job.[1] How much stronger the truth always is than the false!

With warm appreciation and admiration,
                Sincerely yours,   Woodrow Wilson

TLS (Letterpress Books, WP, DLC).
¹ Chamberlain, on January 24, had risen in the Senate on a question of personal privilege to reply to Wilson's statement of January 21. Chamberlain began by having these documents read into the *Record*: Wilson's letter to him of January 20, his reply of January 21, Wilson's public statement, just cited, all of which are printed above at the dates indicated, and Chamberlain's own reply to the public statement. The last two items were reprinted in parallel columns from the *Washington Herald*, Jan. 22, 1918, in *Cong. Record*, 65th Cong., 2d sess., pp. 1194-96. Chamberlain then addressed the Senate to support the position which he had taken and to insert various reports in the *Record*; they emphasized alleged inadequate supplies and medical care for troops in training. He said at one point that he was "very sorry" that Wilson had said that the senators had not consulted him about the proposed legislation, but that he, Chamberlain, and Hitchcock had in fact discussed it with Wilson for an hour, after which Wilson had written his letter of January 11 (WW to G. E. Chamberlain, Jan. 11, 1918, Vol. 45). James then intervened to ask: "Is it not true that the President when he stated that he had not been consulted referred to the 'superior war cabinet' bill and not to the 'munitions ministry' bill?" Chamberlain replied: "That may be so; I think it is susceptible of that construction." James then, with Chamberlain's agreement, had Wilson's letter to James of January 23 (printed at that date in this volume) also read into the record. Further discussion took place, and Chamberlain said that he had not intended "to be understood as questioning the veracity of the President in any way." To this James responded: "I feel sure the Senator did not; but I believe that, upon second thought, the Senator will realize when he reads the letter the President directed to him, together with the letter directed to me, they make it perfectly clear that the President is absolutely right in his statement that he was not consulted." *Ibid.*, pp. 1196-1208.

To Arthur Brisbane

Personal.

My dear Mr. Brisbane: [The White House] 26 January, 1918

Your editorial in the Times night before last on Mr. Roosevelt and his present objects here was a corker.¹ He is certainly not setting forward those purposes of harmony and cooperation which are absolutely essential just now in the counsels and in the action of the country.

Cordially and sincerely yours,   Woodrow Wilson

TLS (Letterpress Books, WP, DLC).
¹ Brisbane's "Today" column in the *Washington Times*, Jan. 24, 1918, referred to recent political attacks by Roosevelt on Wilson as having "encouraged Germany and prolonged German resistance." The editorial (a clipping of which is in WP, DLC) included these statements:
"Mr. Roosevelt comes to Washington as the spokesman of high finance, and acts as the agent of the very rich, organizing a political fight to give the corporations control of the United States Government at the next Congressional election.
"This spectacle of a former President visiting the Capital to organize war against the Government when the nation is at war with Germany is something new, and most original of Theodore Roosevelt's many original ideas. . . ."

To Milton Andrew Romjue

My dear Mr. Romjue: [The White House] 26 January, 1918

I warmly appreciate your letter of yesterday and take pleasure in replying to it.

My attitude with regard to the proposed War Cabinet is that it would add machinery without adding efficiency and that to introduce men inexperienced in the great task we have been working at for ten months and make them masters of that great task would be hardly less than childish.

My opinion with regard to universal military training is exactly that stated by the Secretary of War to the Senate Committee on Military Affairs. It would manifestly interfere with and not advance our present military preparations and activities to add universal military training to our present programme now, and the question whether it should be added after the war is over seems to me to depend entirely upon circumstances which we cannot now forecast. In both these respects I am glad to find my own judgment in accordance with your own.

Very sincerely yours, Woodrow Wilson

TLS (Letterpress Books, WP, DLC).

To John Hollis Bankhead

My dear Senator: [The White House] 26 January, 1918

I warmly appreciate your very generous letter of January twenty-fifth.[1] I received the messages to which you refer and did not for a moment feel that you needed to make any further reply to my suggestion about the Alabama coal operators.

You have rendered a real national service in bringing about the right understanding there[2] and I am warmly obliged to you.

Cordially and sincerely yours, Woodrow Wilson

TLS (Letterpress Books, WP, DLC).
  [1] It is missing.
  [2] A convention of Alabama miners, on December 21, 1917, had accepted working conditions proposed by Richard Rembrandt Peale of the Fuel Administration, and the Alabama Coal Operators' Association also agreed to them in January. John Hollis Bankhead, Jr., president of the Bankhead Coal Company and son of the Senator, was one of the two accredited representatives of the association in the negotiations. For the text of Peale's memorandum of December 14, and for further information, see *United Mine Workers Journal*, XXVIII (Dec. 27, 1917), 6-7, and *ibid.*, Jan. 31, 1918, p. 5. Peale was also president of Peale, Peacock & Kerr, miners and shippers of coal.

To John Henry Fahey

My dear Mr. Fahey: [The White House] 26 January, 1918

I am glad to get the information which your letter of January twenty-fourth brings me about the attitude of the Chamber of Commerce of the United States. Nobody who is not in direct contact with the problems of organization and cooperation as I am daily can realize how imperfectly and crudely such propositions as are now being widely discussed for radical readjustments meet the difficulties and necessities of the case. The faith that some people put in machinery is child-like and touching, but the machinery does not do the task; particularly is it impossible to do it if new and inexperienced elements are introduced.

Cordially and sincerely yours,   Woodrow Wilson

TLS (Letterpress Books, WP, DLC).

To John Sharp Williams

My dear Senator: The White House 26 January, 1918

I have your letter of January twenty-fifth[1] and agree both with you and your correspondent, whose letter I am herewith returning.[2]

In haste, with warm regard and sincere appreciation of your generous championship of the administration,

Cordially and sincerely yours,   Woodrow Wilson

TLS (J. S. Williams Papers, DLC).

[1] J. S. Williams to WW, Jan. 25, 1918, CCL (J. S. Williams Papers, DLC). Williams enclosed a letter from one of Wilson's "most earnest supporters" in Mississippi, who happened also to edit "the most influential paper in the State, that is, influential on your side." He was Frederick Sullens of the *Jackson Daily News*. Williams also commented that the Departments of Justice and of the Interior seemed to appoint "just anybody" whom Senator Vardaman recommended, but that his own suggestions were viewed with suspicion.

[2] Sullens' letter is missing.

To Thomas Watt Gregory

The White House

My dear Mr. Attorney General: 26 January, 1918

I know how difficult it is for you to deal with Senator John Sharp Williams because of the attitude he has taken under a very serious misapprehension, but I quite agree with his judgment that we not only ought to pay no attention to Senator Vardaman's recommendations for office, but that we ought studiously to avoid nominating men whom he picks out.

I haven't thought to discuss this thing with you as I ought to have done, but of course want to do so whenever the occasion arises for making an appointment in Mississippi.

Cordially and faithfully yours,   Woodrow Wilson

TLS (T. W. Gregory Papers, DLC).

To George Washington Goethals

[The White House]

My dear General Goethals: 26 January, 1918

Allow me to acknowledge the receipt of your letter of December twenty-ninth,[1] which has just been laid before me, transmitting the report of the Commission created in accordance with the Act of Congress of September third and fifth, 1916, to observe the operation and effects of the institution of the eight-hour standard work day; and to thank you for the same. I have taken pleasure in transmitting it to the Congress.[2]

With much respect,

Sincerely yours, [Woodrow Wilson]

CCL (WP, DLC).
[1] G. W. Goethals to WW, Dec. 29, 1917, TLS (WP, DLC). In answer to an inquiry by Wilson, Goethals' secretary explained that the dispatch of the letter had been postponed because of delay in printing the report. E. L. Layton to R. Forster, Jan. 28, 1918, TLS (WP, DLC).
[2] The report, which became H. Doc. 690, went to Congress under cover of WW to the Senate and House of Representatives, Jan. 28, 1918, *Cong. Record*, 65th Cong., 2d sess., p. 1365.

To Walter Lowrie

My dear Mr. Lowrie: [The White House] 26 January, 1918

I was honestly sorry to miss you. I was in bed part of yesterday with a severe cold and unfortunately could not see anybody, but I must follow you with this line of sincere congratulation, for you are marrying a young lady whom I greatly admire.[1]

Cordially and sincerely yours, Woodrow Wilson

TLS (Letterpress Books, WP, DLC).
[1] Barbara Armour, daughter of Harriette Foote Armour and George Allison Armour of Princeton, was married there to the Rev. Walter Lowrie on February 9. Shortly afterward, she went with him to Rome, where he continued to serve as the rector of St. Paul's American Church. *Princeton Packet*, Feb. 15, 1918.

From Josephus Daniels

Dear Mr. President: Washington. Jan. 26. 1918.

At the last meeting of the Council of National Defense we talked about a successor of Daniel Willard. My opinion was and is that Mr. Baruch is the best man and that he would serve equally as well as any other man. Moreover he is loyal to the core to your administration, a factor that seems to me should have the greatest weight when other things are equal. Other members of the Council did not agree. With all deference to their judgment I wish you to know my view. You will best determine what to do.

Sincerely   Josephus Daniels

ALS (WP, DLC).

From Gutzon Borglum

Personal & Confidential to the President

My dear Mr President,   Washington, D. C. Jan 26, 1918

Personal needs compel me to return home. I have been here three weeks and am distressed at not being able to place my papers in your hands before leaving.

I do not know what else to say. I believe I understand the great task, world events have thrust upon this young people, and the blessed fortune of having at its head the mind and vision you bring. But never has great opportunity greatly understood more needed incorruptable loyal aids.

I am hurrying home heavy hearted with feelings of impotance. I have pulled the covers from another page of salesmanship, "manufacture[d] by newspaper"—and 'cash register' results, to be informed I must appear before the Senate Military Committee.

I dont like the way this business is drifting rudderless into avoidable entanglements. It's all wrong.

Faithfully & sincerely   Gutzon Borglum

ALS (WP, DLC).

From William Bauchop Wilson, with Enclosure

Dear Mr. President: Washington January 26, 1918.

I am in receipt of a letter from Senator Jones of Washington, with which he incloses copy of a letter to you under date of January 23d[1] relative to an intimation he has received that the Mediation Board is about to recommend to you that the lumber industry on the Pacific coast be placed upon and operated under an eight-hour basis, while this industry in other sections of the country will be permitted to run as it is now run.

For your information I am inclosing copy of my reply to Senator Jones.   Faithfully yours,   W B Wilson

TLS (WP, DLC).
    [1] Jones' letter to W. B. Wilson is missing, but W. L. Jones to WW, Jan. 23, 1918, TLS (WP, DLC), protests strongly against the institution of the eight-hour day in the lumber industry of the Northwest. W. L. Jones to WW, Jan. 26, 1918, TLS (WP, DLC), encloses a telegram of protest from the secretary of the West Coast Lumbermen's Association.

William Bauchop Wilson to Wesley Livsey Jones

My dear Senator: [Washington] January 25, 1918.

I am in receipt of your letter of the 23d instant, calling my attention to the persistent reports that have come to you that I propose to recommend that the eight-hour day be established in the Pacific Northwest in the lumber industry, without its being established in this industry in the other sections of the country.

This is a subject that has had a great deal of attention and concern from me in all its phases. I studied it at first hand during the hearings and deliberations of the President's Mediation Commission held at Seattle and since my return from the West, and if the labor situation was the same in all of the lumber producing sections of the country as it is in the Pacific Northwest, I would have no hesitancy in recommending to the President that the basic eight-hour day be applied to all of the lumber fields of the United States. So far as I am advised at the present time, no other lumber producing district is situated as is the Pacific Northwest in its surrounding circumstances. Nearly all the large industries on the Coast are being operated on an eight-hour work-day, with time and one-half for overtime. The wage rate for all classes of labor is high as compared with the pre-war period. These industries are absorbing large numbers of men. They will not go into the lumber industry on a ten-hour basis when they can secure an eight-hour work-day in the immediate vicinity with as high or higher wages and more comfortable housing conditions and social surroundings. As a result the lumber industry in the Pacific Northwest is short of labor. The spruce production is not more than fifty per cent of the needs of the Government, and I am advised by Mr. Hurley that the Shipping Board is unable to get the fir it needs for ship building purposes.

Under these circumstances I believe it is imperative that the Pacific Northwest lumbermen should accede to a basic eight-hour work-day, with time and one-half for overtime. I know of no other way in which civilian labor can be obtained to secure the necessary production of lumber. In any event, civilian labor, in my judgment, will have to be immediately supplemented by volunteers from the cantonments to promptly bring the lumber production up to the pressing needs of the Government. There is no other lumber producing section in the United States that has to meet these conditions. It would be useless to maintain equality of competitive conditions if they are unable to secure the labor to produce the necessary material to compete with. The lumbermen of the Pacific Northwest are so situated that they must meet the competition for labor as well as the competition for trade, or else the United States Government cannot be supplied with essential material to fill its imperative needs for aeroplanes and ships.

In handling the problem from the standpoint of the effect upon the patriotism of the employer who is required to establish a basic eight-hour work-day while his competitors in distant fields are permitted to continue on a ten-hour day, there must also be taken into consideration the effect upon the patriotism of the workman who is required to work a ten-hour day, while other workmen in the same vicinity doing work requiring similar skill are working but an eight-hour day. There must also be taken into consideration the disturbing effect which would follow the establishment of an eight-hour work-day in lumber districts where the surrounding labor is on a ten-hour day, as compared with the disturbing effect on other labor of establishing an eight-hour work-day where the surrounding labor is also upon an eight-hour work-day.

This is the situation as I found it in the Pacific Northwest, and which impels me to recommend to the President that the basic eight-hour day, with time and one-half for overtime, be instituted in that lumber field.   Respectfully yours,   W. B. Wilson

TCL (WP, DLC).

From Henry Jones Ford

My dear President Wilson: Princeton, N. J. January 26, 1918

I have never doubted that you have the matter constantly in mind, and I note that you made an important step in that direction when you restored the practice of direct personal address to Congress. That is a great point gained, but still it falls below constitutional duty. If our Constitution, like the French Constitution of 1791, made is simply the duty of the Executive to request the legislature to take the subject into consideration, the practice you have introduced would completely satisfy the requirement. But it is the duty of our President to recommend to Congress "such *measures* as he shall judge necessary and expedient." So far as one can judge, the present practice seems to be to request Congress to act, and then, by private negotiation, to recommend the measures to the standing committees.

If you will permit me to offer a suggestion I shall observe that present circumstances are such that it is quite possible to secure the support of the most powerful particular interest in the country in support of direct executive initiative of legislative measures. The railroads are painfully aware of their dismal failure in attempting to control public policy through friends on committees. They are anxious to submit themselves to public control openly administered by experts. It was really railroad influence that established the franchise jurisdiction of the New York Board of Estimates. Steps taken for introducing directly in Congress, measures prepared and recommended by the Inter-State Commerce Commission, would command the support of this same powerful influence.

If any project of the kind should be at any time contemplated I should be glad to cooperate. Young politicians of the class represented by the "Short Ballot Association" and *The New Republic* are solicitous of a lead from you in this direction, and I am often queried as to the prospect of one. I am, as ever

Faithfully yours   Henry J. Ford

ALS (WP, DLC).

Herbert Clark Hoover to Joseph Patrick Tumulty

Dear Tumulty: Washington, D. C. 26 *January 1918*

I enclose herewith a summary of the Rules for conservation[1] which we are proposing to send out tomorrow morning with the President's Proclamation.[2] We have delayed this matter until after the coal storm had blown by in order that we might secure for it proper attention in the press. As these are the rules referred to in the President's Proclamation and as we are sending them out under that caption, I am extremely anxious that they should be laid before the President today.

I apologize for not having had them ready yesterday, but we have been involved in large telegraphic correspondence with our State Administrators in an endeavour to arrive at measures that will take care of local situations.

I do not anticipate any unfavourable reaction of any kind from the country, as the ground work of this programme has been laid and it contains no privation, but rather, a stimulus to patriotic effort. There is in it no curtailment of trade relations of any consequence.

Would you be so kind as to help me out by asking the President if he could go over it during the course of today.

Yours faithfully,   Herbert Hoover

TLS (WP, DLC).

[1] The summary noted that the rules, effective January 28, would depend upon the good will of the American people and their willingness to sacrifice. It stated further: "We have but one police force—the American woman, and we depend upon her to organize in cooperation with our State and local Food Administrators to see that these rules are obeyed by that small minority who may fail. . . ." Among other things, the rules provided that, when buying wheat flour, consumers should buy an equal weight of other cereals, and that bakers would be required to provide Victory bread which contained

not less than 20 per cent of cereals other than wheat. Mondays and Wednesdays were to be wheatless days, and one meal each day a wheatless meal. Tuesdays would be meatless days, and one meal each day a meatless meal. In addition, Saturdays would be porkless days. T MS [Jan. 26, 1918] (WP, DLC). The summary and additional information are printed in the *Official Bulletin*, II (Jan. 28, 1918), 5-7.

² For the text of the proclamation, dated January 18 but released on January 26, see the *New York Times*, Jan. 27, 1918, or the *Official Bulletin*, II (Jan. 28, 1918), 3. The first paragraph reads as follows: "Many causes have contributed to create the necessity for a more intensive effort on the part of our people to save food in order that we may supply our associates in the war with the sustenance vitally necessary to them in these days of privation and stress. The reduced productivity of Europe because of the large diversion of manpower to the war, the partial failure of harvests, and the elimination of the more distant markets for foodstuffs through the destruction of shipping places the burden of their subsistence very largely on our shoulders."

From Robert Lansing

My dear Mr. President: Washington January 27, 1918.

The clear and explicit declaration of war aims contained in your address of January 8th has brought forth no corresponding declaration from the German Government. They have never made a definite statement of terms which would satisfy them, but have preferred to criticize the declarations of their enemies leaving their own aims uncertain. Even in the discussion of the addresses of yourself and of Lloyd George the Imperial Chancellor is, I believe intentionally, ambiguous, vague and careful to avoid making reply to certain propositions which might embar[r]ass Germany with her allies.¹

It seems to me that we are not getting the full benefit of your candid declaration of aims unless we point out that the German Government has never frankly stated their aims and are apparently unwilling to do so. I think that in some way, by an address, a letter or other means, you should challenge them to do this, possibly going so far as to challenge them to answer specific questions such as—What is the German purpose as to Belgium? What reparation will Germany make as to the occupied regions of Belgium and France? What is Germany's aim as to Alsace-Lorraine? What is Germany's attitude as to the independence of Poland, and what territories is it proposed to include in the new nation? What is Germany's aim as to the Baltic provinces of Russia? Does Germany insist that Armenia shall remain under Turkish rule and that Palestine shall be restored to the Turks? Questions such as these if unanswered will place Germany in an unenviable light before the world, and I am convinced that they will be unanswered.

It seems to me that there is an opportunity to weaken very materially the German peace propaganda by showing that, while they seek our war aims, they are unwilling to disclose their own.

Faithfully yours,   Robert Lansing.

TLS (WP, DLC).

[1] Hertling had addressed the Main Committee of the Reichstag on January 24 and had commented briefly, point-by-point, on Wilson's Fourteen Points, except Points 9, 10, and 11, which he left for Czernin to reply to. For one translation of Hertling's speech, see *FR-WWS 1918*, 1, I, 38-42. For other translations, with variations in coverage as well as in language, see the London *Times*, Jan. 26, 1918 (text reprinted in Carnegie Endowment for International Peace, *Official Statements of War Aims and Peace Proposals, December 1916 to November 1918*, James Brown Scott, ed., Washington, 1921, pp. 246-54), and the *New York Times*, Jan. 26, 1918. The German text is printed in *Schulthess' Europäischer Geschichtskalender*, LIX (1918), Part 1, pp. 19-26. For analyses of Hertling's speech, see the memorandum by W. C. Bullitt printed at Jan. 29, 1918, and the Enclosure printed with G. Auchincloss to WW, Feb. 3, 1918.

From William Gibbs McAdoo

Dear Governor,   [Washington] Jany 27, 1918

The appointment of Mr. Stettinius,[1] a member of J. P. Morgan & Co. to have such large control over purchases for the War Department and the suggestion that Mr. Ryan[2] may be appointed Chairman of the War Industries Board prompts me to venture a suggestion.

Confidentially I think the Stettinius appointment very unfortunate. As I have been going over the country I have been impressed with the suspicion of and feeling against the big interests—and J. P. Morgan & Co. particularly as they are believed (and justly, I think) to have made enormous sums through financing and purchasing for the allies prior to our entrance into the War. This is one of the reasons I was so anxious to create the Interally Purchasing Commission here and to get away from the Morgan connection and influence. The masses of the people distrust Morgan & Co. the National City Bank and the so called Copper Trust, just as they do the Standard Oil Trust, which is supposed or is believed to have a large interest in the Amalgamated Copper Co. of which Mr Ryan is President.

Recently Mr. Baker[3] made Mr McRoberts[4] (Vice President of the National City Bank) a Colonel & put him in charge of very important matters. McRoberts is a protege of Armour & Co., I am told, and was put in the National City through their influence. McRoberts & Stettinius are Republicans, and while this alone does not disqualify them, it is not possible to count on their complete loyalty, I fear, when bitter partisan attacks are under way by their party.

Mr. Ryan is a democrat and I like him personally but he is a part of the Morgan, Natl. City Bank, Standard Oil group and if he is appointed, I am afraid the country will believe that the administration has completely surrendered to "big interests" in the War Department where the chief expenditures of the Government are being made. I am sure that it will be a mistake.

There is another side to it which I think you ought to consider. It would be a great injustice to Baruch to put a new man over him— one who knows nothing of the work—when Baruch has been on the job for the past 8 months, knows it thoroughly and is, without doubt, the best qualified and the ablest man for the place. His promotion would be the natural thing. He is absolutely loyal and dependable. He is also the head of the Inter Ally Purchasing Board here—has done all the work—and has been your consistent supporter while Stettinius, the Morgan firm, & the City Bank have been our bitterest enemies.

Mr. Baker once told me he thought that Baruch's reputation as a "Wall St. speculator" disqualified him. I think he overemphasizes if he does not misjudge this point. There have been no bigger Wall St. speculators & manipulators than Morgan & Co. and we take more chances on Stettinius on this score than on Baruch. But Baruch has retired from Wall St. entirely while Mr Stettinius has not, I am told.

I have no interest in Baruch's promotion on personal grounds. I am simply eager for your and Baker's success and the discomfiture of the enemies of the administration. I do not believe it wise or sound policy to put ourselves too fully in the hands of our enemies and the "interests" and take the unnecessary risk of losing the confidence of the masses of the people as well.

If, however, you should decide to put Ryan at the head of the War Industries Board, I think you ought to give Baruch a chance to retire gracefully. I should be glad to put him at the head of the Purchasing Division of the Railroads of the U. S. This is an immensely important piece of work and I will take it up with him if you think well of it. This would hamper the Inter Ally purchasing I fear, but after all we are getting back to what I have believed from the beginning to be the wise plan, a *single* head to buy for the allies and ourselves. So, if Baruch is promoted to Chairmanship of War Industries Board we should get, in effect, the single head for the allies and ourselves. If Ryan is put there, then he should take the ally business as well.

Please dont think I want to interfere in Baker's department. The matter concerns the Treasury as well as the whole Administration & I have felt at liberty therefore to submit my views merely for your information and for what they may be worth.

Affectionately Yours   W G McAdoo

ALS (WP, DLC).
[1] Edward Reilly Stettinius had just been appointed Surveyor General of Supplies in the Office of the Director of Purchases.
[2] That is, John D. Ryan.

From Lincoln Ross Colcord

Dear Mr. President: Washington, D. C. 27 January, 1918.

The other day when Mr. Brougham and I were calling on you,[1] you spoke of liberalism in Germany. Since then the situation there has greatly cleared. Von Hertling has disclosed the weak hand of the militarists, and now Scheidemann has spoken.[2]

The last time that Scheidemann spoke out in this fashion was at the time of the passage of the Reichstag Resolutions in July.[3] On the floor of the Reichstag he threatened the Imperial Government with revolution; but since there was no answer from beyond the borders, he could not go on. The enemies of Germany definitely defeated his best intentions and their own avowed aims. With sound political sagacity he has waited for the pendulum to swing again. He has retained his following, and speaks authoritatively for German liberalism.

I believe with all my heart that you could stop the war now before the spring offensive. I believe that if you would recognize the government of the Soviet in Russia, incorporate into that recognition a statement to the effect that Alsace-Lorraine and similar territorial questions were fitter subject for negotiation than for military decision, repeat that we never could negotiate with German militarism, and in some way acknowledge the present efforts of liberalism in Germany, that liberalism would overturn the Imperial government within a month, and the war for democracy would be won.

Such action, to be frank and effective, might estrange the present governments of England and France, but these governments are in the minority to-day. They must be estranged anyway if liberalism is to be accomplished. I believe that the time to strike has come. The peoples of England and France would complete the task for you. British labor has already spoken in no uncertain language. And the people of France, the soldiers in the trenches, are openly saying that they will not fight for the restoration of Alsace-Lorraine.

The opportunity before you, Mr. President, of uniting the peoples of the world by a master-stroke of liberalism and faith, of clearing out the nests of old governments, and of bringing the war to a triumphant close, has never been so open as it is today. The awful bloodshed of the spring offensive, a bloodshed which will be largely unavailing, can and must be averted. The whole social trend of the war makes it imperative that you save the situation now. The tottering governments of England and France are driving the peoples to their last stand. The spring offensive will not be the clear-cut issue which we commonly contemplate; it will break in revolution on every hand, and may easily pull down society in disaster.

I am taking the great liberty, in this connection, of bringing the name of Raymond E. Swing to your attention. Mr. Swing was the Berlin correspondent of the Chicago Daily News for six years, and knows German liberalism from top to bottom. He is a personal friend of Scheidemann. He thinks in the constructive terms of the new world. Would it be too much to hope that you might spare time to talk with him at this time? I believe he could bring you information which no one else in America possesses.

I am, my dear Mr. President,

Faithfully yours,   Lincoln Colcord[4]

TLS (WP, DLC).

[1] They saw Wilson at the White House on January 16, presumably to talk about Baruch's plan for a newspaper which would present the administration's point of view.

[2] Scheidemann replied to Hertling's speech of January 24 on the same day. Scheidemann said that it was a mistake for the Chancellor to doubt whether Wilson's message was an honest peace effort; eleven of his Fourteen Points were immediately acceptable, and the only questions remaining in dispute were those concerning Alsace-Lorraine and Belgium. The former had to remain German, Scheidemann said, but Belgium should be completely and honorably restored. Scheidemann also criticized the "sword conquerors," who had promised that the submarine warfare and then the army's offensive force would bring victory for Germany. The submarine campaign had had some success, he said, but it had brought the United States into the war, and this would mean long and uncertain combat in the West, with no logical stopping place. Meanwhile, he noted, negotiations with the Russians were lagging, and, at home, German politicians of the Right were saying that the Reichstag's peace resolution of July 19, 1917, had been scrapped. Admiral von Tirpitz had told his supporters: "Have no anxiety. The Fatherland Party and the Chancellor are united. Vital necessities will be guaranteed." Also, Scheidemann continued, food difficulties were certainly as acute in Germany as in Britain and France. He warned the current rulers of Germany that, if they did not bring peace with Russia, they would be hurled from power. London *Times*, Jan. 28, 1918; *New York Times*, Jan. 27, 1918. For the text of Scheidemann's speech, see *Schulthess*, LIX (1918), Part 1, pp. 26-28. About the Fatherland Party, see the memorandum by W. C. Bullitt, Jan. 29, 1918, n. 1.

[3] The so-called "Peace Resolution," about which see P. M. Warburg to EMH, July 15, 1917, n. 1, Vol. 43.

[4] Tumulty attached a note, dated January 29: "Dear Governor: I hope you will be especially careful in replying to this. J.P.T." JPT to WW, Jan. 29, 1918, TL (WP, DLC).

From the Diary of Colonel House

[Washington] January 27, 1918.

Mrs. Wilson telephoned saying the President would like me to come to dinner in order that we might have a conference afterward.

I found the President still suffering from a cold, but able to get about and to dine in the breakfast room. I mentioned to him that he did not seem worried at the attacks being made upon him in Congress and elsewhere concerning the management of the war.

He replied, "You would think they would know me well enough by now to see that they cannot force me to do what I consider unwise."

There was no one at dinner excepting the President, Mrs. Wilson, Miss Bones and myself. After dinner we went to the study, lighted the fire, and began a discussion of the speeches of the German Chancellor and the Austrain [Austrian] Prime Minister.[1] We discussed the advisability of making an answer. My advice was to do nothing for the present; that the situation was becoming more and more favorable for peace, and that no chances should be taken of making a wrong step.

This agreed with the President's view, and it was decided to keep in close touch with the situation and let it develop further before coming to a definite conclusion.

He said he had received a letter from Mr. Bryan which stated among other things that he, Bryan, was preparing for the peace conference with the expectation that the President would make him a commissioner. The President was distressed over this and asked what I would advise. I asked what he had replied to Bryan. He said he had evaded the question by not mentioning it, but writing about the other matters which the letter contained. He wanted to know if I did not think the best excuse would be to appoint officials rather than individuals, and Bryan could be given this as an excuse. I did not believe this would carry very far. I told him I had changed my mind as to the size of the commission. I thought at one time it should not consist of more than himself, or at least, be very small. The Paris Inter-Allied Conference has taught me that this was an impossible working arrangement; that it would be necessary to have sufficient members to go upon the different committees which must be formed to discuss and formulate policies.

The President wondered if I thought five would be sufficient. I thought it would be, but that seven would be better. This would give four democrats and three republicans. He immediately announced his intention of not appointing more than two republicans in any event. I had some difficulty in persuading him that if he went to the conference, he would dominate our representatives, and that he need have no apprehension as to how they would vote. What I have in mind is a unit rule which would make for a united front, therefore, a majority would decide.

Mrs. Wilson said she was disappointed to hear that there would be anyone excepting the President and myself. "I thought that you and Woodrow would go alone" she naively said. The President asked if I had thought of the possible delegates. Much to my surprise he said, "I suppose Lansing would have to go." To which I readily assented. He said, "Lansing with you and myself would make three, and if we have five, it would not be necessary to go outside." If we had more, he wondered what I thought of Baker to represent the War Department. He thought this would give an excuse to Bryan because I was so nearly official, and so closely wrapped up with all his policies and the Afministration [Administration], that my appointment would be expected.

Mrs. Wilson wondered how Root or Taft would do. Again, to my surprise, the President did not seriously object. I thought that Taft would be the better of the two, for the reason that he comes from Ohio and if Lansing went on from New York, we would not want two from that State. I thought also that Taft would be more flexible and tractable, for he is good natured and easily led.

I suggested as a possibility, Senator Johnson of California. The President did not have any opinion of this one way or the other since he did not know Johnson. Neither do I, but I shall look him up and get some idea of his mentality and attitude.

We went over the Foreign Relations Committee of the Senate, but without result. Stone, the Chairman, was utterly out of the question. Lodge, on the other side, was almost as objectionable, because of his narrow and partisan attitude. I wondered if Lawrence Lowell would do. He thought not. He did not think much of college presidents. I was surprised at this, and told him that the last time we talked, he told me the hope of the country he thought was in the universities, by which I assumed he meant the presidents. He replied that he did not, but meant more particularly the factulties [faculties] or people associated directly or indirectly with the universities. I told him the only two college presidents I had met who were equal to the task of being President were himself and Houston. As a matter of fact, I had Mezes in mind also, but I did not consider it wise to mention him because of our relationship.

This led to our talking of the Cabinet. He asked if I thought McAdoo had a chance for the nomination in 1920. I thought he had, and that it was his play to move and to win. I wondered if he had the political sagacity to move correctly. I thought McAdoo might make a dangerous President but, on the other hand, he might make an exceedingly brilliant one. The President thought the responsibility of the office would perhaps meet and overcome the characteristics and criticism I had in mind. I, too, thought it would be a restraining influence.

I felt if Baker made as great a success of the War Department as we all hoped that he, too, would be a formidable candidate.

In the Cabinet he said he had been struck by the fact that no one listened to McAdoo. There was general whispering when he was talking and little or no attention was paid to what he said. This he thought was also true of Redfield of whose good sense he has a high estimate. Houston, he said, usually spoke last upon a subject of general discussion and he found himself nearly always agreeing with what he said. Before we reached this point, however, and while we were talking of candidates for President, I told him that to my mind Houston was the ablest man in the Cabinet as far as sheer intellectuality and good judgment was concerned, but the trouble with him was that he was undiplomatic and lazy. The President was surprised at the last comment, but said that to him to [he] was the most unmagnetic man he had ever met, and he agreed with me that it would be impossible to make him a nominee.

When we were deciding upon the peace delegates, I said it reminded me of when we. used to amuse ourselves by forming his Cabinet during his campaign for his first nomination. The President replied, "I think the only ones definitely decided upon were Bryan and Burleson." As a matter of fact, the President is wholly mistaken in this, for we never decided upon Burleson until long after he, the President, had been elected and was almost ready to be inaugurated, and Bryan was never more than a tentative choice until after the el[e]ction.

We were having such an interesting discussion that I was loath to leave and the President continued to hold me. I had intended to go at ten o'clock but it was twenty minutes after before I left. The President has not been well and I did not like to keep him up since this is the first day he has been out of bed. It was agreed that we had had one of the pleasantest sessions for a long while.

[1] Czernin, in Vienna briefly before returning to Brest-Litovsk, had addressed the Austrian portion of the Parliament on January 24, mostly about the current negotiations with Russia, but also about Wilson's proposals. Czernin had said that the Fourteen Points constituted a peace offer, that Austria-Hungary could "joyfully" agree to some of the points, and that the others could profitably be discussed. He had summed up as follows: "We, therefore, are in agreement in the main. Our views are identical not only on the broad principles regarding a new organization of the world after the war, but also on several concrete questions, and differences which still exist do not appear to me to be so great that a conversation regarding them would not lead to enlightenment and a rapprochement." *New York Times*, Jan. 26, 1918. For the German text, see Ottokar Czernin, *Im Weltkriege* (Berlin, 1919), pp. 395-407. The English translation is printed in *FR-WWS 1918*, 1, I, 54-59.

Czernin's title was not Prime Minister but Minister of Foreign Affairs and Minister of the Imperial and Royal House.

To Frank Lyon Polk, with Enclosure

My dear Mr. Counselor,   The White House. 28 January, 1918.

Thank you for the enclosed. I dare say that for the present we may let this matter stand as it does; but I hope that we shall soon have new material for judgment in the shape of further information from our Ambassador at Tokyo. I do not think that it will be safe or wise to leave the Japanese government in any doubt as to the impression such an attitude on their part makes on us.

Faithfully Yours,   W.W.

WWTLI (SDR, RG 59, 861.00/1047½, DNA).

ENCLOSURE

From Frank Lyon Polk

My dear Mr. President: Washington January 24, 1918.

Mr. Lansing, who will probably be confined to the house for the rest of the week, sent me some memoranda from you in regard to matters in the Department. Among them was the enclosed telegram with your note attached on the subject of possible landing of Japanese in Vladivostok.[1] You may recall that on Saturday, the nineteenth, I sent you the draft of a telegram on this subject to our Ambassador in Tokio, which you approved, and it was forwarded on Sunday, the twentieth. Will you be good enough to let me know whether this telegram which was sent, a copy of which is attached, will be sufficient for the moment, or whether you feel that further action is necessary? It seems that until we hear from Morris this might be enough.

In this connection, I should mention that a Mr. H. Fessenden Meserve, an American citizen, who is a representative of the National City Bank of New York in Moscow, asked for an interview with you and was referred to this Department. He called today and told me he had a personal message for you from the Japanese Minister of Foreign Affairs, and I took the liberty of having him deliver the message to me in order to save your time. It is interesting as bearing on the question under discussion. He said, in the course of a long conversation, that the Japanese Minister asked him to see you and to say that he hoped that this Government would not send troops to Vladivostok or Harbin for the purpose of keeping order, as any such movement on our part would create a very unfavorable impression in Japan. He urged that the matter of keeping order and protecting life in Siberia should be left entirely with the Japanese. The Japanese Minister did not go into any details but rather intimated that if we did land troops the Japanese people would feel that we were doing work which properly belonged to them.

With assurances of respect, etc., I am,

My dear Mr. President,

Faithfully yours,   Frank L. Polk

TLS (SDR, RG 59, 861.00/1047½, DNA).
  ¹ WW to FLP, Jan. 19, 1918, with Enclosure.

To Thomas Watt Gregory

[The White House]

My dear Mr. Attorney General: 28 January, 1918

Thank you very sincerely for your letter about the election of Fred C. Miller as Mayor of Michigan City, Indiana. I am very much interested in the facts as they are recited in your letter. They put a different color on that case from that which it had formerly worn in my mind, and I have no doubt that your judgment is the correct one.   Cordially and sincerely yours,   Woodrow Wilson

TLS (Letterpress Books, WP, DLC).

To Joseph Patrick Tumulty

Dear Tumulty: [The White House, c. Jan. 28, 1918]

Of course, these gentlemen are at liberty to use any statement I have made,¹ but I do not think that it would be proper for me to make any deposition in connection with a trial of this sort. I think the whole country would feel that it was unjustifiable on my part. At the same time, Mr. Ela ought to know that Senator La Follette was one of the men whom I referred to in the statement.

The President.

TL (WP, DLC).
  ¹ Gilbert & Ela, attorneys of Madison, Wisc., were representing the publishers of the *Wisconsin State Journal* and Richard Lloyd Jones, its editor, in a libel suit brought against them by Senator La Follette. Emerson Ela wrote to Tumulty that one of the points which might come up in the action was whether Wilson had intended to imply that La Follette was one of the group of willful men referred to in this statement: "The Senate of the United States is the only legislative body in the world which cannot act when its majority is ready for action. A little group of wilful men, representing no opinion but their own, have rendered the great government of the United States helpless and contemptible." Ela believed that confirmation by Wilson that the statement referred to La Follette would be helpful to the newspaper's defense. E. Ela to JPT, Jan. 22, 1918, TLS (WP, DLC). Wilson's statement is printed at March 4, 1917, Vol. 41.

To Frank Gardner Moore¹

[The White House]

My dear Professor Moore: 28 January, 1918

I am very much complimented that you should be turning anything I have written into Latin.² I hope the boys who have to read it in that language will not dislike me, as some of the young readers of Cicero dislike him, but, after all, the responsibility for that rests on you.

I am very glad to give my permission to you to print such a version, and as for the copyright, I take it for granted that that would belong to you, as of course. The English originals cannot be copyrighted because they are government documents, but I take it for granted that that rule would not apply to the Latin version.

Cordially and sincerely yours,   Woodrow Wilson

TLS (Letterpress Books, WP, DLC).
  [1] Professor of Classical Philology at Columbia University.
  [2] Moore had requested permission to translate into Latin, for use in schools in connection with Cicero's orations, Wilson's speeches of December 4, 1917, and January 8, 1918, printed at those dates in Vol. 45.

From Robert Lansing, with Enclosure

Dear Mr. President: Washington January 28, 1918.

On November 10, 1917, this Government recognized the Polish National Committee with headquarters in Paris and with representatives in France, Italy, Switzerland, Great Britain and the United States. Mr. Paderewski is the representative of the Committee in this country. Previous to recognition by this Government, the Polish National Committee had been recognized by Great Britain, France and Italy. The avowed purpose of the Committee is to further the cause of a united and independent Poland in allied countries and in the United States. The Committee's status cannot be considered that of a Provisional Government. Whatever formal character it may have is the result of recognition by the above mentioned countries.

Up to the present time our recognition of this Committee has been, without doubt, justified at least by the efforts of Mr. Paderewski and his associates in this country.

I attach herewith a letter and a memorandum sent me by Mr. Paderewski concerning, among other things, the recruiting of Poles not subject to the draft in this country.

I have been reliably informed that the efforts of the Polish National Committee in the allied countries have been equally successful along somewhat different lines. Moral support has been secured in England and in Italy for the cause of an independent Poland and in addition to this in France the Committee working in conjunction with the French Government has constituted a small but determined force of men who are willing to fight for the cause represented by the Committee.

The work of this Committee will be seriously crippled unless funds now are provided by the Allies and the United States. Up to the present time the Committee has been financed by private sub-scriptions.

Within the last few weeks I have received several memoranda from the British Embassy requesting to be advised of this Government's attitude towards furnishing financial aid in conjunction with Great Britain to the Polish National Committee for the relief of Polish refugees in Russia, the necessities of the Polish Army and the continuation of the organizations of the Polish National Committee in the allied countries and in the United States. I hesitated to submit the matter to you until I heard direct from Mr. Paderewski.

I attach herewith a letter I received from him a few days ago.

Mr. Paderewski asks for financial assistance for three distinct purposes:

1—Polish National Committee expenses.

2—Relief of Polish refugees in Russia.

3—Five hundred thousand dollars for the purpose of bringing certain Polish officers from Russia to assist in the Polish Army.

If you approve I shall take up (2) with the Red Cross and (3) with the War Department with the recommendation that these matters be promptly investigated and that assistance be extended if it is at all practicable.

I have been informally advised that with respect to (1) the British Government will be glad to share these expenses with this Government. The view of the British Government is that it is highly desirable to keep in close touch with the activities of the Polish National Committee, not only for present purposes, but on account of obvious advantages to be gained ultimately when peace negotiations are being carried on. I entirely agree with this view. At the present time I believe that considerable assistance can be obtained through this organization in securing political and military information concerning the Central Powers for the use of this Government. The agents of the Polish National Committee have peculiar advantages in securing such information on account of their activities in Sweden and Switzerland and at the Vatican.

My thought is that if you are willing to advance from your war fund, say, a maximum of thirty thousand dollars a month to be placed under the control of an agent of this Department who would be attached to the American Embassy at Paris and to be used by him to assist the organizations of the Polish National Committee (a like sum to be provided by the British Government under the supervision of one of its agents), the understanding being that the Polish National Committee in return therefor will secure and place at the disposal of the British Government and this Government all information of a political and military character secured by its agents, great benefit would accrue therefrom both to the Polish National Committee and to the Governments of Great Britain and the United States.

I know of no other way by which the assistance requested by Mr. Paderewski can be furnished by this Government, inasmuch as the Treasury Department is not authorized to lend money except to established governments at war with the Central Powers.

I shall be grateful to you if you can furnish me with your directions with respect to the foregoing.

Faithfully yours,   Robert Lansing.

TLS (SDR, RG 59, 860C.01/84½A, DNA).

E N C L O S U R E

Ignace Jan Paderewski to Robert Lansing

Sir: Washington, D. C., January 19, 1918.

For a long time before the official recognition of the Polish National Committee at Paris, the members of that organization have been carrying out the work of propaganda among the masses of Polish population for the resistance to Germany's political plans. Their endeavors, involving considerable expenditure of energy and money, have been successful. Outside of two members, who cheerfully offered for that purpose all they had possessed, the expenses of the propaganda were covered partly by contributions from the Polish organizations in the United States, partly by private donations from that part of Russian Poland which has not been invaded by the enemy.

The present position of the Polish National Committee at Paris, while greatly enhanced, both politically and morally, through its recognition as an official organization by the Entente Powers and the United States Government, is nevertheless very precarious by reason of the existing financial conditions. Though not adopting, for obvious political reasons, temporarily at least, the name of a provisional government, the Polish National Committee has assumed all the burden of responsibility of such an institution and accepted many of its charges imposed upon it by the very fact of its recognition as an official organization. The already established agencies and offices in Paris, London, Rome, Lausanne and Petrograd with their numerous staffs require the more funds as the members and agents of the Polish National Committee at Paris, handicapped by comprehensible difficulties of correspondence, by letters and wires, are obliged to travel constantly in order to communicate personally. The resources of individuals are now totally exhausted. The contributions from the Polish organizations are being absorbed by charities, especially by the needs of Polish volunteers going to fight in France. The recent social and political disturbances in Russia have completely wiped out all that remained of Polish fortunes there. The Polish National Committee at Paris has practically no financial means whatever.

In view of this distressing situation, the Polish National Committee at Paris, much to its regret, finds itself compelled to appeal to the United States for aid, and most respectfully begs your Excellency to decide whether the President or the Government of the United States would be inclined to grant, in the form of a loan, to the future State of Poland, the financial help as follows:

1. Sixty thousand dollars as a monthly subvention for the maintenance of agencies and offices already existing in Paris, London, Rome, Lausanne, and Petrograd as well as of those which are to be established in neutral countries, for the duration of the war.

2. One million dollars for the immediate relief of Polish refugees in Russia whose situation, under the present regime, is most critical and the number exceeds sixteen hundred thousand.

3. A subsidy of five hundred thousand dollars for the purpose of bringing over from Russia, five hundred experienced Polish officers of all ranks, already promised by the Russian General Staff, and whose presence among the Polish soldiers would greatly increase the value of that fighting material.

The members of the Polish National Committee at Paris, enjoying confidence and respect of an immense majority of our people, there is no doubt that the future State of Poland would gladly redeem this loan which, however important, is only a trifling matter as compared to the unbounded indebtedness of Poland towards the President, the Government, and the people of the United States.

With profound respect, I beg to remain,

Your Excellency's most obedient servant,   I J Paderewski

TLS (SDR, RG 59, 860C.01/84½, DNA).

From Edward Nash Hurley

My dear Mr. President: Washington January 28, 1918.

We have reached a point in the consideration of the problem of housing workmen at the shipyards where we would appreciate your advice and instructions. Personally I have always felt that this problem should not have been thrust upon the Government, but since we must face it we will feel more confident in attempting a solution of it if we know you want us to go ahead.

I am enclosing a memorandum from Mr. Piez,[1] Vice President of the Emergency Fleet Corporation.

There is, of course, a distinct advantage in housing the workmen adequately in that it will aid in securing a more permanent supply of labor. I need hardly tell you that every possible effort was made to induce the shipyards to take care of their employees, as a part of their plant extension, but all such efforts by the Shipping Board, and other departments, have failed.

We have given several months to the matter, constantly striving to cut the program to the bare necessities. If a way could have been found to avoid the expenditure, I believe we would have found it. For a time I thought it might be possible to follow the cantonment idea, but I am convinced that this will not give the results desired— a permanent working force at each yard.

Hog Island,[2] which is one of our chief problems, involves a transportation as well as housing problem. The site which was selected by another administration should not have been selected, but we must work with the tools at hand. If we had a new slate we might have done differently.

Knowing how burdened you are, I am disturbed over the necessity for adding to your cares, but because of the importance of the plan in mind I would not feel free in making any further commitment of the Emergency Fleet Corporation until I could obtain the benefit of your advice.

I sincerely trust your cold has passed away.

Faithfully yours,   Edward N. Hurley

TLS (WP, DLC).

[1] Charles Piez, a Chicago engineer, was president of the Link Belt Co., the Electric Steel Co., and the Illinois Manufacturers' Casualty Co. In his memorandum, Piez pointed to the great concentration of war industries, and the resulting congestion, in the area between Boston and Norfolk, and he recommended various governmental measures to relieve critical housing shortages in shipbuilding areas. C. Piez to E. N. Hurley, Jan. 24, 1918, TLS (WP, DLC).

[2] The American International Corporation, under contract with the Emergency Fleet Corporation, was constructing a fabricating yard for standardized steel merchant ships at Hog Island, Pa., on the Delaware River below Philadelphia. This yard, which was to be the largest facility in the shipbuilding program, had an initial contract to produce fifty 5,000-ton vessels. *New York Times*, Sept. 14 and Nov. 17, 1917.

Two Letters from Herbert Clark Hoover

Dear Mr. President: Washington, D. C. 28 *January 1918*

I am obliged for your letter of January 23rd, in respect to Mr. McAdoo's communication on increased meat purchases.

The $61,000,000 which Great Britain asks should not be intrinsically an addition to their monthly allowances but simply an advance in time as a credit to buy food in excess of the immediate requirements, in our own as well as their interests, and should be so arranged as to relieve pressure later on.

The reasons why this is so, were not stated in the communications from the British Government, and are substantially as follows:

In order to feed our population as well as to feed our associates on the other side at reasonable prices, and in order to ensure that agricultural production in the United States continue at high levels, I conceive that one of the prime functions of the government will be to maintain, insofar as possible, a stability in food prices. Our herds are considerably diminished and must be recuperated.

At this period of the year we always have a large run of cattle and a large run of hogs. We are in the period of accumulation of hog products. In the spring the current supply will fall off, and we may not have enough to keep pace with the demand for ourselves and our associates, unless we attain a large measure of conservation of consumption. But, at the moment the runs are heavy, and we are having an extra large surplus—with a prospect of very deficient supplies later.

The Food Administration asked the British Government to increase its purchases during this period of temporary surplus, so as to reduce their purchases later, in the periods of comparative shortage. And this was particularly important to us so that we should be able to see that the packers paid fair prices to the producers above the minimum limits which we feel would protect recuperation of our herds.

Prices for live animals have dropped perceptibly since the fall, and unless our temporary surplus is absorbed by the foreign demand we shall have a further slump in prices, with consequent discouragement to the producer at a critical period when he is deciding the extent of his future operations. If this further slump in live stock prices came, we should have to withdraw our conservation measures under pressure from the producer, in order to secure the consumption of the surplus amounts in the United States, and thus destroy our whole conservation work. This is markedly true of beef, which is a perishable product. There are no facilities in the United States to preserve any temporary surplus of beef at this time. If it does not go abroad for storage it will simply be eaten here by our people, who at this time have a supply ample for their needs. After spring we will have a long and desperate period to face as to our meat supply, in any event. These difficulties would be doubled if we had to find anew, through a diminished supply, the surplus which we can now offer.

Therefore, if we cannot take care of this temporary surplus we shall have lost the constancy of our people in conservation, we shall have discouraged the producer, and the necessary reaction of a shortage would be higher prices for meat products in the summer and fall, and we shall have lost our hope of maintaining stabilized prices.

As to the financial problem: We assumed that that would be taken care of out of the Allied current income from the United States Treasury. I did discuss the matter with Mr. McAdoo over a month ago, and made a recommendation as to Allied food finances,—in the main that the Treasury should stipulate the setting aside a regular and definite sum for financing the foodstuffs purchased here, instead of allowing their food purchases to become the football of the deficiencies created by the attempts to maintain exchange on neutral centers.

For the last three months we and the Allies own representatives have been totally at sea as to their purchasing power. We receive demands for future food programmes, based upon the necessities of their peoples, and after we adopt measures to meet them we find they are unable to consummate because we are told by their food agencies that their American funds have been diverted to the exchange market. The result has precipitated actual food shortages abroad.

If their representatives and ourselves had a definite budget we might often arrange to finance temporary surpluses such as the present one in meat with our own manufacturers.

Yours faithfully,   Herbert Hoover.

Dear Mr. President: Washington, D. C. 28 *January, 1918*

I am enclosing herewith a letter which I have addressed to Mr. McAdoo today and a letter which I addressed to him on the 6th instant, with regard to food movement in the country.[1] I had hoped that the situation would have ameliorated so as to have relieved me from bringing this additional anxiety to your attention. I do not, however, believe that I should be discharging my duty did I not present this matter to you.

I am   Your obedient servant,   Herbert Hoover.

TLS, (WP, DLC).
¹ Hoover had warned McAdoo in the earlier letter that there was a danger that the acute shortage of grain-carrying railroad cars would gravely damage the Allied cause and the American economy. H. C. Hoover to WGM, Jan. 6, 1918, TCL (WP, DLC). In the second letter, Hoover wrote that the situation had become even more critical, and he suggested that McAdoo consider imposing an embargo on all rail traffic, both passenger and freight, except that which was essential to the War and Navy departments, the Fuel and Food administrations, and the Shipping Board. Hoover added that he had hoped that the situation would already have "disentangled itself" under McAdoo's "fine leadership," but that the recent severe weather conditions now necessitated "action of much more drastic order" than local embargoes and priorities. H. C. Hoover to WGM, Jan. 28, 1918, CCL (WP, DLC).

From William Bauchop Wilson, with Enclosure

My dear Mr. President: Washington January 28, 1918.

I am inclosing you herewith the report of the commission appointed by you to inquire into the industrial conditions in the Rocky Mountain regions and on the Pacific coast, commonly referred to as the President's Mediation Commission. The report was ready for submission some time ago, but owing to the break that took place in the negotiations between the packers and the representatives of their employees it was decided to withhold the report until the difficulties could be overcome and the plan of adjustment outlined carried into effect. That has now been accomplished. After more than a week of negotiations an arrangement was entered into Saturday night by which an agreement was arrived at on twelve of the eighteen demands of the workers and the other six definitely submitted to arbitration.

May I add that, anticipating that you may desire to make the report public, the Department of Labor has had printed 5,000 copies which are available for distribution if you so desire. The work of the Commission having been practically concluded, I would be much pleased if you could find a few minutes between now and Wednesday night to meet them personally.¹

Faithfully yours,   W B Wilson

TLS (WP, DLC).
¹ The Editors have found no indication that such a meeting took place.

ENCLOSURE

REPORT OF PRESIDENT'S MEDIATION COMMISSION TO THE PRESIDENT OF THE UNITED STATES

The President: January 9, 1918.

Your Mediation Commission begs to set forth in this report (1) a summary statement of the results in the specific labor adjustments undertaken by the commission; (2) an analysis, as far as revealed by the limited scope of our investigation, of the difficulties and tendencies making for industrial instability; and (3) recommendations as to the direction that the labor policy of the United States should take, at least during the period of the war.

MEDIATION OF SPECIFIC DIFFICULTIES.

An accumulation of industrial disturbances west of the Mississippi gave rise to national concern and pressed for an understanding of its causes, with a view to the correction of disclosed evils. The immediate anxiety of the Government was the dangerous diminution of the copper supply available for ammunition, due particularly to the strikes in Arizona, and the hampering of the war program, both as to ships and aircraft, because of the disturbed labor conditions in the Pacific Northwest.

Primarily, therefore, the objects of the commission were to open the copper mines of Arizona to their maximum output and so to keep them open for the period of the war, and to bring to pass such a condition in the labor situation of the Pacific Northwest that the shipbuilding and aircraft programs of the Nation may proceed at the required pace and efficiency so far as labor is an element.

To these two specific fields for mediation others were added as other difficulties arose after the commission began its labors. We shall confine ourselves here merely to major difficulties. Of these there were three: (1) A threatened strike in the oil fields of southern California, (2) a threatened and partly executed strike on the telephone lines of the Pacific States, and (3) a threatened tie-up of the packing industry centering in Chicago but affecting the industry of the entire country.

As to each of these situations, and several others not referred to in this report as to which mediation was effected or attempted, the commission has made a detailed report setting forth the existing relation of employers, employees, and community in each of the industries, the causes of the unrest, the history of the strike—where difficulties culminated in strike—the steps necessary for the removal of such causes, the nature of the settlement secured by the commission, where an adjustment was made, and the actual working of such settlement as far as the short time of its operation enabled its ascertainment. A program of industrial policy, either to meet the peremptory needs of war or looking to readjustments beyond, must proceed warily by the light of accredited facts. The intensive studies, directed to the very concrete immediate ends which were the concern of your commission, have at least furnished a considerable volume of important material for the understanding of those complex and subtle phases of modern industry usually called the labor problem. In this report we shall attempt a compact summary.

Disputes in Arizona Copper Districts.

1. About 28 per cent of the total copper output of the United States is produced in the four copper districts of Arizona dealt with by the commission. In the early summer of 1917 strikes became widespread in these centers, resulting, through the total and partial shutdown of the mines extending for a period of over three months, in a loss of 100,000,000 pounds of copper. Necessarily such an industrial disturbance results in continued diminution of output for a considerable time following any settlement of difficulties.

2. The occasions for such shocking dislocations of a basic war industry varied in the different mining camps. Behind and controlling, however, the factors which immediately led to the strikes are the underlying labor conditions of the mining industry of the State, which were devoid of safeguards against strikes and, in fact, provocative of them.

3. Distant ownership, wholly apart from its tendency to divorce income from the responsibility for the conditions under which it is acquired, creates barriers against the opportunity of understanding the labor aspects, the human problems, of the industry, and solidarity of interest among the various owners checks the views of any one liberal owner from prevailing against the autocratic policy of the majority. The resident management of the mines is wholly traditional in its effect, however sincere in its purpose. The managers fail to understand and reach the mind and heart of labor because they have not the aptitude or the training or the time for wise dealing with the problems of industrial relationship. The managers are technical men, mining engineers of knowledge and skill. There is no responsible executive whose sole function it is to deal with labor problems. In fact it has hardly begun to be realized that labor questions call for the same systematic attention and understanding and skill as do engineering problems.

4. The employees, in their turn, present factors of special difficulty. Labor turnover is appallingly large, with all the economic and social evils that such a condition signifies. The striking phenomenon of migratory labor has not been wholly evil in its effects. It has helped to spread ideas of liberalism into our industrial life, however undiscriminating this educative process necessarily has been. But any benefits conferred by migratory labor are wholly offset by its costs, both economic and social. A large migratory working force is economically an intolerable waste. Socially it is a disintegrating element in society. It signifies, too often, men without responsibility of home or home making, men possessed of a feeling of injustice against lack of continuity of employment, serving as inflammable material for beguiling agitators to work upon. This large labor turnover is accepted too much as the plagues of old, something irremediable. There is only the faintest beginning of realization that labor turnover is an evil which can be substantially reduced if not wholly eliminated, and that the responsibility for its elimination is a duty confronting both the industry and the Government.

The polyglot character of the workers adds the difficulty of racial diversities. In one camp 26 and in another as many as 32 nationalities were represented. The industry contains within itself the Balkan problem on a small scale. In other camps, even where there was not great racial diversity, large numbers were non-English speaking, particularly Mexicans. The seeds of dissension among the workers render difficult their cohesion, and the presence of non-English speaking labor tends even to greater misunderstanding between management and men than is normal in American industry. The movement toward Americanization, so fruitful in its results in different parts of the country, has hardly penetrated into these outposts of industry. Next to nothing is done to integrate non-English-speaking labor—citizens and prospective citizens—into our social life.

5. The trade-union movement is the most promising unifying spirit among the workers. The progress of the movement, however, is impeded by the traditional opposition of the companies, by difficulties due to racial diversities and by internal dissensions in the miners' International. The resulting weakness of the organization deprived the industry of the discipline over workers exercised by stronger unions and gave the less responsible leaders a freer field for activity. Thus a numerically small minority could compel a strike because of the solidarity of workmen in time of strike.

6. As is generally true of a community serving a single industry, there was not the cooling atmosphere of outsiders to the conflict.

The entire community was embroiled. Such agencies of the "public" as the so-called "loyalty leagues" only served to intensify bitterness, and, more unfortunately, to the minds of workers in the West served to associate all loyalty movements with partisan and anti-union aims.

7. The labor difficulties were further complicated by factors created by the war. This was particularly true of the situation in the Globe district. Doctrines of internationalism, the conviction that all wars are capitalistic, which before the war had permeated the minds of labor the world over, strongly marked the labor leadership in the Globe district. It led to resolutions of opposition to the war by the miners' local at the outbreak of the war. The situation was further intensified by refusal to display the flag at union headquarters. This incident provoked accusations of disloyalty against the men on the part of the company and its sympathizers. The uncritical opinion of the men that all wars are capitalistic and therefore that ours must be such, was encouraged by the heavy profits of the copper companies resulting from the European war before our entrance into it. The limitation of profiteering through price fixing and taxation had been only too recently accomplished to have made itself felt either in its actual operations or in the understanding of the workmen.

8. This, roughly, is the background against which the copper strikes of 1917 must be projected. To these underlying conditions and to the absence of processes of orderly government in industry the strikes of 1917 must, fundamentally, be attributed. These conditions may not have been left unavailed of by enemies of our war policy nor by exponents of syndicalist industrialism, but neither sinister influences nor the I.W.W. can account for these strikes. The explanation is to be found in unremedied and remediable industrial disorders.

9. Amidst all the diversity of conditions in the four copper districts there were three basic claims urged by the men and resisted by the companies:

(a) While not expressed in so many words, the dominant feeling of protest was that the industry was conducted upon an autocratic basis. The workers did not have representation in determining those conditions of their employment which vitally affected their lives as well as the company's output. Many complaints were, in fact, found by the commission to be unfounded, but there was no safeguard against injustice except the say-so of one side to the controversy. In none of the mines was there direct dealing between companies and unions. In some mines grievance committees had been recently established, but they were distrusted by the workers as subject to company control, and, in any event, were not effective, because the final determination of every issue was left with the company. In place of orderly processes of adjustment, workers were given the alternative of submission or strike.

(b) The men sought the power to secure industrial justice in matters of vital concern to them. The power they sought would in no way impinge on the correlative power which must reside in management. Only by a proper balance of adequate power on each side can just equilibrium in industry be attained. In the minds of the workers only the right to organize secured them an equality of bargaining power and protection against abuses. There was no demand for a closed shop. There was a demand for security against discrimination directed at union membership. The companies denied discrimination, but refused to put the denial to the reasonable test of disinterested adjustment.

(c) The men demanded the removal of certain existing grievances as to wages, hours, and working conditions, but the specific grievances were, on the whole, of relatively minor importance. The crux of the conflict was the insistence of the men that the right and the power to obtain just treatment were in themselves basic conditions of employment, and that they should not be compelled to depend for such just treatment on the benevolence or uncontrolled will of the employers.

10. It was the correction of these underlying conditions making for instability at which the commission aimed in its adjustments. The objective was not merely to open the mines to their full productive capacity as quickly as possible, but to guard against any recurrence of interruption or curtailment of production through labor difficulties, at least during the period of the war.

11. The commission made four specific adjustments in four mining districts. There were variations in detail to suit specific local aspects. In the large, however, the settlements established the framework of sound industrial relations between management and men:

(a) An orderly and impartial process for the adjustment of all grievances inevitable in modern large-scale industry was substituted for the strike. In asking labor, for the period of the war, to forego its ultimate weapon, a compensatory means of redressing grievances had to be supplied. Therefore, there are established in each district United States administrators to decide all disputes where the parties themselves fail of agreement. The commission in effect applied the principle of trade agreements, making the duration of the war the time limit, and, through the mechanism of a United States administrator, provided for the means of determining any claims of breach of the agreement.

(b) Working conditions of industry should normally be determined by the parties themselves. Therefore channels of communication between the management and men were created through grievance committees free from all possible company influence. Through these representative contacts between management and men disputes find expeditious and informal settlement. Still more important, the contact engenders a spirit of mutual understanding and therefore of cooperation.

(c) The right of the men to organize was made effective by providing administrative enforcement for the prohibition against discrimination because of union affiliation.

(d) In view of the dislocation of the labor supply of the country it was important to husband the available man power. Therefore reemployment of the men on strike before employing newcomers was assured, excepting only those—few in number—who were guilty of seditious utterances, who had been proved inefficient, or who were members of any organization whose principles were opposed to belief in the obligation of contract. By casting the burden of reemployment of all the strikers upon the district instead of upon the individual company, the beginning was made toward recognizing the responsibility of the industry as an entirety for the solution of its problems.

12. Administration under this settlement has proceeded in these Arizona districts for over two months, and the results are encouraging. The administrators at once proceeded to their duties. Resourceful energy is needed in the days immediately following a strike in order to prevent misunderstandings and old suspicions from again flaring up. Extremists of both sides have to be diverted. In a word, the problem is to educate the estranged sides to deal directly with one another on the basis of a new faith and a new confidence. This educative process is now being carried out by the administrators with skill and measurable success. Reemployment of the workers was sought to be effected with all practicable speed. Old and new grievances were promptly heard. In one district 250 grievances were disposed of in five weeks. Many of the grievances were found to be trivial or groundless; they were, however, the surviving surface manifestations of the old unhealthy relationship. The prompt disposition of such grievances prevented that balked sense of justice on the part of men which so often leads to the explosion of a strike. Instead of a policy of drift, with intermittent eruptions, there is now the continuous administration of industrial

machinery, which serves as a bulwark for stability. Conditions are by no means fully normal; old feelings and old bitternesses still smolder, but new habits and new hopes of cooperation between management and men are steadily being built.

California Oil Fields Dispute.

1. The oil fields of southern California have an average output of 8,000,000 barrels per month, about one-third of the total oil output of the United States. Eleven companies produce about 95 per cent of this total output. Of these companies the Standard Oil is the largest, employing about 5,000 of approximately 18,000 men in the California field. A strike in the fields of the independents was threatened in the summer of 1917, but averted, and again threatened still more ominously in November last. The country was already embarrassed by oil-fuel shortage, and the commission therefore promptly responded to the call for its intervention to avoid a tie-up.

2. The men presented specific grievances as to hours, wages, and conditions of employment, and sought protection against alleged discrimination because of union membership. The labor employed in this industry, unlike that in most of the industries investigated by the commission, is English-speaking and almost wholly American. A very large proportion of the workers are highly skilled. Nevertheless, it was not until April, 1917, that the men were organized. Their union had grown to include between 9,000 and 10,000 men and is affiliated with the American Federation of Labor.

3. Commissioner Reed, who acted for the commission, found that specific grievances needed correction and that means were required for securing redress of future grievances.

The major specific demands of the men were for an eight-hour day and a minimum wage of $4. In effect they asked that the conditions prevailing at the Standard Oil plants should be introduced by the independents. It was found that the 5,000 employees of the Standard Oil had been on an eight-hour basis since January 1, 1917, and according to the experience of the Standard Oil Co. no loss in efficiency or output resulted from the introduction of the eight-hour day. It was the intention of some of the independents voluntarily to go on the eight-hour basis. Therefore, in providing for an eight-hour day effective January 1, 1918, the commission merely adopted the labor standard as to hours which had been vindicated by experience. To guard against the needs of emergency of the Government in war time, provision was made for a longer working-day if required by the Government. The principle of a minimum wage of $4 on an eight-hour basis, effective December 1, 1917, was likewise introduced. The company further agreed not to discriminate against men because of membership in any union affiliated with the American Federation of Labor.

4. Here, as in the copper districts, machinery of enforcement was essential. Provision was therefore made for Government inspectors to determine the governmental need, if any, for increase in the working hours. Administrators were named for all disputes which the parties can not settle between themselves.

5. The men thus secured betterment in hours and conditions of employment and the means of redress for future grievances. In effect the settlement operated as a trade agreement for the period of the war, and thereby displaced the strike and the lockout. The Government is thus assured stability as to labor conditions in the oil production of California. Opportunities are afforded the men to become disciplined through responsible organization, with resulting increase in efficiency; and the contact between producers and men will make for the healthier relationships between them indispensable to peace and productivity in industry. The response to the Government's needs, once they were made clear to both operators and men, gives full hope for the growth of a cooperative spirit between them. The men showed every readiness to produce the much-needed oil; the operators, both independent and Standard Oil, placed all their resources without stint at the disposal of the Government.

Pacific Coast Telephone Dispute.

1. For several months a tie-up of the telephone system of the entire Pacific coast was threatened. The controversy affected California, Oregon, Washington, Idaho, and Nevada. A strike became actually effective, in November, in Washington and Oregon, and the commission was charged with the adjustment of the entire dispute. Here, as in the other industries, the inability of employers and employees to reach an adjustment of issues between them hampered the country's effectiveness in war.

2. At bottom the failure of the existing industrial system to supply its own prevention against such a breakdown in time of war is attributable to causes of widespread application, but in this telephone industry the commission encountered special features—even if only of detail—which gave rise to their own peculiar difficulties. There was involved a vast network of industry stretching over widespread territory and controlled by one company in itself a subsidiary of a national system. The element of distance, creating managerial

aloofness, thus played a very important part. For the employees the labor policy of "the company" was what the local officials in towns distant from the executive offices made it, and not what the general officers in San Francisco might have wished it to be; distance insulated the general offices from intimate knowledge of industrial relations of the company. The bonds of confidence and cooperation between company and employees were therefore tenuous. Moreover, the fact that the company, despite its bigness, was part of a national system qualified all solutions of labor difficulties by consideration, on the part of the company, of the bearing of such solution, however intrinsically irrelevant, upon other parts of the country. Despite all this, by reason of the skilled character of the employees, the prevailing extent of trade-unions among the men and the resulting practice of collective bargaining between company and men, there was a much healthier tone and a greater basis of stability in industrial relations here than in other industries investigated by the commission.

3. The dispute affected about 3,200 men who construct and keep up the plant and about 9,000 girl operators. These are largely girls between 18 and 20. Because of their immaturity and their normally brief period of employment, they illustrated the familiar difficulties in organizing girl employees. But in the summer of 1917, at a number of points in Oregon and Washington, organization did become effective; the girls formed locals and affiliated with the International Brotherhood of Electrical Workers, the men's union.

4. The recognition of the girls' union became the burning issue in the controversy which culminated in a partial tie-up. The men for the first time—being most favorably situated because of the demand for skilled electricians—made the recognition of the girls' union their controlling principle.

There were two other issues: A demand for an increase of wages and a demand for a closed shop, subsequently modified into a desire for a preferential shop. Wages for men had not increased since 1913, and the cost of living had in the meantime gone up. The men demanded a 25 per cent wage increase; the company offered a 12½ per cent increase. The closed shop demand was used as a leverage in bargaining, but the preferential shop idea was vigorously urged.

5. These were the specific issues that called for adjustment, but they were enveloped in an atmosphere of misunderstanding and suspicion, not only between the company and its employees but also between the northern and southern groups of employees. The dissension among the employees was due partly to the continuance of an old internal union fight, but had been intensified by general

labor conditions in the Northwest leading to more marked radicalism on the part of the northern group. Moreover, a false issue of loyalty had been raised, particularly against the striking girls, which was vigorously repelled. Here as elsewhere the attempt of parties on one side of an economic controversy to appropriate patriotism and stigmatize the other side with disloyalty only served to intensify the bitterness of the struggle and to weaken the force of unity in the country.

6. The commission had to deal with the specific issues as well as with the attendant atmosphere. Its task here, as elsewhere, was to educate all to the realization that the national interest must control the situation. The future as well as the present had to be safeguarded, not merely by the adjustment of specific grievances but by the establishment of a new administrative structure supervised by the Government into which should be built the observance of law and the avoidance of force.

7. Specifically:

(*a*) The girls' locals were included in the trade agreement between the company and the brotherhood. In some other parts of the country the company had heretofore recognized the girls' union, and the plea that this made for inefficiency was the speculation of fear rather than the judgment of experience.

(*b*) Wage increases, obviously necessary, were provided for, leaving the extent of further increases to negotiation between the parties. In default of agreement, the issue was to be determined by an arbiter, to pass upon the complicated facts of a proper wage scale.

(*c*) The recognition of the girls' union, as well as the enforcement of all future grievances, was made effective by the establishment of impartial administrative machinery. United States administrators in the various districts were provided for the settlement of all issues which the parties themselves could not adjust.

(*d*) For the period of the war at least, in place of the resort to strike or lockout, there was thus established an effective peaceful process for the redress of grievances, secured by the authority of the United States Government.

(*c*) [(*e*)] In effect there were involved a reversal of the labor policy of the company. New currents of cooperation were created. It takes some time, however, for such a change of policy to permeate through all the stages of an industrial hierarchy. Partly, therefore, through this delayed adjustment to a new industrial régime on the part of local subordinate officials, partly by reason of obstructive suspicion of some of the radical labor leaders in the Northern States, partly because of the limited facilities for labor administration on the part of the Government, considerable difficulty was experienced in the early days following the ratification of the commission's settlement. The commission was constantly appealed to. The quick exercise of administrative action by the commission and the new administrators, and a strict eye to the enforcement of the settlement in cooperation with the more conservative union leaders and the higher officials of the company, succeeded in tiding over—by a process of flexible administration rather than adjudication—the obstructions and difficulties inevitable in such a situation. Before the commission left the coast signs of a new order of good relationship were already evident. Since then the representatives of the company and the brotherhoods have successfully negotiated a new wage scale without resort to arbitration.

Unrest in the Lumber Industry of the Pacific Northwest.

1. The forests and lumber mills of the Pacific Northwest have a predominant war importance. The raw materials they furnish are indispensable to the execution of the aircraft and shipping programs of the Government. The entire industry employs about 70,000 men. The labor conditions in the lumber industry have their reflex upon all other industry in that territory.

2. Yet this basic war industry suffered a breakdown of several months in the summer of 1917 and is still in a state of seething unrest, woefully short of its productivity. For, while the strike of 1917 was broken and the men went back beaten for the moment, the conflict was only postponed and not composed. Some of the men in fact practice "conscious withdrawal of efficiency," the so-called "strike on the job," and there is every expectation in the minds of those best informed that unless present conditions are changed a complete strike will occur in the spring. This is a situation that must be translated in terms of its significance to the military program of 1918.

3. We are dealing with an industry still determined by pioneer conditions of life. Hardy contact with nature makes certain rigors of conditions inevitable, but the rigors of nature have been reinforced by the neglects of men. Social conditions have been allowed to grow up full of danger to the country. It is in these unhealthy social conditions that we find the explanations for the unrest long gathering force but now sharply brought to our attention by its disastrous effect upon war industries. The unlivable condition of many of the camps has long demanded attention. While large improvements in camp life have recently been made, many of the camps still require much betterment to make them fit human hab-

itations. A number of employers have shown a most commendable understanding of the implications of operating camps unfit for men. Unfortunately, however, the old abuses were so long continued and so widespread that even after physical conditions are bettered a sense of grievance remains. This discontent gradually translated itself into demands not merely for physical comforts but for certain spiritual satisfactions.

4. Partly the rough pioneer character of the industry, but largely the failure to create a healthy social environment, has resulted in the migratory, drifting character of workers. Ninety per cent of those in the camps are described by one of the wisest students of the problem, not too inaccurately, as "womanless, voteless, and jobless." The fact is that about 90 per cent of them are unmarried. Their work is most intermittent, the annual labor turnover reaching the extraordinary figure of over 600 per cent. There has been a failure to make of these camps communities. It is not to be wondered, then, that in too many of these workers the instinct of workmanship is impaired. They are—or, rather, have been made—disintegrating forces in society.

5. Efforts to rectify evils through the trade-union movement have largely failed because of the small headway trade-unions are able to make. Operators claim that the nature of the industry presents inherent obstacles to unionization. But a dominant reason is to be found in the bitter attitude of the operators toward any organization among their employees. This uncompromising attitude on the part of the employers has reaped for them an organization of destructive rather than constructive radicalism. The I.W.W. is filling the vacuum created by the operators. The red card is carried by large numbers throughout the Pacific Northwest. Membership in the I.W.W. by no means implies belief in or understanding of its philosophy. To a majority of the members it is a bond of groping fellowship. According to the estimates of conservative students of the phenomenon a very small percentage of the I.W.W. are really understanding followers of subversive doctrine. The I.W.W. is seeking results by dramatizing evils and by romantic promises of relief. The hold of the I.W.W. is riveted instead of weakened by unimaginative opposition on the part of employers to the correction of real grievances—an opposition based upon academic fear that granting just demands will lead to unjust demands. The greatest difficulty in the industry is the tenacity of old habits of individualism. The cooperative spirit is only just beginning.

6. The unrest, which at bottom is the assertion of human dignity, focuses upon a demand for the eight-hour day. It is almost the only

large industry on the coast in which the basic eight-hour day does not prevail. The operators doggedly opposed the eight-hour day on the ground that they are unable to meet southern competition operating under longer hours. They were unacquainted with the tendencies revealed by the introduction of the eight-hour day in other industries and the experiments of the British ministry of munitions as to the relation between shorter hours and efficiency.

In truth, we can not escape the conviction that with too many opposition to the eight-hour day has become a matter of pride instead of judgment, a reluctance to yield after having defeated the strike. Opposition to the eight-hour day is carried to the point of binding members of an employers' association on the Pacific coast by agreement to discriminate against such mills as introduce the change. On the other hand, the change has been introduced by far-sighted employers, particularly those in the inland empire district, not by way of yielding to threats, but as introducing a wise innovation recognized as a desirable national policy for industry.

7. In the judgment of the commission the introduction of the basic eight-hour day in the Pacific Northwest lumber industry is indispensable as a measure of national need. It is essential in order to assure stability in the industry, efficiency of output, and to obtain an adequate labor supply in the face of better competitive conditions in neighboring industries. Negotiations between the commission and the operators' association on the coast had reached a point where the adoption of the eight-hour day seemed practically assured. Unfortunately, conferences between representatives of the Pacific coast lumbermen and officials in Washington, held contemporaneously with the session of the commission in Seattle, gave rise to advices from such representatives to their associates on the coast which led to a reversal of attitude and to insistence that the eight-hour day must go into operation for the entire country before the Northwest Pacific coast would yield. The principal and certain source of difficulty, therefore, remains. It can be and should be promptly removed by administrative action requiring the basic eight-hour day in all contracts for lumber entering into Government work.

8. Some means of contact between operators and employees as a body is likewise essential. If it is too abrupt a step in the evolutionary process of this industry to deal collectively with trade-unions, some method of representation of the workers collectively in determining the general conditions under which they work and for securing rectification of evils should be devised.

9. With specific grievances removed destructive propaganda extensively preached in the Pacific Northwest will lose its strongest

advocate. Counter propaganda and positive education will then have an easy opportunity to supplant fanatical doctrines.

Packing Industry Dispute.

1. In December a strike radiating from Chicago threatened the meat-packing industry. The issues affected upward of a hundred thousand men. Even more important, the continued meat supply to the allies was involved. The commission was requested to intervene to avert the danger.

2. As is generally true of large industrial conflicts, the roots of the labor difficulty in the packing industry lie deep. The chief source of trouble comes from lack of solidarity and want of power on the part of the workers to secure redress of grievances because of the systematic opposition on the part of the packers against the organization of its workers. The strike of 1903 destroyed the union, and for 14 years the organization of the yards has been successfully resisted. In 1917 effective organization again made itself felt, so that by the end of the year a sizable minority, variously estimated from 25 to 50 per cent, was unionized. It is a commonplace of trade-union experience that an organized compact minority can control the labor situation in an industry. The union leaders felt, and rightly felt, therefore, that their demands had the effective backing of a potential strike. More important than any of the specific grievances, however, was the natural desire to assert the power of the union by asking the packers for union recognition, at least to the extent of a meeting between the packers and the representatives of the unions.

3. This the packers refused to do. They refused to meet eye to eye with the union leaders because of distrust of those leaders. It can not be gainsaid that the absence of a union organization for 14 years, the increasingly large per cent of non-English speaking labor, and the long pent-up feeling of bitterness all tended to make some of the men in whom the leadership for the time being rested somewhat devoid of that moderation in thought and speech which come from long experience in trade negotiations. On the other hand, refusal of the packers to deal with those leaders tended to encourage and intensify those very qualities which dissuaded the packers from industrial contact with them.

4. The two important specific grievances involved low wages and long hours. In fact, two wage increases had, during 1917, been granted to workmen, largely in an endeavor to forestall union activity. Nevertheless the claim was made, and validly made, that the

wage scales, particularly for the great body of unskilled workers, were inadequate in view of the increased cost of living. A further fact that influenced the workers in their wage demand was the belief that the companies had been making excessive profits despite Government regulation of prices. Unfortunately the refusal of the packers to meet the union leaders deprived the packers of the opportunity of explaining away, if possible, the belief entertained by the men that the packers were profiteering.

5. A demand for the eight-hour day in the place of the present ten-hour day had all the momentum furnished by the Nation-wide movement in the direction of the eight-hour day. The companies, in fact, conceded the principle of the eight-hour day. They had been studying the practicability of themselves introducing a change which they realized is inevitable for American industry. They claimed to be obstructed in its adoption by reason of difficulties attending both inbound and outbound shipments. These conditions depend for correction upon action both by the Government and by the industry. The study of the entire matter by the Government is urgent, so that any interferences to this needed measure of social policy may be removed as promptly as possible.

6. The commission's settlement proceeded along the general lines it had taken in other industries:

(*a*) The principle of adjustment through negotiation and arbitration was established to take the place of strike and lockout during the period of the war.

(*b*) Prohibition of discrimination for union affiliation is rendered effective by its enforcement through administrative machinery. It is not sufficient to recognize in the abstract the right of workmen to organize. Therefore, effective means were provided to secure to the union the right to live and to grow.

(*c*) The unfairness of compelling workmen to deal individually with employers of large-scale industries, particularly emphasized in the case of non-English speaking workmen, is recognized in practice by allowing workmen to voice their claims through representatives.

(*d*) The specific demands of the workers as to changes in hours, wages, and conditions of employment were all left for determination by the United States administrator.

7. Here, as elsewhere, a tense situation threatening breakdown of a vital war industry was relieved by establishing machinery for adjustment. Under this machinery the parties are now proceeding to work out their difficulties. The hope is entertained that not only will specific grievances be justly dealt with but healthier permanent

relationships will be created in the very process of seeking to reach adjustments.

CAUSES OF LABOR DIFFICULTIES.

1. The commission had wide opportunities, both as to the extent of territory and the variety of industries investigated, to inquire into industrial conditions in war time. The commission visited Arizona, the Pacific coast, Minneapolis and St. Paul, and Chicago; studied the situation in the copper mines, the telephone industry, the Northwest lumber industry, the meat-packing industry, as centered in Chicago, the rapid-transit situation and the related industrial condition in the Twin Cities, and observed as well other industries in the States adjacent to those it visited. All relevant sources of information were tapped, for close contact was had with workmen on strike and at work; employers and professional men, and Federal and State officials who are brought particularly in touch with labor matters; and in addition, the voluminous official files of Federal and State authorities furnished much knowledge. While undoubtedly each industry presents its own peculiarities, certain underlying general factors applicable to all industry emerge from the three months' work of the commission.

2. Throughout its inquiry and in all its work the commission kept steadily in mind the war needs of the country. The conclusion can not be escaped that the available man power of the Nation, serving as the industrial arm of war, is not employed to its full capacity nor wisely directed to the energies of war.

3. The effective conduct of the war suffers needlessly because of (a) interruption of work due to actual or threatened strikes, (b) purposed decrease in efficiency through the "strike on the job," (c) decrease in efficiency due to labor unrest, and (d) dislocation of the labor supply.

4. These are not new conditions in American industry, nor are their causes new. The conditions and their causes have long been familiar and long uncorrected. War has only served to intensify the old derangements by making greater demands upon industry and by affording the occasion for new disturbing factors.

5. Among the causes of unrest, familiar to students of industry, the following stand out with special significance to the industrial needs of war:

(a) Broadly speaking, American industry lacks a healthy basis of relationship between management and men. At bottom this is due to the insistence by employers upon individual dealings with their men. Direct dealings with employees' organizations is still the minority rule in the United States. In the majority of instances there is no joint dealing, and in too many instances employers are in active opposition to labor organizations. This failure to equalize the parties in adjustments of inevitable industrial contests is the central cause of our difficulties. There is a commendable spirit throughout the country to correct specific evils. The leaders in industry must go further, they must help to correct the state of mind on the part of labor; they must aim for the release of normal feelings by enabling labor to take its place as a cooperator in the industrial enterprise. In a word, a conscious attempt must be made to generate a new spirit in industry.

(b) Too many labor disturbances are due to the absence of disinterested processes to which resort may be had for peaceful settlement. Force becomes too ready an outlet. We need continuous administrative machinery by which grievances inevitable in industry may be easily and quickly disposed of and not allowed to reach the pressure of explosion.

(c) There is a widespread lack of knowledge on the part of capital as to labor's feelings and needs and on the part of labor as to problems of management. This is due primarily to a lack of collective negotiation as the normal process of industry. In addition there is but little realization on the part of industry that the so-called "labor problem" demands not only occasional attention but continuous and systematic responsibility, as much so as the technical or financial aspects of industry.

(d) Certain specific grievances, when long uncorrected, not only mean definite hardships; they serve as symbols of the attitude of employers and thus affect the underlying spirit. Hours and wages are, of course, mostly in issue. On the whole, wage increases are asked for mostly in order to meet the increased cost of living, and such demands should be met in the light of their economic causes. Again, the demand for the eight-hour day is Nation wide, for the workers regard it as expressive of an accepted national policy.

6. Repressive dealing with manifestations of labor unrest is the source of much bitterness, turns radical labor leaders into martyrs and thus increases their following, and, worst of all, in the minds of workers tends to implicate the Government as a partisan in an economic conflict. The problem is a delicate and difficult one. There is no doubt, however, that the Bisbee and Jerome deportations, the Everett incident, the Little hanging,[1] and similar acts of violence

[1] On the situation in the copper mines at Bisbee and Jerome, Ariz., see JPT to WW, July 12, 1917, Vol. 43. Frank Little, an I.W.W. organizer, was lynched in Butte, Mont., on August 1, 1917. Shootings, beatings, and other acts of violence took place in Everett, Wash., in October and November 1916. Norman H. Clark, "Everett, 1916 and After," *Pacific Northwest Quarterly*, LVII (April 1966), 57-64, and Robert L. Tyler, *Rebels of*

against workers have had a very harmful effect upon labor both in the United States and in some of the allied countries. Such incidents are attempts to deal with symptoms rather than causes. The I.W.W. has exercised its strongest hold in those industries and communities where employers have most resisted the trade-union movement and where some form of protest against unjust treatment was inevitable.

7. The derangement of our labor supply is one of the great evils in industry. The shockingly large amount of labor turnover and the phenomenon of migratory labor means an enormous economic waste and involves an even greater social cost. These are evils which flow from grievances such as those we have set forth; they are accentuated by uncontrolled instability of employment. Finally, we have failed in the full use and wise direction of our labor supply, falsely called "labor shortage," because we have failed to establish a vigorous and competent system of labor distribution. However, means and added resources have been recently provided for a better grappling with this problem.

8. It is, then, to uncorrected specific evils and the absence of a healthy spirit between capital and labor, due partly to these evils and partly to an unsound industrial structure, that we must attribute industrial difficulties which we have experienced during the war. Sinister influences and extremist doctrine may have availed themselves of these conditions; they certainly have not created them.

9. In fact, the overwhelming mass of the laboring population is in no sense disloyal. Before the war labor was, of course, filled with pacific hopes shared by nearly the entire country. But, like other portions of the citizenship, labor has adjusted itself to the new facts revealed by the European war. Its suffering and its faith are the suffering and the faith of the Nation. With the exception of the sacrifices of the men in the armed service, the greatest sacrifices have come from those at the lower rung of the industrial ladder. Wage increases respond last to the needs of this class of labor, and their meager returns are hardly adequate, in view of the increased cost of living, to maintain even their meager standard of life. It is upon them the war pressure has borne most severely. Labor at heart is as devoted to the purposes of the Government in the prosecution of this war as any other part of society. If labor's enthusiasm is less vocal, and its feelings here and there tepid, we will find the explanation in some of the conditions of the industrial environment

---

the Woods: The I.W.W. in the Pacific Northwest (Eugene, Ore., 1967), pp. 62-84. For accounts of all these cases, see Melvyn Dubofsky, We Shall Be All: A History of the Industrial Workers of the World (New York, rev. edn., 1975).

in which labor is placed and which in many instances is its nearest contact with the activities of the war.

(*a*) Too often there is a glaring inconsistency between our democratic purposes in this war abroad and the autocratic conduct of some of those guiding industry at home. This inconsistency is emphasized by such episodes as the Bisbee deportations.

(*b*) Personal bitterness and more intense industrial strife inevitably result when the claim of loyalty is falsely resorted to by employers and their sympathizers as a means of defeating sincere claims for social justice, even though such claims be asserted in time of war.

(*c*) So long as profiteering is not comprehensively prevented to the full extent that governmental action can prevent it, just so long will a sense of inequality disturb the fullest devotion of labor's contribution to the war.

RECOMMENDATIONS.

The causes of unrest suggest their own means of correction:

1. The elimination to the utmost practical extent of all profiteering during the period of the war is a prerequisite to the best morale in industry.

2. Modern large-scale industry has effectually destroyed the personal relation between employer and employee—the knowledge and cooperation that come from personal contact. It is therefore no longer possible to conduct industry by dealing with employees as individuals. Some form of collective relationship between management and men is indispensable. The recognition of this principle by the Government should form an accepted part of the labor policy of the Nation.

3. Law, in business as elsewhere, depends for its vitality upon steady enforcement. Instead of waiting for adjustment after grievances come to the surface there is needed the establishment of continuous administrative machinery for the orderly disposition of industrial issues and the avoidance of an atmosphere of contention and the waste of disturbances.

4. The eight-hour day is an established policy of the country; experience has proved justification of the principle also in war times. Provision must of course be made for longer hours in case of emergencies. Labor will readily meet this requirement if its misuse is guarded against by appropriate overtime payments.

5. Unified direction of the labor administration of the United States for the period of the war should be established. At present there is an unrelated number of separate committees, boards, agencies, and departments having fragmentary and conflicting juris-

diction over the labor problems raised by the war. A single-headed administration is needed, with full power to determine and establish the necessary administrative structure.*

6. When assured of sound labor conditions and effective means for the just redress of grievances that may arise, labor in its turn should surrender all practices which tend to restrict maximum efficiency.

7. Uncorrected evils are the greatest provocative to extremist propaganda, and their correction in itself would be the best counter-propaganda. But there is need for more affirmative education. There has been too little publicity of an educative sort in regard to labor's relation to the war. The purposes of the Government and the methods by which it is pursuing them should be brought home to the fuller understanding of labor. Labor has most at stake in this war, and it will eagerly devote its all if only it be treated with confidence and understanding, subject neither to indulgence nor neglect, but dealt with as a part of the citizenship of the State.

	W B Wilson *Chairman.*
Felix Frankfurter,	Verner Z. Reed.
Secretary and Counsel.	E. P. Marsh
Max Lowenthal	John H. Walker
Assistant Secretary.	J. L. Spangler.

Printed report (Washington, 1918).

From Charles Pope Caldwell

Washington, D. C.
My dear President Wilson: January 28, 1918.

I have just left the Senate Military Committee meeting at which the Secretary of War has replied to the attack made upon the Administration's War activities.[1]

While there was but little said other than had been detailed to the House Military Committee by the various heads of Departments and Bureaus that have appeared before us in support of requests for appropriations, I cannot let this opportunity pass without congratulating you upon the magnificent presentation of the facts by Secretary Baker.[2] I believe that a great service has been done to the people in thus giving to the Country a knowledge of the wonderful effort put forth towards accomplishing our purpose.

The frankness with which he has admitted the mistakes complained of where the complaint was justified, the fullness which

* Since this report was written, the direction of the labor administration for the war has been delegated to the Secretary of Labor.

[with] which he has refuted the unfounded charges, and the broad acceptance of responsibility and detailed statement of the steps taken in the discharge thereof, fills me with admiration and makes me proud that I have had the privilege of serving our Country during this time, and glad of the opportunity to add my small effort to the great work.

Permit me, therefore, to pledge anew my confidence in you and your Administration, and again express my willingness to cooperate in every way within my power.

Yours sincerely,   Chas Pope Caldwell.

TLS (WP, DLC).

¹ Responding to recent charges that the War Department had "fallen down in addressing itself to the task of conducting this war," Baker said that the country was entitled to know whether this was true. "Always," Baker said, "there is between the beginning of preparation and the final demonstration of its success a period of questioning, when everybody, you and I and everybody else, goes through searchings of heart to find out whether all has been done that could have been or that ought to have been done." In so large an enterprise as the American military mobilization, there were bound to be some delays and shortcomings, Baker acknowledged, but he and his colleagues had sought to learn from them and to remedy them instead of to repeat them. Baker then "suggested" that Chamberlain's speech of January 24 in the Senate had given many people the impression that the incidents Chamberlain had cited were "characteristic rather than exceptional." Baker asked permission to correct this impression, and, partially in response to the senators' questions, he commented in considerable detail on sanitary conditions in army camps, the supply of ordnance and clothing, construction, censorship, the training and deployment of troops, and related matters. For the text of Baker's remarks, which were widely reported, see the *Official Bulletin*, II (Jan. 29, 1918), 1, 9-30, or *Cong. Record*, 65th Cong., 2d sess., pp. 1411-32.

² A similar comment is recorded in Ray S. Baker, *Woodrow Wilson: Life and Letters* (8 vols., Garden City, N.Y., 1927-39), VII, 503-504: "Secretary Baker spoke for five hours before the Senate Committee on Military Affairs. The large hearing room was packed, for Baker had told the newspaper men. he intended to make an important statement. Throughout the whole time Senator Ollie James, towering in height and bulk, sat on the front row before the speaker, his hands resting on the top of his cane and his chin on his hands. He listened intently until the noon recess came, then hurried from the room, got into a cab and drove to the White House. Rushing into the President's office, he exclaimed: 'Jesus, you ought to see that little Baker. He's eating 'em up!' When the afternoon session began, he was back in his place, ready for the rest of the speech."

To Charles Pope Caldwell

My dear Mr. Caldwell: [The White House] 29 January, 1918

Your letter of yesterday, written after hearing Secretary Baker's statement, has given me the deepest gratification and I want to send you at once this line of warm appreciation. I think the Secretary entirely deserves the praise you bestow upon him. I have found him in every relationship frank, able and courageous, and I am delighted that he has had this chance to show his quality.

Thanking you warmly for your generous attitude,

Cordially and sincerely yours,   Woodrow Wilson

TLS (Letterpress Books, WP, DLC).

Two Letters to Robert Lansing

My dear Mr. Secretary,   The White House. 29 January, 1918.

I think I see this situation as a whole,[1] and of course I am disposed to help in every way possible, but I do not feel at liberty to pledge thirty thousand dollars a month indefinitely. Would the Committee think it fair if I were to limit the pledge to (say) six months, pending developgents [developments]?

And,—another question,— is it not likely that the portion to [the] British Government is to pay would in fact be drawn from our Treasury, by loan? I feel obliged to think of the financial burdens piling up on us.   Faithfully Yours,   W.W.

WWTLI (SDR, RG 59, 860C.01/85½, DNA).
[1] See RL to WW, Jan. 28, 1918, and its Enclosure.

My dear Mr. Secretary,   The White House. 29 January, 1918.

This is a very delicate matter; but while you were away from your office I took occasion to say to the Italian Ambassador (who, oddly enough, had called to thank me in the name of his Government for what I *had* said) that I had limited my statement about Italian rights as I did because I was taking my programme as a whole, including the league of nations through which mutually defensive pledges were to be given and taken which would render strategic considerations such as those affecting the Adriatic much less important. I told him that, failing a league of nations, my mind would be open upon all such matters to new judgments.

I am clear that I could not pledge our people to fight for the eastern shore of the Adriatic; but there is nothing in what I have omitted to say to alarm the Italian people, and it ought to be possible for Orlando to make that plain to his own followers.
      Faithfully Yours,   W.W.

WWTLI (SDR, RG 59, 763.72119/1266½, DNA).

To William Bauchop Wilson

My dear Mr. Secretary: The White House 29 January, 1918

Thank you very much for sending me a copy of the Mediation Commission's report, accompanying your letter of January twenty-eight; and may I not say that I am very much gratified to hear that the controversy between the Packers and their employees is at least in a way to be solved?[1] The delegation who visited me the other day[2] disturbed me very much by their attitude.

If you will be kind enough to have Mr. Creel communicated with and told of the five thousand printed copies of the report which are available for distribution, I will be very much obliged. I find that his committee can time these distributions with relation to other publications, to the advantage of the matter put out.

Cordially and sincerely yours,   Woodrow Wilson

TLS (LDR, RG 174, DNA).
[1] The two sides agreed on January 27 that there should be no discrimination against union members and that questions of hours and wages should be referred to an arbitrator to be appointed by the Secretary of Labor, with the arbitrator's awards to be effective as of January 14. *New York Times*, Jan. 28, 1918.
[2] Wilson had conferred with a delegation representing the various unions in the meat-packing industry at the White House on January 18. See the news report printed at Jan. 18, 1918. Wilson's remark apparently referred to a recent meeting with representatives of the meat-packing industry. However (as in the case of the meeting with the union leaders), there is no mention of the second meeting in the official diaries.

To Gutzon Borglum

My dear Mr. Borglum: The White House 29 January, 1918

It certainly is unfortunate that I should have been confined with a heavy cold just at the time when you had finished your work here and was[1] ready to report to me. I beg that you will not feel this to be an element of discouragement. I would be very much obliged if you could send me the report that you wished to place in my hands, with the data which you have collected to support it. Uncomfortable as I am with this cold, I can go over it at intervals during the day when my head is clear, and would value an opportunity to examine it.   Sincerely yours,   Woodrow Wilson

TLS (G. Borglum Papers, DLC).
[1] Wilson dictated "were also."

To Joseph Patrick Tumulty, with Enclosure

Dear Tumulty: [The White House, Jan. 29, 1918]

This letter will explain itself. It is a matter which will have to be handled very promptly indeed, and I am sending it to you to ask if you will not yourself see or get into immediate communication with the Secretary of the Treasury, the Secretary of War, the Secretary of the Navy, the Secretary of Labor, the Chairman of the Shipping Board, Senator Fletcher, and Congressman Alexander to arrange the conference referred to. It was the Secretary of the Treasury who originated the suggestion out of which the idea of a conference has sprung and if you could arrange this conference at an early date, it would be extremely advantageous.[1]

The President.

TL (WP, DLC).
[1] See the memorandum printed as an Enclosure with WBW to WW, Jan. 30, 1918 (second letter of that date).

ENCLOSURE

From William Bauchop Wilson

My dear Mr. President: Washington January 28, 1918.

Referring to our discussion of the housing problem at the cabinet meeting on January 18th, I called up Senator Fletcher immediately following the meeting and conveyed to him your desire to have a conference before further action was taken on the Senate bill making an appropriation to the Shipping Board for housing purposes. He informed me that the bill had passed the Senate about fifteen minutes before I reached him. It was sent to the House and was referred to the Committee on Merchant Marine and Fisheries which has had it under consideration for several days. At the request of the Committee I appeared before it this morning and, among other things, stated that you desired a conference before final action was taken. The Committee deferred further action until Wednesday morning. The subject is so urgent that I take the liberty of suggesting that you have the conference with the Secretary of the Treasury, the Secretary of War, the Secretary of the Navy, the Chairman of the Shipping Board, Senator Fletcher, Congressman Alexander, and myself at as early a date as it can be arranged.

Faithfully yours,   W B Wilson

TLS (WP, DLC).

To Charles Allen Munn[1]

My dear Munn: [The White House] 29 January, 1918

I am heartily glad you are going to undertake what you outline in your letter of January twenty-fifth.[2] It is not only due to the people of the country that something of that sort should be done, but it is also necessary to the great task we have undertaken that the real facts should stand out for the encouragement and instruction of our own people and of our associates in the war.

I have no doubt that the Secretaries here will be willing to co-operate very heartily and fully.

I hope you will understand me, my dear Munn, when I say that it will not be possible for me to write anything for the number you are projecting. I find it barely possible to do the day's work, and I would not think it wise to publish anything in such a number unless I had been able to give it real thought and make a statement that would be worth your printing by reason of really saying something. You will understand, I am sure, how impossible this is for me just now. I have had to deny myself many privileges of this kind, but it is a stern necessity.

Cordially and sincerely yours,   Woodrow Wilson

TLS (Letterpress Books, WP, DLC).
  [1] Munn, Princeton 1881, was editor of *The Scientific American.*
  [2] It is missing, but it was an invitation to write an article or message to appear in a special "Liberty War Number" of *The Scientific American.* This issue, which was published on April 6, 1918, included articles constituting "A Record of the Actual Accomplishments of the United States During Our First Year of War." Among the authors were Daniels, Baker, W. B. Wilson, Creel, Hurley, Hoover, Garfield, and Grosvenor B. Clarkson, secretary of the Council on National Defense. *The Scientific American,* XCIX (April 6, 1918), 293-336.

To David Lawrence

My dear Lawrence: [The White House] 29 January, 1918

I beg that you will never allow yourself to be hurt by anything I do or do not do.[1] We are working under the sternest conditions that men ever worked under since civilization began. We can't afford to have personal feelings, and for my part I earnestly and sincerely try to exclude them.

You will see, I think, upon reflection how impossible it would be for me to guide even writers like yourself whom I know, and how undesirable, because the facts seem to me to lie patent to everybody and the duty of every man in the United States just now is to look at the facts and not at the color which anybody puts upon them, and look at the facts with a view, not to criticism but to cooperation, to putting everything before the public in a way which will help the public to help the administration by straight thinking on the actual facts.

The plan you have in view seems to me an excellent one of setting forth just how European conditions, which have again and again undergone kaleidoscopic change, necessarily react upon our work and condition it on every side. Since our entrance into the war, we have had to change our plans half a dozen times upon earnest representation upon the other side as to radically altered conditions. Unfortunately, not all of this can be put into the public prints, because to do so would reveal many difficulties and disappointments on the part of the Allies which it is not necessary or desirable that our enemies should know, but the work of interpretation should rest, it seems to me, upon such statements as the Secretary of War made yesterday.

As a matter of fact, all the matter gone over in that report was carefully gone over by the House Committee on Military Affairs when considering the Army appropriations, but the whole scene needed to be described in a single statement, and I am glad that you think as I do that the Secretary of War showed his admirable insight, ability and candor in the way in which he did it.

Cordially and sincerely yours,   Woodrow Wilson

TLS (Letterpress Books, WP, DLC).
  ¹ Lawrence's letter is missing, but presumably it related to his earlier request for an interview. That request is also missing, but Wilson had replied to it on January 19, as follows: "My dear Lawrence: I wish I could see you but my calendar is so jammed just now that I fear it is impossible. May I not make this suggestion to you: You are so close to Tumulty, and have such intimate access to my opinions through him, that I frankly cannot see the necessity of an interview for the purpose of learning my views. With warm regard, Cordially and sincerely yours, Woodrow Wilson." WW to D. Lawrence, Jan. 19, 1918, TLS (Letterpress Books, WP, DLC).

To Whom It May Concern

[The White House]

To Whom It May Concern: 29 January, 1918

The bearer of this letter, Mr. Roy W. Howard, goes to South America upon an errand in which I feel the greatest interest. His purpose is to establish a more extensive and adequate and reliable system of interchanging news between the northern and southern continents, and I hope sincerely that he will receive sympathetic encouragement and assistance. I take pleasure in commending him as a man who can in all respects be depended upon and in whom I feel great personal confidence.

Very sincerely,   Woodrow Wilson

TLS (Letterpress Books, WP, DLC).

From Frank Lyon Polk, with Enclosure

My dear Mr. President: Washington January 29, 1918.

At the request of the Secretary I am sending you enclosed a copy of the secret memorandum received yesterday from the British Embassy, concerning which I believe the Secretary has already spoken to you.

With assurances of respect, etc., I am, my dear Mr. President,

Faithfully yours,   Frank L Polk

TLS (SDR, RG 59, 861.00/1096, DNA).

ENCLOSURE E[1]

Washington January 28, 1918

Memorandum

No. 112 Secret The British Embassy have received a telegram from the Foreign Office stating that recent changes in Russian conditions suggest to His Majesty's Government the necessity for a change in allied policy.

A few weeks ago there appeared to be no political or military forces in Russia outside the area ruled by the Bolsheviki, which could or would do anything to aid the cause for which the Allies are fighting. The whole country presented a spectacle of unredeemed chaos.

Now, however, local organisations appear to have sprung up in South and South East Russia which, with encouragement and assistance, might do something to prevent Russia from falling immediately and completely under the control of Germany. Amongst these the most important are the various Cossack organisations to the North of the Caucasus, and the Armenians to the South. The former control the richest grain growing districts of the country and almost all the iron and coal. The latter, now that the Russian army has ceased to count, will supply the chief bulwark against the Turanian movement.

The advantage of assisting them is, therefore, obvious, but the difficulty is how this shall be done. They cannot be reached effectively by the Baltic or Black Sea, nor through Persia and the South. The Siberian Railway is the one remaining line of communication possible. The British General Staff are strongly of opinion that this line ought to be used and that it could be used if the Japanese would give their assistance. At first sight the great length of the line to be guarded might seem to prohibit the scheme, but a different view is taken by the professional advisers of His Majesty's Government.

Assuming, for the sake of argument, that the scheme is practicable from a military point of view; that the Allies are prepared to invite the Japanese as their mandatories to undertake it; and that the Japanese are ready to accept the invitation; it might perhaps be argued that such a scheme, even if successful, would do more harm than good to the Allied cause in Russia. It would involve the temporary control by foreigners of many thousands of miles of Russian railway, and those foreigners would be drawn from the very nation by which Russia was defeated within recent memory. It might be thought that Russian susceptibility would be deeply wounded by such a project. All the information, however, which

His Majesty's Government have been able to collect, appears to indicate that the Russians would welcome some form of foreign intervention in their affairs, and that it would be more welcome in the shape of the Japanese, engaged as mandatories of the Allies with no thought of annexation or future control, than in the shape of the Germans who would make Russia orderly only by making it German.

The difference from the Allied point of view is very great indeed. While the war continues, a Germanized Russia would provide a source of supply which would go far to neutralize the effects of the allied blockade. When the war is over a Germanized Russia would be a peril to the world. His Majesty's Government think that the scheme outlined above is the only way of averting these consequences and provides the only machinery by which such militant forces as South East Russia still possesses, may be effectually aided in their struggle against German influences on the West and Turkish attacks on the South.

His Majesty's Government desire, therefore, to press the scheme on the favourable consi[d]eration of the United States Government, and would request an urgent decision as events are moving rapidly in Russia.   Colville Barclay

TS MS (SDR, RG 59, 861.00/1096, DNA).
    ¹ The following document was a paraphrase of A. J. Balfour to Lord Reading, No. 538, Jan. 26, 1918, T telegram (FO 115/2445, p. 70, PRO). The telegram was sent also to Paris and to Rome.

From Thomas Nelson Page

Confidential

My dear Mr. President,   Rome January 29, 1918.

    I wrote the Secretary a short time ago giving the situation here up to that time. Things, however, appear to me to be undergoing a certain change here and this change is hard to define, nor can I give precise data to establish its existence. I am, however, sensible of a growing feeling here among some of those who have a strongly definitive part in the Government here and also among a certain class or perhaps party in the country at large that is out of sympathy with Italy and "her aspirations" and interests. This point of view has become much more apparent since the appearance of your last message, which referred to Italy's right to frontiers established along clearly defined lines of nationality. As I have already alluded to this in a number of telegrams since that time, I will only say now that it has become pretty generally accepted here that your expression eliminates a considerable part of what the Italians have been led to believe they might justly claim on the conclusion of peace. The extent of those claims is, of course, known to you and the aspirations are set forth in the secret treaty of the 26th of April between Italy and the Allies, which was published in England in the "New Europe"[1] and has been published in America, I understand in the "Denver Post." The newspapers here have been full of discussion about Italy's rights and claims on the Allies. The greater part of the press demands absolutely all that Italy wishes. An element of the socialistic press, however, declares that peace is the great desideratum, that is, peace with Italy's unquestionable rights satisfied, and that extravagant demands should be subordinated to this. The Vatican press is enigmatic and mainly talks about the equitable nature of the Papal proposals of peace of August first last, and intimates that your suggestions approximate those proposals nearly enough to justify their hope of their being reconciled. Just what is at the bottom of this continued assertion of Italy's claims is not precisely clear, except the desire to obtain all that is possible and the belief that unless she obtains what she aspires to at the conclusion of this war, she is not likely in our time to have another opportunity to enlarge her borders and approximate more nearly the ancient Venetian confines, and that without this the Government may find it difficult to justify its refusal of Giolitti's "parecchio,"[2] which, according to the Italian idea, is about equivalent to "a plenty" as defined by Dr. Johnson, that is, "a little more than enough." So that, in fact, the Government, or at least the Foreign Minister, who has held this post since before the war, will in such case be held responsible for having gained by war less than Giolitti was promised without war.

It is sadi [said] that Orlando's visit to Paris and London was mainly for the purpose of informing the French and British Governments that Italy expected them to stand by the terms of their secret treaty in compliance with which Italy entered the war. He was gazetted to speak at Milan on the 27th and another reason assigned for his leaving Italy at this time was that he had been notified that he would not be allowed to speak there without some danger of a serious disturbance. That is, the intervent[ion]ist war party insisted

---

[1] An English translation of the agreement signed at London on April 26, 1915, was printed in the London *New Europe*, VI (Jan. 17, 1918), 24-27. For the copy of the official text in WP, DLC, see A. J. Balfour to WW, May 18, 1917, n. 1, Vol. 42.

[2] Giovanni Giolitti, former Prime Minister of Italy, had written on January 24, 1915, to his friend, Camillo Peano, a letter which included this statement: "Given the actual conditions in Europe, it is my belief that much may be obtained without going to war." This letter was published by Peano at Giolitti's request. Giovanni Giolitti, *Memoirs of My Life*, Edward Storer, trans. (London, 1923), pp. 391-92. Although Giolitti used the word "molto," the letter became known as the "parecchio" letter.

that if he came he should declare himself very frankly, and the official socialists and anti-war party gave notice that they would give trouble if he should do this. So according to this report, to solve the difficulty, he went to Paris and London. It is probable that both reasons had wieght [weight] with him. It is said further that he and Sonnino were entirely at odds about this visit to England,— that he wished Sonnino to go with him; but Sonnino absolutely refused, saying that he was content with the promise of the two Powers already made and that he felt that they must abide by their treaty. However, Sunday night Sonnino left suddenly for Paris, and although the semi-official press speaks of [his] visit as having been long decided on with a view to uniting in the general council there, it is conjectured here that Orladno's [Orlando's] visit to England and France had not turned out as successfully as had been hoped and that Sonnino has gone to reinforce him.

The publication of the secret treaty has evidently caused considerable embarrassment to the Foreign Office here. I asked Baron Sonnino something about it in an informal conversation Saturday; but he said that he did not wish to talk of it. He said that he would tell me, however, that the clause (fifteen) relating to Italy's attitude to the Pope's intervention at the Peace Congress, when it should come, was not correct.[3] It was changed. I asked him "Is it essentially changed?" and he replied "Yes, essentially"; but this was all he wished to say about it.

There has been in these latter months a strong propaganda carried on in Italy against England and, as I have mentioned on several occasions in my telegrams, this propaganda has been extended recently to stir up feeling against us as well. It is believed by many of those with whom I have spoken on the subject that Germany is at the bottom of this propaganda. I have no doubt that Germany is fostering it with all her power. Although more or less concealed, her power is very great in parts of Italy in certain respects. I find, however, that there is another element besides the German element which is actively, if quietly, at work against us, and I believe that some of those in control are against us, because they fear us. Happily, there are many influential persons who believe in us. Those against us are against us mainly because we represent Democracy. However much they may avail themselves of the term whenever the occasion arises, they represent just the opposite of Democracy. Besides this, they have a fear of America's

[3] The official text, cited above, reads as follows: "Article 15. La France, la Grande-Bretagne et la Russie appuieront l'opposition que l'Italie formera à toute proposition tendant à introduire un représentant du Saint Siège dans toutes les négociations pour la paix et pour le règlement des questions soulevées par la présente guerre."

obtaining so strong a commercial position that she may interfere with their ambitions. They, for the most part, cannot bring themselves to the belief that we are actuated in this war by anything except material considerations and I often hear of men—public men—asking others what we are really aiming at and why we have really come into the war.

Baron Sonnino's attitude towards America is one which has perplexed me as well as surprised me. I do not believe that he has much faith in Democracy. I know that he knows about America so little that it might almost be termed nothing and I do not believe that he is greatly in accord with what is our master motive. I do not say that he does not believe in Liberty, but hardly Liberty as we understand it. He said to me in the last conversation I had with him, when I spoke of my feeling that in everything we and Italy— the Italian people—were believers in Freedom and champions of Liberty; that the Italian people have always felt themselves free— that forms of Liberty have meant little to them and even under the most absolute government they have always felt themselves to be free. For example, he said that in Tuscany, under the government of the Grand Duke, which was absolutely autocratic, the people of Tuscany (he himself is from Florence) never cared about the form of government and if it pressed on them too hardly they simply rose and settled the question. He is undoubtedly a strong patriot and believes in Italy absolutely; works for it with all his powers; is forceful and firm, even to obstinacy. Moreover, he is a man of clear intelligence and more dominative than any one man that I know in Italy. He works almost entirely alone, sees no one except officially, has few personal friends, and by reports is not in the least popular among even his colleagues. His strength is that the people believe him to be honest, strong, and patriotic. Even with these his best asset at present is the fact that the Allies have recognized in him a strong force to pushing to a conclusion the war which he did so much to have Italy join and that if he were supplanted in office his successor might be less inclined than he to fight the war out. He was at one time considered tremendously pro-English and this was used against him by his opponents. Of late, however, it appears as though he were less friendly to England than formerly and as though he were drawing closer to France. Very recently I heard that my French colleague here, M. Barrère,[4] who is the Dean of the Diplomatic Corps, expressed in a company of Frenchmen very critical views of your reference in your message to Italy's war aims and also to France's war aims, the latter, however, on the

---

[4] Camille Eugène Pierre Barrère.

ground that France's war aims were no affair of America's. This view that we have nothing to do with European matters—except of course to come to the aid of the European countries as they may need it—is, I believe, united in by many of those in control in Italy, though I am happy to say that there are some who take a broader view than this. It resolves itself into the same fact of apprehension of the movement of Democracy on the part of those to whom I allude.

I had an Italian intellectual of standing and broad information say to me but the other day that in his judgment the foreign policy of Italy under the present Government is directed with a view to maintaining relations with Germany which can on the conclusion of the war be immediately reestablished and that he believed that there would be an attempt made to reestablish the Triple Alliance as soon as the war ended. I said in reply that I believed that Baron Sonnino is absolutely in earnest about fighting this war through to a victorious conclusion. "Yes," he replied, "but the door has been left open and they always have one eye on Germany." I have had other persons say to me that there are important classes in Italy to-day who are much more friendly to Germany than they are to America and believe in the German ideas more than they believe in the American ideas.

I tell you just what I have heard and undoubtedly there is a certain amount of truth in it.

At bottom, however, the Italian people are sound for Liberty, and Italy under great disadvantages has suffered tremendously and is still suffering more—vastly more—than any of the other western Allies. She has lost something over a million men, of which something like a half million are prisoners in Austria and the rest dead or permanently disabled.

I have wished very much that we could send some troops here, even a small contingent,—a few regiments with a flag,—would have a great effect; but I think it would be necessary to send later on more. You have no idea how often this hope is expressed to me by two classes. I have referred to the propaganda going on against England and now against us. I think that we ought to do something here in the way of having a countervailing propaganda. Our declaration of war against Austria had an immense effect here in Italy among two classes of the people, though Sonnino has never mentioned the fact to me since we declared war, except in his very civil formal note acknowledging my formal note reporting the fact to him.

The Red Cross is doing a great work here and it has, as far as it goes, undoubtedly, an excellent effect as propaganda. Italians themselves, however, are beginning to bring to my attention the importance of our doing something to meet the German propaganda which, they tell me, goes on in Italy with as much intensity as ever, though with more secrecy. I am going to take this matter up with Secretary Lansing, so I will not impose upon you a longer letter; but I consider it a matter of increasing importance.

Believe me, my dear Mr. President, always,

Most sincerely, your friend,   Thos. Nelson Page

TLS (WP, DLC).

From George Creel

MEMORANDUM

My dear Mr. President,   [Washington] January 29, 1918.

I am afraid that there is some feeling that I have acted unwisely in taking Mr. Townley, of the Nonpartisan League, to see you.[1] I can assure you that from that time this organization has been behind you and behind the government.

I enclose an interview got out by Townley, himself, that receives wide publicity in the West.[2] The fight of this League is, fundamentally, the fight of machine politicians.

Respectfully,   George Creel

TLS (WP, DLC).
[1] On November 30, 1917. See White House Staff to WW, Nov. 30, 1917, n. 1, Vol. 45.
[2] Townley said in his statement that he had "absolutely no sympathy for the vicious and unwarranted attacks" which Theodore Roosevelt was making upon the Wilson administration. Townley did not question Roosevelt's right to criticize, but he did regard his motives as political, not patriotic. Delays in war production, were due, Townley added, not to departmental red tape, but to "a desire for extortionate profits." Yet Roosevelt was not complaining about "this piratical profiteering" by munition makers and war contractors. A. C. Townley, T MS dated Jan. 24, 1918 (WP, DLC).

From Thomas William Lamont

Dear Mr. President: New York January 29th, 1918.

Your recent letter to me,[1] in response to mine congratulating you upon your inspiring references to Russia in your address of January 8th last, was so cordial in tone that I am emboldened to write and reiterate the suggestion that may possibly have been made to you, namely, that you try to give a brief appointment to Colonel W. B. Thompson, so that he may have the opportunity of giving to you direct his views as to the present situation in Russia.

Let me explain that Colonel Thompson is an old Exeter school friend of mine, and in the thirty years that I have known him, he has always been sound, discreet and growing in wisdom. He has been tested in many situations, and to my knowledge has never been found wanting. He is a man of unusual ideas and sometimes of unusual and strikingly unique suggestions. But we here have always found his views guided by sanity and thoroughgoing common sense.

When on the other side recently I cabled him to come to London, hoping that he might arrive there before Colonel House's departure. He did not succeed in this. But when he did arrive, it seemed to me that his observations upon the situation in Russia were of such importance to the Allied cause that the British Government should be acquainted with them.

Accordingly, I introduced Col. Thompson to the leading members of the British Government, including of course Lord Reading, Sir Edward Carson and Mr. Lloyd George, and I may say to you without exaggeration that they assured me of the deep impression that Colonel Thompson's views made upon them. Mr. Lloyd George at an interview at which I was present expressed the desire that he give to you by word of mouth a message as to how he regarded the situation.

I am reciting the foregoing so as to make clear that no matter how adequate your sources of information as to Russia may be (and I have no doubt that they are complete), still I would regard Colonel Thompson's presentation to you of real importance. You must realize this to account for this unprecedented request on my part.

Colonel Thompson is actuated I can assure you only by the finest motives of patriotism, neither he nor we having financial interests in Russia.

I myself of course stand in readiness to accompany Colonel Thompson if that should be desired, but that is unimportant: the important thing to my mind is that here is a real man, of great sensibility and earnestness, generous and devoted, who has himself played a not unimportant part in matters over there. I realize how great the burdens are upon you at this time and the necessity, in the interests of the country and of the world, that you should spare your strength; but so pressing is the Russian situation that I venture the hope that Mr. Thompson's story and his personality should come to your personal attention.

May I beg you, my dear Mr. President, to pardon me for this seeming intrusion, and believe me,

Very sincerely yours, Thomas W. Lamont

TLS (WP, DLC).
[1] WW to T. W. Lamont, Jan. 11, 1918, Vol. 45.

Tasker Howard Bliss to Henry Pinckney McCain

Received at the War Department, January 29, 1918 at 5:42 P.M.
Number 15 January 27th.

Your confidential number 14[1] stated that General Pershing had approved the project of 150 of our infantry battalions to serve temporarily with the British but directed me to confer with him before making final arrangements to carry project into effect. General Pershing states that he has never approved this project and in conference with British Chief of Staff, General Robertson, and myself, he insisted that British should bring over six of our complete divisions instead of the 150 battalions. This would give British 72 battalions instead of the 150 which they want. General Robertson telegraphed General Pershing's proposition to Mr. Lloyd George and he has replied to-night asking for an interview with General Pershing and myself at Versailles January 29th. The supreme War Council meets on Wednesday, January 30th. If disagreement is not adjusted in conference with Mr. Lloyd George, I feel sure the question will be taken up following day by Supreme War Council.

Bliss.

TC telegram (WP, DLC).
  [1] Enclosure II with NDB to WW, Jan. 20, 1918.

A Memorandum by William Christian Bullitt

Memorandum for Colonel House,   Washington
Subject: Hertling's Address.   January 29, 1918.

Hertling's address was conceived at the conference of January 14th in which the Kaiser, Hindenburg, Ludendorff and the Chancellor participated. It was then agreed that Hertling should have a free hand to carry out his policy of attaching Courland, Lithuania and Poland to the Central Empires, by means of an imaginary "self-determination," and that annexations on the western front should be limited only by "the national necessities of the German Empire."

But the general strike in Vienna and the riots and threats of the Socialists in Germany compelled Hertling to postpone his address and to disguise his intention. The immediate occassion of the Viennese strike was a reduction in the flour ration; its fundamental cause was the war weariness of the Viennese proletariat. The strike and the accompanying demonstrations were so widespread that no attempt was made to suppress them by force. Although the first demand of the strikers was for peace and bread, they obtained not merely the promise that the Government would adhere strictly to the formula of "no annexations, no indemnities" but also promises of municipal electoral reform, woman suffrage, and the withdrawal of military control from industrial establishments. The entire proletariat manifested bitter hostility towards General Hoffmann and the pan-Germans, whose desire for annexations they considered the cause of the failure of the negotiations at Brest Litovsk. In the words of the reliable Viennese correspondent of the Berliner Tageblatt:

"Enemy countries would take too optimistic a view of the situation were they to suppose that Austria cannot hold out any longer. The population can hold out if need be and will hold out as long as it is necessary to continue the war for self-defense; but it will not hold out for the sake of annexationist aims no matter how concealed."

Meanwhile, the German Socialists nightly were raiding meetings of the Fatherland Party[1] and Scheidemann seems to have hinted that if the Government should announce a program of annexation, the Majority Socialists would join the Minority in bringing about a general strike after the Viennese pattern.

Hertling, therefore, faced the eternal problem of Scylla and Charybdis. If he should announce an annexationist program, the Socialists would call a general strike—the precursor of revolution—and the anti-German feeling in Austria would become uncontrollable. If he should frankly and sincerely adopt the program of "no annexations, no indemnities," Hindenburg and Ludendorff would present their resignations to the Kaiser.

The Chancellor sought safety in the path so often traversed by Bethmann: the path of non-commital ambiguity. As Theodor Wolff ironically puts it in the Berliner Tageblatt, there are many "points where Hertling conceals his interest in clarity of style."

By following this course the Chancellor pleased only the official and semi-official and moderate National Liberal papers, and the editor of Germania,[2] who has become his fidus Achates. The pan-German press flew into paroxysms of rage. The Socialist and liberal press compared his address unfavorably with the address of Czernin, and bemoaned his failure unequivocally to renounce annexations and indemnities, and his lack of clarity in dealing with Belgium, Northern France and Poland. His statement in regard to Alsace-Lorraine alone received unanimous approval.

[1] The Fatherland Party (Deutsche Vaterlands-Partei), founded at Königsberg on September 2, 1917, was headed by the Duke of Mecklenburg, Tirpitz, and Wolfgang Kapp. It united various groups in Germany opposed to the Reichstag's "Peace Resolution" of July 19, 1917, and called instead for a decisive victory over the Allies. For its program, see Schulthess, LVIII (1917), Part 1, pp. 782-85.

[2] August Hommerich.

VORWAERTS wrote: "The speech of the Chancellor might have been a world freeing act *if it had clearly stated that behind German expressions of peace desires there lay concealed no egotistic ambitions for power*. It has not done this, and unfortunately, in parts, was calculated to increase the enemy's distrust in the sincerity of the German peace declaration. *This is especially true of the statements regarding the treatment of Poland and Belgium*. The right of Russia to have a voice regarding Poland actually was recognized in the Brest Litovsk negotiations. *Lasting peace can only come if the whole situation is taken as a basis and any changes based on general sanction. Regarding Belgium, the Chancellor does not even meet the desires of the radical English peace advocates, who demand unconditional return. The conditions under which evacuation of occupied French territory is granted will awaken suspicion in the enemy. Hertling might at least have declared that no aspirations to annex Longwy and Briey existed. The speech of the Chancellor is a master piece of finding elastic formulas into which journalists can read what they want. But of such we have had enough*. Scheidemann in his criticism, pointed out our mistakes and the weakness of the speech and millions of the people support him. When our enemies are ready for a true democratic peace, a premanent [permanent] peace, neither shameful for us or for them, they can count on the immense majority of the German people, who though then will continue to fight for their rights, *want nothing save peace and what was theirs before the war*. The existing current must become strong enough to make resistance to it on the part of those in power impossible."

Minor majority Socialist papers took the same line. The Mannheimer Volksstimme wrote: "*Hertling should have briefly and emphatically declared that Germany still holds to the Reichstag War Aims Resolution*, and, while unable to accept all Lloyd George's and Wilson's proposals, finds them sufficient basis for immediate peace negotiations."

THE SCHWAEBISCHE TAGWACHT wrote: "*Unfortunately it cannot be said that the Chancellor's speech brought the clarity expected by the German people as to whether peace with Russia or general peace was imperilled by annexationist demands. It would have helped matters a great deal if the German Chancellor had given unequivocal expression to the same intentions as Czernin*."

THE CHEMNITZER VOLKSSTIMME wrote: "Czernin's wants peace on the basis that we desire and he wants it soon and sincerely. Hertling wants about the same peace that *we want but we do not know how sincere he is on certain points* although it must be admitted that he did not deliver a war prolonging speech."

THE FRANKFURTER ZEITUNG, leading liberal organ of Germany wrote: *"The speech of the Chancellor has not brought the clarity necessary to thwart the reports of annexionistic politicians.* We greatly regret this, because attempts to force the Government into a policy of *senseless annexations* rob us of internal quiet for the necessary reorganization at home and support the doubts of our enemies as to the good faith of our peace desires. Hertling preserves the hope that it is possible to lead as one all parties of the German people and to postpone the moment of separation. This is a fatal illusion, as he will soon learn. The fact that the German Chancellor and his colleagues in Vienna have discussed and found acceptable part of Wilson's programme and have invited a reconsideration of terms will alienate the Military Party. Therefore it would have been better to have taken the inevitable step and clearly broken away from this party. The Chancellor summarized in three words what Germany expected to gain from the war as a basis of a lasting peace: Integrity of the German Empire, security for our vital interests and the honor of our Fatherland. *We would have wished that he had spoken more clearly relative to Belgium and the occupied portion of France and still more categorically closed the door to the possibility of annexation.* However, our opponents have it in their power to settle once and for all the Belgian problem by guaranteeing the integrity of territory of the Central Powers."

The Muenchner Neuste Nachrichten, the chief paper of Bavaria, a rather liberal organ of the National Liberals wrote:

"The full clarity and precision so necessary after the late occurrences in Berlin is sadly missing in this speech. It omits all mention of the two opposite camps in Germany and gives only the idea of an official peace policy; *but all indications point to the existence of an unofficial peace policy with unknown aims.* * * * *The speech contains no positive statement of war aims and no positive statement regarding Belgium's future and relations to Germany.* Any statesman who would allow such indefiniteness regarding Belgium to shatter peace prospects would undertake a more serious responsibility assuming that Germany's other vital interests are secured."

The Radical Berliner Tageblatt wrote: "Czernin's statement that an exchange of views between Austria and America might form the basis for conciliatory pourparlers between all the nations at war will undoubtedly strengthen the unmistakably increasing peace movements in America and may even suffice to weaken the *obstructive effects of Hertling's speech* and strengthen its parts which make for peace. For it is plain to anybody that there is a long distance between Wilson's points and Hertling's points.

The problems which arise are manifold. *Supposing an exchange of views was commenced with Austria and came to standstill at the points where Hertling conceals his interest in clarity of style.* The effect on Austrian public opinion would have to be considered. However, the egg is laid and we must wait and see what kind of a bird breaks its way out of the shell."

This reception of Hertling's address by the socialist and liberal press makes it highly probable that, if the President should criticize the address from the same standpoint as the Socialists and liberals, he would have the united support of better Germany against Hertling. The fundamental difference between the Chancellor and the common people of Germany and Austria Hungary is that, while Hertling is willing to gamble on the coming offensive, the people of the Central Powers fervently desire peace at once. Hertling's address is open to criticism which would be supported by the German people, first, on the ground of its weakness in conception: The Chancellor still conceives peace as a question of bargaining between individual states. If the President should state that the primary interest of the United States in this war is that out of it should come a more decent international order; that the Chancellor seems to be looking towards a future of state wars and a renewal of the old diplomatic game; that we are primarily interested in the creation of a new world of international decency and that we cannot make peace until the representative[s] of Germany show that they, too, in their hearts desire to create a new world order and are willing to consider the reconstruction of the world in the light of the new order; that, as Vorwaerts puts it, "lasting peace can only come if the whole situation is taken as a basis and any changes based on general sanction"; if the President should place this high conception of peace before the German people he would be support[ed] unanimously by them.

The President almost certainly would be supported by the German liberals and socialists if he should point out: that Hertling also fails to state the details of his program with clarity; that by ambiguous phrases he leaves himself a free hand to annex territory on the Eastern Front under the guise of an imaginary self-determination, and territory on the Western front, if the coming offensive should be successful. The President might point out in the very words of the German liberal and socialist press, that Hertling fails to endorse unequivocally the "no annexations, no indemnities" resolution of the Reichstag of July 19, 1917; that he fails to state frankly that Germany will evacuate Belgium; that he does not even agree to evacuate the occupied departments of France, but utters a sinister phrase in regard to "conditions of evacuation" and leaves the impression that, should it prove possible, he would demand indemnities and annex the Briey-Longwy district; that he declines to discuss the evacuation of Russian territory and g[l]ibly slides over the questions of the Balkans and the subject peoples of the Turkish Empire.

The text of Count Czernin's address had not yet reached the Department. In view of the great sensation it has created in Europe, it seems desirable that the President should delay his reply to Hertling until this address has been received. For it may prove possible to commend heartily Czernin's fundamental conception of peace and thereby point the criticism of Hertling and further widen the breach between Germany and the people of Austria-Hungary.

The common people of the world desire to build a new world of international order. Is it too much to hope that the President may now become the leader of the liberals of Germany and Austria-Hungary as he had become the leader of the liberals of France and England?   Respectfully submitted   William C. Bullitt.

TS MS (WP, DLC).

From the Diary of Colonel House

January 29, 1918.

I have William Bullitt of the State Department gathering expressions from German and Austrian papers concerning the President's speech, and the Chancellor's and Czernin's replies. I am intensely interested as to its reception in the Dual Empire and in Germany. It looks as if the [s]chism which we have tried to create by this speech is more successful than we dared to hope. And this reminds me to say that the President constantly uses the word "we" in reference to that speech.

I lunched with the President and Mrs. Wilson, Miss Bones and Eleanor McAdoo. After lunch the President and I went to his study and went over some data I had gathered since yesterday about the foreign situation. A little later he, Mrs. Wilson and I went motoring. It was the first time the President had been out for several days. He told Mrs. Wilson that "we have tentatively decided to answer the Hertling and Czernin speeches in this way: In reply to Hertling's assertion that differences between Russia and Germany must be settled between the two, and questions between France and Germany should be settled in like manner, we will call attention to the fact that this is the old diplomacy which has brought the world into such difficulties, and if carried to its logical conclusion, Germany and the rest of the world cannot object if England and the

United States should conclude between themselves treaties by which the balance of the world would be excluded from their raw materials." We discussed the best method of making his views public.

This morning when I was with him Lansing suggested that he give out an interview. In mentioning this to the President he[1] disagreed with this conclusion. He said he wanted to make a habit of delivering through Congress what he had to say. I agreed with this procedure because I thought it was in line with open diplomacy and would make a good impression.

He wondered what excuse he could make for going before Congress again. I suggested that he get a member of the Foreign Relations Committee to write him a letter which would call forth a promise to address Congress on the subject upon which he desired information. He objected to this as he did not wish Congress to think they could control him in any way or take part in handling foreign affairs. I then suggested that he state that the questions now pending between the nations were of such importance he felt that every move he made, or contemplated making, or whatever thought he had concerning the international situation, should be communicated through Congress.

I had thought to take the night train home, but having finished everything I concluded to go on the four o'clock. The President therefore drove me directly to Janet's and bade me goodbye there, expressing a hope that I would soon come back. He asked when I thought he should make the speech. My advice was not to be in a hurry, but to prepare it next week, and about Monday or Tuesday of the following week, deliver it. This seemed to meet his approval.

When he left he returned in about five minutes to say that he would send his car back to take me to the train. . . .

One matter I discussed with the President was the appointment of Baruch as Chairman of the War Industries Board. During our ride he told me that W. W. Harris & Co. of Boston, with whom I had put him in touch regarding his investments, wanted him to buy some British bonds which yield 6%. He refused to buy them and for reasons which are apparent. He asked if I saw any objection to his buying Liberty bonds. I told him none whatever. This was apropos of investments in general and of how careful we both needs be.

[1] That is, Wilson.

To Edward Mandell House

My dear House,   The White House. 30 January, 1918.

Please read these despatches; and please tell me how you think a letter like this of Colcord's should be answered?[1] I must give some sort of reply and I do not know what sort would be the best in the circumstances.

It was a delight to have you here and have one or two real talks.
                              Affectionately Yours,   W.W.

WWTLI (E. M. House Papers, CtY).
    [1] House returned the "despatches," whatever they were, and Colcord's letter to Wilson of January 27.

To Charles Homer Haskins

My dear Haskins: [The White House] 30 January, 1918

It was with real pleasure that I received a copy of your book, "Norman Institutions,"[1] and I shall hope for some time of leisure when I may really read it comprehendingly, because it is on a subject on which I have often wished to have more complete and trustworthy information.

It gives me peculiar pleasure, my dear Haskins, to believe that I have been of service to you in your studies.[2] My interest in you and in your career has been very sincere and very great from the first, and it has been a real pleasure to me to see your unusual gifts recognized.

It is delightful to hear that your children and my grandchildren are likely to become chums.[3] I hope that the small people will really get to know each other.

    With the best wishes,
                    Cordially and sincerely yours,   Woodrow Wilson

TLS (Letterpress Books, WP, DLC).
    [1] Charles Homer Haskins, *Norman Institutions* (Cambridge, Mass., 1918).
    [2] Haskins' letter is missing.
    [3] Francis B. Sayre was Thayer teaching fellow at the Harvard Law School during the academic year 1917-1918.

To Margaret Hughes Hughes

                            [The White House] 30 January, 1918

My heart goes out to you in warmest and sincerest sympathy. In the death of your husband I have lost a friend for whom I had the deepest affection and a very genuine admiration.[1]
                              Woodrow Wilson.

T telegram (Letterpress Books, WP, DLC).
  [1] Senator Hughes had died in a Trenton hospital on January 30.

From William Dennison Stephens

Sacramento, California,
My dear Mr. President: January 30, 1918
   Your letter of January 22nd has been received and I note your
interest in the Mooney case.
   This case is now before the Supreme Court of the State on appeal,
and, in consequence, the day of effecting the sentence of the lower
court is automatically set aside. Should the Supreme Court deny
the Mooney appeal then the lower court would name another day.
   The case would not come to the Governor until after the final
judgment by the courts but should it come you may feel assured
that careful consideration will be given to your communication and
to the evidence and findings in the case.
   With best wishes, I am,
                        Yours very truly,   Wm. D. Stephens

TLS (WP, DLC).

From William Bauchop Wilson

My dear Mr. President: Washington January 30, 1918.
   I am glad to be able to write you of the settlement today effected
by your Commission of the labor difficulties in the oil and gas
producing fields of Coastal Texas and the State of Louisiana. The
agreements made provide for the settlement of all disputes during
the period of the war by orderly process, and for the elimination of
strikes and lockouts during that time.
   The district affected has a normal output of three million barrels
of oil per month and employs upwards of eleven thousand men.
   You will be gratified to learn of the fine spirit of cooperation shown
by the representatives of both the operators and the workmen in
their conferences with the Commission and in making concessions
which would permit of a final settlement.
                        Faithfully yours,   W B Wilson

TLS (WP, DLC).

From William Bauchop Wilson, with Enclosure

My dear Mr. President: Washington January 30, 1918.

I am inclosing you herewith a memorandum of the understanding arrived at in the conference on housing held this morning.

I am returning the correspondence from Chairman Hurley and Mr. Piez, which you sent over in connection with the conference.

Faithfully yours, W B Wilson

TLS (WP, DLC).

ENCLOSURE

MEMORANDUM:

At a conference on the housing problem held in the office of the Secretary of Labor Wednesday morning, January 30, 1918, at which Secretary Baker, Secretary Daniels, Secretary Wilson, Senator Fletcher, Congressman Alexander, Chairman Hurley, Assistant Secretary Roosevelt, Mr. Piez and Mr. King[1] were present, the following understanding was arrived at:

First. In view of the immediate need for housing in connection with shipbuilding operations, and of the organization already under way by the Fleet Corporation to handle house-building operations, it was believed that Senate Bill 3389, authorizing the Shipping Board Emergency Fleet Corporation to spend $50,000,000 in providing housing for employes engaged in shipbuilding, should be passed, the housing to be available for employes engaged in industrial operations in connection with the army and navy.

Second. That in perfecting the housing plans of the Shipping Board a representative of the War Department, Navy Department and Labor Department act in an advisory capacity with the representatives of the Shipping Board.

Third. That we should proceed with the object in mind of having the housing problem ultimately administered through the Department of Labor in consultation with the War Department, Navy Department and Shipping Board, but that the housing operations of the Fleet Corporation should not be interfered with unless and until the Department of Labor has an organization and funds which will enable it to take over the housing work of the Fleet Corporation and proceed with it without interruption.

T MS (WP, DLC).
[1] That is, Stanley King.

Hugh Robert Wilson to Robert Lansing

Pontarlier (Berne) Jan. 30, 1918.

2535, For Colonel House. "Hertling's speech not only to quiet Germany's internal troubles started by President's message but opened way for attack on German Government and exposed vulnerable points of Central Powers which apperently make it essential United States strike again through declaration by President. President has accomplished object of his last speech to drive wedge between sections German public opinion, our object now to force issue of war on Germany's terms or peace on our own terms.

Vulnerable points in enemy countries today are: One. Public demand for liberal peace. Two. Open gap between Vienna and Berlin. Three. Difference between pan-German party and rest of Germany. Four. Feeling of uncertainty in Bulgaria and Turkey.

Concerning point one, I suggest agitation in Germany for strikes and demonstrations against Government policies wide spread and Chargé Wilson believes effervescence in Germany has reached highest point at any time since beginning of war. Central Council German labor unions warn workers not to strike because it would increase present internal difficulties and endanger success electoral reform in Prussia. Though this may temporarily prevent strikes unless deep lying causes are removed sentiment in favor of strikes will remain.

Our objects should be to strengthen belief German people that the military leaders are prolonging war, that German Government alone responsible for continued suffering. Suggest advisability pointing out German Government hopes to unite Germany by sacrificing a million German soldiers on western front in attempt to conquer war.

Concerning point two, whether Czernin's reply made with understanding of Germany, it now stands not as important as effect on wide gap between terms of Berlin and Vienna. Apparently Czernin had two objects; A, to aid German liberals and quiet Austro-Hungarians who desire peace at any price, B, to make it possible for America to act as intermediary between Austria-Hungary and Allies knowing that if America showed any interest in proposal, troops of Dual Monarchy might not have to be used on western front.

In Zurich, at request of Chargé Wilson, I met confidential newspaper representative Vienna Foreign Office with consent of BALL-PLATZ. He stated desire to write articles on events in Austria for American newspapers, spoke of Germany as enemy and said his political supporters dissapproved of use of Austrian troops in France and that Foreign Office hoped for confidential discussion of peace terms with America as result of Czernin's speech.

While not recommending confidential discussion with Vienna, I believe if President publicly encourages desire for negotiations in Austria on basis of message, he would indirectly bring pressure to bear on Berlin, would create further dissatisfaction over use of Austrian troops in France and so increase peace sentiment in Austria that it might be possible, if Berlin does not alter aims, to discuss separate peace with Austria at later date.

Regarding point three; Hertling's speech gives another opportunity to attack German Government for not representing people. We could state, if Hertling's words approved by Kaiser, Hindenburg and Ludendorf represent will of German people, peace with this unreformed annexationist Government impossible.

Regarding point four, Bulgaria and Turkey dissatisfied and want peace. Bulgaria will probably agree our terms, Turkey cannot. As you are informed, Bulgaria in strictly confidential and unofficial communication with Legation here. Military operations will have best results in Turkey.

Conclusion: War in decisive period. Peace demanded by all Europe. It may be possible to end war by increasing agitation for peace in Central Powers. Germany tried this in France and England but failed because of Wilson's and Lloyd George's speeches. War today is fought by statesmen to gain enemy peoples. Germany cannot win confidence Entente. They know it but hope by offensive to frighten and force people of France and Italy, if not England, to make peace. In this new warfare we have advantage because President has confidence great mass of enemy peoples. If this confidence can be increased before German military leaders can point to further victory in France, America will have won its first battle in fight to establish democracy in Germany. Signed Ackerman."

Wilson.

T telegram (E. M. House Papers, CtY).

A Message to a Farmers' Conference[1]

[[Jan. 31, 1918]]

I am very sorry indeed that I cannot be present in person at the Urbana conference. I should like to enjoy the benefit of the inspiration and exchange of counsel which I know I should obtain, but in the circumstances it has seemed impossible for me to be present, and therefore I can only send you a very earnest message expressing my interest and the thoughts which such a conference must bring prominently into every mind.

I need not tell you, for I am sure you realize as keenly as I do, that we are as a nation in the presence of a great task which demands supreme sacrifice and endeavor of every one of us. We can give everything that is needed with the greater willingness, and even satisfaction, because the object of the war in which we are engaged is the greatest that free men have ever undertaken. It is to prevent the life of the world from being determined and the fortunes of men everywhere affected by small groups of military masters, who seek their own interest and the selfish dominion throughout the world of the governments they unhappily for the moment control. You will not need to be convinced that it was necessary for us as a free people to take part in this war. It had raised its evil hand against us. The rulers of Germany had sought to exercise their power in such a way as to shut off our economic life so far as our intercourse with Europe was concerned, and to confine our people within the western hemisphere while they accomplished purposes which would have permanently impaired and impeded every process of our national life and have put the fortunes of America at the mercy of the Imperial Government of Germany.

This was no threat. It had become a reality. Their hand of violence had been laid upon our own people and our own property in flagrant violation not only of justice but of the well-recognized and long-standing covenants of international law and treaty. We are fighting, therefore, as truly for the liberty and self-government of the United States as if the war of our own Revolution had to be fought over again; and every man in every business in the United States must

[1] Wilson had intended to be present at the conference of the corn growers and stockmen of Illinois, at the University of Illinois, and a special train had been held in Washington for two days for him. On January 30, however, he sent a telegram to Edmund Janes James, president of the university, as follows: "Regret exceedingly to tell you that my doctor advises that with the sort of cold I am suffering from it would be very imprudent indeed for me to venture on a journey at this time." Wilson asked James to express his regrets to all concerned and added that he was asking Houston to take his place. WW to E. J. James, Jan. 30, 1918, T telegram (IU-Ar); *Wall Street Journal*, Feb. 1, 1918. Houston in turn was "prevented from participating by the tie-up in transportation facilities," whereupon James read Wilson's message to the group. *Official Bulletin*, II (Jan. 31, 1918), 1.

know by this time that his whole future fortune lies in the balance. Our national life and our whole economic development will pass under the sinister influences of foreign control if we do not win. We must win, therefore, and we shall win. I need not ask you to pledge your lives and fortunes with those of the rest of the nation to the accomplishment of that great end.

You will realize, as I think statesmen on both sides of the water realize, that the culminating crisis of the struggle has come and that the achievements of this year on the one side or the other must determine the issue. It has turned out that the forces that fight for freedom—the freedom of men all over the world as well as our own—depend upon us in an extraordinary and unexpected degree for sustenance, for the supply of the materials by which men are to live and to fight, and it will be our glory when the war is over that we have supplied those materials and supplied them abundantly, and it will be all the more glory because in supplying them we have made our supreme effort and sacrifice.

In the field of agriculture, we have agencies and instrumentalities, fortunately, such as no other government in the world can show. The Department of Agriculture is undoubtedly the greatest practical and scientific agricultural organization in the world. Its total annual budget of $46,000,000 has been increased during the last four years more than 72 per cent. It has a staff of 18,000, including a large number of highly trained experts, and alongside of it stands the unique land-grant colleges, which are without example elsewhere, and the sixty-nine state and federal experiment stations. These colleges and experiment stations have a total endowment of plant and equipment of $172,000,000 and an income of more than $35,000,000, with 10,271 teachers, a resident student body of 125,000, and a vast additional number receiving instruction at their homes. County agents, joint officers of the Department of Agriculture and of the colleges are everywhere cooperating with the farmers and assisting them. The number of extension workers under the Smith-Lever Act and under the recent emergency legislation has grown to 5,500 men and women working regularly in the various communities and taking to the farmer the latest scientific and practical information.

Alongside these great public agencies stand the very effective voluntary organizations among the farmers themselves which are more and more learning the best methods of cooperation and the best methods of putting to practical use the assistance derived from governmental sources. The banking legislation of the last two or three years has given the farmers access to the great lendable capital of the country, and it has become the duty both of the men in charge of the Federal Reserve Banking System and of the Farm Loan Banking System to see to it that the farmers obtain the credit, both short term and long term, to which they are not only entitled but which it is imperatively necessary should be extended to them if the present tasks of the country are to be adequately performed. Both by direct purchase of nitrates and by the establishment of plants to produce nitrates the government is doing its utmost to assist in the problem of fertilization. The Department of Agriculture and other agencies are actively assisting the farmers to locate, safeguard, and secure at cost an adequate supply of sound seed. The department has $2,500,000 available for this purpose now and has asked the Congress for $6,000,000 more.

The labor problem is one of great difficulty, and some of the best agencies of the nation are addressing themselves to the task of solving it, so far as it is possible to solve it. Farmers have not been exempted from the draft. I know that they would not wish to be. I take it for granted they would not wish to be put in a class by themselves in this respect. But the attention of the War Department has been very seriously centered upon the task of interfering with the labor of the farms as little as possible, and, under the new draft regulations, I believe that the farmers of the country will find that their supply of labor is very much less seriously drawn upon than it was under the first and initial draft, made before we had our present full experience in these perplexing matters. The supply of labor in all industries is a matter we must look to and are looking to with diligent care.

And let me say that the stimulation of the agencies I have enumerated has been responded to by the farmers in splendid fashion. I dare say that you are aware that the farmers of this country are as efficient as any other farmers in the world. They do not produce more per acre than the farmers in Europe. It is not necessary that they should do so. It would perhaps be bad economy for them to attempt it. But they do produce by two to three or four times more per man, per unit of labor and capital, than the farmers of any European country. They are more alert and use more labor-saving devices than any other farmers in the world. And their response to the demands of the present emergency has been in every way remarkable. Last spring their planting exceeded by 12,000,000 acres the largest planting of any previous year, and the yields from the crops were record-breaking yields. In the fall of 1917, a wheat acreage of 42,170,000 was planted, which was 1,000,000 larger than for any preceding year, 3,000,000 greater than the next largest, and 7,000,000 greater than the preceding five-year average.

But I ought to say to you that it is not only necessary that these achievements should be repeated, but that they should be exceeded. I know what this advice involves. It involves not only labor but sacrifice—the painstaking application of every bit of scientific knowledge and every tested practice that is available. It means the utmost economy, even to the point where the pinch comes. It means the kind of concentration and self-sacrifice which is involved in the field of battle itself, where the object always looms greater than the individual. And yet the government will help and help in every way that is possible. The impression which prevails in some quarters that, while the government has sought to fix the prices of foodstuffs, it has not sought to fix other prices which determine the expenses of the farmer is a mistaken one. As a matter of fact, the government has actively and successfully regulated the prices of many fundamental materials underlying all the industries of the country, and has regulated them, not only for the purchases of the government, but also for the purchases of the general public. And I have every reason to believe that the Congress will extend the powers of the government in this important and even essential matter, so that the tendency to profiteering, which is showing itself in too many quarters, may be effectively checked. In fixing the prices of foodstuffs, the government has sincerely tried to keep the interests of the farmer as much in mind as the interests of the communities which are to be served, but it is serving mankind as well as the farmer, and everything in these times of war takes on the rigid aspect of duty.

I will not appeal to you to continue and renew and increase your efforts. I do not believe that it is necessary to do so. I believe that you will do it without any word or appeal from me, because you understand as well as I do the needs and opportunities of this great hour, when the fortunes of mankind everywhere seem about to be determined and when America has the greatest opportunity she has ever had to make good her own freedom and in making it good to lend a helping hand to men struggling for their freedom everywhere. You remember that it was farmers from whom came the first shots at Lexington, that set aflame the revolution that made America free. I hope and believe that the farmers of America will willingly and conspicuously stand by to win this war also.

The toil, the intelligence, the energy, the foresight, the self-sacrifice, and devotion of the farmers of America will, I believe, bring to a triumphant conclusion this great last war for the emancipation of men from the control of arbitrary government and the selfishness of class legislation and control, and then, when the end has come, we may look each other in the face and be glad that we are Americans and have had the privilege to play such a part.[2]

Message sent by the President to the Farmers' Conference ... (Washington, 1918).
   [2] There is a WWsh outline and a CLST draft of this message in the C. L. Swem Coll., NjP.

To Edward Mandell House, with Enclosure

Dear House,   The White House. 31 January, 1918.

Such symptoms make me uneasy. To my mind they furnish additional arguments why I should presently attempt to show that each item of a general peace is everybody's business. If we have to fight an All-Latin combination, we must fight it. I trust they will have no stomach for such a combination as we could form against them. Is not this the way your mind works on what it [is] to be got from this message of Tom. Page's?

After all, it may be merely the resentment brought about by the prospect that, without our support, Italy cannot get what she went into the war, on cold-blooded calculation, to get.

                    Faithfully,   W.W.

WWTLI (E. M. House Papers, CtY).

E N C L O S U R E

                    Rome. Jan. 29, 1918.

1389. Secret. I am sensible of growing feeling here among men in control that America is becoming too potent and that we are too democratic and too little in sympathy with European interests but I do not believe the people have this idea at all. Newspapers talk of Latin race league or union with Italy as head to counterbalance the power of the Anglo-Saxon peoples and I hear that some leading men have same idea. I hear that French Ambassador is very critical of President's last message apparently resenting that he should take so firm and directive a position in European affairs. This also is, I hear, somewhat Baron Sonnino's private view. They seem now closer than even formerly. Meantime Sonnino opposes sending Italian workmen to France insisting that Italy needs all her men herself but his colleagues overrule him.   Nelson Page.

T telegram (WP, DLC).

Two Letters to William Bauchop Wilson

My dear Mr. Secretary: [The White House] 31 January, 1918

Thank you for your letter of yesterday enclosing the memorandum of the understanding arrived at in the conference on housing held yesterday.

I do not feel that I am entitled to an independent judgment in the matter and I trust sincerely that the agreement arrived at will work out satisfactorily.

Cordially and sincerely yours,   Woodrow Wilson

My dear Mr. Secretary: [The White House] 31 January, 1918

Thank you for your letter of January thirtieth. It is most gratifying to learn that the labor difficulties in the oil and gas producing fields of Coastal Texas and the State of Louisiana have been satisfactorily settled. I congratulate you and I hope that if you have the opportunity, you will express to the representatives of the operators and workmen my appreciation of the fine spirit of cooperation they have shown.   Cordially and sincerely yours,   Woodrow Wilson

TLS (Letterpress Books, WP, DLC).

To Newton Diehl Baker

My dear Mr. Secretary,   The White House. 31 January, 1918.

We are having hard luck with our military attaches at Petrograd, are we not.[1] I should think that being sent to Petrograd would drive most men to drink, but anyone who is so driven is the very man who cannot be trusted to do the real job there, am I not right?

Faithfully Yours,   W.W.

WWTLI (N. D. Baker Papers, DLC).
   [1] That is, in finding a replacement for General Judson, who at this time was on his way to the United States.

To Thomas William Lamont

My dear Mr. Lamont: The White House 31 January, 1918

Thank you for your letter of the twenty-ninth. I have heard a great deal about Colonel W. B. Thompson, and everything that I have heard has attracted me. Some day I hope I shall be able to have a deliberate talk with him, but just at present the changes taking place in Russia are so kaleidoscopic that I feel that information and advice are futile until there is something definite to plan with as well as for.

Cordially and sincerely yours,   Woodrow Wilson

TLS (T. W. Lamont Papers, MH-BA).

From Arthur James Balfour

Private.   Foreign Office, S.W. 1.

My dear Mr. President,   January 31st 1918.

I gather from a message sent by Wiseman that you would like to know my thoughts on the Italian territorial claims under the treaty of London concluded in 1915.

That treaty (arranged of course long before I was at the Foreign Office) bears on the face of it evident proof of the anxiety of the Allies to get Italy into the war, and of the use to which that anxiety was put by the Italian negotiators. But a treaty is a treaty: and we—I mean England and France (of Russia I say nothing)—are bound to uphold it in letter and in spirit. The objections to it indeed are obvious enough: It assigns to Italy territories on the Adriatic which are not Italian but Slav; and the arrangement is justified not on grounds of nationality but on grounds of strategy.

Now I do not suggest that we should rule out such arguments with a pedantic consistency. Strong frontiers make for peace; and though great crimes against the principle of nationality have been committed in the name of "strategic necessity," still if a particular boundary adds to the stability of international relations, and if the populations concerned be numerically insignificant, I would not reject it in deference to some a priori principle. Each case must be considered on its merits.

Personally, however, I am in doubt whether Italy would really be strengthened by the acquisition of all her Adriatic claims; and in any case it does not seem probable that she will endeavour to prolong the war in order to obtain them. Of the three west-European belligerents she is certainly the most war-weary; and if she could secure peace *and* "Italia Irredenta" she would, I believe, not be ill satisfied. Who knows, indeed, whether our difficulty may not be to induce her to go on fighting *even* for "Italia Irredenta"!

Lord Reading who leaves to-morrow morning will give you our last news. The situation changes from day to day. With Russia in dissolution; with Austria, Germany, and Italy measuring with anxious eyes the internal forces which are threatening to shatter their external policy; with France apparently depending on the continued vigour of a man of 76; with some faint signs of unrest even in Britain; with no obvious prospect of decisive military successes for either side in the West,—victory seems likely to be the prize of those nations who have most endurance and the greatest political stability. Since America came in I have never doubted the result!

Yours sincerely,   Arthur James Balfour

P.S. I shall always be delighted to answer with complete frankness any question you care to put to me. But this I think you know already. AJB.[1]

TLS (WP, DLC).
[1] For Wilson's comment on this letter, see Lord Reading to A. J. Balfour, March 18, 1918 (second telegram of that date).

From Edward Mandell House, with Enclosure

Dear Governor: New York. January 31, 1918.

I am returning Colcord's letter. My inclination would be to let Tumulty merely give him a formal answer because I think it is very unfair to present the matter to you in the way he has.

I know Raymond E. Swing, and I am sure you would get nothing of value by seeing him. He is a fine fellow, but not well balanced in his judgments.

I am enclosing a suggestion for Colcord in the event you decide to answer him yourself.[1]

It looks as if things were at last beginning to crack. I do not believe Germany can maintain a successful offensive with her people in their present frame of mind. I hope the Entente will keep still and not do anything, for past experience makes one fearful lest they do the wrong thing. Do you think it advisable for me to get Sir William to warn them? The situation is so delicate and so critical that it would be a tragedy to make a false step now.

Affectionately yours,   E. M. House

TLS (WP, DLC).
[1] It is missing, but see WW to L. R. Colcord, Feb. 4, 1918, which was probably based on House's draft.

E N C L O S U R E

[London] Jan. 30th. 1918.

Instructions have been sent, by telegraph, to Colville Barclay to urge that Japan be asked by the Allies to occupy the Siberian Railway, acting as their mandatory. I hope the scheme will receive very careful consideration in spite of the many serious difficulties it undoubtedly presents. The powerful arguments used in the telegram to Mr. Barclay strengthen this hope. I will not repeat these arguments fully here but I desire to supplement them on two points: the first with relation to Russia and the second with relation to Japan. At first sight the occupation of the Siberian Railway may seem inconsistent with due respect to the rights of the Government now at the head of affairs in Petrograd. It is not our wish to quarrel with the Bolshivic. On the contrary we look at them with a certain degree of favour as long as they refuse to make a separate peace. But their claim to be the Government of all the Russians either de facto or de jure is not founded on fact. Their claim to this position, in particular since the forced dissolution of the Constituent Assembly, is no better than that of the autonomous bodies in South East Russia which it is sought to assist by the occupation of the Siberian Railway: while it is much less probable that they will help to defend the Roumanian Army, to repel the attacks on Armenia or Turkey and to refuse to furnish supplies to the Germans than said autonomous bodies. So much for the situation as regards Russia.

With regard to Japan it is hardly necessary for me to assure you that I fully appreciate the difficulties of the situation. I even doubt whether the proposition will meet with the agreement of the Japanese Government if and when made, but I consider it of real importance that we should do all that is possible to encourage the active participation of the Japanese in the war, particularly at its present stage. The effect of such participation on the ruling military caste in Germany may be considerable. It may be said that Japan's aggrandizement, whether territorially (it might, for instance, prove impossible to get her out of the maritime provinces after she is once established there) or morally, as saviour of the situation as consequence of her successful intervention, would appear to be a grave danger from the point of view of the spectator. There is force in this, but, on the other hand, I would suggest that occupation of the maritime provinces by the Japanese is a question which, in all likelihood, will have to be faced in any case, as conditions in Russia will probably soon make such occupation unavoidable. In such circumstances Japan will, without doubt, act on her own initiative, whatever may be the desire of the Allies. The very fact that Japan will be obliged to come out in the open against Germany and that the respective interests of both countries will come into open conflict, will almost certainly do much to lessen Japanese pressure in other directions. This should be borne in mind when considering Japan's aggrandizement.

I trust you will not mind my putting these considerations before you, but the question is regarded by the Cabinet as one of great military importance. You will realize that it is also one of immediate urgency.

Sir William has just given me this cable.[1] It was sent to me for the purpose of my passing it on to you. E.M.H.

TC MS (WP, DLC).
[1] It is a paraphrase of E. Drummond to W. Wiseman (a message from Balfour to House), Jan. 30, 1918, T telegram (W. Wiseman Papers, CtY). The text as received by Wiseman from London bears the number CXP 506.

From Gordon Auchincloss, with Enclosure

My dear Mr Wilson: [Washington] Jan 31 1918

Mr House asked me to send you this prepared by Bullitt. I am sending him a copy by "Special Delivery"
                              Faithfully yours   Gordon Auchincloss

ALS (WP, DLC).

E N C L O S U R E

Washington
Memorandum for Colonel House   31 January, 1918.
Subject: Political developments in Germany since Hertling's Address.

Each successive cable which reaches the Department indicates more clearly that the President may now make himself leader of the Liberals of Germany and Austria-Hungary. The Liberals and Socialists of the Central Empires no longer suspect the President's good faith. They trust him. The ARBEITER ZEITUNG, organ of the Socialists of Vienna, whose influence to-day is enormous because of the revolutionary spirit in the air of the Austrian capital, calls the President's speech,—"the first and only sincere offer of peace from the ranks of our opponents," and then cries, "The people demand that Czernin shall not let Wilson's peace offer fall, but shall make it the starting point for a general peace."

Scheidemann believes in the President. Haase,[1] leader of the Minority Socialists of Germany, speaks with the same voice, saying, "Threads have already been spun between Austria and America. It is Germany's duty to join Austria. Wilson is plainly guided by a serious wish for understanding, and understanding is possible if our military dictatorship is eliminated." Even so mild a progressive

[1] That is, Hugo Haase.

as Naumann[2] urges: "The German Government must roundly declare that it seeks no sort of annexation. Even if negotiations should fail, Wilson's peace proposals seem to me a serious attempt to work for peace before the decision of life and death, and I would prefer that they should be taken up seriously."

And VORWAERTS writes:

"The resumption of the Brest-Litovsk negotiations is awaited with intense interest. No less tense is the interest with which the whole world awaits the reply to Czernin's call, which will come from across the ocean. The echo which we have heard so far does not count. In Germany, too, the war agitators gave Lloyd George and Wilson a different answer than the Berlin, and, particularly, the Vienna Government. There is no need of surprise at hearing voices warning Wilson not to go into a German-Austrian trap. For this is the unavoidable musical accompaniment between the acts of the great peace drama."

Moreover, the air of Berlin and Vienna is quick with the first stirrings of revolution. Berlin is now in the grip of a general strike similar to the strike which convulsed Vienna ten days ago. From Holland it is reported that, according to the radical press of Berlin, "Five hundred thousand men are on a strike. But there have been no street demonstrations. At a public meeting an organization was formed of delegations of strikers and members of both Socialist groups. A program was drawn up demanding peace without annexations or indemnities on the basis of the right of self-determination, active participation by the workers of all countries in the peace negotiations, seizure of all food supplies in order to effect just distribution, removal of the state of siege and the militarization of factories, liberation of persons imprisoned for political offenses and democratization by the introduction of equal suffrage in Prussia."

Furthermore, VORWAERTS states that the gathering voted by a large majority for the cooperation of both Socialist groups, whose previous hostility to one another has delayed the whole revolutionary movement in Germany.

These risings of the proletariat in Berlin and Vienna may be quieted for the moment by concessions on the part of the Government. But surely they are the final proof that the war has entered the era in which it is no longer a war of rival States, but a world-wide social and political revolution.

The President can lead that revolution. The strikes in Berlin and Vienna were inspired by the example of Petrograd; but neither

---

[2] That is, Friedrich Naumann.

Germany nor Austria has the background of common ownership of land which makes Bolshevikism seem natural to the Russian. The Liberals and Socialists of Germany and Austria are not yet prepared to follow Trotzky. They are prepared to follow the President into a new world of international order and social justice.

How the President can best seize the leadership of the awakened people of Germany and Austria is not yet clear; for Czernin's address is not yet at hand, and the political outcome of the Berlin strike cannot be predicted. But evidence accumulates, from the German and Austrian liberal and socialist press, and from the speeches of the Liberals and Socialists of Germany, that if the President should follow the general line of criticism sketched in the memorandum on Hertling's address previously submitted, he would obtain the united support of Austria and of liberal and socialist Germany.

The question of Alsace-Lorraine alone is filled with difficulty. Even the Minority Socialists are determined that these provinces shall not be cut bodily from the German Empire. But both groups of German Socialists have now adopted a program of "self-determination." That is the principle which more and more is becoming the touchstone by which, to the mind of the common man, the good faith of a nation may be tested. And is it not, indeed, more just and more wise to speak of the wrong done to Alsace-Lorraine in 1871, rather than of the wrong done to France in the matter of Alsace-Lorraine in 1871? The really cruel wrong of 1871 was the wrong done to the inhabitants of the provinces, who have been wrenched from allegiance to allegiance ever since Charlemagne divided his empire into three parts. The suffering of the people of Alsace-Lorraine in 1871 was real anguish of the soul, not a smart of hurt pride, as was the suffering of the rest of France. If it should be considered necessary to mention Alsace-Lorraine at all at the present moment, can we not base our position in regard to these provinces on the simple human ground that the wrong done to the people of Alsace and the people of Lorraine in 1871 must be righted? That formula would find support even in Germany. And self-determination might lead to the return of Lorraine to France.

Now to events after Hertling's address. First, the comment of the Austrian press on the addresses of Hertling and Czernin. The ARBEITER ZEITUNG, courageous organ of the Social Democrats of Vienna, which is, however, not so radical as the young men of the party who led the recent strike, wrote on January 25:

"Czernin's accusation that the strikes attacked him in the back was meant to assure the ruling classes that he had not favored the strikes. *The strikes were in large measure, but not solely, directed against German annexationist desires. Czernin's atti-*

tude at Brest-Litovsk was one of the main causes of the strikes, which bore good fruit by showing that the Austrian people have a will of their own. The attack on Wilson's speech, the first and only sincere offer of peace from the ranks of our opponents, in the official press was due to the influence of annexionist Germany, which has been frustrated by the brave action of the strikers. The German annexionists are more dangerous to Czernin's peace desires that [than] the strikers. Czernin's speech shows, however, important progress. The statement is very welcome that peace without annexations is desired with Russia, which peace the *Austrophile* solution of the Polish problem has endangered. The difference in tone between Hertling's and Czernin's speeches is marked. *Czernin is willing to accept Wilson's speech as a possible basis of discussion while Hertling wishes only to have an alibi for not discussing peace on the basis of Wilson's speech. This is the result of annexationist influence on the German Government. An honest declaration about Belgium is first condition of peace, and Hertling has again refused to make it. His declarations refusing annexations in Belgium or France lack all clearness. The idea that Austria and the United States as the two States whose interests conflict least could start an exchange of opinions leading to general peace, must become a fact. The people demand that Czernin shall not let Wilson's peace offer fall, but shall make it the starting point for general peace. Czernin's statement that Austria will 'defend' her Allies excludes aid in the Western offensive, which would have an annexationist purpose. If Poland is to have the right to determine her own destiny, the same must be true for the Baltic Provinces. The Imperialists and the Military are in power in Germany and, while the speeches of the statesmen sound peaceful, they are without convincing warmth. The road to general peace had [has] been opened and the people must watch that it be not closed."*

Other comments by the Austrian press are of little importance. The FREMDENBLATT official organ of the Foreign Office wrote:

"Czernin's speech is an honest step towards the realization of the speakers ideal of peace. He selected from Wilson's speech all the statements containing possibility of reconciliation, and Hertling also declared in general that the terms of Wilson's speech are acceptable. *The few conflicts between Austria and America should lead to discussion between the two countries and to general peace. Hertling's speech agrees absolutely with Czernin's and the German attitude toward the Belgium question is the same as the Austrian attitude towards the question of territories oc-*

cupied in the southwest. Czernin's speech is patriotic and full of deep conviction, and will not soon be forgotten."

While the famous NEUE FREIE PRESSE, which is "liberal" just in so far as liberalism is compatible with the preservation of all the traditional Austrian bureaucratic abuses, wrote:

"The Entente need only assure the Central Powers that their territory will remain as before the war and peace will come. * * * Both Czernin and Hertling desire a new statement from the Allies and will consider it if made. Wilson must answer this demand, and public opinion in America and the Entente must consider whether it prefers to endure further hardships to return Alsace-Lorraine."

There is little German press comment to add to the excerpts given in the previous memorandum on Hertling's address. The radical BERLINER TAGEBLATT states:

"Hertling did not mention the liberal demand that Alsace-Lorraine should be made a Federal State, and *unfortunately it is known that he does not regard the plan favorably.*"

Vorwaerts adds a criticism worthy of note:

"*The standpoint that the Polish settlement is only an Austrian, German, Polish affair is rather that of a peace of violence than that of a peace of understanding.*"

So much for press excerpts. Now to the addresses of Kuehlmann and the party leaders at the daily meetings of the Main Committee of the Reichstag.

On January 25, Kuehlmann took up the burden of explanation where Hertling had abandoned it the day before. He devoted his entire address to an appeal to the party leaders to stand behind the Chancellor. As ground for asking this support he made the following assertions:

"Conclusion of peace with Finland may certainly be expected within a short time and peace with Ukrainia is probable. * * * Peace with Ukrainia would bring up the Rumanian problem. In my opinion Rumania could no longer resist the will for peace of the Central Powers after peace with Ukrainia and the withdrawal of Ukrainian troops. * * * Our differences with the Maxiamlists [Maximalists][3] relate mainly to application of the right of self-determination. The question is to ascertain the national will of the people concerned. It is undoubtedly true that certain elements in the occupied territory have a superior influence by reason of land possessions or tradition. We consider a vote of a legislative

[3] That is, the Bolsheviks.

body, elected on a broad basis, infinitely more practical than a referendum." Kuehlmann also appeals to the press to remain conscious that "We are bearing the banner of the German Empire and whoever knifes us in the back imperils the national inter[e]sts. Then after saying: *"Austria Hungary has stood at our side in the diplomatic battle in an absolutely loyal manner and will continue to do so. This must prove to those who have stated that our demands are excessive, that our demands are compatible with the most serious and urgent will for peace which prevails in Austria Hungary."*

Kuehlmann concluded:

"What we need and that which we request of you is to do what you can in order that other countries may see that the majority of the representatives of our people stand united behind the policy of the Chancellor."

But Kuehlmann's appeal fell on ears which would not hear. Scheidemann's reply has been reproduced so widely that it seems desirable here to quote only a few of his passionate sentences:

"If you are not able to conclude peace with Russia, go then before you are swept away! Put an end to this policy of ambiguity and vagueness! * * * It will become continually clearer that Austria will not take part in any policy of extension of power. Therefore, you must not attempt in any way to conduct a policy which is antagonistic to the great mass of the German people. Conclude peace with Russia, which you are able to do within twenty-four hours. Peace without any open or concealed annexations! An honest, durable peace without any sub-ideas of extension of territory! And when this peace has been brought about, then go forward with the offensive of the thought of a world peace towards the west! Nobody must be deaf to the increasing desire for peace in the speeches of Wilson and Lloyd George. Hertling has shown that he is perfectly conscious of the significance, especially of Wilson's speech. He said, alas, that nobody speaks so who honestly desires peace. This very much surprised me after all that he had said."

This address of Scheidemann seems to have concluded the proceedings of the Main Committee on January 25. The next day the Main Committee met again, with Kuehlmann in attendance. Count Westarp,[4] leader of the Conservative Party, opened the proceedings by a bitter attack on the Socialists concluding, "There are many signs in the country that the attitude of the Socialists is becoming

---

[4] That is, Kuno Friedrich Viktor, Count von Westarp.

unbe[a]rable. The Conservatives expect that the Chancellor and his advisers will not be influenced by such terroristic tactics."

David,[5] Scheidemann's chief lieutenant, made an excellent speech, saying in part:

"The question of peace with Russia is not hopeless if Germany agrees to a popular vote in the occupied territory on the basis of free democratic suffrage. The Socialists are in the majority in the present Lithuanian Congress which expressed a desire for independence; but the Courland Diet cannot be accepted as representative of the whole people. * * * Peace after this war cannot be made on the basis of any military decision but only on the basis of understanding. Czernin is ready to negotiate with Wilson and now the German Government cannot avoid taking the same ground. *No changes of the war map can make the Reichstag Peace Resolution out of date. A positive statement must now be made about Belgium.* The Flemish people want independence but not from the hand of their enemy. Count Westarp's battle-cry 'Away from the Socialists!' means, 'away from an accom[m]odation peace and away from Prussian Electoral Reform.' The Socialist victory in the Bautzen election[6] is the first reply to the war agitators. We socialists have not threatened but merely warned against the consequences of Pan-German policy which is driving the people to desperation.

Naumann, author of "Mittel Europa," who is a very mild progressive, then took the floor and said:

"The German Government must roundly declare that it seeks no sort of annexation. Even if negotiations should fail, Wilson's peace proposals seem to me a serious attempt to work for peace before the decision of life and death and I would prefer that they should be taken up seriously. Their underlying idea was received in Germany with a sort of unbelieving willingness. No American will be surprised to learn that Germany only negotiated on the basis [of] her own integrity, and the right of the self-determination. Absolute sincerity is necessary, regarding Belgium. If the authorities think the war can be settled by military operations, the present Government must be overthrown and Tirpitz put in command.[7] But those who take the standpoint of self-defense want a peace of understanding. *Hand bills have been distributed among the workers inciting to popular revolution, overthrow of*

---

[5] Eduard David, a leader of the Social Democratic party.
[6] Otto Uhlig, a Social Democrat, was elected on January 25 to the Reichstag from Bautzen, Saxony, a normally safe seat for the German Reform party.
[7] Tirpitz was the actual leader of the annexationist Fatherland party.

the government and the establishment of a German Republic. This is a serious matter and the Conservatives must see that such manifestations are a reaction against attempts to transform a defensive war into a war of conquest."

Haase, leader of the Independent Socialists, then spoke. After criticising the negotiations at Brest-Litovsk and saying:

"The German negotiators are not playing a square game. The occupied territory is still a part of Russia and the people cannot freely express their will as long as foreign troops are present," he continued:

"Hertling's remarks on Belgium are unsatisfactory. It is necessary to say that the economic and military independence of Belgium will be restored. Such a statement would greatly stimulate the peace desire of the English workers. *Is it that Hertling is yielding to the wishes of Hindenburg and Ludendorff when they threatened resignation? If so the coming offensive is to serve to bring about a pan-German peace by force.* Threads have already been spun between Austria and America. It is Germany's duty to join Austria. *Wilson is plainly guided by a serious wish for understanding, and understanding is possible if our military distatorship [dictatorship] is eliminated. The acquisition of Alsace-Lorraine in 1871 cannot be termed disannexation. Their deputies in the French Parliament voted against separation. The French and German Socilaists [Socialists] were agreed before war that Alsace-Lorraine should become a free German state. If it is possible to end the war by granting the population of the Reichsland a referendum, then the concession should be made.* It is irresponsible to pursue a prestige policy in these times. *The Armenians must also be granted their right of self determination.* The Independent Socialists know nothing of the hand bills mentioned by Naumann, but we have never made any secret of our ideal of a social republic. *Can the workers be blamed for exercising the right to strike when the pan-German press threatened the strike of a commanding general?"*

Kuehlmann then made a brilliantly clever address. He omitted all reference to Scheidemann's address of the previous day and plucked from the speech of each man who had preceded him some relatively unimportant points to which he assented. First he dealt in a most friendly tone with the suggestion of Stresemann[8] that German Ministers should make more public speeches! Then he gently chided Count Westarp, saying,

"I believe that his speech came to this: that he supported the

---

[8] Gustav Stresemann, a leader of the National Liberal party.

taking possession of territory on the basis of military successes. As I explained yesterday, very fully, *the choosing of such a standpoint is absolutely impossible for the present Imperial Government in accordance with all its principles and its past.*"

In reply to Gamp[9] he said a kind word for the military authorities.

Then he turned to Ledebour[10] who had criticised the Ukrainian rada and said:

"We take the point of view that Finland as well as Ukrainia have exactly as much right to free diplomatic action towards the outside as any other states."

In reply to Says[11] of the Polish Group he insisted that Trotzky, not he, had objected to the presence of Polish negotiators at Brest-Litovsk. He turned David's criticism by talking about the difficulty of publishing everything "that the Russian deputation proclaims in most certain tones from the housetops." In answer to Naumann he said:

"Naumann referred with a gentleness which I cannot share to the methods of the Maximalists. * * * The Maximalists simply rest upon brute force. Their arguments are cannons and machine guns. * * * What Czernin said about Poland applies to the other frontier nations. We have equally strong confidence in the power of attraction of the free and great German nation on those nations; and German policy will never resort to a mean police pressure or any similar methods, which in the end would only produce an opposite result from what we want, namely, free, sincere, and friendly relations between us and the frontier nations."

In conclusion Kuehlmann politely said:

"I gratefully acknowledge that the debate here in the Reichstag has yielded a firmer and broader basis in this respect than has been the case until now," and retired, having talked very cleverly and committed himself on none of the major issues.

Meanwhile, the German press was debating the report that Czernin had cabled his address in advance to the President. The liberal and socialist papers were rather pleased: the pan-German organs were furious. The jingo National Liberal Taegliche Rundschau, for example, burst forth thus on the 25th:

"Victorious Germany which has borne the heaviest burdens of the war is, therefore, in tow of Austria which is to negotiate a Wilson peace for Germany. Could anything worse be expected of a collapsed Germany? We reject the proposed division of labor,

[9] Karl, Baron von Gamp-Massaunen, a leader of the *Reichspartei.*
[10] That is, Georg Ledebour, a leader of the Independent Social Democratic party.
[11] A garbled reference to Wladislaus Kasimir Seyda, a member of the Reichstag, who had asked why there were Ukrainian but no Polish representatives at Brest-Litovsk. London *Times*, Jan. 29, 1918.

Germany to carry on the war and assume its burdens and Austria to carry on peace negotiations with Wilson—Germany's worst enemy."

It was not until January 28th that the Berliner Tageblatt poured oil on the Troubled waters by saying:

"It would be wrong to take Czernin's statements too literally, and believe that the American President received, directly or indirectly, from Austria a special report on the speech. The facts are as follows:

"A Socialist Delegate requested Czernin to transmit his reply to Wilson through the intermediary of neutral country. Czernin refused, saying: Wilson would get it, the speech, immediately by telegraph. Thus the expression 'at the same hour' is not to be taken literally. With the exception of the Czechs and Socialists, who preferred direct communication to Wilson, all others were satisfied with Czernin's reply. It can be reiterated that there was no direct communication and that the good offices of Neutral Powers were not requested."

The hot words of the Socialist leaders at the meeting of the Main Committee were soon followed by action. But before the strike began there were ominous mutterings in the Socialist press.

Vorwaerts on January 27th wrote:

"The emotion of the masses of Germany's working population arises from deep moral grounds; from the fear that they have been misled. The attitude of the Government is not calculated to disposal [dispose of] doubts and distrust. The German people is known as the quietest and most patient in the world, and *if this people were to be seized with a great unrest* no one should imagine that this resulted from dangerous propaganda. The most dangerous propaganda is innocuous if the masses of the people know that they have all their rights in the country in which they live. The election at Bautzen was a quiet and orderly expression of the voice of the people and every government must respect such voices. Any thought of attempting to force war prolonging aims on the people, aims for which it has never been fighting, or to withhold any of the peoples rights which have been promised *it will have a disastrous effect. This is the great danger today! Remember this Germany!"* On the same day, in another editorial, Vorwaerts said: "Resumption of the Brest negotiations is awaited with tense interest. *No less tense is the interest with which the whole world awaits the reply to Czernin's call which will come across the ocean.* The echo which we have heard so far does not count. In Germany, too, the war agitators gave Lloyd George and Wilson a different answer than the Berlin and, particularly the

Vienna Government. There is no need of surprise at hearing voices warning Wilson not to go into a German-Austrian trap; for this is the unavoidable musical accompaniment between the acts of the great peace drama. It is certain that any visible program of Brest negotiations must strengthen inclinations towards general peace, therefore, the general peace action started by Czernin cannot be better supported than by early removal of all difficulties obstructing peace between Central Powers and Russia. And we must be successful in this, because the Russians have demanded nothing impossible, nothing which offends the conscience of our people, *nothing that could justify return of our diplomats without peace.*"

The Chemnitzer Volkstimme took the same ominous line, saying: *"The Bautzen election is a portent. Perhaps the Government will understand it. It is high time that the Government should stop neglecting important opportunities and sacrificing important German interests merely in order to make death easier for a party doomed to downfall. It is high time that the Government took the position in internal and foreign policy of those without whose help it would have to lay down its arm[s] immediately— the masses of the people. Will the Government heed the portent? Or must the German people speak still more plainly to it?*

The leading papers of the 28th published appeals to the workmen not to strike. The same day the strike began.

Surely this is the dawn of the New World. The forces of reaction in Germany are strong and well entrenched; but "magna est veritas et praevalebit."

                    Respectfully submitted,   William C. Bullitt.

TS MS (WP, DLC).

From William Boyce Thompson

Dear Mr. President: Washington Jan. 31, 1918.

I am in Washington for a few days and am still so vitally interested in the whole Russian situation that it would please me very much if you felt that you could give me a little time to talk with you direct in regard to it. I have been so much impressed with the broadness of your attitude towards Russia that I am anxious to give you some new phases of the situation that appeal strongly to me, and which, I am sure, should be called to your attention.[1]

    I am,   Yours very respectfully,   Wm B Thompson

TLS (WP, DLC).

¹ Wilson dictated the following comment to Swem: "Dear Tumulty: I would be very much obliged if you would explain to Colonel Thompson that my cold still seriously limits my conversation, and tell him I hope on some subsequent visit I can see him, after things become a little more clear from the governmental point of view in the Russian situation. The President." WW to JPT [Feb. 1, 1918], TL (WP, DLC).

From Josephus Daniels

Dear Mr. President: Washington. Jan. 31, 1918.

I am very glad you take the view of the matter you state in your letter with regard to Admiral Sims.¹ There are other reasons why I was going to suggest that Sims do not accept the honorary membership and Admiral Benson holds the same opinion. I am leaving in a few minutes for Annapolis and will see Secretary Lansing tomorrow upon my return. Hope you are better.

                    Sincerely   Josephus Daniels

ALS (WP, DLC).
¹ Wilson's letter about a possible honorary appointment of Sims to the British Board of Admiralty is missing, but the following text is printed in Baker, *Woodrow Wilson*, VII, 514, under date of January 31: "I appreciate fully the spirit in which this honour is offered Sims, and I wish he could accept it; but I am afraid it would be a mistake for him to do so. The English persist in thinking of the United States as an English people, but of course they are not and I am afraid that our people would resent and misunderstand what they would interpret as a digestion of Sims into the British official organization. What do you think?
"I would be very much obliged if you would show this note to Lansing and confer with him about this matter."

From Joseph Patrick Tumulty

Dear Governor: The White House. January 31, 1918

The Vice President asks if you will see Mr. O'Dell,¹ a psychologist who is visiting the city. J.P.T.

What for? Please make inquiries. I should like to please the V.P. if his friend has some errand of real importance W.W.²

Mr. O'Dell is writing an article for the OUTLOOK and is gathering material by interviewing some prominent government officials. He has no wish or intention to quote the President, but desires merely to talk with him in the hope of being aided in the preparation of his article.³

Tell Tumulty my trouble about this is that *The Outlook* is entirely antagonistic, antagonistic in a very ugly way. I do not feel like assisting any of its writers. The journal carries very little weight anyhow, now.⁴

TL (WP, DLC).

¹ The Rev. Dr. Joseph Henry Odell, who had recently visited many of the army training camps and written a series of articles about them for *The Outlook*.
² WWhw on Tumulty's note.
³ T MS (WP, DLC).
⁴ T transcript (WC, NjP) of CLSsh on the above document.

From Charlotte Everett Wise Hopkins[1]

My dear Mr. President: Washington. January 31, 1918.

In response to your interest in the local housing situation I understand that a report has been prepared by the proper governmental agencies recommending the appropriation of the necessary funds for construction and that this report will be passed upon at an early date.

Under the most favorable circumstances it will be at least two months before even temporary structures can be made available and the pressure for suitable rooms for Government employees even now cannot be met. With the twenty-five thousand dollars allowed through the Housing and Health Division of the War Department, existing houses are being equipped and opened as rapidly as possible but these measures at best can only inadequately provide for the emergency, pending such time as the comprehensive program for housing can be carried out. You of course understand that there are clerks—men and women—and officers to be provided for in constantly increasing numbers.

May I therefore again urge upon you the immediate necessity for funds for construction and for authority to secure sites, without delay, for both the temporary and the permanent housing for the war service employees.

With the keenest appreciation of the prompt attention which you have given these matters, I am,

Most sincerely yours,   Charlotte Everett Hopkins

TLS (WP, DLC).
¹ Charlotte Everett Wise (Mrs. Archibald) Hopkins, at this time "chairman" of the Woman's Division of the District of Columbia section of the Council of National Defense.

From William Kent

My dear Mr. President: Washington January 31, 1918.

Permit a note concerning the investigation being had by the Federal Trade Commission in the matter of the Packers.[1]

I have followed it with deep interest knowing the importance of the subject. It is my belief that it will prove far reaching and infinitely beneficial.

You can expect misrepresentation and requests for your interference from all sorts of suspected and unsuspected sources.

I know what some of the facts of the case are from the Packers own admissions.

The investigation will prove the existence of an intolerable lawless conspiracy that has back of it the strength of uncounted millions, endless business connections and no redeeming factors of conscience. If ever you are in doubt in this connection, I shall be glad to furnish you with data that will be convincing.

Secretary Houston knows part of the story.

Yours truly,   William Kent[2]

TLS (WP, DLC).
[1] The F.T.C.'s investigation of the livestock and meat-packing industry had been "abruptly" transferred from Chicago to Washington on the basis of correspondence found by an agent of the commission in the confidential files of Swift & Co., Chicago. This correspondence was said to show that the big packing firms had tried in 1916 to block congressional resolutions to investigate charges by cattlemen that markets were being manipulated. *Washington Post*, Jan. 26, 1918.
[2] In reply, Wilson thanked Kent for his letter and added that he was "very much obliged for the tip." WW to W. Kent, Feb. 1, 1918, TLS (Letterpress Books, WP, DLC).

From Roger Nash Baldwin

New York, January 31, 1918.

Would the President be able and interested to see George Vandeveer, General Counsel for the I.W.W.[1] Friday or Saturday regarding pending trial and widespread industrial unrest due to that prosecution? Please wire reply collect care National Civil Liberties Bureau, 70 Fifth Avenue.   Roger N. Baldwin.

No   W.W.

T telegram (WP, DLC).
[1] George Francis Vanderveer (not Vandeveer), an attorney of Seattle long associated with the cause of labor.

John Joseph Pershing to Henry Pinckney McCain

RECEIVED AT THE WAR DEPARTMENT
Washington, D. C. January 31, 1918. 9. A.M.

Number 555 January 30th.

Confidential. For the Chief of Staff.[1]

Paragraph 1. Reference my cablegrams 487 and 493 and your cable to General Bliss, your conclusion that the proposition to send Infantry battalions for service with British Divisions was recommended by me was erroneous. Have had matter under consideration for some time and am convinced that the plan would be grave mistake. Stated my views fully to Sir William Robertson which resulted in delay until arrival of British Prime Minister yesterday. Following memorandum of our position was presented in conference between ourselves and British and was agreed upon. Memorandum has *approval* of General Bliss.

Subparagraph A. "This memorandum refers to the request made by General Sir Robertson, representing the British War Office, that the American Government send by British shipping to France 150 battalions of Infantry for service in British divisions on the Western front. Replying to this proposal, the following objections appear: First, the national sentiments of the United States against service under a foreign flag. Second, the probability that such action by the United States would excite serious political opposition to the administration in the *conduct* of the war. Third, the certainty of its being used by German propagandists to stir up public opinion against the war. Fourth, it would dissipate the direction and efforts of the American Army. Fifth, difference in national characteristics and military training of troops and consequent failure of complete cooperation would ultimately lead to friction and eventually misunderstanding between the two countries. September 6th, [Sixth,] additional man-power on the Western Front could be provided as quickly by some plan not involving amalgamation.

Subparagraph B "In order to meet the situation as presented by Sir William Robertson and hasten the arrival and training of American troops, it is therefore proposed that the British Government use the available sea transportation in question for bringing over the personnel of entire American divisions under the following conditions; First, that the Infantry and auxiliary troops of these divisions be trained with British divisions by battalions, or under such plans agreed upon. Second, that the artillery be trained under American direction in the use of French materiel as at present. Third, that the higher commanders and staff officers be assigned for training and experience with corresponding units of the British Army. Fourth, that when sufficiently trained these battalions be reformed into regiments and that when the artillery is fully trained all the units comprising each division be united under their own officers for service. Fifth, that the *above* plans be carried out without interference with the plans now in operation for bringing over American forces. Sixth, that question of supply be arranged by agreement between the British and American Commanders in Chief. Seventh, that question of arms and equipments be settled in similar manner."

Subparagraph C. It is recommended that the provisions of the memoranda quoted in subparagraphs A and B be approved.

Paragraph 2. If carried out this arrangement will provide 6 additional divisions to be brought over by British shipping. Details as to available shipping and recommendations as to troops to be selected and their equipment and supply will be submitted at an early date.   Pershing.

T telegram (WP, DLC).
   [1] That is, Maj. Gen. John Biddle, Acting Chief of Staff.

Hugh Robert Wilson to Robert Lansing

Pontarlier (Berne) Jan. 31, 1918

2544. Strictly confidential. Professor Lammasch of Vienna[1] now in Zurich. Department doubtless familiar his personality. He has been a devoted adherent of the idea of a just democratized Austria based on confederation of a[u]tonomous units, each unit comprising one racial group. In other words, an adherent of the ideas stated in my 1476, August 21, Noon outlining Professor Foeruter's [Foerster's] interview with Emperor Charles.[2] Recommend Department reread that telegram.

Lammasch has charged Baron Jongh,[3] Dutch pacifist, to deliver following message to Professor George D. Herron, urging that it be brought to the attention of President Wilson. Lammasch confined to his bed in Zurich with heart trouble so unable to deliver message in person.

Message follows: In August last Emperor Charles offered Premiership to Lammasch but latter refused saying that time was not ripe to put his ideas into execution. Emperor has again urged on Lammasch that he accept task of forming a cabinet. Latter stated that he could only accept under the explicit condition that Austria should not negotiate for peace through Prussia but should make a separate peace. The Emperor unreservedly accepted these conditions. The only thing which prevents Lammasch's immediate acceptance present condition of his health.

Lammasch has just received telegram from Meinl in Vienna, see my 2363, January 7, 9 P.M.[4] stating that if President Wilson will make any public recognition of Czernin speech, in addressing Senate or by any other means, commenting favorably on its tone, it can be counted on with absolute certainty that Austria will continue as follows: One. She will make peremptory demands on Germany to change tone of Hertling's address.

Two. If Germany refuses to do this Austria is prepared to break with Germany and make a separate peace with the Allies through America as mediator.

Jongh reports that Lammasch instructed him to tell Herron "You may assure Herron that what you have told him of Meinl's telegram is absolutely worthy of credence. While we do not trust Czernin absolutely we do trust the Monarch, who is prepared to grant all demands of Democratic Party and is prepared to break with Germany if latter refuses to make peace on basis President Wilson's message. You can go the full length of pledging me to Herron. Do entreat him to get this to President Wilson for if it does it will save democracy in Europe."

Jongh also reports that Lammasch states to him that what Meinl could put in a telegram was only one tenth of the real truth and that real truth went infinitely beyond what would pass the censor.

When questioned on details Jongh indicated that there were two parties in Vienna: one represented by Lammasch with the views above indicated, and the other the Reactionary Court Party including diplomatists and Government officers. The Emperor is prepared to throw over all his former associates and cast in his lot with a nation founded on consent of the governed.

In this connection it seems advisable to report that during the past three days Count Palfy, member of Austrian Legation,⁵ has made repeated and determined efforts to get into conference with Herron and latter has consistently refused as he considered, as I do, inadvisable to get in touch with diplomats of enemy nation accredited here. It seems possible that Palfy, member of aristocracy, has heard some hint of this matter and is endeavoring to ascertain what it amounts to.

When the strength of tradition and the influence of his *educating* [education] are considered, what the Emperor proposes to do seems almost unbelievable that he, a young man, should cut loose from the German-Austrian circles who have always depended on the strength of Germany to maintain their heredity [hegemony], and reach out over them to rest his power on the consent of the people, would demand a breadth of view and a strength of character which would leave me skeptical of the whole matter were it not that it couples [is coupled with] a man of such undoubted integrity as Lammasch.

In view of the prevailing uneasiness in Italy, since President's message, I suggest that if it appears advisable that the President should make any public declaration in sense indicated, France and England be consulted and assurances given and steps be taken in advance to convince Italian Government of our good faith towards her in this proceeding. From members of French Embassy here and well informed Swiss it appears possible that if Italy should hear without warning of any negotiations between America and Austria she might be tempted to hurriedly conclude a separate agreement with the latter power.

Lammasch is arranging for personal interview in a discreet way with Herron as soon as former's health permits, in order confirm this matter from his own lips.

Does Department authorize me to inform French and British chiefs of mission of foregoing?   Wilson.

T telegram (R. Lansing Papers, NjP).
¹ Heinrich Lammasch, author of various works on international law, had been an Austro-Hungarian delegate to the peace conferences in 1899 and 1907 at The Hague, and, since 1900, a judge of the international court there. The Norwegian Nobel Institute had recently published his *Das Völkerrecht nach dem Kriege* (Kristiania, 1917), in which Lammasch had called for international machinery to preserve peace. For additional documents on his cooperation with Meinl, Foerster, and others in various peace efforts, see Heinrich Benedikt, *Die Friedensaktion der Meinlgruppe, 1917-18* (Graz, 1962).
² This telegram summarized a conversation of about July 20, 1917, between Emperor Charles and Friedrich Wilhelm Foerster, Professor of Pedagogy, who was on leave from the University of Munich on account of disagreements with the Faculty of Philosophy over his political views. Foerster at this time resided in Zurich. According to the telegram, the Emperor had discussed eradication of the Prussian military spirit and, as an ideal solution, a voluntary confederation of Austrian and Rumanian states as a counterpoise to Germany, with autonomy for Poland and some acceptance of Bohemia's claims to autonomy. Charles was said to be convinced that such a solution could only be achieved at the behest of the Entente states, many of whose demands he considered reasonable. Foerster, the telegram also reported, was convinced that the Central Powers were more afraid of a future economic boycott than of the American army then in training, and he thought that this fear might soon lead them to sue for peace. P. A. Stovall to RL, Aug. 21, 1917, T telegram (SDR, RG 59, 763.72/6572, DNA). This telegram bears the stamped caption "SENT TO PRESIDENT Aug 24 1917."
³ That is, Jonkheer Dr. Benjamin de Jong van Beek en Donk, a retired senior official of the Netherlands Ministry of Justice and secretary general at The Hague of the Central Organization for a Lasting Peace. He wrote *History of the Peace Movement in the Netherlands* (The Hague, 1915) and related works. Because of his long name, he was familiarly known to American and Entente diplomats as "Ding-Dong." Benedikt, p. 121.
⁴ H. R. Wilson to RL, Jan. 7, 1918, T telegram (WP, DLC).
⁵ Moritz Count Pálffy von Erdöd, Minister in the Austro-Hungarian mission to the Holy See and Agent for Religious Matters, stationed at this time in Bern.

A Memorandum by George Creel

Memorandum for an American Bureau
of Public Information in Europe   [c. Jan. 31, 1918]

Pressure from various quarters has been brought to bear on the Army Authorities to undertake Propaganda along the lines of the different European organizations. Both the British and French maintain bureaus in the allied and neutral countries each one considering its own national interest as well as that of the allied cause.

Thus far, our only "Propaganda" has been through the Press Division of the Intelligence Section of the American Expeditionary Forces which has charge of public relations and of censorship. It has supplied information freely to all who wished it, distributed photographs in allied countries and extended unusual facilities to influential civilians and writers and correspondents for seeing our Army.

Any organization that we may develop in the future should be under Government direction. Volunteer organizations will not only overlap but will assume a semi-official capacity if they receive official assistance necessary for efficiency, and, unless they carry out the spirit of Government's intentions, may produce mischievous results in a work which requires the most delicate possible handling. Dismissing the Volunteer System as impracticable, we may follow one of two courses.

I. The Press Division may extend its work along present lines by an increase of personnel and a small appropriation which might come from the War Department.

II. We might establish a central bureau in Paris where the Press Division already has an office and branch bureaus in London, Rome and Madrid, the Central Bureau being in liaison with the Committee of Public Information in Washington and the Intelligence Section of the Army. Our policy should be to stiffen the moral[e] and determination of the allied countries by the presentation of the immense power which America could exert against the Germans when our preparations are complete. It would counteract German propaganda and other propaganda which has had such serious results in Italy for example, and by the exposition of American thoughts and ideals, remedy the too common scepticism of our motives among the masses in the allied countries who can not conceive that we are not in the war for territorial or commercial gains. After peace negotiations had begun, the organization would still be serviceable in its influence as a means of reflecting our national aims.

The chairman of the central bureau in Paris should be a man of broad European experience, and the branch bureaus in London, Madrid and Rome and the Scandinavian countries should be directed by men who knew the country to which they were assigned sympathetically and spoke the language fluently, including an eminent scholar, a practical man of affairs, an economist, a journalist and others who would reach different institutions and classes of Society. Upon the choice of these men and the character of the chairman would depend the results of the work which would be carried on in a dignified, modest and thorough manner in keeping with the character of the New America as opposed to the America with which Europeans associate boasting, flamboyancy and commercialism.

FIXED CHARGES FOR AN EUROPEAN BUREAU OF
AMERICAN INFORMATION

Annually

Rent of offices in Paris, London, Rome, Madrid,
　　Rotterdam, Berne, Christian[i]a, Stockholm,
　　Copenhagen and Petrograd... $24.000.
Stenographers, clerks and offices expenses................... $50.000.
Salaries of five assistants in each branch
　　at the rate of $250. to $500. monthly......................... $240,000.
　　　　Total of Fixed Charges... $314,000.

The principal assistants would be expected, as a matter of pa-
triotiam [patriotism] as well as of wisdom in the policy of such work,
to give their services for small remuneration. Out of an appropriation of $500,000. say $176,000 would be left for printing, travel
and emergencies of the organization. One assistant at the Central
Bureau should be am [an] accountant who would act as auditor.
All employees would be subject to a month's notice. No moneys
should be spent in such a manner that the record of the expenditure
would not bear public investigation.

1. Sound ethics as well as sound policy apparently require that
our people should be told the truth in some detail of the present
situation of the Allies. The facts had better come from the government now than later from other sources which may play into the
hands of critics.

2. Allied representations of the danger of the Germans winning
a military decision on the Western Front should be considered in
relation to the Allies' desire to have us committed to the war with
our last drop of blood and last dollar to gain ends, which, in some
instances, are not in keeping with our declared purpose in the war.

3. In any event a campaign of education as to the actualities of
the present situation should be inaugurated at home. The only force
which will be convincing to the German General Staff in its survey
of the situation is military force and the building of the bridge across
the Atlantic which will bring military force to bear upon the German
Army. Any preparations, even any public emotion, which is a diversion from this purpose will only play into the hands of the German military party which judges our effectiveness only by its measure of the power of our blows and our potential blows. The response
of our people to the truth should be so determined and concrete in
its warlike intensity that the German Staff will not mistake our
meaning; for this is the best weapon to place in the President's
hands for the earliest possible ending of the war.

4. The French government should be informed of our purpose

in telling our people the facts in order that the French government may, if it chooses, use its censorship in suppressing what may be harmful to French morale while strengthening to our own.

5. It is common talk among the French, and in a lesser degree among the English, masses that we are willing to loan the Allies money[,] to subscribe to Red Cross funds and provide ambulanciers but we are not willing to shed our blood. As the most convincing proof of our determination our trained troops, no matter how small their numbers, should, even at the expense of heavy casulaties [casualties], play a part against any great German offensive on the Western Front which will be well heralded in Europe.

6. In the event of a disaster to the French Army prevision requires that we safeguard our army, and, in the extreme event, join the British Army using British bases for future operations.

7. Such is the character of the French people and such the effect of the strain that they have borne for more than three years that every possible infleunce [influence] should be exerted to stiffen their morale with convicition [conviction] of our strength in order that they may withstand the shock of another great offensive which will undoubtedly be directed against their sector if the German[s] decide to make a supreme effort for a decision on the Western Front.

T MS (WP, DLC).

From the Diary of Josephus Daniels

1918 Thursday 31 January

Page telegraphs that the King wished to make Sims an honorary member of Admiralty—an honor never before given to an American. Lansing (through Polk) seemed to favor it. I opposed. President wrote me a note saying he thought it unwise and later I talked with him about it. Benson opposed and said it would do Sims harm. Officers were saying he was looking too much to English approval. WW: You see he would by such acceptance be tied up to English determination.

A News Report

[*Feb. 1, 1918*]

WILSON SUMMONS SENATORS TO BEAT WAR
CABINET BILL

Washington, Feb. 1.—President Wilson again to-day declared his opposition to the Chamberlain bills to create a War Cabinet and a Director of Munitions. He told a party of Senators who were invited to confer with him that he would rather the objectionable measures were withdrawn and not discussed. He said debate on the legislation would give the impression of a country divided on the war programme.

Mr. Wilson, according to those who attended the conference, reiterated his objections to the proposed legislation and declared he would not consider a compromise on them. He said both bills were obnoxious to him, because they were unnecessary and because they would embarrass and deprive him of authority in prosecution of the war.

The Senators who took part in the conference were Martin of Virginia, Thomas of Colorado, Owen of Oklahoma, Gerry of Rhode Island, James of Kentucky, Robinson of Arkansas, Phelan of California, Underwood of Alabama, Jones of New Mexico, King of Utah and Smith of South Carolina. Other Congressional delegations will see the President within the next few days.

The President is leaving no stone unturned to convince the leaders of the Senate that the measures are absurd. He is making a special appeal to the Democrats. Most of the Republicans, he realizes, will vote for the War Cabinet plan. He has been told by Democratic Senators that Republican leaders would use the passage of such a measure as a campaign argument that the War Department did fail and that another organization had to be created to save the situation.

Senate leaders now say it seems possible to defeat the War Cabinet Bill in the Military Affairs Committee. The one vacancy on that committee caused by the death of Senator Brady[1] is giving Democrats some worry, for the place belongs to a Republican, and if it is filled before a vote is taken, that would give an advantage to Senator Chamberlain and Senator Hitchcock, the two Democrats who are still urging the passage of the bill.

Senator Hitchcock showed signs of yielding to pressure from his associates on the Democratic side some days ago, but it is understood now that he will stand by Senator Chamberlain. He has announced that he will make a speech Monday on the bills. He was preparing his speech to-day and indicated that he would go ahead with his address. Senator Wadsworth of New York is to speak on Tuesday. Administration Senators may adopt the policy of letting the other side speak without replying. This would do away with much debate. They may, however, think it better to present the Administration view.

President Wilson and Secretary Baker believe they have the power to provide a single head of munitions for the War Department, and Senators who visited the White House believe such a plan will be announced within a short while. A centralized control of buying and producing would accomplish the results for which the Munitions Director Bill provides. A reorganization of the War Industries Board is expected, and the name of Bernard M. Baruch, now one of the members of the War Industries Board, is mentioned in connection with the Chairmanship.

The fact that Mr. Baruch conferred with the Secretary of War yesterday and the President to-day is partly responsible for the report. Secretary Baker refused to discuss it.

Senator Chamberlain was impressed with testimony on centralized power for purchasing and distributing war supplies, and it is intimated by Senators friendly to him that he may drop his bill if such a plan is carried out. He told Secretary Baker he would be glad to stop the controversy over his measures, if some satisfactory compromise could be reached. The President said he was not willing to have any compromise through the enactment of additional legislation.

Printed in the New York *World*, Feb. 2, 1918.
   [1] James Hezekiah Brady of Idaho, who had died on January 13, 1918.

To Gutzon Borglum

My dear Mr. Borglum: [The White House] 1 February 1918

   I have your preliminary report and thank you for it most warmly.[1] I will address myself to its consideration at the earliest possible hour.

   In haste   Sincerely yours,   Woodrow Wilson

TLS (G. Borglum Papers, DLC).
   [1] See n. 1 to the Enclosure printed with G. Borglum to WW, Jan. 24, 1918.

To Newton Diehl Baker

My dear Baker: [The White House] 1 February, 1918

Here is Mr. Borglum's preliminary report. Is there not someone entirely disconnected from aeronautics and from those who are prominent in carrying out the aeroplane programme whom you can ask to go over this thing with an unbiased mind and give us his naïve impressions of it? There may be something worthy of our consideration, and suggestions worthy to be adopted.

Cordially and faithfully yours,   Woodrow Wilson

TLS (N. D. Baker Papers, DLC).

To Robert Latham Owen

My dear Senator: [The White House] 1 February, 1918

I have your letter of January thirtieth[1] in which you suggest that the Attorney General frame a law authorizing the trial by court-martial of all alien enemies detected in conspiracy against the law and order of the United States and that citizens of the United States detected in conspiracies involving treason be made subject to the same method of trial.

I shall be glad to consult the Attorney General about this, though I must frankly say, my dear Senator, that my present opinion is that it would be a very serious mistake to put our own citizens under court-martial, for I think it would make an impression with regard to the weakness of our ordinary tribunals which would not be justified.

Just how the law of court-martial would operate in regard to alien enemies detected in conspiracies I do not yet clearly see, but my discussion with the Attorney General will no doubt clear it up.[2]

Cordially and sincerely yours,   Woodrow Wilson

TLS (Letterpress Books, WP, DLC).
[1] It is missing.
[2] The Editors have not been able to find any further letter from Wilson to Owen on this subject, nor any evidence of any discussion between Wilson and Gregory about it.

To Charlotte Everett Wise Hopkins

My dear Mrs. Hopkins: The White House 1 February 1918

I appreciate the gravity of the question you bring again to my attention in your letter of yesterday, and I think it is universally appreciated. My whole attention has for some time been directed to its details, but at present I do not see a way open to the accomplishment of what you suggest. The authority for securing sites must come from Congress, together with an authorization for provision for permanent housing. I have sounded the leaders of the two Houses with regard to this and find that they are averse from the proposition of permanent housing, and I fear that the road we have already started out upon is the only open one.

Cordially and sincerely yours,   Woodrow Wilson

TLS (CU).

From Edward Mandell House

Dear Governor: New York. February 1, 1918.

I have your letter of yesterday enclosing a cable from Tom Page.

The feeling that Page describes is and has always been prevalent in certain circles in every country, but I do not believe it is as serious now as it was before you made yourself the champion of the common people throughout the world. Sonnino as I have told you, is the worst reactionary that I know in Europe, but he does not represent Italian feeling on any subject excepting their desires of Austria.

I agree with you that you should presently show why a just peace is everybody's business. The German Chancellor's speech has given you an excellent opportunity to do this. If a peace conference were held today, and those now in charge of governments were present, I think you would find some envy and resentment at your commanding position. This would make itself felt, more or less, as they dared evidence it in view of your influence with their own peoples.

Unfortunately, the reactionaries are in control of almost all the belligerent governments, but they represent the necessities of their peoples rather than their real sentiments.

I would advise great caution in your next address to Congress, both for the reason I have just mentioned, and because of the disastrous results which a false step made now would have upon the growing demand in Germany for peace.

Affectionately yours,   E. M. House

TLS (WP, DLC).

Two Letters from Newton Diehl Baker

My dear Mr. President: Washington. February 1, 1918.

I do not know what steps have been taken in the Borglum matter since you last spoke to me about it, at which time you told me you planned to write him a letter.

I have heard that he has filed a report with you, but I have not seen a copy of the report. Meantime, I am told that Mr. Borglum is making here and there wild statements about his inquiries and findings, and the Vice-President a few days ago showed me a report, made to him by a friend from Indiana whom Mr. Borglum had invited to go into a company for the manufacture of aircraft, the designs for which he was to procure as confidential data in his investigations of the Aircraft Board, and in which Mr. Borglum himself was to have a stock interest, held in the name of another.

This situation is disturbing for two reasons: In the first place, the morale of the Aircraft Board is seriously impaired by the possibility of thoroughly unjustified statements being made by Mr. Borglum; and in the second place, the very intricate transactions which the Aircraft Board has been obliged to conduct may have weaknesses here and there which experience and reflection has enabled them to amend, but a prejudiced exhibition of those weaknesses in a publicity campaign of attack inaugurated by Mr. Borglum would seriously undermine the public confidence in the effectiveness of the work in that important department. I can not help feel but that Mr. Borglum has grossly abused the confidence which you reposed in him in the letter, and that this disclosure of indirect purposes on his part, while it may be a mad impulse, to organize a company to serve the Government, has yet nevertheless an involvement of a very prejudicial character and ought not to be permitted to proceed upon any theory that the information which Mr. Borglum expects to use in this fashion has been gotten by virtue of the letter which you wrote for the purpose of securing for your information merely the judgment of an outsider upon public business.

As you know, Mr. Eugene Meyer, Jr.,[1] has been acting for me as a liaison officer with the Aircraft Board. He has attended sessions of the Board, is familiarizing himself with its affairs, and his presence there is welcomed by the members of the Board.

Would it not be wise to submit the Borglum report to Mr. Meyer for a critical analysis and, so soon as he shall have gone over it, assuring himself of the portions of it which do recount substantial things and separating out those which are merely speculations based upon insufficient or erroneous data, to have a meeting with

Mr. Borglum at which Mr. Coffin, Mr. Meyer, and I could be present? At such a meeting, after hearing the full story of the analysis of Mr. Borglum's report, you could tell him of your appreciation of so much of the report as was really helpful and of the steps taken to profit by them, and could then tell him that your letter was of course intended only to enable him to have information which would be confidential between you and him, but that his misuse of the letter made it necessary for you to withdraw the confidence which you had originally imposed, and ask him to at once return all papers which had been exhibited to him for the purpose of furthering his inquiry.

I submit this suggestion for your consideration, but without knowledge of the present state of the matter so far as any correspondence between you and Mr. Borglum may have occurred since you last spoke to me about it.

Respectfully yours,   Newton D. Baker

¹ At this time adviser on nonferrous metals to the War Industries Board.

Dear Mr. President: Washington. February 1, 1918.

Mr. Davison of the Red Cross called me on the telephone to say that he had in his possession the original of one of the letters read by Senator Chamberlain in his address to the Senate,¹ and that Mr. Axson had mentioned it to you and you desired a copy of it, which he enclosed to me to send you, and which I herewith enclose.²

I had quite forgotten the fact that Mr. Davison, some days before Senator Chamberlain's speech, had brought this letter into my office and, at the conclusion of a discussion about many other things, had called my attention to it as exhibiting a very beautiful spirit on the part of a father who had lost a son under distressing circumstances. I glanced the letter over at the time and handed it back to him, commenting upon the fineness of the father's spirit and the pathos of the circumstances. When Senator Chamberlain read the letter I did not identify it with the one which Mr. Davison had shown me; nor, indeed, did I then recall that Mr. Davison had shown me any letter. I did, however, immediately after Mr. Davison's call, and no doubt in part because of it, telegraph for Dr. Hornsby,³ one of the greatest experts in the country on hospital administration, to come to Washington so that I might send him as my personal investigator to bring me first-hand information as to hospital conditions at Camp Doniphan⁴ and elsewhere. In the meantime, I instructed the Inspector General⁵ to have his inspectors, who are constantly making general inspections of the camps, to make specific and searching inspections of hospitals and hospital conditions. I had also directed the Surgeon General,[6] as the result of his own personal visit to some of these camps, to leave no stone unturned in the matter of immediate betterment of hospital conditions where any deficiency, either in service or equipment, existed.

I think I now have the names and circumstances of the letters used by Senator Chamberlain, and most thorough-going inquiries are and have been for some time on foot, so that I will be equipped with information both from the Surgeon General's Office and corrective or corroborative information from many independent sources. The reports which come to me now are that the number of nurses in the several hospitals is ample, and that great improvement has already taken place in such of them as were over-crowded or insufficiently officered. There seems to be, though, no safe reliance against emergencies disturbing such conditions, and I am therefore directing the commanding general at each camp to have an officer of his staff specially detailed to make a daily report to him of hospital conditions, thus adding the only safeguard I can think of additional to the professional and civilian inspections already arranged for.

Respectfully yours,   Newton D. Baker

TLS (WP, DLC).

[1] About Chamberlain's address of January 24, see WW to O. M. James, Jan. 26, 1918, n. 1. In the course of his address, Chamberlain read two letters from grieving families, with names omitted, which he said showed that there had been "shameful" neglect of young soldiers who had died in army hospitals. *Cong. Record*, 65th Cong., 2d sess., pp. 1203-1205.

[2] C. D. Hestwood to Henry Justin Allen, Jan. 4, 1918, TCL (WP, DLC). Hestwood was pastor of the Methodist Episcopal Church of Liberal, Kan. Allen was the owner of the Wichita *Daily Beacon* and later (1919-1923) Governor of Kansas. Hestwood's letter about the death of his son, Albert F. Hestwood, was printed in *The Liberal* (Kan.) *News*, Jan. 24, 1918.

[3] John Allan Hornsby, M.D., a distinguished practitioner of Chicago.

[4] Camp Doniphan was at Fort Sill, near Lawton, Okla.

[5] That is, Maj. Gen. John L. Chamberlain.

[6] That is, Maj. Gen. William C. Gorgas.

From Newton Diehl Baker, with Enclosure

Dear Mr President   Washington February 1, 1918

This telegram from Gen Bliss seems to cover the entire situation. If the arrangement meets with your approval I will so notify Gen Bliss.

The second suggestion is submitted for your consideration

Respectfully yours,   Newton D. Baker

ALS (WP, DLC).

ENCLOSURE

Paris January 30th [1918].

Confidential for the Secretary of War.

Number 16 Paragraph 1. The following is in further reference to your number 14 dated January 21st, received in London, and your number 16 dated January 23rd,[1] received in Paris. Your number 14 stated that General Pershing had approved, under certain conditions, the supply to the British of 150 battalions of American Infantry to be transported by British shipping and to serve with the British at the rate of 3 battalions per division, but that this project was contingent upon the supply of tonnage to us from Great Britain to accomplish our agreed minimum military effort of 24 divisions in France by about middle of July. You further directed me to discuss the matter with General Pershing in Paris before taking final action. On January 22nd had conference with Sir Joseph Maclay, British Minister of Shipping. He stated that under no circumstances could Great Britain give us additional tonnage to carry out our 24 division program. I said that in that event I must ask additional instructions before making arrangements to carry out the plans to send 150 battalions to serve with the British. He then said that he would send his principal shipping expert with me to Paris to further discuss the matter with Captain Jacob M. Coward[2] of my staff. After final discussion in Paris, British still declined to give us additional tonnage for our program. Meanwhile, General Pershing told me that he had not approved the plan of sending 150 American Infantry battalions to serve with the British. On further discussion General Robertson, British Chief of Staff, General Pershing and myself, it was proposed by General Pershing that the British bring over the personnel of 6 complete divisions instead of 150 Infantry battalions. This new proposition was telegraphed by General Robertson to Mr. Lloyd George in London, who replied asking an interview with General Pershing and myself yesterday January 29th. On that date the matter was discussed in conference by Mr. Lloyd George, Lord Milner, General Robertson, General Haig, General Pershing, and myself, without definite result. Today the British in a document signed by Mr. Lloyd George accepted our proposition to bring over 6 complete divisions instead of 150 battalions. General Pershing in his number 555 has informed you of the conditions. I recommend immediate approval as the arrangements must be made at once.

Paragraph 2. At today's session of the Supreme War Council, the question came up of utilizing American troops now in France as battalions and regiments in the French and English armies. It was unanimously stated by British, French and Italian representatives that this was the only possible way to utilize American troops in the campaigns of 1918, and that it was vitally necessary to meet the apprehended German attacks. At my request this question was postponed for a short time. British and French insist that this use of our troops is necessary to insure safety of defensive lines in France against growing German attacks. It is probable that Supreme War Council will make demands for this use of all American troops at its present session.

Paragraph 3. The British, French and Italian military representatives have the support of their Prime Ministers and of at least one member their political Cabinets. The American position on the Supreme War Council would be stronger if there were on the Supreme War Council political representation. Would it not be well to designate American Ambassadors at London and Paris as our political representatives, who could be reenforced from time to time by a delegate direct from the administration in Washington? If this is approved, I suggest that immediate action be taken. Bliss.

T telegram (WP, DLC).
[1] H. P. McCain to T. H. Bliss, Jan. 26, *not Jan. 23*, 1918, TC telegram (WDR, RG 407, World War I Cable Section, DNA): "Number 16. Revision of estimates of tonnage required by supply department being made. Will cable results about January 29th."
[2] Jacob Meyer Coward, Coast Artillery Corps, a veteran of the Spanish-American War and formerly a lawyer of Trenton, N. J.

From the Diary of Josephus Daniels

February Friday 1 1918

Baker said stone-cutters were not employed & wondered what Gov. could do to give them employment WW Couldn't they get work on farms? WBW: The unskilled laborers might but the skilled ones, no. They worked with machine tools & could better work in munition factories WW told of a stone-mason at Princeton who had charge of building.[1] His father & four generations had been the consulting masons of the Cathedral of Canterbury. This man (Sutton) was a younger son, could not inherit the place, & so he came to America. He had a triangular piece of white marble. How did he get it? A door to the crypt of Thos. A Becket, moved from above, would not close. The Archbishop told the stone-cutter to cut off piece of marble so door could shut Two triangular pieces were cut off & Archbishop gave them to Sutton. The stone had been brought from Carthage & sent to England as gift from the Pope

Houston—Canada quietly trying to get American labor Lansing to see about it

Gregory Bill in Congress to except Austrians & others from laws against alien enemies. WW opposed it for it would free many enemies from espionage penalties

Talked to Pres. about Blue. He thought I should approve finding in case of Blue. Should take care of his ship.[2]

[1] Sutton, not further identified, had supervised the construction of Seventy-Nine Hall in 1904. See WW to R. Bridges, March 31, 1904, Vol. 15.

[2] A court-martial had sentenced Capt. Victor Blue, who commanded the battleship *Texas* when it ran aground off Block Island in 1917, to a loss of twenty numbers in rank. Admiral Mayo, commander of the Atlantic Fleet, had recommended that this be reduced to ten numbers. *New York Times*, Dec. 18, 1917. Daniels accepted Mayo's recommendation and, in announcing the action, also commended Blue's excellent record. *Ibid.*, March 7, 1918.

Sir William Wiseman to Sir Eric Drummond

[New York] February 1, 1918.

No. 44. Before your Cable CXP.506[1] arrived, BRUSSA [HOUSE] had already told me that ADRAMYTI [WILSON] fears such action might be used by the Germans to consolidate Russians against the Allies. He doubts whether any military advantage can be expected which would justify the political risk which he foresees. I persuaded BRUSSA that, before expressing this to you as their definite opinion, they should cable General Bliss for his advice. This has been done. Unless, however, Bliss cables strongly in favour, I think ADRAMYTI will reject the proposal as far as he is concerned. BRUSSA says he feels sure LUBECK [Lansing?] would not agree.

T telegram (W. Wiseman Papers, CtY).

[1] Printed as an Enclosure with EMH to WW, Jan. 31, 1918.

From Jean Jules Jusserand

Washington, le February 2, 1918.

Having met to-day at Versailles, the Prime Ministers of France, Great Britain and Italy have decided to collectively send the following message to the President of the United States and to request the Ambassador of France to present it on behalf of the three countries:

"The Interallied Wheat Committee reports that:

1st. The bread cereals sent from North America were in December 500,000 tons below the amount fixed by the Paris Conference in November last. In January they have been more than 400,000 tons below the adopted program.

2nd. This deficit of 900,000 tons has been caused by the congestion of railroads and the lack of cars and coal, all of which made worse by the exceptionally severe winter.

These deficits, added to the previous ones, will result in a condition especially serious, throughout the Allied States of Europe, in the forthcoming months of March, April and May. Such a condition can be improved only by the sending of a considerable amount from America in February, March and April.

3rd. The Wheat Committee knows and appreciates the efforts of Mr. Hoover and of the Food Administration in view of helping the Allies at this critical juncture. The Committee is aware that Mr. Hoover realizes the gravity of the situation and agrees with it as to the wants of the Allies.

On the other hand, it begs to point out that the sending of an average of one million tons of grain, which it considers as a minimum, in February and March, necessitates no less efforts on the part of the railroads and the Fuel Administration than on that of the Food Administration. Therefore, the Committee expresses the hope that instructions may be issued for absolute priority to be granted in the United States to those products until the crisis be passed.

It has been decided thereupon that this would be submitted to the President of the United States and that he should be informed that, in the opinion of the three Prime Ministers, the need of cereals in Europe cannot be exaggerated; they express the hope that the President will be so good as to give the necessary instructions. Measures have been taken for supplying the necessary tonnage.

The interested countries have been able to take those measures only by reducing their importations of ammunition in a degree justified solely by the critical character of the food situation.

In the opinion of the Prime Ministers, the dearth of wheat, with the effect it may produce on the morale of the populations (and the important part such a dearth played in the Russian collapse is well known) is at the present time the greatest danger threatening the allied nations of Europe."

T MS (WP, DLC).

From Edward Mandell House

Dear Governor: New York. February 2, 1918.

I assume that you want to talk to Sir William largely about the Russian situation concerning which the British seem so eager.

I have never changed my opinion that it would be a great political mistake to send Japanese troops into Siberia. There is no military advantage that I can think of that would offset the harm. Leaving out the ill feeling which it would create in the Bolchiviki Government, it would arouse the Slavs throughout Europe because of the race question.

Sir William Suggested yesterday that we ask General Bliss what military advantage he thought there would be in such a move. Lansing approved the suggestion and that cable, I believe, has gone to Bliss.

Have you seen the cable No. 2535 from Carl Ackerman?[1] If not, I hope you will do so for it has an important bearing upon your address to Congress.   Affectionately yours,   E. M. House

TLS (WP, DLC).
[1] Printed in H. R. Wilson to RL, Jan. 30, 1918.

From Newton Diehl Baker, with Enclosure

Dear Mr. President: Washington February 2, 1918

The conference summarized in the attached letter was had without committing you in any way as to the person to be chosen as chairman.

Yesterday I discussed the matter with Secretaries Houston, *Lane* (who was not present before) and Daniels[.] Houston was still very sure that Baruch had not the organizing faculty. Lane was doubtful and said he would like to think it over. I confess I do not know where to look for a better suggestion

Respectfully yours,   Newton D. Baker

ALS (WP, DLC).

E N C L O S U R E

From Newton Diehl Baker

My dear Mr. President: Washington. February 1, 1918.

Mr. Baruch and I have discussed at length the suggestion of a reorganization of the War Industries Board. Mr. Baruch believes that the body should be a legal, authoritative, responsible, centralized agency for the purpose of coordinating the demands of the fighting forces. Its object should be to mobilize the resources of the country, to reveal new facilities and additional sources of supply, not alone for the military and naval requirements, but also to the end that the civilian needs be supplied with as little dislocation of industry as possible; that this agency should have power, subject to the approval of the President, to commandeer plants, products, equipment, manufacturing facilities, mines and materials, and the additional power not now granted of distributing materials thus commandeered.

In this general statement I concur. Mr. Baruch believes with me that it takes in, in general terms, the whole program, and that, in all likelihood, some of the features cannot be immediately accomplished; but that ultimately this agency whatever its form will have to exercise substantially these functions.

We agree that the following functions are to be performed:

1. Procurement of military supplies.
2. Conservation of general industrial condition of the country.
3. The determination of prices and compensation.

In order to carry out these purposes it seems to us that the present plan of organization of the War Industries Board is ill-adapted, for the reason, first, that its numbers lead to debate, and delayed decision, and, second, because its power is at present consultative and not final, except by consent.

We recognize that the present question is the appointment of a successor to Mr. Willard, and that the redistribution of power will have to be delayed until the President is empowered by legislation; but the immediate reorganization could begin and suitable distributions of power could then be made when the legislation is secured.

Our suggestions, therefore, would be that a Chairman of the War Industries Board be appointed, that he be directed immediately to reorganize the institution so as to bring about a comprehensive survey by him of the war needs of the government, with power in the Chairman to allocate supplies of materiel and manufacturing facilities, and to determine conversions of industry, both for apportionment to the several war needs reported to him by the purchasing departments of the government, and also with a view to the adjustment of the industrial needs of the government to the general industrial situation of the country, so as to prevent undue dislocation; and to have in view constantly the distribution of labor, transportation facilities of the country, and the general maintenance of industrial standards and facilities, both during and after the war.

Second, the creation of a committee to work in cooperation with the Federal Trade Commission, and to report directly to the President, for the semi-judicial determination of questions of compensation and price. The questions to be considered by this body to be referred to it by the Chairman of the War Industries Board, and its general administrative procedure subject to his general direction.

Such an organization as is herein suggested would, of course, leave the Allied Purchasing Commission in its present state, unless the reorganization of it was deemed advisable; but that could later be determined.

Mr. Baruch believes that it would be easily possible to concentrate this entire purchasing function in one man. If that could be done, and the power were vested in the Chairman the agencies now established could continue to perform all of the work, except the final decisions which would then go to an individual.

The civilian members of the War Industries Board as now composed would be assigned functions in connection with compensation and price determination, and the military and naval members of the Board would, of course, in any event be replaced by those persons who under the reorganizations which have taken place are more appropriate as aids to the Chairman in the solution of his problems affecting the several Departments.

By this process the single representatives of the War, Navy, Allied and Shipping Boards could meet, clear the difficulties, coordinate their needs, and in consultation with the Chairman of the War Industries Board submit their programs for his final allocation, distribution and judgment.

This plan does not contemplate the actual moulding of specifications and contracts, the industrial follow-up, inspection, delivery, storage or distribution of by the Director of War Industries; but leaves those functions to the strongly organized agencies already established in the several Departments, except to the extent which the performance of any of these functions affects the entire program. Where any such question arose the Chairman, by consultation, could easily arrange conditions to overcome the difference.

Respectfully yours,   Newton D. Baker

TLS (WP, DLC).

From Josephus Daniels

Dear Mr. President: Washington. Feb. 2. 1918.

In view of my letter stating my belief that Mr. Baruch is the best man named to succeed Mr. Willard, it is due you to say that Mr. Fahey, former President of the National Chamber of Commerce, tells me that appointment would not be well received by many business men and would be sharply criticized. While the War Council (Super) and the Munition Minister question is under debate in the Senate it might be wise not to make a selection. My own judgment is that in capacity to do the work and in loyalty Baruch is the best man, but whether under all the conditions and prejudices it would be wise to name him now is debatable. Houston, whose judgment is generally good, thinks it would be a mistake. For service, in the long run it would not be, I am sure, but it would not be free from much criticism.

Sincerely yours,   Josephus Daniels

ALS (WP, DLC).

From William Bauchop Wilson

My dear Mr. President: Washington February 2, 1918.

Referring to my letter inclosing copy of letter addressed to Senator Jones relative to the establishment of the basic eight-hour day in the lumber industry of the Pacific Northwest,[1] I have been advised by the Secretary of War that the lumbermen of the Pacific Northwest have stated that they would abide by any directions given by Colonel Disque[2] in the application of the basic eight-hour work-day in that field or any portion of it. Colonel Disque is the representative of the War Department in connection with the production of spruce for aeroplane purposes. If he succeeds in getting a sufficient supply of spruce to meet the needs of the Government, an Executive order such as has been contemplated will not be pressed by me. I have communicated that fact to Senator Jones and other senators and representatives who have made inquiry upon the subject matter.

Faithfully yours,   W. B. Wilson

TLS (WP, DLC).
    [1] That is, WBW to WW, Jan. 26, 1918, and its Enclosure.
    [2] Col. Brice P. Disque, commander of the Spruce Production Division of the Signal Corps, with headquarters at Portland, Ore. Disque had served in the army from 1899 to 1916. He returned to the army in 1917 and was assigned to organize the spruce-production program in the Pacific Northwest. He also organized the Loyal Legion of Loggers and Lumbermen, about which see Tyler, *Rebels of the Woods*; Samuel H. Clay, "The Man Who Heads the 'Spruce Drive'," *American Review of Reviews*, LVII (June 1918), 633-35; and Robert L. Tyler, "The United States Government as Union Organizer: The Loyal Legion of Loggers and Lumbermen," *Mississippi Valley Historical Review*, XLVII (Dec. 1960), 434-51. On Disque's other measures to improve living and working conditions in logging camps and mills, see Brice P. Disque, "How We Found a Cure for Strikes," *System, the Magazine of Business*, XXXVI (Sept. 1919), 379-84.

From Robert Bridges

Dear Mr. President: New York Feb 2 1918

For fear some busy-body should call this *Outlook* guff[1] to your attention I want you to know he is *no relative of mine*, north or south. He was in College when John[2] was there, and used to complain that John got him into scrapes (which is probably true), and is now a New York lawyer. There is also a Bridges³ in this building in the *German* Publication Society who does not belong to the clan. I thought we had a monopoly of the name till the poet-laureate⁴ popped up!

What I really wanted to say is that your whole management of this last flare-up has been consummately fine and right, and you've got them licked. I have no doubt it was a concerted political drive, but why the *Times* fell for it is hard to forgive.⁵

Of course they'll make another drive on some other Cabinet officer—whenever they think he might make a Presidential Candidate! It is a rotten game to pound you when you have such a load to carry.

I have gone to see the Sargent portrait of you three times, and like it hugely.⁶ I can see you getting ready to tell a story, with the quirk to the right side of your mouth. None of the art critics seem to like it—*but for me it's you*—and the real human you that they could not see if they tried! I'd stand on that! What they want is a stern-looking Covenanter with a jaw like a pike. Damn 'em!

Dear Tommy, this is just to say God-speed you—and don't stop to say a word. I just had to relieve my mind—but usually I keep quiet.   Your friend always   Robert Bridges

ALS (WP, DLC).

¹ Henry Wilson Bridges, "Shall We Have a Coalition Cabinet?", *The Outlook*, CXVIII (Feb. 6, 1918), 212.

² That is, John Miller Bridges, a nephew of Robert Bridges, who had been a special student at Princeton in the academic year 1890-1891. Henry Wilson Bridges was a member of the Class of 1893.

³ Unidentified.

⁴ Robert Seymour Bridges, Poet Laureate of England.

⁵ Along with extensive news coverage of congressional and other criticism of Baker and Garfield, the *New York Times*, during January, had made many harsh statements about them in its editorial columns. For example, see the editorials in the *New York Times*, Jan. 12, 14, and 18, 1918.

⁶ By permission of the governors of the National Gallery of Ireland, the portrait was on display at the Metropolitan Museum of Art for one month, beginning January 11.

Robert Lansing to Tasker Howard Bliss

For General Bliss: Washington Feb. 2, 1918

British Government are strongly urging that Japan should be asked by allies to occupy Transiberian Railway in their behalf. From the political point of view I think this would be dangerous and would be used by the Germans to consolidate Russian opinion against the allies. British Government, however, have urged the plan very strongly and before definitely stating I am opposed to it I should like to have your opinion on military advantages, which they think could be secured, in order to help us decide whether these are great enough to outweigh the political objections. Also your opinion of the scheme as a whole.   Lansing.

TC telegram (WDR, RG 120, Records of the American Section of the Supreme War Council, 1917-1919, File No. 318, DNA).

Tasker Howard Bliss to Henry Pinckney McCain

Versailles. February 2d [1918].

Confidential for Acting Chief of Staff.

Number 19. Paragraph 1. As stated in my number 16 the British have agreed to bring over in their own tonnage the personnel of six complete American divisions the last troops arriving not later than June. We have now in France five organized divisions. Yesterday the Supreme War Council adopted a resolution addressed to the four governments stating as an absolutely necessary condition for the safety of the Western front during the year 1918 that American troops must arrive at the rate of not less than two complete divisions per month. This rate of movement must begin at once. If it can be done we will have here 21 divisions by about July. It is of vital importance that this be done. Can you do it? It requires only a moderate increase in troop transports. You can *expect* further assistance in tonnage from the British. Clothing and quartermasters should be provided in time for each division regardless of cost.

Paragraph 2. Can you not hasten action on my number 16 paragraph 1 and General Pershing's number 555 about the six divisions to be transported by the British.

Paragraph 3. First session of Supreme War Council probably concludes today. Will then cable you result.   Bliss.

TC telegram (WP, DLC).

Arthur James Balfour to Sir William Wiseman

[London] February 2nd 1918.

Following is from BALFOUR for COLONEL HOUSE:

I am grateful for your telegram of February 1st.[1] and upon its agreeing as to necessity for caution in dealing with a situation of very great inherent difficulty, and in which this has changed so continuously. Meanwhile we have news that SEMENOV expedition in SIBERIA[2] is making favourable progress and an official telegram will be sent suggesting that the precipitous question of inviting

JAPANESE to occupy TRANS-SIBERIAN RAILWAY should be deferred till we know how SEMENOV fares.

We hope to arrange for money, arms, and ammunition to be supplied to SEMENOV but the latter will have to be provided from JAPANESE sources as no others are available.

T telegram (W. Wiseman Papers, CtY).
  [1] W. Wiseman to E. Drummond, Feb. 1, 1918.
  [2] Capt. Grigorii Mikhailovich Semenov, the Cossack leader who was in command of various non-Bolshevik troops on the Manchurian Railway. He was proposing to obtain control of the Trans-Siberian Railway in the Trans-Baikal province.

From Edward Mandell House

Dear Govenor: New York. February 3, 1918.

I am disturbed at the statement given out by the civil end of the Supreme War Council.[1] It seems to me a monumental blunder. It is the old belligerent tone and will serve the purpose of again welding together the people of the Central Empires back of their governments.

I would not let this deter me from making the statement to Congress you have in mind. I think it is now more necessary than ever. It is a pity that the Entente will insist upon undoing your work, built up with so much care. Until you began the direction of the Allied diplomacy it was hopelessly bad.

Sir William has told me of the substance of your conference today.[2] I agree absolutely with your position. I threshed this subject out in Paris with both the British and French and tried to show them how impossible their position was.
                    Affectionately yours,   E. M. House

TLS (WP, DLC).
  [1] See the Enclosure printed with WW to RL, Feb. 4, 1918 (third letter of that date).
  [2] For Wiseman's report of this conversation, see W. Wiseman to A. J. Balfour, Feb. 3, and W. Wiseman to E. Drummond and A. J. Balfour, Feb. 4, 1918.

From Gordon Auchincloss, with Enclosure

My dear Mr. Wilson: [Washington] Feb. 3rd, 1918.

Mr House has asked me to send you this written by Bullitt.
                    Faithfully yours   Gordon Auchincloss

ALS (WP, DLC).

E N C L O S U R E

Washington February 3, 1918.

Memorandum for Colonel House.

Subject: Comparison of the Addresses of Czernin and Hertling.

Czernin and Hertling undoubtedly discussed the subject matter of their addresses before delivering them. This is proved by the similarity of their replies to all questions which both treated—except the question of Poland—and by the points which each omitted in deference to the other. The apparent differences in the addresses are due almost entirely to the warmth of Czernin's tone. Although he seems to have been bound by previous agreement with Hertling to take the same specific points of view, his sincere desire for immediate peace led him to strive to improve his case by the manner of its presentation, whereas Hertling, who seems to have been willing to gamble on the offensive, made no effort to speak with conciliatory warmth.

Both Czernin and Hertling employed as chief stimulant for their war weary peoples, the prospect of immediate peace with Ukrainia and resultant economic advantages. And it is particularly noteworthy that Czernin adopted the principle of "no annexations, no indemnities" for the Russian front *alone*, and nowhere advocated its general application.

Nevertheless, the following distinctions between the addresses may be made:

1. Czernin made a direct proposal for an exchange of views between Austria-Hungary and the United States.

2. Czernin showed more perception than Hertling of the spirit in which the question of peace must be approached. "Our task is to build a new world," he said, "And to rebuild all that the most trying of wars has destroyed and trampled to the ground." And nowhere did Czernin assert that a question was subject for consideration exclusively by the states immediately involved. Hertling took this position, first, in regard to evacuation of Russian territory; second, in regard to evacuation of French territory; third, in regard to the creation of an independent Poland.

3. Czernin advocated the creation of an independent Poland.

The following table gives a very brief resumé and comparison of the replies of Hertling and Czernin to the President's fourteen proposals:

PRESIDENT'S PROPOSALS.

HERTLING   **CZERNIN**

I.
Open Covenants of Peace
and no Secret Treaties.

HERTLING	CZERNIN
Accepts.	Accepts but considers it impossible to prevent secret treaties.

2.
Freedom of Seas

HERTLING	CZERNIN
Accepts but dislikes President's limitation.	Accepts.

3.
Removal Economic Barriers.

HERTLING	CZERNIN
Accepts.	Accepts.

4.
Reduction of Armaments.

HERTLING	CZERNIN
Accepts. "Discussable."	Accepts. Enthusiastically.

5.
Impartial Adjustment Colonial Claims

HERTLING	CZERNIN
Demands "reconstitution of the world's colonial possessions."	Omits.

6.
Evacuation Russian Territory

HERTLING	CZERNIN
Question concerns only Russia and the four Allied Powers.	Proving with deeds we are ready to create friendly neighborly relationship.

7.
Evacuation and Restoration
Belgium.

HERTLING	CZERNIN
Ambiguous reply. Details to be settled at peace conference.	Omits.

8.
Restoration Invaded Portions France
and wrong done France in 1871 righted.

The conditions and methods of procedure of the evacuation which must take account of Germany's vital interests are to be agreed upon between Germany and France. There can never be a question of dismemberment of Imperial territory.	State of property of our allies before the war we shall defend as our own.

9.
Readjustment Italian Frontiers

Leaves reply to Czernin.	Refuses even to agree to evacuate occupied territory of Italy and speaks of "territorial aquisitions * * * which are now lost forever."

10.
Autonomy for Nations Austria-Hungary.

Leaves reply to Czernin.	Refuses advice as to government of interior of Austria-Hungary.

11.
Restoration Rumania, Serbia and
Montenegro and Access to sea for Serbia.

Leaves reply to Czernin.	Refuses even to agree to evacuate occupied territory.

12.
Autonomy for Subject Nationalities of
Turkey and Internationalization of
Dardanelles.

Will support Turkey in this matter.	Cannot subscribe to violation of sovereign rights of Turkey.

13.
Independent Poland.

Matter for agreement between Germany, Austria-Hungary and Poland.	Accepts.

14.
League of Nations

Will examine basis   No opposition.
for it.

It is still impossible to give a trustworthy estimate of the strikes in Germany. But it is to be noted that the Majority Socialist press is a unit in supporting the strike, and that, while the workers are demanding immediate reform of the Prussian Electoral Laws and a more equitable distribution of food, their primary demand is for immediate peace on the basis of the "No annexations, no indemnities" resolution of the Reichstag.

It seems highly improbable that the strikers will be strong enough to attain control of the Government at once. It is probable that after considerable disturbance the Government will force the strikers back to work. This brings up the question whether it is desirable for the President to launch his reply to Czernin and Hertling while the strike is still in progress or whether it is advisable for him to delay his reply until the strike is settled and the situation has cleared.

There is some danger that if the President should speak at once the opponents of the strikers would be able to employ the President's address as a weapon against them by calling them "the allies of Wilson." But on the other hand, if the President should speak while the strike is still in progress, and should criticise Hertling's address in the very words of the German and Austrian Socialists and Liberals, and should set before them the ideal of a new world of international decency, he would bring courage to their hearts and would be the leader to whom they would look for aid in the days of despair which will follow the crushing of the strike.

This would be particularly true if the President should state that the United States considers the various questions of subject nationalities matters to be decided by negotiation on broad principles of justice, not matters to be decided by military force; and that the United States will adhere to this principle no matter what may be the military outcome of the war and under no circumstances will strive to cut by force pieces from the body of Germany. The chief argument of the opponents of the strikers is that the strikes will make it possible for the enemies of Germany to dismember her. Such a statement by the President would go far towards nullifying the effect of the assertion, for it would enable the Socialists to argue as did VORWAERTS on January 11: "We are protected from annexations by Wilson's promise, 'We do not wish to injure Germany'."

It seems desirable, therefore, that the President should reply to Hertling and Czernin at the earliest possible moment and that he should follow in so far as is practicable the criticisms of the Socialists of Germany and Austria.

In the following list of statements, which it seems desirable the President should make, the actual words of the German and Austrian Socialists are frequently followed:

1. Count Czernin clearly showed a desire to enter into negotiations at once on the basis of the President's statement of war aims. Count von Hertling seemed to desire merely to create an alibi for not entering negotiations before the Spring offensive.

(Vienna ARBEITER ZEITUNG: "Czernin is willing to accept Wilson's speech as a possible basis of discussion; while Hertling wishes only to have an alibi for not discussing peace on the basis of Wilson's speech.")

2. Czernin recognizes that "our task is to build a new world" and seems to recognize that the new world of international order can be created only if the whole situation is taken as a basis and all changes based on general sanction.

(VORWAERTS: "Lasting peace can only come if the whole situation is taken as a basis and any changes based on general sanction.")

3. Hertling still conceives peace as a matter for bargaining between individual states. He even goes so far as to reject general discussion of the questions, of Poland, of the other occupied territories of Russia, and of the occupied provinces of France. The Chancellor seems to be looking towards a future of State wars and to a renewal of the old diplomatic game, and his ambition seems to be to gain improved strategic frontiers, additions of territory and indemnities, rather than to build a new world.

(VORWAERTS: "The standpoint that the Polish settlement is only an Austrian, German, Polish affair is rather that of a peace of violence than that of a peace of understanding.")

4. But the primary interest of the United States in this war is that out of it shall spring a more decent international order; and we shall not make peace with Germany until the representatives of the people of Germany show that they, too, desire to create a new world order and are willing to consider with us the reconstruction of the whole world in the light of the new order. For until the representatives of Germany really desire to cooperate with us in this task there will be no possibility of accomplishing it.

5. It seems most advisable that the President should then picture with daring specification the new era of international coöperation which must arise from the ashes of the war. It would be most desirable to state that the United States wishes to place its economic resources at the service of all the peoples of the world without distinction; also that the United States is ready to accept the prin-

ciple of self-determination for all subject nationalities, not even excluding independence, if desired.

6. It seems most vitally important that the President should state that the United States considers the various questions of subject nationalities matters to be decided by negotiation on broad principles of justice, not matters to be decided by military force; and that the United States will adhere to this principle no matter what may be the military outcome of the war and under no circumstances will strive to cut by force pieces from the body of Germany.

7. The President would receive the unanimous support of the Socialists and Liberals of Germany and Austria-Hungary if he should then criticize Hertling's address on the following specific grounds.

A. The speech of the Chancellor is a masterpiece of ambiguity. Men may read into his elastic formulas whatever they desire. He speaks of the "official German policy"; but his words are so equivocal that they point to the existence of an unofficial policy with unknown annexationist aims.

(VORWAERTS: "The speech of the Chancellor is a masterpiece of finding elastic formulas into which journalists can read what they want.")

(MUENCHENER NEUESTE NACHRICHTEN: The Chancellor gives the idea only of "an official peace policy; but all indications point to the existence of an unofficial peace policy with unknown aims.")

(BERLINER TAGEBLATT: "* * * the points where Hertling conceals his interest in clarity of style.")

B. Count Hertling at no time unequivocally adopts the principle of the "no annexations, no indemnities" resolution of the Reichstag.

(MANNHEIMER VOLKSSTIMME: "Hertling should have briefly and emphatically declared that Germany still holds to the Reichstag War Aims Resolution.")

(DAVID: "No changes of the war map can make the Reichstag Peace Resolution out of date.")

(NAUMANN: "The German Government must roundly declare that it seeks no sort of annexation.")

C. Count Hertling does not even state frankly that Germany will evacuate and restore Belgium, though he knows that an honest declaration in regard to Belgium is the first condition of peace.

(Vienna ARBEITER ZEITUNG: "An honest declaration about Belgium is the first condition of peace and Hertling has again refused to make it.")

(DAVID: "A positive statement must now be made about Belgium.")

(NAUMANN: "Absolute sincerity is necessary regarding Belgium.")

(Haase: "It is necessary to say that the economic and military independence of Belgium will be restored.")

D. He not only refuses to state that Germany will evacuate and restore the occupied provinces of France, but even utters a sinister phrase about "the conditions and methods of procedure of evacuation, which must take account of Germany's vital interests," which leaves the impression that, behind his ambiguous words, lies concealed a purpose to annex the Briey and Longwy districts and to demand indemnities of France.

(VORWAERTS: "Hertling might at least have declared that no aspirations to annex Longwy and Briey existed.")

E. By the use of ambiguous phrases the Chancellor leaves himself free to annex Russian territory under the cloak of an imaginary "self-determination."

(HAASE: "The German negotiations are not playing a square game. The occupied territory is still a part of Russia and the people cannot freely express their will so long as foreign troops are present.")

(Vienna ARBEITER ZEITUNG: "If Poland is to have the right to determine her own destiny, the same must be true for the Baltic Provinces.")

(VORWAERTS: "The right of Russia to have a voice regarding Poland actually was recognized at the Brest-Litovsk negotiations.")

8. Count Czernin's words contain a warmth and clarity which are missing in the words of Count Hertling. His statement that he supports the principle that "an independent Poland should be erected which should include the territories inhabited by indisputably Polish populations," is most welcome.

9. But nowhere in his address does Count Czernin state that he accepts the general principle of "no annexations, no indemnities" for all fronts. On the contrary, he specifically refuses to promise even the restoration of the occupied territories of Italy, Roumania, Serbia and Montenegro, and he applies the formula of "no annexations, no indemnities" only to those territories of Russia which are occupied by Austrian and Hungarian troops.

10. Furthermore, Count Czernin shows no disposition to grant the right to live their own lives, in their own way, to the peoples of Austria, and particularly, to the peoples of Hungary. We have no desire to interfere in the internal politics of Austria-Hungary. But the freest opportunity for autonomous development must be granted to the peoples of Austria-Hungary as well as to the subject peoples of the Turkish Empire, if the structure of world peace is not to be built upon quicksand.

11. It is a step in the direction of a better world that, through the voices of Count von Hertling and Count Czernin, Germany and

Austria-Hungary have committed themselves to support of the principles of open negotiations and unconcealed treaties, freedom of navigation on the high seas, removal of all economic barriers, reduction of armaments and a league of nations.

12. But neither upon these principles nor upon any others can the new world of international order be built until the people of Germany control their own Government and send to represent them men who desire to coöperate with us in building the new world. On the day when the people of Germany send to represent them men who like themselves believe in the principles outlined and are ready to negotiate upon them, on that day they can have peace, but not one day before.

An address by the President which followed these lines would be audacious. But the President would be addressing an audacious, creative, awakened world. In Germany and Austria-Hungary he would be addressing the Socialists who are in revolt. In England he would be addressing the resurgent Labor Party. In France and Italy he would be addressing the Socialists. In Russia he would be addressing the Bolsheviki. These men are the vital spirits of the world to-day. Their principles will be the commonplaces of to-morrow. To unite, to inspire and to lead them, the President should now lay before the world his vision of the future.

Respectfully submitted: William C. Bullitt

TS MS (WP, DLC).

From Newton Diehl Baker

My dear Mr. President: [Washington] February 3, 1918.

I herewith return to you the papers in the Borglum matter, together with a letter to me from Mr. Meyer, and the notes and comments to which he refers in his letter;[1] and which embody the analysis of the Borglum report.

You will observe that in Mr. Meyer's opinion the early appointment of the third civilian member of the Aircraft Board is of very great importance, and Mr. Meyer thinks he ought to be a man whose experience has been in large industrial organization, so that the constant strengthening, which all such bodies as the Aircraft Board need, can be secured through a man of real organizing ability.

It was at Mr. Meyer's suggestion that I wrote you about Mr. Woolley.[2] He now suggests Mr. Charles M. Peek,[3] who is associated with the War Industries Board. He feels that Mr. Peek is exactly the sort of man needed on the Aircraft Board, and that their work is so very much more important than what he is now doing that he should be asked to leave the service of the War Industries Board and go on the Aircraft Board.

My inquiry as to Mr. Jones[4] shows that he is still ill, and the time of his return to Washington is not known.

In addition to this, Mr. Meyer points out that Mr. Borglum's report is really a repetition of much of the comment which has been going around in a more or less suppressed way about Colonel Deeds. A few days ago a New York World reporter came here with a skeleton of the same story. I turned him over at once to General Squier, and he has just written me that he went through all of the facts with General Squier and is satisfied that there is nothing in the story.

In the meantime, in order not to take any chances in the case, I had the whole matter brought to the attention of the Inspector General of the Army with directions to follow the thing through, and leave no possibility unexamined.

The villainy attributed to Deeds is too monumental to be believed, and I suspect that Mr. Borglum has no further information on that subject than the New York World reporter had, which turned out to be without substance. However, I concur in Mr. Meyer's recommendation that a thorough-going inquiry be made into the matter, and a record established, both for the protection of the Department and Colonel Deeds, and I am asking Mr. Meyer to undertake this inquiry.

The last suggestion of Mr. Borglum that the government seize all airplane factories, proceeding itself with the manufacturing of aircraft, would not, in Mr. Meyer's judgment, nor in mine, produce any better results than we are now getting.

It seems to me that these papers are now in the situation where we might with propriety have a meeting with Mr. Borglum, telling him that the organization of the Aircraft Board is being perfected; second, that all the charges which he has suggested against Colonel Deeds and others personally will be investigated both through the medium of Mr. Meyer and the medium of the Inspector General of the Army; third, that his other constructive suggestions will be examined and adopted where valuable; and we might then, I think, ask him to discontinue his inquiries, and submit back to you the letter which ought to be returned.

It happens that Mr. Meyer has known Mr. Borglum for a very long time, and believes that his presence at the interview will have considerable weight with Mr. Borglum in bringing him to a reasonable and proper attitude toward your confidence with regard to the whole subject.

Respectfully yours,   [Newton D. Baker]

CCL (N. D. Baker Papers, DLC).
    [1] Meyer's letter and the notes and comments are missing.
    [2] NDB to WW, Jan. 24, 1918.
    [3] Actually, George Nelson Peek, vice-president of Deere & Co., manufacturers of Moline, Ill., and a member of the War Industries Board and its Commissioner of Finished Products.
    [4] Thomas D. Jones, who had resigned in December 1917 from the War Trade Board.

Sir William Wiseman to Arthur James Balfour

No. 48.   [Washington] February 3, 1918.

A. I lunched today with the President and Secretary of War. The President asked me to send you a cable explaining his views regarding the disposal of American troops in France.

B. The following are the substance of his arguments.

C. In the first place the President is confident you will believe that he is actuated solely by what he considers the best policy for the common good.

D. The President says American troops will be put into the line by battalions with the French or British if it should become absolutely necessary, but he wishes to place before you frankly the very grave objections he sees to this course.

E. Apart from the serious danger of friction owing to different methods, it is necessary that an American army should be created under American leaders and American Flag in order that the people of America shall solidly and cheerfully support the war.

F. The placing of American troops in small bodies under foreign leaders would be taken as a proof that the recent criticism of the War Department was justified and that the American military machine had broken down.

G. The American people would not, he fears, understand the military reasons, and the necessary secrecy would prevent a very full explanation being given.

H. Their resentment would be increased if an agreement was made between the American and British Governments for the disposal of American troops in this way before they left home. It would not have so bad an effect if Pershing as American Commander in Chief, decided after the men arrived in France that it was necessary to place some of them at the disposal of the British in this way.

J. The President therefore hopes you will provide transportation for the six American divisions at present under discussion without making a bargain that they are to be used to reinforce the British Line and that you will agree they are to be used by Pershing as he thinks best.

K. At the same time the President repeats most earnestly that he will risk any adverse public criticism in order to win the war and he has told Pershing that he may put American troops by battalions in the British line, or use them in any way which in his, Pershing's, judgment may be taken by the necessities of the military situation.[1]

L. I would suggest that you send me something in reply to this that I may convey to the President.

T telegram (W. Wiseman Papers, CtY).
[1] Wilson was echoing Pershing's recommendations, conveyed in the Enclosure printed with WW to NDB, Feb. 4, 1918.

To Robert Lansing, with Enclosure

My dear Mr. Secretary,   The White House. 4 February, 1918.

It is very annoying to have this man Robins,[1] in whom I have no confidence whatever, acting as political adviser in Russia and sending his advice to private individuals. I wonder if you feel about it as I do and whether you would be willing to consult with Mr. Davison of the Red Cross with a view to having Robins reminded of his proper functions and their limitations?

Faithfully Yours,   W.W.

WWTLI (R. Lansing Papers, NjP).
[1] That is, Raymond Robins, who, in November 1917, had succeeded William B. Thompson as head of the American Red Cross Mission to Russia. For one view of Robins' importance, see William Appleman Williams, *American-Russian Relations, 1781-1947* (New York, 1952).

E N C L O S U R E

Petrograd, January 23, 1918.

2272. Following from Robins is for Davison, Red Cross:

"10,084, January 23. Deliver the following message to Thompson, 'Eleven. Soviet Government stronger today than ever before. Its authority and power greatly consolidated by dissolution of Constituent Assembly which was led and controlled by Chernoff[1] as permanent President. Acceptance of dissolution as final without important protest general throughout Russia. Chernoff programme not essentially different from Bolshevik industrial and social programme but criticised Bolsheviks as unable to conclude peace. Had control finally rested with this assembly under such leadership the chances are that separate peace would have been concluded without regard to principles controlling Bolshevik leaders. It becomes increasingly evident that present leaders, without regard to consequences, will refuse to abandon principles adopted in negotiations Central Powers. Cannot too strongly urge importance of prompt recognition of Bolshevik authority and immediate establishment of modus vivendi making possible generous and sympathetic cooperation. Sisson approves this text and requests you show this cable to Creel. Thacher[2] and Wardwell[3] concur. Foregoing sent you by open cable today. End of message.' "

T telegram (R. Lansing Papers, NjP).
    [1] Viktor Mikhailovich Chernov, leader of the Social Revolutionary party.
    [2] Thomas Day Thacher, a New York lawyer, at this time a major with the American Red Cross Mission.
    [3] Allen Wardwell, a New York lawyer, at this time a civilian member of the American Red Cross Mission.

To Robert Lansing

My dear Mr. Secretary,   The White House. 4 February, 1918.

As I understand it, our official representative in Petrograd *is* keeping in touch with the Bolshevik leaders informally. Am I not right?   Faithfully Yours,   W.W.

WWTLI (SDR, RG 59, 861.01/14½, DNA).

To Robert Lansing, with Enclosure

My dear Mr. Secretary,   The White House. 4 February, 1918.

There is infinite stupidity in action of this sort. It stiffens every element of hatred and belligerency in the Central Powers and plays directly into the hands of their military parties. These people have a genius for making blunders of the most serious kind and neutralizing each thing that we do. Do you think that anything can be done to hold them off from making fools of themselves again and again? I would very much value your advice.
                                    Faithfully Yours,   W.W.

WWTLI (E. M. House Papers, CtY).

E N C L O S U R E

Paris. Feb. 2, 1918.

3135. Frasier reports to me as follows: "At the final meeting of the Supreme War Council today the French, British and Italian Prime Ministers drafted the following statement of the labors of the conference for simultaneous publication in Paris, London and Rome on Monday the fourth instant, but not to be released before. 'The Supreme War Council gave the most careful consideration to the recent utterances of the German Chancellor and of the Austro-Hungarian Ministry [Minister] for Foreign Affairs but was unable to find in them any real approximation to the moderate conditions laid down by all the Allied Governments. This conviction was only deepened by the impression made by the contrast between the professed idealistic aims with which the Central Powers entered upon the present negotiations at Brest Litovsk and the now openly disclosed plans of conquest and spoliation. Under the circumstances the Supreme War Council decided that the only immediate task before them lay in the prosecution with the utmost vigor and in the closest and most effective cooperation of the military effort of our Allies until such time as the pressure of that effort shall have brought about in the enemy governments and peoples a change of temper which would justify the hope of the conclusion of peace on terms which would not involve the abandonment in the face of an aggressive and unreprentent [unrepentant] militarism of all the principles of freedom, justice and the respect for the law of nations which the Allies are resolved to vindicate.

The decisions taken by the Supreme War Council in pursuance of this conclusion embraced not only the general military policy to be carried out by the Allies in all the principal theaters of war, but more particularly the closer and more effective coordination, under the Council, of all the efforts of the powers engaged in the struggle against the Central Powers. The functions of the Council itself were enlarged, and the principles of unity of policy and action, initiated at Rapallo in November last, received still further concrete and practical development. On all these questions a complete agreement was arrived at, after the fullest discussion with regard, both to the policy to be pursued and to the measures for execution.

The Allies are united in heart and will, not by any hidden designs, but by their open resolve will defend civilization against an unscruperlous [unscrupulous] and brutal attempt at domination. This unanimity, confirmed by a unanimity not less complete both as regards the military policy to be pursued and as regards the measures needed for its execution, will enable them to meet the violence of the enemy's onset with firm and quiet confidence, with the utmost energy and with the knowledge that neither their strength nor their steadfastness can be shaken.

The splendid soldiers of our free democracies have won their place in history by their immeasurable valor. Their magnificent heroism, and the no less noble endurance with which our civilian populations are bearing their daily burden of trial and suffering, testify to the strength of those principles of freedom which will crown the military success of the Allies with the glory of a great moral triumph.' "   Sharp.

T telegram (E. M. House Papers, CtY).

Three Letters to Robert Lansing

My dear Mr. Secretary,   The White House. 4 February, 1918.

I am entirely of Profess[o]r Herron's opinion about this.[1] Bulgaria here appears as playing the most cynically selfish game of dominion. She is brutally frank about it, at any rate; but she can get no "rise" out of us!   Faithfully Yours,   W.W.

WWTLI (SDR, RG 59, 763.72119/1267½, DNA).
[1] H. R. Wilson had reported from Bern on December 28, 1917, about a conversation with Theodore K. Shipkoff, a Bulgarian subject, whose remarks gave the impression that Bulgaria might wish to withdraw from the war. H. R. Wilson to RL, Dec. 28, 1917, printed in *FR-WWS 1917*, 2, I, 512-14. Wilson discussed this conversation with the British Minister in Bern, who informed his government and later said that they were "exceedingly interested" in Bulgaria's attitude toward a separate peace. Wilson proposed to arrange a nonofficial contact with Shipkoff and the Bulgarian Minister in Switzerland, and the State Department approved this course of action. H. R. Wilson to RL, Jan. 2, 1918, and RL to H. R. Wilson, Jan. 5, 1918, both printed in *FR-WWS 1918*, 1, I, 1. Wilson accordingly asked Herron to get in touch with Shipkoff, who then came to his house. Herron gave Wilson a long report of their conversations (G. D. Herron to H. R. Wilson, Jan. 24, 1918, TLS), and Herron sent this by pouch as an enclosure with H. R. Wilson to RL, Jan. 28, 1918, TLS (both in SDR, RG 59, 763.72119/1298, DNA). In the report, Herron described Shipkoff as a financier, "somewhat intimate with King Ferdinand," and head of the monopoly that manufactured attar of roses, "supplying nine-tenths of the world's product thereof." Lansing received H. R. Wilson's dispatch on February 15 and, according to a note on the document, sent it to Woodrow Wilson on the following day.
H. R. Wilson, on January 30, sent a telegram (SDR, RG 59, 763.72119/1219, DNA) which summarized Herron's long and outspoken letter. The telegram, which Lansing sent to Woodrow Wilson on February 2, is printed in *FR-WWS 1918*, 1, I, 65-67, with the following paragraph omitted:
"Herron adopts hostile attitude towards the whole affair, points out inconsistencies in Shipkoff's statements and states that Shipkoff continually emphasizing Great Britain's jealousy of America and endeavoring to sow discontent between the two nations. Herron regards Bulgarian proposals as outlined to be a piece of shameless treachery, an endeavor on the part of Bulgarians to benefit from Germany by having made war on the side of Germany up to the present and to benefit in friendly relations from the Allies by non-participation in war."

My dear Mr. Secretary,   The White House. 4 February, 1918.

I should like, of course, to help the King of Rumania out of his private embarrassments,[1] but I do not think that this Government would be justified in taking any part in this, without legislative action, which could hardly be expected. We are not free in such matters as other governments are.

Faithfully Yours,   W.W.

WWTLI (SDR, RG 59, 763.72/8916, DNA).
¹ Lansing had informed Wilson on February 1 that Charles Joseph Vopicka, Minister to Rumania, Serbia, and Bulgaria, had reported in early December that Ferdinand was seeking to save what was left of his private fortune by having the Allies convert a portion of it into pounds and dollars. His principal investments were in Germany and had been confiscated when his country entered the war. Lansing noted further that the French government was now proposing that France, Great Britain, and the United States "take equal parts in discounting some two and a half million lei of Roumanian securities for the personal account of the King." Vopicka had recommended granting the request, not only because of Ferdinand's personal claims, but also because of political considerations. On the other hand, Lansing pointed out, the Treasury Department held that the United States could make loans legally only to governments, not individuals. In view of these facts, Lansing concluded, he wished to know what answer to give Vopicka and the French government, and whether Wilson would wish to draw on the war fund at his disposal. RL to WW, Feb. 1, 1918, TLS (SDR, RG 59, 763.72/8916, DNA).

My dear Mr. Secretary,   The White House. 4 February, 1918.

I am clearly of the judgment that there is nothing wise or practicable in this scheme¹ and that we ought very respectfully to decline to take part in its execution; but it seems to me that we need, at this juncture, at any rate, give no further reason than this: that our own knowledge of the present attitude and wishes of the Japanese Government convinces us that such a request would be met with a refusal and that, therefore, it seems to us unwise to make a request which would in itself give the Japanese a certain moral advantage with respect to any ultimate desires or purposes she may have with regard to the Eastern Provinces of Siberia.

Faithfully Yours,   W.W.

I understand that you are seeking to obtain General Bliss's judgment of the plan from a military point of view. I am glad of that. That will furnish us with additional data for a judgment.

WWTLI (SDR, RG 59, 861.00/1097, DNA).
¹ See the Enclosure printed with EMH to WW, Jan. 31, 1918.

To Newton Diehl Baker, with Enclosure

My dear Mr. Secretary,   The White House. 4 February, 1918.

How do you think this would do for instructions to General Bliss,— or General Pershing, whichever is the right one to receive them?

That we consider the objections to the plan just those which he states in the enclosed despatch and that in our judgment those objections are final.

That we have no objection to the programme which he here suggests by way of substitute (repeating it), but that our judgment is that the British should undertake to transport six complete divisions across the sea, to be disposed of and trained as General Pershing directs, in conference, of course, with the commanding officers of the other forces.

That we are willing to trust to his judgment upon all points of training and preliminary trying out alike of officers and men, but advise that nothing except sudden and manifest emergency be suffered to interfere with the building up of a great distinct American force at the front, acting under its own flag and its own officers.

Faithfully yours,   W.W.

WWTLI (N. D. Baker Papers, DLC).

E N C L O S U R E

Paris Jan. 31, 1918

3118. For Secretary of State and Colonel House, Frasier reports to me as follows: "At a meeting held between General Robertson and General Pershing yesterday at Versailles General Pershing made the following objections to General Robertson's plan of sending to France by British shipping one hundred and fifty battalions of infantry for service in British divisions on the Western Front. One. The national sentiment of the United States opposed to service under foreign flag. Two. Probability that such acting by the United States might excite serious political opposition to the administration in conducting the war. Three. The certinity [certainty] that it were, would be used by German propagandists to incite public opinion against the war. Four. It would dissipate the effort of the American Army as well as its direction. Five. The danger of differences in national characteristics and military training of soldiers with consequent failure of entire cooperation would undoubtedly lead to frequently and eventual misunderstanding between both countries. Six. Additional man power could be provided as quickly on the Western Front by some plan not entailing amalgamation. General Pershing thereupon made the following counter-proposition which would use both the available tonnage for bringing over the personnel of entire American Divisions to Europe. One. That the infantry and auxil[i]ary troops of these divisions be trained with British divisions be [by] battalions or by some other plan to be mutually agreed upon. Two. Artillery to be trained by using French material as at present but under American direction. Three. That the staff officers and higher commanders be detailed with corresponding units of the British Army for training and experience. Four. That those battalions after sufficient training be reformed as regiments and that after complete training of the artillery all units comprising each division be united for service under their own officers. Five. That plan above mentioned be carried out without interfering with plans now in operation for transporting American forces to France. Six. That the questions of supply be arranged with our advice in concert with American and British Commanders in Chief. Seven. That the questions of equipment and arms be decided in an analogous manner."   Sharp.

CC telegram (N. D. Baker Papers, DLC).

To Josephus Daniels

My dear Daniels: The White House   4 February, 1918

Thank you for your report of your conversation with Mr. Fahey about the chairmanship of the War Industries Board. I do not feel that we can venture to delay that matter very long, but I wish with you to follow the line of action which will bring the least criticism.

I think you will find that members of the two Houses are learning very fast to have a very great confidence in Baruch and, after all, they are our only authoritative critics.

Faithfully yours,   Woodrow Wilson

TLS (J. Daniels Papers, DLC).

To Winthrop More Daniels

Personal.

My dear Daniels: [The White House] 4 February, 1918

Thank you for your letter of February second.[1] I hope with all my heart that Charles E. Hughes will never be connected in any way with affairs down here,[2] he proved himself so absolutely false during the last campaign, but I take it for granted that the majority of the Board will go very slow on putting so untrustworthy a critic in a place where he would have so much opportunity to make mischief.

I know Frederick N. Judson[3] also and he seems to me about the most saturnine man I ever had any dealings with. I think his indigestion must long ago have gone wrong.

Cordially and sincerely yours,   Woodrow Wilson

TLS (Letterpress Books, WP, DLC).
  [1] W. M. Daniels to WW, Feb. 2, 1918, TLS (WP, DLC).
  [2] Daniels had said that Hughes, among others, had been mentioned as a successor to Joseph Wingate Folk as chief counsel of the Interstate Commerce Commission.
  [3] Frederick Newton Judson, lawyer of St. Louis.

To Lincoln Ross Colcord

My dear Mr. Colcord: [The White House] 4 February 1918.

I have read with interest your letter of January 27th.

You may be sure that I am in close touch with the situation and am watching it carefully. Of course, you will realize that you are not in a position to obtain all the information necessary to form a correct judgment, and what seems to you immediately possible and advisable may be, at the moment, altogether impracticable and unwise.   Cordially and sincerely yours,   Woodrow Wilson

TLS (Letterpress Books, WP, DLC).

To Robert Bridges

The White House 4 February, 1918

Bless you, my dear Bobby, for your generous and affectionate letter. It was just what I stood in need of, and my heart responds with the deepest gratitude and affection.

I know Henry Wilson Bridges, a man of extremely light weight and no sort of practical capacity in the field in which he tries to express an opinion in his Outlook article. You need not have feared for a moment that I thought it was anybody even remotely connected with you.

These are certainly times that try the soul, try indeed everything that is in a man, but I believe that what is fair and right will prevail so long as those who are partisans of what is fair and right do not lose heart or let their lines be broken at all.

I am heartily glad you like the portrait. Of course, I do not know what judgment to form of it myself, but the family like it and that is a pretty good test.

With all my heart
                    Your affectionate friend,   Woodrow Wilson

TLS (WC, NjP).

From Newton Diehl Baker, with Enclosure

[Washington, Feb. 4, 1918]

For the Presidents information   Baker

ALS (WP, DLC).

ENCLOSURE

Tasker Howard Bliss to Henry Pinckney McCain

Versailles, received February 4th, 1918 7:13 AM

Confidential. Number 21. February 3d For Acting Chief of Staff.

Paragraph 1. The third session of the Supreme War Council began Wednesday January 30th and continued until final adjournment at noon February 2nd. It considered 14 joint notes of the military representatives and two separate resolutions the full text of which will be forwarded by another conference hand. The action on those of essential importance is indicated below.

Paragraph 2. The approved joint notes numbers 7, 8, 9 and 13 created adoption sub agency(ies) of the Supreme War Council interallied commission on aviation transportation tank(s) and supply.

Paragraph 3 All that follows to be held in absolute confidence: Joint note number 1 and number 12 were on the subject of general military policy for 1918 and general plan of campaign for 1918 respectively. The general military policy approved by the Supreme War Council for 1918 involves a general defensive attitude combined with readiness to take advantage of any opportunity for the offensive. The general plan of campaign for 1918 is to be one of general defense on the western, the Italian, and the Macedonian fronts. The English insisted upon an offensive campaign in Asia Minor with a view to detaching Turkey from alliance with the Central powers. This was supported by the Italians. The French strongly objected. Mr. Lloyd George and Lord Milner said that this offensive campaign would be conducted by British forces now in the Eastern theater and would not divert troops from the Western front. The British military advisers supported this position. The British Commander in Chief and Chief of Staff[1] opposed it. The final action of the Supreme War Council was as follows "The Supreme War Council accept note 12 of the military representative(s) on the plans of campaign for 1918, the British Government having made it clear that, in utilizing in the most effective fashion the forces already at its disposal in the Eastern theater, it has no intention of diverting forces from the Western fronts or relaxing its efforts to maintain the safety of that front which it regards as of vital interest to the whole alliance" In note 12 the arrival in France of at least two American divisions each month is stated as an essential condition on which the plan of campaign is based and is Sine-Qua-Non to safety of the western front. This imposes on us the obligations to provide this monthly minimum and necessary tonnage must be obtained from our own resources.

Paragraph 4. Joint note on note number 14 was on the subject of an inter-allied general reserve for the campaign of 1918 for use according to circumstances on the British French Italian or Macedonian fronts.

Paragraph 5. By the adoption of the first paragraph of note 14 the Supreme War Council decided to establish a general inter-allied reserve. A special executive committee consisting of General Foch, Chairman, and Generals Wilson, Cadorna and General Bliss military representatives with the Supreme War Council of Great Britain, Italy and the United States was created and was charged with the duty of determining the composition and strength of the general reserve and the contributions of each nation thereto; the selection(s) of locality(ies) in which the general reserve is normally to be stationed; the decision(s) and issuance of orders as to time place and period of employment; the determining of the time place and strength of counter offensive and the transfer to the proper Commanders in Chief of troops necessary for the operations.

Bliss.

T telegram (WP, DLC).
¹ Field Marshal Sir Douglas Haig and General Sir William R. Robertson, respectively.

Hugh Robert Wilson to Robert Lansing, with Enclosures

Dear Mr. Secretary: Berne, February 4, 1918.

I do not know through how many hands a despatch must pass before it reaches you and I therefore am taking the liberty of addressing this enclosed despatch to you, marked "Personal and Confidential," in view of its nature. I trust that I am not causing you any inconvenience by so doing.

Very respectfully, Hugh R Wilson

TLS (WP, DLC).

E N C L O S U R E   I

CONFIDENTIAL No. 2321

Sir: Berne, February 4, 1918.

With reference to my strictly confidential cipher telegram No. 2570 of today's date,¹ I have the honor to transmit herewith one copy of a memorandum of the conversation in which Professor George D. Herron reported to me his interview with Professor Lammasch. As the pouch closes tonight I am unable to put this in a more satisfactory form, but beg the Department's leniency in this connection and that it will be remembered when reading this document that it is a shorthand report of the actual conversation of Dr. Herron.

I have the honor to be, Sir,

Your obedient servant,   Hugh R Wilson

TLS (WP, DLC).
¹ H. R. Wilson to RL, No. 2570, Feb. 4, 1918, T telegram (R. Lansing Papers, NjP), an abridged version of the first twelve paragraphs of the following document.

E N C L O S U R E   I I

HIGHLY CONFIDENTIAL.

MEMORANDUM OF CONVERSATION
PROF. GEORGE D. HERRON.

February 3, 1918.

When I got home, so as to try to be sure that I wouldn't forget anything, I made some notes from memory so as to get everything. So I will just follow these because I have got it here in consecutive order.

Well, to begin with, I made it perfectly clear to Lammasch that I had no kind of official mandate, either actual or implied; that he must have that perfectly clear; that I had come at his invitation because he was a friend of a special friend of mine, Professor Foerster; that we wanted to talk it over. Of course he replied then as a matter of courtesy that he had no official mandate, which he proceeded to disprove right away. He told me just how he had come solely for the purpose of this interview. The Emperor, urged on by the Empress, was getting more and more anxious for a change, and they wanted to find some way of getting a confidential message through to President Wilson that would not be known by Germany, or naturally, their other Allies. So not going into details, Professor Foerster is a very generous and loyal friend, and has spoken often about me in an exaggerated way, and so they concluded that the thing to do was to get the interview with me. Of course it is all helped by this irrepressible rumor that I have told you about. So that this actually is directly what the Emperor wants to get through confidentially to President Wilson, and Secretary Lansing of course, and by as narrow a channel as possible so as few as possible shall know of it.

This interview began with the fate of the world hanging on building some kind of a bridge between Vienna and Washington, and considering the way to build that bridge. I told him then that it was best for him to talk and make all of his propositions and let me get clearly before me just what he had to propose, or as he assured me over and over again, that he was really speaking as the Emperor, and then I would say whatever I felt I could say afterwards. So I simply listened to his presentment of the case.

First—as to Czernin's message. He said quite frankly that Czernin was not to be trusted; that Czernin, although he wanted to be liberal in a sense, had no less the Prussian mentality, and was under the influence of Prussia; and that the Emperor personally forced Czernin to make that speech, and also exacted from him a promise that the speech should be transmitted formally to President Wilson from Austria. It was so started and Germany stopped it. Didn't permit it to go out. Germany never told them so, but they know. I said that I only knew what was said yesterday in the papers; that Secretary Lansing said it had not officially reached them. He said he was afraid not, and that Germany didn't probably transmit it. The only possible way to transmit it was through Holland or Denmark, or up that way, and Germany failed to transmit it that way. The Emperor told Czernin very flatly that he must make that speech or resign and give way to somebody that would make it. The speech was a pale and halting presentation of the way the Emperor wanted himself to have it said. It was a case of force majeure. So much for that point.

I brought in there the question about the possibility of his forming a Ministry himself in case some kind of an understanding, or some kind of a preliminary understanding were effected with Washington. He said—no he wouldn't do that under the circumstances; the difficulties would be too great, but he would probably become Secretary of State for Foreign Affairs if the new order of things came. He said that he was personally well acquainted with Secretary Lansing.

Next, getting more definite. The whole heart of the Emperor is in effecting a great change in the constitution of the Monarchy, in getting extricated from Prussian hegemony, and in getting a reorientation, especially with America. He said that the Emperor is honest in this and determined in it, and that he is especially backed up by the Empress whom he describes as extraordinarily clever and forcible.

The plan which Professor Lammasch has worked out with the Emperor then is this: That first President Wilson would make a public address of some kind in recognition of Czernin's address as indicating some sort of preparedness on the part of Austria toward peace. He can address whomever he pleases—The Senate, a labor union, or the high heavens so long as he makes a public recognition. Then the next move would be that the Emperor himself would write a long letter to the Pope, at the same time publishing the letter to the world, in which he would set forth as far as he can under existing circumstances (you will see later what those circumstances are) the desire for the integration and separate development of the people within the bounds of the Austrian Monarchy. He would have to say this in principle rather than geographic details.

Second. The desire for mutual disarmament and the society of nations, exactly as proposed by President Wilson, with the additional statement that if the peace congress would begin with these principles instead of the geographic details, then the questions of the old frontiers would lose their significance and would be easier for arrangement. That is, if the society of nations should be established, and the principle of disarmament agreed upon, every people everywhere, throughout the world or at least within the society of nations should have the right of choice of self-government, or at least autonomy. If the principle were made so that it included, well for instance, by implication, Ireland as well as the irridenta, then it didn't become so important as to what particular governmental centre the different groups of people belong. That if they would begin with these principles, then the questions of Alsace-Lorraine, of the irridenta and all other questions would be easier of negotiation. You can see that there is plenty of room for illusion there, but I am only reporting the Emperor's proposition which he would include in the proposition to the Pope. That would be the second part of the plan.

Then follows Professor Lammasch's scheme for the new Austria which is to integrate, to put together, all the different peoples of Austria, each in separate states. He would group all the Yugo-Slavs that are in the bounds of the Austrian Empire into a new state. That includes Croatia, Slavonia, Bosnia, Herzogovina, Dalmatia into one single state. I know what your questions are. And he would group all the Poles into another state; the Austrians into another state; Transylvania into another, the Magyars or Hungarians strictly speaking into another state; the Italians left within the bounds of the Empire into a province, into an independent province, making Trieste an international port, something like the old free cities.

But this new Austria cannot be created by virtue of any power that the Emperor, or Professor Lammasch or their friends now possess. America must help us to do this. How? As a preface to his answer to "How," we, and I am always speaking of "we" as "Austria," have two great enemies. They are the Magyars, the Hungarians proper, who dominate the whole Empire and whose power is so great that we can do nothing. Our second great enemy, I think maybe equal enemy, is Prussia who because of our internal situation establishes practically a hegemony over us. America must save us from these two enemies. By how? By making it the explicit requirement or condition of peace that Austria shall give integration and autonomy to all the existing national groups within the boundaries of the Austrian Empire.

I naturally said—but this is quite in contradiction to Czernin. Do you mean to say that you would permit us to dictate as to the internal construction of your Empire. His reply was extraordinary: We will not only permit you, we beg you. The Emperor will embrace you. I could hardly believe my own ears. Then follows next. If America will make those explicit conditions of peace to us, we will accept them. We will then confront Germany with the demand that she make peace, and that we accept those conditions. Germany dare not refuse. Of course, I naturally said,—what if Germany refuses. First, Germany dare not refuse, and here came out a secret which he remembered very well but probably wanted me to infer it. If Germany refuses, Bavaria and Wurtemburg and all South Germany will refuse and join us, and, therefore, Germany dare not refuse. It will result in the instant breaking up of Germany. Still, I pressed the question—if she does? Then as a last resort Austria will separate and make her own peace.

He asked me then—of course this was two hours long and I am giving you the naked outline—he asked me then for a frank reply to all this, and I said, of course, you understand I only express my personal opinion, but it is now half past twelve o'clock and we have been together more than two hours, and I would prefer to think over this over night, Professor Lammasch, before I should tell you what I personally think, and then it is getting late and you are tired and ought to rest, and immediately he said,—then we will arrange for tomorrow for the same hour, if you will,—and to that I agreed. He said the house was at our disposal.

Now going on from there. I don't feel I can stop here even now. I must say what I think while it is on my mind, because I wouldn't want to have the responsibility of reporting and presenting all this without, however worthless it might be, saying how it appears to me. I must do that, because you see I gather this from the whole trend of everything. First of all, Austria is not playing Germany's game. Of that I am sure. I am sure that she is trying to use America to get free of Germany. On the other hand she is playing Austria'[s] game, and playing it for all she is worth. Secondly, she is playing the Pope's game. Behind all this nationality conversation that comes out, and he used the expression two or three times—a dream of the young Emperor encouraged in every way by the Pope to restore again in a modernized form the Holy Roman Empire. That I saw as of that the whole pattern was being woven, and I saw it all.

Now Professor Lammasch himself has the motive of: (one) to save Austria; (two) he has a very paternal feeling toward his pupil, toward the young Emperor personally. And that enters into it much more than an outlook upon the condition of the world as a whole so far as Professor Lammasch personally is concerned. That is a kind of a parenthesis.

Now going on again into the Emperor's dream. He sees that the old order passeth, and that whatever the future is it must be by some sort of seizure of the new order. He sometimes used to me the words of the Emperor. I was forced to feel this even though I wanted to feel something else. I went searching for a door as for hidden treasure. My whole attitude was of one wanting to see a door through which a possibility of building a bridge could be seen. But the whole attitude of the Emperor and even of Professor Lammasch, if you submit it to any kind of searching analysis, is that of wanting to capture and use the new order, and not to serve the new order. There is as much difference between the two as between heaven and hell, or black and white. It is the old method by which Constantine adopted Christianity and destroyed it; by which the Roman Catholic Church adopted St. Francis. It is the old method that has prevailed throughout history. And then this idea of handing out in a paternal way as of a benevolent autocrat liberties of a kind to peoples, thereby binding them by better chains, chains with more gold even, to the throne, seemed to me simply reactionism masquerading. I asked him many questions, but after all it was not the interest of these people, it was not actually a true vision of the new order, it was an attempt to really establish a benevolent autocracy in place of the old Habsburg autocracy. In other words across the golden bridge between Vienna and Washington it seemed to me that Austria wouldn't be walking into the future, but America would be walking into the past. That is the picture that came to me in the course of his presentation. And then finally I couldn't even with Professor Lammasch see anything but an almost greedy, evil, or in one sense parochial point of view. Good man that he is, I couldn't see that he understood, that there was anything that indicated he understood the programme which President Wilson had presented to the world of wanting, of literally making the world a world of democratic peoples, of free, self-governing peoples. I couldn't see that either he or the Emperor, as he presented it, had grasped that with mentality, that after all it was only a somewhat glorified and yet no less masquerading and sordid self-preservation that they were seeking for.

We could take advantage of this situation and make separate peace with Austria. Of that I am sure. I am also sure that if we did it, in the end the last state of the world might be worse than the first, but we would betray, and without meaning to, the hopes of all these peoples of the world that are looking to us. Even in this conversation it came out that not in the whole history of the world has the world so looked to a nation as it now looks to America. Looks to us, it trusts us. It looks to us to make good our platform of a world democracy and people in fellowship with each other. And so the world has never looked to a man as it now looks to President Wilson and has never trusted a man as it trusts President Wilson. And I came away feeling what I didn't want to feel. I wanted to find an open door, you see. I came away feeling that with all that I had in hand at that moment—we must let Austria wait, we must keep on. We really would destroy by this compromise, if we come to a measure of compromise, that faith that is rising in the hearts of all these peoples in the world, and I have been thinking ever since I left him that, terrible as it is, and I tell you ever since I have seen you last I have sweated blood every night over this, to say that is real, if it costs all these millions of our lives and actually breaks up and smashes the old world, and makes a new one, it is worth it. I came away with the feeling that this is a case of Satan appearing as an angel. You know the old expression. This is what I am saying to you. I haven't said anything to him.

T MS (WP, DLC).

Sir William Wiseman to Sir Eric Drummond and Arthur James Balfour

[Washington] February 4, 1918.

No. 49. Most Secret. Further notes on my interview with the President and Secretary of War, which lasted about three hours and covered various subjects. BAKER only stayed during discussions on military matters.

They discussed recent attack on War Department: BAKER's confidence is somewhat shaken, but the President is quite unmoved.

(A). President was entirely frank and showed a willingness to discuss any subject and listen to views opposed to his own. I am more than ever confident that he is most willing to cooperate with us, and is single-minded in his desire to win the war.

(B). I believe he will agree to have some American troops used with British in France. For political reasons, which in my opinion are sound, he feels that public opinion here must be carefully considered in carrying out such a scheme. It must not be said here that, instead of an American Army, the Americans are only depot battalions for British troops used thus to avoid trouble the British Government may have with their Labour Party on man-power. If it is done it must be shown as an effort on America's part additional to raising her national Army—as an emergency and temporary measure adopted by the American Commander-in-Chief in France. May I suggest a cable from you to the President appreciating difficulties with national sentiment here, and asking if we transport the six divisions mentioned we can rely on their being used in any way our Staff shows PERSHING to be necessary? I could get HOUSE to cable BLISS on the subject if you like.

(C). During the discussion I pointed out very plainly that it would be worse than useless to have an American Army in France too late—that is, if the line was broken. And equally useless to have an American Army if there was not sufficient shipping to carry supplies and food for civilian populations. Also that I did not think the American higher commands and staff would be sufficiently experienced this year to handle a large force, that is, half-a-million to a million men, even if the men and supplies were there. An inexperienced American Staff with however fine an army would be object of special attack by Germans and probably lead to disaster, terrible for the Allies but even worse for United States. The American failure to provide the estimated tonnage must now mean a readjustment of Allied plans on an important scale, and further emergency measures and sacrifices by America. I added READING would be here in a few days with definite proposals to lay before them, and begged that they should listen to him most carefully and act promptly on his suggestions in order to avoid the unthinkable failure of the Allied cause owing to lack of proper American co-operation.

(D). To all this the President and Secretary listened without taking offence and agreed there was much truth in it; also expressed themselves anxious for READING's advice and assistance.

(E). With reference to the proposed JAPANESE co-operation in Russia, I think President can be persuaded to agree if you persuade BLISS that the military end is practicable and likely to have substantial results and if the Japanese are approached confidentially and carefully sounded as to their attitude. The President is particularly anxious not to appear as obstructing any of your schemes.

(F). The Secretary of War wants to go to Europe on tour of

inspection in order to learn needs of situation at first-hand, and will do so if and when he feels the Senate enquiry into War Department has been satisfactorily answered.

(G). GENERAL LEONARD WOOD was sent abroad by Administration in the sincere desire to use even their most bitter political enemies if they could serve the country, but they regret to hear that he has been freely criticising the Administration and casting doubt on their ability to make any satisfactory showing. Unfortunately he has found sympathisers among highly-placed French and British persons whom he has quoted indiscreetly. BAKER points out that Wood has not the necessary information to speak with authority.

(H). The President told me he was thinking of again addressing CONGRESS on WAR AIMS in answer to HERTLING and CZERNIN. He wants to take the heart out of the German offensive by showing that German Government are sacrificing their soldiers for conquest, and that the Germans are not fighting a defensive war. He would say all questions at issue must be settled on basis of common sanction of all belligerents and not between any two. He remarked that as far as he was concerned he would not allow IRELAND to be dragged into a Peace Conference. He is anxious to reaffirm most strongly the doctrine "No annexations and no punitive indemnities," with (he says) the accent on "punitive." He proposes to point out the difference between Austrian and German aims, and say he would listen to any proposal from Austria but it would have to be made in public. He will not hold secret conversations. This would not be intended as offer of separate peace between America and Austria, but as the United States leading the way to a separate peace between Austria and the Allies.

(I). He asked my views: I urged that before addressing Congress he should exchange views with you informally and generally. He replied that he was always glad to exchange views with you and get your criticisms.

(J). His insistence on "No annexations" made me think of Colonial questions, which, however, we did not discuss, but I pointed out the danger of Germany purposely misinterpreting "No annexations" and accepting it as an offer to return to the statu quo. Also there might be some danger in publicly offering separate peace to Austria owing to ITALIANS who might consider such peace would be made at their expense. He took the first point, but is not very sympathetic to ITALIAN aims.

(K). Shortly after I left White House a cable was received giving text of SUPREME WAR COUNCIL message from Paris. I learned today that President was not altogether pleased or quite in agreement with the tone of message. He may make it clear in future that United States is represented on Supreme War Council only as far as military matters are concerned.

(L). From what he said I gather he wishes to make a practice of sending for me for similar conversations. I propose, with your consent, to inform him that this will be undesirable so long as LORD READING is in the country.

T telegram (W. Wiseman Papers, CtY).

Sir William Wiseman to Sir Eric Drummond

Washington Feb 4th. 1918

Yesterday President explained to me his views on proposed scheme for Japanese cooperation in Russia.

His judgment is against the proposal because

(a) He feels sure from conversation he had with Ishii that the Japanese will not agree to the proposition at any rate not in the way or on the scale which would make for success.

(b) He doubts if any military advantage which is likely to be achieved would justify the risk of our actions creating a serious anti-Allied and even pro-German sentiment in Russia.

On my suggestion President agreed to refer the proposition to General Bliss for his advice on the military part of the proposed undertaking and President will keep an open mind until he hears from Bliss.

He wants you to feel that he is anxious to cooperate in any scheme for improving conditions in Russia which in his judgment the U. S. can join with any reasonable hope of success.

Hw telegram (FO 115/2445, PRO).

From Edward Mandell House

Dear Governor: New York City. February 5, 1918.

I suppose you have seen that the London Daily News and some of the other liberal papers are attacking the statement made by the Supreme War Council.

A representative of the News came to see me about it and the mere fact that I refused to say anything was significant. I think you will find that the incident will have some elements of advantage to you. When you make your address there will be an immediate response and of such warmth that Lloyd George will hesitate to repeat such a blunder. Another effect will be to place the leadership more firmly in your hands.

It is not altogether a bad thing our not having a civil representative on the Supreme War Council. If I had been there this statement would not have been issued. Nevertheless, it would have been difficult to have kept them from doing something of a similar nature. They tried this repeatedly when I was in Paris, and my mere statement that the United States would not join them, and my cordial advice to them to go ahead alone, always had the desired effect. They pointed out that since the United States had a representative sitting, it would look very badly to issue a statement in which we did not join. I agreed that this was true, but I hoped they would use their own judgment.

Affectionately yours,   E. M. House

TLS (WP, DLC).

From Bernard Mannes Baruch

My dear Mr. President: Washington February 5th, 1918.

Actuated solely by my deep interest in the public good, may I presume to ask that before you come to a decision on the reorganization of the method of purchases you give me the opportunity to be heard.[1] With all the facts before you, I have unbounded confidence in your judgment.

In my opinion, much not alone of our naval and military efficiency and, therefore, success, but the unification and solidification of the people behind the war, depends upon this method. Great confusion has already taken place and more is taking place and will continue to take place, unless steps are taken to correct it.

Sometimes things go so far that it becomes humanly impossible to correct without much unnecessary suffering. If it were solely a question of business, I would not ask to be heard, but the increasing confusion and consequent loss of confidence are bound to have an effect far reaching and perhaps disastrous.

Sincerely yours,   Bernard M Baruch

TLS (WP, DLC).
[1] Wilson saw Baruch on February 7.

From Newton Diehl Baker, with Enclosure

Dear Mr. President: Washington. February 5, 1918.

I have just received the enclosed note from Mr. Baruch, which I pass along to you so that you can note the only doubt he has about the letter which I sent you as being expressive of his views and mine in the matter of the future organization and functions of the War Industries Board.

Respectfully yours,   Newton D. Baker

TLS (WP, DLC).

E N C L O S U R E

Bernard Mannes Baruch to Newton Diehl Baker

My dear Mr. Secretary: Washington February 4th, 1917 [1918].

I received this morning a copy of your letter addressed to the President. I am wondering whether the letter was definite enough as to our thoughts that this agency should be an individual who decentralizes the execution of his authority. In the letter you speak of it as a body, which gives the impression that we thought it should be a board, whereas I understood we were both agreed it should be one man.   Sincerely yours,   B M Baruch

TLS (WP, DLC).

From William Gibbs McAdoo

CONFIDENTIAL.

Dear Mr. President: Washington February 5, 1918.

Senator J. T. Robinson's enemies in Arkansas are trying to induce somebody to enter the forthcoming primary against him. The Senator is such a warm friend and strong supporter of the Administration and is needed so much in Washington, that it would be unfortunate if he was obliged to devote any part of his time to an unnecessary campaign in Arkansas. He has been somewhat in doubt about making the race.

I was talking to him the other day, and it seemed to me that if you would write the Senator a letter saying in effect that you learn with regret that he is somewhat in doubt about seeking a reelection to the Senate and that you hope sincerely this is not true because it would be a misfortune to the country if it should lose his valuable services in the Senate, it would be of great service to the Senator and might forestall a hostile move.

I told the Senator that I would ask you if you would feel at liberty to write such a letter. I hope you may see your way to do it.

Cordially yours,   W G McAdoo

TLS (WP, DLC).

Hugh Robert Wilson to Robert Lansing

Pontarlier (Berne) Feb. 5, 1918.

2578. Strictly confidential. Supplementing my 2570, Feb. 4, 10 a.m.[1] Interview therein described was held in a house near Berne belonging to Von Muehlon[2] formerly director of *Maceration*[3] works. He became believer in international disarmament and resigned in 1910. Kaiser begged him to retain position which he did until July 1914 at which time he repudiated action Germany, declared himself squar[e]ly against Kaiser and left Germany and has since lived in retirement in Switzerland.

He informed Herron, on whom he made great impression for ability and character, that while Lammasch had not confided in him yet he knew what was going on and desired to tell Herron that the whole thing was a delusion since neither Emperor Charles, Lammasch, Foerster or any of those men, good men though they were, were able to put through such a program.

Muehlon's opinion This man may be secret agent of Kaiser. If so, this just what he would say.[4]

He urged strongly that America hold out and declared that not until February second had he realized that a revolution is possible in Germany. He has seen friends straight from Germany and he now knows that a revolution is possible. He told Herron to inform President Wilson that a revolution is preparing and is actually under way in Germany and that it will be a real one. The revolution is springing up out of the earth like the French revolution. The Socialist leaders have lost control of the working men and are trying to prevent revolution but cannot control it. He does not think that Kaiser or Junkers or Socialist leaders can now stop the movement. He therefore urges that America hold on. He stated you do not need to make a great offensive or even great demonstration. Just hold fast, do not let Germany break through and let German people see that Germany cannot break through.

Maybe German subterfuge to prevent dealing with Austria otherwise why oppose what would aid German revolution?

He analyzed the spirit in Germany and declared that ten years before the war he felt that his country would be the ruin of humanity. Germany must repent and acknowledge her wrong doing or she will continue to menace humanity. She must repair the wrong of Belgium and the wrong of Alsace Lorraine.

He then informed Herron that on July 15, 1914, he had a conversation with Helferich[5] in which latter outlined program for beginning of war. Von Muehlon has written a memorandum of this conversation and has attempted in vain and is still attempting to get it published in some German paper over his signature. He gave Herron a copy for transmission to the President but with the understanding that the President keep it confidential until such time as Muehlon advises him that the obligations for secrecy is removed. He will remove obligations if he fails in his last attempt to get it printed within Germany.[6] Translation of memorandum follows in subsequent telegram. In view of highly confidential and important nature this document I am transmitting it in dekic code.[*]

Wilson.

[*] Mixed Blue Code.

T telegram (R. Lansing Papers, NjP).

[1] See n. 1 to H. R. Wilson to RL, Feb. 4, 1918, printed as Enclosure I with H. R. Wilson to RL, Feb. 4, 1918.

[2] Dr. Wilhelm von Muehlon, a lawyer from Bavaria, had been an official of the German Foreign Office in 1907 and 1908. On Chancellor Bernhard von Bülow's recommendation, he was employed in 1908 by the Krupp firm in Essen, where he became private secretary to Gustav Krupp von Bohlen und Halbach. Muehlon was appointed to the Krupp company's board of directors in 1911. He was involved in diplomatic negotiations in the Moroccan crisis of that year and in buying wheat from Rumania in 1914. He resigned from the Krupp firm late in 1914 and moved to Switzerland in 1916. At this time he lived at the Chateau Hofgut at Gümligen, near Bern.

[3] Probably a garble for Krupp or one of its components.

[4] Marginalia RLhw.

[5] Karl Theodor Helfferich, who in 1914 was the Director of the Deutsche Bank, was at this time in charge of coordinating the German government's work in formulating economic peace terms.

[6] Muehlon's memorandum, "The Viennese Ultimatum to Serbia," was published in the *Berliner Tageblatt* on March 21, 1918, and an English translation was printed in the *New York Times* on April 21, 1918. For further details about Muehlon's disclosures, see G. D. Herron to WW, May 31, 1918, n. 8.

Frank Lyon Polk to Arthur Hugh Frazier

Washington, February 5, 1918.

3149. Strictly confidential. For Frazier.

Department is not entirely satisfied with the liaison established for reporting the activities of the Supreme War Council and, accordingly, requests that in future the following procedure be adhered to:

(1) Cables pertaining to matters considered by Supreme War Council should be sent by code clerk (Byars)[1] in code given General Bliss by Department, except when resolutions are quoted and these should be quoted in blue. The contents of these cables should be known only to General Bliss, Byars and yourself and in case cables are very confidential you should do first coding yourself. You should

advise General Bliss that this is the fact so that he will feel perfectly free to cable most confidentially to the Secretary of State.

(2) Cable reports should be much fuller and should contain not only resolutions adopted by Council but also as much information as it is possible for you to obtain privately concerning the views of the military and civil members of the Council; also substance of discussions preceding adoption of resolutions and confidential comment that you may secure from influential persons concerning activities of Council.

(3) If possible forecasts of probable future action of Council should be cabled Department. In this connection, Department points out that in your 3088, January 24, 4 p.m. you stated, QUOTE It is now probable that the Prime Ministers will not sit at War Council meeting on twenty-ninth instant UNQUOTE. Department received no notice of change of plan until your 3117, January 31, 6 p.m., announcing meeting on January thirtieth at which French, British and Italian Prime Ministers were present.

(4) Colonel House has asked Department to cable you that he does not wish you to send him cables in code through French Consul General in New York. Colonel House states that it is exceedingly inconvenient for him to decode these messages, and, accordingly, he wishes any messages that you may have for him to be sent through Department.

(5) Your 3134, February 2, 8 p.m. indicates to Department that British, French and Italian Prime Ministers do not fully understand that the United States Government has no diplomatic or political representative on War Council and that General Bliss's function is purely military. Department's impression in this respect is confirmed by your 3135, February 2, 11 a.m., containing statement authorized for publication by Supreme War Council. This statement begins, QUOTE The Supreme War Council gave the most careful consideration to the recent utterance, et cetera UNQUOTE. What must have been meant was that the British, French and Italian Prime Ministers gave the most careful consideration, et cetera. Further, the text of the official statement of the Conference states prominently that QUOTE Mr. A. H. Frazier, First Secretary of the United States Embassy at Paris was present during the political discussions UNQUOTE. No mention was made of the capacity in which you were present. Department is most particular that in future it be clearly understood that you attend the meetings of the Council simply for the purpose of reporting its proceedings, but with no voice in the political discussions. You should make it very clear to the members of the Council that this Government objects to the publication by the Supreme War Council of any statement

of a political character which carries with it the inference that the United States Government, on account of your presence and the presence of General Bliss, has been consulted and approves of such statement. You should point out to the members of the Council that statements issued by the Supreme War Council upon which the United States Government has a military representative naturally carry the inference that they are issued with the approval of the United States Government. The United States Government objects to the issuance of such statements by the Council as may in any way be considered political unless either (1) the text of the statement is first referred to the President for his approval or (2) it is expressly stated in the statement that it is made upon the authority of France, England and Italy and that it has not been submitted to the Government of the United States.

(6) What is meant by language in your 3135, February 2, 11 a.m. to the effect that QUOTE The functions of the Council itself were enlarged, et cetera UNQUOTE. Does this mean anything further than that subcommittees mentioned in your 3014, January 10, 3 p.m. and 3088, January 24, 4 p.m. were provided for and that control of reserve mentioned in your 3061, January 18, 6 p.m. was agreed to.

(7) The Department is cabling Ambassador Sharp modifying Department's No. 2996, of December 29, 1917.[2] In the future you will devote all your time to the work of the Supreme War Council in the capacity of diplomatic liaison officer to General Bliss. Department trusts that, relieved of your duties at the Embassy, you will be in position to keep Department much more fully informed of the political and military proceedings of the Council. The importance of these proceedings and of the informal discussions held outside regular meetings requires in the opinion of the Department daily reports by you. You should advise Department promptly if you require further assistance in your work and if you fully understand views of Department as expressed above.   Polk Acting

TLS (SDR, RG 59, 763.72Su/17b, DNA).
[1] Winfield Scott Byars.
[2] This telegram is missing in the State Department's files.

To Joseph Patrick Tumulty[1]

Dear Tumulty: [The White House, c. Feb. 6, 1918]

It is very clear to me that the commercial travelers of the country can be of the utmost service to the Government and in that way to the whole world by taking pains to acquaint themselves with the real facts of governmental activity and of governmental policy, facts which the Committee on Public Information will, I know, be glad to supply them with in perfectly unpartisan form, and then making themselves agents to see to it that everybody they run across gets straightened out as to what the facts really are and so gets in an attitude of support and cooperation rather than of criticism and pulling-apart.

For example, if they would make themselves thoroughly familiar with the recent statement of the Secretary of War, they would be equipped to discuss the preparations of the Government as they could be equipped in no other way. They could then read, as they chose, the testimony taken before the Military Affairs Committee of the Senate with a view to getting the mistakes and delays into proper perspective and relation to the work as a whole.

I almost envy them their opportunity to do work of this sort, because I want the people of the country ready to know and understand. When they do know and understand, I am sure their enthusiasm in supporting the Government will be increased and confirmed. The President.

TL (WP, DLC).
¹ Tumulty had passed along to Wilson a letter transmitted by Allen Towner Treadway, a Republican congressman from Massachusetts. The letter, from Ralph E. Bullard, senior counselor of the Springfield Council No. 12 of the United Commercial Travelers of America, stated that commercial travelers met and conversed with all classes of people all over the country, including the cracker-barrel orator, the soap-box spellbinder, and "all sorts of 'isms' and 'ists.' " Bullard asked whether Treadway could get Wilson to state "in just a few words one thing we Commercial Travelers as good Americans can do to help 'Win the War.' " Treadway offered to forward to Bullard any statement that Wilson might choose to prepare. A. T. Treadway to JPT, Feb. 4, 1918, TLS, enclosing R. E. Bullard to A. T. Treadway, Feb. 1, 1918, TL, both in WP, DLC.

To John Sharp Williams

My dear Senator: The White House 6 February 1918

Thank you for having let me see Mr. Erving Winslow's letter.¹ I appreciate the force of what he suggests about Russia, and I do not know that I have ever had a more tiresome struggle with quicksand than I am having in trying to do the right thing in respect of our dealings with Russia.

With the deepest appreciation of your fine speech of the other day,² Cordially and sincerely yours, Woodrow Wilson

TLS (J. S. Williams Papers, DLC).
¹ J. S. Williams to WW, Feb. 5, 1918, TLS (WP, DLC), enclosing E. Winslow to J. S. Williams, Feb. 2, 1918, ALS (J. S. Williams Papers, DLC). Winslow, who wrote on stationery of the Anti-Imperialist League, New Haven, Conn., had declared that a speedy victory in the war was necessary to forestall the serious menace of anarchy arising from war weariness and the example and propaganda of Russia. That country despised and rejected any alliance with orderly government, Winslow added, and "Heaven forbid"

any recognition by the United States. One hopeful possibility, in his view, would be to arrange free passage for Japanese troops to take up an offensive on an (unspecified) eastern front, with some "territorial gift" to Japan, while Russia was left to settle its own affairs. This, however, might mean an "Eastern Question" later on.

² Williams' speech of February 4 was in reply to one by Hitchcock, who had addressed the Senate to explain why the Committee on Military Affairs had recommended passage of the Chamberlain bills.

Williams, who had interrupted Hitchcock several times, responded that "any man ought to know who has any sense at all" that "Congress or a committee can not carry on a war and can not furnish the brains to anybody else to carry it on." Referring to the bill's requirement that the President appoint "three distinguished men of demonstrated ability," Williams then asked: "If the President is a fool, how are you going to give him brains by an act of Congress? If the President of the United States is not a fool, what is the need of your legislation?"

Shortly afterward, Williams rejected "this idle talk about passing a bill for a war cabinet 'in order to strengthen the arms of the President.'" To this he replied: "I should think when it came to the question of somebody strengthening my arms or holding up my hands, I would be the best judge; and I imagine the President is the best judge of whether he wants that sort of strengthening or not. You know that is not the intention of it, as well as I do; you know it is a usurpation by the legislative of executive authority; and, if you are lawyers, you know that it is absolutely unconstitutional.

"Do you know what I would do if I were President of the United States and you dared pass that war cabinet bill on me? I would veto it first; and then if you passed it by a two-thirds majority, I would utterly refuse to obey it, upon the ground that the Constitution invested certain duties and liabilities in me, and that I could not forsake them." *Cong. Record*, 65th Cong., 2d sess., pp. 1607-19.

To Joseph Taylor Robinson

My dear Senator: [The White House] 6 February, 1918

I have been distressed to hear that you were somewhat in doubt about seeking a reelection to the Senate. I hope with all my heart that there is no foundation for this impression. I should deem your retirement from the Senate a real national loss. My close and confidential association with you has taught me to value your counsel and your support in these trying times in a very unusual degree, and I am writing this as an earnest and friendly protest against any thought you may have had of retiring. This is a time when it is necessary that men who know each other's talents and principles and objects, and who feel themselves united in a common cause, should stand together not only, but keep together. I know that is your own thought and spirit, and it is because I have found your aid and counsel so exceedingly valuable that I am making this appeal to you.

Cordially and sincerely yours,   Woodrow Wilson

TLS (Letterpress Books, WP, DLC).

From Edward Mandell House

Dear Governor: New York. February 6, 1918.

I hear that Stet[t]inius is being thought of as head of the War Industries Board.

McAdoo and Tumulty think it would be a mistake and I am inclined to agree with them. I am afraid it will look too much like the Morgans are running things. Could he not be used to the same advantage under someone else? I merely make the suggestion without thoroughly knowing the situation.

Affectionately yours, E. M. House

TLS (WP, DLC).

From Newton Diehl Baker

Dear Mr. President: [Washington] February 6, 1918

Both of these letters are interesting.[1]

General Wood went to France, just as one of thirty-two division commanders, to see what he should teach his troops here. Had he not gone there would have been a storm here, as it is he immediately begins a plot, over there, to undermine Gen Pershing. Would it not be wise for you to talk to Lord Reading a bit, so as to prevent the possibility of Mr Lloyd George embarrassing us by any request for a return of Gen Wood, via London?

Respectfully, Newton D. Baker

ALS (N. D. Baker Papers, DLC).
[1] They are missing.

From Charles Scribner

Dear Mr. President: New York Feb. 6, 1918.

Messrs. Harper & Brothers have written to us requesting that we transfer to them the right to publish "An Old Master."[1] You may remember that in 1912, when you were Governor of New Jersey, we wrote suggesting a republication of the book but you did not think at that time that such a republication was desirable as an independent book, though you did write that at some time it might come into a set of your collected works unaltered. Without hesitation we have given to the Harpers the right to publish the book in such a collected set but they desire the complete transfer. As we have never given up the hope that in connection with some new material the book might be reissued under our imprint, we are reluctant to abandon all claim to it, though on every ground we shall be governed by your wishes in the matter. If you do not think that your interests would be sufficiently met by the inclusion of the book in the collected works and prefer now that we give up any idea of a future reissue, a note from you will be sufficient and not misunderstood. It seems to us that a volume of literary essays in our hands would in no way interfere with a collected set and would extend the circulation and influence of your work, though we can appreciate the desire of Messrs. Harper & Brothers to become your exclusive publishers.

Please give this question your consideration and let us have a line from you directly at your convenience. I do hate to bother you with any personal question: my excuse is that this is a matter in which you also are personally interested.

Yours sincerely   Charles Scribner

TLS (WP, DLC).
[1] That is, Woodrow Wilson, *An Old Master and Other Political Essays* (New York, 1893).

From Frank Latimer Janeway[1]

My dear President Wilson: New York City February 6, 1918

Next Monday morning Chaplain Frazier U.S.N.[2] is going to present me, with some others, to Secretary Daniels as a candidate for a commission as Chaplain in the Navy. As you may know Chaplain Frazier is in charge of the bureau for recruiting men for the chaplaincy.

Would you be so kind as to grant me your endorsement as I apply for this position? When I was Secretary of the Philadelphian Society at Princeton you knew my work intimately. You knew somewhat of my work when I was minister of the Church at Dartmouth College, and on one occasion at the suggestion of Professor Miller[3] you offered me a position at Princeton under your administration there. For the last six years I have been the associate minister at the Brick Church here in New York. On the strength, therefore, of your knowledge of my work and in remembrance of the many courtesies you showed me in the days when I was placed in intimate association with your leadership, I presume to make this request.

Might I ask that the reply be sent c/o Hotel Raleigh, Washington D. C. "to be called for."

Thanking you sincerely for your consideration of this request, with warm personal regard, I am

Very respectfully yours,   Frank Latimer Janeway

TLS (WP, DLC).
[1] The Rev. Frank Latimer Janeway, Princeton 1901, associate minister of The Brick Presbyterian Church of New York.
[2] Capt. John Brown Frazier, U.S.N.
[3] That is, Lucius Hopkins Miller.

Hugh Robert Wilson to Robert Lansing

Pontarlier (Berne) Feb. 6, 1918.

2582, Highly confidential. At the end of conversation reported my 2570, February 4, 10 A.M. Lammasch requested from Herron expression of latter's views on proposal. In view duration of conversation and Lammasch's ill health, Herron agreed on his own initiative to return and give his views at subsequent interview.

Herron thereupon reported to me first conversation and sketched what he intended to reply. He declared that he had received impression running through entire conversation that primary object of Emperor and Lammasch in proposal which latter had outlined was to save and glorify Hapsburg dynasty and to establish a modernized Holy Roman Empire by a form of imperial *gift*. Herron stated that after considering carefully Lammasch's statements he felt that it was based on uprighteous [unrighteous] compromise with old order and medievalism and that Emperor should throw himself upon generosity of his people and take step spontaneously recognizing liberty and autonomy of racial units without outside pressure from President or Pope.

While I recognize that Herron's solution was ideally the best, I pointed out to him practical difficulties and that what Emperor and Lammasch propose was in reality a great step in advance and that it was but hardly humanly possible to expect more at the present time. I advised Herron that if he desired to reply to Lammasch outlining his obligations he should prelude his remarks not only by a statement of his entire unofficial position but a declaration sufficient to convince Lammasch of that unofficial position.

At subsequent interview, acquiescing in my request to make his position clear, Herron began by stating that he had informed me literally and accurately as possible Lammasch's proposal for transmission President Wilson. Herron continued stating Lammasch must understand Herron could not even attempt to guess what President's decision would be. About that he had absolutely nothing to say. Herron stating plainly that in this case he had acted only as a reporter and that what he was about to say was literally and absolutely an expression of his personal views alone.

Herron then pointed out danger of spread of Bolcheviki doctrines

Probably correct[1]

and that in Europe there was utter lack of leadership. No great man had arisen to meet occasion. Further, Europe bound up with obsolete diplomacy entirely inadequate to meet present situation.

Herron then endeavored to show that Emperor's proposal was really founded in unrighteousness and begged Lammasch to endeavor to persuade Emperor not to try to save Austria but to really try to save Europe; to seize this opportunity to take a great historical initiative. The opportunity will be short lived and Emperor should take whole measures and not half way ones. In present conditions it is the improbable that is most probable and that what may seem fantastic and great act of daring is the only thing that can save Europe from catastrophe, from a long war with America, or perhaps both. He urged Lammasch to appeal to a higher sort of ambition in the Emperor to act on his own initiative and give liberty of choice to his subjects as an act of faith rather than relying on external pressure.

Lammasch questioned as to attitude toward nationalities, what could be done with Italians. Herron replied, "Could not you create of the Irrendenta an Italian province giving Trieste the university that it wants and giving this Italian province autonomy without string to it, asking it to remain within the Empire for short time but agreeing after five or ten years of this experiment to have a plebiscite to decide what they wish?

This example of Herron's typifies the idea that he endeavored to bring home to Lammasch, for the entire Empire.

Affected by his appeal Herron declared that he was sure if Emperor would voluntarily take such a step not only the President but America as a whole would rise up and acclaim him. The Emperor need not bargain. Lammasch seemed much moved and stated he would do his utmost to present the case adequately to the Emperor.

Questioning why the Pope could not take the initiative Herron replied that America and England in large percentage are protestant and would only have faith if the Emperor, the ruler of the nation, took the step.

Then Lammasch inquired, relative to the point on which Herron had laid so much stress (that Austria must take initiative) as to whether Herron saw any objection in the President making just some kindly recognition of what Czernin had said and then have the Emperor act according to the program which Herron outlined. Herron again emphasized the fact that he could not answer for the President but that he could see no possible objection to it but the matter was, of course, entirely for the President's decision.

Lammasch begs that if President decides to give this cue it be done at the earliest possible moment because it will have perhaps a very decided effect upon the terrible *chemical* offensive which the Germans are proposing.[2] If he gives the cue and then Austria can respond and something is under way such action will, if it does nothing else, limit the vitality of the offensive to some extent.

I feel that Professor Herron has sketched the ideal solution for this tremendous question but I do not feel that because the Lammasch solution falls short of the ideal, it necessarily be discarded when it represents as I believe this does a vast step in advance for all the oppressed racial units of Austria-Hungary. Admitting that the Emperor is striving for the glorification of his dynasty his manner of achieving this end is such that it would give to the subject races a far higher form of political freedom than they have enjoyed under the Empire and as great a measure of autonomy as many desire. It must be considered that the agreement by the Emperor to take this step on his own initi[a]tive without being able to offer the hope of immediate peace as recompense will very possibly plunge his country into civil war with a foreign enemy with Irredentist dreams still on its flank. While there is no reason to make a pact of devious diplomacy with the Austrian Government, one might at least extend a helping hand in expressing recognition of the change in tone of the Austrian statesmen.

As for the feasibility of the plan outlined by Lammasch, I fail to see how America can lose by a first declaration such as the Emperor desires. Obviously if it works out according to their hopes we will gain thereby. Equally obviously if the plan fails and civil war in cooperation with the difficulties with Germany result it will contribute by so much to the weakening of the resistance of Central Powers. Furthermore the fact that Austria-Hungary and America were growing closer together would render it excessively difficult for the pan-Germans to whip up the flagging energies of the German people into a new offensive. It must be borne in mind, however, that the Emperor and Lammasch will encounter tremendous opposition which may be so strong as to render impossible the realization of any portion of their program.

Respectfully suggest that the four telegrams 2544, January 31, 4 P.M., 2570, February 4, 10 A.M. 2571, February 4, 11 A.M.[3] and this be considered as a unit in order to gain comprehensive view of conversations.

Lammasch returned last night to Vienna.   Wilson.

T telegram (R. Lansing Papers, NjP).

  [1] RLhw.

  [2] German newspapers were at this time boasting that the German army now possessed a new and "more deadly gas," which it would use with terrible effect in its forthcoming offensive on the western front. *New York Times*, Feb. 21, 1918.

  [3] An error by H. R. Wilson, or in transmission, or by the decoder. Wilson undoubtedly meant Telegram No. 2578 of February 5.

To Frank Irving Cobb

Personal.

My dear Mr. Cobb: The White House 7 February, 1918

Your editorial, "Vicious and Unconstitutional,"[1] I had seen and it is certainly unanswerable. But, after all, answers do not reach these gentlemen no matter how overwhelming and convincing. Their purpose is not to help but to take the management of the war out of my hands. Senator Chamberlain is in conference much more often with systematic opponents of the administration than with its friends, and is particularly exposed to be used by those Republicans who find it intolerable that this war should be under Democratic direction. They seem apparently to believe that the only real executive ability in the country is possessed by Republicans and that the country is unsafe so long as Republicans do not dominate the guiding counsels of the country. They are a singularly provincial and small-minded coterie, representing not the great body of Republicans in this country, but only certain preconceived notions and small privileged groups.

Cordially and faithfully yours,   Woodrow Wilson

TLS (IEN)
[1] The New York *World* had printed two editorials under the heading "Vicious and Unconstitutional," the first on January 22, the second on February 3, 1918. Both strongly opposed Chamberlain's "War-Cabinet" bill.

To Joseph Patrick Tumulty

Dear Tumulty: [The White House, c. Feb. 7, 1918]

I am very sorry but I can't do this,[1] because, while I enjoyed the play and thought it very beautiful, there were some things about Mr. Barrymore's acting which did not seem to me an interpretation of the real Peter Ibbetson. The book[2] upon which the play is founded happens to be one with which I am especially familiar, because it fascinated me, and I could not write about the play without a criticism which would be entirely useless, now that it has been on so long and the method of its presentation so firmly established in the habit and conception of the players themselves. Personally, I enjoyed it very much.   The President.

TL (WP, DLC).
[1] The Wilsons had seen *Peter Ibbetson* (book by John N. Raphael), with Constance Collier and John Barrymore in the leading roles, at the Belasco Theater on February 1, and Miss Collier wrote the next day to Tumulty to ask if there was "the slightest hope" that Wilson could spare the time to write her "a little note to say if he liked it or not?" "I need hardly tell you," she added, "how tremendously I shall value it." Constance Collier to JPT, Feb. 2, 1918, TLS (WP, DLC).
[2] George Du Maurier, *Peter Ibbetson* (London and New York, 1891).

To Howard Alexander Smith[1]

My dear Mr. Smith:　　　　[The White House] 7 February, 1918

I have read your letter of yesterday with genuine interest.[2] It is upon a subject which has given me a great deal of thought first and last. I do not know whether your interesting suggestion is feasible or not, because when I made a different sort of attempt to organize and concentrate such activities I ran upon many difficulties, but I will take pleasure in discussing the matter with the Secretary of State, and thank you for your thoughtful interest.

Cordially and sincerely yours,　Woodrow Wilson

TLS (Letterpress Books, WP, DLC).
　[1] At this time, an assistant to Hoover in the Food Administration.
　[2] See n. 1 to the following document.

To Robert Lansing

My dear Mr. Secretary:　　　The White House 7 February, 1918

Here is a suggestion from an old acquaintance of mine which I would like to have you consider and give me an opinion about.[1] I have written to him that the matter presents a multitude of difficulties but that I would be very glad to discuss it with you.

Cordially and sincerely yours,　Woodrow Wilson

TLS (WP, DLC).
　[1] H. A. Smith to WW, Feb. 6, 1918, TCL (WP, DLC). Smith compared "a suffering and dying Europe and an America in comparative comfort and plenty," and he urged that the "highest destiny" of the United States was "to preserve life rather than destroy." American aid to suffering nations had been generous, he continued, but it had been "spasmodic, unscientific and local," and it had come essentially from individuals. Not all foreign needs were the same, and there were many complications. For this reason, he recommended "the nationalization of these endeavors and their public finance," with the appointment of an additional Assistant Secretary of State in charge of all relief activities. This post called for the "largest visioned man in the United States available." He would have "the most glorious opportunity to serve his country and the world that history has ever presented," and the United States would "intelligently and constructively" fulfill its national destiny.

From Gordon Auchincloss, with Enclosure

My dear Mr Wilson:　　　　　[Washington] Feb 7th, 1918

Mr. House asked me to send you this written by Bullitt.

Faithfully yours　Gordon Auchincloss

ALS (WP, DLC).

ENCLOSURE

Memorandum for Colonel House.

Subject: The Strikes in Germany.   Washington February 7, 1918

The strikes of the German workers began on Monday, January 28; reached their greatest extent on Thursday, January 31 and subsided on Saturday, February 2. The primary cause of the strikes was the failure of the German Government to obtain peace, which the strikers attributed to the refusal of the Government to offer peace on the basis of no annexations, no indemnities. The chief contributing causes of the strikes were: 1. The suppression of all peace meetings of the Independent Socialists and the readiness of the Government to allow the annexationist Fatherland Party to hold its meetings unhindered by the police. 2. The Prussian Diet's obstruction of the bill for reform of the Prussian Electoral Franchise. 3. Faulty distribution of food.

The strikes were brought into being by the Independent Socialists, who distributed secretly pamphlets urging the workers to strike as the only means of expressing their determination to have a peace of understanding at once.

At Berlin the strikes began on January 28. Conservative estimates placed the number of strikers on this day at 400,000. By January 31, the strikes had broken out in Hamburg, Cologne, Kiel, Ludwigshaven, Danzig, Mannheim, Nurenberg, Chemnitz and many other cities. At least 1,000,000 workers were striking on this day. The strikers were orderly; there were few riots and almost no lives lost. It was unnecessary in most cities for the police and military authorities to make good their threats to put down disturbances with an iron hand. The threats alone sufficed to drive the laborers back to work. By Saturday, February 2, the backbone of the strike had been broken and on Monday, February 4, work had been resumed by the majority of the strikers.

Although the strike was instigated by the Independent Socialists alone, the Majority Socialists at once supported it. They took the ground that they would not have started the strike, but that as it was a fait accompli and as they approved its purposes, there was no reason why they should oppose it. The stated purpose of the strikers was to force the Government to adopt the following program:

1. Peace without annexations or indemnities on the basis of the right of self determination.

2. Active participation by the workers of all countries in the peace negotiations.

3. Seizure of all food supplies in order to effect just distribution.

4. Removal of the state of siege and of militarization of the factories.

5. Liberation of persons imprisoned for political offenses.

6. Democratization by the introduction of equal suffrage in Prussia.

The strikes were condemned by the entire press except that of the Socialists; but there was a decided line of cleavage between the method of dealing with the strikers advocated by the annexationist press and the method advocated by the liberal press. The Conservative press and the jingo papers of the National Liberals and the Centrum advocated immediate suppression of the strike by military means. The FRANKFUERTER ZEITUNG, the BERLINER TAGEBLATT and the MUENCHENER NEU[E]STE NACHRICHTEN, on the other hand, advised the government to accede to the demands of the strikers for immediate Electoral Reform and for an immediate declaration of Germany's readiness to make peace on all fronts without annexations or indemnities on the basis of the right of self-determination.

The Government adopted the course desired by the annexationists. The Secretary of State for the Interior[1] refused to meet the strikers' executive committee of seventeen. Hindenburg issued appeals and threats. The commanders of the army corps on duty in cities where the strikes had broken out forbade under heavy penalties all meetings to discuss political matters of any sort and threatened all strikers with immediate service at the front. Dittmann,[2] a member of the strikers executive committee of Berlin, was arrested and condemned to five years imprisonment. The police broke up all attempted street demonstrations. As a result the strikers were cowed into submission. And the Government made no concessions.

But, as the BERLINER TAGEBLATT wrote on February 3, after the strikes had been crushed: "Even if the strike is soon ended, the attitude of the Government towards the workers is bound to have serious political consequences. The Fatherland party was countenanced in many ways; but when the workers requested a conference, formal objections were raised. The Government tactics are short-sighted. *A movement of this sort can be stifled; but that is not the point. The workers must be kept in the humor to work for the commonwealth. We fear the Government's circuitous policy will reduce its parliamentary basis, cause radicalization of the Socialist Majority, as well as of the Labor Unions, and leave a sting in the working classes.*"

This brief resumé of the events in Germany during the past ten days is drawn from cables to the Department. Press dispatches indicate that the Government is punishing with great severity many persons connected with the strike. It is further reported that the Reichstag is to meet on February 19 to debate the events of the past ten days.

Before the Reichstag meets the President must give the German Socialists new ammunition for their attacks on the Government. If the Socialists should be confined to defending their actions during the strike, they would be wholly on the defensive, and might lose much of the power they have to-day. And this is particularly true because of the Versailles Declaration:[3] No blow at the German Socialists, no blow at world liberalism, has ever been better timed than that declaration. No words have ever been more welcome to the German Government. The Versailles Declaration renders ridiculous the demands of the German Socialists for a conciliatory attitude on the part of the German Government. And unless the President shall deliver another great liberal statement before the meeting of the Reichstag, the German annexationists may well succeed in their present attempt to discredit the Socialists utterly in the eyes of the non-Socialist liberals of Germany.

But if the President does reply in the most liberal spirit to the statements of Hertling and Czernin, the temporary defeat of the Versailles Declaration may be retrieved. Czernin is about to return to Vienna without the peace with Ukrainia which he promised his war-weary people. How have the people of Austria reacted to the military suppression of the German strikes? Their bitter hatred of the German annexationists must have been further inflamed. If the President should take the general line indicated in previous memoranda, in his reply to Hertling and Czernin, he might produce another revolt of the weary, disillusioned Viennese proletariat and in consequence, a great renaissance of the strike spirit in Germany. For the spirit of the Socialists in Germany is by no means dead. They are for the moment defeated and dispirited. But they are sore and angry. New inspiration from the President and new events in Austria will restore their courage and their fighting spirit.

But the Versailles Declaration and the return of Czernin to Vienna empty handed make it supremely desirable that the President should speak soon.   Respectfully submitted: William C. Bullitt

TS MS (WP, DLC).
[1] Max Wallraf (Ludwig Theodor Ferdinand Wallraf), former Mayor of Cologne.
[2] Wilhelm Friedrich Dittmann, a member of the Reichstag and of the Independent Social Democratic party.
[3] That is, the statement by Clemenceau, Lloyd George, and Orlando, printed as an Enclosure with WW to RL, Feb. 4, 1918 (third letter of that date).

From Joseph Patrick Tumulty

Dear Governor: The White House 7 February 1918.

Since our little talk a few days ago with reference to Bernard Baruch, I have thought of the effect upon the country of the selection of the man you have in mind. I refer to Mr. S.[1] I am surprised to find already a disaffection among a great many of our friends who are wondering about the consequences of such an appointment. For instance, this point of view has been brought to me by persons who, I know, are friendly to us: As you well know, the German propagandists in this country are very anxious not only to provoke our laboring men but also the masses generally, by making them believe that this is a capitalists' war. Your Administration has been singularly free from any possible suggestion of this sort. Will we not play into the hands of the bolsheviki not only in this country but abroad? Will we not also weaken the hand of Mr. Gompers who will be accused of working hand in glove with a Morgan partner?

Then too there is another side of it that appeals to me. It is a well known fact that our industries benefitted considerably in the two years prior to the entrance of the United States into the War. We have been accused of "bleeding" our Allies. It is also a well known fact just how the purchases were made and a great many people have not hesitated to say that the fiscal agents of the Allies were so closely linked up with the other corporations in this country as to make many people apprehensive as to whether the same inter-corporation arrangements will not be in vogue once more when the same man does the purchasing for us. As I have often told you, I would not have suggested Baruch six months ago if I had not heard praise of him on every side. Just the other day a friend of mine was talking with Chandler Anderson who is, as you know, a Republican. Anderson has been inside of Baruch's organization for the last several months, and he told this friend of mine that Baruch had a very splendid system and was doing great work. One thing is certain,—that we know where Baruch stands because he has been with us from the start. We are sure of Baruch's vision, loyalty and generous sympathies. Are we sure of the other man? Can we take a chance?
                    Sincerely yours,   J P Tumulty

TLS (WP, DLC).
[1] That is, Edward R. Stettinius.

From John Miller Baer[1]

My dear Mr. President: Washington, D. C. Feb. 7, 1918

I want to offer to you the services of the Nonpartisan League to help remove whatever impression on the public mind, may have been caused by newspaper reports of criticisms of the Administration's war policies and administrations.

I have a letter from Mr. A. C. Townley, the President of the League, asking me to make this specific offer of services to you. It has always been the purpose of the League to support you and your Administration. This is the plain fact, though it has been the earnest effort of our political enemies to make things appear otherwise. It is true that there has been some dissatisfaction among farmers about what they think to be the "half-way" method of price fixing. But as your aims are understood that dissatisfaction has disappeared. We want to help to make those aims even more plainly understood.

In the Northwest it seems to us that the powers that be in that territory are striving, industriously, to undermine your Administration under the guise of "constructive" argument. We really believe that our experience in meeting such attacks, as they have been directed by partisan politicians in an effort to destroy our organization, makes us particularly able to help you.

The Nonpartisan League has great strength in thirteen (13) states. It has hundreds of speakers and organizers travelling and talking to the people all the time. The people in our territory are mostly farmers who have confidence in our organization. It is their own. Will you use us? We have an enthusiastic desire to use our influence in any way that you or any Governmental Department may suggest.

Sincerely and respectfully yours,   J. M. Baer[2]

TLS (WP, DLC).
  [1] Congressman from North Dakota, the first Nonpartisan Member of Congress.
  [2] See WW to J. M. Baer, Feb. 18, 1918.

A Memorandum by Colville Adrian de Rune Barclay

Feb 7, 1918
Handed to me by Br. Charge. FLP
Washington, February 6th, 1918.

MEMORANDUM.

No. 153 SECRET. With reference to their memorandum no. 112 Secret of January 28th,[1] the British Embassy have received a further telegram from the Foreign Office directing them to suggest to the United States Government that if it is decided to approach the Japanese Government on the subject, the opinion of the latter should be invited as to the feasibility of the occupation of the Trans Siberian Railway and further as to whether they would be willing to undertake this operation.

His Majesty's Government are of the opinion that, provided the means of transport are available, it would be in the power of the Japanese Army to occupy the whole Trans Siberian Railway, as they are informed that no organised military opposition is to be expected.   Colville Barclay

TS MS (SDR, RG 59, 861.00/1098, DNA).
   ¹ Printed as an Enclosure with FLP to WW, Jan. 29, 1918.

Arthur James Balfour to Edward Mandell House[1]

For E.M.H. from Balfour.   [London, Feb. 7, 1918]

I should be very grateful if you felt able to communicate following to the President as a personal message from me.

We have received the following information from a source in touch with Count Czernin and there is every reason to believe that it has been communicated to us under instructions.

Count Czernin is understood to be in favor of a separate peace but wishes to find a pretext for breaking with Germany such as that his hand has been forced by the Austrian nation. Public opinion in Austria is wearied by the way in which peace negotiations with Russia are being spun out without results. The Emperor of Austria himself is in favor of a speedy peace as he fears the red wave. Tension between Austria and Germany is greater now than at any time during the last four years. Germans are furious with Czernin and reproach him with having acted in such a conciliatory way as to cause the President to make peace proposals as if latter were victorious. If Austria could be given to understand that in concluding a separate peace she would obtain from America the financial assistance which is absolutely indispensable to her, public opinion would be strong enough to impose such a peace even on partisans of a "war to the end." The expediency of America acting as an intermediary between Austria and the Entente is especially emphasized. This is the first authentic suggestion we have received that Austria is contemplating the possibility of a separate peace. It may be due to a passing mood. It may be part of some scheme to divide Entente powers. In any case however we are disposed in principle that matter should not be allowed to drop and that for many reasons the American Government is the one best able to deal with it effectively. If they are willing to do so I would venture very respectfully to suggest that while on one hand it is important that Count Czernin should not feel his message has been ignored so on the other hand no haste should be shown in coming to closer quarters with Austrian negotiatiors. All our accounts go to prove that the condition of Austria is very bad not merely economically but socially and if violent suppression of strikes in Germany stimulates revolutionary feeling in Austria, as well it may, this will probably combine with and reinforce Slav, Bohemian and Polish National aspirations which are threatening the unity of the Austrian-Hungarian Empire.

We know by experience that mere rumour of negotiations in Vienna on the basis of an undivided Austria not only causes great alarm in Italy but is at once used by Austrian diplomats as a proof that the Entente has abandoned the cause of all the subject nationalities under the Hapsburg rule, a support [report] which greatly weakens our friendship[s] and heartens our enemies. These however are considerations which are as familiar to U.S.G. as to ours and though they show the extreme delicacy of the questions to be solved they indicate that of all the Entente powers America is in the best position to solve them.

HwC telegram (WP, DLC).
   ¹ Another copy of this document is E. Drummond to W. Wiseman, Feb. 7, 1918, T telegram (W. Wiseman Papers, CtY).

Sir Eric Drummond to Sir William Wiseman

[London] February 7, 1918.
Your telegram No. 48: Following from BALFOUR:
Please express to ADRAMYTI [WILSON] my gratitude for the exposition of his views regarding the disposal of AMERICAN troops in front. I appreciate highly the frankness of this communication, and I have never for a moment doubted that he is actuated in this, as in all other questions, solely by consideration for the common good.

Speaking for myself, I attach the greatest weight to his arguments. American soldiers must feel that they belong to an American Army fighting under American flag. It is only on these terms that the best can be got out of them, or that they can count on the enthusiastic support of the American people. I know that these views were strongly pressed by GENERAL PERSHING at Versailles, but I understand proposals were there made which in his view would enable small American units to train, and, if need was considerable, to fight in the immediate future in companies with French or English troops without interfering with or delaying the creation of a great American army. If so, early and much needed assistance would be given us on the Western front without hindering the realization of legitimate American ideals. I hope I am right.

I need hardly add that I am entirely at the President's disposal if anything I can do can help to make the position easier.

T telegram (W. Wiseman Papers, CtY).

An Outline of an Address to a Joint Session of Congress

[c. Feb. 8, 1918]

THE CONDITIONS OF A GENERAL PEACE.

Czernin's utterances gratifying as conceived in a humane and statesmanlike spirit, but afford no defined ground for conference and seem to contemplate separate pourparleys with the U. S.

The thing at stake now is *the peace of the World.*

All must be participants in the discussion of that.

Every item in that becomes the business of all.

Hertling's reply is the very negation of general peace and makes one fear he has no conception of how it can be brought about.

If separate discussions and agreements about territorial changes which in fact affect the peace of the whole world, then separate discussions and agreements about raw materials and trade arrangements and opportunities.

The United States has no desire to interfere in European affairs or to act as arbiter in European territorial disputes, but she has entered the world war (for such it has become) and cannot see her way to peace until the causes of that war are removed and its renewal rendered unlikely.

And is quite ready to be shown that the settlements she has outlined are not the best or the most enduring.

The only way that can be done is by seeing to it that Justice is made the rule of every settlement; and that includes

The reasonable satisfaction of national aspirations;

The unqualified acceptance of the principle that peoples and provinces are not to be handed about from sovereignty to sovereignty as if they were chattels and subjects of bargain and sale;

A clear recognition of the principle that all settlements are to be made in the interest and for the benefit of the peoples concerned and not as parts of an adjustment and compromise of claims amongst rival governments.

Are the Central Empires ready for a general peace erected upon such foundations?

If not, they can have no separate peace.

WWT MS (WP, DLC).

A Draft of an Address to a Joint Session of Congress

[c. Feb. 8, 1918]

GENTLEMEN OF THE CONGRESS: On the eighth of January I had the honour of addressing you on the conditions of a general peace which I took to be necessary in the view of our people. The Prime Minister of Great Britain had spoken in similar terms on the [blank] of January. To these addresses the German Chancellor replied on the [blank] and Count Czernin, for Austria, on the [blank] It is gratifying to have our desire that all exchanges of view on this important matter should [be] made in the hearing of all the world so promptly realised.

Count Czernin's reply, which is directed chiefly to my own address of the eighth of January, is uttered in a very friendly tone. He finds in my statement a sufficiently encouraging approach to the position of his own Government with regard to a final accommodation to justify him in expressing, as he does very courteously, the opinion that it furnishes a basis for a more detailed exchange of views between the Government of the United States and the Government of Austria-Hungary. He is represented to have intimated that the views he was expressing had been communicated beforehand to me and that I was aware of them at the time he was uttering them; but in this I am sure he was misunderstood. I had received no intimation of what he intended to say. There was, of course, no reason why he should communicate privately with me. I am quite content to be one of his public audience.

Count von Hertling's reply was in a very different tone and apparently of an opposite purpose. It confirmed, I am sorry to say, rather than removed, the unfortunate impression made by what we had learned of the conferences at Brest-Litovsk. His discussion of general principles, we are given to understand, has no practical application to the particular items which must constitute the substance of any final settlement between the nations now at war. He is jealous of international action and of international counsel. He accepts, he says, the principle of public diplomacy, but he insists, nevertheless, that the several questions upon whose settlement must depend the acceptance of peace by the eighteen nations now engaged in the war must be discussed, not in general council, but severally by the nations most immediately concerned by interest or neighbourhood. He agrees that the seas should be free, but looks askance at any limitation to that freedom by any international action in the interest of the common order. He would be glad to see economic barriers removed between nation and nation, for that could in no way impede the ambitions of the military party with whom he seems constrained to keep on terms. He raises no objection to a limitation of armaments. But the German colonies must be returned without debate. He will discuss with no one but the representatives of Russia what disposition is to be made of the peoples and the lands of the Baltic provinces; with no one but the Government of France what shall be done with French territory and with no one what shall be done with regard to Alsace-Lorraine, and only with Austria what shall be done with Poland. In the determination of what shall be done with regard to all Balkan questions he defers to Austria and Turkey, Germany's allies, and with regard to the agreements to be entered into concerning the non-Turkish peoples of the present Turkish Empire to Turkey the Ottoman authorities themselves. Austria and Italy must settle for themselves the questions at issue between them. After a settlement all around effected in this fashion, by individual barter and concession, he would have no objection, if I correctly interpret his statement, to a League of nations which would undertake to hold the new balance of power at a stable equilibrium.

It must be evident to everyone who understands what this war has wrought that no general peace, no peace worth the infinite sacrifices of these years of tragical suffering through which the peoples of the world are now passing, can possibly be arrived at in any such fashion. The method the German Chancellor proposes is the method of the Congress of Vienna. We cannot and will not return to that. What is at stake now is the peace of the World. Is it possible that Count von Hertling does not see that, does not grasp it, is in fact living in his thought in a world dead and gone? He has utterly forgotten the Reichstag Resolutions of the nineteenth of July. They spoke of the conditions of general peace, not of national aggrandizement or arrangements between state and state. The peace of the world depends upon every item of the settlement which I proposed in my recent address to the Congress. I of course do not mean that the peace of the world depends upon the acceptance of any particular set of suggestions as to the way in which those items I then set forth are to be dealt with. I mean only that those problems each and all affect the whole world; that unless they are dealt with in a spirit of unselfish and unbiassed justice, with a view to the wishes, the natural connections, the racial aspirations, the security and the peace of mind of the peoples involved no permanent peace will have been attained. They cannot be discussed separately or in corners. None of them constitutes a private or separate interest from which the opinion of the world has been shut out. Whatever affects the peace that is to end this war affects mankind.

Is Count von Hertling not aware that he is speaking in the court of mankind, that all the awakened nations of the world now sit in judgment on what every public man, of whatever nation, now says on the issues of a conflict which has spread to every region of the world? The Reichstag Resolutions of July accepted the decisions of that court. There shall be no annexations, no contributions, no punitive damages. Peoples are not to be handed over from one sovereignty to another by an international conference or an understanding between rivals and antagonists. National aspirations must be respected; peoples must be dominated or governed only by their own consent. 'Self-determination' is not a mere phrase. It is an imperative principle of action, which statesmen will ignore at their peril. We cannot have general peace for the asking, or by the mere arrangement of a peace conference. It cannot be pieced together out of individual understandings between powerful states. All the parties to this war must join in the settlement of every issue anywhere involved in it; because what we are seeking is a peace that we can all unite to guarantee and maintain and every item of it must be submitted to the common judgment whether it be right and fair, an act of justice, not a bargain.

The United States has no desire to interfere in European affairs or to act as arbiter in territorial disputes. She is quite ready to be shown that the settlements she has suggested are not the best or the most enduring. They are only her own sketch of the principles that ought to be followed. But she has entered this war because she was made a partner, whether she would or not, in the wrongs which it inflicted, and the conditions of peace will touch her as nearly as they will touch any other nation to which is entrusted a leading part in the maintenance of civilization. She cannot see her way to peace until the causes of this war are removed, its renewal rendered as nearly as may be impossible.

This war had its origin in the disregard of the rights of small nations and of nationalities which lacked the union and the force to make good their claim to determine their own allegiances and their own forms of political life. Covenants must be entered into which will render such things impossible for the future and those covenants must be backed by the united force of all the nations that love justice and are willing to maintain it at any cost. If territorial settlements and the political relations of great populations are to be determined by the contracts of the powerful governments which consider themselves most directly affected, why may not economic questions also? It has come about in the altered world about us that justice and the rights of peoples affect the whole field of international dealing as much as access to raw materials and fair and equal conditions of trade. Count von Hertling wants those essential bases of commercial and industrial life to be safeguarded by common agreement and guarantee, but they cannot be if the other matters to be determined by the articles of peace are not handled in the same way as items in the final accounting. He cannot ask the benefit of common agreement in the one field without according it in the other. I take it for granted that he sees that selfish compacts with regard to trade and the essential materials of manufacture would afford no foundation for peace. Neither, he may rest assured, will separate and selfish compacts with regard to provinces and peoples.

Count Czernin sees this fundamental element of peace with clear eyes and does not seek to obscure it. He sees that an independent Poland, made up of all the Polish peoples who lie contiguous to one another is a matter of European concern and must of course be conceded; that Belgium must be evacuated and restored, no matter what sacrifices and concessions that may involve; and that national aspirations must be satisfied in the common interest of Europe and mankind. He is silent about questions which touch the interest and purpose of his allies more nearly than they touch those of Austria only, I suppose, because he feels constrained to defer to them in the circumstances. Seeing and conceding these things, he naturally feels that Austria can respond to the terms of peace proposed by the United States with less embarrassment than could Germany or Turkey and Bulgaria. He could probably have gone much farther had it not been for the embarrassments of Austria's alliances and of her dependence on Germany.

It is not clear whether, in inviting a further comparison of views between the United States and Austria he meant to suggest that that exchange should be made privately and confidentially or made publicly and before all the world. He will realize, I am sure, that the United States can confer with regard to these great matters which concern all only in the presence of all. She could conform sincerely to her own fundamental condition of peace in no other way. And, after all, the test of whether it is possible to go any farther in such comparisons of view is very simple. Count von Hertling seems disposed to accept some of the fundamental conditions of peace in principle, but he rejects them in fact. Does Count Czernin think that his Government and the people for whom it speaks would be willing to accept these principles and would wish, fearlessly and impartially, to apply them?

First, that peoples and provinces are not to be handed about from sovereignty to sovereignty as if they were chattels and pawns in a game, even the great game, now forever discredited, of the balance of power; but that,

Second, every territorial settlement involved in this war must be made in the interest and for the benefit of the populations concerned and not as a part of any mere adjustment or compromise of claims amongst rival states; and,

Third, that the utmost satisfaction must be accorded all well defined national aspirations that can be satisfied without introducing new elements of discord and antagonism that would be likely in time to break the peace of Europe and consequently of the world?

A general peace erected upon such foundations can be discussed. No other peace can be. No separate peace would be worth while if it did not manifestly constitute part of such a general peace, in which there was no other rule but justice and fair dealing to all concerned.

I would not be a true spokesman of the people of the United States if I did not add that we have entered this war upon no small occasion. We have great resources and a resolution that never turns back from a course chosen upon principle. Our resources are in part mobilized. Our armies are rapidly going to the fighting front, and will go more and more rapidly; and behind the million and a half men now in training or ready for the line of battle there are ten million more. All our resources and all our men will be put into this war of emancipation,—emancipation from fear and the mastery of selfish groups of autocratic [masters,]—whatever the difficulties and present partial delays, even if we have to build every ship that is to take them over and make them effective across the sea. No reverses can dismay us or divert our purpose. We are indomitable in our power of independent action and can in no circumstances consent to live in a world governed by intrigue and force. We beli[e]ve that our own desire for a new international order under which reason and justice and the common interests of mankind shall prevail is the desire of enlightened men everywhere. Without that new order the world will be without peace and human life without tolerable conditions of existence and development. Having set our hands to the task of achieving it, we shall in no circumstances turn back.

I hope that it is not necessary for me to say that no word of what I have said is intended as a threat. That is not the temper of our people. I have spoken thus only that the whole world may know the true spirit of America,—that men everywhere may know that our passion for justice and for self-government is no mere passion of words but a passion which, once set in action, must be satisfied. The power of the United States is a menace to no nation or people. It will never be used in aggression or for the aggrandizement of any selfish interest of our own. It springs out of freedom and is for the service of freedom.[1]

WWT MS (WP, DLC).
[1] There are occasional WWsh notes of a few paragraphs of this document in WP, DLC. As House notes in the extract from his diary printed below, Wilson did not make a shorthand draft.

A Petition[1]

The President: Washington, D. C., February 8, 1918.

Desiring earnestly to support and assist the Government of the United States in winning the war, we, representatives of the Federal Board of Farm Organizations and other farmers' organization, whose names will be found appended, including in all more than 3,000,000 organized farmers, have assembled in Washington to discuss ways and means for increasing the production of food at the coming harvest.

As set forth in the memorial of the Federal Board of Farm Organizations, submitted to you on January 22, 1918,[2] a reduction in the amount of the coming crop is certain and unavoidable unless certain causes, all of them beyond the control of the farmers, are recognized and removed. We speak with all respect, but definitely, because we know the facts of our own knowledge, and because the time during which effective action can still be taken to increase the coming crop is short.

The chief obstacles which must be removed before the farmers of America can equal or surpass this year the crop of 1917 are:

1. Shortage of farm labor.

2. Shortage of seed, feed, fertilizers, farm implements, and other agricultural supplies.

3. Lack of reasonable credit.

4. Prices often below the cost of production.

5. The justified belief of the farmer that he is not regarded as a partner in the great enterprise of winning the war.

Farmers by themselves are powerless to remove these obstacles. Unless the Government grasps the vital seriousness of the situation and forthwith takes steps to help, a crop shortage is certain in spite of any and all things farmers can do to prevent it.

The Government, we understand, will spend some $4,000,000,000 to assist commercial enterprises to produce munitions of war. We approve of this action, recognizing that it is necessary. Assistance for food production in this crisis does not involve any such vast expenditure. But without such assistance, vigorously and promptly given, it will remain impossible for farmers to grow the crops required. The Government should not hesitate to assist in the production of one sort of supplies essential to win the war when it has already spent vast sums to assist in the production of others.

We deem it our duty to advise the Nation of these facts in order that the threatened danger may be minimized if not entirely prevented, and we respectfully suggest the following remedies:

1. As to labor, the parole of trained farm workers back to the farm, to remain there so long as their services are considered by the Government to be more useful in productive agriculture than in the Army. The last classification of registrants under the present selective draft, we are informed, is not being uniformly enforced, and in particular we understand that skilled farm workers, farm foremen, and bona fide farmers are being placed in class 1. We ask for such an interpretation of the rule as will make such cases impossible. We welcome the assistance of all organizations that are helping to furnish labor in the production of food, and we believe that their services should be employed as fully as possible.

We ask for such interpretation of the selective draft as will secure to the Nation the services of all of its citizenship where those services are of most value to the Nation, and for binding instructions to be issued to all boards to that effect. Especially do we ask that the definition of a skilled farm laborer be a man who is actually engaged in productive agriculture, and is supporting himself in it, without regard to college or university training.

2. As to farm supplies, provisions should be made for furnishing to producing farmers who need them such seeds, feeds, fertilizers, and farm machinery at cost as may be actually necessary to maintain their production or to increase it within practicable limits. We urge the transportation of farm products and supplies by the most economic routes and the prompt movement of perishable crops in their season.

We urge that in carrying out the measures to win the war farmers' cooperative societies be given the same consideration that is given to other commercial organizations.

3. As to credit, steps should be taken by the Government to promote aggressively and in all practicable ways short-time loans to farmers for the purpose of financing the production of crops.

4. As to prices, should the policy of price control prevail, then we ask that it shall be applied as much to what the farmer buys as

to what he sells, to the end that consumer and producer be protected from exploitation.

5. As to representation, we recommend the immediate appointment of a farm commission, to consist preferably of nine farmers actually engaged in the business, to be selected by the President from men representative of and satisfactory to the great farm organizations of America, and to report directly to him on all questions that affect the increase of agricultural production and distribution. Such a commission should be authorized to secure information from all Government sources, and all departments of the Governments should be instructed to cooperate with it. It should be in uninterrupted session at the city of Washington, and provision should be made for necessary quarters and expenses by Federal action. The commission should be required, as its first task, to report at once upon all matters necessary in the immediate execution of recommendations Nos. 1 to 4 above.

Such a commission is needed first of all to give to the farmers of America a sense of partnership in the conduct of the war to which they have a right. The occasional consultation with farmers called to Washington or the occasional appointment of a farmer to a subordinate place does not amount to fitting participation in the conduct of the war on the part of one-third of the population of the United States, and all the more when that third produces the one form of supplies which is the most essential.

This plan would be in harmony with the procedure already adopted by the Government in other essential industries. The creation of such a commission would convince all farmers that their viewpoint was fully represented in Washington and always accessible to the President, and would inspire and encourage them as nothing else could.

Immediate and vigorous action is imperative.

Printed in *Cong. Record*, 65th Cong., 2d sess., pp. 1979-80.
[1] Wilson, on February 8, received this petition from a delegation from the Federal Board of Farm Organizations, which represented seventeen national organizations. The spokesman was A. C. Davis of Gravette, Ark., national secretary of the Farmers' Union.
[2] There is a brief note about this "memorial" in the *New York Times*, Jan. 23, 1918. If this document reached the White House, Wilson probably never saw it, and it was not saved.

Remarks to Farmers' Representatives

Gentlemen: 8 February, 1918.

I cannot, of course, off hand answer so important a memorial as this, and I need not tell you that it will receive my most careful and respectful attention. Many of the questions that are raised here have been matters of very deep and constant concern with us for months past, and I believe that many of them are approaching as successful a solution as we can work out for them. But just what those steps are, I can't now detail to you. You are probably familiar with some of them.

I want to say that I fully recognize, as Mr. Davis has said, that you gentlemen do not mean that your utmost efforts will be dependent upon the acceptance of these suggestions. I know you are going to do your level best in any circumstances, and I count on you with the utmost confidence in that. There has never been a time, gentlemen, which tested the real quality of folks as this time is going to test it, because we are fighting for something bigger than any man's imagination can grasp. This is the final struggle between the things that America has always been opposed to and was organized to fight and the things that she stands for. It is the final contest, and to lose it would set the world back, not a thousand, but perhaps several hundred years in the development of human rights. The thing cannot be exaggerated in its importance, and I know that you men are ready, as I am, to spend every ounce of energy we have got in solving this thing. If we cannot solve it in the best way, we will solve it in the next best way, and if the next best way is not available, we will solve it in the way next best to that, but we will tackle it in some way and do it as well as we can.

I am complimented by a visit of so large a representation and thank you for the candid presentation of this interesting memorial.

T MS (WP, DLC), with corrections from a reading of the CLSsh notes in the C. L. Swem Coll., NjP.

To Joshua Willis Alexander, with Enclosures

My dear Judge: The White House 8 February, 1918

Since Senate Bill #3387 raises some difficult questions in which may lurk considerable danger, I am taking the liberty of sending you the enclosed memorandum of the Attorney General regarding it. I know that you will be willing to give that memorandum your careful consideration.

With warmest regard,

Cordially and sincerely yours,   Woodrow Wilson

E N C L O S U R E   I

From Thomas Watt Gregory

Dear Mr. President: Washington, D. C. February 7, 1918.

I comply with your request made at the last meeting of the Cabinet at which I was present by sending you a memorandum to be made the basis of a letter addressed by you to Judge Alexander, Chairman of the House Committee on Merchant Marine, in regard to Senate Bill 3387.

You will note that this bill has already passed the Senate and is now before the House, having been reported out by the House Committee on Merchant Marine on January 29th with certain amendments which appear in italics in the copy of the bill herewith enclosed.[1] I am informed that the bill may be taken up by the House at any time.   Faithfully yours,   T. W. Gregory

TLS (photostats in RSB Coll., DLC).
[1] It is missing.

E N C L O S U R E   I I

Washington, D. C. February 7, 1918.

MEMORANDUM ON SENATE BILL NO. 3387.

This bill deals with two distinct subjects, namely, (a) the power to establish "a military or war zone" within defined areas surrounding any shipbuilding plant and (b) the power of the Government to acquire shipbuilding plants by condemnation, purchase, etc. The latter of these two subjects is not discussed in this memorandum.

The first section of the proposed bill, providing for the establishment of military or war zones reads in part as follows:

"That the President of the United States of America, as Commander in Chief of the Army and Navy, be, and he is hereby authorized and empowered from time to time to create and establish within the defined areas within and surrounding any shipbuilding plant, where vessels are under construction for the United States of America a military or war zone in order to protect the safety of such plant and to secure the successful prosecution of the work therein; that such designated area shall be directly under the control of the President with the right and authority to treat such area as if it were a fort, camp, or other military establishment of the United States of America, and that all laws applicable to forts, camps, or other military establishments shall be applicable to the zone or area so designated; and any person, persons, firm, or corporations who shall violate any such law shall be punishable in the manner therein provided."

The phase "military or war zone" has no fixed meaning or significance in civil law and its use in this proposed statute presents the serious question whether the courts would hold that civilian laborers working within such shipyard military zone would be subject to the rules of military law.

While the decisions are not without conflict, it has generally been held that civilians working in forts, camps and other stations of a permanent character, are not subject to the rule of military tribunals, even in war time. On the other hand civilian workmen or other civilians accompanying an army actually engaged in military operations in the field are subject to the Articles of War, (See R. S. Sec. 1342, Art. 2, Par. d). This distinction between civilians engaged in *camps* and military establishments of fixed location, as distinguished from civilians engaged with armies in the *field*, apparently rests on the theory that in war military operations in the field disorganize the local civil government and of necessity the military authorities must preserve order there by military law.

If Congress intends to leave the Civil Courts in control of shipyard areas then the provision here discussed is meaningless. If on the other hand, the courts should conclude that Congress meant to change the present status of shipyards by using the phrase "military or war zone," it is possible that the courts might rule that Congress intended by this to subject laborers within shipyard areas to military law. In either event, it is apparent that the enactment of the statute would cause great uneasiness and apprehension among laborers within these proposed shipyard zones. Large numbers of unskilled laborers are necessarily employed in these yards and the effect of such a bill could not be otherwise than disastrous in disrupting business organization.

This bill may be aimed at entirely different results, namely, either to provide military patrols for shipyards or to lay the foundation for promulgating vice and liquor regulations in and near shipyards. Legislation is not necessary in order to place shipyards under military guard. The President, by virtue of his power to regulate the conduct of enemy aliens, has already authorized the War Department to establish military patrols for the enforcement of alien enemy regulations in water-front areas and by similar action he can at any time authorize the War Department to establish military patrols surrounding other barred zones. If the intention of this measure is to lay the foundation for establishing liquor and vice zones in areas surrounding shipyards this can be accomplished in a simple and expeditious manner by adding appropriate brief amendments to Sections 12 and 13 of the Selective Service Act of May 18, 1917.

T MS (photostat in RSB Coll., DLC).

To Charles Scribner

My dear Mr. Scribner: The White House 8 February, 1918

No apology was needed for your kind letter of February sixth. I am heartily glad that you should have such a desire as you express about publishing for me again something in addition to my little volume, "An Old Master," but as I look forward to my tasks, even after the end of my term as President, I must admit that I see little opportunity or prospect ahead for writing any essays which I could use for additional volumes. All my life I have had a definite plan in mind with regard to what I wanted to write,[1] which has been set aside and postponed by one task after another, and if this office does not entirely wear me out, I want to turn to that as soon as I can.

I am very much gratified that you should be willing to turn the little volume, "An Old Master," over to the Harpers. I believe that their intention is to use it only as a part of an edition of my collected writings, and as I see no prospect of adding to it in kind, I should suppose that was the only part it would play in my future publications.   Cordially and sincerely yours,   Woodrow Wilson

TLS (WC, NjP).
[1] His ill-fated "Philosophy of Politics."

To Charles Ashford Greathouse[1]

[The White House]
My dear Mr. Greathouse: 8 February, 1918

When the Democratic Editorial Association of Indiana meets on the twenty-fifth, will you not convey to the Association my very cordial greetings? The editors of the country have a great responsibility at present, the responsibility of holding the attention of the country steady to the truth. Extraordinary efforts are being made, I am afraid, to mislead the people with regard to the actual facts of the war administration, and there is a particularly strong effort being made to take the direction of the war out of the hands of the constitutional authorities. The best way to meet such efforts and to neutralize unfair opposition is to bring the actual truth constantly to the attention of the people. The things that are wrong must and will be corrected, but the things that are right must and will be maintained, and the cure for all distempers is in every instance the real facts. These I shall always be rejoiced to have the people of the country know, and I am sure I can count on the loyal editors of the country everywhere and of whatever party to put upon those facts the true and just interpretation.

A task of unparalleled magnitude and dignity is now imposed upon the United States and I for one have supreme confidence in the wish and power of our people to rise to the great opportunity.

Cordially and sincerely yours,   Woodrow Wilson

TLS (Letterpress Books, WP, DLC).
¹ Greathouse, the secretary and treasurer of Bookwalter-Ball Printing Co. of Indianapolis, was chairman of the Democratic State Central Committee of Indiana. He had served three terms as State Superintendent of Public Instruction.

To Frank Latimer Janeway

My dear Janeway: [The White House] 8 February, 1918

I have your letter of February sixth and am writing today directly to the Secretary of the Navy. I hope with all my heart your desire to serve as a chaplain may be gratified.

With the warmest regard,

Cordially and sincerely yours,   Woodrow Wilson

TLS (Letterpress Books, WP, DLC).

To Josephus Daniels

My dear Daniels: The White House 8 February, 1918

Frank Latimer Janeway, now the Assistant Pastor of the Brick Presbyterian Church of New York, is anxious, I learn, to get a commission as chaplain in the Navy. If there is a vacancy available, I hope sincerely he may get it. He was a pupil of mine at Princeton and is one of the finest fellows I have ever known. It is delightful to see such men turn to this service.

Cordially and faithfully yours,   Woodrow Wilson

TLS (J. Daniels Papers, DLC).

To Edith Kermit Carow Roosevelt

[The White House] February 8, 1918

May I not express my warm sympathy and the sincere hope that Mr. Roosevelt's condition is improving?[1]

Woodrow Wilson

T telegram (Letterpress Books, WP, DLC).
[1] Roosevelt had undergone minor surgery on both ears on February 6 and immediately developed a serious infection of the left inner ear. On the following afternoon, his condition was reported to be "serious but not critical." Roosevelt remained in the Roosevelt Hospital in New York until March 4. *New York Times*, Feb. 8 and March 5, 1918.

From Edith Kermit Carow Roosevelt

New York, February 8, 1918.

Many thanks for your kind message.

Edith K. Roosevelt.

T telegram (WP, DLC).

From John Sharp Williams

My dear Mr. President: [Washington] February 8, 1918.

I hope you won't misunderstand my forwarding you Mr. Erving Winslow's letter. Of course you are having "a tiresome struggle with the quicksands of the Russian situation." Don't go too fast about it. We are fighting for the liberties of the English speaking race; to go a step further, we are fighting for liberty, equality and fraternity, but we are not fighting for the universal license for everybody to rob everybody else. It may sound a bit impertinent right now to mention anything that I would do if I were the President of the United States, but if I were, there is one thing I would *not* do: I would not get mixed up in that Russian situation until I clearly knew what that Russian situation was.

Our political enemies very much ridiculed your policy of "Watchful waiting" with regard to Mexico. I do not hear much criticism of it now. A little "watchful waiting" with regard to Russia would not be "patience misapplied." It might even be patience very well applied. Of course the present situation is very much more quickening,—even soul quickening,—than the other in Mexico but the general principle to be found in the modification of moderation still applies.

I thank you for what you say about my speech the other day. I think it was the poorest speech I ever made during my entire political life. I had just come back from Billy Hughes' funeral,—sick, tired, worn out, cold to the point where the marrow in the bones had been nearly frozen,—and when I came into the Senate I found that Senator Hitchcock was speaking. I attempted to answer him. Nobody is more utterly aware of the fact that I did not completely answer him than I am. I struck him and his allies only in the high places. I did not go into details, first, because I did not have sufficient knowledge of the details; second, because I scorn details in the present situation. When it comes to converting an army of 200,000 men on paper into a million and a half of men and adapting all the executive instrumentalities of the Government to the work, everybody, not an ass, knew before hand that there would be multitudinous failures and inefficiencies, and that no one human mind could possibly correct them all, and furthermore, that no nine, or nineteen or thirty-nine human minds added to the one human mind, sitting in council as a board or a directorate, could act much better than one human mind could, if any better at all.

Very frequently it is better *to make a mistake quickly than to arrive at the right conclusion too late.* I do not regard myself as a fool exactly, but I frankly acknowledge that if I had been in Mr. Baker's place I could not have done as well as Baker has done. Suppose that in equipping, munitioning and supplying a million and a half of men, Chamberlain and Hitchcock and their ilk could be able to designate 100 cases in which there have been abuse, oppression, cruelty, disorganization, stupidity, and everything else. Suppose I, or somebody else, could disprove their contention in 75 of the 100 cases. Suppose that we could not disprove them in the balance. They would still have the better of the argument *as a matter of detail.* That is the reason why, in the speech which you were kind enough to praise, although it was the poorest production of my entire political existence, I did not go into details at all. Nobody has ever been able to count the specks on the sun they are so many, but the sun still shines, and it has just about as many specks on it in August as it has in December.

With every expression of regard, I am,

Very truly yours,   John Sharp Williams

TLS (WP, DLC).

From Bernard Mannes Baruch

My dear Mr. President: Washington February 8th, 1918.

I shall presume again to make the suggestion that when you have made your selection of the man to head the direction of purchases, as temporary Chairman of the War Industries Board, if you address a letter to him substantially covering the statement of your views as expressed to me yesterday, it would have a very helpful effect, not alone from the military and naval but also from the industrial and financial standpoint.

Some emphasis might be made of the maintenance of a standard of wages, hours and sanitary conditions and the direction of the placing of orders, so there shall be as little dislocation and congestion as possible through competition for the same materials and facilities.

Even if all orders were not directed by this central agency, copies of all orders placed should be sent to him in order that someone would know, not alone what materials and facilities we had but to what extent they had been drawn upon by all consumers.

Very truly yours,   Bernard M Baruch

TLS (WP, DLC).

From Louis Freeland Post

My dear Mr. President: Washington February 8, 1918.

May I offer a personal suggestion?

Now that the conscription law has been vindicated, would it not be desirable in the public interest, voluntarily to grant a blanket pardon to such of the persons early convicted under its provisions as were not consciously disloyal in their opposition to the law?

Such a pardon, with the reasons stated as you could state them— the fact that the law was a novelty to them, that it seemed inconsistent with their notions of American democracy, that their imaginations had not yet visualized to them our actual participation in the war, that theirs were first cases under a law that will be rigorously enforced in all future cases, and that they were not actuated by treasonable motives—would, I am confident, have a stimulating effect upon a large body of confused but nevertheless patriotic sentiment.

With great respect I am

Faithfully yours,   Louis F. Post

TLS (WP, DLC).

From the Diary of Colonel House

The White House, Washington, D. C. February 8, 1918.

Gordon called me over the telephone this morning at ten o'clock to say that the President was eager for me to come down as soon as possible. Through the assistance of Joseph Nye of the Secret Service I succeeded in getting off comfortably on the 11.08 train.

I reached Washington practically on time and drove first to 1827 Nineteenth Street to see Janet and Louise. I then came to the White House where the President was awaiting me. We immediately went into conference.

We first cleared the decks by reading all the despatches bearing on foreign affairs that had come during the day, and by reading the address to Congress which he had prepared and was holding for my criticism.

We did not finish and start to dress until seven minutes of seven. I walked out of my room at seven o'clock to find that the President had beaten me by a half minute. Both he and Mrs. Wilson are rapid dressers.

After dinner we went into executive session and continued until bedtime. I did not interrupt while he read the draft of the message, but I made mental notes of changes I thought necessary. When he had finished I praised it most cordially. I felt that it was a remarkable document, but I knew that much of it would have to be eliminated. I nearly always praise at first in order to strengthen the President's confidence in himself which, strangely enough, is often lacking, and it was particularly so of this address.

After I had praised it as a whole, we agreed to go over it in detail and criticise. Mrs. Wilson keeps the original manuscripts of these speeches. The President said he had departed from his usual custom and did not first write the address out in shorthand but had typed it from the beginning, and had written it disjointedly and in sections. He usually devotes hours at a time to these messages, but in this instance, on account of the pressure of affairs, he did not do so. The original typewritten manuscript will doubtless some day be published, and when published, the eliminations made will be seen. I have never advised a quarter as many eliminations in any previous address as in this one. He had something about Alsace and Lorraine which I asked him to cut out and explained why. He did so without comment. He did not argue with me at all when I pointed out changes. This in itself, showed that he was not confident.

The main eliminations were toward the end of the message. I objected to his stating that we had 1,500,000 men ready to go to

Europe and that we had 10,000,000 men that would go if necessary. I asked him to eliminate such statements because it seemed like boasting, and I thought the whole world knew, as well as he or I, of the resources of the United States, both in men and wealth. He accepted this quite cheerfully.

I objected to his making positive statements as to Czernin's opinions. In one instance I asked him to use the expression "it seems" rather than the more positive one which he used concerning Czernin. When we had finished polishing it off we went to bed with no conversation upon other subjects.

A Revised Draft of an Address to a Joint Session of Congress[1]

[Feb. 8-10, 1918]

GENTLEMEN OF THE CONGRESS: On the eighth of January I had the honour of addressing you on the ⟨conditions of a general peace which I took to be necessary in the view of⟩ *objects of the war as* ⟨*conceived by*⟩ our people *conceive them*. The Prime Minister of Great Britain had spoken in similar terms on the *fifth* of January. To these addresses the German Chancellor replied on the *twenty-fourth* and Count Czernin, for Austria, on the ⟨twenty-⟩ *same* ⟨*date*⟩ *day*. It is gratifying to have our desire *so promptly realized* that all exchanges of view on this ⟨important⟩ *great* matter should *be* made in the hearing of all the world ⟨so promptly realized⟩.

Count Czernin's reply, which is directed chiefly to my own address of the eighth of January, is uttered in a very friendly tone. He finds in my statement a sufficiently encouraging approach to the ⟨position⟩ *views* of his own Government ⟨with regard to a final accommodation⟩ to justify him in expressing ⟨, as he does very courteously, the opinion⟩ *the opinion*, that it furnishes a basis for a more detailed ⟨exchange of views between the Government of the United States and the Government of Austria-Hungary⟩ *discussion of purposes by the two Governments*. He is represented to have intimated that the views he was expressing had been communicated ⟨beforehand⟩ to me *beforehand* and that I was aware of them at the time he was uttering them; but in this I am sure he was misunderstood. I had received no intimation of what he intended to say. There was, of course, no reason why he should communicate privately with me. I am quite content to be one of his public audience.

[1] Words in angle brackets deleted by Wilson; words in italics added by him to the original draft.

Count von Hertling's reply ⟨was⟩ *is, I must say, very vague and very confusing. It is full of equivocal phrases and leads it is not clear where. But it is certainly* in a very different tone *from that of Count Czernin,* and apparently of an opposite purpose. It confirm⟨ed⟩s, I am sorry to say, rather than remove⟨d⟩s, the unfortunate impression made by what we had learned of the conferences at Brest-Litovsk. His discussion and acceptance of general principles ⟨, we are given to understand, has no practical application to the particular⟩ *leads him to no practical conclusions. He refuses to apply them to the substantive* items which must constitute the ⟨substance⟩ *body* of any final settlement between the nations now at war. He is jealous of international action and of international counsel. He accepts, he says, the principle of public diplomacy, but he ⟨insists, nevertheless, that⟩ *appears to insist that it be confined, at any rate in this case, to generalities and that the several particular questions of territory and sovereirgnty,* the several questions upon whose settlement must depend the acceptance of peace by the ⟨eighteen nations⟩ *twenty-three states* now engaged in the war must be discussed *and settled,* not in general council, but severally by the nations most immediately concerned by interest or neighbourhood. He agrees that the seas should be free, but looks askance at any limitation to that freedom by any international action in the interest of the common order. He would *without reserve* be glad to see economic barriers removed between nation and nation, for that could in no way impede the ambitions of the military party with whom he seems constrained to keep on terms. ⟨He raises no⟩ *Neither does he raise* objection to a limitation of armaments. *That matter will be settled of itself, he thinks, by the economic conditions which must follow the war.* But the German colonies, *he demands,* must be returned without debate. He will discuss with no one but the representatives of Russia what disposition ⟨is to⟩ *shall* be made of the peoples and the lands of the Baltic provinces; with no one but the Government of France ⟨what shall be done with French territory and with no one what shall be done with regard to Alsace-Lorraine⟩ *the "conditions" under which French territory shall be evacuated*; and only with Austria what shall be done with Poland. In the determination of ⟨what shall be done with regard to all Balkan questions⟩ *all questions affecting the Balkan states* he defers, *as I understand him,* to Austria and Turkey, Germany's allies; and with regard to the agreements to be entered into concerning the non-Turkish peoples of the present ⟨Turkish⟩ *Ottoman* Empire to ⟨Turkey⟩ the ⟨Ottoman⟩ *Turkish* authorities themselves. ⟨Austria and Italy must settle for themselves the questions at issue between them.⟩ After a settlement all around, effected in this fashion, by individual barter and concession, he would have no objection, if I correctly interpret his statement, to a League of nations which would undertake to hold the new balance of power ⟨at a stable equilibrium⟩ *steady against external disturbance.*

It must be evident to everyone who understands what this war has wrought *in the opinion and temper of the world* that no general peace, no peace worth the infinite sacrifices of these years of tragical suffering ⟨through which the peoples of the world are now passing⟩, can possibly be arrived at in any such fashion. The method the German Chancellor proposes is the method of the Congress of Vienna. We cannot and will not return to that. What is at stake now is the peace of the World. *What we are striving for is a new international order based upon broad and universal principles of right and justice,—no mere peace of shreds and patches.* Is it possible that Count von Hertling does not see that, does not grasp it, is in fact living in his thought in a world dead and gone? ⟨He has⟩ *Has he* utterly forgotten the Reichstag Resolutions of the nineteenth of July⟨.⟩ *or does he deliberately ignore them?* They spoke of the conditions of general peace, not of national aggrandizement or *of* arrangements between state and state. The peace of the world depends upon ⟨every⟩ ⟨each item of⟩ the *just* settlement ⟨which I proposed in⟩ *of each of the several problems to which I adverted in* my recent address to the Congress. I of course do not mean that the peace of the world depends upon the acceptance of any particular set of suggestions as to the way in which ⟨those items I then set forth⟩ ⟨the several⟩ *those problems* are to be dealt with. I mean only that those problems each and all affect the whole world; that unless they are dealt with in a spirit of unselfish and unbiassed justice, with a view to the wishes, the natural connections, the racial aspirations, the security, and the peace of mind of the peoples involved no permanent peace will have been attained. They cannot be discussed separately or in corners. None of them constitutes a private or separate interest from which the opinion of the world ⟨has been⟩ *may be* shut out. Whatever affects the peace ⟨that is to end this war⟩ affects mankind, *and nothing settled by military force, if settled wrong, is settled at all. It will presently have to be reopened.*

Is Count von Hertling not aware that he is speaking in the court of mankind, that all the awakened nations of the world now sit in judgment on what every public man, of whatever nation, ⟨now says⟩ *may say* on the issues of a conflict which has spread to every region of the world? The Reichstag Resolutions of July *themselves frankly* accepted the decisions of that court. There shall be no annexations, no contributions, no punitive damages. Peoples are not to be handed

⟨over⟩ *about* from one sovereignty to another by an international conference or an understanding between rivals and antagonists. National aspirations must be respected; peoples ⟨must⟩ *may now* be dominated ⟨or⟩ *and* governed only by their own consent. 'Self-determination' is not a mere phrase. It is an imperative principle of action, which statesmen will *henceforth* ignore at their peril. We cannot have general peace for the asking, or by the mere arrangement of a peace conference. It cannot be pieced together out of individual understandings between powerful states. All the parties to this war must join in the settlement of every issue anywhere involved in it; because what we are seeking is a peace that we can all unite to guarantee and maintain and every item of it must be submitted to the common judgment whether it be right and fair, an act of justice, ⟨not a bargain⟩ *rather than a bargain between sovereigns.*

The United States has no desire to interfere in European affairs or to act as arbiter in *European* territorial disputes. *She would disdain to take advantage of any internal weakness or disorder to impose her own will upon another people.* She is quite ready to be shown that the settlements she has suggested are not the best or the most enduring. They are only her own *provisional* sketch of the principles that ought to be followed. But she ⟨has⟩ entered this war because she was made a partner, whether she would or not, in the wrongs ⟨which it inflicted,⟩ *committed by the military masters of Germany against the peace and security of mankind*; and the conditions of peace will touch her as nearly as they will touch any other nation to which is entrusted a leading part in the maintenance of civilization. She cannot see her way to peace until the causes of this war are removed, its renewal rendered as nearly as may be impossible.

This war had its ⟨origin⟩ *roots* in the disregard of the rights of small nations and of nationalities which lacked the union and the force to make good their claim to determine their own allegiances and their own forms of political life. Covenants must *now* be entered into which will render such things impossible for the future; and those covenants must be backed by the united force of all the nations that love justice and are willing to maintain it at any cost. If territorial settlements and the political relations of great populations *which have not the organized power to resist* are to be determined by the contracts of the powerful governments which consider themselves most directly affected, *as Count von Hertling proposes*, why may not economic questions also? It has come about in the altered world ⟨about us⟩ *in which we now find ourselves* that justice and the rights of peoples affect the whole field of international dealing as much as access to raw materials and fair and equal conditions of trade. Count von Hertling wants these essential bases of commercial and industrial life to be safeguarded by common agreement and guarantee, ⟨but they cannot be⟩ *but he cannot expect that to be conceded him* if the other matters to be determined by the articles of peace are not handled in the same way as items in the final accounting. He cannot ask the benefit of common agreement in the one field without according it in the other. I take it for granted that he sees that *separate and* selfish compacts with regard to trade and the essential materials of manufacture would afford no foundation for peace. Neither, he may rest assured, will separate and selfish compacts with regard to provinces and peoples.

Count Czernin *seems to* see ⟨s this⟩ *the* fundamental elements of peace with clear eyes and does not seek to obscure ⟨it⟩ *them*. He sees that an independent Poland, made up of all the *indisputably* Polish peoples who lie contiguous to one another, is a matter of European concern and must of course be conceded; that Belgium must be evacuated and restored, no matter what sacrifices and concessions that may involve; and that national aspirations must be satisfied, *even within his own Empire*, in the common interest of Europe and mankind. He is silent about questions which touch the interest and purpose of his allies more nearly than they touch those of Austria only, ⟨I suppose,⟩ because he feels constrained *I suppose*, to defer to them in the circumstances. Seeing and conceding these things, he naturally feels that Austria can respond to the ⟨terms⟩ *purposes* of peace proposed by the United States with less embarrassment than could Germany ⟨or Turkey and Bulgaria⟩. He ⟨could⟩ *would* probably have gone much farther had it not been for the embarrassments of Austria's alliances and of her dependence on Germany.

⟨It is not clear whether, in inviting a further comparison of views between the United States and Austria he meant to suggest how such exchanges should be made that that exchange should be made privately and confidentially or made publicly and before all the world. He will realize, I am sure, that the United States can confer with regard to these great matters which concern all only in the presence of all. She could conform sincerely to her own fundamental condition of peace in no other way.⟩

⟨And⟩ After all, the test of whether it is possible *for either government* to go any farther in ⟨such⟩ *the* comparisons of views is ⟨very⟩ simple *and obvious*. ⟨Count von Hertling seems disposed to accept some of the fundamental conditions of peace in principle, but he rejects them in fact.⟩ Does Count Czernin think that his Government and ⟨the people for whom it speaks would be willing to accept these principles and would wish, fearlessly and impartially, to apply them?⟩ *his people are ready to take an attitude sharply contrasted with that of Count von Hertling and accept not only the general principles I have enunciated in the name of the people of this country but also the practical conclusions to which they lead? Those principles are:*

First, that peoples and provinces are not to be ⟨handed⟩ *bartered* about from sovereignty to sovereignty as if they were chattels and pawns in a game, even the great game, now forever discredited, of the balance of power; but that,

Second, every territorial settlement involved in this war must be made in the interest and for the benefit of the populations concerned, and not as a part of any mere adjustment or compromise of claims amongst rival states; and,

Third, that ⟨the utmost satisfaction must be accorded all well defined national aspirations that can be satisfied⟩ *all well defined national aspirations shall be accorded the utmost satisfaction that can be accorded them* without introducing new *or perpetuating old* elements of discord and antagonism that would be likely in time to break the peace of Europe and consequently of the world?

A general peace erected upon such foundations can be discussed. ⟨No other peace can be. No separate peace would be worth while if it did not manifestly constitute part of such a general peace, in which there was no other rule but justice and fair dealing to all concerned.⟩

Until such a peace can be secured we have no choice but to go on. I would not be a true spokesman of the people of the United States if I did not ⟨add that⟩ *say once more that* we ⟨have⟩ entered this war upon no small occasion. ⟨We have great resources and a resolution that never turns back from a course chosen upon principle.⟩ *We can never turn back from a course chosen upon principle.* Our resources are in part mobilized *now, and we shall not pause until they are mobilized in their entirety.* Our armies are rapidly going to the fighting front, and will go more and more rapidly ⟨; and behind the million and a half men now in training or ready for the line of battle there are ten million more⟩. ⟨All our resources and all our men⟩ *Our whole strength* ⟨and all our wealth⟩ will be put into this war of emancipation,—emancipation ⟨from fear, and the⟩ *from the threat and attempted* mastery of selfish groups of autocratic ⟨masters,⟩ *rulers*— whatever the difficulties and present partial delays. ⟨even if we have to build every ship that is to take them over and make them effective across the sea.⟩ No reverses can dismay us or divert our purpose. We are indomitable in our power of independent action and can in no circumstances consent to live in a world governed by intrigue and force. We beli[e]ve that our own desire for a new international order under which reason and justice and the common interests of mankind shall prevail is the desire of enlightened men everywhere. Without that new order the world will be without peace and human life ⟨without⟩ *lack* tolerable conditions of existence and development. Having set our hand⟨s⟩ to the task of achieving it, we shall ⟨in no circumstances⟩ *not* turn back.

I hope that it is not necessary for me to ⟨say⟩ *add* that no word of what I have said is intended as a threat. That is not the temper of our people. I have spoken thus only that the whole world may know the true spirit of America,—that men everywhere may know that our passion for justice and for self-government is no mere passion of words but a passion, which, once set in action, must be satisfied. The power of the United States is a menace to no nation or people. It will never be used in aggression or for the aggrandizement of any selfish interest of our own. It springs out of freedom and is for the service of freedom.

WWT MS (WP, DLC).

From the Diary of Josephus Daniels

1918 Friday 8 February

Cabinet—Baker brought up that John Mitchell and certain other miners had been cited to appear before Supreme Court for contempt.[1] They had been adjudged guilty because they had tried to organize labor in a factory where the employes had been coerced into signing an agreement that they would not join the union. Mahlon Pitney had written the decision of the court in the face of the fact that the Clayton anti trust act had exempted labor from the provision. The act charged was committed prior to Clayton act. W.W. spoke contemptuously of Pitney & lawyers who had learned nothing & did not know the age they are living in. Wilson to see Gregory and see if same course—postponing till after war—could not be taken as in case against Harvester and other trusts.[2]

Leonard Wood had sought to supplant Pershing by telling French & English if he were in command he would divide Am. troops up in companies & have them lost or united with English & French divisions.[3] Reading expected to request Wood to go to Europe. If he does, "I will not reply in diplomatic language" said WW

Morally not straight & not truthful

[1] A suit in equity, Hitchman Coal & Coke Co. *v.* Mitchell, Individually, *et al.*, had begun in the United States circuit (afterwards district) court for the northern district of West Virginia

on October 24, 1907, when Mitchell was president of the United Mine Workers. In 1918, Mitchell was no longer an officer of the union; he was chairman of the New York State Industrial Commission and president of the New York State Food Commission. Mitchell was not an "answering defendant" in the case, nor was William Bauchop Wilson, who had also been named in the original suit.

The facts of the Hitchman case are stated in detail in the opinion of the Supreme Court, delivered by Justice Pitney on December 10, 1917, and in the dissenting opinion by Brandeis, in which Holmes and Clarke concurred. The majority opinion upheld the "yellow dog" contract, that is, a written pledge by an applicant for a job that, as a condition of employment, he would not join a union. The plaintiff in this case, Pitney said, was entitled to protection, through the court's injunction, against union organizers. The case was remanded to the district court for further proceedings in conformity with the opinion. 245 U. S. 229.

The Supreme Court, on January 14, 1918, ordered President Frank J. Hayes, Vice-President John L. Lewis, Secretary-Treasurer William Green, and seven other members of the United Mine Workers to show cause why they should not be declared in contempt of court for violating an injunction restraining representatives of the U.M.W. from attempting to organize employees of the Hitchman company. The company had argued that intimidations and threats had reduced its work force. The court ordered the union officials to appear in court at noon on March 4. *New York Times*, Jan. 15, 1918.

[2] Gregory, on January 2, had asked the Supreme Court to defer argument on seven pending antitrust suits until the next term of the court. Gregory's brief stated that, during the war emergency, the government wished to avoid competition from private enterprises in its financial operations and that the dissolutions which were sought would require financial operations on a large scale. *New York Times*, Jan. 3, 1918.

[3] Daniels, quoting later from his diary, corrected this sentence as follows: "Leonard Wood had sought to supplant Pershing by telling the French and English that if he were in command he would divide American troops in companies and have them united with English and French divisions." Josephus Daniels, *The Wilson Era: Years of War and After, 1917-1923* (Chapel Hill, N. C., 1946), p. 290.

Three Letters from Robert Lansing

My dear Mr. President: Washington February 9, 1918.

The subject of which Mr Smith writes[1] is one which has by no means escaped the attention and earnest consideration of men of vision who look forward with concern to the mighty task which will be imposed upon the world after this war is ended. I have had numerous letters upon this subject, some very much in line with the one written by Mr. Smith, others based on an international credit system, and still others on private charities. The problem is a most difficult one and it cannot be readily solved, as every proposal has serious difficulties.

In the proposal of Mr. Smith the idea would require primarily the sanction of Congress. It could not be carried out without legislation, whether the funds were to be given or advanced as loans to the impoverished countries or nationalities. It would require enormous sums to make an impression on rebuilding the waste places. I doubt very much if Congress has attained that generous spirit which would insure legislation of that sort or whether the people would sanction it.

As to the machinery necessary to carry through efficiently so vast a scheme of restoration, that too would require Congressional action, and until the plan proposed is adopted in a general way I do not think that it would be especially advantageous to consider the agency.

The experience of this Department in relief work in the various countries occupied by Germany shows the problem to be one of great intricacy requiring a large and well-organized staff of individuals to insure economy and efficiency. To form such an organization before the work is determined upon in detail would be impossible.

Whether this work should be done under the Department of State I am not prepared to say until Congress has practically determined on the character and extent of the work. While it has to do with foreign relations in a measure I am rather disposed to think it would come more properly under an independent board, as it would require the aid of the Treasury and the Department of Commerce as well as the Department of State. In any event an additional Assistant Secretary would hardly be the method and I am quite sure Congress would never approve of creating such an office for temporary work of this nature.

Strongly as the humane purpose of Mr. Smith's idea appeals to me I doubt very much the practicability of attempting to act upon it at the present time.

I am returning Mr. Smith's letter herewith.

Faithfully yours,   Robert Lansing

TLS (WP, DLC).
[1] That is, H. A. Smith to WW, Feb. 6, 1918, about which see WW to RL, Feb. 7, 1918, n. 1.

My dear Mr. President: Washington February 9, 1918.

In reply to your inquiry concerning the relationship of the Embassy with the Bolsheviki,[1] on December 6th the Department cabled the Embassy that it desired the American Embassy to withhold direct communication with the Bolsheviki Government;[2] on the 11th of December the Department disapproved the Consul at Petrograd conferring informally with Trotsky,[3] and on the 15th the Department circularized the European missions, also Tokyo, Peking and Bangkok, instructing them to have no official relations with Russian diplomatic officers who were recognized or appointed by the Bolsheviki Government.[4]

On December 28th, the Department informed the Embassy that it had not modified its decision to avoid intercourse with the Bolsheviki Government.[5] On January 11th we also reiterated to the Embassy our decision to avoid relations with the Bolsheviki.[6]

Recently the Ambassador has used Mr. Robins, the head of the American Red Cross Mission in Russia, as a channel of information. In a telegram dated January 31st, Mr. Francis says that he is endeavoring through Mr. Robins to have Lenine revoke the appointment of John Reed as Bolsheviki representative here.[7] In order to save the Roumanian Minister, it appears that Ambassador Francis went direct to Lenine and again to the Foreign Office.[8]

In a further telegram it appears that Mr. Francis has acknowledged a communication from the Bolsheviki as follows:

"The American Embassy has the honor to acknowledge receipt of communication from the Russian People's Commissariat for Foreign Affairs dated January 29th, 1918."[9]

The Ambassador, therefore, has begun on his own initiative to make use of Robins further than to secure information and is also finding it necessary to come in touch personally with the Bolsheviki authorities. As we have never modified our instructions to him and it is evident that he feels the necessity of keeping in touch with the authorities, it might be wise to instruct him accordingly, leaving to him the selection of the channel through which he may desire to communicate.[10]

With assurances of respect, etc., I am, my dear Mr. President,
Faithfully yours,   Robert Lansing

Approved by President 2/12/18

TLS (SDR, RG 59, 861.00/4212a, DNA).
[1] WW to RL, Feb. 4, 1918 (second letter of that date).
[2] RL to D. R. Francis, Dec. 6, 1917, TS telegram (SDR, RG 59, 861.00/796a, DNA); printed in FR 1918, Russia, I, 289.
[3] Missing in the State Department files, but see RL to D. R. Francis, Dec. 6, 1917, T telegram (SDR, RG 59, 861.00/796A, DNA).
[4] RL to Diplomatic Representatives in European Countries, Japan, China, and Siam, Dec. 15, 1917, T telegram (SDR, RG 59, 861.01/9a, DNA); printed in FR 1918, Russia, I, 317.
[5] Missing in the State Department files.
[6] Missing in the State Department files.
[7] D. R. Francis to RL, Jan. 31, 1918, T telegram (SDR, RG 59, 861.00/1053, DNA); printed in FR 1918, Russia, I, 363. Georgii Vasil'evich Chicherin, the newly appointed Deputy Commissar for Foreign Affairs, had informed Francis on January 29 that Reed had been appointed Soviet consul in New York. Reed had solicited an appointment as diplomatic courier so that his papers might be safe from search and/or seizure. Trotsky had proposed the consulship instead. Francis, Sisson, Robins, and Alexander Gumberg, a Russian-American who often served as go-between with the American colony and the Bolshevik regime, all worked to have Reed's appointment reversed. Apparently at Lenin's behest, the appointment was canceled some time during the first week of February. Kennan, Russia Leaves the War, pp. 405-10.
[8] The Soviet authorities, on January 13, had arrested the Rumanian Minister to Russia, Count Constantine J. Diamandi, and four members of his staff in retaliation for alleged attacks on Russian troops by units of the Rumanian army in Moldavia. Francis, as dean of the diplomatic corps in Petrograd, convened a meeting of all the diplomatic representatives on the following morning. They agreed to demand the immediate, uncon-

ditional release of the Rumanian diplomats in a joint note of protest to the Soviet government. Francis suggested that they go as a body to the Smolny Institute to present the note to Lenin and requested an audience at 4 P.M. that day. The meeting occurred at the time and place requested, and the American and French ambassadors and the Belgian and Serbian ministers took the chief roles in the discussion. Late that evening, Francis received word that Diamandi and his colleagues would be released; they actually were freed on January 15. *Pravda* declared on the same day that Francis had agreed to make formal protest to the Rumanian government for its treatment of Russian troops in return for the release of Diamandi. Francis heatedly denied this assertion, both at the time and later. For Francis' reports about the incident, see *FR 1918, Russia*, I, 477-82. For many additional details, see Kennan, *Russia Leaves the War*, pp. 330-42.

9 Not found.

10 RL to D. R. Francis, Feb. 14, 1918, TS telegram (SDR, RG 59, 861.00/1064, DNA); printed in *FR 1918, Russia*, I, 381. Lansing here instructed Francis as follows: "Department approves your course and desires you gradually to keep in somewhat closer and informal touch with Bolshevik authorities using such channels as will avoid any official recognition. This Government is by no means prepared to recognize Bolshevik Government officially. Department's previous instructions are modified to this extent." The missions in London, Paris, Tokyo, Peking, and Jassy were advised of the contents of this cable.

My dear Mr. President: Washington February 9, 1918.

With reference to your inquiry[1] in regard to the telegram of January thirtieth from the Consul General at Moscow, in which it is requested that additional consular officers be sent to Russia as soon as possible,[2] I take pleasure in saying that three consular officers have already been ordered to report to the Consul General at Moscow and it is believed that in a day or so several others can be detached from their present duties and sent to Russia. In view of the distribution of control over Russia among different political factions and the interruption in the ordinary means of communication, it has seemed to this Department that the appeals from the Consul General for additional assistance should be granted, as far as available men permit, in order that he may be given a sufficient staff to keep the Department and the Embassy fully and promptly informed in regard to developments in all parts of Russia.

Faithfully yours,   Robert Lansing

TLS (WP, DLC).

1 Probably a verbal one.

2 Not found.

From Robert Lansing, with Enclosures

My dear Mr. President: Washington February 9, 1918.

I am enclosing a memorandum which Mr. Long and Mr. Williams prepared at my request, after conversation this morning, relative to the possibility of Japanese Military operations in Siberia.

I also enclose drafts of telegrams to London and Tokio on the subject.

Would you be good enough to let me have your views as to the advisability of sending the telegrams as drafted, or, if you disapprove, in what way they should be amended?

Faithfully yours,   Robert Lansing.

TLS (SDR, RG 59, 861.00/1097, DNA).

ENCLOSURE I

MEMORANDUM

February 9, 1918.

The Japanese Government has asked that the task of occupying the Chinese Eastern and Amur Railway be left to her alone (from Tokyo, January 17, 5 p.m., attached).[1] Japan has also definitely requested that the British Government agree to this (do). The British Government in secret memorandum left with the Department January 28th, (attached),[2] requests this Government to accede to the proposition to make Japan the mandatory of the Allies in occupying the Chinese Eastern Railway (that part of the Trans-Siberian Railroad which crosses the Chinese Province of Manchuria), and the Amur Railway (which is another branch of the Trans-Siberian Railroad).

France has instructed her Ambassador at Tokyo to join his British Colleague in acceding to the request of the Japanese Government (from Tokyo, February 8, 10 p.m.).[3]

These requests are made conditional upon the contingency that it shall become necessary to intervene, but nevertheless are direct requests to the Governments of Great Britain, France and the United States.

The British Government in a supplemental secret memorandum received by the Department, February 7th,[4] invites the Government of the United States to consider permitting the Japanese Army to occupy the whole of the Trans-Siberian Railway (memorandum attached).

Mr. Maklakoff,[5] Russian Ambassador at Paris, in a conversation with Mr. Sharpe, stated that he believed that the threatening of Russian territories by the armed forces of the Allied Powers, and particularly by Japan, would have a disastrous effect not only on his own country but upon the cause of the Allies and would arouse throughout Russia sentiments unitedly hostile to the allied cause (#3138, February 3, 10 p.m., from Paris, attached).[6]

The attached proposed telegrams to London, Paris, Tokyo and Peking,[7] and the attached memorandum[8] in answer to the two secret memoranda from the British Embassy are predicated upon the belief that it would be inadvisable to accede to the request of Japan to be put in sole control of the Trans-Siberian Railway, or to occupy any portion of Siberian or Chinese territory, and suggest instructions which would direct the policy of this Government in the premises. B.L. ETW BM

[1] R. S. Morris to RL, Jan. 17, 1918, *FR 1918, Russia*, II, 29-30.
[2] Printed as an Enclosure with FLP to WW, Jan. 29, 1918.
[3] R. S. Morris to RL, Feb. 8, 1918, *FR 1918, Russia*, II, 44.
[4] British Embassy to Department of State, Feb. 6, 1918, *ibid.*, p. 38.
[5] Vasilii Alekseevich Maklakov.
[6] W. G. Sharp to RL, Feb. 3, 1918, *ibid.*, p. 37.
[7] For the telegrams as sent, see RL to WHP, Feb. 13, 1918, and the other telegrams cited in n. 2 thereto.
[8] Enclosure II below. The substance of it was also transmitted to the French and Italian embassies on February 14 and to the Chinese and Belgian legations on February 18.

ENCLOSURE II

MEMORANDUM.[1]

Washington, February 8, 1918.

The Department of State has given careful consideration to the secret memoranda of His Britannic Majesty's Embassy, No. 112 and 153, received respectively on January 28th and February 7th, 1918, which communicate the opinion of His Britannic Majesty's Government that recent changes in Russian conditions suggest the need for a change in allied policy that certain local organizations appear to have sprung up in South and South-east Russia which, with encouragement and assistance, might do something to prevent Russia from falling immediately and completely under the control of Germany. His Britannic Majesty's Government call attention furthermore to the fact that the only way in which assistance can be given these organizations is over the Siberian Railway and state that the British General Staff are strongly of opinion that this line ought to be used and that it could be used if the Japanese would give their assistance.

The information collected by His Britannic Majesty's Government appears to indicate that the Russians would welcome some form of foreign intervention and that it would be more welcome in the shape of the Japanese engaged as mandatories of the Allies with no thought of annexation or future control than in the shape of the Germans who would make Russia orderly by making it German.

The later memorandum No. 153 communicates the suggestion

of His Britannic Majesty's Government that if it is decided to approach the Japanese Government on the subject, the opinion of the latter should be invited as to the feasibility of the occupation of the Trans-Siberian Railway, and further as to whether they would be willing to undertake the operation. The memorandum states further that His Britannic Majesty's Government are of the opinion that, provided the means of transport are available, it would be in the power of the Japanese army to occupy the whole Trans-Siberian Railway.

The information in the possession of the American Government does not lead it to share the opinion of His Britannic Majesty's Government that any form of foreign intervention in the affairs of Russia would be welcomed by the people of that country. It is believed on the contrary by the Government of the United States that any foreign intervention in Russian affairs would, at the present time, be most inopportune.

The American Government is not indifferent to the effect which the unfortunate condition of Russia at the present time is having upon the plans of the Allies, but it has not lost hope of a change for the better to be brought about without foreign intervention. Should such intervention unfortunately become necessary in the future, the American Government is disposed at present to believe that any military expedition to Siberia or the occupation of the whole or of a part of the Trans-Siberian Railway should be undertaken by international cooperation and not by any one power acting as the mandatory of the others.   B.L. ETW BM

TI MSS (SDR, RG 59, 861.00/1097, DNA).
  [1] Sent to the British embassy on February 8, with Lansing's signature.

From Herbert Clark Hoover

Dear Mr. President: Washington, D. C. *9 February 1918*

I send the following response to your desire for a memorandum as to our cereal food position for your consideration of the cable from the Premiers of England, Italy and France:[1]

1. At the Paris Conference a definite cereal world programme was drawn up for the provisioning of the Allied countries during the year. I attach herewith a copy of the programme there agreed upon.[2] The following table is a summary of the actual experience with this programme for the months of December, January and February, from which you will see that the failure in shipment

  [1] J. J. Jusserand to WW, Feb. 2, 1918.
  [2] "Estimated Shipments of Cereals (Excluding Oats) to All Allies, Table No. 1, Position on 10th December 1917," CC MS (WP, DLC).

amounts to 1,144,000 tons of cereals and of this failure,—35 per cent. falls upon Canada, 37 per cent. on the United States and 29 per cent. upon other countries, such as the Argentine, India, et cetera. You will therefore observe that the failure in delivery falls, as to 64 per cent, outside of the United States. The problem, however, is one of practical character and simply means, in view of

	December 1917 000 tons		January 1918 000 tons		February 1918 000 tons		TOTAL
Canada Programme	335		425		465		1,225,000
Actual Shipment	290		346		250		886,000
Deficiency		45		79		215	339,000
United States Programme	465		575		675		1,715,000
Actual Shipment	201		353		650		1,204,000
Deficiency		264		222		25	511,000
Other Countries Programme	220		350		300		870,000
Actual Shipment	131		235		210		576,000
Deficiency		89		115		90	294,000
Total Programme	1020		1350		1440		3,810,000
Total Shipments	622		934		1110		2,666,000
Total Deficiency		398		416		330	1,114,000

their statement, that we must increase our shipments to at least partially take care of this deficiency.

2. It must also be a prime consideration to protect our own population, as well as to increase the shipments to the point desired by the Allies. The following is a rough summary of our food situation.

a. We have apparently a sufficiency of corn to meet both domestic and export requirements provided we do not lose it. On the other hand, the corn crop this year is anything up to 50 per cent. soft corn and much of it will be lost if not moved within six weeks. Inasmuch as some of the corn will probably not keep beyond the end of March the farmers are naturally desirous of selling it in preference to their better qualities. If it can be re-moved from the farms to the terminal elevators and dried, a great deal of it can be saved. This situation, however, has created a blockade in trade because the country dealers will not buy and store this corn on account of its dangerous condition, unless they can have complete assurance in advance, of railway cars for its instant removal. With the general car shortage and their repeated failure to secure cars, we have thus developed a complete block in its movement. I understand Mr. Houston's view is that it is desirable that the farmer should keep this corn and feed it on the farms and ship the better qualities of corn which he is now holding in reserve. I see no way to induce the farmer to bring out this better quality of corn.

b. In the matter of wheat, although we have exhausted our export surplus, we are continuing to supply the Allies with flour from approximately 12,000,000 bushels of wheat per month in the hope that we can reduce the consumption in this country by that amount. I am fearful, however, that with the general de-generation in the distribution of other foodstuffs, such as corn and potatoes, we will not be able to secure this conservation. This again becomes a question of car supply to get a sufficient distri-bution of the substitutes for wheat. In any event, I understand that you approve of the policy that we should ship this amount of wheat at least until the critical situation of the Allies has passed, regardless of the risk to our supplies later in the year.

c. We have an ample supply of oats of good quality and the problem is simply one of transportation.

d. Our stocks of rye are practically exhausted as we have but a small crop in any event and the drainage abroad has been very large.

e. The American people are today eating large quantities of barley in substitution for wheat. At the same time the Allies are buying large supplies in America partially for bread and partially for brewing purposes. Also, our own brewers are trying to ac-cumulate large stocks of barley for fear that it will be absorbed by the other two markets. The consequence is, the price of barley has gone to unheard-of figures and is causing great discontent throughout the country. I believe it is necessary to seriously con-sider some repression of the use of barley for brewing. We are now investigating what measures can be taken in this direction and I have the feeling, in the situation in which we find ourselves, that—with a subnormal wheat crop and with a corn crop that, through loss, is likely to be subnormal—neither we nor the Allies are warranted in the continued use of cereals for brewing purposes. I do not however believe that we should take any action in this matter unless similar action is taken in the Allied countries. Altogether, I feel, despite the short wheat crop and the probable loss of corn, we can feed our own people and the Allies through the year. The Allies however must draw every grain possible from the Argentine and we also may need to import. I cannot disavow the fact that we may have a period of extreme domestic difficulty later in the harvest year.

3. Any study of our food situation will develop the fact that the domestic situation is in critical condition as the cumulative result of transportation failure for the last three months. The following table of arrivals of four of the principal cereal commodities at terminals will indicate to you the degeneration of our cereal food distribution.

TOTAL CARS MOVED
(Interior and seaboard terminal receipts)
Wheat, corn, flour, oats.

	This year	*Last year*
November	94,202	116,849
December	75,120	96,073
January	64,945	112,065
	234,267	324,987

The result has been exorbitant prices for the uncontrolled corn and oats in the consuming centers and the danger of loss of the corn untransported. A further illumination of the domestic difficulty may be found in the volume of potato movements.

[4.] On the first November we had in the principal potato raising territory, 138,000 carloads of potatoes, the distribution of which should be accomplished equally over a period of eight months, or approximately 17,000 carloads per month. The actual movement, however, was:

November—12,934 cars
December— 6,798 "
January — 9,841 "

Leaving a balance of over 23,000 cars per month which must be moved if we are not to lose a considerable portion of the potato crop. The incidental effect of a short supply of potatoes has been two-fold: to drive the population to eat more bread and cereals and to lift the price of potatoes in all of the consuming centers, yet to demoralize the price in producing centers so that today the farmer is clamorous to sell his potatoes at $1. a hundred, whereas the city populations are paying $2. and $2.25 per hundred when there should not be a differential of more than 40 cents.

5. A further indication of the lack of movement of our foodstuffs lies in the situation of our warehouse stocks. The following table shows the stocks of wheat, oats and corn in our terminal storage at the first of each of the months shown, by which you will observe that we have not at any time during this period had more than 30 per cent. of our normal reserves for immediate distribution. The failure does not arise in any difficulty with the farmer in marketing his material for a stock-taking at the end of January of the cereals lying in country elevators shows 170,000,000 bushels of grain awaiting transportation to the terminals.

TOTAL IN TERMINALS
of
Wheat, Oats, Corn

	This year	Last year
November 1st—	21,291,000	89,462,000
December 1st—	27,138,000	89,656,000
January 1st—	31,885,000	89,130,000
February 1st—	30,957,000	82,802,000

I think the above figures clearly indicate the great degeneration in transportation and they illuminate the economic situation in the country at the present time in our growing areas of short supply among the consuming centers, in the shortages of stocks in the larger cities and in the exorbitant prices of the uncontrolled cereals, that is, corn and oats. The price level in these grains are at such a basis as to stifle the livestock industry and to force rises of price in animal products, dairy products, et cetera.

6. Mr. McAdoo's assistants entirely agree that the fundamental dislocation is a very great shortage in cars available for the movement of grain in the western territory and that the prime cause for this shortage lies in the fact that the empty cars for this service are blocked in the eastern section. Measures have now been instituted to give preferences in the use of box cars for grain and grain products movement and measures of co-operation have been established with the Food Administration through which I hope for some amelioration and that we may be able to meet the present Allied demands. I and my associates have felt that these measures should go even further than now proposed but I entirely agree that their efficacy should be tested for a few days. I am confident that the degeneration in transportation would have been stemmed when the railways were taken over and Mr. McAdoo placed in charge but the weather has so far been insuperable. On the other hand the cumulative result makes it a serious consideration as to whether

measures which might have been successful on January 1st will save the situation on February 9th.

I beg to remain

Your obedient servant,   Herbert Hoover

TLS (WP, DLC).

From William Cox Redfield

My dear Mr. President: Washington February 9th, 1918.

There is a matter that I venture to think requires immediate care—concerning which days are precious—which has, I fear, been lost to sight in the volume of current work and which seems to need a word from you to get the prompt action required.

For months now the question of restricting exports has been discussed. The Shipping Board in the person of Dean Gay[1] has given it much thought. You have kindly allotted us funds with which to assist Dean Gay. The importance of the subject is recognized by everybody yet it is a fact that so far no single definite step has been taken by the restriction of any import to actually release one ship from that work and turn it over to the military authorities for their use. There may have been (I know of none) sporadic cases of the kind but no concerted action and no result thus far of the efforts making. No one has consulted the records of this Department on imports to know what is possible in that respect and, so far as I am able to learn, the matter is still in the reporting and discussion stages while we are crying for ships.

I do not pretend to know why the delay nor have I any thought of criticism because I do not know what causes it. I venture to think, however, that the fact of the delay should be brought to your attention in view of the grave national importance of getting as many ships into use as possible.

Yours very truly,   William C. Redfield

TLS (WP, DLC).

[1] Edwin Francis Gay, Dean of the Graduate School of Business Administration of Harvard University, who had just been appointed director of the Division of Planning and Statistics of the Shipping Board.

From Samuel Gompers, with Enclosure

Sir: Washington, D. C. February 9, 1918.

Mr. William English Walling and I have had several conferences, particularly in these past few days, at which was discussed the situation as it exists in Russia and Germany.

As a result, he has prepared a statement which I have gone over with him. It fully represents our views of the situation. It is our opinion that the statement should be presented to you for your consideration and I, therefore, take the liberty of enclosing it herein in the hope that it may be a contribution of some helpfulness to your thoughts on the subject.

Respectfully yours,   Saml. Gompers.

TLS (WP, DLC).

E N C L O S U R E

THE CHIEF DANGER OF REVOLUTIONS AND REVOLUTIONARY MOVEMENTS IN EASTERN EUROPE: REVOLUTIONS IN WESTERN EUROPE.

Revolutions can succeed or cause serious trouble more easily in free countries than in military autocarcies [autocracies]. Hence, free countries have more to fear than military autocracies from international revolutionary movements like that of the Bolsheviki or the German Minority Socialists.

The Governments of America and Great Britain are doing everything possible to encourage the German Minority Socialists and are apparently inclined to recognize the Bolsheviki as the de facto Government of Russia, which they undoubtedly are. But such recognition, or any friendly steps, would be taken by the Bolsheviki in Russia and all other countries as an acknowledgement of partial defeat by the "imperialist" governments of Great Britain, France and America, against which they have declared a world wide class war (with violence and a reign of terror, according to Lenine's last speech to the Soviet).[1]

The German and Austrian pseudo-revolutionary strikes in reality proved the helplessness of the German and Austrian workers unless aided by widespread military revolt. But, occurring as they did at the same time with the Bolshevik conquest at Kiev, Odessa and Orenburg, they have immeasurably strengthened Bolshevik confidence—until the slightest concession, or anything but a continuation of complete outward indifference, would be taken by them as showing that they are conquering the Entente countries also, and that we are becoming afraid of pacifist strikes similar to the Austrian and German ones.

The direct objective of our government in "establishing a better understanding" with the Bolsheviki is not to encourage them either in their home or their foreign policy but solely to delay and restrict their approach to Germany and above all to encourage their efforts to revolutionize the peoples of Central Europe. We are also endeavoring to appeal directly to these peoples to revolt. Both policies have the over-whelming approval of the Entente peoples. But we forget that the continuing success of Bolshevism in Russia and the growing strength of pacifist strikes in Germany and Austria immensely aid the already dangerous pacifist movements among the working-men of France, England and Italy—movements united in the demand for a Stockholm conference to bring about "an immediate democratic peace." As we have seen with the Bolsheviki, the emphasis is on the "immediacy" which involves a recognition of the war map and of the military situation at the time the conference is held. This is proved nearly every time a Stockholm advocate gets up to speak or write. "This awful war must end at once." That is the avowed purpose of the Conference, which proposes to deal with "realities."

Entirely independently of German victories, brutal German peace terms, Bolshevik surrenders, or other events, the Stockholm movement grows—without the slightest check or interruption. I have watched carefully for the influence of events. It is nil. No German victory or ultimatum can affect the underlying cause, war weariness—accompanied by Utopian dreams fanned into new life by the Russian revolution.

The Stockholm movement grows apace. Sooner or later delegations may steal from the Entente countries (or be chosen from persons residing abroad) and the conference will occur—or an agreement will be reached without it. The conference will contain one minority demanding German peace terms and another standing for the equal rights of all peoples, but the over-whelming majority will be for those terms upon which an immediate peace can be obtained. And if the conference is not held a Labor and Socialist entente, including all the parties of Europe will probably soon be formed and will reach the same conclusion.

The current in this direction is steady and rapid, and is accelerating. The French Socialists are unanimous and the labor unionists nearly unanimous for Stockholm, while a clear majority have already subordinated the question of peace terms to the proposition that an immediate peace can and should be attained. In Italy the situation was similar until the great defeat. After that there was a short revival of the fighting spirit; all later reports indicate a rapid tendency for Socialists and unionists to resume their previous revolutionary pacifist activities. The situation in England is not very much better. For the first time a full third of the labor unions have adopted the whole pacifist program, while Henderson, a leading spokesman of British Labor repeats almost daily that an international Socialist and Labor conference can bring an early end to the war. There is no danger that an international revolutionary strike to end the war will begin in England, but there is a very grave danger that such a movement may spread to England from Italy or France. The danger is not immediate. But if Bolshevism continues to succeed, and the German Socialists' strikes become more prolonged and menacing, a few months more may produce movements far more threatening to the French and Italian armies than are Bolshevism and German Socialism [to] the armies of Germany and Austria. Such a general European movement would almost certainly spread to England. Nor could it fail to have an effect on Chicago, New York, San Francisco and our other foreign industrial centers in this country.

Even if—in the midst of such a crisis—the German government were overthrown and the war brought to an end, Germany would keep a very large part of the advantages she has won.

For the danger is that these widespread strikes will begin before the power of America has been fully developed, that is before Germany has lost anything whatever of her conquests. The German Socialists might voluntarily and magnanimously surrender surrender [sic] a certain part of the German gains. But even the Haase and Liebknecht[2] programs do not offer to relinquish German domination over Germany's present allies, nor her economic domination over Russia and all surrounding small nations. Nor does the Haase program offer any solution of the questions of German and Austrian Poland and Alsace-Lorraine or propose any compensation for the vast destruction done by the Kaiser—except very vaguely—and insufficiently—in the case of Belgium.

But it is far more probably [probable] that any revolutionary movement in Germany, before her military defeat—would prove either partial or abortive. The result would then be that Germany would have been less weakened by her own upheaval than Italy, and France—and, perhaps, less weakened than England.

The peace then offered would be even worse than that of Haase, namely Erzberger's and Czernin's Teutonic and adaptation [Teutonic adaptation] of the status quo ante and "no annexations, no indemnities" formula, with neighboring nations bound by coerced economic treaties and "readjustments of the frontiers."

To aid the German Socialists (positively) and the Bolsheviki (negatively) is not only playing with fire, it is almost certain to end the war before German defeat or American victory—with all the consequences that must inevitably follow such an indecisive outcome.

T MS (WP, DLC).
[1] Actually, Walling was here combining and oversimplifying remarks on class struggle and world revolution which Lenin had made in the course of three separate speeches before the Third All-Russia Congress of Soviets of Workers', Soldiers', and Peasants' Deputies on January 24, 25, and 31, 1918. For the full texts of these speeches, see Vladimir Il'ich Lenin, *Collected Works*, trans. Yuri Sdobnikov *et al.* (45 vols., Moscow, 1960-70), XXVI, 455-82.
[2] That is, Hugo Haase and Karl Liebknecht.

From the Diary of Colonel House

February 9, 1918.

The President and I went over the message again today and made some minor changes. Contrary to his usual custom, he had Schwem [Swem] write the address in its entirety after we finished the corrections.[1]

He called in Lansing today around twelve o'clock and read it to him. Lansing made two or three suggestions as to changes of words which the President adopted and which I think added to its strength. I saw Lansing vefore [before] he went over and told him about what was in the message. I also had a general talk of a very satisfactory nature with him. The President, I told him, was exceedingly pleased at the cordial way he, Lansing, worked with me, and he expressed admiration at the broad spirit in which he acted. Lansing assured me that what he desired was accomplishment and it did not matter to him how it was done, through me or through himself.

In talking to the President of this I told him that Lansing was constantly urging me to come to Washington and that if I came as often as he wishes, I would be there all the time. The President smiled and replied "I suppose he has found out that the only time he knows anything of what is going on is when you are here." I am much more frank with Lansing than the President is, and I have such confidence in his discretion that I do not hesitate to tell him anything.

In talking to the President today about matters in general, I told of my sense of humiliation as a member of the human family that there was so much malicious scandal and gossip going about, and that people of refinement, of education and of standing were willing to repeat obvious lies against public men and against one another. I wondered if it was peculiar to the upper stratum of society. If it was, I wondered whether it was a good thing to try to lift people in general up to the so-called top. The President thought it was largely a question of having leisure. Busy people and the people who were doing things worth while have neither the time nor the inclination to go to the sewers for topics of conversation. He cited stories he had heard of Garfield. One was if Garfield had not been assassinated when he was a scandal of a grievous nature would have been brought out. He also told one of Washington. There was a story current that Washington caught his death by crossing the Potomac in an open boat on a winter's night in order to go to the house of his mistress, a colored woman who lived on the other side of the river. The absurdity of such stories is apparent, but doubtless many evil minded people believe them. The President thought stories of this nature about public men, and he included himself, rose and fell with their popularity. He noticed that scurrilous letters and criticisms came in when he was attacked most vigorously by Congress. When he was on the crest of the wave, they almost or entirely ceased. I can confirm this because I get the reflex action in the same ratio as the President's popularity is strong or weak.

The President, Mrs. Wilson, Eleanor McAdoo and I went to the National Theater to see "Pollyanna."[2] The President and Mrs. Wilson went to a charity ball afterward and wished me to join them, but I preferred to return to the White House after taking Eleanor home.

[1] This draft is in WP, DLC.
[2] "Pollyanna: The Glad Girl," a comedy by Catherine Chisholm Cushing, adapted from the popular novel *Pollyanna* (Boston, 1913) by Eleanor Emily Hodgman (Mrs. John Lyman) Porter.

From William Lea Chambers

My Dear Mr President   Washington Feby 10th, '18

You have always been so friendly with me, and shown such personal interest in our afflicted daughter[1] that I feel you would expect me to let you know when the supreme moment of our sorrow came. The dear long suffering child is spending her first Sabbath today with the Angels, her beautiful untouched spirit having left as the bright new day was coming.

Sincerely yours   W. L. Chambers

ALS (WP, DLC).
[1] Louise Lanier Chambers, who died on February 10 at the age of thirty-one.

A Memorandum by Robert Lansing

MEMORANDUM on DR HEINRICH LAMMASCH.

February 10, 1918.

Professor Heinrich Lammasch of Vienna was the President of the Tribuman [Tribunal] in the arbitration of the North Atlantic Coast Fisheries which sat at The Hague from June to September, 1910.[1] His mind was acute and not of the legalist type. He was more of a legal philosopher than a strict legalist. His endeavor was to seek common ground for compromise rather than to do legal justice. Throughout he was striving to find the line of least resistence and employed the subtleties of the law for that purpose. While his method was hardly conducive to a final conclusion of the controversy in that particular case, it indicated a spirit of conciliation and a political rather than a judicial attitude in the adjustment of international disputes.

I knew Dr. Lammasch very well and I believe him honest and sincere, lacking entirely the ability or inclination to engage in intrigue. In fact I would not suspect him of intentional deceit or misstatement. He has from the beginning of the war been opposed to it and in search of a means to restore peace. In fact early in the war Dr. Lammasch wrote me that he hoped the United States would find some way to bring about an adjustment which would stop the useless slaughter which was taking place. After the accession of the Emperor Karl I heard from sources, which I cannot recall, that Lammasch was very influential with the young ruler and that his influence would be directed to a restoration of a peace.

In fact my personal view is that Lammasch is entirely sincere in all that he says, that he believes that if his suggestions are followed, Austria will make peace regardless of Germany's attitude, and that Austria would openly break with Germany if the latter refused to make peace along the lines laid down by the President. Whether the Emperor Karl would dare to do this or be able to resist the political power of the Austrian statesmen under German influence is open to serious question, but I am convinced that Lammasch firmly believes that he possesses the power.

Convinced of Lammasch's honesty of purpose, I am sure that he would not have spoken as he did unless he was acting under authority of the Emperor Karl. When we realize that the Hapsburgs whose house is more ancient and imperial than the Hohenzollerns and look upon the latter as upstarts and resent their assumption of superiority, I think the attitude of the Austrian Emperor is easier of comprehension. Furthermore we know from reports received after the death of Franz Josef and before we had broken relations with Austria-Hungary, that the new Emperor was most democratic which he showed by abolishing many of the imperial and ancient formalities, even riding in civilian dress in the tram-cars to hear what the people were talking about. Everything that has come to us indicates a sincere purpose on his part to reestablish the Empire on democratic principles. All this fits in with the statements of Lammasch.   Robert Lansing

TS MS (WP, DLC).
    [1] Lansing had served as counsel for the United States during this arbitration.

From the Diary of Colonel House

February 10, 1918.

I did not arise until late and then motored to Go[r]don's and with him, Janet and Louise, rode for an hour an[d] a half in the country. I stopped on the way back at Gregory's whose mother[1] died yesterday. I walked from there to Gordon's to meet Richard Washburn Child. I was interested to hear Child say that he found the Washington atmosphere intolerable and intended leaving to take an apartment in New York.

Senator Hiram Johnson, of California, lunched with us. I found him almost everything I expected not to find. He seemed to put himself out to be pleasant, and naturally I received a favorable impression. I am looking him over for the purpose of suggesting his name to the President as a possible commissioner to the peace conference. After lunch I drew him out on the European situation to find how his mind functioned there. I explained a great many things about our foreign relations of which he was ignorant.

I explained the President's January 8th speech, to some parts of which he took exception. He thought the speech committed us to a policy of helping European countries to territorial acquisition. He was gratified to hear the President's real views upon this subject. He declared the President would find him supporting him in his peace program when that came about. Much to my surprise, he appeared modest and not self-assertive. Whether this was his natural manner or an excessive desire to please, I cannot determine by this one interview.

I told the President of my interview with Johnson and of my intention to see Senators and Representatives from time to time and try and get them in a happier frame of mind toward the administration. He approved, but does not realize that no one but himself can do this effectively.

Herbert Hoover followed Johnson. As usual he was full of pessimism. He spoke well of McAdoo, but thought he should resign from the Treasury and give his entire attention to the railroads. He complained that as it was, McAdoo "was merely a megaphone" expressing the opinions which the railroad experts unloaded on him. He went into the food situation at considerable length and also the question of the distribution of coal. He had a plan which he wanted Garfield to adopt and which he wanted me to approve and take to the President to force on Garfield.

In talking to the President later he said it was disagreeable to have interviews with Hoover because of his excessive pessimism. Nothing was ever being done right. I expressed the thought that Hoover and McAdoo were much alike in desiring all the power in sight in their own hands, but the difference between them was that McAdoo had much charm and magnetism, while Hoover had none.

Louise and I walked to Gregory's again after Hoover left. While I was there the President came in and I returned with him to the White House. I was glad I did so because it gave me the opportunity to express my feeling that his address to Congress still lacked something, and the something I thought it lacked was the focusing of the world's attention on the military party in Germany. I thought he should say that the entire world was now in substantial agreement as to a just peace with the exception of this small group who seemed determined to drive millions of men to their death in order to have their will.

The President caught at my suggestion and took a pad and pencil and began to frame a new paragraph. This paragraph begins: "a general peace erected upon such foundations can be discussed," and ends with the sentence, "the tragic circumstance is that this one party in Germany is apparently willing and able to send millions of men to their deaths to prevent what all the world sees to be just."[2]

He had the word "thousand" to which I objected and suggested "millions" to which he readily assented.

I thoroughly approve the message as it now stands. The President is not enthusiastic about it, but I have told him time and again that he need not worry for I was certain it would meet with almost universal approval.

I had expected to meet Lord Reading at the station when he arrived at six o'clock but I was unable to do so because of this change in the address which we had under discussion.

Margaret[3] had Mr. and Mrs. Crampton of New York[4] for the week end. I was struck with the extreme courtesy of the President toward them. He took as much trouble to entertain them, and was as deferential as I am sure he was to the Duke and Duchess of Devonshire who were recently his luncheon guests. The President's inate refinement is always striking.

After dinner I went to see McAdoo. He usually goes to bed at eight o'clock, has his dinner in bed, and does what work there is to be done there. He came down in his pajamas to the drawing room to see me. I tried to leave in a half hour, but it was almost an hour before he finished with his budget. He insisted again that he was not a candidate for the Presidency, and I almost think he believes it. His reason is that he has no money which, of course, is no reason at all, for if he remains in the Cabinet, the drain will be from that position, not as a candidate and not as President should he be successful.

I returned to the White House at half past nine o'clock and the President and I had a short conference until ten. The President desired his speech re-written by Swemm, and the question was how it could be done without giving any intimation to the Executive Office. He had the White House usher, Hoover's understudy,[5] take a message to Swemm cautioning him not to mention to anyone in the Offices anything concerning the address. I cannot understand why the President will continue such an intolerable state of affairs. It hampers him in every direction. It has come to the point where he will trust the flunkies around the White House rather than his own Secretary.

We went to bed early because of the day the President has before him tomorrow.

[1] Mary Cornelia Watt (Mrs. Francis Robert) Gregory had died, after a month's illness, at her son's home in Washington.
[2] Wilson typed this revised paragraph and pasted it into Swem's draft. Wilson also retyped and pasted in the portion of the text beginning "I would not be a true spokesman" through "Our whole strength will be put."
[3] That is, Margaret Wilson.
[4] David Henry Crompton and Lillian Sheridan Crompton. He was president of Booth & Co., which dealt in sheepskins.
[5] Unidentified.

An Address to a Joint Session of Congress[1]

Reading copy, 11 Feby, 1918[2]

Gentlemen of the Congress: On the eighth of January I had the honor of addressing you on the objects of the war as our people conceive them. The Prime Minister of Great Britain had spoken in

[1] Wilson addressed a joint session of Congress in the House chamber at 12:30 P.M. The two houses had been notified of his desire to address them only a short time before noon. *New York Times*, Feb. 12, 1918.
[2] WWhw.

similar terms on the fifth of January. To these addresses the German Chancellor replied on the twenty-fourth and Count Czernin, for Austria, on the same day. It is gratifying to have our desire so promptly realized that all exchanges of view on this great matter should be made in the hearing of all the world.

Count Czernin's reply, which is directed chiefly to my own address of the eighth of January, is uttered in a very friendly tone. He finds in my statement a sufficiently encouraging approach to the views of his own Government to justify him in believing that it furnishes a basis for a more detailed discussion of purposes by the two Governments. He is represented to have intimated that the views he was expressing had been communicated to me beforehand and that I was aware of them at the time he was uttering them; but in this I am sure he was misunderstood. I had received no intimation of what he intended to say. There was, of course, no reason why he should communicate privately with me. I am quite content to be one of his public audience.

Count von Hertling's reply is, I must say, very vague and very confusing. It is full of equivocal phrases and leads it is not clear where. But it is certainly in a very different tone from that of Count Czernin, and apparently of an opposite purpose. It confirms, I am sorry to say, rather than removes, the unfortunate impression made by what we had learned of the conferences at Brest-Litovsk. His discussion and acceptance of our general principles lead him to no practical conclusions. He refuses to apply them to the substantive items which must constitute the body of any final settlement. He is jealous of international action and of international counsel. He accepts, he says, the principle of public diplomacy, but he appears to insist that it be confined, at any rate in this case, to generalities and that the several particular questions of territory and sovereignty, the several questions upon whose settlement must depend the acceptance of peace by the twenty-three states now engaged in the war, must be discussed and settled, not in general council, but severally by the nations most immediately concerned by interest or neighborhood. He agrees that the seas should be free, but looks askance at any limitation to that freedom by international action in the interest of the common order. He would without reserve be glad to see economic barriers removed between nation and nation, for that could in no way impede the ambitions of the military party with whom he seems constrained to keep on terms. Neither does he raise objection to a limitation of armaments. That matter will be settled of itself, he thinks, by the economic conditions which must follow the war. But the German colonies, he demands, must be returned without debate. He will discuss with no one but the representatives of Russia what disposition shall be made of the peoples and the lands of the Baltic provinces; with no one but the Government of France the "conditions" under which French territory shall be evacuated; and only with Austria what shall be done with Poland. In the determination of all questions affecting the Balkan states he defers, as I understand him, to Austria and Turkey; and with regard to the agreements to be entered into concerning the non-Turkish peoples of the present Ottoman Empire, to the Turkish authorities themselves. After a settlement all around, effected in this fashion, by individual barter and concession, he would have no objection, if I correctly interpret his statement, to a league of nations which would undertake to hold the new balance of power steady against external disturbance.

It must be evident to everyone who understands what this war has wrought in the opinion and temper of the world that no general peace, no peace worth the infinite sacrifices of these years of tragical suffering, can possibly be arrived at in any such fashion. The method the German Chancellor proposes is the method of the Congress of Vienna. We cannot and will not return to that. What is at stake now is the peace of the world. What we are striving for is a new international order based upon broad and universal principles of right and justice,—no mere peace of shreds and patches. Is it possible that Count von Hertling does not see that, does not grasp it, is in fact living in his thought in a world dead and gone? Has he utterly forgotten the Reichstag Resolutions of the nineteenth of July, or does he deliberately ignore them? They spoke of the conditions of a general peace, not of national aggrandizement or of arrangements between state and state. The peace of the world depends upon the just settlement of each of the several problems to which I adverted in my recent address to the Congress. I, of course, do not mean that the peace of the world depends upon the acceptance of any particular set of suggestions as to the way in which those problems are to be dealt with. I mean only that those problems each and all affect the whole world; that unless they are dealt with in a spirit of unselfish and unbiased justice, with a view to the wishes, the natural connections, the racial aspirations, the security, and the peace of mind of the peoples involved, no permanent peace will have been attained. They cannot be discussed separately or in corners. None of them constitutes a private or separate interest from which the opinion of the world may be shut out. Whatever affects the peace affects mankind, and nothing settled by military force, if settled wrong, is settled at all. It will presently have to be reopened.

Is Count von Hertling not aware that he is speaking in the court of mankind, that all the awakened nations of the world now sit in judgment on what every public man, of whatever nation, may say on the issues of a conflict which has spread to every region of the world? The Reichstag Resolutions of July themselves frankly accepted the decisions of that court. There shall be no annexations, no contributions, no punitive damages. Peoples are not to be handed about from one sovereignty to another by an international conference or an understanding between rivals and antagonists. National aspirations must be respected; peoples may now be dominated and governed only by their own consent. "Self-determination" is not a mere phrase. It is an imperative principle of action, which statesmen will henceforth ignore at their peril. We cannot have general peace for the asking, or by the mere arrangements of a peace conference. It cannot be pieced together out of individual understandings between powerful states. All the parties to this war must join in the settlement of every issue anywhere involved in it; because what we are seeking is a peace that we can all unite to guarantee and maintain and every item of it must be submitted to the common judgment whether it be right and fair, an act of justice, rather than a bargain between sovereigns.

The United States has no desire to interfere in European affairs or to act as arbiter in European territorial disputes. She would disdain to take advantage of any internal weakness or disorder to impose her own will upon another people. She is quite ready to be shown that the settlements she has suggested are not the best or the most enduring. They are only her own provisional sketch of principles and of the way in which they should be applied. But she entered this war because she was made a partner, whether she would or not, in the sufferings and indignities inflicted by the military masters of Germany, against the peace and security of mankind; and the conditions of peace will touch her as nearly as they will touch any other nation to which is entrusted a leading part in the maintenance of civilization. She cannot see her way to peace until the causes of this war are removed, its renewal rendered as nearly as may be impossible.

This war had its roots in the disregard of the rights of small nations and of nationalities which lacked the union and the force to make good their claim to determine their own allegiances and their own forms of political life. Covenants must now be entered into which will render such things impossible for the future; and those covenants must be backed by the united force of all the nations that love justice and are willing to maintain it at any cost. If territorial settlements and the political relations of great populations which have not the organized power to resist are to be determined by the contracts of the powerful governments which consider themselves most directly affected, as Count von Hertling proposes, why may not economic questions also? It has come about in the altered world in which we now find ourselves that justice and the rights of peoples affect the whole field of international dealing as much as access to raw materials and fair and equal conditions of trade. Count von Hertling wants the essential bases of commercial and industrial life to be safeguarded by common agreement and guarantee, but he cannot expect that to be conceded him if the other matters to be determined by the articles of peace are not handled in the same way as items in the final accounting. He cannot ask the benefit of common agreement in the one field without according it in the other. I take it for granted that he sees that separate and selfish compacts with regard to trade and the essential materials of manufacture would afford no foundation for peace. Neither, he may rest assured, will separate and selfish compacts with regard to provinces and peoples.

Count Czernin seems to see the fundamental elements of peace with clear eyes and does not seek to obscure them. He sees that an independent Poland, made up of all the indisputably Polish peoples who lie contiguous to one another, is a matter of European concern and must of course be conceded; that Belgium must be evacuated and restored, no matter what sacrifices and concessions that may involve; and that national aspirations must be satisfied, even within his own Empire, in the common interest of Europe and mankind. If he is silent about questions which touch the interest and purpose of his allies more nearly than they touch those of Austria only, it must of course be because he feels constrained, I suppose, to defer to Germany and Turkey in the circumstances. Seeing and conceding, as he does, the essential principles involved and the necessity of candidly applying them, he naturally feels that Austria can respond to the purpose of peace as expressed by the United States with less embarrassment than could Germany. He would probably have gone much farther had it not been for the embarrassments of Austria's alliances and of her dependence upon Germany.

After all, the test of whether it is possible for either government to go any further in this comparison of views is simple and obvious. The principles to be applied are these:

First, that each part of the final settlement must be based upon the essential justice of that particular case and upon such adjustments as are most likely to bring a peace that will be permanent;

Second, that peoples and provinces are not to be bartered about from sovereignty to sovereignty as if they were mere chattels and pawns in a game, even the great game, now forever discredited, of the balance of power; but that

Third, every territorial settlement involved in this war must be made in the interest and for the benefit of the populations concerned, and not as a part of any mere adjustment or compromise of claims amongst rival states; and

Fourth, that all well defined national aspirations shall be accorded the utmost satisfaction that can be accorded them without introducing new or perpetuating old elements of discord and antagonism that would be likely in time to break the peace of Europe and consequently of the world.

A general peace erected upon such foundations can be discussed. Until such a peace can be secured we have no choice but to go on. So far as we can judge, these principles that we regard as fundamental are already everywhere accepted as imperative except among the spokesmen of the military and annexationist party in Germany. If they have anywhere else been rejected, the objectors have not been sufficiently numerous or influential to make their voices audible. The tragical circumstance is that this one party in Germany is apparently willing and able to send millions of men to their death to prevent what all the world now sees to be just.

I would not be a true spokesman of the people of the United States if I did not say once more that we entered this war upon no small occasion, and that we can never turn back from a course chosen upon principle. Our resources are in part mobilized now, and we shall not pause until they are mobilized in their entirety. Our armies are rapidly going to the fighting front, and will go more and more rapidly. Our whole strength will be put into this war of emancipation,—emancipation from the threat and attempted mastery of selfish groups of autocratic rulers,—whatever the difficulties and present partial delays. We are indomitable in our power of independent action and can in no circumstances consent to live in a world governed by intrigue and force. We believe that our own desire for a new international order under which reason and justice and the common interests of mankind shall prevail is the desire of enlightened men everywhere. Without that new order the world will be without peace and human life will lack tolerable conditions of existence and development. Having set our hand to the task of achieving it, we shall not turn back.

I hope that it is not necessary for me to add that no word of what I have said is intended as a threat. That is not the temper of our people. I have spoken thus only that the whole world may know the true spirit of America,—that men everywhere may know that our passion for justice and for self-government is no mere passion of words but a passion which, once set in action, must be satisfied. The power of the United States is a menace to no nation or people. It will never be used in aggression or for the aggrandizement of any selfish interest of our own. It springs out of freedom and is for the service of freedom.

Printed reading copy (WP, DLC).

To William Gibbs McAdoo

My dear Mac: [The White House] 11 February, 1918

I do not think it would be wise to appoint Crosby a member of the Supreme War Council.[1] I have a very clear conception of the relations of the Inter-Allied Council and the Inter-Allied Shipping Board to the Supreme War Council. That Council can and will at any time call in the chairman or other representatives of these two bodies for consultation upon the matters which should be concerted through the instrumentality of those who are conducting them. I was having a talk the other day with House about the practice of the Supreme War Council in this matter (he is a member of it, you know) and he confirmed my impression that they freely consulted with anybody, Cabinet officers, members of consultative bodies, or any others, whenever it was necessary to coordinate information and effort, and this is as it should be. If I made Crosby a member of the Supreme War Council, I would have to make Stevens[2] also, who has gone over to represent us in the shipping matters, and this would be inconsistent with any practical development and is, moreover, I am convinced, unnecessary.

I utter these opinions confidently because I have given the matter a great deal of thought, and I am sure you will understand that I am not dismissing the suggestion hastily.

Always   Affectionately yours,   Woodrow Wilson

TLS (Letterpress Books, WP, DLC).
  [1] Wilson was replying to WGM to WW, Feb. 6, 1918, TLS (WP, DLC).
  [2] That is, Raymond B. Stevens.

To Louis Freeland Post

Personal.

My dear Mr. Secretary: [The White House] 11 February, 1918

Your suggestion about pardoning the men who at first resisted the conscription interests me very much and appeals to me not a little, but I think perhaps it is unwise to show such clemency until we have got such a grip on the whole conduct of the war as will remove all doubts and counteract all cross currents. I don't feel that I can follow my heart just now.

Cordially and sincerely yours,   Woodrow Wilson

TLS (Letterpress Books, WP, DLC).

To William Lea Chambers

[The White House]

My dear Judge Chambers: 11 February, 1918

I was touched to the quick when I read your letter of yesterday telling me of your daughter's death, and my heart goes out to you in the warmest and sincerest sympathy. The beautiful spirit in which you take your loss assures me that you know the only Source of comfort, but as your sincere friend I want to add, if I may, such comfort as heartfelt sympathy can bring.

Cordially and sincerely yours,   Woodrow Wilson

TLS (Letterpress Books, WP, DLC).

From Joseph Irwin France

Dear Sir: Washington, D. C. February 11, 1918.

I have desired to seek an interview with you to talk over the subject matter which I here present, but knowing the many demands now made upon your time, I take the liberty of writing you upon this vital problem of our war preparations. You have already eloquently appealed to the Nation with the words,—"We must all speak, act, and serve together," and now we need the machinery for such cooperation. Evidences are accumulating that a better national organization for the winning of the war is imperative.

I urge upon your consideration the enclosed Bill[1] which is practically a universal national service act. This Bill was drawn to bring this principle of national organization to the attention of the Senate in concrete form. I feel that we can conquer the German organization only by means of a better organization. I hope also that we may seize this war as an opportunity for a better integration of the Nation. I do not feel that coercion or compulsion in any impolitic or un-American way will be necessary under such an Act. The embodiment of this principle of universal service in proper legislation would, however, afford an opportunity for the latent capacity of our people for cooperative effort to find such expression in active service as would make possible very quickly a nation both efficient and invincible.

Trusting that this, the large and central problem of the war, is receiving your careful consideration, I am,

Very respectfully,   Joseph I. France

TLS (WP, DLC).
¹ 65th Cong., 2d sess., S. 3440, *A Bill to Authorize the President to further mobilize the Federal forces and to increase temporarily the Military Establishment of the United States* (WP, DLC). This bill, introduced by France on January 9, authorized the President, during the existing national emergency, to enroll the entire male population of the United States between the ages of eighteen and forty-five and to select from the rolls thus created men either for military service or for service in occupational categories vital to the war effort. Those persons selected would be deemed to be in the service of the United States until dismissed or discharged. The bill also authorized the President to create the organizational structure necessary to carry out this program.

From David Starr Jordan

Stanford University, Calif., Feb. 11, 1918.

Congratulations on exalted outlook in world's statesmanship.

David Starr Jordan.

T telegram (WP, DLC).

Robert Lansing to the American Legation, Jassy, Rumania

Washington, February 11, 1918.

Referring your 178 and 201, this Government is very much disposed to help the King of Roumania in his personal embarrassment and the delay in answering your telegrams has been due to our endeavor to find some means of obtaining the necessary funds. It now appears that an undertaking of the character you suggest could not be justified without legislation. This would entail debate in Congress and a considerable amount of publicity. Unfortunately, we are not free in such matters as other Governments are and if occasion offers, you should so inform the King, expressing to him at the same time our full appreciation of his difficult situation and that we are fully alive to the sacrifices which his unswerving courage and loyalty have entailed.   Lansing

T telegram (SDR, RG 59, 763.72/8686, DNA).

From the Diary of Colonel House

February 11, 1918.

The Postmaster General was my first caller at the White House. He arrived at nine o'clock. He is in a belligerent mood against the Germans, against labor, against pacifists etc. He is now the most belligerent member of the Cabinet.

After he left I started to the State Department but received word that the President would like to see me in his study. He had a letter from McAdoo enclosing a cable from Oscar Crosby. Crosby suggested that it would be a good idea for him to sit in the Supreme War Council, and McAdoo in his letter approved. He also wished Crosby made High Commissioner. The President handed me the letter without comment, asking my opinion as to how he should answer it. I advised making Crosby a high commissioner if he, Crosby, desired it, but I would not allow him to sit in the Supreme War Council. I thought it would be a dangerous experiment. The President said he not only would not have him sit in the Supreme War Council, but he would not make him a high commissioner. He did not believe in these high sounding titles, besides he was not doing more important work than Stevens, and it would cause trouble to have one a high commissioner and the other not. As for the Supreme War Council, he would not allow anyone to sit in it other than myself.

I asked him what was in his mind regarding my going over and sitting in it. Personally, I was opposed to any civilian sitting in that Council, and believed it should be made up of purely military members. He disagreed with this and thought the civil representatives should sit in with the military as we could not secure close cooperation otherwise. As to my going over, he thought we had better wait and see what his message to Congress accomplished. If things settled down again, and the war was likely to go on through the summer, then he thought I should go over again. This follows out my original suggestion that I should go around the first of April.

After leaving the President I went to the State Department and saw Polk, Fletcher, Baruch and several others. When I returned, Mrs. Wilson, Mrs. Bolling, Margaret and Janet, whom Mrs. Wilson had invited to go with us, went to the Capitol to hear the President's address delivered at half past twelve o'clock.

The President was in fairly good form and seemed anxious to impress Congress with the importance of his speech. They applauded some of the points, but they were not enthusiastic. He was talking over their heads and but few of them knew what it was all about or what his purpose was in addressing them again at this time.

On the return from the Capitol I drove with the President. He was only half pleased with his reception and only scantily hopeful of the success of his speech. I differed with him and was enthusiastic, which seemed to hearten him.

After lunch I drove to Lord Reading's. He has re-taken his old quarters at No. 2315 Massachusetts Avenue. I was delighted to hear him say, "I would have given a year of my life to have made the last [half] of the President's speech." I said I was sure he would want to know why the last half. The reply was that the first half was merely a reiteration of Czernin's and Hertling's positions, but the last half was a noble itterance [utterance], both from an oratorical viewpoint and from that of a statesman.

Sir William Wiseman who was with Lord Reading and Gordon, who took lunch there, pronounced it the best address the President has yet delivered.

I drove from Reading's to see Janet and Louise, and then returned to the White House where the President was waiting to hear if I had any news from Reading. He was delighted when I told him what Reading, Wiseman and Gordon had to say. He was more cheerful and more hopeful about the result of the speech. Neither he nor I consider it as highly as they do. I regard the President's January 22nd speech of 1917, and his January 8th speech of this year the greatest he has made. In speaking of the January 8th speech I told the President that that was a great adventure. He stood to win or lose by it, while this speech was a perfectly safe proposition.

Both the President and Mrs. Wilson urged me to remain over until tomorrow. There is to be an exhibition of Navy pictures this evening at the White House and they thought I would enjoy them. I had made my arrangements, however, to take the four o'clock and did so. Mr. and Mrs. Edward S. Martin,[1] Margaret Wilson and her friends, the Cramptons, and Sir William Wiseman came over with me. Someone called my attention to the fact that there were two large engines attached to the train. This recalled McAdoo's promise last night that I should get to New York on time. At the rate we ran in some places, I felt that he should have added, "If you get there at all."

[1] Julia Whitney (Mrs. Edward Sandford) Martin.

To Edward Nash Hurley

My dear Hurley: [The White House] 12 February, 1918

Will you not permit this suggestion? I make it because of a dispatch which has turned up among those sent me by the State Department in which it appears that the Dutch Government is very much embarrassed in coming to the agreements with us which we are pressing upon it by the publication of such announcements as appeared under the Washington date of February ninth, for example, in the New York Times, headed, "Will free ships for our troops."[1] The suggestion is this: Such publicity is in itself, of course, legitimate and useful enough, but everything ramifies in every direction now apparently and I hope that it will be possible to direct the publicity matter in such a way as to avoid similar collateral embarrassments. It unfortunately happens that what is good news for our people is sometimes bad news for our State Department, using the word "bad" in two very different senses. It occurs to me that it would be feasible for your representative on the War Trade Board to confer with the representative of the State Department on that board with regard to such matters.

I know you will recognize how legitimate and important this suggestion is.

Cordially and faithfully yours,   Woodrow Wilson

TLS (Letterpress Books, WP, DLC).
[1] Wilson referred to a clipping in WP, DLC, which appeared in the *New York Times*, Feb. 10, 1918. The article mentioned the fact that the Shipping Board was negotiating for the purchase of neutral ships which would add 1,000,000 tons for overseas service in nonhazardous areas.

To Joshua Willis Alexander

My dear Judge: The White House 12 February, 1918

Thank you for your kind note of the ninth[1] about the memorandum of the Attorney General concerning Senate Bill No. 3387.[2]

I entirely agree with you that it is highly important that liquor and vice zones should be established in the areas surrounding shipyards and I have no doubt you are quite right that this can be accomplished in a simple and expeditious manner by adding the proper brief amendments to sections 12 and 13 of the Selective Service Act of May 18, 1917. I wonder if you would be kind enough to confer in this matter with Mr. Dent, the Chairman of the Committee on Military Affairs, whose committee I assume would deal with such amendments. I do not like to have this important matter fall between stools, and would be very glad to confer with Mr. Dent about it if he expresses a wish that I should do so.

Cordially and sincerely yours,   Woodrow Wilson

TLS (photostat in RSB Coll., DLC).
  ¹ It is missing.
  ² Enclosure II with WW to J. W. Alexander, Feb. 8, 1918.

To Bernard Mannes Baruch

My dear Baruch: The White House 12 February, 1918

Thank you for your letter of February eighth. The suggestion is a good one and I will certainly act on it.

Cordially and faithfully yours,   Woodrow Wilson

TLS (B. M. Baruch Papers, NjP).

From William Julius Harris

My dear Mr. President: Washington 12 February, 1918.

Having become convinced that a large majority of the true and loyal patriots of Georgia desire me to become a candidate for United States Senator to succeed Senator T. W. Hardwick, I herewith tender my resignation as a member of the Federal Trade Commission, to become effective on the thirty-first day of May, 1918. I have fixed this date, as this will enable me to complete the consideration of important matters pending before the Commission which have been under my special charge.

Sincerely yours,   Wm J. Harris

TLS (WP, DLC).

From Josephus Daniels

My dear Mr. President: [Washington] 12 February, 1918.

I have your letter concerning Reverend Frank Latimer Janeway. I was pleased to meet Mr. Janeway yesterday and I have directed his appointment as a Chaplain in the Naval Reserve Force with the rank of Lieutenant.   Faithfully yours,   [Josephus Daniels]

CCL (J. Daniels Papers, DLC).

From Henry Means Pindell

Peoria, Ill., February 12, 1918.

Your message yesterday was worth a million fresh troops on the western front. You struck a might[y] blow for peace, you[r] old friends are mightly proud of their early relationship with you. I hope you are well.   Henry M. Pindell.

T telegram (WP, DLC).

From Paul Samuel Reinsch

Dear Mr. President: Peking. February 12, 1918.

For some time I have not written you, because I know that your thought and work, which I follow day by day, are necessarily given directly to the European situation and the part we are taking there. But affairs in this part of the world are also closely connected with those efforts to save the world for peaceful life and free government, which our men are dying for in Europe. I am enclosing a depressing report on the present situation in China.[1] There is so much that is good, strong and promising here, that it is hard to have to send so gloomy an account; but we must recognize the full extent of the evil before we can do anything helpful. It is my hope that the impulse for free government in China may not die for want of any encouragement from the liberal nations and because of obstruction from other sources. I fully know that you feel that our ideals and our safety are bound up with a free, self-governing China. In my telegram of February 11th,[2] which I requested the Secretary of State to communicate to you, I pointed out some ways in which the liberal Powers may be of assistance here without raising any difficult political problems at this time. That our country should be able to do something to help the cause of free government and national independence in China, is our hope: it is to our institutions that progressive China is looking for models, to our active sympathy for encouragement.

With heartfelt wishes for your continued strength to meet the overpowering problems confronting your Government, and for your health and well-being, I remain,

Faithfully yours,   Paul S. Reinsch.

TLS (WP, DLC).
  [1] P. S. Reinsch to RL, Feb. 12, 1918, TCL (WP, DLC).
  [2] P. S. Reinsch to RL, Feb. 11, 1918, T telegram (SDR, RG 59, 893.00/2767, DNA). Reinsch reported that the political situation in China was deteriorating. There was growing friction between northern and southern China, and the Japanese were encouraging the divisive forces. He urged that the Allies and the United States "give some

attention to China in order to avoid surprises and dangers." The United States and the Allies should appoint a joint commission to assist China to mobilize its resources in such areas as shipbuilding and the production of food. Reinsch also suggested that the United States announce its readiness to "support" a Chinese military expedition to Europe "as soon as internal unity in China shall have been restored and national action made possible." Extracts from this telegram, from which references critical of Japan are omitted, are printed in *FR 1918*, pp. 83-84.

Gutzon Borglum to Joseph Patrick Tumulty

My dear Mr. Tumulty: [Washington] February 12th, 1918.

I have hoped and tried to see you a couple of times since I had the few minutes with you last week, but I understand today that you are down with a cold. I am sorry on your own account and on mine.

I must now return home, so must leave this beautiful city, and with you for the President, the result of the preliminary inquiry. I cannot help but feel that whatever there is good in this or may come out of it as good for the country belongs in part to you. For had you not acted upon that short note, which I sent you, nothing would have been heard of this until too late. I doubt very much that anyone else would have borne the petty abuses, insults, and intrigue that have been thrown across my path in trying to meet the President's request.

There's a man's job here and it has been tangled up between little vain people and big interests with adroitly placed agents carrying our country's uniform and playing the devil with its money and its future. You know I am not a Democrat and my politics are independent and I have seen a good deal of political activity and perhaps I see, and hear, and know things that can only reach you indirectly, and I tell it to you with a good deal of concern that our President is not going to get through the job he has laid out, without bitter, unprincipled interference by interests that are still powerful and are resorting to any means of silently involving or defeating his purpose.

I would like to have had a talk with you but there seems so little time and so much else of importance in hand. Good luck to you, and let me congratulate you before I close, on your admirable stand with regard to the New Jersey Senatorship.[1] It would be little short of a calamity if you, with your long experience and information, should at this time for any reason, leave the side of the President.

Very sincerely yours,   Gutzon Borglum

TLS (WP, DLC).
[1] Tumulty had announced on February 7 that he would not be a candidate to succeed the late Senator William Hughes. *New York Times*, Feb. 9, 1918. See also John M. Blum, *Joe Tumulty and the Wilson Era* (Boston, 1951), p. 156.

The British Embassy to the Department of State

Washington February 12, 1918

Memorandum

The British Embassy present their compliments to the Department of State and have the honour to inform them, under instructions from His Majesty's Government, of the following outline of policy which His Majesty's Government propose to adopt in regard to Palestine:

Through the channel of the provisional military administration they are acting with the object of securing:

1. Religious equality for all concerned.

2. Equal laws as regards the Allies of the United Kingdom.

3. The settlement with the religious chiefs, whether Christian or Moslem, through official or other intermediaries, of all questions relating to the Holy Places.

4. The maintenance by a civil police force of order in the Holy Places, this force to be recruited from the various denominations which have a religious interest in their custody, and to be under British control.

5. The return to Jerusalem in the near future of the heads of the various religious denominations but not of Consular or Political Representatives.

6. The reduction to as small a number as possible of the European personnel, and the employment of local functionaries and officials, whenever this is feasible, no special community being favoured.

7. The maintenance of Zionism on right lines, taking care that the safety of Christian and Moslem Holy Places shall not be prejudiced, and the granting of full facilities for the reconstruction and establishment of institutions and colonies.

8. The removal of German influence.

9. The establishment of a regime of religious equality, justice and fair play for all.

CC MS (FO 115/2421, pp. 404-05, PRO).

Sir William Wiseman to Lord Reading

[New York] February 12, 1918.

SECRET. SUBJECT: RECOGNITION OF BOLSHEVIC GOVERNMENT.

I told BRUSSA [HOUSE] the sense of the two Russian cables you showed me yesterday. He immediately remarked that he and ADRAMYTI [WILSON] had been discussing the same thing and had come to the conclusion that the United States ought to recognise the Bolshevic Government.

He suggests that he shall send the following cable to FALSTERBO [BALFOUR], but would like your judgment first:

Proposed Cable:

"I have in mind to recommend ADRAMYTI that the United States should recognize the Bolshevic Government in Russia. Our objects in doing this would be:

"(a). To encourage the Liberal parties in Germany and Austria;

"(b). To prevent the Germans from saying that we were helping the reactionary party in Russia and thereby consolidating Russian opinion against the Allies, and increasing German influence in Russia.

"Before taking this matter up with ADRAMYTI I should like to have your views on the subject."

T telegram (W. Wiseman Papers, CtY).

Two Letters to Robert Lansing

My dear Lansing: The White House 13 February, 1918

Just a memorandum. The passage we were looking for was not in one of the regular dispatches but in the message[1] which House showed you in manuscript and of which there was only one copy.
                    Faithfully yours,   Woodrow Wilson

TLS (R. Lansing Papers, NjP).
[1] The preceding document.

My dear Mr. Secretary: The White House 13 February, 1918

I wish you would read (it deserves a very careful reading) the enclosed paper by Mr. William English Walling which Mr. Gompers was kind enough to send to me. It seems to me to speak an unusual amount of truth and to furnish a very proper basis of the utmost caution in the conduct of the many troublesome affairs that we are from time to time discussing.

I would be very much obliged to you if you would be kind enough to return the paper after you have read it.
                    Cordially and sincerely yours,   Woodrow Wilson

TLS (WP, DLC).

To William Julius Harris

My dear Mr. Chairman: [The White House] 13 February, 1918

It is with the deepest regret that I see you withdraw from the Federal Trade Commission, but I know the motives under which you are acting and do not feel at liberty to argue against them. I, therefore, accept your resignation as you request, to become effective on the thirty-first day of May next, in order that you may be able to complete the consideration of important matters now pending before the Federal Trade Commission which have been under your special supervision.

May I not say how warmly I have appreciated the way in which you have performed the difficult and often delicate duties assigned to you in the Trade Commission? I am sure that I am expressing the general feeling when I express my regret at your withdrawal.

Cordially and sincerely yours,   Woodrow Wilson

TLS (Letterpress Books, WP, DLC).

To Charles Warren

My dear Mr. Warren: [The White House] 13 February, 1918

It was certainly very kind of you to prepare the statement in which the extreme language used and the bitterness of the attacks made on Mr. Lincoln in Congress are shown so strikingly.[1] I have looked it through with the greatest interest and with no little astonishment. I knew that the attacks had been of the extremest sort, but I did not realize how extreme they had been.

I wonder if I am at liberty to keep this copy which you have sent me, and whether you have it in mind to make any public use of the document? I think interest in it would be very wide, and the publication of it might serve to clear the air a good deal just at this moment when it is thick.

With warm appreciation,

Cordially and sincerely yours,   Woodrow Wilson

TLS (Letterpress Books, WP, DLC).
[1] C. Warren to WW, Feb. 12, 1918, TLS (WP, DLC). The statement is missing.

To David Franklin Houston

My dear Houston: [The White House] 13 February, 1918

Here is the memorial which the farm delegation left with me the other day.[1] It contains practically nothing in addition to what the previous memorial of another group contained but I send it to you because I want you to see all that I see, and also because I would very much like to know what your opinion is as to the council of farmers to have some official standing and sit at our elbow here. It is only too clear to me how it would be made up if made up not by our choice but in the way suggested.

Cordially and faithfully yours,   Woodrow Wilson

TLS (Letterpress Books, WP, DLC).
  [1] Printed at Feb. 8, 1918.

To Robert Scott Lovett

My dear Judge: [The White House] 13 February, 1918

I have your letter of February tenth proposing certain prices for zinc and take pleasure in approving the proposals of the War Industries Board in that matter.[1] I have authorized the issuance of the statement which you so kindly had prepared and which accompanied your letter.

Cordially and sincerely yours,   Woodrow Wilson

TLS (Letterpress Books, WP, DLC).
  [1] R. S. Lovett to WW, Feb. 7, 1918, TLS (WP, DLC).

To Ellen-Duane Gillespie Davis

My dear Friend: [The White House] 13 February, 1918

Still you continue to be exceedingly generous and I hope you know how genuinely grateful we are for the delicious eggs and butter which you have sent us.

I am heartily sorry to hear[1] that you and E.P. feel that it is best to sell the farm, not, I beg you to believe, because we have benefitted so deliciously from its products, but because it has been so clear to us that your heart was in it, and we know how much your pleasure and probably your health was served by it. But the reasons you give are certainly conclusive and I don't doubt that your judgment is right.

Mrs. Wilson joins me in warmest regard and affectionate appreciation.   Faithfully your friend,   Woodrow Wilson

TLS (Letterpress Books, WP, DLC).
  [1] Her letter is missing.

From Newton Diehl Baker, with Enclosure

Dear Mr President   [Washington, c. Feb. 13, 1918]

Gen Pershing seems to have worked out a satisfactory arrangement. The details and dates have not yet been received here. The[y] shall include one or two divisions of the National Army (drafted men) in the number taken over by the British

Respectfully   Newton D. Baker

ALS (WP, DLC).

E N C L O S U R E

From H A E F February 12th [1918].

Number 596 Confidential. For the Chief of Staff.

Reference paragraph one your 735,[1] British military authorities are in complete accord with the proposals outlined in subparagraphs A and B my cablegram 555.[2] Under these arrangements the personnel with equipment C of *four* combat two replacement divisions of a corps should be sent * * * Conference is in progress with the French military authorities with regard to the necessary artillery and artillery ammunition, wagon transportation and necessary replacements in clothing and equipment except for artillery will be supplied by the British employing their own tonnage. The course of training including tour in front line trenches will cover a period of about ten weeks after which complete divisions will be ready for service in American sector but our own transportation must begin to arrive in France not later than May 15th in our own tonnage to make these divisions ready for service with us. In this connection it is possible that British may be able to furnish us permanently the wagon transportation for all of these troops but reliance should not be placed on this possibility and arrangements for furnishing transportation should be made as above provided, but shipments should be delayed until further notice. French are considering possibility of furnishing draft horses for the artillery and also for other arms. Report will be made later as to their decision. All corps troops not included in the combat and replacement divisions should be sent by our own sea transports in such manner as to complete the corps upon the termination of the training. Second sentence paragraph 2 your 735 "They will join with transportation, machine guns, pistols, artillery etc." reference to transportation not understood. Transportation should be handled as herein indicated. Information requested as to number and type of machine guns contemplated. Recommend advance agents of each division be sent to France ahead of their divisions to arrange necessary details.

Pershing.

TC telegram (WP, DLC).
    [1] Not found.
    [2] J. J. Pershing to H. P. McCain, Jan. 31, 1918.

From Robert Lansing

My dear Mr. President: Washington February 13, 1918.

I have attached two recent telegrams from the American Consul at Vladivostok[1] which lead me to suggest that Admiral Knight might return for a short visit to observe conditions at that port. The American colony is small. On the other hand there are large stocks of various supplies, including munitions, of American origin or ownership accumulated at Vladivostok which we should not fail to safeguard from falling into German hands or serving German purposes.

I should be glad to have the Admiral's views of the situation which is somewhat complex, and am inclined to agree with the Consul that his visit would emphasize the friendly attitude which this Government has manifested consistently towards the Russian people without regard to parties.

Faithfully yours,   Robert Lansing

TLS (SDR, RG 59, 861.00/1048, DNA).
    [1] John Kenneth Caldwell to RL, Jan. 31 and Feb. 4, 1918, FR 1918, Russia, II, 36, 37-38.

From Edward Nash Hurley

My dear Mr. President: Washington February 13, 1918.

Please let me express my appreciation of the characteristically kind spirit of your note received this morning. I can readily understand how the newspaper articles you mention were a source of embarrassment to the State Department.

I am deeply distressed over these articles because part of one of them at least was based upon a brief answer which I made to one of the newspaper men whose inquiry was directed towards substantiating Senator Hitchcock's assertion on the floor of the Senate that Secretary Baker could not possibly send 1,500,000 men to France by the end of the year.

My whole thought was to indicate that Secretary Baker's prediction could be fulfilled. The pointed questions that are asked cannot always be avoided, but after reading your note this morning I felt that my foot had slipped.

You can rest assured that I have taken your injunction to heart and will avoid the possibility of such embarrassment in the future. I can't help saying, however, that the kindly manner in which you point the way is deeply appreciated.

Sincerely yours,   Edward N. Hurley

TLS (WP, DLC).

Frederick Asbury Cullen[1] and Others to Joseph Patrick Tumulty

Dear Sir: New York February 13, 1918.

A petition to the President asking that he extend executive clemency to the five Negro soldiers of the Twenty-fourth Infantry recently sentenced to death by court martial at Fort San [Sam] Houston is now being circulated among the citizens of New York. It is expected that there will be ten thousand or more signers to this petition; and it is our wish to place it directly in the hands of the President. We are writing to ask if you will not use your good offices to secure a brief audience with President Wilson on Wednesday, February 20th, or at his earliest convenience thereafter, for a delegation of three that will bring the petition to Washington.[2]

Yours very respectfully,   Rev F A Cullen.
Edward W. Daniel
John E. Nail.[3]

TLS (WP, DLC).
[1] Pastor of the Salem Methodist Episcopal Church of New York and president of the New York branch of the National Association for the Advancement of Colored People.
[2] Wilson received the delegation on February 19. See WW to NDB, Feb. 19, 1918, n. 1.
[3] The Rev. Edward W. Daniel was vice-president of the New York branch of the N.A.A.C.P.; John E. Nail, a real estate dealer, was treasurer.

Robert Lansing to Walter Hines Page

Washington, February 13, 1918.

CONFIDENTIAL American Ambassador at Tokyo has cabled that his French colleague has received instructions from his Government to join his British colleague in acceding to the request of the Japanese Government that the latter be allowed free hand in the event of intervention in Siberia. He also states his British colleague has as yet received no reply from his Government.[1]

The British Embassy here has presented confidential memoranda suggesting: First, that Japan, acting as the mandatory of the Allies, be asked to occupy the Chinese Eastern and Amur Railways, and, second, that the Government of the United States consider the practicability of having Japan occupy the whole Trans-Siberian Railroad.

The Government of the United States would be very glad to coincide with the position which may be taken by the Government of Great Britain and which probably has been taken by the Government of France, if the United States Government did not feel that the request made by the Japanese Government, if acceded to, might prove embarrassing to the cause of the powers at war with Germany. There are several elements which contribute to this determination: First, It is considered inadvisable to take any steps which will unnecessarily antagonize at this time any of the various elements of the people which now control the power in Russia. Second, The necessity for intervention has not in the opinion of this Government arisen and decision concerning it may be postponed in order that it may be further considered in the light of circumstances as they may develop. Third, If the necessity for intervention should arise it may become expedient in the circumstances then existing to have military cooperation to that end by the parties at war with Germany, or by such of them as may feel they should be asked to cooperate. Fourth, Unless the matter is broached to the Government of China and consented to by it, this Government may deem it advisable to consider whether harmonious cooperation might not be promoted if such part of the Trans-Siberian Railroad as crosses the territory of China should be guarded and protected by the military forces of China.

The Government of the United States considers that it would be particularly unfortunate to do anything now which would tend to estrange from our common interests any considerable portion of the people of Russia, and that circumstances do not seem to warrant at this time a decision to take steps in Siberia which would, in its opinion, have the effect of arousing Russian opposition and resentment.

You will please make an opportunity to lay the matter orally before the authorities of the Government to which you are accredited. You will express the hope that that Government will in consideration of the views expressed agree with the Government of the United States that it will be for the best interests of the powers at war with

Germany and Austria to adopt the course of action suggested and avoid a commitment at the present time. Lansing[2]

T telegram (SDR, RG 59, 861.00/1066, DNA).
[1] R. S. Morris to RL, Feb. 8, 1918, T telegram (SDR, RG 59, 861.00/1066, DNA).
[2] The same telegram was sent to the embassy in Paris, and the embassy in Tokyo and the legation in Peking were informed of its contents.

David Rowland Francis to Robert Lansing

Petrograd Feb. 13, 1918

2365. For the Secretary. My 2354,[1] mainly framed by Sisson on documents procured by myself and sent at his instigation to prove relation which I thought existed from the beginning of the last revolution until my conviction shaken by Robins who said after thorough investigation, was convinced that Lenin and Trotsky received no German money. Am now satisfied they did accept it but recent developments demonstrate they did their work too well and were making inroads in Germany and Austria. They felt justified in accepting money from Germany as they promote the chances for their world wide social revolution for which they are constantly working, being willing to sacrifice any country therefore. Kolontai[2] and three other prominent Bolsheviks leaving for Stockholm bent on international revolutionary propaganda; watch them. Provisional Government probably unaware that money used; such information possibly withheld by Halpern,[3] its trusted official, whom British now suspect although he was then their legal adviser.

Separate Ukraine peace negotiated with Bourgeois Rada which Soviet army successfully fighting;[4] Sweden and Germany aiding Bourgeois element in Finland which Russian Red Guard fighting; reported arrests by Bolshevik of Baltic province German sympathizing land owners because Germans threatening Revel and Petrograd, all indicate that Bolchevik sincerely opposing Germany and consequently aiding Allies but unintentionally. Difficult to believe that declaration that state of war ceased is part of frame up with Germany.[5] Army demobilization part of program to prove Bolshevik not continuing imperialistic war while organizations of Red Guard volunteer legion to defend revolution not inconsistent.

Meantime Alexieff, Korniloff, organizing army in south avowedly to preserve order in Russia when Soviet Government overthrown as now generally predicted inevitable. A's representatives here declare he not fighting Bolshevik but pleased by their success in Ukraine.

Situation is difficult problem. Immediate solution impossible.

Trotsky and other peace commissioners returned to Petrograd and Trotsky will address central Soviet committee evening of fourteenth. Francis.

T telegram (WP, DLC).

¹ D. R. Francis to RL, Feb. 9-13, 1918, T telegram (SDR, RG 59, 862.20261/53, DNA), printed in *FR 1918, Russia*, I, 371-78. This lengthy telegram, transmitted in sections over five days, consisted of the texts, with some running commentary, of the first group of what came to be known as the Sisson Documents. These were copies of letters, telegrams, and circulars, procured from various Russian sources, including the Bolshevik headquarters in the Smolny Institute in Petrograd, which purported to show that Lenin, Trotsky, and other Bolshevik leaders had been in the pay of the German government since before the outbreak of war in 1914 and had continued to accept German funds even after the November Revolution. Edgar Sisson, greatly intrigued by this first group of documents, began to devote himself full-time to procuring additional material from the shadowy underground agents who had provided the original papers and to establishing the authenticity of all the documents. For Sisson's own discussion of the materials, see Edgar G. Sisson, *One Hundred Red Days: A Personal Chronicle of the Bolshevik Revolution* (New Haven, Conn., 1931), pp. 291-401 *passim*. For a much fuller and impartial discussion of the acquisition and significance of the documents, see Kennan, *Russia Leaves the War*, pp. 413-20, 441-54. Many American and British diplomats and governmental officials doubted the authenticity of the materials from the first. Kennan has proved beyond reasonable doubt that most of the documents were forgeries. See Kennan, "The Sisson Documents," *Journal of Modern History*, XXVIII (June 1956), 130-54.

² Aleksandra Mikhailovna Kollontai, Commissar of Public Welfare, the only female member of the Council of Commissars. The mission to Sweden was intended to establish commercial and diplomatic contacts for the Bolshevik regime.

³ He cannot be identified.

⁴ The Ukrainian Central Rada was a regional representative body which had come into being following the revolution of March 1917. It claimed, somewhat tenuously, to hold supreme political authority in the Ukraine and demanded and received from the provisional government in Petrograd a large measure of regional autonomy. "Bourgeois" is an inaccurate term to describe the members of the Rada; most were socialists of one variety or another. However, because of their nationalistic aspirations, they were unable to reach a satisfactory accommodation with the Bolshevik regime following the November Revolution. In late December, the Petrograd authorities established a Bolshevik government in the Ukraine with its seat at Kharkov, and, shortly thereafter, undertook military operations against the Rada, by then located in Kiev. Meanwhile, the Rada sent its own representatives to Brest-Litovsk in the hope of negotiating a separate peace between the Ukraine and the Central Powers. Both movements reached culmination almost simultaneously. The Bolsheviks took Kiev on February 8 and a by then largely meaningless German-Ukrainian peace treaty was signed at Brest-Litovsk on the following day. See Kennan, *Russia Leaves the War*, pp. 165-66, 183-86; Richard Pipes, *The Formation of the Soviet Union: Communism and Nationalism, 1917-1923*, rev. edn. (Cambridge, Mass., 1964), pp. 53-73, 115-26; and John W. Wheeler-Bennett, *Brest-Litovsk: The Forgotten Peace, March 1918* (London, 1938), pp. 154-221 *passim*.

⁵ This was a reference to Trotsky's famous formula, "No war—no peace." That is, the Soviet government declared that Russia was no longer at war with the Central Powers and would demobilize its armies on all fronts at once; at the same time, it refused to sign the peace treaty proposed by the Central Powers. Trotsky had persuaded Lenin to agree to this *démarche* in conferences in Petrograd in late January. It was left to Trotsky to decide upon the psychological moment to announce the policy. He did so in a well-known speech to the peace conference at Brest-Litovsk on February 10, following which the Soviet negotiators immediately left the conference. See *ibid.*, pp. 183-97, 207-28. Trotsky's speech is printed in Jane Degras, ed., *Soviet Documents on Foreign Policy* (3 vols., London and New York, 1951-53), I, 43-45.

To Joseph Irwin France

Personal.

My dear Senator: [The White House] 14 February, 1918

Thank you for the courtesy of your letter of February eleventh. I have read the bill which accompanied your letter, S. 3440, with close attention. It amounts, does it not, to a universal draft, industrial as well as military, and constitutes a departure from the policy of the Government, and indeed of the governments of other free states, which is so radical that I take the liberty of saying that I do not think it would be wise even if it were possible.

The working men of this country are very warmly opposed, and I think quite justifiably opposed, to being drafted and subjected to compulsory labor. The labor difficulties are many and it is not at all clear how some of them are to be overcome, but I believe that it would be a very serious mistake to depart from the methods which are already available. I mean that the men must be sought out and the conditions of labor must be acceptable, and that we must accomplish the results we desire by organized effort rather than by compulsion.

I speak frankly about this matter, because my conviction with regard to it is very deep-seated, and I beg that you will not regard my expression of this judgment as in any way subtracting from my appreciation of your courtesy in consulting me.

Sincerely yours,   Woodrow Wilson

TLS (Letterpress Books, WP, DLC).

To the Duke of Devonshire

[The White House] 14 February, 1918

May I not thank you earnestly for the courtesy of your message[1] informing me of the death of Sir Cecil Spring-Rice[2] and beg that you will convey to Lady Spring-Rice for Mrs. Wilson and myself our profoundest sympathy for the death of her husband whom we had come to esteem as a friend and admire as a man and for whose loss we personally grieve.   Woodrow Wilson.

T telegram (WP, DLC).
   [1] It is missing.
   [2] Spring Rice had died of heart failure in the early morning of February 14 at Government House in Ottawa, where he had been a guest of the Duke of Devonshire.

From Robert Lansing

My dear Mr. President: Washington February 14, 1918

I enclose a copy of a telegram from Mr. John F. Stevens dated at Harbin, February 10th,[1] and another from the Ambassador at Tokio, dated February 8th,[2] which present conditions bearing on the question of whether the Russian Railway Service Corps shall return to America or proceed to Siberia; the men are now at Nagasaki.

I believe the importance of keeping the Siberian Railway in operation to be very great. The friendly purpose which originally prompted us to put these experienced American railway men at the disposal of Russia has not, in my mind, been qualified by later developments. I believe we should take prompt affirmative action on Mr. Stevens' report. To assist you in forming your own conclusions on this question perhaps you will allow me to recall some of the circumstances.

The Russian Railway Service Corps was organized on the recommendation of Mr. Stevens after conference with the Provisional Government of Russia. It consists of two hundred and thirty American railway operators, including division superintendents etc., and about fifty skilled railway mechanics. The men sailed for Vladivostok in early November, but when they arrived there December 14th, conditions were not favorable to their landing, especially as they had brought no reserve food rations. They accordingly proceeded to Nagasaki where, it was agreed after conference with Russian authorities in this country they should be held for a reasonable period.

Six weeks and more have now elapsed and Mr. Stevens has returned to Harbin, under instructions from the Department, to make a final report as to whether the Corps should go into Siberia or return home.

The original plan was that the expenses of maintenance and salaries should be paid from Russian credits here until the men reached Russia, when they would be taken over by the Russian Ministry of Ways and Communications to serve as instructors and advisers. They are specially commissioned by the Secretary of War as officers of the "Russian Railway Service Corps" in grades from second lieutenant to colonel, and they wear the uniform of American army officers of corresponding rank.

At the present time it would appear that only about one hundred thousand dollars remain from the Russian credits originally allocated to the expenses of this Corps. It is possible that additional

Russian funds may prove obtainable here or through the Russian railway authorities in Siberia, but this cannot be certain. If the men go in, they must not be abandoned through lack of foresight on our part. On that account, any decision to send them into Russia should include a consideration of the possibility of having ourselves to supply means for their further maintenance. The aggregate monthly pay-roll of the Corps is about $70,000. It was estimated that the cost of keeping the men in the field for a year, including salaries, transportation to Russia, telephone apparatus and equipment, etc., would approximate $1,500,000. The men have been picked, by a careful process of selection, from our various railways and their salaries are necessarily proportionate; I understand that Mr. George Emerson, who is in charge of the Corps with the rank of Colonel, receives compensation at the rate of $20,000 a year.

I have given you these details to recall the very considerable effort which was made in getting these men together and sending them to Russia and the importance which was consequently attached to the undertaking at that time. Mr. Stevens thinks the original plan can be carried out if we act now.

Faithfully yours, Robert Lansing

TLS (SDR, RG 59, 861.77/770b, DNA).
[1] J. F. Stevens to RL, Feb. 10, 1918, TC telegram (SDR, RG 59, 861.77/770b, DNA). Stevens briefly outlined a scheme to put the members of the Russian Railway Service Corps to work in and around Harbin on the Chinese Eastern Railway, a branch of the Trans-Siberian Railway. He urged the necessity of immediate approval of the plan in Washington: "If you disapprove my decision wish to say frankly I can do no more."
[2] R. S. Morris to RL, Feb. 8, 1918, TC telegram (SDR, RG 59, 861.77/770b, DNA), printed in FR 1918, Russia, II, 42-43. Morris reported that Stevens had telegraphed him, saying: "Prospect dubious. The situation in my opinion grave. The Allies should act vigorously or they may later on be at war to hold north [route] across the Pacific." More important, Morris stated, the Japanese government was "seriously discussing some plan of immediate action" in regard to Siberia, but it desired approval by the United States and the Allies. He then summarized a conversation which he had had on February 5 with the Japanese Foreign Minister, Viscount Ichiro Motono, in which the latter had hinted broadly that the Japanese would take control of the area along the lines of the Trans-Siberian and Chinese Eastern railroads between Vladivostok and Chita.

From Herbert Clark Hoover

Dear Mr. President: Washington, D. C. *14 February 1918*

Three different bills have been introduced into Congress during the last few days, looking toward an increase in the minimum guarantee for 1918 wheat, from the $2.00 under the Food Bill to various sums up to $3.00. One of these has been introduced by Senator McCumber, another by Senator Gore and still another by Congressman Norton.[1] There has also been organized in Washington a group of agricultural representatives called the "Wheat

Growers Protective Association," whose energies are directed towards accomplishing this legislation.

It does seem to me that determinations of this type should be left to commissions to be appointed by yourself, to make necessary and proper inquiry in which all complexions of such problems can be considered and it was in our mind to suggest to you—some time next June—to assemble such a commission as sat last year, and obtain from them a view as to the price to be paid over and above the guaranteed minimum for 1918 wheat if in their view any increase was desirable. My present purpose, however, of addressing you is to express my extreme anxiety as to the results that will come from the agitation of such legislation. About 125,000,000 bushels of 1917 wheat are still in the hands of the farmer and we are depending upon this supply for the bread of our people for the months of April, May and June. An agitation of this character will surely create hopes in the minds of the farmer that he will receive a larger price next year for his wheat than is being paid this year ($2.20) and he will certainly hold his present wheat with the hope of mixing it with his 1918 wheat and securing the larger return. I feel absolutely certain that if such legislation is passed or even pressed, one of two alternative courses will have to be pursued by the Government.

The first alternative is to stop all Allied shipments instantly and to use force to secure at least a sufficient portion of the 1917 wheat from the farmer to complete our domestic supplies at the price that was established by the commission under your direction and which price was stated to be constant for the year. The second alternative would be to at once raise the price of wheat to the level of the enlarged guarantee. In so doing we will not only be acting unfairly to all of the agricultural community who have marketed their wheat on the assurance that it was a fixed and constant price for the year, but further than this, we would be practically helpless to prevent the same rise in the price of some 90,000,000 bushels of wheat in the hands of the thousands of country elevators and mills and some 20,000,000 barrels of flour in the hands of the distributing trades in the country. In other words, in such an event a tax of anything up to $200,000,000 will be placed upon the consuming community without one penny's benefit to the producer and to the sole benefit of the distributing trades. It is hopeless for us to expect to prosecute the 300,000 concerns engaged in the distribution of wheat and flour for profiteering, or to determine which of their particular stores were based on the old price and which upon the new.

You are perhaps aware that there has been planted this year 42,000,000 acres of winter wheat as against 40,000,000 acres last year and as against 33,000,000 pre-war normal. I take it that this has been planted because of the stimulation of the $2.00 guarantee and it is evidence in my mind—and I think in Mr. Houston's—that the guarantee is ample to produce the results desired. Moreover, the world food situation has developed to a point where it is almost a matter of indifference as to what cereal is planted. The Allied peoples are now eating such a mixture of wheat, corn, rye and barley that if the farmers in this country should decide that any other cereal is preferable to planting spring wheat, it would make but little difference in the world food supply.

I have every desire that justice should be done to the American farmer, that he should receive every stimulant possible to the utmost exertion, but I believe that our anxiety should be equally directed towards the position of the American consumer, for if the price of flour should be raised during this winter by $5. per barrel it would mean a rise of at least two cents a pound in the price of bread and, as you know, already our anxieties are sufficiently great as to tiding over our industrial populations with the present range of prices without disturbances.

I am   Your obedient servant,   Herbert Hoover

TLS (WP, DLC).
¹ Patrick Daniel Norton, Republican congressman from North Dakota.

Louis Seibold to Joseph Patrick Tumulty

My dear Joe: [New York] February 14, 1918

Answering your note of the other day:

The inspiration of the Non-Partisan League was undoubtedly an honest attempt to secure needed reforms of an agrarian character for the benefit of the farmers of the Northwest, particularly North Dakota, who felt themselves the victims of discriminations practiced by the railways, the milling interests and other corporation agencies.

The extraordinary success of the movement, whetted the avarice of the promoters of it, who seemed to have entirely lost sight of their original ideals and responded (for their own profit) to many extravagant ventures proposed by the rapidly increasing membership—now approximately 150,000 at $16 a head per year.

The original program of the League was consequently modified and adopted to permit the reflection of both open and veiled hostility to the Government's war policy, as illustrated by the speeches of the League leaders and the Editorial utterances of its organ when the President urged the Selective Military Draft Law, the initial

Liberty Loan and the other projects that he wisely deemed necessary for the welfare of the country. In other words, the League played to strong pacifist and anti-American elements, which is undoubtedly very substantial in that section of the country.

These expressions of dissent and disloyalty were continued until the meeting held under the auspices of the League in St. Paul in September, at which Senator La Follette delivered the speech that aroused a great storm of protest throughout the country and resulted in a demand from the people of Minnesota for his expulsion from the Senate.[1]

The League then ceased its open antagonism to the Government though its recantation was disingenuous and not convincing; nor is it yet. The present utterances of its spokesmen are evasive rather than frankly loyal.

The propaganda of the League is of the Bolsheviki sort—against moneyed and other corporate interests which are embraced in the slogan of the League "Down with the dollar-cursed Atlantic Seaboard." The D.C.S.[2] is alleged, by the League's spokesmen to control the Government, now as in past administrations.

My conclusions after a month's study of the operations of the League (and which I hope are impartial) is that the movement, primarily commendable, has degen[e]rated into an opportunist venture designed to advance the personal interests of the general offices of the close corporation that controls it.

Its program of expansion, recently announced by Mr. Townley, the League's president, calls for alliances with the elements of discord in labor organizations and other elements of industrial and agricultural life, with a view of recruiting a sufficient following to secure the balance of power in politics.

The encouragement given the I.W.W. movement is an instance of this ambition.

The control of the executive and lower legislative branch of North Dakota by the League, during the last two years has not resulted in the adoption of any of the reforms contained in the League platform.

In a word, I regard the venture which as said, was genuinely an attempt to bring about commendable reforms, as little less in its present stage, as a get-rich-quick scheme of its clever, though personally uninteresting creators.

The most complete and ac[c]urate information of a detailed character regarding the League and its activities has been collected by Mr. C. W. Ames,[3] a member of the Minnesota Committee of Public Safety, who has conducted an exhaustive and impartial inquiry into the subject.

I hesitate to impose upon the already heavily overtaxed shoulders of the President, so am confining my response to your letter to these general terms. He has my good wishes always, and if there is any service which I may perform to lighten them, he has but to command such skill or abilities as I may possess no matter what the extent of personal sacrifice.

To you I send my best wishes and I assure you that no one can grieve more deeply for Billy Hughes than I. It was a real privilege and joy to have known such a man.

With my best regard to the President and his family and to your own, I am,   Faithfully yours,   Louis Seibold

TLS (WP, DLC).
¹ La Follette had addressed, extemporaneously, a conference of the Nonpartisan League in St. Paul on September 20, 1917. His main topic was the financing of the war. He argued that persons who profited from the war should bear the main burden of financing the war effort. However, the most controversial portions of his address were some rather incidental references to his opposition to the entrance of the United States into the conflict. The gravamen of his remarks was that, while the United States had had some grievances against Germany, they were insufficient to justify America's entrance into the European bloodbath. As one historian has pointed out, even accurate news reports of La Follette's speech would have set off a furor. As it happened, the Associated Press reported that the Senator had said that the United States had had no grievances against Germany and that the sinking of *Lusitania* had been justified. The published reports of the speech created a storm of denunciation against both La Follette and the Nonpartisan League. The Minnesota Commission of Public Safety conducted an investigation of the speech and, as a result, petitioned the United States Senate to expel La Follette. Similar demands came from many parts of the country. Senator Frank B. Kellogg introduced a resolution to expel the Wisconsin Senator. The resulting senatorial investigation continued until after the Armistice, when it was finally dropped. Some eight months after La Follette's address, the Associated Press admitted that its original dispatch on his speech had been seriously in error. See Belle Case La Follette and Fola La Follette, *Robert M. La Follette, June 14, 1855-June 18, 1925* (2 vols., New York, 1953), II, 761-71, 771-919 *passim*, and Carl H. Chrislock, *The Progressive Era in Minnesota, 1899-1918* (St. Paul, Minn., 1971), pp. 149-52.
² That is, the "Dollar-Cursed Seaboard."
³ That is, Charles Wilberforce Ames.

From Robert Lansing

My dear Mr. President: Washington February 15, 1918.

I have read the enclosed memorandum on Revolutions in Europe by Mr. William English Walling with great interest and care, and throughout the reading I felt that Mr. Walling had a keen appreciation of the forces which are menacing the present social order in nearly every European country and which may have to be reckoned with even in this country. It is really a remarkable analysis of the dangerous elements which are coming to the surface and which are in many ways more to be dreaded than autocracy; the latter is despotism but an intelligent despotism, while the former is a despotism of ignorance. One, at least has the virtue of order, while the other is productive of disorder and anarchy. It is a condition which cannot but arouse the deepest concern.

I think that Mr. Walling's views in regard to the Bolsheviks are helpful and sound, and after reading them I am more than ever convinced that our policy has been the right one and should be continued. In talking with the French Ambassador yesterday about Russia he said that he considered our course had been the wisest and that the other Governments had failed in dealing with the situation.

We will soon have to face this proposed socialist meeting at Stockholm and determine upon the attitude we should take in dealing with it. We must decide whether or not we are to permit Americans to obtain passports to attend the meeting there or anywhere else it may be held. The meeting of this element of society, imbued with the idea of an international social revolution, might become a very real menace to all existing forms of government, democratic as well as monarchical. And yet, if we prevent Americans from attending there is danger of seemingly confirming the charge that this nation is controlled by a capitalistic class. I see no middle course. No avoidance of a decision. I think that the subject ought to engage our attention because we should have a very definite policy determined before the time for action arrives.

I thank you for letting me see Mr. Walling's memorandum which is most instructive and of which I have taken the liberty to make a copy for future reference and in order to give to it more critical study.   Faithfully yours,   Robert Lansing.

TLS (WP, DLC).

From Edward Mandell House

Dear Governor: New York. February 15, 1918.

I am enclosing you a letter from Weigand.[1] I hope you will read it for I think he gives the true situation and it will be useful to keep in mind.

I am also enclosing a few newspaper comments which may have escaped your observation.[2] I am a little surprised at the warmth with which the French received your address. There seems not to have been a dissenting voice.

Many of the correspondents of the English papers have been to see me within the last day or two, and it is the general opinion that your speech was necessary, and that it will be of great benefit in holding English sentiment steadfast.

The press comments that we have so far from Germany and Austria are less favorable than we hoped, but I am sure the message will do the work intended.

The effect upon our people has been and will continue to be of the best. You have gone to the limit, and if you receive an unfavorable response from the Central Powers, American people of every shade of opinion will feel that you have done all that was possible.

The proceedings in the House of Commons the other day were made to look favorable to the Lloyd George Government.[3] As a matter of fact, quite the contrary is true. We will talk of this later.

Affectionately yours,   E. M. House

TLS (WP, DLC).

[1] K. H. von Wiegand to EMH, Feb. 14, 1918, TLS (WP, DLC). Von Wiegand cautioned against the common assumption that the recent Austrian peace moves were indicative of a rupture in the Austro-German alliance. His interviews with various Austrian officials in the last few years indicated that the Austrians had long felt that they, because less odious to the Allies than the Germans, would have to take the initiative when the time for peace talks came. The Germans, Von Wiegand believed, had recently come to a reluctant acquiescence in this view. He also suggested that the American press was placing too much "emphasis and hope" on the prospects for revolution in Austria and Germany.

[2] These enclosures are missing.

[3] For some time, Lloyd George had been maneuvering to have General Sir William R. Robertson either removed as Chief of the Imperial General Staff or rendered powerless if he remained in that post. The Prime Minister's professed reason for this activity was to reassert civilian control over the military establishment. By early February, it appeared that a stalemate had been reached since Robertson refused either to leave the War Office or have his powers diluted. Lloyd George then decided to dismiss the General. Herbert H. Asquith, who was aware of the impending dismissal, brought up the subject in the House of Commons on February 12. He demanded, on behalf of the House, an assurance that no change was contemplated in the authority and power of either Robertson or Sir Douglas Haig, the British commander in chief in France. Lloyd George responded with an implicit threat of a dissolution and a general election. "If the House of Commons and the country," he said, "are not satisfied with the conduct of the War, and if they think there is any Government which can conduct it better, then it is their business, in God's name, to put that other Government in." As it turned out, House's comment on the significance of the proceedings was a bit premature. Robertson's "resignation" as Chief of the Imperial General Staff was made public on February 18. Lloyd George's government stood the test in Parliament largely because Haig had at the last moment decided to stand with the Prime Minister rather than to back Robertson. For a careful account of this intricate affair, see William Maxwell Aitken, Baron Beaverbrook, *Men and Power, 1917-1918* (London, 1956), pp. 186-216.

From Ralph Pulitzer

My dear Mr. President,   [New York] Feb 15th [1918].

After giving very careful and, I confess, painful consideration to what you said to me yesterday I decided that, in the face of your judgment as well as that of Secretary Daniels, the responsibility for carrying out my desire to go on foreign service was greater than I was able to assume.

I have, therefore, acquiesced in the suggestion of the Secretary that I be transferred to Intelligence work in New York, and the transfer has been ordered.

In a situation which represented a dilemma of sacrifices I hope and think you will believe that I have subjected myself to by far the greater sacrifice. I can only hope that it will be justified by the results although that is something that I suppose can never be known.

I pay you the compliment, Sir, of not thanking you for any kindness to me in this matter of duty, and yet I feel I must write to express my appreciation of the advice which has ended my perplexities.

Please do not trouble to answer this letter, which I am sure you will understand, is not one of those written for the sake of its reply.

With sincere regards I am

Faithfully yours   Ralph Pulitzer.

ALS (WP, DLC).

Tasker Howard Bliss to Robert Lansing

Versailles, France. February 15, 1918

Your special blue to me dated February 2 was not received until today. Subject matter is now under discussion by Military Representatives on Supreme War Council and I expect to cable their joint view to you on Monday.   Bliss.

TC telegram (WDR, RG 120, Records of the American Section of the Supreme War Council, 1917-1919, File No. 317, DNA).

Hugh Robert Wilson to Robert Lansing

Pontarlier, (Berne), February 15, 1918.

2647. CONFIDENTIAL. At my request Ackerman has arranged, in his capacity as correspondent for PHILADELPHIA EVENING LEDGER, with an Austrian correspondent of considerable ability to receive ten telegrams a month from Vienna on political affairs. Correspondent has enough influence to get his stuff past censor and so far it has been excellent.

He is ready at Ackerman's telegraphic request to interview any statesman on any given subject. This is brought to Department's attention so that if it desires to submit questions on any subject to Czernin or others the means is provided to do so unofficially and without Austrians realizing interest of our Government therein. Ackerman requests that as much of this information as may be expedient be brought to attention of Whaley[1] of EVENING LEDGER and that instructions be given him concerning routing these telegrams to United States for publication. H.P.D.[2]   Wilson.[3]

T telegram (SDR, RG 59, 763.72/8873, DNA).
    [1] Percival Huntington Whaley, editor of the *Philadelphia Evening Ledger.*
    [2] Perhaps "High Priority Dispatch."
    [3] There is an RLhw notation on this letter which reads as follows: "Prest says—Not be done. 2/19/18 RL."

Robert Lansing to Hugh Robert Wilson

[Washington] February 15, 1918

1500. SECRET FOR WILSON ALONE TO DECODE.

Concerning the possible need of Austria to obtain financial aid after the war under certain conditions I think that it would be wise at this time to convey secretly, unofficially and orally to Lammasch or his agent that, in the event of Austria being deprived of German financial support through acting contrary to the wishes of the German Government in independently arranging a cessation of hostilities and negotiations for peace at the present time, person conveying information has strong impression amounting to conviction that Government of the United States will exert its influence to the end that financial assistance may be obtained in the United States as nearly as possible to the extent that Germany would have furnished it if there had been no breach in their relations.

As to the most expedient channel to convey this secret and unofficial information to Lammasch I rely wholly upon your discretion, though I think that it would be unwise to employ Herron, whose relationship with Lammasch should in no way be embarrassed by making him the agent of delivery of even the most unofficial message. Herron has acted so wisely and shown such discretion his future usefulness must in no way be endangered. Please act promptly and discreetly in this matter and report fully.   Lansing

T telegram (SDR, RG 59, 763.72119/8184a, DNA).

Lord Reading to the Foreign Office

Washington. 15th February 1918.

No. 624. (K). *Secret.* I have had a long interview with President to-day, who received me very cordially:

(1). Disposition of American troops. I referred to urgent need of assistance of American troops and I was proceeding to press arguments in favour of Sir W. Robertson's scheme when President informed me that he understood this matter had now been settled and that within the last 24 hours, General Pershing had informed United States Government immediate arrangements had been made which President gathered satisfied both British and French Military authorities.

He said he had taken the opportunity within the last few days of testing public opinion of various well informed and well disposed quarters in America and opinion was unanimous that it would be a grave error to send American troops under any bargain or understanding with British Government that these should be used to supplement British army instead of for purpose of forming an American army. He added that there was a section of public and in Congress, which was not pro-British, but (?indeed) was anti-British, which was regrettable, but sentiment nevertheless existed and must be considered. He stated General Pershing had fullest powers to make any necessary disposition of American troops and if he thought it necessary to use American troops with British or to supplement British brigades with American battalions, it was left to his judgement as Military Commander and he added General Pershing seemed now to have come to a conclusion.

I have had no intimation of any change in the situation since I left England save telegrams which passed while I was on the seas. President himself was not fully seized[1] of details and referred me to Secretary Baker. I therefore did not press the matter further, but expressed satisfaction with news he had given me.

(2). Mexico.

I read to President material portions of three despatches from you, numbers 861, 872, and 885, which I received this morning as I was about to leave for the White House. He said that throughout his experience of Mexican affairs he had repeatedly received information that Carranza intended to interfere with situation at oil wells, which had not been followed by action (?specified). He believed present situation arose from desire of Carranza to substitute his troops for those of Pelaez at oil wells and thus obtain whatever benefits in money or otherwise were available.[2] He requested me to procure further information as to nature of agreement concluded by Carranza, and as to enemy agents with whom it had been made in order that United States Government might investigate matter.[3]

---

[1] That is, apprised.

[2] About the continuing domination of the oil-producing region around Tampico by General Manuel Peláez and the brief and unsuccessful attempt by the Carranza government to dislodge him in February 1918, see Robert Freeman Smith, *The United States and Revolutionary Nationalism in Mexico, 1916-1932* (Chicago, 1972), pp. 102-104, 118.

[3] Undoubtedly, Wilson's request was the result of one of the recurring rumors that

I promised to forward his request. He seemed to be unconvinced of reliability of statement. I called his attention to an article in "Washington Post"[4] of to-day stating an agreement had been drawn up between President Wilson and Carranza, which was mutually satisfactory to both Governments and would be formally signed within a few days. The terms of agreement are stated with an appearance of precision and naming persons who have taken part in negotiations. I told the President that I had not heard of any agreement or negotiations until I read "Washington Post" this morning. He said that was exactly his position and that he knew nothing of it and that so far as he was concerned, it was without foundation, but that State Department might be negotiating some minor arrangement of which he was not aware. I am hoping to see Secretary of State to-morrow and will again cable you.

(3). Japan.

I referred to answer from (?State Department) to the effect that United States Government did not think it advisable that Japan should act as mandatory of Allies, but that there should be International co-operation. I pointed out we could not send a force there, neither could French or Italians, and asked whether President intended to send American troops. He said he meant by International co-operation, landing of sailors and marines, but that he thought matter one of academic interest only as he was sure Japanese would not undertake task of guarding railway. Moreover he was of opinion that effect upon Russians of landing of Japanese troops in Siberia, would be that middle class and moderate parties in Russia might be as glad to have the protection of German intervention which was closer at hand than Japanese. My impression is that American Government is against any intervention by Japanese in Siberia with Allies or for Allies, and would prefer if Japan should intervene at Vladivostock, that she should do so on her own initiative thus leaving it open for America and Allies to make any representations they may hereafter think fit to Japan. I placed British Government's views before him, but it had little if any effect as his attitude was that nothing would result as Japan would not agree to carry out any such plan. End of K.

---

the Carranza government had concluded some kind of political and/or economic agreement with Germany. Wilson was skeptical of the "reliability of statement." The most thorough modern study of German-Mexican relations concludes that, while Carranza was somewhat pro-German and certainly anti-Ally and anti-United States, he did refuse all German efforts to negotiate a political alliance and refused to reach an economic agreement because he was unwilling to accept the conditions demanded by Germany. Friedrich Katz, *The Secret War in Mexico: Europe, the United States and the Mexican Revolution* (Chicago and London, 1981), pp. 387-524 *passim*.

[4] Albert W. Fox, "Carranza Has Made Terms with Wilson," *Washington Post*, Feb. 15, 1918.

(4) Food.

I explained seriousness of situation as regards food and very urgent necessity of greater supplies being transported to Seaboard. He stated he fully appreciated situation and was doing everything possible to meet it and that Mr. MacAdoo had all necessary powers and Government was doing everything possible to expedite forwarding of supplies. I cabled yesterday substance of my interview with Mr. MacAdoo.

(5). Shipping Construction.

I said I was very concerned about position so far as I had been able to ascertain it and that there seemed a possibility of further serious delay.

He said this was a labour question and was also occasioning him much concern.[5] Demands were pressed by workmen for large increases in wages which, if granted, would he believed, decrease instead of increase production, as men would work fewer hours. We discussed possibility of utilizing services of labour mission headed by Mr. Appleton,[6] and it was finally left that I should see Mr. Hurley the President of Shipping Board about it. President Wilson is considering labour problem as a whole and more particularly with regard to shipyards as situation is undoubtedly serious.

(6). Criticisms upon United States Government.

President discussed with me criticisms which had been levelled at United States Government. He thought it was of advantage to have had them and they had enabled Government to give explanations and statements to rebut reckless observations which had

[5] William Levi Hutcheson, president of the United Brotherhood of Carpenters and Joiners of America, had long been reluctant to go along with the government's program for labor-management cooperation for the duration of the war. In particular, he had refused to sign the agreement creating the Shipbuilding Labor Adjustment Board. He objected to the agreement principally because it in effect banned the closed shop. In late 1917, the board had reached an agreement with carpenters on the West Coast which provided large wage increases in return for the abandonment of the closed shop. This led to great discontent among carpenters on the eastern seaboard. In early February 1918, Hutcheson and the board reached an impasse in negotiations to head off a strike on the East Coast; the board demanded that Hutcheson sign the agreement which had created it before he could negotiate wages and other issues; Hutcheson still refused. On February 11, carpenters and joiners in shipyards on Staten Island and Shooters Island in New York Harbor took matters into their own hands by going on strike and demanding large wage increases and the closed shop. They were joined by their co-workers in Baltimore on February 14. In several public statements, Edward N. Hurley directly blamed Hutcheson for the strikes and demanded that the strikers return to work and allow the board to work out a settlement. Hutcheson in reply insisted that he had tried to prevent the walkouts but that he could not persuade the strikers to return to work unless their demands were met. See Robert A. Christie, *Empire in Wood: A History of the Carpenters' Union* (Ithaca, N. Y., 1956), pp. 217-27, and the *New York Times*, Feb. 13-16, 1918.

[6] That is, William Archibald Appleton, secretary of the General Federation of Trade Unions of Great Britain and a member of the British Labor Mission, which had recently come to the United States at the invitation of the American Federation of Labor to provide the American organization with the benefit of its wartime experience.

been made in some quarters. My own impression from all I have learnt is that criticisms and investigations have had effect of stimulating and quickening Government's activities in some respects although general situation is still in some confusion. I will report later more fully upon this.

(7). No mention was made by President or by me of difference of views between him and British Government as to true meaning of Count Czernin's speech or as to policy to be pursued. I had discussed matter with Secretary of State who attributed no importance to it. I thought it inadvisable therefore to raise it with President unless I heard that you wished it.

T telegram (FO 371/3486, PRO).

To Robert Lansing

My dear Mr. Secretary,   The White House. 16 February, 1918.

This[1] is, indeed, extremely interesting, and confirms my impression of Herron. I agree *in toto* with his analysis and conclusions!
Faithfully yours,   W.W.

WWTLI (SDR, RG 59, 763.72119/1300½, DNA).
[1] Enclosure II printed with H. R. Wilson to RL, Feb. 4, 1918.

From Robert Lansing

My dear Mr. President: Washington February 16, 1918.

If you will allow me I should like to refer again to the question of sending the Russian Railway Service Corps into Siberia.

All supplies and equipment have been furnished. The only possible charges I had in mind, in my letter of February 14th, were the salaries of the men and the expenses of their ultimate return to this country. We may be able to devise means to provide for both these items from Russian funds—indeed I am hopeful that we can. But, meanwhile, we should be certain that any final shortage in the Russian funds can be made up by ourselves.

This seems to me to be one of those bridges that we ought to make sure in advance that we shall be able to cross if we have to do so.   Faithfully yours,   Robert Lansing

TLS (SDR, RG 59, 861.77/770, DNA).

To Robert Lansing

My dear Mr. Secretary,   The White House. 16 February, 1918.

If your impression is right in this matter and all that we have to pay is the salaries of the men actually engaged in this work and the expenses that will be incident to their return to this country, I am of course willing to bear those charges, provided they are really accompli[s]hing something and the charge is not of indefinite duration. Their message referred to other and very much greater expenditures.   Faithfully Yours,   W.W.

WWTLI (SDR, RG 59, 861.77/770, DNA).

To Robert Lansing, with Enclosure

My dear Mr. Secretary,   The White House. 16 February, 1918.

This makes me exceedingly uneasy. Our views and Francis's have not in the least agreed as to the use that should be made of money in Russia and I hope that you will let him know that we cannot (under the terms under which moneys are put at our disposal) accept drafts of this kind. It may be necessary to accept this one (I leave that to your judgment) but this should not be repeated, of that I am clear.   Faithfully Yours,   W.W.

WWTLI (SDR, RG 59, 124.614/89, DNA).

ENCLOSURE

Petrograd, February 11, 1918.

2359. Have occasion to use money for objects which I cannot trust to cables, consequently shall draw for not exceeding total of twenty-five thousand dollars, disposition of which I shall advise later. My 2354[1] explains partly. Other Embassies have such funds; and Sisson appears to have unlimited amount.   Francis.

T telegram (SDR, RG 59, 124.614/89, DNA).
[1] See D. R. Francis to RL, Feb. 13, 1918, n. 1.

From Robert Lansing, with Enclosure

My dear Mr. President: Washington February 16, 1918.

A copy of this message has been sent to you and I am sure that it causes you the same concern that it does me.

I think that resolutions of this sort are valueless and tend to give an impression that we recognize a certain measure of force in acts of the Bolshevik Government. This seems to me unfortunate. In any event I think it unwise for Mr. Crosby to act in a matter which is chiefly political rather than financial. Do you not think it would be well to speak to Secretary McAdoo about this and see if something cannot be done to offset this unauthorized action on the part of Mr. Crosby?   Faithfully yours,   Robert Lansing

TLS (SDR, RG 59, 861.51/272, DNA).

ENCLOSURE

London, Feb. 14, 1918.

8656. For McAdoo from Crosby. At meeting of Finance Section of Inter-Ally Council on Friday, Bonar Law and Klotz both being present, Klotz proposed following resolution which was adopted: "The Finance Section of the Inter-Ally Council on War Purchases and Finance, referring to the statement put forward by the Diplomatic Conference of London on February 18, 1831, regarding Belgian affairs 'It is a principle of commanding nature that treaties do not lose their value whatever be the changes that intervene in the interior organization of peoples,' Recommends for the consideration of the Governments represented the following statement:

"Whereas, The Imperial Russian Government when it contracted liabilities undoubtedly represented Russia and definitely obligated it:

"Whereas, This obligation cannot be repudiated by any authority whatever governing or which should eventually govern in Russia without shaking the very foundations of the law of nations:

"Whereas, There would be in that case no more security in the relations States and it would be impossible to enter into a contract over any long period of time on account of the risk of such a contract being eventually ignored.

"Whereas, Such a policy would mean the destruction of the credit of States as much from a political as from a financial view point.

"Whereas, A State could not borrow money under normal conditions if the lenders only guarantee was the maintenance of the constitution under which the borrowing Government as representing the country puts out a call for credit.

"Whereas, No principle is more clearly settled than the one according to which a nation bears the responcibility of the acts of its Government and the liabilities incurred are not affected by any change in authority.

"Whereas, The obligations of Russia bind and will bind the new

State or the group of new States that represent or will represent Russia now.

"Therefore, The Allied Powers will take into consideration the principles above mentioned in every negotiation relating to the recognition of the new State or new States that are eventually to be constituted in Russia."

In voting for the resolution, Chancellor of the Exchequer and myself were moved by consideration that being only a recommendation of the general principle to our respective Governments we were not in any way conpromising [compromising] their action and at the same time, according to Klotz representations, might, if the Governments accept the recommendation, aid him in some of his great difficulties. Due to the vast amount of Russian obligations held in France my own opinion is that the paragraphs defining the general principle of responsibility of succeeding Governments for debts of predecessors has been already so often stated that repetition scarcely necessary. Most important part has to do with suggestion that no recognition of new States carved out of original Russian territory should be made without provision for adoption of part of general debt."   Page.

T MS (SDR, RG 59, 861.51/272, DNA).

To Robert Lansing

My dear Mr. Secretary,   The White House. 16 February, 1918.

I was indeed very much disturbed by this message. I will speak to McAdoo about the impropriety of Crosby's taking part in any such action in the future. The Inter-Allied Board was certainly not constituted to give political advice.

And this leads me to beg that you will communicate with the Governments of Great Britain, France, and Italy to the following effect,—referring to the recent action of the Supreme War Council with regard to conditions of peace and to this action of the Inter-Allied Board with regard to the recognition of the Bolshevik authorities:

That the President wishes very respectfully but very earnestly to urge that when he suggested the creation of the Inter-Allied Board and gave his active support to the creation of the Supreme War Council it was not at all in his mind that either of these bodies should take any action or express any opinion on political subjects. He would have doubted the wisdom of appointing representatives of this Government on either body had he thought that they would undertake the decision of any questions but the very practical questions of supply and of the concerted conduct of the war which it was understand [understood] they should handle. He would appreciate it very much if this matter were very thoroughly reconsidered by the political leaders of the governments addressed and if he might be given an opportunity, should their view in this matter differ from his, to consider once more the conditions and instructions under which representatives of the United States should henceforth act.

This is, it may be, a bit blunt, but I think it imperative that we should safeguard ourselves in this all-important matter. Perhaps you will think it best to communicate these views through the diplomatic representatives here, so that they may put it in their own language after being given to understand how grave our objection is.[1]   Faithfully Yours,   W.W.

WWTLI (SDR, RG 59, 763.72Su/32½, DNA).
[1] Lansing communicated Wilson's message with minor variations in separate letters to Jusserand, Reading, and Macchi di Cellere on February 18, 1918 (SDR, RG 59, 763.72Su/32½, DNA). He also sent the message on the same date to the American ambassadors in France, Great Britain, and Italy for their own information but not for communication to the governments to which they were accredited. FR-WWS 1918, I, 1, 125.

From Edward Mandell House

Dear Governor: New York. February 16, 1918.

I want to suggest that you caution the Department of Justice concerning the selection of the man who is to investigate Hog Island affairs.[1]

I did not know who was involved, and hardly knew it was going on until it was brought to my attention by influential men connected with the work. Because of the character of the men involved I should be surprised if there was much in it. However, if they have been guilty of over-reaching the Government there is no punishment too severe, for there is nothing that would create so much suspicion and distrust in the eyes of our people.

It is evident that every possible influence will be brought to bear in this case. Perhaps you know this, but fearing lest you may not, I thought I would send a word of warning so you may personally look into the personel of those who will undertake the investigation.

The man selected should be of such known integrity and freedom from corporate interest that his report will be accepted without question.   Affectionately yours,   E. M. House

TLS (WP, DLC).

¹ See E. N. Hurley to WW, Jan. 28, 1918, n. 2. At Hurley's request, Wilson, on February 13, had requested the Attorney General to make a thorough investigation of the alleged waste and extravagance in the construction of the Hog Island facility. WW to TWG, Feb. 13, 1918, TLS (Letterpress Books, WP, DLC). This was to be in addition to the investigation by the Senate Commerce Committee already under way. Gregory announced on February 19 that the investigation would be carried out by George Carroll Todd and Mark Hyman, both assistants to the Attorney General. *New York Times*, Feb. 15 and 20, 1918.

From Edward Nash Hurley

My dear Mr. President: Washington February 16, 1918.

The carpenters' strike, as you are aware, is very serious. But it is serious only because it reveals the fact that ordinary appeals to patriotism among these men now striking are ineffective.

The Carpenters' Union has suggested the appointment of a wage commission to settle the dispute. But what is the use of establishing a new arbitration agency if the men won't recognize the present Wage Board or wait for decisions or agree to abide by them when they are handed down?

The present Wage Adjustment Board is composed of trustworthy men—Mr. Macey,¹ whom you appointed; Mr. Berres,² whom Mr. Gompers appointed; and Mr. Coolidge,³ whom I appointed, and who is serving with Mr. Gompers' Welfare Committee. Yet the carpenters would not wait until the present board looks into their grievances and makes a just decision.

We of the Shipping Board have gone through so much in the last six months, and have yielded so much to labor, and have been so disturbed with the recurrence of demands for higher wages and still higher wages, that I cannot help feeling that we must take a stand for fundamental decency.

We are working on a plan to conscript all capital invested in the shipyards, forcing the owners to surrender all profit. On the other hand, there can be no question of our liberality to labor.

But we must build ships and we cannot do the job if we must face some new threat of a strike, or what is worse, a strike without notice, somewhere every day, as we have in the past six months. We cannot yield to the demand that shops be closed because that would mean the conscription of human labor by the labor unions. I am a union man myself, but I hope we will never reach the point where we will deny the citizen the right to work in a yard solely because he has not joined the union.

The carpenters, alone of all organizations employed in the building of ships, refuse to submit their grievances to the Shipbuilding Labor Adjustment Board. Any concessions to this one union at this time would be a serious injustice to the other organizations that are loyally submitting their difficulties to the Adjustment Board and would be putting a premium on striking rather than orderly hearings.

I think we have gone as far as we should, as far as we can, in making concessions. It will be better, I think, to suffer a little delay now, while public opinion is brought to bear, rather than to settle the trouble by yielding and thus continue the encouragement of the spirit which demands but is never satisfied.

There has been a suggestion of a national wage scale for all the yards, but I fear this would upset the country generally, spreading to every industry. My own thought is that there is nothing to do but to appeal to the country and let the carpenters go back to work and await the decision of the Labor Adjustment Board, as every other shipyard craft and even some of the carpenters' locals have done.

I am enclosing copy of a telegram which is self-explanatory, also copy of the demands made by the Carpenters' Union on the Emergency Fleet Corporation calling for the closed shop for carpenter, together with my comments thereon.[4]

I am writing you frankly how I feel, in the hope that you may advise me in this matter of the highest national importance, and will await your advice and counsel.

Very faithfully yours,   Edward N Hurley

TLS (WP, DLC).
  [1] That is, V. Everit Macy.
  [2] Albert Julius Berres, secretary-treasurer of the Metal Trades Department of the American Federation of Labor.
  [3] Louis Arthur Coolidge, treasurer of the United Shoe Machinery Co.
  [4] W. Pigott to J. O. Heyworth, c. Feb. 16, 1918, TC telegram (WP, DLC); "MEMORANDUM of working conditions to be established . . . ," n.d., CC MS with E. N. Hurley typed comments in margin (WP, DLC).

From Franklin Delano Roosevelt

My dear Mr. President: Washington February 16, 1918.

As Mr. Daniels is away today, and as I did not have an opportunity of talking to him before he left about the strike of the carpenters' organization in New York and Baltimore, which threatens to spread to other points along the coast, may I give you a short statement showing in what way the Navy is affected?

First, this strike does not at the present time affect wood-workers in the Navy Yard, as they are living up to their agreement with me of last October, which put into effect a scale of wages good for one year from last November. This scale is nearly two dollars a day less than their present demands against the Fleet Corporation. There is, however, the danger that if the trouble spreads it may also affect the Navy Yards.

Second, the Navy Department is working in complete harmony under an agreement with the Shipping Board and the Federation of Labor, signed by Mr. Gompers and seventeen Presidents of important international unions, with the exception of the carpenters. The carpenters refused to sign principally because they insist on recognition of the principle of the closed shop.

Third, under this agreement, the Shipbuilding Labor Adjustment Board has already settled all labor difficulties on the Pacific Coast, and will announce tomorrow its wage scale for the Delaware River District, covering wage scales and conditions of employment. Further, this Board is now engaged in hearings covering the whole Southern Coast, and has fixed a date for hearings in New York.

Fourth, the important point, in my judgment, is that this Board has already accomplished much and is the duly authorized medium for the settlement of all labor questions affecting the shipbuilding industry. You will remember that you appointed the Chairman of this Board, Mr. V. Everett Macy, to represent the public. Every important trade in the shipbuilding industry, with the exception of the carpenters, is working under agreement with this Board, and I feel very strongly that if negotiations are opened by any other government agency looking to a settlement with a *single trade* along lines different from the regular agreement with the Federation of Labor, the whole situation will become very much involved and it may lead to a total disruption of the existing satisfactory agreements.

The Labor Adjustment Board stands ready, of course, to include the carpenters in the same agreement under which all the other important trades are working.

I only write you this because of the danger that the whole situation may again become demoralized, and that such demoralization would, of necessity, affect the Navy work also.

Faithfully yours,   Franklin D Roosevelt

TLS (WP, DLC).

From William Levi Hutcheson

My dear Mr. President: New York, February 16, 1918.

The situation now existing in the shipyards is of a nature that requires immediate attention. I, as President of the United Brotherhood of Carpenters and Joiners of America, endeavored to reach an understanding with the officials of the United States Shipping Board but was unable to do so. I feel that if given the opportunity to lay the matter fully before you that a solution should be quickly arrived at. I desire to inform you my dear Mr. President, that I as a patriotic citizen am desirous of rendering every assistance to you and our country to carry on the work necessary to bring about a successful conclusion of the world war in which we are engaged. Yours most respectfully and sincerely,

William L. Hutcheson, General President
United Brotherhood of Carpenters and Joiners
of America.

T telegram (WP, DLC).

Thomas Nelson Page to Robert Lansing

Rome, February 16, 1918.

1423. SECRET. In conversation with Baron Sonnino this morning he expressed great satisfaction at coming of our military commission. Spoke of strong moral support our sending troops Italy would have.

Talked informally of Vatican position on peace moves and on clause fifteen of the secret treaty just published here.[1] He says he hears the Vatican has taken some sort of steps to try and get Germany to take some action, at least, regarding Belgium which will affect President Wilson's views. The Vatican has just printed the secret treaty with interpellations and discriminations on clause fifteen in the British House of Commons and Italian Chamber and with notes substantially charging falsehood in denials of existance of pact to exclude Vatican from action touching peace. Sonnino expressed view which he has always held that the admission of the Vatican to peace council would raise very embarrassing questions and that internationalization of Vatican would produce troublesome results and diminish spiritual power of Pope. He is evidently very desirous President's view should prevail with us and in my judgment his views on this point are sound. He declares that Italy did not expel the Central Empires' Representatives at the Vatican; they left on their own accord after the Royal Italian Government had given its assent to their remaining. He mentioned that the approaching Socialist Conference in London will ask that internationalist socialism shall be represented at the peace council board and he expressed a hope that only the Governments of belligerents

would be represented. Any other arrangement will he thinks produce endless confusion. Nelson Page.

T telegram (WP, DLC).
¹ That is, the Treaty of London. For the text of Article 15, see T. N. Page to WW,
Jan. 29, 1918, n. 3.

To William Levi Hutcheson

[The White House] 17 February, 1918.

I have received your telegram of yesterday and am very glad to
note the expression of your desire as a patriotic citizen to assist in
carrying on the work by which we are trying to save America and
men everywhere who work and are free. Taking advantage of that
assurance, I feel it to be my duty to call your attention to the fact
that the strike of the carpenters in the ship yards is in marked and
painful contrast to the action of labour in other trades and places.
Ships are absolutely necessary for the winning of this war. No one
can strike a deadlier blow at the safety of the nation and of its forces
on the other side than by interfering with or obstructing the shipbuilding programme. All the other unions engaged in this indispensable work have agreed to abide by the decisions of the Shipbuilding Wage Adjustment Board. That Board has dealt fairly and
liberally with all who have resorted to it. I must say to you very
frankly that it is your duty to leave to it the solution of your present
difficulties with your employers and to advise the men whom you
represent to return at once to work pending the decision. No body
of men have the moral right in the present circumstances of the
nation to strike until every method of adjustment has been tried to
the limit. If you do not act upon this principle you are undoubtedly
giving aid and comfort to the enemy, whatever may be your own
conscious purpose. I do not see that anything will be gained by my
seeing you personally until you have accepted and acted upon that
principle. It is the duty of the government to see that the best
possible conditions of labour are maintained, as it is also its duty
to see to it that there is no lawless and conscienceless profiteering
and that duty the government has accepted and will perform. Will
you cooperate or will you obstruct? Woodrow Wilson

T telegram (Letterpress Books, WP, DLC).

From William Levi Hutcheson

My dear Mr. President: New York, February 17, 1918.

Your telegram requesting our members to return to work at hand. In reply I am instructing our representatives to go among the men of our craft and use their influence to have the men return to work at once. I have exhausted every effort to reach an adjustment with the Shipping Board. I have no power to sign the agreement of the Adjustment Board which would deprive our members of their constitutional rights. Being desirous of reaching a conclusion whereby a cessation of work may be prevented in the future I most respectfully request that you notify me as to when I can meet with you, as I feel that is the only way in which to solve the question.

Yours most sincerely and respectfully,

Wm. L. Hutcheson.

T telegram (WP, DLC).

From Edward Mandell House

Dear Governor: New York. February 17, 1918.

Frank Cobb and Sam Blythe took lunch with me yesterday in order to discuss the plan for bringing into service the great writers of this country, so that the people may better understand what the Government has done and is trying to do in the war.

I consider this one of the most important moves on the board at present, and Cobb and Blythe have a very concrete idea as to how it should be done. I have steered them away from any conflict with Creel, and they understand that it is necessary to in no way encroach upon his field.

They desire to associate with them three others, and they wish to lay before you not only the names they have in mind, but also the general plan. Will you not make an appointment for them to see you sometime this week after Wednesday? If they can do what they think they can do, I believe you will find it one of the most potential aids yet enlisted in the Administration's behalf.

Will you not let me know when you can see them.

Affectionately yours, E. M. House

After you have accepted the plan I will look after the matter for you.

TLS (WP, DLC).

To Herbert Clark Hoover

My dear Mr. Hoover: The White House 18 February, 1918
   I have your letter of the fourteenth and agree with you that the agitation of legislation for a higher price of wheat is a very serious mistake just now. I will see what I can do, though it is practically impossible, I fear, to prevent agitation of this sort.
          Cordially and sincerely yours,   Woodrow Wilson

TLS (H. Hoover Papers, HPL).

To Asbury Francis Lever

My dear Mr. Lever: [The White House] 18 February, 1918
   I am taking the liberty of sending you a copy of a memorandum which I have just received from Mr. Hoover, the Food Administrator. He makes a very strong case indeed, it seems to me, against the agitation of legislative action to secure higher prices for wheat while the existing crop is unhandled and unsold. There could hardly be a more dangerous field of agitation than this, and I am writing to ask if it would not be possible to check such agitation in some kind and tactful way.
   The food situation in the world is one of the most serious that we have to face, and one of the most difficult to handle. We are handling it with reasonable success, and I should look with peculiar apprehension upon anything that would disturb the present comparatively even course of affairs.
   I am confident in the hope that you will regard this matter as of such critical consequence as to justify my calling it to your attention in this way.
          Cordially and sincerely yours,   Woodrow Wilson[1]

TLS (Letterpress Books, WP, DLC).
   [1] WW to T. S. Martin, Feb. 18, 1918, TLS (Letterpress Books, WP, DLC), is the same letter, *mutatis mutandis.*

To Ollie Murray James

My dear Senator: [The White House] 18 February, 1918
   That was a corking good speech you made the other day[1] and I would be indeed insensible if I did not send you a line of very warm and grateful thanks for your generous attitude towards myself. It is delightful to have such whole-hearted champions, friends that

really stand up and are counted in every time of crisis, and my heart goes out to you in the warmest and deepest appreciation.

Cordially and sincerely yours,   Woodrow Wilson

TLS (Letterpress Books, WP, DLC).
[1] James had spoken in the Senate on February 14 in response to Senator Chamberlain's speech in New York on January 19, about which see WW to G. E. Chamberlain, Jan. 20, 1918, n. 1. James noted the adverse effects which such speeches could have on public opinion in Europe; he then devoted most of his address to a refutation of Chamberlain's contention that the American military establishment had broken down. He argued that, given the vast and unprecedented problems involved, America's war mobilization to date had been a tremendous success. He concluded with a strong tribute to Wilson's war leadership by comparing it to Washington's and Lincoln's. *Cong. Record*, 65th Cong., 2d sess., pp. 2095-2103.

To Newton Diehl Baker

My dear Mr. Secretary,   The White House. 18 Feb'y, 1918

Pray pardon me. I ought long ago to have returned these important confidential papers.[1]   Woodrow Wilson

ALS (N. D. Baker Papers, DLC).
[1] See NDB to WW, Feb. 6, 1918.

To George Creel

Dear Creel: The White House 18 February, 1918

I wish you would read this.[1] I am getting evidence from many quarters that the activities of the Non-Partisan League are in many respects questionable and its leaders self-seeking and untrustworthy. It might be worth your while to learn what Mr. Ames, of the Minnesota Committee on Public Safety, who is referred to on the third page of this letter, knows about the League and its leadership.

Faithfully yours,   Woodrow Wilson

TLS (G. Creel Papers, DLC).
[1] That is, L. Seibold to JPT, Feb. 14, 1918.

To John Sharp Williams

Confidential

My dear Senator: The White House 18 February, 1918

Thank you for letting me see the enclosed letter from Mr. Erving Winslow.[1] I was in hopes that men like Mr. Winslow would realize that in discussing the utterances of the German and Austrian Ministers I was acting upon considerations and information which did not lie upon the surface but were derived from the many confidential sources of information which the Government must use. I am, therefore, not in the least afraid that I am walking into a German trap or that I am playing into the hands of the pacifists and pro-Germans. Nobody can be more wary of those groups than I wish to be, and I think it is rather a pity to discountenance, as Mr. Winslow seems to try to do, all processes of diplomacy even in the midst of arms.

Cordially and faithfully yours,   Woodrow Wilson

TLS (J. S. Williams Papers, DLC).
  [1] E. Winslow to J. S. Williams, Feb. 14, 1918, ALS (J. S. Williams Papers, DLC). As Wilson's letter indicates, Winslow had expressed the fear that recent Austro-German peace feelers were a "trap" into which the United States Government was in danger of falling.

To John Miller Baer

My dear Mr. Baer: [The White House] 18 February, 1918

Your letter of February seventh brings me a very gratifying message. I am always glad, you may be sure, to learn of such work as you speak of. Support of the Government just now and the correct interpretation of its policies and purposes are of the utmost consequence not only to the United States but to the world, and the work of the sort you outline contributes to the universal cause.

Sincerely yours,   Woodrow Wilson

TLS (Letterpress Books, WP, DLC).

To Ralph Pulitzer

My dear Mr. Pulitzer: [The White House] 18 February, 1918

You very graciously and considerately bid me not to reply to your note which I have just had laid before me, but I would be denying myself a pleasure if I did not write just a line or two to say how admirable I think the spirit in which you have acted and what a pleasure it was to me to be of any, even the least, service to you in deciding a question of the very greatest perplexity. I think you have decided it right.

Cordially and sincerely yours,   Woodrow Wilson

TLS (Letterpress Books, WP, DLC).

To Lucy Marshall Smith

My dear Cousin Lucy: [The White House] 18 February, 1918

It was most cheering and delightful to get your letter,[1] and after Edith and I had read it I felt almost as if I had had a little glimpse of you and Cousin Mary. Stockton had just been telling us of his little visit to you and delighting us by telling us how well you both looked and seemed, and so our hearts are gladdened every way.

We are pegging along here, weathering the storms that come from Capitol Hill as well as we can and praying that sober thought and sanity may get and keep the upper hand.

Poor Helen is just now confined in a sort of quarantine because of an attack of pink-eye, which, fortunately, is not painful; it has no physical result except making a hermit of her! Margaret has gone again to New York to get ready for some concerts she is going to give at the various cantonments within reach of us here; and Nell is the only member of the family who is laid up for repairs, she having made the mistake of contracting a case of tonsilitis.

This is our bulletin for the present, but this letter goes to you not as a health report, but as a love message from us all.

Affectionately yours,   Woodrow Wilson

TLS (Letterpress Books, WP, DLC).
  [1] Lucy M. Smith to WW, Feb. 13, 1918, ALS (WP, DLC).

To Robert Bridges

My dear Bobbie: The White House 18 February, 1918

Here are two poems by Bertha Bolling, Mrs. Wilson's sister, which I hope you will read and, if you like either of them, consider publishing it in the magazine. I am also sending you, clipped from the Red Cross Magazine, her Red Cross poem recently published, so that you may have a sufficient taste of her quality.[1]

I know I can send you these, my dear Bobbie, without making you feel under the slightest compulsion to publish either of them if you don't want to. Her flights are short, but sometimes they are distinct flights.

In haste   Affectionately yours,   Woodrow Wilson

TLS (WP, DLC).
  [1] One of these poems was Bertha Bolling, "The Yellow Curtains of Rome," *Scribner's Magazine*, LXIII (June 1918), 740. A second poem, Bertha Bolling, "The Vision," Hw MS, is attached to a carbon copy of Wilson's letter in WP, DLC. Obviously, it was returned by Bridges.

From Robert Lansing

Dear Mr. President: Washington February 18, 1918.

I beg to return herewith your note of February 16th in regard to Ambassador Francis's #2359, February 11, 12 p.m., and, in order that you may have all the information in the case, also attach copies of the Ambassador's telegrams #2354 referred to in his #2359.

In view of the very important information which the Ambassador has reported in these telegrams, I believe that he should be furnished with funds to obtain the originals or photostats of the documents mentioned by him, as I feel that this and additional information of the same nature is of vital importance to us at this time.

It is presumed that the Ambassador will draw against me in an amount not to exceed $25,000. Consequently, the fund used for this purpose will be the one available to me and not the one at the disposal of the Bureau of Information.

While the Ambassador does not state exactly the sources from which he will obtain the originals or photographs of the documents mentioned in his #2354, I am inclined to think that he has been able to get in touch with Mr. Bourtseff, who was placed by Kerensky at the head of the "contre-reziedka" mentioned in Section I of the Ambassador's telegram #2354, paragraph 3.[1] The "countre-reziedka" was Kerensky's counter-espionage department. The Yoffe document was possibly obtained from some minor official in the Smolny Institute,[2] who may be anti-Bolshevik at heart and possibly a former official of the Kerensky government, or perhaps of the Imperial Government. We happen to know that there are members of the former Imperial Secret Police now in the Smolny Institute.

Under the circumstances, I think it would be a great pity if the Ambassador were not provided with all the funds necessary to obtain the information mentioned by him, as well as the additional information set forth in the secret message despatched to him today, a copy of which is attached hereto.[3]

Faithfully yours,   Robert Lansing.

The President is satisfied with this explanation. RL 2/19/18

TLS (SDR, RG 59, 124.614/89, DNA).

[1] Vladimir L'vovich Burtsev, Russian historian and publicist, who was known as "the Sherlock Holmes of the Russian Revolution" for the part he played in exposing czarist *agents provocateurs* among the revolutionaries. One of the most vociferous opponents of the czarist regime, Burtsev had been repeatedly imprisoned and had been forced into exile in 1905. He returned to Russia in 1914 and was immediately arrested, but was later released. During the war, he demanded a cessation of all revolutionary activity until the defeat of Germany had been accomplished. After the outbreak of the Bolshevik revolution, he was again arrested because of his opposition to the Soviet regime, but he was released in the spring of 1918 and managed to flee to Paris. From there, he continued his fight against the Bolsheviks and called for the establishment of a united front of all Russian parties for the liberation of Russia. See the *New York Times*, Oct. 30, 1942.

² The headquarters of the Bolshevik government in Petrograd.

³ RL to D. R. Francis, Feb. 18, 1918, T telegram (SDR, RG 59, 862.20261/53, DNA), printed in *FR 1918, Russia*, I, 381-82. Lansing asked Francis to provide authentication of the documents cabled by Francis in No. 2354 (about which see D. R. Francis to RL, Feb. 13, 1918, n. 1), including, if possible, either the original documents or photographs of them. He also requested additional documentation of a similar nature. Lansing expressed "great interest" in the documents so far received and urged Francis to "make every endeavor to obtain further evidence not only of German intrigue with Bolsheviki but also with members of former governments particularly Stuermer." He added the further comment: "Department agrees with you that the case must be completed before publication can even be considered. Department is not inclined to think publication at this time desirable."

For an explanation of and commentary on the "Yoffe" (Joffe) document, see Francis' No. 2354 and Kennan, *Russia Leaves the War*, pp. 415-16.

From Robert Lansing, with Enclosures

My dear Mr. President: Washington February 18, 1918.

The Ambassador of France has received an urgent telegram from his Government urging that Great Britain, France, Italy and the United States make an immediate declaration to the following effect in regard to Roumania:

1. That the Allies conclude no peace without Roumania's integrity being restored.

2. That in case the King is forced to withdraw from from [*sic*] his country he and his dynasty will be restored to the throne.

3. That the King and Government of Roumania take part in the final negotiations for peace, whatever happens, even if they be forced to leave Roumanian territory.

4. That all means necessary for the carrying on of the Roumanian Government, financial and otherwise, will be furnished the Government, the King, the army and the Parliament, even though they be outside the territorial limits of Roumania.

5. That all that may be done in the invaded territory of Roumania (presumably by the enemy) will be considered as null and void.

6. That an energetic military action will be maintained on all the Allied fronts.

7. That we will try everything possible to smooth over the difficulties between the Roumanians and the Bolsheviki.

It is urged that this declaration be made by the United States as well as by other countries, even though the American Government is not a party to the Treaty of Bucharest, of August, 1916.[1]

To present this matter clearly for your consideration, I have prepared a note to the Ambassador of France transmitting the text of a telegram to the American Minister at Jassy, authorizing him to make independently certain representations to the King and Government of Roumania, as I think that we should pursue in this case our policy of avoiding joint action with the Allied Governments.

The situation of Roumania is unquestionably desperate and the unswerving loyalty and courage of the people and of the King in their struggle against the Central Powers justifies our putting heart into them by giving them such assurances as we properly may as to the future. I shall be glad to know how far you approve making the representations embodied in the proposed instructions to Jassy, in view of your message to the King, which you will recall and of which I enclose a copy, dated November 28, 1917.

Faithfully yours,   Robert Lansing.

TLS (SDR, RG 59, 763.72/9025, DNA).
    ¹ That is, the secret treaty between Rumania and France, Great Britain, Italy, and Russia, signed on August 17, 1916, under the terms of which Rumania was to enter the war against Austria-Hungary in return for a free hand to annex large portions of the Austro-Hungarian Empire, including all of Transylvania. There is no copy of the Treaty of Bucharest in WP, DLC.

E N C L O S U R E   I

Washington, February 21, 1918.

AMLEGATION JASSY.

It has been represented to this Government that the Governments of Great Britain, France, Italy and the United States should make a declaration to the King of Roumania defining specifically the principles which they have determined to adopt in view of the grave conditions which confront the Roumanian people in spite of their unswerving loyalty and courage in maintaining the struggle against the Central Powers.

You are accordingly instructed to represent to the King and to the Government of Roumania that this Government is unwilling to unite in a joint declaration as suggested but that acting independently it desires to give assurance that it will, so far as it may, give support to the following propositions:

First, that in any treaty of peace to which the United States is a party, the political and territorial integrity of Roumania shall be adequately safeguarded.

Second, that the people of Roumania shall have entire freedom in the determination of their Government.

Third, that the Government of the United States will consider with the governments of its co-belligerents the furnishing of financial and other means necessary to maintain the Roumanian Government and Roumanian army whether the same are located within or outside the national territorial limits of Roumania.

Fourth, that measures or actions by the Central Powers or their Allies in the invaded territory of Roumania will be considered as null and void in so far as they adversely affect the title or authority of Roumania and its Allies.

Fifth, that the United States is determined to continue with all its resources of men and of national wealth, its struggle against the Central Powers until the principles for which it entered the war have been attained.   Lansing[1]

T telegram (SDR, RG 59, 763.72/9025, DNA).
[1] This is the only copy of this telegram in the State Department's files.

E N C L O S U R E   I I

[Washington] November 28, 1917.

Amlegation, Jassy.

91. Referring to your 161 of November 17, 8 P.M. please convey the following message to the King of Roumania from the President of the United States:

The people of the United States have watched with feelings of warmest sympathy and admiration the courageous struggle of Your Majesty and the people of Roumania to preserve from the domination of German militarism their national integrity and freedom. The Government of the United States is determined to continue to assist Roumania in this struggle.

At the same time I wish to assure Your Majesty that the United States will support Roumania after the war to the best of its ability and that, in any final negotiations for peace, it will use its constant efforts to see to it that the integrity of Roumania as a free and independent nation is adequately safeguarded.   Lansing

TC telegram (SDR, RG 59, 763.72/9025, DNA).

From Robert Lansing, with Enclosure

PERSONAL AND CONFIDENTIAL:

My dear Mr. President: Washington February 18, 1918.

I send you a letter which I have just received from Ambassador Page at Rome which voices a fear which I have had in regard to Italy. I wonder how soon Secretary Baker intends to have the Military Commission in Italy? It seems to me that that is the next best move we can make.   Faithfully yours,   Robert Lansing.

ENCLOSURE

Thomas Nelson Page to Robert Lansing

Confidential

My dear Mr. Secretary: Rome January 29th, 1918.

I have sent by this pouch a long letter to the President,[1] but there were a number of matters which I did not discuss with him, or discuss at least as fully as they require.

The expressions in the President's message and in Lloyd George's speeches relating to Italian war aims fell so far short of what Italy desires and what her Government and Press have led her people to expect that there has been a tremendous stir here about Italy's aims and claims, at least on the part of the people who write and talk about such things. This has resulted in strong currents of critical feeling about America and England, and the propaganda which has been going on for months against England is, I learn, now sufficiently broadened to include America also. I believe that this is a part of the almost universal German propaganda which covers the world, but undoubtedly a good many Italians are being drawn in to take part in it. Happily for us, a great many Italians have been equally aroused to resist this propaganda. These last, however, are continually bringing to our attention the importance of our taking some steps ourselves to countervail this anti-American anti-Democratic propaganda. And I agree with them fully in thinking that it is a matter of great importance that we should set ourselves seriously to this work. I have on a number of occasions sent telegrams about this matter, more or less urgent, but so far I have apparently had little success in impressing my views on whoever the matter has been referred to at home. I suggested making an appropriation of funds, reasonable enough one would think; for in the beginning I suggested something like $2.500. Later I suggested the great effect that it would have to send a Military Mission, or a Mission of Military Observers to the Italian Front. The response was a suggestion of sending a distinguished newspaper or war correspondent just made into a Reserve Captain to represent America where all the other Allies were represented by trained military men in Commissions of from six to a dozen members each with Generals, or at least Colonels at their head. This was far worse than nothing, and would undoubtedly have been considered by the people here as a slight and possibly an intentional slight. The absence of a Mission of Military Observers here is often commented on, though naturally not to me, by Italians who say they have enrolled a greater number of men to their population than France has done;

that they have lost over a million men; that they have until just recently borne a greater weight thrown against them per kilometer of front without any assistance whatever than any other of the Allies; that they have suffered more than any of the Western Allies in privation, and as much in battle losses.

A great part of this is true. The Italian people have suffered and are suffering tremendously. Moreover, another claim which they put forward insistently is well-founded: that Italy's front is as important to the Allied cause as the French Front; that if Italy's front should be broken and Italy forced to make peace France would be lost as definitely as if the French front were forced. Now the security of Italy's front rests upon first her troops at the front, and secondly the endurance of her people, and it is this endurance which the propaganda to which I have alluded above is addressed on the part of the Germans and of those Italians who allow themselves to be used in this German propaganda. The military situation appears for the present to be very good, although I understand the propaganda is again working to some extent even in the trenches. The dangerous point is the failure to meet the economic situation in Italy with sufficient food supplies, coal supplies and other supplies of the necessaries of life.

I have sent you by this mail a letter written by David Lubin,[2] the American Representative at the International Institute of Agriculture, giving the views of a number of important Italian public men on this point, and I commend those views to serious consideration. The number of men at present under arms in Italy, is I believe somewhat exaggerated, though I learn that Italy has enrolled about 4,300,000 men of which she has lost about a million, one half of them, about, being prisoners in Austria. But the main facts stated by these men is the importance of saving Italy to the Allied cause. And whatever may be said of certain elements who are against Democracy and who are at heart more friendly to Germany, if reports are to be believed, than they are to America, the Italians at large beginning with the King and concluding with the great body of the plain people are believers in Liberty. And it is to stand by them and to overthrow those who are carrying on the German propaganda that we should take effective steps, the most effective in our power.

The declaration of war against Austria was a tremendous stimulus here. There was an element undoubtedly which was far from wishing us to take this step and which has resented our doing so, but the Italian people and many of their best leaders know what it has done for Italy, however the press may be engaged at present in fomenting criticism of us because the President did not go further in his message, and announced that Italy ought to have all her Government has claimed. The sending of troops here would be the greatest propaganda that could be started. Even a small number of troops with the flag would count for much. But undoubtedly there would be expectations that that small number would ultimately be increased. I could not tell you how many men have said to me personally what I have heard several say in public speeches: If America would only send her flag—her starry flag it would be a symbol not only to Italy but to the world that America recognizes that Italy is fighting for freedom, for Liberty and has the same ideals that America has.

Believe me, Mr. Secretary, it would have an immense moral effect. It would have an immense effect not only for the present and while the war lasts,—but for years to come.

I know the difficulties that stand in the way of sending troops here, but it is well worth all the trouble. It will bind Italy to America in a way that nothing else on earth will.

Meantime, I ought to have the means placed in my hands to carry on a reasonable propaganda here in Italy to show the Italians what America and Americans are doing for Italy. We are doing it and it is now [not] known as it should be known. The other Allies are engaged in pressing upon the attention of the Italians what they are doing for them. We have no means here of showing what we are doing, and about all they know is that we are lending them money, selling them supplies by no means as much as they need, or think their due proportion, and helping the other Allies with everything including armies.

I urge you to have this matter given the most serious consideration. No money could be spent which would bring so rich a return. There are many more things which I would like to write you about, but for the present I forbear

Believe me always most sincerely yours,

Thos. Nelson Page

TLS (SDR, RG 59, 763.72/8706½, DNA).
    [1] T. N. Page to WW, Jan. 29, 1918.
    [2] Agricultural economist and retired merchant of Sacramento, Cal. He was largely responsible for the founding of the International Institute of Agriculture at Rome in 1910 for the purpose of pooling agricultural information for the benefit of all farmers of the world. His letter cannot be found in the files of the Department of State.

From Edward Nash Hurley

My dear Mr. President: Washington February 18, 1918.

I am more sorry than I can tell you that I was not in my office to show my appreciation of your call. I was at the British Embassy, conferring with the four British representatives of labor, and with Lord Redding and Mr. Gompers.

Incidentally, you have probably observed with the same satisfaction which I have felt that the carpenters have returned to their work. Your statement of yesterday was inspiring. It strengthened the hearts of all of us and aided Union labor itself. The whole country has responded. I will shortly submit to you our plan for ending even the possibility of profiteering in the shipyards.

This morning with Mr. Piez, the General Manager of the Fleet Corporation, I called on Mr. Gompers at his office, and we had a most satisfactory chat. There is no question of Mr. Gompers' helpfulness. His attitude has been one of the most encouraging factors in this situation.

We are trying to work out some way at the present time to make Mr. Hutcheson feel that he has taken the right course in asking the men to go back to work. I think the whole matter will be worked out, with good feeling all around. The Wage Adjustment Board's attitude will be approved generally by the men and by the public.

Sincerely yours,   Edward N. Hurley

TLS (WP, DLC).

From William Gibbs McAdoo, with Enclosure

Dear Governor,   [Washington] Feby 18, 1918

Referring to the attached—you will doubtless recall that I rebuked Crosby, at your request, for appearing to go outside of his specific task,—hence his desire for express instructions in cases where his advice is sought concerning matters not specifically under his jurisdiction.   Affectionately yrs   W G McAdoo

ALS (WP, DLC).

E N C L O S U R E

From William Gibbs McAdoo

Dear Mr. President: Washington February 18, 1918.

I hand you herewith a letter dated January 16th which I have received from Mr. Crosby and which I think you will be interested in reading.[1] As the letter is of a confidential character, I have thought it better not to have it copied and since I desire to refer to it again I hope you will return it to me. In addition to the very interesting and intelligent account of financial and general matters contained in this letter, I wish to call your attention to the fact that Mr. Crosby has been consulted by Ambassador Page in connection with the Swedish negotiations, by Mr. McCormick and Mr. Sheldon[2] in connection with the Swiss negotiations, and by Mr. Auchincloss in connection with certain Polish matters but has hesitated to intervene in these affairs in the absence of instructions from here. If you approve, I should like to direct Mr. Crosby to give such advice and assistance as may be desired in connection with these or other matters which concern the financial problem.

Cordially yours,   W G McAdoo

TLS (WP, DLC).
   [1] It is missing in all collections.
   [2] Louis Pendleton Sheldon, representative in London of the War Trade Board and the Food Administration.

From Frederick J. Wilson[1]

Dear Mr. President: New York February Eighteen 1918

On February 15th, the International News Service was permitted by representatives of the British Government to announce that it had been restored to the mails and cables privileges of Great Britain, its colonies, and its allies. I know that we owe this to the friendly attitude of your Administration. We are grateful. We are grateful because it not only will inure to our advantage but will put the International News Service in a better position to serve the United States and its President.

I am   Very sincerely,   Fred. J. Wilson

TLS (WP, DLC).
   [1] General manager of the International News Service.

John R. Shillady[1] to Joseph Patrick Tumulty

Dear Sir: New York City February 18, 1918.

I am in receipt of yours of February 14 informing us that the President had referred to the Attorney General our appeal for a word of condemnation of the torturing and burning at Estill Springs, Tenn., of a colored man accused of murder.[2] This morning we have a letter from the Attorney General, by William C. Fitts,[3] Assistant Attorney General, informing us that "under the decisions of the Supreme Court of the United States, the Federal Government has absolutely no jurisdiction over matters of this kind; nor are they connected with the war in any such way as to justify the action of the Federal Government under the war power."

On February 15 we telegraphed Governor Rye[4] of Tennessee, a copy of which is attached.[5] On the 14th Governor Rye is reported in the Knoxville Journal and Tribune and other Tennessee papers as saying that he did not know what authority he had in the matter. No reply or acknowledgment of our appeal to the Governor of Tennessee has yet been made.

In view of this statement of the Attorney General and the silence of the Governor of Tennessee, we beg you to lay this matter again before the President lest the laws be flouted and justice denied. A statement from the President at this time, if he would be disposed to make it, would have a tremendously stimulating effect on the morale of the colored people whose sons are preparing to give their lives for America and who in sadness of heart and some disturbance of mind are looking apprehensively toward Tennessee to see whether in our own nation law or mob violence is to be supreme.

The President's inspiring moral leadership as a man, no less than his position as President, gives him the opportunity, and may we suggest respectfully, the responsibility, of speaking out. Hundreds of thousands of colored soldiers in the army and millions of their fathers, mothers, sisters and brothers would receive a new baptism of devotion to their country if it were made clear that the equal protection of the laws was to be afforded all men, whether white or black.

If the President would see fit, while receiving the delegation of colored men from New York Tuesday afternoon, to allude to this question, we believe profoundly that the nation would be stirred as by nothing else to renewed respect for law.

This Association wishes it understood that it does not and will not condone the crimes nor apologize for the offenses of colored men.   Sincerely,   John R. Shillady

TLS (WP, DLC).

[1] Secretary of the National Association for the Advancement of Colored People.

[2] The lynching of Jim McIlherron took place on February 12. For some gruesome details, see the *New York Times*, Feb. 13, 1918.

[3] William Cochran Fitts.

[4] Thomas Clark Rye.

[5] J. R. Shillady to T. C. Rye, Feb. 15, 1918, TC telegram (WP, DLC). Shillady, on behalf of the N.A.A.C.P., appealed to Rye to "take action to bring to justice the perpetrators of the foul wrong."

Roger Nash Baldwin to Edward Mandell House, with Enclosure

Dear Col. House: New York, Feb. 18, 1918

Thank you for your reply in regard to the Administration's policy in relation to liberal and radical opinion, about which we sent you a memorandum at your suggestion.

Our committee, which discussed the whole problem again today, felt that any statement we might send direct to the President would not get serious attention from his Secretarial staff. Unless you think it of enough importance to send to him yourself, we are inclined to the view that we had better not press it further on him.

We do feel, however, that it is important to modify the policy of the Postoffice Department and the Department of Justice, in the interest of the President's policies, and we should feel that the next best approach would be through Congressional action. We are reluctant to attempt that move, and hope that you might be willing to forward our memorandum to the President.

With best wishes,   Sincerely yours,   Roger Baldwin.

TLS (WP, DLC).

E N C L O S U R E

Memorandum for Col. House   *January 24, 1918.*

The liberal and radical forces, which were for the most part opposed to the entrance of the United States into the war, are now of a mind, for the most part, to back the President's war aims.

But the policy of suppression of the radical press and the general terrorization of public opinion by over-zealous officials makes it exceedingly difficult for these forces to speak. The result is that the function of discussion of war policies and war aims is now largely in the hands of the "Tories."

In order that the liberal and radical forces may be released to perform their natural function of backing up a democratic international program, two things are necessary:

1. That the President indicate clearly in the near future the line which in his mind can be properly drawn between those matters which can be fully discussed without prejudice to the country's interest, and those which cannot;

2. That the policy of the postoffice department in suppressing liberal and radical papers, without indicating in what way they offend, be modified and definite regulations adopted instead; and

that the Department of Justice instruct local District Attorneys not to proceed against citizens and organizations unless there is deliberate and direct incitement to law-breaking. Definite regulations thus adopted by the postoffice department and the Department of Justice should replace the present confusing uncertainties, due to the vague language of the Espionage Act.

T MS (WP, DLC).

A Petition[1]

[[Feb. 19, 1918]]

We come as a delegation from the New York Branch of the National Association for the Advancement of Colored People, representing the twelve thousand signers to this petition which we have the honor to lay before you. And we come not only as the representatives of those who signed this petition, but we come representing the sentiments and aspirations and sorrows, too, of the great mass of the Negro population of the United States.

We respectfully and earnestly request and urge that you extend executive clemency to the five Negro soldiers of the Twenty-Fourth Infantry now under sentence of death by court martial. And understanding that the cases of the men of the same regiment who were sentenced to life imprisonment by the first court martial are to be reviewed, we also request and urge that you cause this review to be laid before you and that executive clemency be shown also to them.

We feel that the history of this particular regiment and the splendid record for bravery and loyalty of our Negro soldiery in every crisis of the nation give us the right to make this request. And we make it not only in the name of their loyalty, but also in the name of the unquestioned loyalty to the nation of twelve million Negroes—a loyalty which today places them side by side with the original American stocks that landed at Plymouth and Jamestown.

The hanging of thirteen men without the opportunity of appeal to the Secretary of War or to their Commander-in-Chief, the President of the United States, was a punishment so drastic and so unusual in the history of the nation that the execution of additional members of the Twenty-Fourth Infantry would to the colored people of the country savor of vengeance rather than justice.

It is neither our purpose nor is this the occasion to argue whether this attitude of mind on the part of colored people is justified or not. As representatives of the race we desire only to testify that it does exist. This state of mind has been intensified by the significant fact that, although white persons were involved in the Houston affair, and the regiment to which the colored men belonged was officered entirely by white men, none but colored men, so far as we have been able to learn, have been prosecuted or condemned.

We desire also respectfully to call to your attention the fact that there were mitigating circumstances for the action of these men of the Twenty-Fourth Infantry. Not by any premeditated design and without cause did these men do what they did at Houston; but by a long series of humiliating and harassing incidents, culminating in the brutal assault on Corporal Baltimore,[2] they were goaded to sudden and frenzied action. This is borne out by the long record for orderly and soldierly conduct on the part of the regiment throughout its whole history up to that time.

And to the end that you extend the clemency which we ask, we lay before you this petition signed by white as well as colored citizens of New York; one of the signers being a white man, president of a New York bank, seventy-two years of age, and a native of Lexington, Kentucky.

And now, Mr. President, we would not let this opportunity pass without mentioning the terrible outrages against our people that have taken place in the last three-quarters of a year; outrages that are not only unspeakable wrongs against them, but blots upon the fair name of our common country. We mention the riots at East St. Louis, in which the colored people bore the brunt of both the cruelty of the mob and the processes of law. And we especially mention the savage burnings that have taken place in the single state of Tennessee within nine months; the burnings at Memphis, Tennessee; at Dyersburg, Tennessee; and only last week at Estill Springs, Tennessee, where a Negro charged with the killing of two men was tortured with red-hot irons, then saturated with oil and burned to death before a crowd of American men, women, and children. And we ask that you, who have spoken so nobly to the whole world for the cause of humanity, speak against these specific wrongs. We realize that your high position and the tremendous moral influence which you wield in the world will give a word from you greater force than could come from any other source. Our people are intently listening and praying that you may find it in your heart to speak that word.

Printed in James Weldon Johnson, *Along This Way: The Autobiography of James Weldon Johnson* (New York, 1933), pp. 323-24.

    [1] Read to Wilson by James Weldon Johnson, who, with the Revs. Frank M. Hyde, George Frazier Miller, and Frederick Asbury Cullen, represented the Harlem branch of the N.A.A.C.P. A fragment of the copy of the petition is in WDR, RG 165, No. 114575, DNA. This file includes all the letters, telegrams, and petitions received by the White

House and the War Department relating to the court-martial cases of members of the 24th Infantry.

² Charles W. Baltimore, who had allegedly been beaten at the time of his arrest in Houston on August 23, 1917. He had been hanged in the first group of convicted men on December 11, 1917. Haynes, *A Night of Violence*, pp. 1-7, 96-97.

To Newton Diehl Baker

My dear Baker: The White House 19 February, 1918

This document, which was left with me today, accompanied by a gigantic petition, that is, gigantic in the bulk of its signatures, has I must say moved me very much.¹

I hope you will have time to read at any rate the portion which concerns the soldiers in the 24th Infantry. I believe I have already said to you that I would like very much to participate in the reconsideration of the cases of both the men who have been condemned to death and the men who have been condemned to life sentence.

Cordially and faithfully yours,   Woodrow Wilson

TLS (WDR, RG 165, No. 114575, DNA).

¹ Johnson described the meeting as follows: "The presentation of the petition was finished; the President did not rise, and I retook my seat. He talked with us about the mission that had brought us to the White House. We were surprised when he admitted that he had not heard of the burning at Estill Springs. He asked us to give him the facts about it; and declared that it was hard for him to think that such a thing could have taken place in the United States. We pressed him for a promise to make a specific utterance against mob violence and lynching. He demurred, saying that he did not think any word from him would have special effect. We expressed our conviction that his word would have greater effect than the word of any other man in the world. Finally, he promised that he would 'seek an opportunity' to say something.

"Mr. Wilson talked on with us in a sociable manner. He sat with his knees straight, his elbows resting on the arms of his chair, his hands joined at the tips of his fingers and thumbs, and pointing in front of him in the shape of a wedge. I had seen him only once before, and then at a distance, when he had marched in a preparedness parade in New York; now I was sitting within six feet of him and regarding him intently. I had thought of him as an extremely austere man; as he talked, I realized that the official air had been dropped, and that he was, as we say, very human. His head, no longer inclined forward, rested back easily, and the sternness of his face relaxed and, occasionally in a smile, became completely lost. He asked us questions about the colored people, and we answered them as wisely as we could. He chatted a short while longer, even recounting one or two slight reminiscences of his youthful days in the South. We had been with the President a few minutes longer than a half-hour when he rose, signifying that the interview was at an end. We left with a last plea in behalf of the condemned man of the Twenty-Fourth Infantry. When I came out, it was with my hostility toward Mr. Wilson greatly shaken; however, I could not rid myself of the conviction that at bottom there was something hypocritical about him." Johnson, *Along This Way*, pp. 324-25.

Two Letters to Herbert Clark Hoover[1]

My dear Mr. Hoover: [The White House] 19 February, 1918

May I not call your attention to this important point:

There is pressing need of the full co-operation of the packing trade, of every officer and employee, in the work of hurrying provisions abroad. Let the packers understand that they are engaged in a war service in which they must take orders and act together under the direction of the Food Administration if the Food Administration requires.

Cordially and sincerely yours,   Woodrow Wilson

TLS (Letterpress Books, WP, DLC).
[1] The first letter is an expansion of a draft by Hoover dated February 19, 1918, T MS (WP, DLC).

My dear Mr. Hoover: The White House 19 February, 1918

The men who brought me the enclosed memorial[1] struck me as sincere and straightforward, and they made the very definite statement that they were losing so much per head on the cattle they were raising and they ascribed as the reason the entire control of the price by the packers. I would be very much obliged if you would look over these papers and make any comments upon them that occur to you and any suggestions of practicable courses of action, because manifestly our supply of meat depends upon the solution of just such questions as this.

Cordially and faithfully yours,   Woodrow Wilson

TLS (H. Hoover Papers, HPL).
[1] Dwight B. Heard et al. to WW, Feb. 13, 1918, TLS (WP, DLC), enclosing "RESOLUTIONS adopted at the TWENTY-FIRST ANNUAL CONVENTION of the AMERICAN NATIONAL LIVE STOCK ASSOCIATION AT SALT LAKE CITY, UTAH, JANUARY 14, 15, and 16, 1918," T MS (WP, DLC). The resolutions were set forth under the following headings: "Pledging Support to Our Government, Urging Increased Production of Live Stock and Food Products, Indorsing the Federal Trade Commission Investigation, Indorsing a National Organization of Producers," and "General Statement and Presentation of Resolutions."

From George Creel

My dear Mr. President: Washington, D. C. February 19, 1918.

With regard to the attached letter, I have written to Mr. Ames, asking him to send me all the data that Seibold mentions. This Committee has no connection of any kind with the Non-Partisan League, nor has it ever given it approval of any kind. It was simply the case that this League, controlling the state of North Dakota and with powerful organizations in several other states, was fighting

Hoover, fighting the war, and making grave statements with regard to your own attitude.

I made it my business to see Townley, brought him into touch with Hoover, and as a result of our interviews, the League is today one of your foremost supporters, is backing the war, and is backing Hoover. This was our only concern in the matter. The result was accomplished without any endorsement or without embarrassment to the Administration.

The democratic politicians to some extent, and the republican politicians to a very large extent, hate this League and are trying to destroy it, and much of the attack springs from this antagonism. I have not concerned myself with its industrial and economic views, simply making it a point to get them behind the war, instead of being against the war.   Respectfully,   George Creel

TLS (WP, DLC).

From Robert Lansing

My dear Mr. President: Washington February 19, 1918.

I have talked with Mr. Boris Bakhmeteff about sending the Russian Railway Service Corps into Siberia. He not only favors continuing the original plan for these men, but tells me he can take care of the entire charges of the Corps for three or four months, by which time it may be possible that we may find additional funds available in the settlement of Russian obligations.

I have communicated this to Mr. Stevens and authorized him to return to Harbin with Colonel Emerson and the men of the Corps. They will begin work in cooperation with the railway authorities of the Chinese Eastern Railway and will operate eastwards toward Vladivostok and also westwards to Manchuria Station and gradually to Irkutsk.

I have attached a copy of a telegram from the Ambassador at Tokio,[1] expressing Mr. Stevens urgent views that he should be authorized to carry out the work on the Siberian Railway.

          Faithfully yours,   Robert Lansing

TLS (SDR, RG 59, 861.77/309, DNA).
[1] R. S. Morris to RL, Feb. 17, 1918, TC telegram (SDR, RG 59, 861.77/309, DNA).

Hugh Robert Wilson to Robert Lansing

Pontarlier. (Berne), February 19, 1918.
2676. STRICTLY CONFIDENTIAL.

My cipher telegram 2544, January 31, 4 p.m., and succeeding telegrams. Jong Vanbeek[1] has received telegram from Meinl in Vienna which in translation reads as follows:

"Heinrich met with a favorable reception for his proposals. He also has transmitted your long telegram addressed to me February second. He thinks a business agreement with the chief of our legal adviser highly probable. Please inform him."

To understand this telegram which is in guarded language to escape Austrian censor Heinrich is to be interpreted as Lammasch, legal adviser is George D. Herron, and chief is President Wilson. The long telegram referred to is explained in my despatch number 2356, February eighth. It was sent by Jong to Meinl and conveyed in disguised language of business terms Herron's views as to necessary reforms within Empire.

Telegram quoted above appears to indicate that Lammasch found Emperor favorably disposed towards ideas advanced by Herron and that Lammasch considers peace through America highly probable.

Wilson.

T telegram (R. Lansing Papers, NjP).
[1] That is, Jonkheer Dr. Benjamin de Jong van Beek en Donk.

William Graves Sharp to Robert Lansing

Paris, February 19, 1918.

For the Secretary of State and Colonel House. General Spiers,[1] British Liaison officer on General Foch's staff, showed me today in confidence a paper which had been submitted by the British War Office to the French General Staff for its consideration.[2] The subject of this paper was Japanese intervention in Siberia and it was dated the fifteenth instant. The substance is as follows: A resolute Japanese intervention in Siberia by taking possession of the Trans-Siberian railway from Vladivostok to Tcheliabinsk would: One. Reenforce the national element in Russia and Siberia to the detriment of the forces of anarchy. Two. Would save Roumania. Three. Would prevent the Germans from withdrawing their troops to the Western front.

The Japanese are ready to act and would require only six and one half divisions. They only stipulate that they shall be allowed to act alone in order to obtain the consent of the nation to this oper-

Marching in the Red Cross Parade in New York, May 18, 1918.
Cleveland H. Dodge (with cane) is to the far left.

Lord Reading

William B. Wilson

General Enoch H. Crowder

General Pershing and Secretary Baker in Bordeaux

Count Ottokar Czernin von und zu Chudenitz

Count Georg F. von Hertling

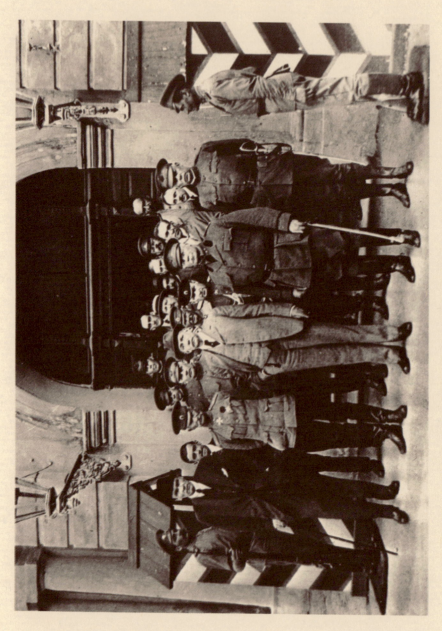

The Russian Commission. In the front row, from the left: Mikhail I. Tereshchenko, General Aleksei A. Brusilov, Elihu Root, and General Hugh L. Scott

ation. Great Britain and France have accepted the principle of the operation and are desirous of overcoming the attitude of hesitation on the part of the United States.

The paper opposes the argument that the appearance of Japan troops in Siberia would unite all Russian elements against the invaders by the statement that according to information from Siberia and Russia described as certain all the orderly elements in these two countries demand an energetic intervention and that all classes of Russian society have appealed for a Japanese intervention. Many Russian officers have even asked to serve with the invading Japanese forces.

The paper concludes with the observation that if German domination over Russia and Siberia is a great danger, a German-Japanese domination over the entire world would be a still more formidable peril which could be eliminated by bringing Japan effectively and directly in opposition to Germany, a thing which the Japanese seem to have avoided since the beginning of the war. As a disadvantage the paper admits that Japanese prestige would be increased at the expense of French, British and American prestige in the Orient by such intervention but that Japan would gain no material benefit as her people are not psychologically constituted to dominate or administer foreign populations as the history of the Japanese occupation of Corea and Formosa demonstrates. In this connection I heard yesterday from a reliable source that France is contemplating sending a special Ambassador to Siberia. Frazier.

Sharp

T telegram (WP, DLC).
    [1] Brig. Gen. Edward Louis Spiers (he changed his surname to Spears later in 1918), head of the British Military Mission in Paris.
    [2] R. S., "Russia, Japanese Intervention. SECRET," Feb. 14, 1918, TI MS (WP, DLC). Frazier paraphrases this document as does Bliss in his telegram printed below.

Sir William Wiseman to Sir Eric Drummond

[New York] February 19, 1918.

No. 55. (Very Secret): Certain influences near ADRAMYTI [WILSON] are urging him to recognise or otherwise support Bolsheviki Government. If you will give me your views I could probably get ADRAMYTI to adopt them before he comes to any other decision.

T telegram (W. Wiseman Papers, CtY).

Lord Reading to the Foreign Office

Washington February 19th 1918.

No. 681 URGENT SECRET.

This morning I received a letter addressed to me as Ambassador by the Secretary of State in the following terms: . . .[1]

The French and Italian Ambassadors received letters in identical terms. Upon receipt I saw Mr. Lansing and observed that the letter came as a great surprise. He said the letter was a personal one addressed by him to me and was not a formal communication. I replied that its contents made it necessary that I should communicate it textually to my government. In acknowledging the letter I stated my ignorance of the action of the Inter allied Board to which reference is made.

From all I have learned it is undoubted that the action of the Supreme War Council caused the President considerable annoyance particularly as he was not consulted before the public announcement and the U.S.G. had taken no part in the political deliberations. The wording of the press communication created the impression that the U.S.G. was a party to the declaration, which was couched in language which the President did not approve. It is clear to my mind that he made the last speech to congress partly for the purpose of dissoc[i]ating himself from this declaration.

But I do not believe that the President when directing this communication to the three Ambassadors appreciated its full importance. My two allied colleagues have cabled the text to their governments and are much disturbed. If I had known what had happened I would forthwith have asked for an interview with the President. Save for the newspaper publication of the declaration of the Supreme War Council which I saw upon arrival in the U. S. I have heard nothing except what the French Ambassador and Tardieu tell me.

Please give me promptly full information of your views so that I may see President particularly as Colonel House will be here Friday. May I impress upon you the imperative necessity of keeping me very fully informed. end.

T telegram (W. Wiseman Papers, CtY).
  [1] Here Reading repeated the text of WW to RL, Feb. 16, 1918 (fourth letter of that date), beginning with the second paragraph, "referring to the recent action . . . ," and continuing to the end of the third paragraph.

Tasker Howard Bliss to Henry Pinckney McCain

Versailles February 19th [1918].

Very Confidential. Number 32

For The Secretary of State, The Secretary of War and The Chief of Staff. Please deliver copy to the Secretary of State with as little delay as possible.

Paragraph 1 Reference dispatch of February 2d from Secretary of State received by me February 14th and my dispatch to the Secretary of State February 15th I submit the following.

Paragraph 2 The permanent military advisers yesterday and today carefully considered the question of Japanese intervention in Siberia by their occupation of the Trans-Siberian railroad in behalf of the allies. They adopted joint note number 16 addressed to the Supreme War Council and embodying the following resolution.

Paragraph 3 "The military representatives are of the opinion, first, that the occupation of the Siberian Railroad from Vladivostok to Harbin, together with both terminals, presents military advantages that outweigh any possible political disadvantage. Second, that they recommend this occupation by a Japanese force, after obtaining suitable guarantees from Japan, together with a joint allied commission. Third, the question of the further occupation of the railroad shall be to *determine whether or not* (Determined by?) the allied governments concerned according(ly) as circumstances develop."[1]

Paragraph 4. My comments follow. First, practically the only military advantage from proposed action is securing military supplies at Siberia and Harbin and preventing them being sold to Germans and preventing Germans from using Asiatic coasts for submarine bases. This loses much of its weight since Germany resumed yesterday status of war with Russia. Second, British military men seem to favor combined occupation of Siberian railroad from Vladivostok to Cheliabinsk. A secret memorandum was shown me yesterday by the British military section in which the following views appear. They think it is the last chance of saving Russia for the allies and of preventing withdrawal of German troops from Russian front. By occupying the railroads as far west as Cheliabinsk they hope to consolidate the orderly Russian sentiment in Siberia against the anarchist sentiment. They say that the Japanese have all their plans ready and demand only that the operations should be left to them to execute alone and that they shall not have the humiliation and pin pricks in the shape of allied "Show the Flags" detachments to contend with in obtaining the willing consent of their people. They further say that the Japanese Expeditionary Force will seize Vladivostok and the maritime provinces when they like;

that now that the United States are in a fair way to being armed to the teeth a very different complexion is *placed* on our Japanese question; that although a German domination of Russia and Siberia would be a danger, a German-Japanese domination of the world would be a greater one, and that the latter could probably be avoided by bringing the Japanese out into the open, a course which they have studiously avoided since the beginning of the war. It is evident foregoing views cannot be realized by stopping occupation of railroad at Harbin. However British say movement can be pushed to Cheliabinsk if desired. The question is whether this will play into the hands of the Germans. The latter yesterday resumed status of war against Russia, that is to say against the Bolshevicks. The Germans as the declared enemies of the Bolshevicks may be as likely to consolidate in their own favor the anti-Bolshevick sentiment as the Japanese are to consolidate it in favor of the allies. Again, will inviting Japanese intervention in Siberia "bring the Japanese out into the open" as the British seem to think. May not the Germans make a deal with them as to respective spheres of influence that will give Germany all she wants in Western Russia. Third, the second paragraph of above resolution is based on belief that joint allied forces to occupy Siberian railroads can not be formed. The joint allied mission is to be composed of political and military men who will keep the Governments concerned fully informed.

Paragraph 5 *I think* that the project of Japanese intervention in Siberia involves possible grave danger and that the resulting purely military advantages will be small. But [while] writing above dispatch I have consulted my English and French Colleagues and I agree with them that some chance must be taken. I believe that all the immediate purely military advantages that can be secured will be obtained by the occupation of Vladivostok. The danger will be minimized if no attempt is made to proceed further than Vladivostok or at the most Harbin until effect on Russian sentiment both Bolshevick and anti-Bolshevick is ascertained.   Bliss.

T telegram (WP, DLC).

¹ This sentence in Bliss' copy reads as follows: "Third, the question of the further occupation of the Railway shall be determined by the Allied Governments concerned according as circumstances develop." T. H. Bliss to H. P. McCain, Feb. 19, 1918, T telegram (WDR, RG 120, Records of the American Section of the Supreme War Council, 1917-1919, File No. 315, DNA).

Two Letters to Robert Lansing

My dear Mr. Secretary: The White House 20 February, 1918

I am very glad to receive this information, and glad that the work of the Russian Railway Service Corps can go on.

In haste   Faithfully yours,   Woodrow Wilson

TLS (SDR, RG 59, 861.77/309, DNA).

My dear Mr. Secretary: The White House 20 February, 1918

Representatives of the International News Service (Hearst's) are writing to me thanking me for the influence they suppose me to have exerted to obtain the removal of the ban put upon the Service by the British Government in the use of the mails and cables, but, of course, I had absolutely nothing to do with it. I am, however, anxious to find out how it did happen. Do you know?

Cordially and faithfully yours,   Woodrow Wilson

TLS (RSB Coll., DLC).

To William Gibbs McAdoo

My dear Mac: [The White House] 20 February, 1918

Thank you for letting me see the enclosed letter from Crosby. I have never had any objection to him giving any advice he is asked for concerning financial matters. What I have been made uneasy about was his participation in political matters. For example, just the other day he joined his colleagues of the Inter-Allied Board in advising us not to recognize the Bolshevik Government. That, it seems to me, was a very serious departure from his instructions. The fact is that in my view neither the Supreme War Council nor the board of which Crosby is chairman has any business to formulate political opinions and give political advice. Their doing so has already complicated the European situation very seriously and nullified much of what we have been attempting to do. I have even gone so far as to make representations to this effect to the other governments in an informal way.

The utterance of the Supreme War Council the other day in Versailles has played into the hands of the Germans in a way that is most discouraging.

In haste   Affectionately yours,   [Woodrow Wilson]

CCL (WP, DLC).

To William Gibbs McAdoo, with Enclosure

My dear Mac: The White House 20 February, 1918

The situation stated by Mr. Hoover in the enclosed letter has been presented to me from various quarters. I know that you will wish to know about it and that you will make every possible effort to get cars into the West. I know that Mr. Hoover does not exaggerate when he says that the situation is extremely critical, and while I cannot judge the practical aspects of the matter, his contention is that if the empty cars were got out of the East into the West and there distributed throughout the grain regions, they would relieve the situation as much as it can be relieved.

Always   Faithfully yours,   Woodrow Wilson

E N C L O S U R E

From Herbert Clark Hoover

Dear Mr. President: Washington, D. C. *19 February 1918*

I addressed you last on the 8th instant as to our domestic transportation of foodstuffs.[1] Since that date, by a preference in the use of box cars for grain in the western territory, there has been some acceleration in the movement of some of the grains to the terminals. On the other hand the number of cars have not been sufficient to maintain the food traffic from the west into the east and have not been sufficient to move Allied supplies of cereals and meat products. In consequence, we are faced not only with a renewed failure in Allied shipments, but also, our stocks of foodstuffs in the eastern states are steadily diminishing. The Allied Purchasing Commission reports to me that the situation has become now the most critical in which they have found themselves since the beginning of the War. There are still great numbers of box cars on the eastern lines which belong to the west and the movement in the eastern territory is still far below the necessities of the case.

I cannot but feel that we are approaching a very serious crisis and I feel greatly discouraged over the entire situation.

I am   Your obedient servant,   Herbert Hoover.

TLS (W. G. McAdoo Papers, DLC).
 [1] He meant February 9. See H. C. Hoover to WW, Feb. 9, 1918.

From Robert Lansing, with Enclosure

My dear Mr. President: Washington February 20, 1918.

In connection with the appeal of the International Committee of the Red Cross,[1] concerning which I spoke to you yesterday, together with Secretary Baker—whose Department is opposed to any such arrangement—I send you herewith a draft of a communication which I had then prepared for transmission to our Embassies at London, Paris and Rome.

Upon returning to the Department I found that Mr. Barclay of the British Embassy had seen Mr. Phillips and under instructions from his Government orally asked whether the appeal of the International Committee should not be answered in identic terms and also whether we would not agree that the reply be framed in Paris.

Pursuant to Mr. Barclay's communication I propose sending the enclosed telegram to Paris,[2] before sending out the one which is directed to London.

Will you kindly indicate your wishes in the matter?

Faithfully yours,   Robert Lansing

TLS (SDR, RG 59, 703.72116/532, DNA).
[1] Conveyed in H. R. Wilson to RL, Feb. 11, 1918 (SDR, RG 59, 763.72116/533, DNA), printed in *FR-WWS 1918*, 2, pp. 779-81.
[2] RL to W. G. Sharp, T telegram, Feb. 21, 1918 (SDR, RG 59, 763.72116/533, DNA), printed in *FR-WWS 1918*, 2, pp. 781/82: "Department has received an appeal from the International Committee of the Red Cross at Geneva for the discontinuance by all the countries at war of the use of poisonous, asphyxiating and other gases. The British Embassy here reports a suggestion from the French Foreign Office that identic reply be framed in Paris. You may consult your British colleague unofficially and telegraph Department the tenor of suggested reply."

ENCLOSURE

Washington. February 18, 1918.

Please inform the British Government that this Government has received the open appeal of the International Committee of the Red Cross at Geneva protesting against the use of poisonous, asphyxiating and other gases in warfare and has received a suggestion from the British Embassy that an identic reply should be returned by all the Allied powers. The Department concurs in this view and suggests that such an identic reply be formulated along the lines of the following text. Please ascertain whether the British Government shares the views of this Government and inform the Department what alterations if any are proposed. Am also consulting the French and Italian Governments. The matter should be regarded as of extreme urgency:

Quote. "The Government of the United States has received with gratification the appeal of the International Committee of the Red Cross at Geneva, Switzerland, dated February 6, 1918, protesting against the use of poisonous, asphyxiating and other gases in warfare and has noted with satisfaction the open demand of the Committee that this method of warfare be renounced. After an exchange of views with the Governments of its co-belligerents the Government of the United States makes on its own behalf the following reply.

"War, by its very nature, cannot be altogether disassociated from physical and mental suffering; the destruction of human life on the battle field is inseparable from pain and must leave in its wake the distress of broken family ties and disrupted homes. These are the recognized penalties of war and must continue until the progress of civilization evolves conditions under which war can no longer be forced upon unwilling peoples.

"But in times of peace the nations have continually sought to formulate standards whereby war, if it should occur, would be rendered less cruel, less inhumane than in the past; whereby the conduct of warfare would be brought into accord with the advance of civilization and whereby humane sentiment rather than brutality would rule on the field of battle. Repeatedly have representatives of the powers met and agreed upon rules of war which, by their general acceptance, have been incorporated into the law of nations, and confirmed by the most solemn international covenants.

"Among the rules thus adopted, none can be more effectively aimed at avoiding the hideous suffering and cruelty which modern science has rendered possible than those which forbid the employment of poison or poisoned arms and which ban the use of weapons, projectiles or materials calculated to cause needless suffering. There can be no question that poisonous, asphyxiating and other gases fall under this provision. This Government has been given unhappily ample opportunity to witness their effect, and fully concurs with the International Committee of the Red Cross in its description of the terrible sufferings and cruel deaths caused by their use. To all of the statements of the Committee regarding the criminal and barbarous nature of this practice, and to the prospects of its future development, the Government of the United States most earnestly subscribes.

"The use of such measures is abhorrent to the Government of the United States. It is not the wish of this Government to adopt them and it could do so only with great reluctance. Yet it cannot permit the enemy to obtain unequal advantage; the American forces in the field must protect themselves by meeting such tactics by similar tactics. They will do so with the greatest repugnance but with equal energy.

"Nevertheless the United States stands ready at any time to give practical expression to this repugnance by entering into a solemn and reciprocal agreement with its enemies, as proposed by the International Committee of the Red Cross, to renounce the practice of using poisonous, asphyxiating and other gases in warfare. It only remains for the International Committee of the Red Cross to obtain a similar expression from the Imperial German Government and the Governments of the other Central Powers to effect this most worthy proposal.

"Should such an agreement be unanimously subscribed to by the warring nations and duly brought into faithful observance, the Red Cross will have achieved another victory for civilization and will have won for itself enduring honor in the name of mercy and humanity, in whose noble cause it has so constantly devoted its unsparing labors." Unquote.

T telegram (SDR, RG 59, 703.72116/532, DNA).

Two Telegrams from Walter Hines Page

London, Feb. 20, 1918.

8748. MOST SECRET. For the Secretary and the President.

Admiral Hall informs me that he had just learned through the source* indicated in my 7276, of September 27th last,[1] that on the 18th instant the Austro-Hungarian Minister of Foreign Affairs at Vienna sent a cipher message to his Ambassador at Madrid[2] of which the following is a translation.

"On behalf of His Highness, Your Excellency is requested to communicate the following words without delay to the King of Spain and to hand it to him in writing:

'The European situation has been materially cleared up by Mr. Wilson's public speech on the one hand and by Count Czernin's on the other and the points at issue have been reduced to a certain minimum hence the time seems to have come when a direct discussion between one of my representatives and one representing Mr. Wilson might clear up the situation to such an extent that no further obstacle would stand in the way of a world's peace congress.

'Your magnanimous desire so frequently expressed to pronounce proposals for peace at such a time prompts me to request you to

* Wireless from Madrid.

forward the following message through a secret channel to President Wilson:

'In his speech of February twelfth President Wilson expressed four main principles as the foundation of an understanding to be hoped for. My position in regard to these four principles I can sum up as follows:

'In point one President Wilson demanded, according to the German text before me, "that each part of the final settlement must be basic for the essential justice of that particular case and upon such adjustments as are most likely to bring a peace that will be permanent." With this guiding principle I am in agreement. Every man of principle and intellect must desire a solution which assures lasting peace and it is only a just peace, securing vital interests, that can afford such a solution.

'Points two and three belong together and are to the effect that "peoples and provinces are not to be bartered about from sovereignty to sovereignty as if they were chattels and pawns in a game, even the great game, now for ever discredited, of the balance of power, but that every territorial settlement involved in the war must be made in the interest and for the benefit of the populations concerned and not as a part of any mere adjustment or compromise of claims among the rival states."

'The question of territory I believe will resolve itself very simply if all governments expressly declare that they renounce conquests and annexations. Of course all states would have to be placed on the same footing. If the President will endeavor to bring his allies into line in this respect Austria will do everything in her power to induce her own allies to take up this position. As regards what might be accomplished in respect of possible frontier modifications in the interest and in favor of the peoples concerned similar friendly conversations may be carried on between state and state for, and this seemed to be the opinion of the President too, a lasting peace could scarcely be promoted if in a desire to avoid a forcible transference from the sovereignty of one power to another we wished to prevent a corresponding territorial settlement in other parts of Europe where hitherto there has been no fixity of frontiers as in the case of the part of (undecipherable group) inhabited by Bulgars. However the principle must remain that no state shall gain or lose anything and the pre-war possessions of all states be regarded as inviolable.

'Point four "all well defined national *aspersions* (aspirations?) shall be accorded the utmost satisfaction that can be accorded to them without introducing new or perpetuating old elements of discord and antagonism that would be likely in time to break the peace of Europe and consequently of the world."

'This statement too so clearly and aptly put by the President is acceptable as a basis. Again I lay the greatest stress on the fact that any fresh settlement of conditions in Europe should not increase the risk of future conflict, but rather diminish it. Wilson's sincerity in saying "that the American Government was quite ready to be shown that the settlements she has suggested are not the best or the most enduring," arouses in us a high hope that we may in this question too reach some agreement. In this exchange of opinion we shall be in a position to furnish conclusive proof that there are national demands the satisfying of which would be neither good nor enduring nor would they provide for the grievances which are continually put forward a solution which would meet the wishes of the states affected. We shall be able to establish this in the case of the national claims of Italy to the part of the Austrian Tyrol inhabited by Italians by means of the proof of indisputable manifestations and expressions of the popular will in this part of the Monarchy. I must therefore for my part most strongly urge that my representative discuss with the President every possible means of preventing fresh crises. In the principle already enunciated of an entire renunciation of annexations the demand for the complete surrender of Belgium is apparently also included. All questions of detail such as Serbia's access of the sea, the granting of the necessary commerce and navigation outlets for Serbia and many other questions, could be certainly cleared up by discussion and prepared for a peace conference.

'The second main principle which the President had already established consists in the unconditional avoidance of a future war. With this I am in complete accord.

'As regards the third point laid down by the President, the main purport of which is general disarmament and freedom of the seas for the prevention of future world wars, there is no difference of opinion between the President and myself. In view of all this I hold that there exists such a degree of harmony between the principles laid down by the President on the one hand and (? myself) on the other that results might be expected from an actual conference and that such a conference might bring the world considerably nearer to the peace fervently desired by all states.'

'If you will be good enough to forward this reply to Mr. Wilson I believe you would render the cause of peace in general and the whole human race the greatest service in the power of any benefactor. Signed. KARL.'

"Your Excellency is requested to communicate the result of your demarche. Signed. CZERNIN." Page.

[1] WHP to RL, Sept. 27, 1917, T telegram (SDR, RG 59, 862.20235/103, DNA).
[2] Karl Emil, Prince zu Fürstenberg.

London. February 20.

8749. Most secret. My immediately preceeding telegram.

It should be observed that the Emperor Karl's message is to be communicated in writing to the King of Spain, which makes it appear certain that it is sent with the knowledge and approval of the German Government.

The Emperor Karl proposes preliminary discussions without mentioning terms, in anticipation of a final World's peace conference. This is what the Germans have aimed at from the beginning, notably, the encouragement of attempt last September, also through Madrid, to bring about preliminary discussions with the British authorities without the knowledge of Great Britain's Allies.

Page.

T telegrams (SDR, RG 59, 763.72119/7725 and 7726, DNA).

From Newton Diehl Baker

My dear Mr. President: Washington. February 20, 1918.

I have had repeated cablegrams and letters from General Pershing urging that I visit our Expeditionary Forces in France, and as our plans have gone forward I have come more and more to realize the need of an actual inspection of ports, transportation and storage facilities and camps of our overseas Army.

Of course, we are constantly having officers of the several Armies returning from France with information and recommendations; but they frequently serve only to illustrate the impossibility of securing a complete view of the situation by any other course than a personal inspection.

In addition to this, the relatives and friends of our soldiers are deeply concerned to know the conditions under which these soldiers live and the environment in which they find themselves. It will be of importance if I can give comforting assurances as the result of an actual visit to the camps; and it may be that I can suggest betterments as the results of our experience here where great encampments have been built up, and a most wholesome and helpful environment provided with the cooperation of all the helpful and sympathetic agencies which the people of the country have placed at our disposal.

The various reorganizations in the War Department have now progressed to a place where I feel that they will proceed uninterruptedly with their task, and I can with more comfort than would have been possible at an earlier time, be absent for a brief time. I am writing, therefore, to ask your consent to my absence long enough to pay a hurried visit to France for such an inspection trip as I have herein outlined. My plans would carry me to France, and would include a thorough inspection of our ports, lines of transportation and communication, and camps, with a brief visit to Paris and London.   Respectfully yours,   Newton D. Baker

TLS (WP, DLC).

From Herbert Clark Hoover

Dear Mr. President: Washington, D. C. 20 *February 1918*

I have not the remotest doubt but that the operations of the Grain Division of the Food Administration will come up for assault or investigation by Congress sooner or later, and it occurs to me it might be worth while taking time by the forelock and having an investigation of our own. I am wondering if you would mind my appealing to Dr. Taussig to secure assistance and make an investigation of the entire operations and write a report—this report to be made to yourself. We could then be armed to use it the minute we saw that such an investigation was brewing. I would not propose to make any public announcement.

I am   Your obedient servant,   Herbert Hoover

TLS (WP, DLC).

From William Royal Wilder, with Enclosure

My dear Wilson: New York February 20, 1918.

I have two reasons for not following my usual course and sending the enclosure direct to Mr. Lansing,—*quod valeat.*

The greatest crisis of the war is upon us. Unless the Poles are utilized and helped to secure their own independence and straighten out affairs in Russia, they will lose their hope of independence, and the Germans will absorb some and dominate the rest of Russia. I know something of the situation for it has occupied every moment of my leisure time for over a year, and I am very much in earnest about it.

I also send the enclosure to you on account of the personal reference to myself in it. I have not the honor of Mr. Lansing's acquaintance and he may misunderstand it. The members of the Polish National Defense Committee are my friends, and my inclusion is, of course, complimentary. You and I know that "number 2" on the list had better be omitted, or better yet, be filled in by the name of some one in the State Department who knows infinitely more about the subject than I do. My usefulness will begin and end in starting such a conference and stating my views and holding myself ever in readiness to give such information and assistance as I possess. Please see to it that Mr. Lansing gets no wrong notion about my connection with the matter by reason of the friendship and devotion of the Poles, which have been inspired by my interest in their country and in them.

I can add but little to the enclosure except by way of reiteration, and to urge upon you, Mr. Lansing and the Allies the importance of declaring at once the independence of the Poles, and morally now and physically and materially as soon as possible, aid them. A strong buffer Republic will tend to democratize Germany and enable Russia to reorganize herself.

The present anarchy in Russia is really due to the effort of the various nationalities formerly held in subjection by the Czar, to realize their racial and national ideals. No one regrets more than I the fact that the Polish National Defense Committee is not acting in harmony with what may be known as the "Paderewski Party." This is due somewhat to American politics, but more to the fact that the former represents the lower middle classes in Poland and the element composing the emigrants to this country, while the latter connotes the clerical, reactionary and well to do Poles both here and in Europe. It is our business to utilize *them all* for their and our common good.

It will give me much pleasure to wait upon you and Mr. Lansing at any time.   Sincerely yours,   Wm. R. Wilder

E N C L O S U R E

From Alexander N. Debskí and Bronislaw D. Kulakowski

Dear Mr. President: [New York] February 18, 1918.

The Polish question is approaching a critical point. All Poland has been outraged at the news that the Central Powers have ceded to the Ukraine Republic without the knowledge and consent of the inhabitants the Chelm (Kholm) Province, a large portion of Poland. At the receipt of this sinister news there arose a synchronous protest throughout the country in spite of the fact that Poland is divided into military zones of occupation and in spite of the fact that intelligence communication by telephone, telegraph and mail is under the control of government officials of the Central Powers, and no one is allowed to travel without a German passport. This protest took on various forms in various places. The cities displayed black flags, theatres and performances were closed, factory workmen, despite privation, joined in one day's demonstration strike, the Polish Cabinet at Warsaw[1] submitted its resignation, the Polish Club of the Parliament of Vienna turned into opposition to the Government of Austria and Poles occupying prominent places in the Austrian service resigned.

Count Szeptycki, the Military Governor General of the part of Poland occupied by Austria, Mr. Madeyski, the Count's deputy for foreign affairs,[2] Mr. Ignace Rosner, the Austrian envoy at Warsaw, have all resigned, sacrificing their individual careers to their Polish patriotism.

On the eastern borderlands of Poland, the Polish contingents of the former Russian armies, the only troops that remained undemoralized, reacted against Russian anarchy and debauchery as well as against the German annexation lust by raising the Polish war banners. A large territory of the eastern domains of the former Polish Republic, together with the cities of Minsk, Rohaczev, Bychov, Mohilev, Orsza and Smolensk with their supplies fell into the hands of the Polish troops commanded by General Dowbor-Musnicki[3] who in spite of German vigilance succeeded in communicating with the Polish Government at Warsaw. A Berlin dispatch to the Frankfurter Zeitung (New York Times February 17) states that: "Reports in Warsaw papers that Polish regiments of the Russian Army have offered to place themselves at the disposal of the Warsaw Government are causing serious anxiety in political circles in Germany." And the New York Times correspondent adds: "The report thus mentioned seems to suggest that the Poles have suddenly appeared as an important military factor."

The above news is highly significant. It confirms the correctness of the argument of the Polish National Defense Committee presented in the memorials and communications addressed to the State Department and particularly that of August 1917 handed to Mr. Lansing by Messrs A. Debski, Stanislaus Rayzacher and Bronislaw D. Kulakowski,[4] also in the letters of December 1 and 14, 1917,[5] to Mr. Wilder which were subsequently forwarded to the Secretary of State.

The thing we most desired has happened: All factions have recognized the Polish Government and the Polish army in Russia has submitted to its command. The Polish Nation has found itself united in a final struggle against the Germans.

Time is pressing. Poland fighting in its isolation may succumb, *as did Serbia, if not properly reenforced.* The Germans may conquer the whole of North Russia and drawing upon the food resources and its mineral wealth may establish a permanent foothold over a tremendous area of the globe stretching across to Vladivostok. They will then be able to afford the loss of African colonies.

We turn to you, Sir, in this moment for active help in the situation. You alone of all the great leaders of the world have strengthened the Polish spirit speaking in the name of America for an independent Poland. We realize the difficulties with which American action on behalf of Poland is beset. We reckon with this condition and do not request things impossible of realization.

We ask only for your moral support and for the initiative in putting the United Polish element in touch with the representatives of the United States and the Allied Nations. We ask you for this friendly act toward our people, which act does not involve any responsibility with regard to anyone.

To avoid mistakes and to exploit timely the situation that arose in Poland we take the liberty of suggesting to you the desirability of calling a conference to Washington in order to make possible coordinated action.

We respectfully recommend that the following persons be asked to participate in such conference:

(1) A representative of the State Department;

(2) Mr. William R. Wilder of New York, a devoted friend of Poland;

(3) A representative of the British Embassy;

(4) A representative of the French Embassy;

(5) A representative of the Italian Embassy;

(6) Major Joseph Kozlowski, head of the Polish-French Military Mission;

(7) Mr. Ignace I. Padarewski, Gotham Hotel, New York, N. Y.;

(8) Professor Zowski[6] of the University of Michigan;

(9) Dr. Stanley Stanislaus, an American of remote Polish descent, Lock Haven, Pa.;

(10) Dr. E. H. Lewinski Corwin[7] of the New York Academy of Medicine, New York;

(11) Mr. George J. Sosnowski of Poland, 59 Wall Street, New York, N. Y.;

(12) Mr. Alexander Debski, personal friend of General J. Pilsud-

ski, who is now held prisoner by the Germans, 75 St. Marks Place, New York, N. Y., and

(13) Mr. B. V. Kulakowski, the editor of the official organ of the Polish Defense Committee, 2788 Broadway, New York, N. Y.

This conference is to have no authoritative character whatsoever. Its purpose is to afford an opportunity for an elucidation of the situation in Eastern Europe and for considering the magnitude of the Polish forces which can be placed at the disposal of the contemplated joint action.

The calling of such a conference in the near future will be a great step forward. We are certain that such a conference will dispel many erroneous views and opinions, will move the Polish question from its present deadlock position and will lay the foundation for the resumption of military activities on the Eastern front.

We fear that the superhuman efforts of the Polish nation fighting alone against the might of Germany will resolve itself into fruitless heroism if joint action on the part of the United States and the Allies will come too late or if it be *one-sidedly developed.*

As the representatives of the Polish National Defense Committee remaining since 1912 in contact with General Pilsudski, and as the Polish democrats devoted to the United States and desirous at all times of following your political leadership, we beg you to make an early decision in this matter. Should you possibly have any doubts or should you desire further preliminary explanations, we suggest that you use the good offices of Mr. William R. Wilder.

We beg you to receive the assurances of our high esteem and of our readiness to be at your service.

THE POLISH NATIONAL DEFENSE COMMITTEE,

By Alexander N. Debskí

Bronislaw D. Kulakowski

TLS (SDR, RG 59, 860C.01/144, DNA).

[1] The cabinet headed by Jan Kucharzewski, which administered that portion of Poland then occupied by the Austrian army. See Arthur J. May, *The Passing of the Hapsburg Monarchy, 1914-1918* (2 vols., Philadelphia, 1966), II, 503-10.

[2] Stanislaw Szeptycki and Jerzy Wiktor Madeyski.

[3] Józef Dowbor-Muśnicki, a former general of the czarist armies, at this time commanding the First Polish Army Corps formed out of Polish elements in the Russian army, which claimed to be an army of independent Poland. See Piotr S. Wandycz, *Soviet-Polish Relations, 1917-1921* (Cambridge, Mass., 1969), pp. 54-57.

[4] See the Enclosures printed with WW to RL, Aug. 21, 1917, Vol. 44.

[5] W. R. Wilder to RL, Dec. 1 and Dec. 17, 1917, TLS, with enclosures (SDR, RG 59, 860C.01/52 and 57).

[6] Stanislaus Jan Zowski (Zwierzchowski), Professor of Hydro-Mechanical Engineering at the University of Michigan.

[7] Edward Henry Lewinski Corwin, Ph.D., expert on public health, executive secretary of the committee on public health relations of the New York Academy of Medicine. Author of *The Political History of Poland* (New York, 1917).

To Robert Lansing

My dear Mr. Secretary,   The White House. 21 February, 1918.

I must say I am afraid of *any* expression of policy framed jointly at Paris. There has been none yet that seemed to me even touched with wisdom. I see that you have sought to suggest and safeguard, but I am afraid that statesmen like our friend L-G. will not care to be guided and will rather rejoice in a somewhat crude and cynical rejoinder to the Red Cross.

I approve the despatch to Sharp, however, and am quite willing to subscribe to a proper reply if they will let us see it beforehand. Sharp can cable it, and the delay will not be serious.[1]

Faithfully Yours,   W.W.

WWTLI (SDR, RG 59, 763.72116/532, DNA).
    [1] Lansing's proposed telegram was not sent. Instead, Lansing informed Sharp that the British embassy in Washington had received a suggestion from the French Foreign Ministry that an identic reply to the International Red Cross be framed in Paris. Lansing instructed Sharp to consult with his British colleague and to telegraph to the State Department the "tenor of suggested reply." RL to W. G. Sharp, Feb. 21, 1918, *FR-WWS 1918*, 2, pp. 781-82. Discussions about the matter dragged on to the end of the war.

To Joseph Patrick Tumulty

Dear Tumulty: [The White House, c. Feb. 21, 1918]

I would be very much obliged if you would intimate to the Secretary of State the real character and activities of Father Kelly[1] and say that, while of course I am glad to have his enclosure[2] acknowledged in my behalf with appreciation, I hope that Father Kelly's request for a personal message will simply be overlooked, not only so far as I am concerned but so far as members of the Cabinet are concerned.   The President.

TL (WP, DLC).
    [1] Msgr. Francis Clement Kelley, not Kelly, president of the Catholic Church Extension Society of the United States of America. For Wilson's earlier contacts with him, see the index references in Vols. 32 and 33 of this series. Lansing, in RL to JPT, Feb. 20, 1918, TLS (WP, DLC), had enclosed F. C. Kelley to RL, Feb. 14, 1918, TLS (WP, DLC). Kelley had requested a "personal message" from Wilson encouraging national unity in wartime, and similar messages from Baker and Daniels, to be printed in a future issue of *Extension Magazine*, the organ of the Catholic Church Extension Society.
    In his note transmitting Kelley's letter (JPT to WW, Feb. 21, 1918, TL [WP, DLC]), Tumulty had reminded Wilson that Kelley was "the gentleman who took issue with me when I attempted a defense of your Mexican policy." "He is a bitter partisan Republican," Tumulty continued, "and is also disposed to help us when we do not need his friendship." About Tumulty's public exchange with Kelley in 1915, see John M. Blum, *Joe Tumulty and the Wilson Era* (Boston, 1951), p. 92.
    [2] Kelley had enclosed in his letter Leopoldo Ruiz and Francisco Plancarte to WW, Feb. 10, 1918, TLS (WP, DLC). This letter, written by two archbishops on behalf of all the Mexican Roman Catholic bishops and archbishops in exile in the United States, firmly denied published reports that any of them favored the Central Powers or that they had in any way encouraged intervention by the United States in Mexico. On the contrary, they insisted, they had maintained a strict neutrality in all such matters and were principally concerned with the issue of religious freedom in Mexico.

To George Creel

My dear Creel,   The White House. 21 February, 1918.

Please read this and then destroy it.[1] I am sending it to you only that you may consider the feasibility of doing what Reinsch suggests in the portion of the message which I have marked.

                              Faithfully Yours,   W.W.

WWTLI (G. Creel Papers, DLC).
    [1] P. S. Reinsch to RL, Feb. 19, 1918, T telegram (SDR, RG 59, 861.00/1124, DNA). What was probably the marked portion reads as follows: "It is to be feared that unless constructive action can be taken Siberia may be controlled by Bolshevik and Germany. All information indicates urgent necessity for systematic efforts to dispelling [dispel] great ignorance and prejudice of Russian population relating to America. American motives and institutions have been constantly misprinted [misrepresented], American coldness, aloofness[,] failure to come in touch with the Russian people and the leaders of the United States. For instance the Japanese in Siberia are systematically cultivating Russian good will through personal consummation [communication] and propaganda, are preparing for political influence and industrial concessions. What America needs is full newspaper discussion and lectures on American affairs as well as contact with people. I consider it of the greatest importance immediately to send organizers. . . . They could establish organization of Russian teachers close to people engaging them for lectures on the war, thirty roubles expenses per month. Cost relatively insignificant, results of immense importance can be obtained."

To Herbert Clark Hoover

                                        The White House
My dear Mr. Hoover: 21 February, 1917 [1918]

If Mr. Taussig has the time, I should entirely approve of his investigating the grain division of the Food Administration as you suggest in your letter of yesterday.

          Cordially and sincerely yours,   Woodrow Wilson

TLS (H. Hoover Papers, HPL).

To Mrs. F. C. Foley[1]

My dear Mrs. Foley: [The White House] 21 February, 1918

It is with unusual appreciation that Mrs. Wilson and I receive the splendid turkey you were kind enough to send,—the remarkable turkey which was sold on New Year's day at the Red Cross auction. We shall, I am sure, enjoy the turkey tomorrow, but I want you to know that the best thing about it will be the flavor of friendship which accompanies it.

          Cordially and sincerely yours,   Woodrow Wilson

TLS (Letterpress Books, WP, DLC).
    [1] Of Newell, Ia. She cannot be further identified.

From Robert Lansing

My dear Mr. President: Washington February 21, 1918.

I have your inquiry in regard to the removal of the British ban on the International News Service.

Mr. Balfour, when he was here, and afterward other British representatives have said to me that if this Department would request the removal of the ban it would be done. From first to last I have replied that we would make no such request. When I went away last summer I told Mr. Polk the policy I had adopted and he says that he followed the same course.

Mr. Polk tells me that recently he learned from British sources that Treasury officials had interested themselves in the matter, but of course he did not and I do not speak from actual knowledge. I do not think that the British representatives have mentioned the matter to me within the past four months.

Faithfully yours,   Robert Lansing

TLS (WP, DLC).

From Henry Pomeroy Davison

Dear Mr. President: Washington, D. C. February 21, 1918.

Brigadier-General William V. Judson, Military Attache and head of the American Military Mission to Russia for the past eight months, arrived in Washington yesterday direct from Petrograd, and has this morning presented to me a letter of introduction from Raymond Robins.

In conversation, General Judson expresses a very high opinion of the work Robins is doing, going so far as to say that no American in Russia is better posted as to the situation there, or doing more important work. Because of the nature of his remarks, I deemed it wise to advise him that we were asking Robins to absent himself from Russia to attend a conference in Paris. He at once expressed the opinion that this would be a very unfortunate move, that when he left Petrograd some of the present government officials interpreted his leaving as evidence of lack of sympathy on the part of the United States, and that for Robins to leave, even temporarily, would be regarded by Lenine and Trotsky as significant, and, therefore, in General Judson's opinion, it would be better to stop all shipments and leave Robins than it would be to withdraw Robins and continue the shipments.

Before meeting General Judson I had visited the State Department to confer with them relative to shipments to Russia and had told Counsellor Polk of our proposed cable to Robins. After my talk with General Judson, I thought it advisable to again confer with Mr. Polk and get his opinion as to the advisability of having Robins leave Petrograd in view of the statements of General Judson. Mr. Polk expressed the opinion that perhaps it would be unfortunate and, therefore, better for Robins to remain. This is my own judgment so far as I can form any with the meagre information at hand.

I am writing to inform you in order that you may not be under the impression that Robins is leaving Petrograd, and I am, therefore, not sending the cable as I contemplated doing. Should you have any different opinion or should conditions so develop that you believe it wise to have him leave temporarily or permanently, you will, I trust, promptly advise me and action to that end will be taken.

Sincerely yours,   H. P. Davison

TLS (WP, DLC).

From William Gibbs McAdoo

PERSONAL.

Dear Governor: Washington February 21, 1918.

Yours of the 20th re Crosby just received, and I agree with you fully as to the impropriety of the Supreme War Council and the other councils participating in political matters or attempting to formulate political policies. I shall caution Crosby against any such tendencies or action.   Affectionately yours,   W G McAdoo

TLS (WP, DLC).

From Herbert Clark Hoover

Dear Mr. President: Washington, D. C. 21 *February 1918*

I have received your letter of the 19th enclosing the memorial presented to you by Mr. Hurd[1] and his associates. Most of these gentlemen have already discussed these matters at length with us. I do think, however, that it is desirable to set out this situation on the points raised by these gentlemen so far as we are able to penetrate into it. I therefore attach rather a full memorandum to that end[2] and upon which you may desire to secure Mr. Secretary Houston's views before using, as it concerns production matters.

In addition to the statement contained therein with regard to the packers, I would like to say that, as you know, I have no great love for the packers and they have been very difficult to deal with. They do control prices in the sense that every group of middle-men operating in large units control prices to some extent, that is, they control prices more or less from day to day and in the particular sense as to the price they pay for individual cattle and sheep and the prices at which they make individual sales. On the other hand, in the long run, even they cannot control the great forces of supply and demand. By the methods which we have employed in limiting their profits we have endeavoured to restrain the large ones from driving the little ones out of business, and have tried by our large buying orders for abroad to keep the plants, both large and small, running at full capacity. We have not detected, and we are certain they have not been making excessive profit since November 1st, although they appeared to have made very large profits prior to that date. Their sworn statements to us as to their monthly operations show that they have operated at a very small margin, or even a loss, for the last two months. We are anxious that the Federal Trade Commission should give us the use of their staff of accountants to check up these statements as it is a very involved and complicated matter in which their own staffs have already had valuable experience. This work is in the nature of cost accounting similar to that in certain branches of the government and I understand, if some direction were given by you to the Federal Trade Commission they would place their staff at our service. I am wondering if you would be so kind as to instruct them to undertake this work.

It is only fair to say with regard to the packers that they have performed an indispensable service for war purposes. We have studiously kept away from discussions as to their previous career and private character and I can say that they have advanced very far during the last three months in performing a work of national service.   Yours faithfully,   Herbert Hoover

TLS (WP, DLC).
    ¹ That is, Dwight B. Heard.
    ² "Memorandum," Feb. 20, 1918, T MS (WP, DLC), an analysis of the various factors affecting the supplies and the prices of beef, pork, mutton, and lamb in the American market.

From George Creel

My dear Mr. President: Washington, D. C. February 21, 1918.

Proper world circulation for your addresses is being defeated by these difficulties:

(1) We are not able to negotiate in advance with the cable companies for special service.

(2) We are not able to inform our foreign representatives in advance that the messages are coming.

(3) The addresses are delivered at the worst possible time of the day for secruing [securing] textual publication in Europe. They do not reach the Continental offices until after midnight, when there is not time for translation and when the papers, of necessity, are compelled to print short extracts.

Is it not possible for me to have the address the night before the day of its delivery? We can then make arrangements with the cable companies for special service and put it on the wires at nine o'clock in the morning, holding it in Paris and London for release. I can guarantee an absolute secrecy.

Respectfully,   George Creel

TLS (WP, DLC).

Charles Richard Crane to Joseph Patrick Tumulty

New York, February 21, 1918.

Please look over the telegram in today's Times from Harold Williams and especially the one from Moscow.[1] I should like to have the President and postmaster general see them as they are undoubtedly authentic. Cordial greetings.   Charles R. Crane.

T telegram (WP, DLC).

[1] There were two telegrams from Harold Williams in the *New York Times*, Feb. 21, 1918: "Russia Expiring Under Reds' Rule," datelined Petrograd, February 18, and "Moscow Is Become a City of Despair," datelined Moscow, February 13. The first dispatch asserted that the Bolsheviks were rapidly conquering almost all of Russia, more through the power of their revolutionary ideology than through military force. Williams gave as an example the case of General Alekseev's army in the Don River region, which easily defeated Bolshevik forces in combat but was being undermined from within by skillful Bolshevik propagandists. Williams believed that all Russia would become Bolshevist before a reaction would begin to set in. He repeated this theme in the second dispatch, in which he pictured Moscow as a temporary refuge for the middle class and intellectuals driven from power by the Bolsheviks. But even in Moscow, political and economic anarchy was setting in. Profiteers were making fortunes through their control of vital foodstuffs, and everyone was in fear of his life. Moscow was an example of the hopeless condition that would prevail throughout all Russia until the Bolsheviks had run their course.

Walter Hines Page to Robert Lansing

London, February 21 1918.

8764. MOST SECRET.

My 8748, February twentieth. Furstenburg sent the following message to Czernin yesterday:

"As soon as the text, which has been mutilated in several places, has been definitely established I shall ask His Majesty to receive me in order that I may deliver the message to him tomorrow evening, February twenty-first."

The Austro-Hungarian Minister of Foreign Affairs has sent the following supplementary message to the Ambassador at Madrid:

"If Mr. Wilson assents to the King's proposal and sends a representative to discuss matters with me he should send some one who speaks either French or German as I do not know English well enough to discuss such weighty matters."   Page

T telegram (SDR, RG 59, 763.72119/7727, DNA).

Hugh Robert Wilson to Robert Lansing

Pontarlier, (Berne), February 21 1918.

2694. STRICTLY CONFIDENTIAL. Department's 1500, February 15, 11 p.m., was decoded personally by me.

Lammasch has no agent in Switzerland and I hesitated to confide this message to any neutral. It was therefore imperative to confide it only to a person of confidence who could deliver the message secretly, orally and unofficially to Lammasch in Vienna.

I therefore summoned York Steiner an Austrian who often calls at the Legation in connection with the sale of the vessels of the Austro-American line to Phelps Brothers. He is a close friend and warm admirer of Lammasch and a disciple of his in political matters. He is known personally to Grew in the Department and has always been found worthy of confidence both by the former Embassy at Vienna and this Legation; furthermore he is an ardent admirer of President Wilson, an opponent of German domination in Austria, and has come to Switzerland to devote himself to furtherance of mutual understanding between Austria and the United States.

I asked him whether he could proceed to Vienna on a confidential mission of benefit to his country. He replied that he could proceed as soon as the necessary three days of passport formalities had elapsed. I told him to obtain the necessary vise and then return to me. He returned on the nineteenth instant having obtained permission to visit Vienna on the ground of his desire to bring his daughter back to Switzerland; a reason which really exists and a mission which he will accomplish.

I then delivered your message which he repeated to me in exact wording. He expressed himself as profoundly moved by this opportunity to be of service to his country and assured me that having delivered his message he would wipe it from his memory. He has arranged to inform me by a harmless telegram to his wife on Tuesday, who will know nothing of its import, when message has been delivered.

Dulles[1] and I are ciphering this message and matter is known to no one else.   Wilson.

T telegram (R. Lansing Papers, NjP).
[1] Allen Welsh Dulles, Second Secretary of the American legation in Bern.

To William Gibbs McAdoo

My dear Mac: [The White House] 22 February, 1918

I have received several letters of thanks recently for the removal of the British ban on the International News Service (Hearst's). Inasmuch as I had made it a principle to have nothing to do with the dealings of the British Government with any news service, I, of course, had nothing to do with this. When Mr. Balfour was here, and afterwards when other British representatives have said to us that if the State Department would request the removal of the ban, it would be removed, we have invariably replied that we would make no such request. I have, therefore, been inquiring what influence, if any, was exerted from Washington, and I have been told that Treasury officials had something to do with it. I can't believe this, but I wish you would be kind enough to make inquiry and let me know.

In haste   Affectionately yours,   Woodrow Wilson

TLS (Letterpress Books, WP, DLC).

To George Creel

My dear Creel: The White House 22 February, 1918

Yes, if I can finish the next address in time, I will certainly see that the experiment is tried of complying with the suggestions of your letter of yesterday. Those suggestions are entirely reasonable. I have realized the difficulties you have contended with. You know, I am sure, the only reason why I have embarrassed you. We will see next time if the thing can be done secretly when so many people are concerned.

Cordially and faithfully yours,   Woodrow Wilson

TLS (G. Creel Papers, DLC).

Two Letters to Newton Diehl Baker

My dear Mr. Secretary: The White House 22 February, 1918

I have your letter of February twentieth and concur in your judgment that General Pershing's repeated requests that you should visit our expeditionary forces in France should be complied with. I believe that it will add to the morale, not only of our forces there, but of our forces here, to feel that you are personally conversant with all the conditions of their transportation and treatment on the other side, and I believe that it will be serviceable to all of us to have the comprehensive view which you will bring back with you.

I sincerely hope that your journey will be safe. We shall look for your return with impatience, because your guidance is constantly needed here.

Cordially and sincerely yours,   Woodrow Wilson

Private.

My dear Baker: The White House 22 February, 1918

I think it would be of the greatest service so far as the spirit of things is concerned if you would visit Italy and get in touch, if even for a very brief time indeed, with the military people there. It would gratify them deeply and would show our interest in the best way in which we can show it for the present.

Faithfully and cordially yours,   Woodrow Wilson

TLS (N. D. Baker Papers, DLC).

To Henry Pomeroy Davison

My dear Mr. Davison: [The White House] 22 February, 1918

Thank you for your letter of yesterday about the advice of General Judson with regard to Mr. Robins' remaining in Petrograd. I dare say that General Judson's advice is good; at any rate, I am quite content to see it accepted for the present until things clear up a bit in that unhappy country.

Cordially and sincerely yours,   Woodrow Wilson

TLS (Letterpress Books, WP, DLC).

From Robert Lansing

My dear Mr. President,   Washington February 22, 1918.

I told you after cabinet meeting on Tuesday, the 19th, of my interview that morning with Lord Reading and his perturbation over your attitude as to the Versailles declaration and the resolutions of the Inter-Allied Council of which Mr. Crosby is president. I think his chief fear was that the matter would become public and be used by the political enemies of Lloyd George for I understand that since the parliamentary crisis is passed he is less disturbed.

Day before yesterday, the 20th, Jusserand came to see me. He was far more excited than Lord Reading and showed considerable irritation that he had not been warned beforehand. He said that you had received him recently and had never mentioned the matter to him nor had you done so to Reading, a fact which he considered most unfortunate. He said that he was sure that "your rebuke" would be very badly received.

I told him that the Prime Minister must have known that this Government did not consider that the Supreme War Council had to do with political subjects, that we had no political representative on the Council and had no intention of having one, and that it seemed an extraordinary proceeding to issue a statement at Versailles which would give the impression that the War Council had approved. I told him that, in the event that the three Allied Governments considered your assertion as to the scope of the two councils to be a rebuke, they had no one to blame but themselves, and that you had no other course but to state plainly your views.

This did not seem to satisfy Jusserand at all, though his chief ground of complaint seemed to be that you had not consulted him about the matter.

Yesterday (Thursday) I had an interview with the Italian Ambassador. I found him in a very different temper from the other Ambassadors. He agreed that your attitude was quite correct, that Baron So[n]nino fully understood it, and that the latter had resisted so far as he was able any joint action without first consulting this Government.

This is a brief resumé of my interviews.

                              Faithfully yours   Robert Lansing.

ALS (WP, DLC).

From Herbert Bayard Swope

Dear Mr. President: Washington, February 22, 1918.

Accept my thanks for the signed photograph you were good enough to send me. I shall prize it highly always.

Acting upon the permission you gave me when I saw you last, of making suggestions pertinent to matters in hand, I beg to submit the outline of an idea that you may find to be not wholly without value:

Today this country, under your leadership, is the foremost exponent of true international morality. Today this country through you is preaching (and seeking to put into practice) a world democracy. Today, through your inspiration, the war has taken on the character of a spiritual crusade, instead of remaining, as it was, largely a struggle for material domination.

These points admit of no dispute among fair-minded men. But sometimes I think that the people of the country ask themselves if the war cannot bring answers to problems other than those of a political nature; if the war cannot be used to determine matters of an immediate and personal sort instead of having the outcome more or less restricted to matters that are, to certain classes, seemingly abstract and remote.

I believe that Labor is constantly asking itself the question, What new social order is peace to bring forth? What part shall we play in the reorganization that is to follow the war? What does the war mean to us, apart from the need of defeating the Prussianization of the world?

It may be true that these questions have been answered from time to time, but in this country there has been no definitive reply made from the one man whose reply would carry conviction with it—yourself. I believe that a statement from you on these points would bring certainty to the workers of the unity of their interests with those of all other elements making up our people. A statement of this sort will once more show those whose concern is chiefly with themselves that you are thinking of them when you think in terms of world justice.

On Monday next there is to be a conference in the office of the Secretary of Labor on labor relations. It is to be participated in by employers and employes. I understand that the discussion is to be limited to conditions coterminous with the war, but it seems to me that an opportunity will be presented to lay a foundation for after-war relations as well. With that thought in mind, it occurs to me that the appropriate moment for a definition of the country's attitude toward the workers is at hand. I believe that there would be a highly favorable public reaction were you either to address a letter to the conferees, or, better still, appear before them in person and speak to them about what the future holds for the workers in this country. I can think of nothing more important, for the matter goes to the very root of their existence.

Those who know you, know what a passion you have always felt for the many as against the few. Your life has been marked by real devotion to the cause of the people. Would it not be wise now to make a reaffirmation of this faith; to visualize for those who see in your [you] their friend and leader those conditions of life that the new order is to create?

In such an exposition there could be included such points as:

Living wage; hours of labor; representation of labor in the direct[or]ate of the undertaking in which it is engaged; profit-sharing; pension system; old age, health and employment insurance; national labor exchanges; housing; welfare conditions; the right to change employment without sacrifice of pension interest (with which goes the connotation of reward for continuous and efficient service); plans for the transitional period of demobilization; greater ease of land purchases; elasticity in loaning operations; readjustments of taxation; the development of a deeper national and community interest.

This is but a rough outline of the points that might be encompassed in such an address as I have in mind. Some of them, perhaps, are visionary and impractical, but I am including them because even if they are not susceptible of immediate achievement they belong, properly, in such a vision of the future as you, best of all, could paint. You have done it for the world. Why not draw in the details for America?

If I am unduly bold in submitting this plan, I am certain that you will excuse it because of the sincerity of my desire to be of help, in a small way, to you who are of such great help to all who seek to make life better.

With regard and respect,

Faithfully,   Herbert Bayard Swope

TLS (WP, DLC).

From Rollo Ogden

Dear Mr. President: [New York] February 22d, 1918.

I have been revolving in my mind the question whether we have not a powerful weapon against Germany not yet used. I mean an economic weapon. It is not the boycott after the right kind of peace that I am thinking of, but rather the threat of a boycott in order to bring about the right kind of peace. We all know that bankers and industrialists in Germany are extremely anxious about future recuperation and trade relations. Might it not possibly have a great effect upon them and their government if the clear prospect of commercial isolation were held up by this country unless the German rulers should presently agree to just terms of peace?

I will put my suggestion bluntly and crudely in order to be brief. Let us suppose that Congress enacted an actual statute to the general effect that unless Germany agreed within a period of say two months to evacuate and restore Belgium and to quit northern France, for a term of let us say ten years no German ship should be admitted to an American port, no German goods allowed entry, directly or indirectly, through American custom houses, and no German subject be permitted to set foot on our shores. I have talked with several persons rather intimate with financial and manufacturing opinion in Germany, and their belief is that some such peace ultimatum by our government would be certain to have a marked effect. It would frankly be a war measure, but the threat of non-intercourse would be only contingent and would be automatically removed by a reasonable attitude on the part of the German government in regard to the ending of the war.

I dislike to intrude my thoughts upon your crowded days, but perhaps you will glance at this letter and give it such weight as it may deserve.

Believe me, with great respect,

Sincerely yours,   Rollo Ogden.

TLS (WP, DLC).

Walter Hines Page to Robert Lansing

London, Feb. 22, 1918.

8780. Most Secret. My 8764, February 21. A message from Furstenberg to Czernin just intercepted indicates that the interview took place as arranged and soon the King undertook to telegraph the Emperor's message to Washington.   Page

T telegram (SDR, RG 59, 763.72119/7728, DNA).

Arthur James Balfour to Lord Reading

[London] d. 22 February 1918.

No. 1008 URGENT Your tel. No. 681.[1]

As regards statement issued by Supreme War Council at Versailles, I do not think that I can do better than to send you an extract from a speech I made in House of Commons on Feb. 13th (see my following tel.)[2]

I am not quite clear to what action of Inter-Allied Board with regard to recognition of Bolsheviki President refers in his letter.

I think that it must be resolutions passed at meeting of military representatives on December 23rd.

History of matter is as follows. War Cabinet in order to take a decision as to policy which they should pursue in Russia asked military representatives to give their opinion as to whether Southern Russia and Roumania were effectively able to resist Bolsheviki forces assisted and controlled by Germans. This was clearly a question on which expert military views were indispensable, and they were recorded in resolutions referred to. Resolution did not in any way bind Governments as regards policy but were purely informative. When Supreme War Council met on February 1st they simply took note of resolutions passed by military representatives. They were neither approved nor rejected.

I trust that these explanations will clear away misapprehensions felt by President and you may embody them in a personal letter to Secretary of State.

T telegram (W. Wiseman Papers, CtY).
  [1] Reading to the Foreign Office, Feb. 19, 1918.
  [2] The telegram is missing, but, in a debate upon another instance in which the Supreme War Council had made an allegedly "political" statement, Balfour made the following comment: "As the House is aware the Council consists, besides the military advisers, of the Prime Minister from each of the countries concerned with another Minister—that is, as far as Europe is concerned. America is represented at it only by a military adviser. America therefore, it is quite obvious, could not and did not deal with this question at Versailles in the sense in which hon. Gentlemen appear to think it was and ought to have been dealt with." *Parliamentary Debates: Commons*, 5th Ser., Vol. 103, col. 170.

Sir Eric Drummond to Sir William Wiseman

[London] Feb. 22nd. 1918.

No. 52. Your telegram of Feb. 19th. I do not consider I can do better than give you substance of telegram to LOCKHART[1] who was sent as our agent to Petrograd to conduct semi-official relations with Bolsheviki authorities. Begins:

"There appears to be some slight misconception about our policy with regard to Government at Petrograd. Internal affairs in Russia are no concern of ours. We only consider them in so far as they affect the war. If at this moment large parts of the country accept particular type of socialism favoured by Bolsheviki this is the affair of Russia not of Britain and it appears to us quite irrelevant to the problem of diplomatic recognition. Full and complete recognition of Bolsheviki Government is at present impossible and a complete rupture is very undesirable. So long as it is understood that our diplomatic relations remain semi-official and informal we see no reason why you should not act as recognized representative at British Embassy. We are prepared to eneter [enter] into relations with de facto Bolsheviki Government at Petrograd exactly as we have entered into relations with de facto Governments of Finland, Ukraine etc.

We do not of course desire at this moment to go back on past-broken treaties, repudiated debts, abandoned military stores, declaration of war against Roumania[2] and so forth. But confining oursleves [ourselves] to the present and future there are evidently certain fundamental questions with regard to which we cannot grant what Bolsheviki desire and they cannot grant what we desire. We want them to abstain from Bolshevik propaganda in Allied territory. They want us to abstain from giving aid or encouragement to any political or military movement in Russia which has not their approval. First course would require Bolsheviks to abandon their loudly advertised principles, second would require us to abandon our friends and Allies in those parts of Russia where Bolshevism cannot be regarded as de facto Government. There are however many very important questions on which judicious diplomacy might prove most valuable. Foremost among these at present moment is to induce Petrograd Government not to make a separate peace with Germany and to abandon their attitude of hostility towards Roumania. We therefore assent to your suggestion that your position should be henceforth that of a recognized intermediary. We do this without making conditions because directly we begin to discuss conditions we shall reach a hopeless impasse. We shall stop Bolshevik propaganda in this country as far as we can, and if official Bolshevik agents behave outrageously we shall r[e]quire them to leave this country exactly as we would representatives of any other Power which began to interfere in our domestic affairs. Monsieur Trotzky will presumably reserve same right but if he is to induce us to cease relations with Cossacks and Caucasians it can only be by proving that he is de facto authority in those countries.

Finally I believe that whatever our differences, there is one point on which we are agreed. We both desire to overthrow militarism in Central Europe. If so there may well be questions of policy on which cooperation is possible. I may instance, on Trotzky's part, refusal to Germany of supplies which would assist her in prolonging war and facilitate efforts of military party to crush popular movements in favour of a democratic peace.

On our part we would await his suggestions as to how we could best help in such circumstances either by essential supplies or otherwise." Ends.

In a further telegram to LOCKHART sent on Feb. 21st. in reply to one from him recording a conversation which he had had with Trotzky on Feb. 16th, Mr. Balfour adds:

"If Trotzky has made peace with the Central Powers as appears in the Press, this would seem to have so altered conditions in Russia as to render useless all further discussions on previous lines. Rumour, however, may be untrue or misleading, in which case we may still be able to cooperate with Trotzky's Government. Such cooperation must, however, be, I agree, one of calculation not of love. In so far as Bolsheviki are opposing or embarrassing our enemies their cause is our cause. In so far as they endeavour to foment revolution in this or in any other Allied country we shall thwart them to the best of our ability. In so far as they are dealing with internal politics in those parts of the country where there are de facto rulers we have no desire to interfere. Very principles which induce us to cooperate with Bolsheviki urge us to support any forces in Russia which seem likely to offer resistance to our enemies or aid to our friends. It was on these grounds and these grounds alone that we have done what we could for Cossacks and for trans-Caucasia. Facts are we did our best for Ukraine and for Cossacks because we deemed it necessary to grasp at even the most shadowy chance for helping Roumanian Army. It seems now to be clear that Rada has thrown in its lot with our enemies and that Cossacks are worthless.[3] There is no likelihood, therefore, that we shall do anything on their behalf to which Trotzky would object. But we cannot pledge ourselves to abstain from such action in other parts of Russia as may in our opinion help to win the war though we have not the slightest intention of indulging in any anti-revolutionary propaganda. I am entirely in favour of some kind of commercial agreement, but care must be taken to prevent any supplies we may send to Russia joining hundreds of thousands of tons already sent which have benefitted no one but the Germans."

T telegram (W. Wiseman Papers, CtY).

[1] Robert Hamilton Bruce Lockhart, former acting British consul-general in Moscow, who had taken up his new duties in Petrograd in early February.

[2] Although there was no formal declaration of war by the Soviet government against Rumania, relations between the two regimes had continued to deteriorate after the

Diamandi incident (about which see RL to WW, Feb. 9, 1918, second letter of that date, n. 8). Trotsky announced the severance of diplomatic relations with Rumania on January 26, and, on January 28, Diamandi and his staff were given ten hours to leave Russia. The Rumanian army began an advance into Bessarabia and was soon fighting Bolshevik forces. The Soviet government on February 17 sent an ultimatum demanding that the Rumanians evacuate Bessarabia. *New York Times*, Jan. 29-31, Feb. 18-20, 1918.

[3] About the Ukrainian Central Rada and its peace treaty with Germany, see D. R. Francis to RL, Feb. 13, 1918, n. 4. The Cossack military forces of the Don River region had proved unable to cope with the Bolshevik military groups sent against them. Their defeat was hastened by the defection of several Cossack regiments which had repudiated the government of the Don Territory headed by the Cossack General, Aleksei Maksimovich Kaledin. Faced with defeat from both without and within, Kaledin committed suicide on February 11. Bolshevik troops seized Rostov, the largest city of the Don region, on February 24 and took Novo-Cherkassk on the following day. See William Henry Chamberlin, *The Russian Revolution, 1917-1921* (2 vols., New York, 1935), I, 373, 377-82.

To Albert Sidney Burleson

My dear Burleson: The White House 23 February, 1918

I gladly comply with Mr. Crane's wish expressed in the enclosed telegram and send you this interesting and distressing clipping.

Always   Faithfully yours,   Woodrow Wilson

TLS (A. S. Burleson Papers, DLC).

To Joseph Patrick Tumulty

Dear Tumulty: The White House [c. Feb. 23, 1918].

Mr. Strunsky has entirely misinterpreted the spirit and principles of this Government if he thinks it possible for it to propose to interfere with the form of government in any other government.[1] That would be in violent contradiction of the principles we have always held, earnestly as we should wish to lend every moral influence to the support of democratic institutions in Russia and earnestly as we pray that they may survive there and become permanent.   The President.

TL (WP, DLC).
[1] Simeon Strunsky, "Memorandum on Russia," [c. Feb. 23, 1918], T MS (WP, DLC). Strunsky, an editorial writer for the New York *Evening Post* who had been born in Russia, declared that the "outstanding motive force" in Russia since the first day of the revolution in March 1917 had been the fear of a return to a reactionary regime. This fear even explained the rise of the Bolsheviks to power and the absence thus far of any strong opposition to their rule since the Russian people preferred even Bolshevik anarchy to reaction. Strunsky argued that the only way to save Russia for freedom and for the Allied cause was "by an outspoken guarantee from this Government to the people of Russia, that whatever happens in that country short of her taking active part with our enemies, the United States will see to it that the rule of autocracy shall never be reimposed upon the Russian people; a guarantee, in other words, to Russia, of democratic institutions."

To Herbert Bayard Swope

My dear Swope: The White House 23 February, 1918

Your letter of yesterday interests me very deeply, I need hardly say, and furnishes much material for constructive thinking, but my present judgment is that this is not the time for formulation. If we were dealing with only one class, a statement could be made which I think would guide and stimulate rather than disturb, but just so certainly as such a statement was attempted at this time, there would spring up a grand controversy in which the selfish and exclusive interests of the country would speak loudest because through the largest number of the journals and magazines. I am afraid that, while we could easily hold our own in such a debate, this is not the wise time to start a debate which would distract attention from the matters immediately in hand and pressing for the right solution. Don't you think there is something in that?

Cordially and sincerely yours,   Woodrow Wilson

TLS (received from Bruce Gimelson).

To William Gibbs McAdoo

My dear Mac.,   The White House. 23 February, 1918.

Please scrutinize this proposal and the terms in which it is put[1] very carefully and critically before making your recommendation to me as to the action our government should take. I cannot forget our own feelings and our own ineffectual protests when we were neutrals against the constant extension, arbitrary step by step, of this questionable form of embargo; and I shall wish to be very clear about this step before I commit our government to joining in it.

Affectionately Yours,   W.W.

WWTLI (TDR, RG 56, Office of the Secretary, General Corr., 1917-1932, DNA).
    [1] This proposal to tighten the financial blockade of the Central Powers was embodied in O. T. Crosby to WGM, Feb. 20, 1918, T telegram (TDR, RG 56, Office of the Secretary, General Corr., 1917-1932, DNA). The plan, already approved by the French government and under consideration in Great Britain, called for the creation of a "White List" of banks in neutral countries. To be admitted to this list, a bank would have to agree, by an as yet unspecified future date, to accept certain restrictions upon its dealings with banks of the Central Powers. After that date, banks in the Allied countries would be instructed to deal only with banks on the White List. The restrictions were designed to prevent the transfer of funds or securities from the countries of the Allies to those of the Central Powers, to prevent the Central Powers from raising funds in neutral countries, and to prohibit banks in neutral countries from transmitting letters and documents to or from the Central Powers. McAdoo decided not to accept the proposal in principle at that time, although he reserved judgment for the future. For Crosby's "confidential information," McAdoo also quoted the second sentence of Wilson's letter to him just printed. WGM to O. T. Crosby, March 11, 1918, T telegram. For a clarification of the proposal and its implications, see also Albert Strauss, "Memorandum for the Secretary of the Treasury," March 1, 1918, TS MS. These two documents are located in the file cited above.

From Robert Lansing

My dear Mr. President: Washington February 23, 1918.

I thought over last night what course we should take in dealing with the communication which we have been warned will arrive via Spain. It seems to me we might do this: Give the text to our principal cobelligerents and say to them that through the same channel as we received the communication we intend to reply by asking whether the document has been submitted to the German Government and, if so, whether it meets with its approval as no answer could be made until we are advised of German knowledge or ignorance of Austria's action.

This would furnish an acknowledgement to Austria without saying we have the communication under consideration, and I cannot see how it would arouse any suspicion or cause any offense among the Allies. Then whichever way Austria replies we will be in a position to do as we please for either reply offers possibilities since we can avoid giving any indication which one we desire.

                    Faithfully yours,   Robert Lansing

TLS (WP, DLC).

From William Gibbs McAdoo

CONFIDENTIAL.

Dear "Governor":   Washington February 23, 1918.

I have your letter of the 20th, enclosing letter addressed to you by Mr. Hoover on the 19th. Unfortunately, Mr. Hoover deals in generalizations and his letter is far from accurate, so far as the transportation situation is concerned. Of course, I am impressed with the seriousness of the situation, and I am doing everything possible to relieve it. I am sure that it can be shown that the railroads are doing their part with great effectiveness at this time. I shall send you shortly a resume of facts which I hope you will read because you will get a better idea of the true situation and I think your anxieties may be largely relieved.

On the morning of the 22d Mr. Hoover gave out a most unfortunate, and I think unjustifiably alarming, statement to the country.[1] To my mind it is open to five principal criticisms:

(1) While anyone who reads the statement from end to end sees that a measure of credit is given to the Railroad Administration for its present work, the general reading public will undoubtedly get nothing beyond a blurred but all-pervading notion that the railroads

have been and still are broken down. This general impression is incorrect and unjust.

(2) Since the general impression made by the statement is that all difficulties as to the food supply are due to past and still existing defects in rail transportation, the result is that every other agency which is charged with any legal or moral responsibility for trying to aid the food situation will feel relieved from that responsibility. A man who otherwise would feel some obligation either to hurry his food supplies to market or to aid otherwise in accomplishing effective results, will have his disposition to act greatly impaired by the feeling that no matter what he does the situation cannot be remedied because Mr. Hoover has indicated that the railroads, even under Government control, cannot carry the food to the destinations where it is needed.

(3) Mr. Hoover, having created by this article the impression that there is a desperate domestic food shortage and that the railroads are so defective as to be unable to remedy it, has given a wide and far-reaching stimulus to the disposition to hoard food supplies and thereby create an artificial shortage, even if an actual shortage does not exist.

(4) Mr. Hoover's widely advertised statement that there is a critical food shortage will, of course, have the effect of encouraging the farmers and others who control large quantities of food supplies to hold them back with the expectation that much higher prices will be obtained, instead of sending them forward promptly to the markets.

(5) Such statements as Mr. Hoover's not only unduly disturb the country, but seriously affect its morale. I need not point out that such statements, if they reach the enemy, give genuine aid and comfort.

Upon reading Mr. Hoover's statement, I addressed a letter to him (copy attached marked A).[2] Mr. Hoover replied as per copy attached marked B,[3] to which I replied as per letter marked C.[4]

I am anxious to cooperate with Mr. Hoover and everyone else to do the big job the country has in hand with the utmost effectiveness and expedition, but I do think that constant statements unduly alarming the country and inexcusably inaccurate ought to be stopped.

As I stated in my letters to Mr. Hoover, I will guarantee the transportation on the railroads of all the food supplies he can collect in this country if he will only tell me where such supplies are located and their destination.

I have read statements in the papers that ships were being detained in New York because the railroads were not supplying the necessary cargoes. I have the following telegram from Mr. A. H. Smith,[5] Regional Director, New York City:

"The situation as regards movement provisions, flour grain and supplies to ships New York Harbor is unchanged, as reported to you my wire yesterday. No steamers being reported as waiting delivery of such commodities. This is confirmed by the British Ministry shipping board."

Mr. C. H. Markham,[6] Regional Director, Atlanta, Georgia, advises me as follows:

"There has been a material increase in the movement of grain through the port of New Orleans, but no congestion in the elevators, which are only about one-third full. On the 18th there were 20 ships in port, and only sufficient grain and other food supplies to provide about one-half lading. The shortage of tonnage at the port of New Orleans is not due, however, to failure of the railroads to provide necessary transportation."

This is an illustration of the fact that while the railroads have ample transportation to carry grain to New Orleans, the grain is not supplied. The railroads, as you know, can only furnish transportation. They cannot produce the supplies nor take supplies belonging to others and move them at will. Mr. Hoover must tell us where the supplies are and where he wants them shipped if we are to act effectively.

Please be assured that I am most eager to do everything in my power to help. I should like to see a spirit of cooperation on the part of others charged with an important part in this work, but we cannot get it through the newspapers and by the making of rash and inaccurate statements. I speak somewhat feelingly about this matter because I do think the Administration is being seriously injured by those who so constantly air their views and theories, not always well matured, through the press of the country.

Affectionately yours,   W G McAdoo

P.S. I made a special request this evening of the newspapermen that they need not make it appear that there is a controversy or a row on between Mr. Hoover and myself, because there is nothing of the kind. I am simply trying to pin Mr. Hoover down so that we can deal with specifics and thus get the benefit of real cooperation.

I enclose copy of telegram just received from A. H. Smith, showing that the bunkering situation at New York is in good shape.[7]

TLS (WP, DLC).

[1] "Most Critical Food Situation in the Country's History Will Come Within Next Sixty Days, Says Administrator Hoover," *Official Bulletin,* II (Feb. 23, 1918), 1, 3. Hoover's argument was concisely summarized in the subheading: "Railroad Congestion, Mr. Hoover States, Has Jeopardized Safety of Perishable Foodstuffs, Disturbed Prices, In-

creased Cost of Feeding Cattle, Reduced Reserve Supplies, and Restricted Supplies for Allies."

² WGM to H. C. Hoover, Feb. 22, 1918, TCL (WP, DLC), also printed in *ibid.*, p. 1. McAdoo guaranteed that the railroads could and would move food supplies destined for the Allies, subject only to delays caused by weather, provided that Hoover would inform him of the locations of the supplies and the port or ports from which they were to be shipped. He also said that he wished "to reassure the country by saying that so far as transportation is concerned, there is no danger of suffering from a serious food shortage in the Eastern part of the country."

³ H. C. Hoover to WGM, Feb. 23, 1918, TCL (WP, DLC), also printed in *ibid.*, Feb. 25, 1918, p. 1. Hoover expressed "great relief" that the railroads would be able to move promptly the foodstuffs needed both at home and abroad.

⁴ WGM to H. C. Hoover, Feb. 23, 1918, TCL (WP, DLC). McAdoo acknowledged Hoover's letter of the twenty-third and pointed out that Hoover had ignored his statement that the railroads would move food for the Allies if Hoover would supply the necessary information about locations and destinations.

⁵ Alfred Holland Smith, president of the New York Central Railroad, at this time regional director of railroads for the eastern district.

⁶ Charles Henry Markham, president of the Illinois Central Railroad, at this time regional director of railroads for the southern district.

⁷ A. H. Smith to WGM, Feb. 23, 1918, TC telegram (WP, DLC).

Two Letters from Newton Diehl Baker

My dear Mr. President: Washington. February 23, 1918.

This is to lay before you a memorandum of the six special services which the Council of National Defense felt ought to be entrusted to the War Industries Board.

6¹1. Priorities (including such arrangements as are necessary to insure priorities established, to secure the concurrence of Food, Fuel, Transportation, and War Trade Board to the extend [extent] necessary to prevent conflicts of priority. The purpose of this coordination being to enable a project once approved to be carried through without the possibility of interruption by the failure of another agency to recognize the priority granted by the centralizing body.).

1 2. The creation of new facilities.

2 3. The conversion of existing facilities to new uses.

3 4. The conservation of resources by commercial and industrial economies.

4 5. Advice to the several purchasing agencies of the Government regarding prices.

5 6. The making of Allied purchases.

Respectfully yours,   Newton D. Baker

TLS (WP, DLC).

¹ This and other numbers in this column WWhw.

My dear Mr President: Washington. February 23, 1918

The enclosed is too long to read,[1] but if you are to be visited by any more delegations of farmers you will find the full operation of the draft on the agricultural population set forth here. The statistical facts show at least some of the complaints to be unjustified

Respectfully,   Newton D. Baker

ALS (WP, DLC).
[1] E. H. Crowder, "Memorandum for the Secretary of War. *Subject*: Uniformity of administration of draft boards respecting agricultural exemptions," TS MS (WP, DLC). Crowder wrote that, while absolute uniformity in the administration of the military draft laws and regulations was impossible, the system as then constituted was as fair and impartial as it possibly could be.

Hugh Robert Wilson to Robert Lansing

Berne, Feb. 23, 1918.

2708. McNally[1] sends the following:

"The wife of a German general is responsible for the statement that Count Hertling recently said to her 'My hands are out towards President Wilson in his peace efforts and my government will, in furtherance of this desire, agree to vacate all enemy territory now occupied by ourselves including Belgium which will be handed back without any reservation whatever. In return we shall expect to hold and to have returned to Germany all territory held by her before this war and that we will under no circumstances entertain possibility of relinquishing Alsace Lorraine to France.'

The lady gave it as her opinion that if Germany became hard pressed she might agree to converting Alsace Lorraine into an independent state similar to Bavaria and Wurtemburg. It is reported by the same person that Conrad Haussmann, member of the German Reichstag, who recently has returned to Germany from Switzerland there, declared that he had had a conversation with Professor Herron of Geneva in which the latter had said to him as a representative of President Wilson that unless Germany was ready to return Alsace Lorraine to France the United States would not enter peace negotiations of any kind with Germany. Is Professor Herron a representative in Switzerland of President Wilson?"

Wilson

T telegram (R. Lansing Papers, NjP).
[1] James Clifford McNally, United States Vice Consul at Zurich.

William Graves Sharp to Robert Lansing

Paris, Feb. 23, 1918.

11. CONFIDENTIAL. The French Minister for Foreign Affairs[1] sent for me this morning and showed me a telegram just received from Mr. Jusserand which I saw at a glance embodied the President's note as communicated to the Embassy in Department's telegram number 3197 of the eighteenth instant. The Minister for Foreign Affairs said he could not understand the objection of the President to the resolution of the Supreme War Council of February second as the latter had expressed practically the same sentiments in his address to Congress of the eleventh instant. I repeated to him the communication which I was instructed in the Department's number 3149, February fifth, to make to the military representatives at Versailles;[2] it was plain that he saw the force of the argument but he stated that it would be very dangerous if the Central Powers thought that the Allies were divided in matters of policy. I replied that this danger could be obviated in the future by submitting resolutions to the President for his approval in advance of their publication or by an explicit statement that they represented the views of only such of the Allies as had political or diplomatic representative[s] present. The Minister for Foreign Affairs said he had no idea when the next meeting of the political representatives of the Supreme War Council would take place but thought, in deference to the wishes of Mr. Lloyd George, the meeting would be held in London. The contents of this telegram are known to myself only. Frazier.   Sharp

T telegram (WP, DLC).
[1] That is, Stéphen Jean Marie Pichon.
[2] See F. L. Polk to A. H. Frazier, Feb. 5, 1918.

From the Diary of Colonel House

Washington, D. C. February 23, 1918.

Frank Andrews, of Texas,[1] took breakfast with us this morning. I left on the 11.08 train for Washington. The train arrived on time and I went immediately to Gordon's where I am to stop this time. Their dinner guests were Secretary and Mrs. Lane, the Swiss Minister and his wife, Henry White, Sir William Wiseman, John Saltonstall[2] and Mrs. Ames.[3]

Justice Brandeis had been telephoning Gordon that it was important for him to see me at once upon my arrival so I gave him a half hour before dinner. He is disturbed over the conduct of the War Department and Secretary Baker's trip to Europe. He wants

Baker or the President to make General Crowder acting Secretary of War while Baker is away instead of Assistant Secretary Crowell. He does not believe Crowell can do the work efficiently. He also believes that Baker is exhausted physically and that "his mind does not function properly." I promised to see Crowder in the morning and to take the matter up with the President later if I thought it advisable. I cannot quite understand why a Justice of the Supreme Court should bother about other peoples business as Brandeis does.

[1] Lawyer and Democratic party leader of Houston.
[2] John Lee Saltonstall, former stockbroker of Boston, at this time a lieutenant in the naval reserve on duty in the office of the Chief of Naval Operations in Washington.
[3] She cannot be identified.

A Statement

[[Feb. 24, 1918]]

Under the food control act of August 10, 1917, it is my duty to announce a guaranteed price for wheat of the 1918 harvest. I am, therefore, issuing a proclamation setting the price at the principal interior primary markets.[1] It makes no essential alteration in the present guaranty. It is a continuation of the present prices of wheat, with some adjustments arising from the designation of additional terminal marketing points.

This guaranteed price assures the farmer of a reasonable profit even if the war should end within the year and the large stores of grain in those sections of the world that are now cut off from transportation should again come into competition with his products. To increase the price of wheat above the present figure, or to agitate any increase of price, would have the effect of very seriously hampering the large operations of the Nation and of the allies by causing the wheat of last year's crop to be withheld from the market. It would, moreover, dislocate all the present wage levels that have been established after much anxious discussion and would, therefore, create an industrial unrest which would be harmful to every industry in the country.

I know the spirit of our farmers and have not the least doubt as to the loyalty with which they will accept the present decision. The fall wheat planting, which furnishes two-thirds of our wheat production, took place with no other assurance than this, and the farmers' confidence was demonstrated by the fact that they planted an acreage larger than the record of any preceding year, larger by 2,000,000 acres than the second largest record year, and 7,000,000 acres more than the average for the five years before the outbreak of the European war.

It seems not to be generally understood why wheat is picked out for price determination, and only wheat, among the cereals. The answer is that, while normal distribution of all our farm products has been subject to great disturbances during the last three years because of war conditions, only two important commodities, namely, wheat and sugar, have been so seriously affected as to require governmental intervention. The disturbances which affect these products (and others in less degree) arise from the fact that all of the over-seas shipping in the world is now under Government control and that the Government is obliged to assign tonnage to each commodity that enters into commercial over-seas traffic. It has, consequently, been necessary to establish single agencies for the purchase of the food supplies which must go abroad. The purchase of wheat in the United States for foreign use is of so great volume in comparison with the available domestic supply that the price of wheat has been materially disturbed, and it became necessary, in order to protect both the producer and the consumer, to prevent speculation. It was necessary, therefore, for the Government to exercise a measure of direct supervision and as far as possible to control purchases of wheat and the processes of its exportation. This supervision necessarily amounted to price fixing, and I, therefore, thought it fair and wise that there should be a price stated that should be at once liberal and equitable.

Those peculiar circumstances governing the handling and consumption of wheat put the farmer at the very center of war service. Next to the soldier himself, he is serving the country and the world and serving it in a way which is absolutely fundamental to his own future safety and prosperity. He sees this and can be relied upon as the soldier can.

The farmer is also contributing men to the Army, and I am keenly alive to the sacrifices involved. Out of 13,800,000 men engaged in farm industries, 205,000 have been drafted, or about 1.48 per cent of the whole number. In addition to these there have been volunteers, and the farmers have lost a considerable number of laborers because the wages paid in industrial pursuits drew them away. In order to relieve the farming industry as far as possible from further drains of labor the new draft regulations have been drawn with a view to taking from the farms an even smaller proportion of men, and it is my hope that the local exemption boards will make the new classifications with a view of lightening the load upon the farmers to the utmost extent. The Secretary of War has asked for authority to furlough soldiers of the National Army if conditions permit it, so that they may return to their farms when assistance is necessary in the planting and harvesting of the crops. National and local agencies are actively at work, besides, in organizing community help for the more efficient distribution of available labor and in drawing upon new sources of labor. While there will be difficulties, and very serious ones, they will be difficulties which are among the stern necessities of war.

The Federal Railway Administration is cooperating in the most active, intelligent, and efficient way with the Food Administration to remove the difficulties of transportation and of the active movement of the crops. Their marketing is to be facilitated and the farmers given the opportunity to realize promptly upon their stocks.

The Department of Agriculture and the Food Administration will continue to cooperate as heretofore to assist the farmers in every way possible. All questions of production, of the marketing of farm products, of conservation in the course of production, and of agricultural labor and farm problems generally will be handled by the Department of Agriculture, while all questions of distribution of food supplies to the allies and of conservation in consumption will be handled by the Food Administration; but the chief reliance is upon the farmer himself, and I am sure that the reliance will be justified by the results. The chief thing to be kept clearly in mind is that regulations of this sort are only a part of the great general plan of mobilization into which every element in the Nation enters in this war as in no other. The business of war touches everybody. It is a stern business, a cooperative business, a business of energy and sacrifice, a business of service in the largest and best and most stirring sense of that great word.   Woodrow Wilson.[2]

Printed in the *Official Bulletin*, II (Feb. 25, 1918), 1-2.
    [1] It is printed in the *Official Bulletin*, II (Feb. 25, 1918), 3. The guaranteed prices ranged from $2.00 a bushel for Salt Lake City, Great Falls, Mont., Spokane, and Pocatello, Idaho, to $2.28 for New York.
    [2] There is a WWsh outline of this statement in WP, DLC.

Edward Mandell House to Arthur James Balfour

[The White House, Feb. 24, 1918]

In view of the intercepted message from the Emperor of Austria to the King of Spain and your recent message to the President through me which I received on the eighth,[1] the President would very much appreciate any comments or suggestions you may be kind enough to make. The actual message has not yet been received from Spain. How far would you think it necessary to go in apprising the Entente Governments of the character of the message from Austria?[2]

WWT MS (E. M. House Papers, CtY).
  [1] A. J. Balfour to EMH, Feb. 7, 1918.
  [2] This was sent in W. Wiseman to E. Drummond, Feb. 24, 1918, T telegram (W. Wiseman Papers, CtY).

To Douglas Smithe[1]

[The White House] 24 February 1918.

It is not a memorial service of private grief that you are holding in honor of the two boys of your community who died on the TUS-CANIA.[2] The nation whom they were defending honors them with you, and it should be some consolation to remember that they have died for humanity in a cause so exalted that it may well mitigate grief and make even death itself less pitiful.

Woodrow Wilson.

T telegram (Letterpress Books, WP, DLC).
  [1] Secretary of the chamber of commerce of Strawn, Texas.
  [2] The British liner *Tuscania*, then in charter service to transport American troops, was torpedoed and sunk as she neared the Irish coast on February 5. According to an official estimate by the War Department, released on February 21, the ship had been carrying 2,179 American officers and men. Of these, 1,971 were saved, 127 were known dead, and eighty-one were missing and presumed dead. The two men from Strawn, Texas, were Daniel W. Trowbridge, known to be dead, and Elton L. Edmondson, missing. *New York Times*, Feb. 7-9, 16, 22, and 27, 1918.

From Gutzon Borglum

Stamford, Connecticut
February 24 1918

My dear Mr. President:

Enclosed is a copy of my letter to the Secretary of War,[1] together with his reply.[2] They explain themselves. I said nothing of what had become of my report, nor does he appear to know. I agree with the urgency indicated in his letter but it will be extremely delicate for me to meet Mr. Baker and deal with this subject frankly as it must be dealt with until you and I have an understanding in this matter. Please advise me by wire.

I do not wish to become involved in and shall avoid all side issues until this, the most potential military machine at our disposal, is clean of corruption and Germans and engaging the honest attention of our great manufacturing interests and we are free from intrigue and are headed right in production.

Very sincerely yours, Gutzon Borglum

P.S. I feel I ought to tell you that our aeronautic conditions have been investigated—organization, personnel, character and record of men in charge—by the Allies. Two of these investigators I have direct reports on and they are fearful of informing their governments of the real situation.

I'm very unhappy about this whole business. It looks bad now for our nation, for our world credit, and it is looking bad for our government. Please realize that for months I have been looking into the ways and means of aircraft production. I have seen its workings and I have burdened you with only a small part of the conditions that are murdering our country's potentiality and eating into the moral conscience of the nation. How long must I, knowing this, sit and see the time pass, which each day becomes less and less, more and more precious and necessary to heal the wounds that have struck humanity to her knees, and which we—in name at least—appear officially opposed to. Even since I left my report (two weeks ago) at the White House, the enemy of the world has acquired, potentially, territory and people exceeding all America, saved his economic future[,] broken "the ring" and thrown us into guerilla warfare. This should give us pause.

I think I have indicated with clearness that I could save, within a fortnight, something over a hundred millions. Not that I care for that, but if the price of five Hog Island ship yards could be combed from the loot of a single department of our administration and at once add to production, there must be something deserving a people's attention. With that money I could have built a fleet of air planes capable of driving the Germans inland in the time I have spent examining the records of incompetent, corrupt officers, German in origin or under German control.

Private information came to me Thursday that armoured German planes had appeared. One of these will handle a dozen of ours. (Informant a British aviator just landed). This was suggested to our board six months ago.   G.B.

TLS (WP, DLC).
    ¹ G. Borglum to NDB, Feb. 17, 1918, CCL (WP, DLC). Borglum informed Baker that his preliminary inquiry into the production of military aircraft had been completed. He declared that his investigation had been hampered from the beginning by "petty intriguing methods."
    ² NDB to G. Borglum, Feb. 20, 1918, TLS (WP, DLC). Baker stated only that it would give him "great pleasure" to see Borglum in Washington at his early convenience and to give him "all the time necessary" to have a full and complete report of the work that Borglum had been doing.

From the Diary of Colonel House

February 24, 1918.

The President telephoned at ten o'clock asking me to go to church with him and to lunch afterward. I tried to evade the church part of it but he seemed so disappointed that I gave way. He and Mrs. Wilson called at ten minutes before eleven and we motored to the unfinished Episcopal Cathedral where they are holding services in a chapel. We had seats directly under the pulpit and it looked as if the rector[1] was about to preach a sermon showing up the deficiencies of the War Department. I was relieved when he switched off into a different direction. Both the President and I thought he might have preached a different sermon had the President not been there. The vicar's[2] prayer was for "the President of the United States and his counsellor."

In dictating this my secretary wonders how long such things can continue without causing trouble. I wonder too.

When we returned to the White House we had time before lunch to discuss the Austrian Emperor's note to the President sent through the King of Spain, which the British have intercepted and already given us. We agreed that it would be well to ask Balfour's opinion of it and we outlined the following cable. The President wrote it on his typewriter and it is attached.

"To, A. J. Balfour:

In view of the intercepted message from the Emperor of Austria to the King of Spain and your recent message to the President through me which I received on the 8th, the President would very much appreciate any comments or suggestions you may be kind enough to make. The actual message has not yet been received from Sprain. How far would you think it necessary to go in apprising the Entente Governments of the character of the message from Austria?"   (Signed) Edward House"

When we had finished this we discussed the English Labor program recently announced at Nottingham.[3] Much to my surprise,

---

[1] The Rev. Dr. George Carl Fitch Bratenahl, Dean of the Cathedral of St. Peter and St. Paul.

[2] It is not clear whether House here refers to Bratenahl or to the Rev. Dr. William Levering De Vries, Canon of the Cathedral.

[3] At the party conference at Nottingham, January 23-26, 1918, the Labour party considered a new constitution, drafted largely by Arthur Henderson and Sidney Webb, and a comprehensive statement of policy, *Labour and the New Social Order*, which was primarily the work of Sidney Webb. The constitution was designed to convert the Labour party from a loose coalition of trade unions and socialist groups into a strong national party with local branches and individual memberships which could make an effective bid for national political control. However, it also contained a famous clause setting forth the principal objective of the party: "To secure for the producers by hand or by brain the full fruits of their industry, and the most equitable distribution thereof that may be

he said he did not disagree with it further than the minimum wage which he confessed to know little about and he had not thought of any visible way by which it could be maintained.

We discussed the trend of liberal opinion in the world and came to the conclusion that the wise thing to do was to lead the movement intelligently and sympathetically and not allow the ignoble element to run away with the situation as they had done in Russia. He spoke of the necessity of forming a new political party in order to achieve these ends. He did not believe the Democratic Party could be used as an instrument to go as far as it would be needful to go and largely because of the reactionary element in the South. I disagreed with him. I thought it would be unwise to attempt the building of a new party without first seeing whether the Democratic Party could be forced into the direction we thought advisable. I did not believe the people of the South would sustain the reactionary element provided the President came out strongly enough against them. I do not know whether I convinced him but at least he stopped arguing against my opinion.

Again let me say that the President has started so actively on the liberal road that I find myself, instead of leading as I always did at first, rather in the rear and holding him back. He turned to me and said almost pathetically, "that is a big program for a tired man to think of undertaking."

I asked if he remembered how we used to say that we would put through everything during the first term, as rapidly as it was possible to do, so that if a second term was not to be had, we would have at least made a shining mark. The pathos of it is that I used to spur him on to get through in the early part of his administration in order that he might rest during the latter part, but the farther we go the less rest there is in sight.

He said he remembered quite well this attitude and that it reminded him of a farmer who had a sick bullock and concluded to yoke himself up with the remaining one. The bullock ran awat

---

possible, upon the basis of the common ownership of the means of production and the best obtainable system of popular administration and control of each industry and service." The new constitution was adopted at a later session of the conference on February 26, 1918. Webb's statement of policy was adopted with modifications at a party conference in June 1918. It called, among other things, for a national policy designed to assure to every citizen a minimum standard of civilized life, including full employment and a living wage. It demanded the common ownership of the nation's land and the nationalization of many systems of transportation and public utilities. It also called for progressive income and inheritance taxes, the proceeds of which were to be redistributed in a comprehensive system of social services. The program served as the basis of Labour party policy for the next thirty years. See George D. H. Cole, *A History of the Labour Party from 1914* (London, 1948), pp. 39-40, 44-81, and Ross McKibbin, *The Evolution of the Labour Party, 1910-1924* (Oxford, 1974), pp. 91-106.

[away] at a terrible pace down the road the farmer yelling "for God's sake why does'nt some damn fool stop us."

While we were talking, McAdoo telephoned to say he had received a letter from the President rebuking him for meddling with the restoration by the British and French Governments of the International News Service, and requesting me to explain to him how it happened. I undertook to do this, telling the President the whole story. He replied that McAdoo was never satisfied with letting other people's business alone; that the matter was absolutely a function of the State Department, but as usual, McAdoo had "butted in." I tried to explain that it was done "unofficially." He said, "well that may be, but with you and McAdoo telling them to do it, it does not sound very unofficial."

The President said, as far as he was concerned, he did not wish Hearst to be under any obligations to him and upon receipt of letters from the Hearst people thanking him for what had been done, he immediately replied that he had done nothing and knew nothing about it and did not approve.

I told him Melville Stone was offended because he had asked for an appointment upon two separate days and he had declined to see him. The President replied, "You may tell Stone I never expect to receive him, for I do not believe in him, and want nothing to do with him." Mrs. Wilson who was sitting by turned to me and said, "are you going to tell him that?" To which I replied, "you know well enough I am not going to tell him any such thing." She asked what I would tell him. "That," I said, "I will decide later, but it will not be the message the President has sent." The President listened to this and smiled broadly.

While we were on the newspaper question, I thought I would cover it all. I therefore brought up the New York Times' outline of a way by which that situation might be righted.[4] Again he said "I do not care what The Times said, for it is not of the slightest importance since they represent an element for whom I have no respect and would as soon have them against me as for me." From my viewpoint he is wrong in all these matters. I would use the newspapers to help the Government rather than to hinder it.

We decided to go out in the motor, and we motored more than fifty miles into Maryland. They asked me to dine at the White House but I returned to Gordon's because there were many matters to

[4] The Editors have found no editorial or article on news censorship, the role of newspapers in the war effort, or any related topic in the *New York Times* for January or February 1918. Perhaps the outline was conveyed orally to House by a representative of the *Times*; however, if so, there is no mention of the matter in House's diary for January or February.

attend to. During the drive we talked of various things. Among them the offer of Harper Brothers and the difficulty of his discharging his duties as President if he were at the peace conference. He did not think he could get bills from Congress over in time to veto them within the ten day limit, and he wondered if he might be able to do it by cable.

I found he had completely forgotten the engagement I asked him to make with Frank Cobb and Sam Blythe. He set it for Thursday and I will notify them. While we were driving he declared that when he was out of office he would follow warm weather. He spoke of Bermuda as a "Lotus Land." He said if it belonged to the United States he would like to live there permanently.

When they left me at Gordon's a rush of callers began. Gregory, Polk and many others came. McAdoo had me on the telephone frequently.

I dined with Lord Reading. There was no one else present excepting Lady Reading,[1] Sir William Wiseman and Reading's immediate staff. I asked him to send a cable recommending Commander Gaunt for a K.C.B. He promised to do so.

He told me of an interesting conversation he had with Cardinal Gibbons, pledging me to secrecy. It seems the Pope wishes to sit at the peace conference. Reading thought it was to regain temporal power. Gibbons denied this. Reading then thought it was to help Austria and Gibbons only half-way denied this.

We discussed the Versailles statement which Reading agreed was ill advised. I gave him, in confidence, the context of the President's note to Lansing on this subject and let him know that it was Lansing's *faux pas* and not the President's that such a curt document was sent Great Britain, France and Italy.

Reading spoke of Lloyd George's characteristics and said that of all our public men McAdoo reminded him most of George. He said George seldom went deep into any subject, but he quickly obtained a superficial knowledge which enabled him to discuss it intelligently, though superficially; that whenever an attempt was made to drive him into a subject greater than his depth, he evaded it and adroitly led the conversation away into different channels.

[1] Alice Edith Cohen Isaacs, Lady Reading.

From the Diary of Josephus Daniels

1918 Sunday 24 February

At 6 p.m. went to White House to see the President. Baker also present. We discussed the new regulations or chart for War Industry Board. He will make BMB[1] the Chairman with large powers.

WW wished to discuss now because Baker is going to Europe. With two or three suggested amendments we approved Presidents draft as wise & applicable. Judge Lovett wishes to get off. From racial or other reasons the Judge does not like Baruch & would not serve under him. He is a prima donna said WW. Necessary for McAdoo to find a good RR man to replace him. Lord R. was told by the Pres. that unless all allied countries agreed upon a Commander in chief we could not consent to our troops being under any but American command. Baker was told to say that to George & Clemenceau. George removed Robertson & made Parliament believe it was as result of Allied War Conference & due to paper of Gen Bliss. Baker was instructed to see Bliss and ascertain what Bliss wrote. Believes George is playing politics & does not tell the truth. Petain also criticized Pershing because he would not merge American soldiers with French commands. Will not stand for that. English Gen objected because orders agreed upon in Versailles Council were sent direct by Gen Foche & not through British Commander. WW expressed hatred of red tape.

Colored man told "Obey nobody but men with stripe on their shoulders[."]

¹ That is, Baruch.

To Franklin Knight Lane

My dear Mr. Secretary: [The White House] 25 February, 1918

I sincerely hope that you may be successful through the Bureau of Education in arousing the interest of teachers and children in the schools of the United States in the cultivation of home gardens. Every boy and girl who really sees what the home garden may mean will, I am sure, enter into the purpose with high spirits, because I am sure they would all like to feel that they are in fact fighting in France by joining the home garden army. They know that America has undertaken to send meat and flour and wheat and other foods for the support of the soldiers who are doing the fighting, for the men and women who are making the munitions, and for the boys and girls of Western Europe, and that we must also feed ourselves while we are carrying on this war. The movement to establish gardens, therefore, and to have the children work in them is just as real and patriotic an effort as the building of ships or the firing of cannon. I hope that this spring every school will have a regiment in the Volunteer War Garden Army.

Cordially and sincerely yours,   Woodrow Wilson

TLS (Letterpress Books, WP, DLC).

From Alfonso XIII

EMBAJADA DE ESPAÑA EN
WASHINGTON [Feb. 25, 1918].

Mr President

I have received the following message from His Majesty the Emperor of Austria, who asks me to transmit it to you with all secrecy; and as the subject on which it verses is one which interests us all, for the sake of humanity, I do not hesitate in meeting the wishes of my Cousin by transmitting his petition:

"The speeches pronounced on solemn occasions, on one side by Mr Wilson and on the other by Count Czernin, have cleared essentially the situation of Europe, and reduced to a certain minimum the principal points under discussion. It seems to me therefore, that the moment has arrived in which a direct explanation between one of my Representatives and Mr Wilson might clear the situation in such a manner that no obstacle would be raised in the road leading to the reunion of a Congress for the peace of the World.

Your noble and generous purpose, many times demonstrated, in granting your valuable support to the currents in favor of peace, in this historic moment, has induced me to request of you, that you will transmit to President Wilson the following message, by the most strictly secret means:

In his message of February 12, the President of the United States exposed four fundamental principles as conditional to the settlement, to the attainment of which we should aspire.

My attitude in respect to these four principles may be condensed in the following form:

As regards the first of them, the President of the United States, according to the German translation which we have here, demands: 'That each part of the final settlement be based upon justice applicable to the particular case, and upon an agreement, from which it may be hoped, within the limits of probability, that a lasting peace may ensue.'

I accept this initial principle, as every reasonable man, possessed of ethic sentiments, must wish for a solution which may guarantee a lasting peace; and only a just peace, which establishes an equilibrium between the opposing interests, can offer a solution of this kind.

The second and third points complete each other and are thus conceived: 'That peoples and provinces cannot be transferred, (I take it from one Sovereignty to another) as if they were chattels or pawns in a game, even if this game be the great game of the equilibrium of force, which has been discredited for ever; and therefore, every solution of a territorial problem, to which the present war has given rise, must be given in the interest and in favor of the population interested in it, and not as part of a mere settlement or compromise between the aspirations of rival States.'

The territorial problem can, I think, be very easily solved. All the States will declare expressly that they renounce conquests and indemnities. Of course it goes without saying that it would be indispensable that all the States should accept the same principle. If the President of the United States were disposed to induce his Allies to accept this principle, Austria Hungary would do everything in her power to induce her German Ally to accept it also. What would subsequently have to be done as regards the modification of frontiers, perhaps precisely in the interest and in favor of populations interested in the matter, might be arranged by means of a friendly agreement between State and State; and this also seems to be the opinion of the President of the United States. It would surely not be efficacious, for the purpose of ensuring a lasting peace, to prevent the solution of the territorial problem in that part of Europe, where up to now the situation has not been sufficiently consolidated in this respect, as for instance in the part of the Balkan Peninsula inhabited by Bulgaria, in order to give rein to the desire of avoiding the exchange of peoples from one Sovereignty to another. Nevertheless, the principle which must be maintained is that no State should gain or lose, admitting as a standard the territorial situation of all the States before the war.

The second fundamental principle, which the President has already exposed, consists in the absolute necessity of preventing an economic war in the future. I adhere to it absolutely.

As regards the third fundamental principle established by the President, and which refers to the plan of general disarmament and to the liberty of the seas, in order to avoid a future economic world war, there does not exist any difference of opinion between the President and me.

The fourth point says: 'That all national aspirations which are clearly defined must meet the most ample satisfaction that may correspond to them, without admitting new factors of division and of hatred, which might shortly again disturb the peace of Europe and of the whole world.'

This principle also, such as it has been clearly and ably exposed by the President, is acceptable as a fundamental basis.

'I naturally also attribute the greatest importance to the new settlement of the European situation not increasing but on the contrary diminishing, the risk of future conflicts. The United States would willingly recognize, if was so demonstrated to them, that the solutions proposed by them were not the best or the most lasting.'

There is a hope in my mind that we will also come to an understanding on this point. In this exchange of ideas we will be in a position to produce evidence that there exist national aspirations, the satisfaction of which would not bring the good and lasting solution in accordance with the desires of the populations interested, of certain problems which each moment are placed in the foreground; as we are in a position to do, for instance regarding the national aspirations of Italy to Austrian territory, as declared by Italy, who invokes a considerable number of manifestations and of desires, freely expressed by the people of that part of the Monarchy.

On my part, I would also attribute the greatest importance to my Representative discussing with the President of the United States all the possible means of preventing future conflagrations.

In the principle before alluded to, of complete renunciation to all annexations, is naturally comprised the demanded restoration of Belgium. Every other special question, such as that of the access of Servia to the sea, the concession of the necessary economic facilities to Servia and to other states, the incorporation to the Metropolis of the Bulgarian groups which are separated from it, are certainly susceptible of being cleared up by discussion, and of being prepared for the Peace Congress.

In view of the aforesaid, I think that between the fundamental bases mentioned by the President on one side and my aspirations on the other, there exists the requisite degree of coincidence to be enabled to hope that a positive result may come from a direct exchange of views, and that this exchange of views might make peace, so desired by all, come nearer to the world.   Charles."

The President of the United States already knows that for the humanitarian and sympathetic cause of the approximation of the end of the war, by means of a possible agreement between the belligerents, he can count upon my Country, upon my Government and upon my most enthusiastic Cooperation.

your very sincere friend   Alfonso R.

TL (WP, DLC).

Two Letters from William Gibbs McAdoo

Dear "Governor":   Washington February 25, 1918.

The War Finance Corporation Bill[1] is going to pass, and we shall have to appoint four Directors, who, with the Secretary of the Treasury, will compose the Board of that Corporation. I must secure not only thoroughly able men, but men who are loyal to the Administration and who will work in harmony with me. The handicap of differences among those from whom cooperation must be had is greater than all the other load that is upon me or could be imposed upon me.

Baruch would be an invaluable man on the Board of the War Finance Corporation or as the Director of the Division of Purchases of the Railroad Administration. I should like very much to have him for either one of these places. Would you be willing to relieve him of his other work? I believe he can render greater service to the Government in either one of the positions I have described than in the position he now fills.

Affectionately yours,   W G McAdoo

[1] Wilson signed the War Finance Corporation Act on April 5, 1918. It established a government-owned corporation under a board of directors which consisted of the Secretary of the Treasury, *ex officio* chairman, and four additional members appointed by the President with the advice and consent of the Senate. The W.F.C. was empowered to make advances for from one to five years, through the medium of banks, to industries essential to the war effort or, in exceptional cases, to make such advances directly to such industries; to make advances to savings banks; and to buy and sell government bonds, especially Liberty bonds. Funds with which to make these advances were to be obtained from subscription by the government to the capital stock of the corporation to the extent of $500,000,000, and further provision was made to raise funds, if required, through the sale of bonds of the corporation to a maximum of $3,000,000,000. For a discussion of the War Finance Corporation and its operations from May 20, 1918, until its demise in April 1929, see Woodbury Willoughby, *The Capital Issues Committee and War Finance Corporation* (Baltimore, 1934).

Dear Mr. President: Washington February 25, 1918.

Referring to your note concerning the International News matter, I took no official action whatever in this connection. I asked Colonel House, who happened to be at the White House yesterday, to tell you how this came about.

Affectionately yours,   W G McAdoo

TLS (WP, DLC).

From the White House Staff

Memorandum: The White House. February 25, 1918

The Director of Housing asks for the pen with which the President signs the Housing Bill.[1]

T MS (WP, DLC).

[1] Senator Fletcher, chairman of the Senate Committee on Commerce, on January 5 had introduced S. 3389, a bill to empower the Emergency Fleet Corporation to purchase, lease, requisition, or otherwise acquire improved or unimproved land, houses, buildings, and for other purposes. The bill was passed, and Wilson signed it on March 2 as Public Law 102. The pen which he had used was sent to J. Rogers Flannery, manager of the general service division of the Emergency Fleet Corporation.

Representative Clark of Florida, chairman of the House Committee on Public Buildings and Grounds, introduced, on February 26, a wider bill, H.R. 10265, to authorize the Secretary of Labor to provide housing, local transportation, and other community facilities for war needs. This bill was enacted as Public Law 149, approved May 16, 1918.

From the Diary of Colonel House

February 25, 1918.

I have seen a multitude of people today. Gifford,[1] Admiral Benson, Lansing and Jusserand were the most important. Gifford suggested a plan by which the President should form the Secretaries of the Treasury, War and Navy, Chairmen of the Shipping, War Industries, Food and Coal Boards into a War Board. His idea is to have them meet at the White House once a week and have the President sit with them. He thought it would have a fine effect upon the country, and would enable those mentioned to function better. He gave me charts showing the deficiencies in the different departments. It is a chart easily understood and shows in what industries we are behind at present and those in which we are not. It also shows, at a glance, the shipping, coal and other situations.

I dined with the President and outlined the plan to which he agreed. He said he might give up one Cabinet Day for this purpose and meet with them as suggested.[2] I urged him to do this.

Benson gave all the Naval information to date which was interesting and which I later transmitted to the President. He feels, as I do, that before the year is out, we will have the submarines largely curbed.

In talking to Lansing, I was surprised to have him tell me that sometime ago the President called his attention rather sharply to a statement which appeared in the newspapers to the effect that I was not going abroad again, but that he, Lansing, would probably go in my stead. Lansing explained to the President that he had merely told the newspaper people that he knew of no plan for my going at present. The President remarked, "You had better leave the newspaper men alone." It is in such ways that W.W. shows his affection for me.

Ambassador Jusserand was in an excited mood when we first began to talk. He had received the President's abrupt demand of the Allies regarding the giving out of political statements from the Supreme War Council. I gave him the same explanation I did to Reading with which he was delighted. I cautioned him, however against mentioning it, for I did not want to get Lansing into any trouble. Jusserand agreed that Lansing was a fine fellow and ought to be protected even if now and then he let his foot slip. There were a lot of other matters he wished to go into but I had no time to do more than touch them lightly.

After dinner with the President and Mrs. Wilson we went into executive session, finishing up a lot of matters about which the President desired an opinion. He had a letter from W. F. McCombs asking permission to serve in some capacity, with or without salary.[3] He also asked for an interview with the President. I advised seeing him and putting him at work where he could give no trouble. The President said he would see him, but he did not intend permitting him to get in a position where he could give more trouble than he had already done.

We discussed the advisability of not sending Elkus to Switzerland at the present time. I thought if it were done, it would be impossible to make the Entente believe he had not been sent over for the purpose of discussing peace with Austria.

We discussed, at great length, the question of Japanese intervention in Siberia, but came to no conclusion. There are arguments both for and against it. My thought was that unless Japan went in under a promise to withdraw, or at least be subject to the disposition of the peace conference, the Entente in backing her would place themselves in exactly the same position as the Germans now occupied toward Western Russia, to which there is such vociferous objection among the Western Powers.

I left early as I was tired and I thought the President was also.

[1] That is, Walter S. Gifford.

[2] This was the inception of the so-called War Cabinet or War Council, an unofficial body which met with Wilson regularly on Wednesdays beginning March 20, 1918. Those usually present were Baker, McAdoo, Daniels, Hurley, Hoover, McCormick, Garfield, and Baruch, or their deputies. See Daniel R. Beaver, *Newton D. Baker and the American War Effort, 1917-1919* (Lincoln, Neb., 1966), p. 173; and Edward N. Hurley, *The Bridge to France* (Philadelphia and London, 1927), pp. 319-21.

[3] McCombs' letter of February 20 is missing. On April 3, thinking that it might not have reached Wilson, he sent Wilson a copy. W. F. McCombs to WW, Apr. 3, 1918, TLS (WP, DLC), enclosing W. F. McCombs to WW, Feb. 20, 1918, TCL (WP, DLC). McCombs' name was on Wilson's appointment calendar for March 2, but his arrival from Hot Springs, Ark., was delayed, and he did not see Wilson at that time. W. F. McCombs to WW, March 2, 1918, ALS (WP, DLC).

To Edward Mandell House

Dear House, [The White House] Feby 25/18

Will you not read the enclosed papers against our next talk.

The Borglom letter[1] is one of a series. I think he is crazy—and therefore, perhaps, all the more dangerous. W.W.

ALI (E. M. House Papers, CtY).
[1] G. Borglum to WW, Feb. 24, 1917.

To Newton Diehl Baker

My dear Mr. Secretary: The White House 25 February, 1918

Thank you very much for the memorandum about the accommodation of the draft, so far as possible, to the necessities of agricultural labor. The memorandum will be very serviceable to me indeed.   Cordially and faithfully yours,   Woodrow Wilson

TLS (N. D. Baker Papers, DLC).

To William Gibbs McAdoo, with Enclosure

My dear Mac: The White House 26 February, 1918

Please read carefully the enclosed copy of a letter I have just received from Judge Chambers, the United States Commissioner of Mediation and Conciliation. He raises a very interesting point about labor troubles on the railways, and my present judgment is that it would not be wise in any circumstances to reject or dislocate the instrumentalities we have been at such pains for many years to build up. I do not anticipate that there will be any necessity for meeting this question, but we ought to have it in mind and do the wise thing with a view always to *afterwards*.

Affectionately yours,   Woodrow Wilson

TLS (W. G. McAdoo Papers, DLC).

E N C L O S U R E

From William Lea Chambers

My dear Mr. President: Indianapolis, Indiana, Feb. 23, 1918.

In conformity with the practice of the Board of Mediation to keep you informed of the progress of its work from time to time I assume that you will be pleased to know that its mediation work has been progressing without interruption and with the same measure of success since Government control of the railroads began as when the railroads were operated under their own management. Since the Wage Commission was appointed, established as I understand it as an advisory body to the Director General, the Board of Mediation has declined to take up wage controversies, and that will be the policy of the Board until the Wage Commission reports to the Director General and he replies to the demands of the Employees. It is to be hoped that his action will settle the general question of wages. But suppose the employees decline to accept his decision, what then? In the meantime the Board of Mediation is constantly receiving requests for services, and its members are in different parts of the country holding conferences, employing their best endeavors in the adjustment of controversies other than wages; but we wish you to know that it is our purpose to aid in every possible way in promoting the highest efficiency in transportation. There are innumerable questions of controversy constantly arising between employees of railroads and the managements that do not directly affect the question of wages and such controversies, unless they are speedily adjusted, necessarily interfere with the operation of the railroads, to the serious detriment of the parties concerned, and especially of the public interests.

The services of the Board of Mediation have unquestionably borne very fruitful results. When it is recalled that in not a single instance has there been an interruption of interstate railway service, caused by labor disputes, since the passage of the Act of Congress of July 15, 1913, where the services of the Board of Mediation have been invoked in advance of a break in negotiations between the parties, does not the question force itself upon our consideration as to whether any other method of adjusting such controversies can be safety substituted?

Perhaps the highest testimonial to the merits of the present law and its administration is the comparatively small number of cases that have reached final adjustment through arbitration. Practically all of them have been adjusted in mediation. When it is considered that these methods are entirely unsupported by any mandate of law and that neither party is compelled to seek the services of the Board of Mediation or to accept its counsel the results are even more remarkable.

Notwithstanding these facts it is known to members of the Board, as doubtless to yourself, that there is opposition to the mediation law and to present methods in certain quarters, confined however, in my belief, to a comparatively few persons. Substantially all the managing officials of the railroads and the representatives of the brotherhood employees, who have had actual personal connection with the mediation work, and the administration of the law, cordially support the law and its administration. It will be interesting to you, if you had the time to review the volume of testimonials in support of this statement which are on file in the office of the Board at Washington.

I am in the midst of mediation conferences here between certain employees and the C.C.C. and St. L. Railroad,[1] with fair prospect of adjusting all points satisfactorily, leaving out the question of wages which I have submitted to the Director General for his approval. From here I am proceeding to Denver, Colorado, to fill an appointment agreed upon for mediation of controversies between the Denver and Rio Grande Railroad and certain of its employees; following which I have a request for services that may take me to Portland, Oregon, and other cases are awaiting me at Dallas, Texas. Assistant Commissioner Hanger has several assignments on important eastern roads at Detroit, Cleveland and New York City.

Very respectfully yours,   W. L. Chambers

TLS (W. G. McAdoo Papers, DLC).
  [1] The Cleveland, Cincinnati, Chicago and St. Louis Railway Co., which was controlled by the New York Central Railroad Co.

To William Gibbs McAdoo

My dear Mac: The White House 26 February, 1918

I am mighty sorry but I can't let you have Baruch for the Finance Corporation. He has trained now in the War Industries Board until he is thoroughly conversant with the activities of it from top to bottom, and as soon as I can do so without risking new issues on the Hill I am going to appoint him chairman of that board.

This is entirely confidential.

Affectionately yours,   Woodrow Wilson

TLS (W. G. McAdoo Papers, DLC).

To William Lea Chambers

My dear Judge: [The White House] 26 February, 1918

Thank you for your letter of February twenty-third from Indianapolis. Such reports and indications of the pending situation are always most welcome.

Cordially and sincerely yours,   Woodrow Wilson

TLS (Letterpress Books, WP, DLC).

To Edward Mandell House

My dear House: The White House 26 February, 1918

Would you be generous enough to convey the substance of what follows to Harper & Brothers?

(1) I would not feel justified now in making any decisions with regard to the literary work that I am to do after the expiration of my term, or the conditions under which I am to do it. My own

expectation is that I shall wish to be absolutely free. I none the less appreciate the generous suggestions of Harper & Brothers.

(2) The only item with regard to the programme for a collected edition of my works which seems to call for comment is that concerning the little book, AN OLD MASTER and OTHER ESSAYS, which the Scribners publish. I had a letter from Mr. Charles Scribner, and indicated to him that I would be very glad to see him comply with the request of Harper & Brothers with regard to it.

With regard to CONGRESSIONAL GOVERNMENT and MERE LITERATURE, published by Houghton Mifflin and Company, of Boston: I believe that the sale of MERE LITERATURE has been comparatively small of late, but the sale of CONGRESSIONAL GOVERNMENT has been maintained at a steady, though not high, level ever since the early years of its currency. The publishers of these two volumes were my first publishers, they treated me with unusual generosity as a newcomer into the field when I was a youngster, and I don't like to insist upon anything that they think will be to their disadvantage. I, therefore, do not like to make the request of them suggested by Mr. Hitchcock.[1] I take it for granted that they would be willing to disclose to a representative of Harper & Brothers the full commercial value of the books, but, as I understand it, the objection is on sentimental rather than on commercial grounds.

Affectionately,   Woodrow Wilson

TLS (E. M. House Papers, CtY).
  [1] James Ripley Wellman Hitchcock, a member of the board of directors of Harper & Brothers, had proposed that the house get out a complete edition of Wilson's works and had asked Wilson to request a transfer of the copyright of books published by other firms to Harper & Brothers. J. R. W. Hitchcock to JPT, July 19, 1917, TLS (WP, DLC).

To Helen Woodrow Bones

Dear Helen,   The White House [c. Feb. 26, 1918].

I have attached the note which should be returned to Mrs. Petty.[1]

Please, when you write, say that I did not desire any interest and tell her that I hope that when she pays the balance remaining of the three hundred dollars she will subtract the fifteen dollars interest she includes in her present cheque, sending only one hundred and thirty-five.   W.W.

WWTLI (WP, DLC).
  [1] May Randolph (Mrs. Calvin H.) Petty of Cranbury, N. J., was an old friend of Wilson and his family. She had written to him in October 1915 to congratulate him on his engagement to Mrs. Galt and in September 1916 to express sympathy on the death of his sister, Annie Josephine Wilson Howe, whom, she said, she had not seen for many years. Mrs. Petty, in March 1916, had thanked Wilson for some photographs of his daughters, presumably sent to replace others that had been lost in a fire suffered by the Pettys. May R. Petty to WW, Oct. 9, 1915, Sept. 23, 1916, and March 28, 1916, all

ALS (WP, DLC). The Editors have found no record of the origin of Wilson's loan to Mrs. Petty, but Miss Bones, in returning the first note for $300, expressed to her the hope that things would be easier for her "from now on." Helen W. Bones to May R. Petty, Feb. 26, 1918, CCL (WP, DLC). Later in 1918, the Pettys moved to Princeton, where Calvin Petty became manager of Hugh L. Scott's farmlands. May R. Petty to WW, Nov. 25, 1918, and July 12, 1919, both ALS (WP, DLC).

From Robert Lansing

Dear Mr. President: Washington February 26, 1918.

I beg to inform you that on January 11th at the instance of Senators Swanson and Ransdell certain American citizens having interests in Costa Rica came to the Department of State and set forth their position before Mr. Polk relative to the overthrow of the Gonzalez Government in Costa Rica by Tinoco. The Americans present included Minor C. Keith,[1] First Vice-President of the United Fruit Company and President of the Northern Railroad Company of Costa Rica, who spoke in his own behalf and in behalf of the United Fruit Company, Bradley W. Palmer,[2] General Counsel of the United Fruit Company, Crawford Ellis, Vice-President of the Fruit Company, S. G. Schermerhorn,[3] Executive Vice-President of the United Fruit Company, who spoke in behalf of the United Fruit Company and John N. Popham,[4] President of the Costa Rica Union Mining Company and General Manager of the Abangarez Gold Fields, who spoke in his own behalf.

The substance of the statements of Mr. Keith were to the effect that he had no knowledge of the intention on the part of Tinoco to overthrow the Government of Gonzalez and that he had no interest in this coup d'etat. The representatives of the Fruit Company set forth in their statements that the policy of the United Fruit Company had been for many years not to take part in local politics in any Central American country. They further deposed that they knew nothing of any contemplated revolution in Costa Rica in January 1917, until after the revolution had occurred and that to the best of their knowledge and belief neither the United Fruit Company or any of its officials had anything whatever to do with such a revolution.

Mr. Popham stated that he never had anything to do with Costa Rican politics until March 1917, and that after that date his activities related to combating German influences and advancing American interests in connection with the war situation. He claimed that the Gonzalez regime in Costa Rica was under German influence and that Tinoco had freed Costa Rica from that influence.

These gentlemen requested that their statements be transmitted to you for your disposition and they were informed by Mr. Polk that if they were presented to the Department in proper form he would have a digest made to be sent to you.

In accordance with Mr. Polk's promise, I beg to enclose herewith a digest of the statements made by the above-mentioned American citizens in regard to the revolution in Costa Rica of January 1917.[5]

Faithfully yours, Robert Lansing.

TLS (WP, DLC).
[1] Minor Cooper Keith.
[2] Bradley Webster Palmer.
[3] Sheppard Gandy Schermerhorn.
[4] John Nichols Popham.
[5] Department of State, "In the matter of the hearing of the American Interests of Costa Rica, in their exoneration of the charge or imputation made against them of complicity in the change of government made in Costa Rica by the abdication of Gonzales, and the assumption of provisional power by Tinoco. Before Hon. Frank Lyon Polk, Counsellor for the Department of State. State Department, Washington, D. C. Friday, January 11, 1918. . . . ," T MS, WP, DLC.

From Robert Lansing, with Enclosure

My dear Mr. President: Washington February 26, 1918.

In connection with the Siberian question I enclose a memorandum which I found on my desk on returning from Cabinet meeting relative to a statement made to Mr. Miles by a representative of the French Ambassador. I do not see that it changes our proposed policy but would be obliged if you would give me your views.

Faithfully yours, Robert Lansing

TLS (WP, DLC).

E N C L O S U R E

MEMORANDUM Washington February 26, 1918

Subject: Inquiries from French Embassy *in re* Russia

1. The French Government informs the Ambassador here that it regards the question of intervention in Siberia as of grave urgency. They say reports from "Irkutsk, Harbin and Vladiv[o]stok show conditions to be extremely serious" with prospect of the railway being wholly interrupted. The French believe it of utmost importance to keep the railway open as being the only access for counteracting German efforts, whether political or military.

2. The French have reports that stores of munitions at Archangel are in danger; that the local authorities there are only willing to release stores or to allow ships to sail on condition that civilian supplies—shoes, cloths, or foodstuffs—be exchanged. The Ambas-

sador asks whether we will allow two ships to proceed to Kola or Archangel with such supplies and load for return with munitions?

3. The French Government has received an urgent request from the Bolshevik Government to return to Russia the 20,000 Russian troops sent to the French front, who mutinied and are now dispersed in detention camps. French have apparently replied "yes" provided that Oolish [Polish], Czech, and other troops be allowed to leave Russia for French front.

At the same time the French Government is urgent to know if we will now consider favorably former proposal to return these troops. General Pershing endorsed a proposal to send them to Panama and there transship them into Japanese vessels for Valdivostok [Vladivostok]. Our reply was that the carrying out of this plan should be dependent on the approval of the Russian Government—which approval, it is suggested, has now been received in the demand of the Bolshevik Government on France.

Could you have Mr. Crane[1] telephone me if this statement is inadequate.   Basil Miles

TS MS (WP, DLC).
[1] That is, Richard Crane.

From Newton Diehl Baker, with Enclosure

Dear Mr. President: Washington. February 26, 1918.

I enclose copies of two cablegrams from General Bliss.

The shorter one you will observe shows that the Italian Supreme Command based its request on General Wood's expressed desires.[1] I have directed General Biddle to notify General Pershing that we have been informed of the statement of the Italian Supreme Command with regard to General Wood, but believe it important for him to return to this country as the other generals have done who have been sent to inspect the Western Front and, therefore, to make no change in his orders, which are for his immediate return to this country.   Respectfully yours,   Newton D. Baker

TLS (WP, DLC).
[1] T. H. Bliss to H. P. McCain, No. 38, Feb. 26, 1918, TC telegram (WP, DLC).

ENCLOSURE

Versailles February 25th.

Number 52 Confidential.

For the Acting Chief of Staff and the Secretary of War.

Paragraph 1. Reference your number 25[1] I have represented to my colleagues the view of our government that the subject matter of joint note number 16 transmitted in my number 32[2] involves political and diplomatic questions that must be settled by the governments concerned and the hope that the military representatives on the Supreme War Council will refrain from urging the views expressed in second and tenth paragraphs of said joint note number 16.

Paragraph 2. My view remains as suggested in my number 32. But there seems to be among military men generally as well as politicians a very strong feeling that some sort of intervention in Siberia will be necessary. This was expressed in an interview I had yesterday with General Foch. He told me he had given an interview that day to the representative of New York Times on this subject. I believe this interview represents view of French Government. The English are especially anxious for intervention. General Rawlinson[3] lately commanding 4th British Army in Flanders has taken the place of General Wilson as British Military representative on the Supreme War Council. He believes that there must be intervention. Therefore likely that strong pressure will be brought to bear on the United States. But if so this pressure will come from Governments concerned and not from the military representatives here.

Paragraph 3. Further reference to your number 25 following is procedure adopted by Supreme War Council in a resolution at its recent third session with reference to joint notes of its military representatives. Resolution follows: "The head of each government represented on the Supreme War Council undertakes to notify the military representatives of the Supreme War Council as soon as possible whether any joint note presented by them has been accepted by his government, or whether he wishes them reserved for discussion at the next meeting of the Supreme War Council. If a joint note is accepted by all the governments concerned, it shall, as from that date, be treated as a decision of the Supreme War Council." This procedure is intended to facilitate action as the time approaches when prompt action will be vitally important. The joint note of the military representatives must be unanimous. To secure unanimity each representative sometimes must yield points which he does not consider of vital importance. When joint note is agreed upon each representative cables it to his government for final action.

Our notes relate only to the military phase of a question although that question may involve political and diplomatic phases. In the latter case it is assumed that the governments concerned * * * [take up][4] the political questions among themselves through diplomatic channels. After that is done each government informs its military representative on the Supreme War Council that it approves the joint note or that it disapproves it or that it desires to reserve its final decision until it learns of the action taken by the Supreme War Council on that occasion.   Bliss.

T telegram (WP, DLC).
   [1] "Your number 32 received. Secretary of War agrees thoroughly with your comments in paragraphs 4 and 5 and urgently hopes that your associates will regard the matter as involving political and diplomatic questions to be settled by the governments and to that end will refrain from urging views set forth in resolution in paragraphs 2 and 3. McCain." H. P. McCain to T. H. Bliss, No. 25, Feb. 22, 1918, CC telegram (WDR, RG 407, World War I Cable Section, DNA).
   [2] T. H. Bliss to H. P. McCain, Feb. 19, 1918.
   [3] Maj. Gen. Sir Henry Seymour Rawlinson.
   [4] Addition from copy in WDR, RG 407, World War I Cable Section, DNA.

From Thomas Nelson Page

Confidential

My dear Mr. President: Rome February 26th, 1918

As my telegrams will have informed you, the Chamber closed on Saturday evening in a sort of burst of glory. Sonnino, Orlando, (the Premier) and several other Ministers having made important addresses, among them the Minister of War, the Minister of Transports, the Minister of Finance,[1] which carried the Chamber and brought a Vote of Confidence in favor of the Government by a majority distinctly firmer than on the last Vote. The actual Vote was 340 to 44 which represented the ultra-Socialist Vote. Orlando's speech was a great success and he is said to have received the greatest ovation that any man has received in twenty years. The importance of all this lies in the fact that it represents a distinct amelioration in political conditions here as the reception of these speeches showed a reflection of feeling in the country.

Meantime the economic condition of the country is certainly very serious, chiefly because of the scarcity of food and of coal. The spirit of the Army rests at last on the spirit of the people and the spirit of the people, however high, is undoubtedly dependent upon the ability to secure food enough. The scarcity of food together with the scarcity of coal on which depends keeping the shops open for the manufacture of munitions especially, and keeping the railroads

   [1] Gen. Vittorio Alfieri, Riccardo Bianchi, and Filippo Meda, respectively.

going, constitutes the grave peril of the moment and this peril is very grave because it is undoubtedly known to the enemy and, as is believed here by those who are well informed, has given the enemy the conviction that Italy presents the most vulnerable point in the Allies' front. The reports say that the Germans have withdrawn all of their Divisions but two, and undoubtedly the British and the French apprehend that the great push which the Germans are evidently preparing to make will take place in France or Flanders, or perhaps both. I find, however, that the Italian officials, the men charged with the responsibility of Italy, have the conviction that the attack will be made on the Italian Front and pushed with as much tenacity as was shown at Verdun. Moreover, they are labouring under the greatest anxiety. They speak to me with much more frankness than they used to do before we declared war on Austria and although they put on a bold enough face, the anxiety as to the result taken in connection with the present conditions in Italy is unmistakable. Also I feel that there is good ground for it. The present coal situation, for example, is one which gives reason to fear an absolute collapse of everything. Italy's normal coal consumption in peace times is about 23,000 tons per day. Under great urgency she has been able to get from the Allies promises of 15,000, but about 9,000 is the most she has been able to obtain and it is not coal such as she has always had, but is of a quality which is burning out the railway engines in such a way as to require their being stopped several times on any long run to be cleaned out. I received to-day information from a most responsible man that even so the present supply in Italy is so small as to constitute an immediate peril. The average supply ahead is about enough to run Italy for fifteen days, that is the average in the war zone which is given precedence over the rest of the country, but the supply in Rome and the supply in Naples are reported to be only about one day ahead, and the peculiar geographical situation of Italy with long runs from the ports where coal can be brought in renders the problems much more grave than might appear on the surface. The Minister of War has explained to me personally how the geographical situation of Italy and the relation of the railroads thereto increased the difficulties of distribution, even where there appeared on the surface a supply adequate for the immediate future. I mention all this in order that you may understand how much more serious the situation is than one might think from reading published reports.

All of the foregoing has an intimate connection with the possibility of Italy's being able to hold out. If the spirit of her people gives way she will not be able to keep on and everything that tends to inspire her people to keep up their courage is of service to our common cause. It is for this reason immediately that I am so glad to have had a Military Mission sent here and certainly I trust that General Swift's Mission which has come will not be taken away.[2] I shall not believe until I am officially so informed that anything so unwise could possibly occur as to withdraw this Mission from Italy. It has been received with more than cordiality. It has had every attention shown it and the expressions of appreciation made to me personally has been far more earnest than anything formal could have been. As soon as the Mission arrived I gave the Members a dinner at which General Alfieri, the Minister of War was present and he has to-day given the Mission a luncheon at which all the Members were present and all the high officials of the Ministry of War were present as well and at which the Minister of War proposed a toast to yourself and to America and made a little address full of real feeling, in which he expressed the confidence in the aid which America's entry into the war has brought to the Allied Cause, whose sincerity cannot be doubted. I might give you in some detail just how earnest he was in his expression of appreciation of America and of your part in the great work, but the translation of his earnest phrases into English, at the same time that I was trying to transpose a few American ideas into Italian to reply to him in proposing the health of the King was too much for me. I will only say that I feel sure he was sincere when he declared that all he had said came from his heart, as well it might.

I do not think it is too much to say that the Italian people, I am not speaking of the Government, are looking to America at this moment as their absolute hope. They feel that England and France are strained to the utmost and they feel that we are the hope of their salvation.

General Swift and his Staff leave for the Front tomorrow. Every arrangement has been made for them and I for one feel that nothing better could have been done than to send them here. I hope very much also that before a great while it may be possible to send some troops here. I do not mean a great number of troops—I know that would be impossible—but one or two regiments. As I telegraphed you, once Sonnino said to me personally, if you could send 5,000 troops with the flag it would have a great moral effect; and it would. Undoubtedly they would want more in the future; that would be natural; but to meet the present exigency the sending the Flag is

---

[2] Maj. Gen. Eben Swift was chief of the American military mission and commander of United States forces in Italy from February to August 1918. Other members of the mission were Col. John McAuley Palmer, General Staff, Lt. Col. Robert Urie Patterson, Medical Corps, and Capt. Fiorello Henry La Guardia, Air Service.

the thing that will have its effect. The flag with the Corporal's guard would represent for the people to the Italian people the fact that America wishes to fight for Italy on Italian soil as much as she wishes to fight for any of the other Allies. Such an act will never be forgotten and if we do not send the Flag here, but send it only to France for the French Front and to the British Front, this fact will never be forgotten either. Not all the money we can lend them, nor all the provisions we can send them will have on the Italian people the effect that it will have to send the American Flag here. If you send it you have in the future a hold on the Italian heart which nothing else on earth will give you.

It has been suggested to me that even if at present we have no troops to send to the Italian front, if we would send a Brigade or two to be trained here it would have a great moral effect; then they could be used in the future where occasion might seem to demand their presence.

I present this matter to you with such earnestness because I know this people and I know their present situation, and I feel profoundly that there is a situation here in which we can be of great service to the common Cause. I do not venture to talk of the military phase of the matter, though I know its difficulties, but there is also the phase of which I am speaking: the political effect which, how[e]ver it may not be possible to recognize on the part of the military authorities in France, is here at least too intimately bound up with the military question for us not to look it squarely in the face.

I devote so much space to talking about things here in Italy that I leave unsaid to you many things which I would like to say, especially about my appreciation of the burdens which you carry and of the manner in which you bear them. I will leave it to you, however, to know without my saying so how much I appreciate all that you have done and are doing.

Orlando in the Chamber on Saturday turned to the Socialists who had claimed that you had got your idealism from Zimmerwald[3] and had used the Zimmerwald formula, and reading a passage from

[3] An international conference of left and center socialists, held at Zimmerwald, Switzerland, September 5-8, 1915. Lenin, a leader of the Zimmerwald left, regarded this group as the beginning of a new international movement to challenge the Second International. The manifesto adopted by the conference was a compromise. Addressed to the proletariat of Europe, it declared that the war had been caused by imperialism and capitalistic greed. It criticized the Majority socialists, moreover, and appealed to the working classes to restore international solidarity. The manifesto was signed by German, French, Italian, Russian, Polish, Rumanian, Bulgarian, Swedish, Norwegian, Dutch, and Swiss delegates. It called for "the self-determination of peoples," "no annexations, open or concealed," and "no forced economic affiliations." For the text, see Horst Lademacher, ed., *Die Zimmerwalder Bewegung: Protokolle und Korrespondenz* (2 vols., The Hague, 1967), I, 166-69. A translation is printed in Olga Hess Gankin and H. H. Fisher, *The Bolsheviks and the World War: The Origin of the Third International* (Stanford, Cal., 1940), pp. 329-33.

your message in which you declared that America has devoted all of her resources to the cause of Democracy and Liberty, exclaimed: "This is Idealism—Idealism put in practice."

But my letter is already too long, and I will only add a word to tell you that our little regimental band of youngsters in kahki uniforms, thirty-two in number, playing "The Star-Spangled Banner" and two or three other American tunes has been received with an appreciation which could not have been exceeded had they been grand orchestras in gaudy uniforms and numbered two hundred and fifty each like the British and French bands.

Always, my dear Mr. President,
                    Most sincerely your friend,   Thos. Nelson Page

TLS (WP, DLC).

Two Letters from George Creel

Dear Mr. President: Washington, D. C. February 26, 1918.

As I explained to you, we have organized the Swedish population of the country with really wonderful results. Edwin Bjorkman,[1] our organizer, feels that the whole movement can be given great impetus by your generous action in connection with the following facts:

In June, 1917, about one hundred young Swedes of Rockford, Illinois, were sentenced by Federal Judge Landis[2] to one year in the House of Correction for failure to register.

As a result of a very painstaking investigation, Bjorkman is convinced that in at least ninety-five per cent of the cases the offense was largely technical and unintentional.

The lawyer who represented them was not a very able person, and all pleaded guilty. They have since explained to Bjorkman that they thought that this simply meant that they had failed to register, but that they did not intend to say that they were opposed to the legislation or that they had refrained willfully from registration. Few of them spoke good English, or had any large understanding of the proceedings. All were given a maximum punishment.

You will recall that Cattell,[3] the son of Professor Cattell in New York, deliberately refused to register, violating the law intentionally and definely [defiantly], yet he was given a sentence of one day only.

These Swedes have served seven months, and many of them are entirely willing to go in the Army, and some of them are married and the fathers of families.

What I suggest, is the informal appointment of some one like

John Lynn [Lind], or Justice Olson[4] of Chicago, to talk with these boys, and to make recommendations to you based upon the careful investigation of each individual case.

Respectfully,   George Creel

[1] Edwin August Bjorkman, a writer, editor, and translator of New York, was director of the Scandinavian bureau of the Committee on Public Information and secretary of the John Ericsson League of Patriotic Service.

[2] That is, Kenesaw Mountain Landis.

[3] Owen Cattell, son of J. McKeen Cattell of Columbia University, was found guilty on June 21, 1917, of conspiracy to obstruct the operation of the selective-service law. He and his co-defendant, Charles Francis Phillips, were among the leaders of the Collegiate Anti-Militarism League. Both were fined $500, deprived of their rights as citizens, and sentenced to serve one day in the Tombs prison on the conspiracy charge, and Phillips was sentenced to serve five additional days for failure to register. *New York Times*, June 22 and July 13, 1917.

[4] Harry Olson, chief justice of the Municipal Court of Chicago.

Dear Mr. President: Washington, D. C. February 26, 1918.

The enclosed letter[1] has been given some publicity, and will be given a great deal more unless I stop it. There is much in the letter that is good, but there are some paragraphs, which I have marked, that involve questions of policy. May I have your views on this?

Respectfully,   George Creel

TLS (WP, DLC).

[1] This letter is missing, but Wilson's reply to Creel of February 28 identifies it as a letter from Philander P. Claxton, the Commissioner of Education, which opposed the suppression of the teaching and study of the German language in American high schools and colleges. The American Defense Society, the American Patriotic League, the National Security League, other organizations, and some state and local officials were calling for severe restrictions on the teaching of German. Earlier, in at least one letter and a public statement, Claxton had declared that the study of the German language was now more important than before the war. Charles Lee Lewis, *Philander Priestley Claxton: Crusader for Public Education* (Knoxville, Tenn., 1948), pp. 204-205. Another letter by Claxton of March 12 on the same subject was published in the *Official Bulletin*, II (March 19, 1918), 4, obviously with Creel's approval. This letter of March 12, addressed to Robert Lincoln Slagle, President of the University of South Dakota, began: "In reply to your letter of February 26, I must say that I can not agree with those who would eliminate German from the high schools and colleges of the United States at this time. It is, of course, desirable now, and always is, that nothing should be taught in any language in our schools or elsewhere that would tend to create a spirit of disloyalty to our country or to the American ideals of freedom and democracy." However, Claxton stood his ground on the main issue. "The United States," he wrote, "is at war with the Imperial Government of Germany and not with the German language or literature. . . . After the war is over intercourse with the German people will be re[e]stablished, probably not immediately and fully, but our relations with them will no doubt be more important as the years go by. Germany may even yet become one of the leading nations for the preservation of the peace of the world." Claxton added that he had "reason to believe" that these views were "fully in harmony with those of the administration in Washington."

From George Creel, with Enclosure

Dear Mr. President: Washington, D. C. February 26, 1918.

Hamilton Holt is very insistent in the attached matter. I am sending it, however, because I thought you might be interested in seeing the Lincoln interview. It is rather interesting. If you will indicate your wishes to Mr. Swem, I will write Mr. Holt myself.

Sincerely,   George Creel

E N C L O S U R E

To the President: New York February 20, 1918

In going over the old files of The Independent the other day, I stumbled across a very interesting article published September 24, 1864, entitled "A Talk With Abraham Lincoln." It was written by the Rev. John P. Gulliver of Norwich, Conn., and in it President Lincoln sheds much light on how he came to acquire his remarkable power of expression in both his speeches and his writings. I am enclosing you a copy of this article.

I want to reprint this article side by side with a similar article which will tell in a somewhat similar way how you acquired your equally lucid literary style and capacity for noble and forceful statements.

I realize, of course, that you might have compunctions which would prevent you from writing such an article under your signature, even if you had the time. But I wonder if it would not be possible for you to let me or some more expert interviewer have a talk with you some time in which you would informally express some of your views, and let the interviewer write it up in his own way as his own article, as the Rev. Mr. Gulliver did.

Printing the two articles side by side would really prove of great interest to the American public, especially to the thousands of young men and women in our high schools and colleges who are now studying The Independent as a text book in current events.

I talked the matter over with Mr. Creel, and he expressed his willingness to present the matter to you, and I am, therefore, sending this letter to you through him.

Very respectfully yours,   Hamilton Holt

TLS (WP, DLC).

From Herbert Clark Hoover, with Enclosure

Dear Mr. President: Washington 26 *February 1918*

Please find enclosed herewith a letter that I have addressed today to Lord Reading with regard to the March programme of Allied shipments. I wish you to know that this shipment amounts to a very considerable diversion from our domestic demands and will sooner or later precipitate us into difficulties with our own supplies. We felt, however, that it was your wish that we should take care of their pressing necessities.

Yours faithfully,   Herbert Hoover

TLS (WP, DLC).

ENCLOSURE

Dear Lord Reading: [Washington] 26 *February 1918*

With respect to wheat for March, we will, in the course of today or tomorrow, pass to the Railway Administration the location of 5,000,000 bushels of wheat—125,000 tons—in the Pacific Northwest, and are asking them to undertake its transportation to the Gulf for March loading. This, together with the 300,000 tons of flour arranged for—subject to the movement of certain wheat to the mills—is, I feel, all that we can do on the wheat line at the moment and this involves some bread shortage in this country. Our Grain Division have great hopes of the arrangements made for buying of corn in the terminal markets. They feel that it should be possible to buy up to 15,000,000 bushels of corn for March loading, or, say 400,000 tons, if present railway movement maintains. This of course will also be accomplished with a great deal of jeopardy to the domestic trade, but it is a risk we will take. If these totals are accomplished it will, according to Mr. Robson's[1] letter of February 20th, give a total of 1,285,000 tons—or a margin of safety of 185,000 tons.   Yours faithfully,   [Herbert Hoover]

CCL (WP, DLC).
[1] Herbert Thomas Robson, chairman of the Wheat Export Co., which the British government had established in 1916 to purchase wheat in the United States.

From Charles Doolittle Walcott[1]

Dear Mr. President: Washington, U.S.A. February 26, 1918.

My attention has been called to the fact that the typewriting machine upon which you have personally prepared many of your state papers is about to be replaced with a new one, and I venture to inquire if it is possible to secure this interesting object for permanent preservation with the historical collections of the National Museum.

Through its intimate association with the epoch-making documents produced in connection with one of the most stirring periods of American and world history, this machine has become of very great national interest and your consent to its acquisition for the purpose stated would be very greatly appreciated.

Very respectfully yours,   Charles D. Walcott

TLS (WP, DLC).
[1] Secretary of the Smithsonian Institution.

From William Byron Colver

My dear Mr. President: Washington February 26, 1918.

In the absence of Chairman Harris and Mr. Davies, reply to your letter of February 22d[1] enclosing letter from Mr. L. F. Swift (which is returned herewith)[2] awaited the return of Governor Fort this morning.

We are sending you, herewith, brief extracts from a report of progress made by Mr. Heney as being a succinct summary of the present situation in the packing inquiry.[3]

Mr. Heney is convinced that the packers, knowing that our appropriation is nearing exhaustion, are seeking by every means to obstruct and delay us in the hope that the exhaustion of the fund will force an end to the investigation.

Mr. Swift says that Swift & Company, has violated no law and been party to no illegal actions. The fact as to that is in rapid process of determination.

Mr. Swift says that "innocent and irrelevant facts, having no material bearing upon the subject matter under investigation, have been read into the proceedings with unjust characterization and sinister inference."

The fact as to that is, that facts and acts innocent appearing and seemingly irrelevant when taken alone, are sinister and relevant when fitted together with other similar facts.

The fruits of the Commission's labors will soon appear. Today we are taking action looking to the preservation of a reputable Philadelphia concern which, after a business history of forty years, was being ruthlessly crushed out of existence. This proceeding is the result of the evidence secured at Governor Fort's hearing during the holidays.

As we have assured you before, this work while directly under Mr. Davies, has had the constant consideration of each of the Commissioners. Each step is carefully taken.

Mr. Davies, having been compelled to leave Chicago, Governor Fort is going there tonight to continue the public hearings. We feel that the Governor's presence guarantees the fairness and bona fides of the hearings as Mr. Davies' presence has guaranteed them heretofore.

As you know, the process of the Commission is being resisted by the packers in court proceedings. The United States District Court has upheld the Commission and the matter comes up on the packers' appeal in the United States Circuit Court on Friday, March 1st.

As to your reply to Mr. Swift, may we suggest that, in view of the situation, the proceeding is in the public interest, and that you see no warrant for interfering with the judgment of the Commission.

For the Commission,

Yours respectfully,   William B. Colver
Acting Chairman

TLS (WP, DLC).
  1 WW to W. J. Harris, Feb. 22, 1918, CCL (WP, DLC).
  2 L. F. Swift to WW, Feb. 19, 1918, TLS (WP, DLC).
  3 "Extracts from Mr. Francis J. Heney's Memorandum Dated Chicago, 4 February 1918," T MS (WP, DLC). Heney at this time was a special attorney for the Federal Trade Commission in charge of an investigation of the high cost of living, with special reference to the packing industry. In this report, Heney reviewed various transactions in the packing industry and stated that he was "fully convinced" that an examination of certain files would furnish "conclusive evidence" that Armour & Co., Swift & Co., Morris & Co., and Wilson & Co., were in an "unlawful combination" which had for its ultimate object "the monopolization of practically all the food products of the United States, and particularly of cattle, sheep, and hog products and their by-products, and also grain, poultry, eggs, cheese, butter, and dairy products generally, as well as fish, including those of the Great Lakes and Alaska salmon, and also including canned vegetables and canned fruits generally, as well as fertilizers, concentrated dairy feeds, leather and other things too numerous to specify." Heney noted the support which the National Cattlemen's Association had given to the continuation of the commission's hearings, and he concluded by stating that a "complete exposure of the nefarious practices of the big packers, followed by speedy and vigorous remedial action on the part of the Government," would do much to stimulate the production of food supplies.

From Joseph Alfred Arner Burnquist

St. Paul, Minnesota, February 26, 1918.

(Personal)

Minnesota, in response to request from your administration and as patriotic duty produced thirty three million bushels of potatoes last year. Stop. Thirteen million bushels on hand spoiling for want of market, but principally for want of refrigerator cars to move same.

Stop. Cannot supply division quartermasters department furnish immediate outlet for large part of same and director of railways furnish transportation to move this enormous supply of valuable food stuff? Stop Failure to do so at once means destruction of supply and small acreage this year. Stop All other sources of relief but your good self have been appealed to without success. Stop. Here is an opportunity to cut red tape and produce results. Stop. May we hear from you at once? Stop. If promises could have accomplished desired result the potatoes would have moved long ago. Stop. What can we expect and when? Stop. The situation is a critical one both as effecting immediate stock on hand and acreage to be planted this year. Stop.

Minnesota Commission of Public Safety,
by J. A. A. Burnquist, Chairman and
Governor.

T telegram (WP, DLC).

Sir William Wiseman to Sir Eric Drummond

[Washington] Feb. 26th. 1918.

MOST URGENT. MOST SECRET.

No 60. Further to my telegram 59.[1] A message was delivered yesterday afternoon to Adramyti [Wilson] by Spanish Ambassador practically identical with the intercepted one you have seen. Adramyti thinks he ought not to delay answer. Adramyti and Brussa [House] are inclined to encourage further discussion. I have begged them to await your view, pointing out that Berlin may know of Vienna's action and the danger of being drawn into a conference which Sundgan [Reading] describes in his cable to you to-day. I am keeping Sundgan fully informed but please reply through me in New York as position with Adramyti and Brussa is very delicate. If Adramyti consults Sundgan he must also consult Jusserand.

T telegram (W. Wiseman Papers, CtY).
[1] "Adramyti feels he must decide promptly regarding message mentioned in my last cable. Brussa is here in consultation with him. Please cable your views immediately." W. Wiseman to E. Drummond, No. 59, Feb. 26, 1918, T telegram (W. Wiseman Papers, CtY).

Lord Reading to Arthur James Balfour

Washington. 26 Feb. 1918.

SECRET.

No. 793 I have seen Mr. Lansing and communicated substance of your telegram No. 1008[1]

My intention has been throughout not to exaggerate but to minimise the importance of Mr Lansing's letter[2] and all that has happened since convinces me that this is the best policy to pursue. My impression is that had it not been for the resolution of the Inter Allied Council on War Purchases and Finance the letter never would have been written. The President had made his answer to the Supreme War Council declaration. Although he was annoyed by the apparent inclusion of America in the views expressed by the Supreme War Council upon Count Czernin's speech, I doubt much whether further notice would have been taken by him.

It is obvious from your telegram No. 1008 that you did not understand the reference in Mr Lansing's letter to the Inter Allied Board and the recognition of the Bolshevik Government. At my request Mr. Lansing produced the Boards Resolution to me and I now know the inner history that led to his letter.

This resolution of the Board which contained the recommendations on the policy to be pursued by the Government was introduced by Mr. Klotz and was apparently approved by the Chancellor of the Exchequer and Mr. Crosby with an explanation from the latter that as the resolution contained only recommendations to the Government and did not decide policy the Board could accept it.

The President had always feared that his representatives on councils, however limited their jurisdiction might encroach upon matters of policy with which they were not concerned and this resolution in his view showed that his fears were amply justified. The result was that he wished to make it plain again in a communication to the Allies that the authority of the different U. S. representatives on missions was limited and did not extend to political matters.

Having upon receipt of the letter from Mr Lansing once expressed to him my view as to its importance I have pursued the policy of minimising it and I am sure that this is what the Administration prefer. I have seen Mr Lansing and made a verbal communication to him to the effect that you had explained the matter in the House of Commons. I explained that the inference I drew was that the declaration was intended to deal with military matters only but that these could not be determined without due regard to the political situation: With Germany and Austria as disclosed by recent speeches it so happened that the three Prime Ministers were present and I conceived that there could be no possible objection by the President to their expressing their views on the speeches of Hertling and Czernin when discussing military policy.

Mr. Lansing agreed and said that no question could have been raised if the interpretation had been stated to be that of the three Prime Ministers without having the appearance of including the President: I said this was not intended and had only appeared because the War Council was declaring its military policy. I am sure he was pleased to have an end of the matter and he said at once that the explanation was completely satisfactory. I said that I should not write it unless he wished it. He was of the same view and thought it quite unnecessary and that all he would ask was that I should send him a copy of the part of your speech as cabled to me that he might show it to the President with the explanation I had made. I subsequently sent him a copy of the extract from your speech as cabled.

I think the incident is ended provided our allies do not magnify its importance. Before seeing Mr Lansing I communicated with my French colleague and told him the substance of my intended statement and I also communicated it to my Italian colleague who will take the same view.

Great care must be taken that the Inter Allied Council on War Purchases and Finance does not present the appearance of coming to conclusions on political matters. I know the difficulty and that it is not introduced by us. It is one however that I have always feared. The American Administration are very sensitive about any such action and even though a resolution recommending political action or a policy may be merely a pious expression of opinion it in their view embarrasses the Administration and will certainly, if it recurs, lead to a recall of particular representatives and possibly to a change of policy.

I have been in active consultation with Colonel House since Saturday and will communicate further with you later. I cannot however too strongly impress upon you the imperative necessity of taking the U. S. Government into your confidence and more particularly of informing them beforehand of any action or declaration on your side which may produce the impression in America that the Administration have approved an action or declaration. You will appreciate their difficulty. They say that if they allow the declaration or action to pass they are exposed to criticism here. If they dissociate themselves from it they produce an appearance of want of unity. There is not the slightest sign of weakening in their determination to continue to the end and I am convinced that the President is quite resolute to do everything possible more particularly at this moment when the Russian situation appears so depressing for the Allies.

I would suggest as the policy to be pursued that we should consult the President even though at times it might not be strictly necessary. It will show an intention of the closest co-operation with the President and will avoid the recurrence of such a situation as that recently created.

I am doing utmost to work in closest accord with French and Italian colleagues.

CC telegram (W. Wiseman Papers, CtY).
  [1] That is, A. J. Balfour to Lord Reading, Feb. 22, 1918.
  [2] About which, see WW to RL, Feb. 16, 1918 (fourth letter of that date).

From the Diary of Colonel House

February 26, 1918.

I have not been very fit today and have tried to keep quiet, but it has been impossible. The President sent me a note and a lot of papers to go through about which he wanted advice.

I lunched with McAdoo alone. We had a long conversation concerning current affairs relating to the Treasury and to the railroads. I found it difficult to get away from him as he was so full of talk.

I have seen Wiseman constantly while here. At my request he has remained in Washington until I go home, for we are taking up various matters confronting our two Governments, particularly the Austrian-Spanish note.

This afternoon, the Spanish Ambassador asked for an audience, and handed the President the note from the Emperor of Austria. The President said he had difficulty in composing his face and in trying to look surprised.[1] He has written a memorandum in reply to Emperor Charles which he read to me last night and which I thoroughly approve.[2] It is non-committal and seeks further information.

No one can know the amount of discussion the President, Lord Reading, Sir William Wiseman, Lansing, Gordon and I have had concerning what action the President should take regarding this note from the Emperor of Austria, and what attitude he should assume toward the Entente in regard to it. As I told the President last night, it is one of the most delicate and difficult situations with which he has yet had to deal. There is so much involved; it is not only the Austrian-German situation, but also, the question of the Entente and our relations with them.

Sir William Wiseman dined with us tonight. Janet left on the four o'clock for New York. I had planned to go with her, but at the President's request, I remained. He seemed so loath to have me go at this critical time. He desired me to wait until Balfour's reply came to the despatch I sent him tonight.[3]

¹ Page reported from London on March 6 that he had just learned (i.e., from intercepted telegrams) that Alfonso had informed Charles that Riaño y Gayangos had delivered Alfonso's letter to Wilson on February 25. Page's report continued:
"The Ambassador had stated that the President read it with care and remarked that it was transcendental but that its receipt placed him in a somewhat embarrassing position as he had expressed himself as opposed to secret negotiations. He welcomed the King's intervention. He would have to examine the communication with care before replying. The Ambassador had added that while it was difficult to penetrate the President's reserve he was left with the impression that the receipt of the communication was an enormous surprise to the President.
"The above is a summary of a translation which probably suffered by being several times removed from the language in which the interview took place." W. H. Page to RL, March 6, 1918, printed in FR-WWS 1918, 1, I, 149.
² See the draft printed at Feb. 28, 1918.
³ House undoubtedly referred to the two telegrams from Wiseman to Drummond, just printed.

From the Diary of Josephus Daniels

1918 Tuesday 26 February

Cabinet. Discussed policy of rehabilitation of soldiers & decided to give the task to the Vocational Educational Board that had been studying the plan. McAdoo inclined to opinion that it ought to be under the War Insurance Board, but it was decided to prepare the bill & let all cabinet members give their opinion.

To Charles Doolittle Walcott

My dear Doctor Walcott: [The White House] 27 February, 1918

Thank you for your letter of yesterday about my typewriter. Evidently you have been reading some more of the fiction that constantly appears about my typewriting machine. I have been several times represented as pounding away on a worn-out machine that is an interesting antique, when, as a matter of fact, I have a perfectly able-bodied machine of recent manufacture, with all the appliances and new notions which the manufacturers have seen fit to add to their newer machines, and I am not by any means through with it. It is likely to see many more years of work. I should be very much distressed to put a new one in its place.

I am none the less obliged to you for your suggestion about the interest that would attach to this particular machine and feel very much complimented that you should have wished it for the museum.   Cordially and sincerely yours,   Woodrow Wilson

TLS (Letterpress Books, WP, DLC).

To Hamilton Holt

My dear Mr. Holt: [The White House] 27 February, 1918

Creel has sent me your letter of February twentieth. I am, of course, deeply complimented that you should wish to put me alongside of Lincoln in any kind of brace, but what you propose is, I beg you to believe, impossible. It is impossible because I couldn't for the life of me tell you how I got my training in writing, except that it was superintended by a very wonderful father, and, besides, the thing I have always made a terrible fist of is talking about myself or analyzing any process of my own development.

With much appreciation,
                    Cordially and sincerely yours,   Woodrow Wilson

TLS (Letterpress Books, WP, DLC).

To Thomas Watt Gregory

                                          The White House
My dear Mr. Attorney General: 27 February, 1918

I should like to do something like what Creel proposes in the enclosed,[1] but I don't like to do it unless it has your approval. What do you think?
                    Cordially and sincerely yours,   Woodrow Wilson

TLS (JDR, RG 60, Numerical File, No. 186233-1011-8, DNA).
[1] G. Creel to WW, Feb. 26, 1918 (first letter of that date).

To William Gibbs McAdoo

My dear Mac: The White House 27 February, 1918

I have received a number of appeals like the one enclosed for refrigerator cars. What is the situation about them? I should like to give the best and most reassuring reply to this telegram that the facts justify.   Affectionately yours,   Woodrow Wilson

TLS (W. G. McAdoo Papers, DLC).

From Lord Reading, with Enclosures

My dear Mr. President,   Washington Febry 27/18

I have the honour to enclose copies of the two telegrams about which I spoke this morning.

I have the honour to be with the highest respect
My dear Mr. President

Your obedient Servant   Reading

ALS (WP, DLC).

E N C L O S U R E   I

SECRET.

Telegram from Mr. Balfour to Lord Reading
February 26th 1918.

Recent events in Russia render, in the considered opinion of the British Cabinet, the adoption of the policy outlined in my recent telegram to Paris a matter of great urgency.[1]

The most important Allied interests in Siberia are: (1) The preservation of the military stores now lying at Vladivostock which were bought with our money, and (2) the denial to the enemy of the vast agricultural resources available to the west of Lake Baikal.

His Majesty's Government do not doubt, after a full consideration of all the information at their disposal, that the former point will be dealt with by Japan with or without our consent. It would neither be difficult nor dangerous nor costly for her to occupy the junction of the Amur and Siberian Railways, as she is both anxious and ready to do. This would provide for Japanese security at the present moment, and satisfy that portion of Japanese public opinion which cherishes ambitions in Siberia for the future. It could, however, obviously do nothing to hinder the exploitation of the cornfields in West Siberia by the Germans, which, if the information of His Majesty's Government be correct, is the most important source of supply that is to be found anywhere in Russia under existing conditions.

It would only be possible to induce the Japanese Government to adopt the larger scheme if we were to appeal to their duty to their Allies, offer them a mandatory, and, should it prove necessary, assist them financially.

The possibility of this policy's uniting Russian national feeling against the Allies and of its throwing Russia into the arms of Germany, is the main argument against it. National feeling in Russia seems, however, to be non-existent for the moment. If it still survives it seems incredible that any of it should support the Bolsheviki in view of the absolute bankruptcy of their foreign policy. The fact would be proclaimed by the mandatory of the Allies that they do not propose to imitate in Siberia the policy of conquest which is being carried out by the Germans in European Russia. Moreover, according to the information of H. M. Government, Japanese troops, in the event of their being accompanied by commercial travellers, who might be of other nationalities, who brought with them such commodities as clothing and boots, would be welcomed from Vladvistock to Omsk as benefactors.

His Majesty's Government have reluctantly arrived, however, at one conclusion, which is indeed of secondary importance. Though a mandatory is desired by the Japanese, co-operation will not be tolerated by them. In their view the presence of small Allied forces, such as those which are accompanying General Allenby[2] in Palestine, not only give no assistance, but imply distrust. It seems immaterial whether this view be reasonable or not. In the view of H. M. Government it should not be contested, since it is certain to be adhered to. Ill feeling might easily be produced by argument, and H. M. Government feel confident that conviction would never be produced.

I can only add that it is with the United States that the final decision appears now to rest. France is eager for the decision. It is favorably regarded in Italy. Since the complete surrender of the Bolsheviki,[3] the British Government believe that there is no other alternative open. Common action will of course become impossible if a different view is taken by the United States. In that event, however, it is much to be feared that action will be taken by Japan alone and that, in taking action, sufficient extension will not, on the one hand, be given to her plans, nor, on the other, will she carry them out under the safeguards that would be provided by an Allied mandatory.

To sum up: the suggestion which I make on behalf of His Majesty's Government is;

(1) That the United States should join Great Britain, France and Italy in immediately inviting Japan to occupy the Siberian Railway;

(2) That this occupation should be extended, if possible, to Chiliabinsk and, in any case, as far as Omsk;

(3) That a declaration should accompany the occupation, from all the Allies, in which it should be explained that it was only a temporary measure rendered necessary, in the interests of Russian independence, which was left at the mercy of German militarism as a result of the collapse of the Government at Petrograd.[4]

[1] That is, the statement of policy proposed in the memorandum printed as an Enclosure with FLP to WW, Jan. 29, 1918.

[2] Gen. Sir Edmund Henry Hynman Allenby, Commander in Chief of the Egyptian Expeditionary Force.

[3] Following Trotsky's declaration of "no war-no peace" and the departure of the Soviet negotiating team from Brest-Litovsk on February 10 (about which see D. R. Francis to RL, Feb. 13, 1918, n. 5), the German High Command decided to renounce the armistice with Russia and resume hostilities. General Max Hoffmann notified the Soviet government on February 16 that the armistice would end on February 18. On the latter date, the German armies began a rapid advance all along the eastern front and met almost no resistance from the demoralized and largely disbanded Russian armies. The principal objectives of the German army were to occupy Latvia, Estonia, and the Ukraine. At Lenin's instigation, the Soviet government, late on February 18, sent a telegram to German headquarters accepting the peace terms which the German government had earlier proposed. After some delay to permit their armies to make further gains, the Germans presented new and harsher terms in the form of an ultimatum which was delivered to Petrograd on February 23. Under the threat by Lenin that he would resign from the party and the government if the ultimatum was not accepted, the Soviet regime capitulated on February 24. The negotiators reassembled at Brest-Litovsk on February 28, this time without the presence of Trotsky. Although the German ultimatum allowed three days of discussion, beginning on March 1, the Russians showed no inclination to haggle over details, and the final peace treaty was signed on March 3. The treaty required, among other things, the immediate, full demobilization of all Russian armies, including the embryonic Red army; the cessation of all revolutionary propaganda; Russian renunciation of all claims to the territory lying west of a line running from the Gulf of Riga to the northwest corner of the Ukraine; the return of Turkish territories captured by Russia during the war; the recognition of the independence of the Ukrainian People's Republic, and Russian evacuation of Estonia, Latvia, and Finland. Wheeler-Bennett, *Brest-Litovsk*, pp. 228-75, 403-408.

[4] This was a paraphrase of A. J. Balfour to Lord Reading, No. 1080, Feb. 26, 1918, T telegram (FO 115/2445, pp. 85-86, PRO).

E N C L O S U R E   I I

SECRET.

Telegram from Mr. Balfour to Lord Reading.
February 26th, 1918.

Since the despatch of my previous telegram we have learned that the enemy prisoners in Siberia are being organised with a view to cutting the Railway. This demonstrates the extreme urgency of action by the Japanese. Could instructions be sent to Mr. Stevens in the meantime to do anything that he can to protect the lines with or without the assistance of General Semenoff?[1]

T MSS (WP, DLC).

[1] This was a paraphrase of A. J. Balfour to Lord Reading, No. 1083, Feb. 26, 1918, T telegram (FO 115/2445, p. 91, PRO).

From Walter Hines Page

London. February 27, 1918.

8826. Personal. Secret For the Secretary and President only.

My 8815[1] of yesterday. I have had a long private and wholly unofficial conversation with Balfour. He left the impression clearly on my mind that he regards the Austrian approach made separately to the United States as another class [case] of the German policy of trying to create trouble between the Allies. It is admitted in Furstenberg's telegram of February twenty third that the German Government is essentially a partner in this approach and Hertlings speech also makes this partnership plain. Balfour pointed out that there are several ways in which conversation between the United States and Austria at this stage of the war and without a more specific basis of discussion might be hoped by Germany to create dissension. One way is this. The British and French treaty with Italy which is regrettable, but by which Great Britain and France are in honor bound cannot be overcome to square with the President's just conditions of peace. If this fact leaked out in a conversation and be made known by Germany, Italy might abandon the war. Balfour thinks that this unfortunate treaty will not give trouble in the end, but any premature discussion or even mention of it might * trouble.

Another possible unfortunate effect might be a dampening of war spirit in the United States if it became known that peace conversation was going on and the Germans would make it known if it suited their purpose.

Mr. Balfour pointed out other possible troubles that might be caused. He remarked that nothing could bring disagreement between the United States and Great Britain but that many complications might arise with other Governments. Then he said "I suppose of course that the President would prefer House as his spokesman. If House came to Europe now to discuss peace the whole world would blaze * expectations with discouraging effect in all Entente Countries."

He spoke of ? [Smuts'] private and unsuccessful errand to Switzerland which became known to Great Britain's embarrassment against the greatest precautions.[2]

He knows that Austria is most eager for peace, but in this move through Madrid the hand of Berlin is visible. The real wishes of Austria are much more clearly set forth in the Herron conversations in Switzerland than in the Emperor's message to the King of Spain.

I sought this conversation with Balfour on my own initiative in the hope of extracting from him some intimation of his views for your information. I disapprove of [assume?] what he said was consciously designed for communication to you, but his conviction and feeling were clear. It is certain that he hopes that the President will decline to discuss a general peace with Austria alone.

Page

T telegram (SDR, RG 59, 763.72119/10497, DNA).
    [1] WHP to RL, Feb. 26, 1918, FR-WWS 1918, i, I, 138-39, which quoted a report from Fürstenberg to Czernin about his audience with Alfonso XIII and the dispatch of Charles' message to Wilson.
    [2] About this matter, see R. H. Campbell to EMH, Jan. 2, 1918, n. 3, Vol. 45.

From Robert Lansing, with Enclosure

My dear Mr. President: Washington February 27, 1918.

I have had, this afternoon, interviews with the British and French Ambassadors in relation to Japan's desire to occupy Siberia with a military force.

Lord Reading informed me that he had seen you and had given you a copy of a secret telegram which he had received from Mr. Balfour and of which I received a copy this morning and append to this letter.[1]

The French Ambassador gave me the substance of a telegram which he had received from his Foreign Office containing a summary of a telegram they had received from their Ambassador[2] at Tokio. This latter is to me of especial interest in view of the avowal of Motono to declare publicly the disinterestedness of Japan and also the pledge to carry on military activities as far as the Ural Mountains—that is, to the confines of Asia. This memorandum I also enclose.

I also would call your attention to the enclosed telegram from Stevens, at Yokohoma, which may not have attracted your attention, but bears directly on the present subject.[3]

In discussing the matter with the French Ambassador, who was my first caller, I told him that I fully appreciated the attitude of the Allied Governments in regard to Japan and that it would appear Japan intended to act in any event. If that was so it was merely a question as to whether it was better to make Japan the mandatory of the other powers or to permit her to act independently, as I doubted the advisability of protesting in case she sent a military force into Siberia.

The Ambassador asked me in case it was decided that Japan should act at the request of the other powers whether the United States would be a party.

I told him I thought there was serious difficulty in the way—

chiefly that such an agreement as was proposed would amount to a treaty and that would have to be submitted to the Senate, where there were several strongly anti-Japanese Senators who would oppose it. I said further that in case action was taken by the Allied Governments I felt we should not be asked to take any part.

The Ambassador seemed disappointed at first but he said finally that he fully understood the difficulty and also the opinion which I urged that it was better for us and more in accord with our general policy to not join in such an agreement.[4]

When Lord Reading called I told him substantially what I had told the French Ambassador. He seemed to feel that in view of the telegram which the French Ambassador had received a new phase was put upon the problem and that if Japan was willing to make public such a declaration it might be the best policy to make her the mandatory of the Allied Powers.

He said further that he fully agreed with my view as to the inadvisability of an agreement on our part which would compel Senatorial consent.

Since we talked over this matter yesterday I do not know as the conditions have materially changed, but certainly the French telegram has thrown a new light upon it and I think we should carefully consider whether or not we should urge the Allied Governments not to make Japan their mandatory.

My own belief is that Japan intends to go into Siberia anyway and that it might be a restraint upon her if she should make a declaration such as Motono proposed. So far as this Government is concerned I think all that would be required would be a practical assurance that we would not make protest to Japan in taking this step.

As the whole matter is of vital importance and requires immediate action if any is to be taken I would be gratified if you would give me your views and guidance at the earliest possible moment.

Faithfully yours, Robert Lansing.

TLS (WP, DLC).
[1] That is, another copy of the telegram printed as Enclosure I with Lord Reading to WW, Feb. 27, 1918.
[2] Eugène Louis Georges Regnault.
[3] This telegram has not been found in the State Department files.
[4] J. J. Jusserand to the Foreign Ministry, No. 234, received Feb. 28, 1918, CC telegram (État-Major de L'Armée de Terre, Service Historique, 16 N 3012, FMD-Ar), is a report on this conversation. Lansing's summary was correct; however, he did emphasize to Jusserand the importance of involving the Chinese where Manchuria was concerned.

ENCLOSURE

Substance of a Telegram received February 27, 1918 by the FRENCH AMBASSADOR from his Government: being a summary of a telegram from the FRENCH AMBASSADOR at TOKIO.

Immediate consent to the Japanese arrangement concerning Siberia is indispensible. Mr. Motono has seen the French Ambassador and has shown himself ready to promise disinterestedness and even to say so publicly. He also declared that he was ready to pledge his country to act so far as the Ural Mountains.[1]

T MS (WP, DLC).
[1] This summary was typed on stationery of Lansing's office.

From Robert Scott Lovett

My dear Mr. President: Washington February 27, 1918.

I received this morning your letter of yesterday and confidential copy of your proposed letter to Mr. Baruch, for which I thank you.[1] I immediately sought an interview with Mr. McAdoo, and have just returned from a conference with him respecting the matter you asked me to discuss with him. He is writing you his views, in which I entirely concur.

Upon announcement of the reorganization, there would seem to be no further obstacle to my retirement from the War Industries Board, with suitable explanation; and my railroad work really requires it. It is of course true that the last thing I would desire would be to seem to be retiring because of the reorganization. May I venture to suggest, therefore, that when the reorganization is announced from the White House, it also be stated in substance that I am retiring pursuant to an understanding when I came that after January first I might retire from the Board to resume more actively my railroad duties, but that pending reorganization of the Board, I had agreed to continue until it should be completed?

Mr. McAdoo has under consideration a plan that may call for my services in his organization here in a way that will also permit me to do what I have to do for the Union Pacific; and this he tells me he will decide tomorrow. If he should desire my services, then of course the above suggested statement would be unnecessary.

May I renew assurances of my sympathetic interest in your task and of my readiness to assist wherever I can be of real service?

Very respectfully,   R. S. Lovett

TLS (WP, DLC).
¹ Both letters are missing in WP, DLC, and in the W. G. McAdoo Papers, DLC. For the letter as sent to Baruch, see WW to B. M. Baruch, March 4, 1918.

Two Letters from William Gibbs McAdoo

Dear Mr. President: Washington February 27, 1918.

Judge Lovett has showed me your letter of yesterday to him and copy of your proposed letter to Mr. Baruch enclosed therewith, and I have discussed with him the subject about which you asked him to confer with me.

I am very strongly of opinion that it would be a mistake to constitute, in connection with the War Industries Board, a Priorities Committee to determine questions of priority in transportation or delivery. Perhaps you are not aware that Judge Lovett has not been dealing with priorities in transportation since the Government took control of the railroads. He agreed with me that the taking over of the railroads completely changed the situation in that respect and, at my request, he issued an order on December 31st suspending indefinitely all priority orders then outstanding. Since that time questions of priority have been determined by me and by my organization as the circumstances required from time to time. I have detailed a traffic expert to the War Department, to the Navy Department, to the Food Administration, etc., to handle these questions under the general direction of my immediate assistants and the plan is working most successfully. I urge, therefore, that this plan should not be changed, at least for the present, and I am convinced that to operate with any Priorities Committee in connection with the War Industries Board would introduce new difficulties in the transportation situation. My suggestion, therefore, is that you omit from your proposed letter to Mr. Baruch the following paragraph at the end of page two, viz.,

"In the determination of priorities of delivery when it must be determined who should be assisted when necessary in addition to the present Advisory Priorities Organization by the advice and cooperation of a Committee constituted for the purpose and consisting of official representatives of the Food Administration, the Fuel Administration, the Railway Administration, the Shipping Board and the War Trade Board, in order that when a priority of delivery has been determined there may be common, consistent and concerted action to carry it into effect."

and strike out in earlier paragraphs reference to priorities of "delivery," thus confining the operations of the Priorities Division of the War Industries Board to questions of priority in production, as at present.

Judge Lovett concurs fully in the views herein expressed.

Cordially yours, W G McAdoo[1]

[1] Another copy of this letter bears the T notation: "Dictated by Judge Lovett." WGM to WW, Feb. 27, 1918, CCL (W. G. McAdoo Papers, DLC).

My dear Mr. President: Washington February 27, 1918.

Referring to the attached in regard to movement of potatoes from Minnesota producing points to markets:

Mr. Hoover's estimate of potatoes remaining in Minnesota of 1917 crop recently made is 9,500,000 bushels. The Department of Agriculture's daily report of 25th inst., copy of which I attach for your information, shows loading in Minnesota 87 cars, the largest of any State. It also shows for producing points:

"Maine, demand slow."

"Colorado, demand limited."

"Wisconsin, demand poor, market weaker."

It further shows adequate supply in the principal consuming markets of the country, and that Colorado, Idaho, California, Oregon and Minnesota are shipping to Texas markets, and Idaho, Colorado, Wisconsin and Minnesota shipping to markets East of Chicago.

Since the weather began to moderate there has been an increased demand for refrigerator cars for loading all kinds of perishable food products. If we were able to fill all orders for cars the result would certainly be overstocking of markets and lowering of prices to ruinous figures. You can realize how difficult it is to fill all orders for cars when all shippers desire to forward shipments at the same time. Special attention, however, is being given to the movement of this class of traffic at this time.

Cordially yours, W G McAdoo

TLS (WP, DLC).

From George Creel, with Enclosure

Memorandum

Dear Mr. President: [Washington] February 27, 1918.

As you can see from the attached letter, Doctor Mott is in need of funds again. All of his accounts have been checked, and every cent has been expended intelligently and properly.

Respectfully,   George Creel.

TL (WP, DLC).

E N C L O S U R E

John R. Mott to George Creel

Dear Mr. Creel: New York February 8th, 1918.

Of the $2,000,000 which you have thus far had forwarded to me on account of the $4,000,000 for the work in Russia, France and Italy, I find today that we have on hand only $150,758.88. We shall have to make large remittances within the next few weeks. I write, therefore, to ask whether you cannot kindly arrange to have sent to me within a week or two an additional installment of $1,000,000.[1]

I have had most gratifying reports of what our men are accomplishing in Russia. When Colton[2] and MacNaughten[3] with their party get through (they are now in Stockholm) with the films, a much larger service can be rendered, and yet you will be more than pleased when I see you and report on exactly what the men already in Russia have accomplished. From what Red Cross and other men who have returned from Russia say, it is the best thing being done along the lines which you and I have at heart, with the exception of what Sisson himself is accomplishing. The work for the French Army is advancing by leaps and bounds and was not projected by us one day too soon. Apparently we at last got the right man to head affairs in Italy—Dr. Nollen[4]—and his preliminary reports show that we are there in the nick of time.

With best wishes,   Very sincerely yours,   J R Mott

TLS (WP, DLC).
    [1] Wilson, in WW to WGM, Feb. 27, 1918, TCL (WP, DLC), instructed McAdoo to pay the $1,000,000 requested from his war emergency fund.
    [2] Ethan Theodore Colton, Associate General Secretary of the Y.M.C.A.
    [3] Edgar MacNaughten, a Y.M.C.A. worker since 1904, had gone as a representative of its international committee to Austria-Hungary in 1916 to assist prisoners of war, most of whom were Russians, and had remained there until October 1917 as acting secretary of the war-prisoner service. During part of 1918, he was the divisional Y.M.C.A. secretary for the Rainbow Division in France.
    [4] John Scholte Nollen.

From Robert Russa Moton

Tuskegee Institute, Ala.
My dear President Wilson: February 27, 1918.

I am venturing to write you about a matter which, in my opinion, should be brought to your personal attention. I have asked Mr. Scott[1] to present it to you in person.

There are thousands of colored people throughout this country who are deeply interested in the Negro Republic of Liberia. There are certain things about the situation that should be said bearing not only upon our own efforts in this country to hold the colored people to a straight line of patriotic cooperation, but as to how Liberia may be encouraged, and thereby, by reaction, influence Negro Public opinion in this country in the right direction.

The purpose of this letter then is to ask if you would be willing to meet a small committee of only three or four men—Mr. Scott, now serving in the War Department; Mr. William H. Lewis,[2] who is making a series of wonderfully fine addresses under patriotic auspices, and myself, some afternoon or evening, after office hours, no announcement to be made before or after said conference, and nothing to be said with the idea or purpose of making any kind of capital out of the conference, except, as above stated, to help Liberia, if possible.

The Negroes of the country are deeply stirred by Liberia's plight, and as President Roosevelt and President Taft exhibited an interest in the little Black Republic ten years ago, I am thinking, Sir, you may not object to such a conference as here suggested in connection with the present situation.

I know how busy you are and would not add one bit to your own burdens, but I am of the opinion that great good can be accomplished by such a conference.[3]

Yours very respectfully,   R. R. Moton

TLS (WP, DLC).

[1] That is, Emmett Jay Scott, secretary of the Tuskegee Institute, now serving as special assistant to the Secretary of War to advise on matters affecting Negro soldiers.

[2] William Henry Lewis of Boston, Assistant Attorney General of the United States from 1911 to 1913.

[3] Wilson suggested the date of March 8. However, Tumulty's letter of March 2 to Moton informing him of this date arrived too late for Moton to make arrangements with his committee. Moreover, Moton had another engagement on March 8. R. R. Moton to JPT, March 6, 1918, T telegram, and R. R. Moton to JPT, March 6, 1918, TLS, both in WP, DLC. Apparently the meeting never took place.

From Roger Nash Baldwin, with Enclosure

Dear Mr. President: New York, Feb. 27, 1918.

Although we appreciate that your attention has been called several times to the possible desirability of a change in the government's policy of handling the I.W.W., we venture to renew the suggestion that the present indictments be dismissed and that the whole matter be turned over to the Department of Labor, as an administrative problem.

In view of the appro[a]ching trial, and the increase of industrial unrest in the western states, it seems to us of the highest importance to the country that some such action should be taken.

We beg to submit the enclosed memorandum, which puts the case as we see it.   Very sincerely yours,   Roger Baldwin.

TLS (WP, DLC).

E N C L O S U R E

Industrial Unrest in Relation to the Pending Trial of 166 I.W.W. Leaders and Organizers.

Memorandum by the National Civil Liberties Bureau, New York, Feb. 1918

The arrest and imprisonment, pending trial, of several hundred officials, organizers and sympathizers of the I.W.W. is already producing considerable labor unrest in the west. The leading case, which will come to trial during the next two months, will undoubtedly increase strikes and unrest; first, because of the widespread publicity which will be given to the trial, (which will last for several months at least); second, because of the increased feeling of hostility both to the government and employers aroused by the attack that will inevitably be made by the I.W.W. defense on the industrial conditions which make the I.W.W. possible.

The theory of the government in prosecuting the I.W.W. was to stop labor agitation and strikes among the great body of unskilled migratory workers in the west, led for the most part by I.W.W. groups. It is already demonstrated that the indictments have had exactly the contrary effect.

The I.W.W. has been indicted ostensibly because its activities interfered with the conduct of the war. As a matter of fact, the indictment is directed against the essential operations of the I.W.W. as a labor organization. The same indictment could have been brought against many other of the old-line trade unions during the war. The problem is an administrative matter which should in our opinion be handled by the Department of Labor. It cannot be successfully solved by prosecutions.

The matter has already been fully presented to Secretary of War Baker, to the President's Mediation Commission, to the Secretary of Labor and to Mr. Justice Brandeis. We feel certain that if recommendations from the Mediation Commission were asked, or if the opinion of the Secretary of War were sought, that they would be along the lines of the suggestion here made.

NATIONAL CIVIL LIBERTIES BUEARU [BUREAU].

T MS (WP, DLC).

Lord Reading to Arthur James Balfour

Washington February 27, 1918

Urgent Tel: No: 828
Your tels: Nos: 1080 & 1083.[1]

Immediately upon their receipt I saw the President. He desired to have the documents for consideration and I sent him paraphrases. He discussed the matter freely and said he was anxious you should not think that if he raised difficulties it was because of any objection to Japan but because of his conviction that the Russian people would regard any manifesto of disinterestedness on the part of the Allies on a par with similar manifestos issued by the Central Powers in European Russia, and that the Allies would consequently lose the moral force of their position. He wished however, time for consideration.

Subsequently I saw Sec. of State who informed me that French Ambassador had made a communication to him to the effect that the Japanese Govt. were willing to entertain suggestion of undertaking to occupy the railway as far as the Ural Mountains and to issue a declaration of disinterestedness.

I told Mr. Lansing of my conversation with the President. He said he thought the situation was altered by the news communicated to him by the French Ambassador. He would see the President this afternoon and communicate with me as soon as a decision was reached.

Hw telegram (FO 115/2445, pp. 93-94, PRO).
[1] The Enclosures printed with Lord Reading to WW, Feb. 27, 1918.

Arthur James Balfour to Edward Mandell House

[London] Feb 27th [1918].

Very urgent No 53 [54].[1]

The following is for Col House from Mr Balfour.

Please express to President Wilson my very high appreciation of his confidence.

My views about Austrian Minister for Foreign Affairs' message are as follows for what they are worth.

A) I am profoundly impressed by the decided difference between Austrian Minister for Foreign Affairs' official utterance conveyed through the King of Spain and personal policy of Emperor of Austria as embodied in a conversation between Professor Lammasch and Dr. Herron of which we had an account from our Minister in Berne. First does not appear to go beyond a suggestion for a return to the Status Quo Ante except that Bulgaria is to obtain a great deal that she did not possess before the war, while Servia is to get something and to lose something, balance of loss and gain being on the whole against her. These proposals are known to the German Emperor and doubtless represent his policy. They amount to a victory for the Central Powers and can hardly be reconciled with the Presidents public declarations on the subject of peace terms.

B) The proposals of Professor Lammasch through Dr. Herron are of a very different nature and I presume represent opinion of the Emperor of Austria (in his then mood) unaffected by German influences. Professor Lammasch lays down with great emphasis and in quite clear language the right of peoples to choose their own form of Government and the Emperor is reported as expressly desiring to see this principle applied to his own Dominion.

As far as it goes this scheme is in harmony with the principles laid down by the President and might therefore form a starting point for discussions. But there are two very serious objections. In the first place it ignores Italy and in the second place, unless it is very carefully handled it may alienate the subject races of Austria whom the President desires to help. Various Slav peoples have so often been fooled by the phrase "self government" that they will be disposed to regard all schemes which are so described as giving them the old slavery under a new name. They will draw no distinction between what the President desires to give them and what they have already. What they have already leaves them completely subject, in Austria to a German minority, in Hungary to Magyar one.

C) I need not insist on the dangers both from the Italian and Austrian side which conversations begun on Lammasch basis must

carry with them. The future of the war largely depends on supporting Italian enthusiasm and on maintaining anti-German zeal
of Slav population in Austria. Both Italians and Slavs are very easily
discouraged and are quick to find evidence in foreign speeches that
their interests are forgotten or betrayed.

I fear that Austrian statesmanship will not be above using any
indications that the President has a tenderness for the Austrian
Empire as a means of convincing the Slavs that they have nothing
to hope for from the Allies and had best make terms with the Central
Powers.

d) Some risk, however, must be run and, if the President feels
strongly that it is really essential not to close the door to further
discussions, it seems to me that it might be worth while to take
steps to ascertain if the Lammasch conversations really represented
the mind of the Emperor and whether he would be prepared to
treat them as a basis for discussion. Austro-German proposals to
the King of Spain appear so completely inconsistent with the Presidents public declaration that it is hard to see how any discussion
round a table could bridge the differences between them.

In answer to the question which the President asks me about
taking the Allies into his confidence I suggest it must largely depend
on the policy he intends to pursue. When the German proposals
for a conference last summer were conveyed to me by the King of
Spain I called the Ambassadors of the Great Belligerents, including
Japan, to the Foreign Office and informed them of everything that
had occurred.

This, in the circumstances, was quite easy and avoided all occasion for suspicion. It may not be so easy now. But my advice
would be to follow the same course *if the Austrian Minister for
Foreign Affairs' proposals are in question*—, but, if, on the other
hand, the President means to follow up the Lammasch-Herron line
I should, in his place, content myself with telling the Allies very
confidentially that I was carrying on informal conversations with
Austria and would communicate further with them if occasion arose.

e) I offer these suggestions with the utmost diffidence and only
in consequence of the direct request which you were good enough
to convey to me from the President.

HwC telegram (WP, DLC).
    ¹ The number was changed in A. J. Balfour to W. Wiseman, Feb. 27, 1918, T telegram
(W. Wiseman Papers, CtY). Another copy of this telegram is in FO 115/2388, pp. 106-
108, PRO.

Sir William Wiseman to Sir Eric Drummond

[Washington] February 27, 1918.

No. 61. Reference your No. 52 of the 22nd:

ADRAMYTI [WILSON] and BRUSSA [HOUSE] have abandoned any idea of recognising Bolsheviki Government at present. Your arguments, however, will be useful if the question arises again.

T telegram (W. Wiseman Papers, CtY).

From the Diary of Colonel House

February 27, 1918.

Henry P. Davison and Mr. Case[1] of the Red Cross called yesterday. They wished advice as to Russia; and whether to continue to send succor there. I advised sending it. Davison said he was leaving for Europe this week. I congratulated him upon the splendid work the Red Cross was doing under his direction.

I dined with the President and Mrs. Wilson and we went to the theater. Eleanor McAdoo came into the box during the evening. Just before and during dinner we discussed matters of interest pending and the developments since we were together. After the theater, The President insisted upon taking Eleanor and me home before going to the White House. While these theater parties are the most restful diversions he has, I am fearful of them. I am afraid that some day someone will try to assassinate him.

The President complained of being tired. Though he looks better than upon my last visit, I can see indications of fatigue. He does not remember names as well and he does not think to do the things we decide upon. Grayson was talking of this yesterday. He said that while he gave the impression to everyone that the President worked day and night, he and I knew that eight hours work a day was about all he was equal to. I will say this, however, that I believe the President can do more in eight hours than any man I know. He wast[e]s no time in talking or useless argument or energy of any sort. McAdoo has more energy and staying powers, and works perhaps twice as many hours as the President, but he does not accomplish as much because he wastes so much energy in talking.

[1] George Bowen Case, a member of the War Council of the American Red Cross and a prominent lawyer of New York.

A Draft of a Telegram to Alfonso XIII[1]

The White House [Feb. 28, 1918].

I am ⟨of course⟩ gratified that my recent statement of the principles that ought to be observed in formulating terms of peace should ⟨receive⟩ in so large a measure by [be] accepted by His Majesty the Emperor of Austria and that His Majesty should ⟨wish for⟩ *desire* a more particular comparison of views between the two governments and I would be very glad if His Majesty felt at liberty to be more explicit ⟨about⟩ *concerning* the application of the *four* principles I outlined in my address to the Congress of the United States on the eleventh of February last. My address of the eleventh of February merely undertook to state, perhaps more clearly than I had stated them before, the principles which I had sought *definitely* to apply in my address to the Congress on the eighth of January preceding. In that previous address I ⟨did⟩ set forth ⟨very⟩ *with* definite⟨ly⟩ *particularity* the way in which I thought those principles ought to be carried out in action. ⟨The⟩ *I assume that the* Emperor ⟨therefore already has⟩ *has my address of the eighth of January and that he has already* before him the detailed programme ⟨as I now think it ought to be formulated⟩ *which I think should form the basis for a general peace stated* in as clear and specific terms as any personal representative of mine could ⟨present the⟩ *state* it. It would, ⟨therefore,⟩ greatly aid me in determining whether a more intimate personal comparison of views would be worth while if I might have, as nearly as possible, an equally explicit programme from him. His Majesty says, in the message which you have been kind enough to transmit to me, that he believes that he has convincing evidence in his possession that certain settlements which have been proposed in connection with the complicated Balkan situation would be less acceptable to the peoples concerned and more likely to breed further antagonisms than the settlements which Austria herself would propose, and that certain settlements desired by Italy would be unacceptable to the populations most directly concerned, but he does not give ⟨us⟩ *me, what I greatly desire,* the benefit of his own affirmative suggestions. ⟨I have said, of course, most sincerely, that I was quite ready to be shown that the settlements I have proposed might be advantageously set aside for others more likely to produce the satisfactions of national and racial opinion and feeling which must underlie a desirable and permanent peace.⟩ I can ⟨, therefore,⟩ assure His Majesty of my entire willingness to consider any solutions he may have in mind ⟨and to frankly compare them with my own suggested programme⟩. I would in particular like to know how His Majesty would propose to compose the uneasiness and satisfy the national aspirations of the Slavic peoples who are so near neighbours to his own country and so closely related by ties of blood with great bodies of his own subjects; what dispositions he would suggest with regard to the Adriatic lit[t]oral; how the rivalries and antagonisms of the Balkan states, rendered more acute than ever by this war, might in his judgment best be ⟨composed⟩ *allayed*; what concessions exactly he would think it right to make to Italy; and what protection he would think it feasible to throw around the non-Turkish peoples now subject to the Ottoman Empire. I understand him to be practically of my own ⟨opinion and purpose⟩ *purpose and opinion* with regard to Belgium and Poland. In the light of such specific particulars it will be possible to judge of many points of action and the whole question of conference much better than I am now able to judge. I beg ⟨once more⟩ to assure His Majesty (if the assurance is necessary) that I am seeking no strategic advantage, no advantage of any kind, but only a just settlement which will give the world ⟨peace⟩ a righteous and therefore lasting peace.

WWT MS (WP, DLC).
[1] Words in angle brackets deleted by Wilson; words in italics added by him.

From the Diary of Colonel House

February 28, 1918.

When I awakened this morning I heard Sir William in the next room taking down a message from Balfour which was being repeated to him from my apartment in New York over the private telephone which now runs through the State Department and to Gordon's house. His secretary, knowing of this private wire, telephoned Sir William at Lord Reading's and told him the despatch had arrived. Wiseman came to Gordon's a little after seven o'clock and took down the message. The despatch is appended and is in reply to mine of Sunday.

It is about as I expected and does not alter the situation in any way. After seeing two or three people and discussing the matter with Wiseman and Gordon, I went to the White House at 11.30 and was with the President for an hour before his appointment with the French Ambassador. We concluded that there was nothing in the message which prevented the President from carrying out our plan of sending the message he had prepared to the Austrian Emperor.

I asked the President last night if he had cautioned Secretary Baker, who is on his way to Europe, about talking pacifism. It is one of the matters he had forgotten, but he said he would send a wireless to him at once. Gordon prepared one which I reviewed and which the President approved, and it was sent to the Secretary by Admiral Benson later in the day.[1]

The President asked me to take his reply to the Austrian Emperor and show it to Lansing while he, the President, was with Jusserand. Lansing came to the White House and approved the text with the exception of one paragraph. In submitting it to the President later he asked if I agreed with Lansing. Upon receiving an affirmative reply, he cut out the paragraph without further discussion. In my opinion, the paragraph had better been left in if the Entente had not objected.

The President was pleased with his interview with the French Ambassador. He expected rather a stormy time because he intended to tell him of his communication to the Austrians. Jusserand thought he was acting wisely. The Ambassador said that his Government had picked up some information which led them to believe that the two Kaisers, Wilhelm and Karl, had gotten the Apostolic Delegate in Munich[2] to take their peace terms to Rome for the purpose of having the Pope use his good offices toward peace. I have my doubts as to the correctness of this information, but the French seem to credit it.

Besides the family, McAdoo, Doctor Axson and Vance McCormick were at lunch. McAdoo and I talked for nearly an hour afterward. I went from the White House to the State Department to see Lansing and Gordon. Since William Phillips is sick and Frank Polk is away, Lansing and Gordon are doing all the work. The Secretary and I discussed the Japanese intervention proposal and the question as to whether the President should make known to the Entente the exact context [contents] of his message to the Emperor of Austria. Lansing was strongly in favor of doing so and I agreed with some mental reservations.

Sir William Wiseman called at 4.30 to say he had advised Lord Reading of the context [contents] of the President's message which I had requested him to do, but asked Reading not to cable his Government until he had official information. I told Sir William

[1] The draft prepared by Gordon Auchincloss, "For Secy Baker from The President," was strictly confidential and was to be deciphered by the ship's captain. It began with a reference to General Leonard Wood and read as follows: "In view of the visit of a certain high officer of the U. S. Army to England and France and the spreading by him of false reports concerning the inefficiency of the War Dept and of allegations to the effect that you personally were a pacifist, I suggest that you let it be known to British, French and Italian officials with whom you may come in touch, and in any public statement you may be called upon to make [to make] it emphatically clear that it is the determination of this Govt to bend all its energies to the vigorous prosecution of the war and to devote all its resources to that end." EMHhw MS (E. M. House Papers, CtY).
[2] The Most Rev. Eugenio Pacelli, Archbishop of Sardi, later Pope Pius XII.

that Lever of the British Treasury Department, who is now on Reading's staff, was *persona non grata* to McAdoo and he wished for a change. I urged Wiseman to attend to this promptly, giving the reasons for McAdoo's attitude.

Wiseman saw Reading and the change was agreed upon, Reading endorsing McAdoo's opinion of Lever. I had a half hour with Reading at six when he called to say goodbye and to discuss pending matters.

I forgot to say that before lunch today the President thought I should not leave Washington at present; that the situation was critical, and he hoped I would think best to remain. He puts such requests so nicely that I hate to disagree with him, and yet I think it best for me to leave. I promised to return soon. He remarked that my coming created so much comment that he wondered if it would not be better for me to come oftener and remain longer rather than to come infrequently and cause a sensation.

I dined at the White House. Dr. Axson and one of Mrs. Wilson's brothers[3] were present. The President wanted me to go to the theater but I declined. After dinner we settled some pending questions. I told him Hoover had asked me to recommend someone to represent the Food Board on the Interallied Council and I wondered whether he wished to send someone in that capacity. Upon asking for my advice, I thought he had better do so since he had accepted the principle of sending representatives of the Treasury and of the Shipping Board.

Dr. Axson is now working as Secretary of the Red Cross under Harry Davison. He asked if I did not think Davison a fine, lovable fellow. The President was amused at my reply that "he seemed to be." I did not commit myself further. And this reminds me that last night at dinner, the President, Mrs. Wilson and I were discussing how ubiquitous Jews were; one stumbled over them at every move and they were so persistent that it was impossible to avoid them. I thought it surprising in view of the fact that there were so few in the world. This brought on an argument as to how many there were. I thought not more than fifteen million—twenty millions at the outside. Mrs. Wilson guessed fifty millions and the President one hundred millions. To settle it he sent the butler for a World's Almanac and was greatly surprised to find that in Europe there were less than ten millions, in Asia about a half million and in this country about three millions. He could not believe it even after he saw the figures. The reason I happened to hit the mark was that I remembered having read somewhere that one tenth of the Jews

---

[3] John Randolph Bolling.

of the world were living in New York City. While I knew this was not strictly true, I thought it somewhere near the truth.

I drove with the party to the theater and then went to Nineteenth Street where Gordon, David Miller and I had a pleasant evening together until Wiseman called in the Ambassador's car to take Miller and me to the midnight train.

At the theater the other evening, the people sitting in the box next to us moved baco [back] so far in order not to obstruct our view that I called the attention of the President to their consideration. The President immediately got up and went over to the edge of our box and asked if they would not move forward; that while he appreciated their action, it was unnecessary because we could see perfectly well if they, too, made themselves comfortable. This shows the President's great consideration in such matters.

One of the most important things I did while in Washington was to suggest to the President, and got him to agree, to ask Congress to pass a law giving our Government the right to place an embargo upon raw materials for a period of five years after the war, the law not to mention any specific nation, but to authorize the Government to use it against any or all governments at will. I thought unless he did this he would not have any potent weapon in his pocket to deal with the Central Powers at the Peace Congress. It was no use to threaten, I thought, besides a peace conference was no place to make threats, and even if he made one it was not certain he would be able to carry it into effect. He saw the point; made a memorandum and declared he would do it at once.

I have arranged with Sir William Wiseman to cable his Government to do likewise. I have mentioned this before in writing of an interview I had some weeks ago with André Tardieu.

I had Wiseman write a cable to Balfour in reply to the one I received from him this morning. I brought out clearly some points I wanted the British to know so they could better appreciate the President's position. I am sending this despatch without the knowledge of the President but I am confident of his entire approval.[4]

[4] See W. Wiseman to E. Drummond, March 1, 1918.

To William Gibbs McAdoo

My dear Mac: [The White House] 28 February, 1918

I don't agree with you about the paragraph in the War Industries Board reorganization to which you refer in your letter of yesterday, because I think you have mistaken its purpose. I do not wish to disturb the existing methods of conference and cooperation with regard to priorities of shipment, but there are matters "of delivery" very much larger than mere questions of transportation. The Shipping Board must be brought in and, even more necessarily, the War Trade Board, because they control all movements in and out of the country by their control over both exports and imports, and it is in my judgment absolutely necessary to have a supplementary body of regular constitution which will be available to see to it that all obstacles may be removed from the free movement of articles, not only within the country but out of it and into it.

Affectionately yours,   Woodrow Wilson

TLS (Letterpress Books, WP, DLC).

To Robert Scott Lovett

My dear Judge Lovett: [The White House] 28 February, 1918

You always excite my admiration by the way you do things, and I am sincerely obliged to you for your two letters.[1] I am disposed to think that your suggestion about Mr. Parker[2] is an excellent solution of the question as to who shall take your place as priorities member of the War Industries Board.

You may be sure I will manage the mention of your retirement as you suggest, and I want to add how glad I am to hear that there is likely to be work which you will have time to do here in connection with the Railway Administration in addition to the work you must undertake for the Southern Pacific.

Cordially and sincerely yours,   Woodrow Wilson

TLS (Letterpress Books, WP, DLC).
  [1] The second letter is missing.
  [2] Edwin Brewington Parker, a lawyer of Houston.

To George Creel

My dear Creel: [The White House] 28 February, 1918

I agree with Doctor Claxton that the opposition to teaching German in our schools is childish, but this letter is certainly most unwise in the passage which you have marked and if you can do anything to restrict its circulation, I will be very glad indeed.

Cordially and sincerely yours,   Woodrow Wilson

TLS (Letterpress Books, WP, DLC).

From William Kent

My dear Mr. President: Washington February 28, 1918.

I am intensely interested in the work of the Federal Trade Commission. That Commission is one of the most powerful instrumentalities of Government for good or ill. If it clearly and bravely sees and does its work, it furnishes a means of correcting the business evils which if uncorrected must necessarily lead to turmoil if not to revolution.

On the other hand, if it falls into unreliable hands it can be used to whitewash and to grant immunity baths to the malevolent powerful interests. I do not believe you have before you any more critical domestic problem than in filling the vacancies on that Commission with men whom the public can fully trust; and geography should not be considered, nor should any more attention be paid to party politics than the law specifically provides.

I do not believe you can realize the conscienceless pressure and the limitless temptation that will be applied to this Commission. No perfunctory endorsements or petitions, no matter how numerously signed, should have weight. Selection of Commissioners should be as careful as those of Cabinet Members and, in every case, a detailed history of men's attitude and public service should be investigated by the most trustworthy and careful examiners.

I am informed that Mr. Bracken,[1] at present Secretary of the Commission, is a leading applicant for appointment. Mr. Bracken will not do at all, as you can easily learn by consultation with the present Commissioners and with others that know of his bent. As merely an indication of his attitude, permit me to quote from a letter from McManus,[2] attorney for Swift & Co., writing to his superior, Mr. Veeder,[3] about August 14th, 1916, the letter being taken from the packers' files.

Alluding to Congressman Doolittle's[4] formal complaint, upon which the Federal Trade Commission was empowered to act, Mr. McManus states that

"such complaint is privileged under the Federal Trade Commission practice and is not available to the public. However, it is as follows:" (whereupon the Doolittle complaint is quoted).

Mr. Bracken admitted to those in charge of the investigation that he, Secretary of the Commission, had handed this confidential document to McManus, the rough working attorney of Swift & Co.

If you desire, I can send you a statement of quotations in the record from the packers' files that show the packers' inside views and statements concerning the attitude of the Administration.

Of course I know what your position has been and also know the position of Secretary Houston who was naturally your nearest adviser in this matter, but I believe it would be interesting and profitable to you to know what these people said about it. I should not intrude this citation on you without your request.

Yours truly,   William Kent

TLS (WP, DLC).
¹ Leonidas Locke Bracken, a lawyer from Muncie, Ind., secretary of the Federal Trade Commission since 1916.
² Robert C. McManus, a lawyer of Chicago.
³ Henry Veeder, a lawyer of Chicago.
⁴ Dudley Doolittle of Kansas, a Democrat.

To William Kent

My dear Kent: The White House 28 February, 1918

Thank you for your letter of this morning. It expresses my own views with regard to the critical importance of appointments to the Federal Trade Commission.

If I don't ask you to let me see the evidence to which you refer, I mean the evidence of the attitude of the packers, it is only because I don't want to see red. I am sure you will understand.

In great haste   Sincerely yours,   Woodrow Wilson

TLS (W. Kent Papers, CtY).

From Robert Lansing, with Enclosure

My dear Mr. President: Washington February 28, 1918.

The Zionist Committee, through its secretary, has sent me the letter which I attach hereto. This Committee makes two requests:

1—That passports be issued to representatives of the Committee to proceed to Palestine via London or Paris as a part of a Commission composed of representatives of the Zionist organization of England which is acting with the sanction of the British Government.

2—That this Department recognize a Zionist Medical Unit composed of from thirty-five to forty-five persons. This Unit is to proceed to Palestine to render service to the civilian population there.

I hesitate to accede to these requests in view of the following considerations:

1—This Government has never accepted Mr. Balfour's pronouncement with reference to the future of Palestine and has expressly refrained from accrediting consular agents to that territory, in which action the British Government has entirely acquiesced.

2—This Government is not at war with Turkey.

3—A possible embarrassment may arise on account of the presence in Palestine of individuals, even though their errand is one of mercy, sponsored by an organization having distinctly political aims.

I should be grateful to you if you would advise me of your views with reference to this communication from the Zionist Committee.

Sincerely yours, Robert Lansing.

Pres. authorized the unit. FLP March 3, 18

E N C L O S U R E

Jacob de Haas to Robert Lansing

Sir: Washington, D. C., February 27, 1918.

On behalf of the Zionist organization, I earnestly request you to authorize the issuance of passports to E. W. Lewin-Epstein,[1] Mary Fels,[2] and such others as may be named by my Committee, all being loyal American citizens of creditable reputation, said passports to be issued to them personally on their appearing before the designated official, so as to enable them to proceed to Palestine, via London or Paris. Together, the persons named and to be named will go as part of a Commission representing our Zionist organization, joining a Mission composed of representatives of the Zionist organizations of England and other countries, which together will form a Mission proceeding with the sanction of the British Government under the direction of Dr. Weitzmann[3] to Palestine. The objects of the Mission are outlined in a cable, signed Weitzman Frankfurter, copy of which I attach.[4]

MEDICAL UNIT

Further in connection with the proposed sending of a Zionist medical unit to Palestine, which matter has been before the Department in various forms, I now beg, in the first place, to call your attention to the following message from the British Embassy, and earnestly request the State Department to recognize our unit, which will comprise from thirty-five to forty-five persons, in the form requested by the British authorities, which I understand from representatives of the British Embassy, is in accord with the precedent established by the British Government in the recognition of various units that have rendered service during the war for special purposes. Under the convention proclaimed February 28, 1910, between the United States and other powers for the adaptation of the principles of the Geneva Convention, it is necessary that the unit receive an official commission from the United States, and that the

Government notify the names of the personnel to the Central Powers.

I may add that the British authorities clearly understand that our unit is to render much needed service to the civilian population in Palestine, which is at present practically denuded of doctors and nurses required for the normal purposes of any country. May I ask, upon such recognition being accorded to us, the Department authorize the issuance of the passports in the usual way and enable us to purchase medical supplies, etc. The message from the British Government reads:

"Mr. Jacob de Haas, Secretary of Zionist Committee,
      44 East 23rd Street, New York.

We are informed that there will be no objection to despatch of Zionist Medical Unit to Palestine as one of the American Medical Units provided American Government will recognize it and will in accordance with Geneva convention notify enemy of their recognition.

        Reading."

                Very truly yours,   Jacob de Haas

TLS (SDR, RG 59, 867N.01/14½, DNA).
   ¹ That is, Lewis Epstein (Eliahu Ze'ev Halevi Lewin-Epstein).
   ² Mary (Mrs. Joseph) Fels, widow of the soap manufacturer of Philadelphia, was active as a lecturer in the single-tax movement and had organized the Joseph Fels Commission to carry on her husband's work for the Zionist cause.
   ³ That is, Chaim Weizmann.
   ⁴ C. Weizmann and F. Frankfurter to L. D. Brandeis, Feb. 27, 1918, TC telegram (SDR, RG 59, 867N.01/14½, DNA).

From George Creel, with Enclosure

Memorandum

My dear Mr. President: [Washington] February 28, 1918.

I send you a further memorandum, showing Dr. Mott's need.
              Respectfully,   George Creel.

TL (WP, DLC).

ENCLOSURE

John R. Mott to George Creel

Dear Mr. Creel: New York February 26th, 1918.

I trust that by this time you have been able to arrange matters so that the third installment of a million dollars can be sent to me this week, because I am holding up matters of the greatest impor-

tance, especially in connection with the demand for the rapid expansion of our work in the French Army. Since I saw you, I have
received from our two head workers in the French Army of over
three million men a cablegram reading as follows:

"Clemenceau Petain urging organization ten new foyers daily Minimum weekly requirement twenty five virile native Americans
Cannot accept foreigners as representatives Include athletic directors Sympathy energy adaptability culture count more than
language Highest standard of American leadership in foyers essential to win war insist France and America"

You will agree with me that this is a most remarkable appeal. Think
of our being asked to open up this helpful work at ten new points
each day during the coming weeks and to dispatch to France twenty-
five able workers each week. You will see at a glance the imperative
need of our having the funds so that we may not tie up this indispensable piece of work at the most critical period.

Very cordially yours,   J. R. Mott

TLS (WP, DLC).

From Thomas Watt Gregory

Dear Mr. President: Washington Feb. 28, 1918.

I am very grateful to you & Mrs. Wilson for the exquisite flowers
sent when my Mother died. We took them with her to Miss. where
she was laid by the side of my Father,[1] who died in the Confederate
Army 55 years ago. She was almost eighty years old & one of the
things she most often spoke of was her pride in having known you
& come in contact with the great constructive work of your administration.

Her life was a long one & useful to the last & she left many
friends behind.   Sincerely Yours   T. W. Gregory

ALS (WP, DLC).
[1] Capt. Francis Robert Gregory, M.D., a native of Mecklenburg County, Va.

A Draft of an Address

[c. March 1, 1918]

The address of Count von Hertling, made to the German Reichstag on the twenty-fifth of February last,[1] inasmuch as it is in so
large part intended as a reply to my address to the Congress of the
eleventh of February, clearly calls for a rejoinder on my part, not
only because it is by intention addressed to this Government, but

also because it is, I fear, based upon certain misapprehensions which may seriously darken counsel unless they are promptly cleared away.

Count von Hertling seems to be under the impression that in my address of the eleventh of February I intended in some way to soften or alter the statements with regard to the attitude and objects of the United States which were contained in earlier addresses, and that I am seeking, now here now there, for some ground of rapprochement and accommodation. If that is his impression, I am very sorry, for it is an entirely erroneous impression. The position of this Government has in no respect shifted or altered. If I confined myself in my address of the eleventh of February to a statement of principles only, I did not for a moment intend to be understood as modifying what I had said on the eighth of January. In that earlies [earlier] address I explicitly applied to each chief item of the greater questions involved in this war the principles which I simply summarized in the later address. The address of the eighth of January contained, and still contains, our terms of peace. We have not altered those terms. They stand until others are proposed which are better, until some other definite programme of justice and freedom is as explicitly outlined which will lead more certainly and more directly to a righteous and permanent peace.

We are not seeking peace. We are not casting about for means of accommodation. We are seeking justice and the firm establishment of the rights of all free men. Only the road to this can for us be the road to peace. We have stated our own conception of where that road lies, and we are asking What programme of right and justice has the Imperial German Government in mind? That, and that alone, is the question for which we are seeking an answer. So far as we are concerned, the war cannot end or slacken until that question is answered fully and frankly and in terms of justice to weak and strong alike which are as fair and acceptible as ours, or better and more enlightened. We are not tired. We have no reason to be discouraged[.] We have only begun to take our part in action. We shall play that part with ever increasing energy and ardour. And the spirit of our associates is the same. But we wish a clear air of purpose in which to fight, and we ask the German Government to be as outspoken and explicit as we have been. I take it for granted there is nothing that they are ashamed to avow.

The German people have no doubt become keenly and painfully aware of the impression their military masters have made upon the rest of the world,—and sometimes even upon their own allies. They are believed to be seeking an arrogant dominion in Europe and Asia. They are believed to be seeking to carry out the extraordinary and far-reaching "Pan-German" programme of annexation and control which so many of their partisans so frankly set forth by book and pamphlet and address in the years which immediately preceded the outbreak of the war. The spokesmen of the Imperial Government deny this and declare that they are fighting in defence of the Fatherland against those who would destroy it or rob it of its rightful place of influence and power among the nations. We can see no such issue in the war. We have several times solemnly assured the German people that we have no thought of aggression, no wish to injure Germany. If in the terms of peace we have laid down there is anything which seems to have such an object, it is proposed only to rectify wrongs formerly done to one or another party to the present war which constituted no settlement at all even and, when they were consummated, but only embittered and perpetuated strife and makes settled peace impossible, the peace and safety of Germany as well as of Europe itself.[2]

WWT MS (WP, DLC).
    [1] Hertling acknowledged that Wilson's address of February 11 might perhaps represent a small step toward a mutual rapprochement [gegenseitige Annäherung] and that he, Hertling, could, with one reservation, agree with many of the principles which Wilson had stated. The reservation stipulated that these principles had to be recognized, not just by Wilson, but by all states and nations. A league of nations was "an aim devoutly to be desired," Hertling went on, but that aim had not yet been reached, and England's war aims were "thoroughly imperialistic." England talked of self-determination but did not apply that principle to Ireland, Egypt, or India. "Our war aims from the beginning," Hertling went on, "were the defense of the fatherland, the maintenance of our territorial integrity, and the freedom of our economic development." Even in the East, Hertling added, German military operations were defensive and in no way were aimed at conquest. For the text of Hertling's speech, see *Schulthess' Europäischer Geschichtskalender*, LIX (1918), Part 1, pp. 86-91. English translations are printed in the *New York Times*, Feb. 27, 1918, and in *FR-WWS 1918*, I, I, 135-38. For further comment on Hertling's speech, see the Enclosure printed with G. Auchincloss to WW, March 7, 1918.
    [2] There is a WWsh draft of this document in WP, DLC.

A Draft of An Aide-Mémoire

JAPAN-SIBERIA
Handed me by Prest noon 3/1/18[1]
The White House.

The Government of the United States is made constantly aware at every turn of events that it is the desire of the people of the United States that, while cooperating with all its energy with its associates in the war in every direct enterprise of the war in which it is possible for it to take part, it should leave itself diplomatically free wherever it can do so without injustice to its associates. It is for this reason that the Government of the United States has not thought it wise to join the governments of the Entente in asking the Japanese government to act in Siberia. It has no objection to that request being made, and it wishes to assure the Japanese government that it has entire confidence that in putting an armed force into Siberia it is doing so as an ally of Russia, with no purpose but to save Siberia from the invasion of the armies and intrigues of Germany and with entire willingness to leave the determination of all questions that may affect the permanent fortunes of Siberia to the Council of Peace.

WWT MS (SDR, RG 59, 861.00/1246, DNA).
[1] RLhw.

From Robert Lansing, with Enclosures

My dear Mr. President: Washington March 1, 1918.

I enclose to you, in accordance with your suggestion, an elaboration of Minister Reinsch's plan as to an International Commission relative to the measures which should be taken for the military participation of China in the War.

Faithfully yours,   Robert Lansing.

TLS (B. Long Papers, DLC).

E N C L O S U R E   I

[Washington] February 21, 1918.

To: The Secretary.
Subject: An International Commission to China.
Resumé: A Plan outlined at the request of the President. China entered the war at the invitation of the United States and has adopted the attitude of the United States towards other Powers at war with Germany and Austria. China, therefore, deserves our attention. Her desire to be of assistance is thwarted by Japan. The best method of utilizing her vast resources of men and raw materials is by the organization of an International Commission to investigate and recommend measures.

China should invite Powers each to send a commission. These should unite with a commission appointed by China in an international organization. There should be special experts in politics of the Far East, in military matters and in certain industrial lines.

The situation in Siberia makes urgent the need of preparing China for participation in the war.

T MS (B. Long Papers, DLC).

E N C L O S U R E   I I

Edward Thomas Williams to Robert Lansing

MEMORANDUM.

Dear Mr. Secretary: [Washington] February 21, 1918.

Mr. Reinsch in his telegram of February 11, seven p.m.,[1] suggests the appointment by the governments of the nations at war with Germany and Austria of a joint commission "to assist China in constructive work for the common purpose."

The President has asked that the Department outline a plan for the organization of such a joint commission.

The following is respectfully submitted for consideration.

China entered the war upon the suggestion of the United States and has followed the United States in the attitude adopted towards the anti-Teutonic Allies.

China has vast resources in men and raw materials and desires to make some substantial contribution towards the success of the cause which she has espoused. She is hampered by the constant efforts of the Japanese to stir up internal trouble and otherwise to cripple her and prevent her attaining such a position as would give her a standing in the Peace Conference and a voice in the disposition of her own territories.

The Powers at war with Germany and Austria need China's assistance. That can best be obtained by the organization of an international commission to visit China, investigate conditions and recommend measures to be taken. This would harmonize efforts of the Powers to utilize China's resources and would tend to check any selfish plans of Japan. China should invite certain powers each to send a commission. These should join with a commission appointed by China in an international organization. Each commission should have in its membership certain political and industrial and military experts. It is suggested that there should be in each at least one man familiar with Far Eastern political questions, one military expert, one mining and one agricultural expert and one person of wide experience in business enterprises.

The reasons for the appointment of such persons are briefly that:

1. The relations between China and Japan, between Japan and Russia and between China and the European Powers are so delicate that no chance should be taken of creating friction by offenses unwittingly given. The appointment of some one familiar with political questions in the Far East becomes, therefore, a matter of importance.

2. There is very slight prospect of sending Chinese troops to

Europe but the situation in Siberia is so critical that it may become necessary for China to defend her own territories or to take part in a joint expedition to Siberia. Her military forces should, therefore, be properly equipped and trained for such purposes.

3. The vast mineral resources of China ought to be rendered available to the nations at war with Germany and Austria. Hence the need of a mining expert.

4. There is some doubt as to the possibility of obtaining in China proper any food supplies for use in Europe, but there is no doubt whatever about the possibility of bringing under cultivation great stretches of virgin soil in Manchuria and Mongolia. An agricultural expert would be of service in this connection.

5. Questions of manufacture, transportation and of effective organization and business management in general are sure to arise and suggest the need of some person of wide business experience to give advice upon these matters.

It is suggested that the invitation to form such a joint commission should come from China. If Japan or any other power declines, they can scarcely object to being left out. If they accept they will have to coöperate in some practical scheme. It is not believed that Japan would positively decline to assist in such a plan. With the advice of many experts of different nationalities the chance of China's falling entirely under Japanese domination is lessened and Japan's interests are also sufficiently well guarded.

Chinese troops under foreign officers could do excellent service in Siberia should military operations become necessary there and such activity on China's part would tend to lessen factional strife and unite the country and win a standing before the world that would deserve a place in the Peace Conference.

If the United States should prove to be the only Power accepting the invitation, even then we ought not to draw back. I beg to suggest that it be intimated to the Chinese Minister in an informal way that his Government would do well to issue such invitations.

E.T.W.

TLI (B. Long Papers, DLC).
¹ See P. S. Reinsch to WW, Feb. 12, 1918, n. 2.

From Herbert Clark Hoover

Dear Mr. President: Washington, D. C. *1 March 1918*

You will recollect that I discussed with you the fact that Mr. C A Spreckels was raising difficulties over the signing of the contract for purchases of Cuban sugar. All the other refiners in the United

States have signed this contract. It has been signed by the representatives of the Allied governments and by the representatives of the Cuban government. We have arranged a loan of $100,000,000 to finance the Cuban sugar crop and the American bankers have loaned the money on the faith of this contract. Mr. Spreckels has not, so far, refused to sign the contract, but he has raised one quibble after another and in a patient desire to settle the matter amicably, he has been supplied with sugar since the first of January pro rata with the other refiners.

I enclose herewith copy of his last communication.[1] I would be glad—if you could see your way to do so—if you would now direct me—if he does not at once sign the contract—to give the necessary instructions to the War Trade Board and to the Shipping Board, to cease the issuance of licenses to him on one hand for import, and to cease providing him with transportation on the other. The necessity for this whole arrangement is receiving daily demonstration, as, for instance, owing to the shortage in overseas transportation, sugars have accumulated to large quantities in Cuba and were it not for this arrangement and the finance behind it, the price of sugar would have absolutely collapsed in Cuba before this, the mills would have been shut down,—with all the possibilities of disturbance and dislocation—to say nothing of the total jeopardy of our sugar supplies not only this year but next year as well.

I may mention, for your own information, that the points Mr. Spreckels raises in the latter part of his letter are also quibbles. Every refiner has the right to act as a wholesaler if he so wishes, provided he complies with the regulations as to wholesalers. So far as purchases of sugar in Cuba are concerned, these are in the responsibility of the Cuban government who are managing that end of the work and not upon us.

As to two-cent extra freight rates to his refineries, you will also find enclosed letter of February 5th, addressed to Mr. Spreckels, which shows the dishonesty of this paragraph of his letter, for on this date the matter was settled as he wished.

Yours faithfully,   Herbert Hoover

TLS (WP, DLC).
[1] Hoover's enclosures are missing in all collections.

From Charles Doolittle Walcott

Dear Mr. President: Washington, U. S. A. March 1, 1918.

That typewriter will wear out some day and then it will be of still greater interest. In the future, I hope it may be deposited in the Museum.

We think of you these days, not only as *our* Leader, but the Leader of all of humanity that believes that Right makes Might in the conduct of the affairs of mankind.

With all best wishes,

Sincerely yours,   Charles D Walcott.

TLS (WP, DLC).

From Edward Nash Hurley

My dear Mr. President: Washington March 1, 1918.

I am sure you will be glad to know the progress we are making in the matter of electrically welding ships—let me say that your interest in this subject has stimulated us all.

The preliminary investigations are such as to justify my authorizing that a sample center section of one of our hulls be electrically rivetted together. I am calling on the best brains to aid and feel much encouraged to believe that a great increase in speed and other advantages will follow. You will be interested to know that some of the best welders are young women.

The new system has great merit in that shipments of material can thereby be made direct from the steel mills to the shipyards, eliminating the present railroad journey from the mill to the fabricating shop. Furthermore, as no holes are required in the plates there is an additional saving in time and expense. I am confident that within a few weeks I will be able to submit to you another report that will be most encouraging.

Sincerely yours,   Edward N. Hurley

TLS (WP, DLC).

From David Franklin Houston

Dear Mr. President: Washington March 1, 1918.

I have carefully considered Mr. Hoover's memorandum dealing with the memorial presented to you by Mr. Dwight B. Heard and his associates.[1] I think that, in the main, his observations are sound. They perhaps need slight qualifications. The discussion is based somewhat too largely on the outcome for those cattlemen who make a business of purchasing and feeding cattle and who therefore have to buy large quantities of feedstuffs. It should be noted that the greater part of the live stock of the country is produced under different conditions, that is, on the ranges or on the farms where the grazing furnishes a large part of the feedstuffs or where the farmers owning the live stock produce the feedstuffs. The fact that only about 26 per cent of a normal corn crop leaves the farm will throw light on the situation. Out of a total corn crop, therefore, of 2,700 million bushels, not over 600 millions find their way to nearby or distant markets. It is the judgment of experts of this Department that, for the great body of cattlemen, that is, for those who are not merely "feeders," the conditions during the last year have been very favorable. They are of the opinion that they are, in relation to other farm producers, not only in a fairly satisfactory position but perhaps in a better position than they have been for a long time. It is true that many of the feeders, and especially those who highly finish animals, have suffered hardship. This arises in no small measure from the fact that many of them, anticipating that the quality of the corn crop might not be satisfactory, bought considerable supplies of feedstuffs at high prices.

In reference to the attempt to stabilize the price of hogs by fixing a ratio between hogs and corn, I may say that at the outset I pointed out to Mr. Hoover the difficulties involved, expressing the view that it might prove to be impracticable. However, the effort was made and there is a sort of moral obligation outstanding to corn producers to attempt to keep the value up. Because of a considerable increase in feedstuffs last year and especially of the large volume of soft corn and of the tremendous efforts made by the Department and other agencies to control animal diseases, the number of all classes of live stock, especially of hogs, very considerably increased. It may therefore require unusual action to maintain the price of hogs. This simply emphasizes the difficulty of attempting to regulate prices to farm producers and of singling out any one product for consideration. All farm products are so interrelated that it is impossible to deal with one of them without disturbing every other; and wholesale price fixing of a great variety of products, over a continent like this with its six or seven million producers, is impracticable.

What I have said bears directly on the resolutions of the live stock people, especially on that part where the hardships of the cattlemen are pictured and the apprehensions of the committee as to the future of the industry are revealed. Their statements under resolution No. 5 would convey the impression that, because of adverse conditions, the number of live stock in the country had decreased and that the financial position of the cattlemen was generally unsatisfactory. I have already called your attention to the fact that, notwithstanding all the difficulties last year, the number of live stock increased in 1917 as follows: horses and mules, 453,000; milch cows, 400,000; beef animals, 1,800,000; sheep, 1,300,000 (For the first time in over thirty years there was an increase in the number of sheep); and hogs, 3,800,000.

The thing that seems to have disturbed the cattlemen and farmers generally rather more than anything else is the impression that the Government, either directly or indirectly, has undertaken to restrict or to hold down the prices of farm products to producers. There has been so much talk about the price of wheat that the impression has been conveyed to some minds that a restrictive price instead of a *guaranteed* price to insure the wheat producers against loss has been established. As you know, the sole aim of the guaranteed price is to stimulate production. Wheat was the only commodity in respect to which the Government had power to deal directly with price. Some have interpreted the efforts of the Food Administration under the licensing power and under its informal agreements to control unwholesome speculation and to prevent profiteering in distribution as being an effort to hold down prices to producers. I have not understood that this was the aim of the Food Administration. Mr. Hoover's recent statement[2] that he has had in contemplation in the matter of price handling only wheat, sugar, and hogs, and that he has undertaken rather to furnish safeguards and to stimulate production in reference to wheat and hogs and to prevent speculation in sugar, should go far towards correcting existing misapprehensions. The committee which presented the memorial to you came to see me and expressed the general view that there should be no effort to fix prices to farm producers. Later, they seem to have got the impression that it would be a good thing to have some sort of price fixing, provided the prices for their products could be increased, or provided the prices of feedstuffs could be lowered. I told them that the latter proposition would not appeal with any great force to the five or six million producers of feedstuffs. I think it would be well to continue to make clear just what the attitude and policy of the Government is with reference to price control to farm producers.

I have not received from any of these gentlemen many valuable, constructive suggestions for the betterment of agriculture. However, I am of the opinion that it would be desirable once more to call representative producers into conference. Therefore, Mr. Hoover and I have arranged to constitute an advisory committee made up of representative producers whom we shall invite from time to time to conferences in Washington. We may get some useful suggestions from them and, in any event, we shall, I hope, do much to create a better state of mind. I suppose we shall continue for some time to have "gas attacks" in this field.

Faithfully yours,   D. F. Houston

TLS (WP, DLC).
[1] See WW to H. C. Hoover, Feb. 19, 1918 (second letter of that date), n. 1, and H. C. Hoover to WW, Feb. 21, 1918, n. 2.

² Hoover's statement was printed in the *New York Times*, Feb. 26, 1918, and in the *Official Bulletin*, II (March 5, 1918), 10, 12.

From William Gibbs McAdoo

Dear Mr. President: Washington March 1, 1918.

I have just received your letter of February 28th in which you say that you do not agree with me about the paragraph in the War Industries Board reorganization, referred to in my letter of February 27th.

If what you have in mind is the constitution of a committee which will determine the question of priority of deliveries as between the various governmental departments and agencies but will not determine priorities of transportation, I see no objection, but it will be impossible for me or anyone to run the railroads successfully if an outside committee undertakes to determine priorities of transportation, because that is the power to operate the railroads themselves. The railroads are suffering today from the effort of outside agencies to do this very thing.

I should be very happy, therefore, if you would modify the paragraph in the War Industries Board reorganization to which I have referred, so as to make it clear that after priorities of delivery have been determined upon, priorities of transportation must be dealt with by the Director General of Railroads. As the paragraph now stands I think it is susceptible to the construction that the proposed committee will determine priorities of transportation.

The plan will be workable if this is done.

                    Affectionately yours,   W G McAdoo

TLS (WP, DLC).

Lord Reading to the Foreign Office

                    Washington March 1. 1918

Urgent and Secret No. 859 After careful consideration the U.S.G. have come to the conclusion that they could not join the other Allies in requesting Japan to act as their mandatory in Siberia, as such an arrangement would be in the nature of a Treaty which would have to be submitted to the Senate for approval, & they are not prepared to risk the opening of the whole Japanese question in a public debate at this time. They have however no objection to H.M.G. & the French Govt. requesting the Japanese govt. to act in Siberia and upon learning from us that such a request is being made they will send to the U. S. Ambassador at Tokyo the telegram the text of which is given in my immediately following telegram.

Counsellor of State Dept read this text to French Ambr. this afternoon & will also communicate it to Italian Ambr. tomorrow.

The attitude of the U. S. is no doubt to a great measure dictated by the apprehension of opposition in Congress on the ground of departure from their traditional policy of "no entangling alliances" & of keeping their hands diplomatically free.   R.

Hw telegram (FO 115/2445, pp. 97-98, PRO).

Sir William Wiseman to Sir Eric Drummond

[Washington] March 1, 1918.

Following for FALSTERBO [BALFOUR] from BRUSSA [HOUSE]

No. 64. VERY SECRET.

ADRAMYTI [WILSON] has asked me to thank you for your message.[1] We waited until it arrived before coming to a decision. AD-RAMYTI is glad to find (as he fully anticipated) your view is substantially in accordance with his own. He has replied to the King of Spain's message[2] in a way which will not close the door to further discussion, but rather develop and probe what the Emperor of Austria has in mind. We feel that if this message indicates a genuine desire to meet the just demands of the Allies, it ought not to be rejected; and if, on the other hand, it is merely designed to cover annexationist schemes, it can be best met by demanding that the Central Powers shall apply the principles they profess to hold to concrete cases. If the Germans are not sincere in their expressed desire for peace, is it not of the highest importance to expose this before whole world—the German people themselves if they will listen; certainly before the neutrals and any of those in Allied countries and the United States (particularly in Labour and Socialist circles) who may still believe in German professions? If any further conversations take place the United States will at the same time redouble her efforts to equip her own forces and assist the Allies. ADRAMYTI is well aware that an efficient army is at the present moment the best guarantee against the intrigues of German militarism. He cannot, of course, in any sense commit the Allies by these conversations, but he wishes to assure you that he has no intention of allowing the United States to be committed to any further steps unless the Central Powers are prepared to translate general principles into frank and concrete assurances.

ADRAMYTI will inform the Allied Ambassadors in the general sense of the above. He has considered most carefully and is bearing in mind the very just observations you make in your message.

T telegram (W. Wiseman Papers, CtY).
   [1] That is, A. J. Balfour to EMH, Feb. 27, 1918.
   [2] For the message as sent, see Prince zu Fürstenberg to O. Czernin, March 5, 1918.

An Aide-Mémoire

INFORMATION.   The White House [c. March 1, 1918].

The President has received from the Emperor of Austria a message in which the Emperor expresses agreement with the four principles of peace which were formulated by the President in his address to the Congress on the eleventh of February last and in effect invites a further comparison of views through personal representatives. In reply the President has asked the Emperor for as definite a programme for the application of the four principles as the President himself made public in his address to the Congress on the eighth of January last. The President hopes in this way that he may possibly obtain what has so long been desired a definite programme of the war aims of the Central Powers. He feels at liberty while making this effort to accede to the wish of the Emperor of Austria that this interchange of messages be personal and private.[1]

WWT MS (R. Lansing Papers, NjP).
   [1] Presumably a response to A. J. Balfour to EMH, Feb. 27, 1918, to be read to Lord Reading. A. J. Balfour to EMH, March 7, 1918, which is printed as Enclosure II with EMH to WW, March 8, 1918, might well have been a commentary on Wilson's aide-mémoire.

From the Diary of Josephus Daniels

March Friday 1 1918

The President told us he was tired & when he was tired he first felt it by being unable to find language. Story of Rusty Pat he kicked out of recitation room. "That's me Professor."[1] Said when he lectured he poured everything of himself into the lecture & afterward was so tired he would not recognize his best friend. Had no command of language "I guess I had used up all language I had."

Why not join Japan & go into Russia? B & W[2] said if Japan went in she would never come out & we ought to join No said WW. "We have not ships to send soldiers and besides if we invade Russia will not Germany say we are doing exactly what she is doing. We will lose our moral position.["]

IWW. Should all alien IWW be interned[?] Wilson thought only those who were leaders. Lumbermen in Wash[.] refused the 8 hour[-

day] & to make better conditions for labor, & they enrich the soil on wh. IWW propagates. WBW told to see them & War Dept. & tell them to accept 8 hr law before calling on Gov. to use strong arm.

[1] This was probably the incident referred to in this account: "It was later related that when Wilson first arrived at Princeton he was suspected of effeminacy because he had taught at Bryn Mawr. The students soon tested his mettle by bringing a drunken Irishman into the classroom. Wilson noticed him and inquired, 'Who asked you to come here, sir?' 'The shtoodents invoited me in.' 'Well,' said Wilson, 'I'll invoite you out again.' Taking him by his coat collar, he hustled the intruder downstairs, then returned to the classroom as though nothing had happened. From then on he had the class tamed." Henry W. Bragdon, *Woodrow Wilson: The Academic Years* (Cambridge, Mass., 1967), p. 205.
[2] Burleson and W. B. Wilson.

From William Bauchop Wilson

My dear Mr. President: Washington March 1, 1918.

You will be very much interested in knowing that since returning to the Department today I have received a telegram from Dr. Suzzallo, of the University of Washington,[1] informing me that the lumber operators of Washington and Oregon have decided to put the eight-hour workday into effect today.

I am sending you a copy of the telegram herewith.[2]

Faithfully yours,   W B Wilson

TLS (WP, DLC).
[1] Henry Suzzallo, President of the University of Washington and chairman of the Washington State Council of Defense.
[2] H. Suzzallo to WBW, Feb. 28, 1918, TC telegram (WP, DLC).

To Charles Doolittle Walcott

My dear Doctor Walcott: [The White House] 2 March, 1918

I warmly appreciate your kind references to myself in your letter of yesterday. They cheer me very much.

Cordially and sincerely yours,   Woodrow Wilson

TLS (Letterpress Books, WP, DLC).

To William Bauchop Wilson

My dear Mr. Secretary: [The White House] 2 March, 1918

It certainly is singular that immediately following our conversation in Cabinet the other day the lumbermen of the Northwest should institute the eight-hour day. I am heartily glad and have telegraphed Colonel Disque to the following effect:

"I am sincerely glad to hear of the action of the lumbermen in instituting the eight-hour day. I think that they will find this an act not only of wise policy but of good sense from every point of view."[1]   Cordially and sincerely yours,

CCL (WP, DLC).
[1] WW to B. P. Disque, March 2, 1918, T telegram (Letterpress Books, WP, DLC).

To Edward Nash Hurley

My dear Hurley: [The White House] 2 March, 1918
    I am heartily glad to hear about the progress in electrical welding. I believe it is going to mean a great deal.
    Thank you for reporting.
                    Cordially and faithfully yours,   Woodrow Wilson

TLS (Letterpress Books, WP, DLC).

From Frank Lyon Polk

My dear Mr. President: Washington March 2, 1918.
    The enclosed despatch from Mr. Wilson, at Berne, has just arrived, enclosing the report of Professor Herron's conversation, and I hasten to send them on to you.[1] While Mr. Wilson's telegrams gave the substance of these conversations, I assume you will be interested in the more detailed report.
                    Yours faithfully,   Frank L. Polk

TLS (WP, DLC).
[1] H. R. Wilson to RL, Feb. 4, 1918, TLS (WP, DLC), enclosing H. R. Wilson to RL, No. 2321, Feb. 4, 1918, TLS (WP, DLC), and G. D. Herron, memorandum of conversation with H. Lammasch, Feb. 3, 1918, T MS (WP, DLC).

A Memorandum by William Christian Bullitt[1]

Memorandum for Mr. Polk.   Washington March 2, 1918.
Subject: Our Policy in regard to Japan's proposed invasion of Siberia.
Substance: The moral position upon which our whole participation in the war is based will be irretrievably compromised unless we protest publicly against Japan's invasion of Siberia.
    Japan pretends that she must at once invade Siberia in order to

[1] At the top of the page: "Dear Mr President: Mr House asked me last night to send you this Faithfully yours Gordon Auchincloss"

prevent the supplies which are at Vladivostok and other points from falling into the hands of the Germans. The Germans are at present 2,550 miles away from Vladivostok. The workingmen and women of Russia are still maintaining a front against the German advance. Japan's plaint that the Germans are about to establish themselves in eastern Siberia is simply dust for the eyes of the ignorant.

We are about to assent tacitly to Japan's invasion of Siberia. Why? Because we fear that if we oppose Japan, she will switch to the side of Germany. We believe that Japan will take this step because of her desire to annex eastern Siberia, which she covets so intensely that if she can not obtain it with the consent of the Allies she will take it with the assistance of Germany.

Our fear that Japan may join Germany is, therefore, admission that desire to annex eastern Siberia is at the bottom of Japan's proposed invasion. We know that Japan is an autocratic imperialistic state in which the forces of liberalism and decency are far weaker than even in Germany. We now propose to assent to an invasion of Siberia by this autocracy. It is clear that if a "new world order" is to be created at the end of this war Japan must be cast out of Siberia. In assenting to Japan's invasion we are, therefore, permitting without protest the creation of another great obstacle to a more decent international order. We shall have to throw Japan out of Siberia some day unless we are willing to compromise on all the principles for which we are asking our soldiers to die.

Why not publicly oppose Japan now? We would not have the support of the Governments of France and England in our action. But we would have the support of the peoples of France and England. We would have the support of the Liberals and the new and mighty Labor Party in England. We would have the support of the Unified Socialists in France. And these men represent the great mass of Englishmen and Frenchmen. From their ranks will be drawn the governments of France and England of to-morrow. The MANCHESTER GUARDIAN, the ablest organ of British liberalism, wrote yesterday:

"Some of the French newspapers and now General Foch (the noted French strategist) seem to be confident that Japan should and will occupy Vladivostok, Harbin and generally as much of Russian far eastern territory as she can conveniently lay hands on. Such action is represented as a high service to the allied cause. It is suggested that the Germans might pass through Russia, absorb Siberia and place themselves on the Pacific as a menace to Japan.

"Such military operations would be most fantastic. Even if there were any substance in the hypothesis Japan would not counter such a German move by settling down in Vladivostok and Harbin, which still would leave practically the whole of European and Asiatic Russia exposed. If Japan should decide to take Vladivostok, Harbin and Russia's territory in the extreme east it will not be to please the French or to help the Allies; it will be because Japan has long desired to possess those places and thinks that Russia's adversity is her opportunity.

"In France this may be regarded as just punishment for the repudiation by the Bolsheviki of the national debt and for the separate peace made with Germany, but if Japan does to Russia's eastern frontier even more cynically what Germany is doing to Russia's western frontier, how can the Allies approve it without losing the claim to a higher standard of principles than their enemies?

"To encourage or not to repudiate any such action on the part of Japan would be a gross error and would be a flat contradiction of the whole policy of President Wilson. Is it not time that President Wilson took the diplomacy of the war effectively in hand? Speeches will not do it."

President Wilson should answer that call.

What course of action would the Japanese pursue if the President should publicly declare against any invasion of Russia. Assume the worst. Japan might go in, regardless of the President's words, supported by the Governments of France and England. But the Governments of France and England would be likely to fall on the issue and opponents of the Japanese invasion of Siberia would be likely to come into power. Again assume the worst. The Japanese Government might then begin to dicker with the German Government and to educate public opinion for a switch to alliance with Germany. Japan might join her sister imperialism,—Prussia. But then the fight would be the cleanest thing in the world. The democracies of America, Russia, England and France would be arrayed against the imperialistic autocracies of Germany and Japan. And in that fight, not a few persons in Germany and Austria-Hungary would be on our side. That fight would, indeed, be for a new world order. We should have held to our faith, and win or lose we should face history with a clean, uncompromising record. And I believe that we should win.

What is the alternative? If we stand aside while Japan invades Siberia with the assent of the Governments of England and France, the President's moral position as leader of the common people of the world will be fatally compromised. Take the first concrete case which he will have to meet. If the United States assents to the Imperial Japanese army invading territory controlled by the Bolsheviki, for the ostensible purpose of restoring order, the United States cannot object to the Imperial German army invading territory controlled by the Bolsheviki for the ostensible purpose of restoring order. What shall we reply to Hertling? We CAN act one way in one case and another way in the other. But our excellent legal distinctions will not carry conviction to the mind of the common man in England and France or in Germany and Austria-Hungary.

In Russia to-day there are the rudiments of a government of the people, by the people and for the people. The latest news indicates that the Bolsheviki are maintaining their power throughout Russia. Unless the Soviet Government is overthrown by enemy imperialists it will continue to control Russia. Are we going to make the world safe for this Russian democracy by allowing the Allies to place Terauchi[2] in Irkutsk, while Ludendorff establishes himself in Petrograd?

The President must oppose invasion of Siberia by Japan in the name of democracy and liberalism. He must act, or his position as moral leader of the liberals of the world will be lost. We cannot stand aside and maintain our moral integrity. We cannot wash our hands of this matter. Unless we oppose, we assent. Pontius Pilate washed his hands. The world has never forgiven him.

Respectfully submitted: William C. Bullitt

TS MS (WP, DLC).
[2] Count Masatake Terauchi, Prime Minister of Japan.

A Memorandum by Breckinridge Long

[Washington] March 2, 1918.

MEMORANDUM OF CONVERSATION HAD WITH MR. JOHN SOOKINE.

Mr. Sookine, formerly Secretary at the Russian Embassy, called this afternoon. He said that he had come at the urgent request of his Ambassador who could not come himself because [he] had gone to New York to lay the same matter before Colonel House.

He opposed the sole intervention by Japan in Siberia on the grounds,

First, that it would alienate the people of Siberia and Russia in general, and the population of the districts which were occupied by Japanese in particular, from the Allied cause;

Second, that the distrust which the people of Russia felt for Japan was greater than the antipathy which they had towards Germany.

He stated that it would facilitate the German economic and political control of Russia,

(a) By inducing the people to accept German organization and control rather than Japanese;

(b) By offering an argument for Germany to use against the allied cause and Japan by holding up the spectre of Japanese control of Siberia and, possibly, Russia.

He advocated a military political expedition into Russia to be composed of two Japanese armed corps and such fragmentary military units as the United States, France and England could send, even if the British contingent was composed of Indian troops and the French contingent composed of such soldiers as may now be in Chochin, China. He advocated a political head of this expedition to be a committee of the Allies, or an American diplomatic representative, especially designated who, or which,[1] would be in control of the expedition.

He argued that, while the better element of the Russian people were still opposed to Germany, he feared that Germany would diplomatically proceed in her entrance into Russia by restoring order and by bringing about organization, upon which she would predicate the argument that she desired peace, that she wanted co-operation with Russia, that she desired peaceful economic and industrial intercourse and development and could say that the only objection and obstacle to peace was the ambition of the military powers opposing Germany on the western front. He said that he feared that the Russian people might be seduced into accepting the situation and that he believed, from his interpretation of Hertling's most recent speech, that that would be the German policy.

He argued that Germany's policy in Russia would be not only military but a diplomatic endeavor to influence and control the social, economic and industrial elements of the country. He argued that the way to off-set and counter-act the success of this movement would be to establish a political base as close to the eastern side of the Ural Mountains as possible and to conduct from such a base, supported by the military expedition, a campaign against the German campaign of diplomacy and propaganda.

He realized the physical difficulties preventing any military co-operation on the part of the United States and fully realized the danger consequent to the arming, releasing and organizing of the German and Austrian prisoners near Irkutsk and in Trans-Baikal, particularly with regard to destroying the railroad, or sections of the railroad, or bridges. There is one bridge right near the border of Manchuria which is one of the longest and highest bridges in the world and which, if destroyed, would break completely the line of communication and which it would take two years to rebuild.

The impression which I received from him was that he and Mr. Bakmetieff feared the intervention of Japan as the mandatory of the Allies but were slowly coming to realize the imminence and the necessity for that particular kind of intervention but that they were endeavoring to do everything in their power to subordinate Japan to the actual supervision and control of the Allies while Japan should be in Siberia. Irrespective of this interpretation, there is considerable force to his argument and a great deal of merit in the suggestion that a political base be established in western Siberia or in eastern Russia to combat, as far as possible, the diplomatic and commercial intrigues and the propaganda of Germany. Of course, this political base would have to be supported by a large military force, much greater than two army corps, which should stretch along, protect, guard and hold the only line of communications to the eastward, which is the Trans-Siberia Railroad.

Breckinridge Long

TS MS (SDR, RG 59, 861.00/1246, DNA).
  ¹ Wilson transposed this phrase to read: "which, or who."

A Memorandum by Franklin Knight Lane

March 2 [1918].

Yesterday, at Cabinet meeting, we had the first real talk on the war in weeks, yes, in months! Burleson brought up the matter of Russia, . . . Would we support Japan in taking Siberia, or even Vladivostock? Should we join Japan actively—in force?

The President said "No," for the very practical reason that we had no ships. We had difficulty in providing for our men in France and for our Allies, (the President never uses this word, saying that we are not "allies"). How hopeless it would be to carry everything seven or eight thousand miles—not only men and munitions, but food!—for Japan has none to spare, and none we could eat. Her men feed on rice and smoked fish, and she raises nothing we would want. Nor could the country support us. So there was an end of talking of an American force in Siberia! Yes, we were needed—perhaps as a guarantee of good faith on Japan's part that she would not go too far, nor stay too long. But we would not do it. And besides, Russia would not like it, therefore we must keep hands off and let Japan take the blame and the responsibility.

The question is not simple, for Russia will say that we threw her to Japan, and possibly she would rush into Germany's arms as the lesser of evils. My single word of caution was to so act that Russia, when she "came back," should not hate us, for there was our new land for development—Siberia—and we should have front place at that table, if we did not let our fears and our hatred and our contempt get away with us now.

Printed in Anne W. Lane and Louise H. Wall, eds., *The Letters of Franklin K. Lane, Personal and Political* (Boston and New York, 1922), pp. 266-67.

From Edward Mandell House, with Enclosure

Dear Governor: New York. March 3, 1918.

The enclosed letter was prepared by Justice Brandeis and Rabbi Wise for your information although addressed to me.

I hope you may find it possible to permit them to send their medical unit to Palestine for they seem so earnest in their desire to do so.

If you do not think it advisable to let them go to Palestine, they would be fairly content if they might be permitted to have passports which would take them to Egypt. Surely there could be no objections to that.

If you will let the State Department know your decision in response to Lansing's letter about the matter,[1] it will answer all purposes without replying to this.

Affectionately yours,   E. M. House

TLS (WP, DLC).
[1] That is, RL to WW, Feb. 28, 1918.

E N C L O S U R E

Stephen Samuel Wise and Jacob de Haas to Edward Mandell House

My dear Col. House: New York March 2, 1918.

In furtherance of our telephonic conversations of yesterday, I beg to lay before you the following facts in connection with our request for passports to enable our representatives to join the Weitzman Commission to Palestine and for recognition of our Medical Unit to render service in that country:

Our Organization has been invited, with the approval of the British Government, to appoint representatives who are to co-operate with Dr. Weitzman and his colleagues in tasks with which you are fully cognizant, and the purposes of the Commission are compatible with the aims and purposes of our Government.

The dispatching of a Medical Unit to Palestine, which has the sanction of the British Government, is a continuation and enlargement of work begun prior to the war and continued throughout the war through the generous facilities placed at our disposal in various ways by the Government. The service to be rendered is of a character similar to that performed by the Red Cross.

Passports for the Members of the Commission. We beg to suggest that no political significance attaches to the issuance of a passport, which merely serves to identify the holder as an American citizen entitled to all the priveleges and immunities of such citizenship.

During this war two classes of persons have been denied passports: (a) those having no business in the countries to which they desire to be admitted and who would therefore require shipping facilities, which, because of the tonnage shortage, could be used to better advantage, or (b) persons who may be guilty of acts hostile to this country or its associates in the war.

The approval and sanction by the British Government of co-operation on the part of American citizens in the Weitzman Commission must necessarily exclude such citizens from both of these classes, and entitles them to the normal rights incident to such citizenship.

The Zionist Medical Unit. With respect to the request for recognition of the Zionist Medical Unit there is a seeming additional difficulty.

Under the Geneva Convention every medical unit, to be entitled to protection from the enemy, must be officially designated by the belligerent and the enemy must be notified by the Government that the unit is designated as a medical unit. As long as the Government is satisfied that the purpose of the unit is to afford aid to the wounded, sick and needy, the personnel of that unit are entitled to be respected as such and to be exempt from capture.

The Government in recognizing the Zionist Medical Unit is merely continuing along other lines the attitude it adopted in affording the Zionist Organization facilities for distributing money, drugs and food for the relief of the people of Palestine.

All that is sanctioned by the Government granting a Commission to the Unit and notifying the enemy according to the Geneva Convention is the relief to be afforded. If the Government is satisfied that the Zionist Organization honestly intends to afford relief and that its action will be beneficial, the Commission (which affords only exemption from capture, as is the case with the Red Cross and other units) should issue.

Trusting that this will meet with your agreement, I am

Yours very truly,   Stephen S. Wise

Jacob de Haas.

TLS (WP, DLC).

Two Letters from Edward Mandell House

Dear Governor: New York. March 3, 1918.

Professor W. E. Dodd of the Chicago University desires to be considered for a vacancy on the Federal Trade Commission. I do not know how well fitted he is for it but if you wish I will look him over with that in mind.

He speaks of himself as a "student of our economic and social history of twenty years standing." He has written most appreciatively of you in some of his recent books.[1]

Senator Root is coming to see me this afternoon to talk, I take it, about Russia. This Siberian-Japanese question is of such serious import that it might have a good effect throughout republican circles if you would ask Root to come to Washington to see you. McAdoo suggests this, giving as his reason that it would produce a find [fine] effect among republicans in Congress.

If you had sent a democrat at the head of the Russian Mission there would probably have been a great outcry by now concerning their failure to bring about better results.

Affectionately yours,   E. M. House

[1] William E. Dodd, *The Social and Economic Background of Woodrow Wilson* (Chicago, 1917).

Dear Governor: New York. March 3, 1918.

Senator Root has just left. He agrees with you and with me as to the danger of the proposed Japanese intervention in Siberia. He thinks that even if Japan should announce her purpose to retire when the war was over, or at the mandate of the peace conference, the racial dislike which the Russians have for the Japanese, would throw Russia into the arms of Germany.

The Russian Ambassador, whom I saw yesterday, is of a like opinion.

We are treading upon exceedingly delicate and dangerous ground, and are likely to lose that fine moral position you have given the Entente cause. The whole structure which you have built up so carefully may be destroyed over night, and our position will be no better than that of the Germans.

I cannot understand the fatuous determination of the British and French to urge the Japanese to take such a step. Leaving out the loss of moral advantage, it is doubtful whether there will be any material gain.

The French have come to hate the Russians and do not care what ill fate befalls them and for reasons which are obvious. The

English that are in power have such an intense hatred for Germany that they have lost their perspective.

Affectionately yours,   E. M. House

TLS (WP, DLC).

From the Diary of Colonel House

March 3, 1918.

Senator Root was my most interesting caller. He came with Bertron, who was also a member of the Mission to Russia, to discuss the Japanese-Siberian situation. Root agrees with the Russian Ambassador that it is a mistake for the Japanese to go in, giving the same reason as Bakhmateff gave yesterday, and to which I fully agreed.

The President and I discussed this backward and forward during the last week and, as a matter of fact, we have discussed it intermittently since my return from Europe. While I was in Europe, as the diary will show, it was almost a daily topic between the British, French and myself. I have never changed my mind as to the inadvisability of Japanese intervention, and my letter to the President of today, which is a part of the record, will explain more fully my position.

Miss Beatty,[1] who has just returned from Russia, was another interesting caller, and so was Richard Washburn Child who submitted an article he has written for Collier's. He, too, wanted to discuss and give his views on the proposed Japanese intervention. He differs from the rest of us in as much as he believes with certain guarantees it is a proper and desirable action.

[1] Bessie Beatty, formerly of the editorial staff of the San Francisco *Bulletin*, who had been in Russia for eight months.

A News Report

[March 4, 1918]

PRESIDENT SPEAKS AT PLAY'S PREMIERE

Washington, March 4.—President Wilson attended the premiere at the New National Theatre tonight of a new war play entitled "Friendly Enemies," presented with Louis Mann and Sam Bernard as joint stars in the main roles. Between the second and third acts the President was called upon by Louis Mann from the footlights for a speech, and responded with a few words of appreciation complimentary both of the play and the players. It was the first time within the memory of the oldest first-nighter that a President had made a speech from a stage box between the acts of a play.

Both Bernard and Mann had been called upon for speeches, and toward the end of what he had to say Mr. Mann mentioned that the President was present. Walking toward the stage box he expressed a desire that the President say something. The remarks of the actor were so worded that it would have been difficult for the President not to respond, and he did so very graciously.

"Friendly Enemies," written by Samuel Shipman and Aaron Hoffman, and staged by Robert Milton, is an American comedy drama, the story of which is built around the character of two Americans of German descent, one of whom, Henry Block, played by Bernard, is very patriotic, but the other, Karl Pfeifer, played by Louis Mann, is distinctly pro-German in his views, until news comes telling of the loss of his son, who had volunteered for service in the army, when an American transport was reported torpedoed. This brings out the Americanism of Karl Pfeifer. After that the son turns out not to have been lost and the play ends happily.

In the company supporting Mann and Bernard are Mme. Mathilde Cottrelly, Miss Regina Wallace, Eugene Ward, Richard Barbee, and Natalie Manning.

Printed in the *New York Times*, March 5, 1918.

To Bernard Mannes Baruch

My dear Mr. Baruch: The White House 4 March, 1918

I am writing to ask if you will not accept appointment as Chairman of the War Industries Board, and I am going to take the liberty at the same time of outlining the functions, the constitution and action of the Board as I think they should now be established.

The functions of the Board should be:

(1) The creation of new facilities and the disclosing, if necessary, the opening up, of new or additional sources of supply;

(2) The conversion of existing facilities, where necessary, to new uses;

(3) The studious conservation of resources and facilities by scientific, commercial, and industrial economies;

(4) Advice to the several purchasing agencies of the Government with regard to the prices to be paid;

(5) The determination, wherever necessary, of priorities of production and of delivery and of the proportions of any given article to be made immediately accessible to the several purchasing agen-

cies when the supply of that article is insufficient, either temporarily or permanently;

(6) The making of purchases for the Allies.

The Board should be constituted as at present and should retain, so far as necessary and so far as consistent with the character and purposes of the reorganization, its present advisory agencies; but the ultimate decision of all questions, except the determination of prices, should rest always with the Chairman, the other members acting in a cooperative and advisory capacity. The further organization of advice I will indicate below.

In the determination of priorities of production, when it is not possible to have the full supply of any article that is needed produced at once, the chairman should be assisted, and so far as practicable guided, by the present priorities organization or its equivalent.

In the determination of priorities of delivery, when they must be determined, he should be assisted when necessary, in addition to the present advisory priorities organization, by the advice and cooperation of a committee constituted for the purpose and consisting of official representatives of the Food Administration, the Fuel Administration, the Railway Administration, the Shipping Board, and the War Trade Board, in order that when a priority of delivery has been determined there may be common, consistent, and concerted action to carry it into effect.

In the determination of prices the chairman should be governed by the advice of a committee consisting, besides himself, of the members of the Board immediately charged with the study of raw materials and of manufactured products, of the labor member of the Board, of the chairman of the Federal Trade Commission, the chairman of the Tariff Commission, and the Fuel Administrator.

The chairman should be constantly and systematically informed of all contracts, purchases, and deliveries, in order that he may have always before him a schematized analysis of the progress of business in the several supply divisions of the Government in all Departments.

The duties of the chairman are:

(1) To act for the joint and several benefit of all the supply departments of the Government;

(2) To let alone what is being successfully done and interfere as little as possible with the present normal processes of purchase and delivery in the several Departments;

(3) To guide and assist wherever the need for guidance or assistance may be revealed: for example, in the allocation of contracts, in obtaining access to materials in any way preempted, or in the disclosure of sources of supply;

(4) To determine what is to be done when there is any competitive or other conflict of interest between Departments in the matter of supplies: for example, when there is not a sufficient immediate supply for all and there must be a decision as to priority of need or delivery, or when there is competition for the same source of manufacture or supply, or when contracts have not been placed in such a way as to get advantage of the full productive capacity of the country;

(5) To see that contracts and deliveries are followed up where such assistance as is indicated under (3) and (4) above has proved to be necessary.

(6) To anticipate the prospective needs of the several supply departments of the Government and their feasible adjustment to the industry of the country as far in advance as possible, in order that as definite an outlook and opportunity for planning as possible may be afforded the business men of the country.

In brief, he should act as the general eye of all supply departments in the field of industry.

Cordially and sincerely yours,   Woodrow Wilson[1]

TLS (B. M. Baruch Papers, NjP).
[1] There is a WWT draft outline of this letter in WP, DLC.

To David Franklin Houston

My dear Mr. Secretary: The White House 4 March, 1918

I am taking the liberty of sending you a letter which I have just addressed to Mr. Bernard Baruch.

I am sending you the letter for your information not only, but in order to afford myself the opportunity of asking if you will not be kind enough, whenever the occasion arises, to afford the War Industries Board the fullest possible cooperation of your department.

I have the lively hope that this reorganization of the War Industries Board will add very considerably to the speed and efficiency of our action in the matter of war supplies.

Cordially and sincerely yours,   Woodrow Wilson[1]

TLS (D. F. Houston Papers, NjP).
[1] Wilson sent the same letter, *mutatis mutandis*, to the other members of his cabinet; to the chairmen of the Federal Trade Commission, of the War Trade Board, and of the United States Shipping Board; to the Food Administrator; to the Fuel Administrator; and to the Director General of Railroads. These letters were sent, on or about March 4, 1918, as WW to RL, WW to JD, WW to FKL, WW to WCR, WW to WBW, WW to W. J. Harris, and WW to V. C. McCormick, all CCL (Letterpress Books, WP, DLC); as WW to WGM (as Secretary of the Treasury), WW to WGM (as Director General of Railroads), and WW to ASB, all TLS (WP, DLC); as WW to NDB, TLS (N. D. Baker Papers, DLC); as WW to TWG, TLS (T. W. Gregory Papers, DLC); WW to H. C. Hoover, TLS (H. Hoover Papers, HPL); WW to E. N. Hurley, TLS (E. N. Hurley Papers, InNd); and WW to H. A. Garfield, TLS (H. A. Garfield Papers, DLC).

To Robert Somers Brookings

My dear Mr. Brookings: [The White House, March 4, 1918]

It has seemed best (I think to all of us) that we should follow out to a logical conclusion the gradual, practical development which has been taking place in the whole matter of securing supplies for the Government, and I have tried in the letter of which I am taking the liberty of enclosing you a copy to put the logical outcome in as concrete terms as possible with regard to the War Industries Board.

I am writing this letter to express my very warm appreciation of the services you have rendered as a member of the War Industries Board, and to express, also, the hope, which I do with entire confidence, that you will be so generous as to cooperate to the fullest extent in the new administration. I have followed your own particular course in the Board with a great deal of admiration and very genuine appreciation and am constantly glad that we should have your disinterested service and advice.

Cordially and sincerely yours,   [Woodrow Wilson]

CCL (Letterpress Books, WP, DLC).

To Hugh Frayne

Mr dear Mr. Frayne: [The White House, March 4, 1918]

It has seemed best (I think to all of us) that we should follow out to a logical conclusion the gradual, practical development which has been taking place in the whole matter of securing supplies for the Government, and I have tried in the letter of which I am taking the liberty of enclosing you a copy to put the logical outcome in as concrete terms as possible with regard to the War Industries Board.

I am writing this letter to express my very warm appreciation of the services you have rendered as a member of the War Industries Board, and to express, also, the hope, which I do with entire confidence, that you will be so generous as to cooperate to the fullest extent in the new administration.

Cordially and sincerely yours,   [Woodrow Wilson][1]

CCL (Letterpress Books, WP, DLC).
[1] Wilson sent this letter, *mutatis mutandis*, on March 4, 1918, to F. F. Fletcher and P. E. Pierce, both TLS (Letterpress Books, WP, DLC).

To Robert Scott Lovett

My dear Judge: [The White House, March 4, 1918]

You were generous and gracious enough to say that you would wait for an intimation from me as to when you were free to act upon your desire to return to the active administrative duties of your road, and I am writing now to say that inasmuch as it is necessary to effect an immediate reconsideration of the functions and constitution of the War Industries Board, I want you to know just what is in contemplation beforehand and to choose the time of your retirement as you think best, because I know that the last thing you would desire would be to seem to be retiring because of a reorganization. I send you a copy of a letter I have just written to Mr. Bernard M. Baruch.

Under the present administration of the railroads, I think that your judgment will be what mine is, that the priorities member of the Board should hereafter be an official representative of the Railway Administration, and I would be very much obliged if you would be kind enough to take the matter up with Mr. McAdoo and give me the benefit of your joint advice as to who your successor should be.

With the highest respect and the most grateful acknowledgment of your kindness and service.

Cordially and sincerely yours,   [Woodrow Wilson]

CCL (Letterpress Books, WP, DLC).

To William Gibbs McAdoo

My dear Mac: [The White House, March 4, 1918]

Judge Lovett, as you know, is about to retire from the War Industries Board, and I have given him his own choice of time so that he may not seem to be retiring because of the reconstitution of the Board. I think that it would be well to constitute the priorities member of the Board (Judge Lovett's successor) an official representative of the Railway Administration. I have asked Judge Lovett to consult with you as to who his successor should be, and I would like very much a nomination from you.

Always   Affectionately yours,   [Woodrow Wilson]

CCL (Letterpress Books, WP, DLC).

To Benedict Crowell

My dear Mr. Secretary:　　　[The White House] 4 March, 1918

I am very much distressed that the sentence quoted in the enclosed telegram should have been contained in the draft instructions to the medical advisory boards.[1] They, of course, represent a view absolutely contrary to that of the administration and express a prejudice which ought never to have been expressed or entertained. In all of this I am sure you will agree with me, and I hope that you will be kind enough to make an immediate excision of these sentences and instruct the medical advisory boards accordingly, letting it be known, if you will be kind enough, to the senders of the enclosed telegrams that you have done so.[2]

I am making this request with all the greater confidence because I am sure you will sympathize with my point of view in the matter.

Cordially and sincerely yours,　　[Woodrow Wilson]

CCL (WP, DLC).

[1] This telegram, from Louis Marshall of New York, president of the American Jewish Committee, called Wilson's attention to the following statement in the manual of instructions for medical advisory boards: "The foreign born, and especially Jews, are more apt to malinger than the native born." Marshall's telegram is missing, but B. Crowell to WW, March 4, 1918, TLS (WP, DLC), and its enclosures convey the content of Marshall's telegram.

[2] Crowell's letter to Wilson, just cited, enclosed a copy of new instructions to medical advisory boards. The sentence concerning the foreign born had been excised.

To Edward Beale McLean

My dear Mr. McLean:　　　[The White House] 4 March, 1918

You have kindly given me leave to make suggestions as to any way in which the Post can help in the conduct of the war,[1] and I am, therefore, going to take the liberty of saying to you that I am almost daily distressed by the articles of Albert W. Fox[2] appearing in the Post. This morning, for example, there is an article headed, "The President to Speak," which, like many of his other articles, is absolutely without foundation.[3] Mr. Fox is apparently in the habit of formulating policies for me at his pleasure, and this is so serious in the effect it might have even upon the international policy of the Government that it might become necessary, if Mr. Fox's articles of this sort were continued, for me to make a public statement that they were without authority and that the man was absolutely inventing what he chose to put into my mind and to represent as my purpose. I, of course, would be extremely loath to do this because of the injury it might do the paper and because I do not believe that Mr. Fox's articles are consistent with your own attitude and intention.

Cordially and sincerely yours,   [Woodrow Wilson]

CCL (WP, DLC).
   [1] See WW to E. B. McLean, July 12, 1917, and E. B. McLean to WW, July 14, 1917, Vol. 43.
   [2] Albert Whiting Fox had been a reporter for the *New York Herald* in Washington, Berlin, and London from 1907 to 1915 and came to the *Washington Post* in 1916.
   [3] This article began as follows: "With President Wilson believed to be ready to address Congress on the international situation in general, and the Russian situation in particular, there are plain intimations that this next utterance will definitely dissipate the false impressions which pacifists and peace-by-compromise advocates have given of the President's last message. A ringing American message, true to the ideals for which the nation is now shedding its blood and giving its treasure, is expected."
   Fox also stated that there was "undoubtedly a growing feeling of disapproval over the President's speech of February 11, due chiefly to the fact that pacifists and peace-by-bargain supporters have seized upon it here and abroad for a renewal of their activities." In conclusion, Fox found "a fervent hope now in many quarters" that the influence of the "peace-parleying advocates" would not rise again, at least not while Americans were dying daily on the battlefields. These advocates had had their innings, he wrote, and henceforth the nation under Wilson's leadership was to concentrate on the war. *Washington Post*, March 4, 1918.

To Kate Trubee Davison[1]

My dear Mrs. Davison: [The White House] 4 March, 1918

Allow me to acknowledge the receipt of your letter of March first.[2]

It does, I admit, go very much against one's heart to advise that no mourning be worn for those whose lives are lost in the war, and yet I agree with you that it is a counsel of wisdom that it should not be, because, as you say, it would produce in the long run a universal aspect of gloom which would be quite out of keeping with the fine spirit in which the courageous mothers and fathers of the country have given their sons to the great cause.

I find myself sympathizing with the suggestion that some badge be adopted, and the color you suggest, royal purple, with some insignia upon it, seems to me eminently appropriate, but I do not think that it would be wise to make an official suggestion about it. It occurs to me that if some patriotic body like the Daughters of the American Revolution were to make this public suggestion and take some active steps to have the suggestion made widespread, it would accomplish the purpose and accomplish it much better by making the whole thing spontaneous and unofficial.

I wonder how this suggestion commends itself to you?

With much respect,

Cordially and sincerely yours,   Woodrow Wilson

TLS (Letterpress Books, WP, DLC).
   [1] Mrs. Henry Pomeroy Davison.
   [2] Kate T. Davison to WW, March, 1, 1918, ALS (WP, DLC).

From Edward Beale McLean

My dear Mr. President: Washington D. C. March 4th, 1918.

I have just received your letter, and have taken up the subject with Mr. A. W. Fox.

I regret that anything should have appeared which is a cause of annoyance to you, and I assure you that I shall take pains to see there is no reoccurrence of such utterances.

Very truly yours,   Edward McLean

TLS (WP, DLC).

From Bernard Mannes Baruch

My dear Mr. President: Washington March 4, 1918.

It will give me great pleasure to accept the appointment you have offered me as Chairman of the War Industries Board. It is my every desire to do whatever is in my power to assist in the prosecution of the war.   Very sincerely yours,   Bernard M Baruch

TLS (WP, DLC).

From Breckinridge Long, with Enclosure

My dear Mr. President: Washington March 4, 1918.

May I submit to you a memorandum on Russia and Siberia— containing a thought as to what the Government might do?

As some of the matters touched upon are outside the strict field of activity of the State Department, I take the liberty to divert it from the natural course and submit it directly to you.

Please do not bother to acknowledge it.

Your obedient servant,   Breckinridge Long

TLS (WP, DLC).

E N C L O S U R E

MEMORANDUM

To drain Germany of her gold supply will bring economic ruin to Germany and detract from the effectiveness of her influence in the territory now being occupied by her and will nullify any advantage she may now have.

Germany will obtain supplies in Russia. That we cannot prevent.

The extent to which she will be able to obtain them depends upon the extent to which the people of Russia will be sympathetic and friendly to Germany and upon the efficiency of the economic and industrial organization which she will set up throughout the territory over which she will exert an influence.

While we cannot prevent Germany obtaining supplies in Russia we can try to arrange that she pays gold for what she does get. This can only be attempted through a political base. The place to establish such a base would be in European Russia or as near the eastern side of the Ural Mountains as possible.

There will be portions of the population of Russia which will not be reconciled to German control nor easily amenable to German influence. These peoples, if left entirely to the exploitation of Germany, will sooner or later become pacified by and subjected to German influences, whereas, if there was a political base, a well directed anti-German activity, a source of encouragement and aid to the dissatisfied portions of the population, subjection of these peoples by Germany would be more difficult and longer delayed. A political base could be made a nucleus around which would gather and to which would naturally gravitate individuals and factions which would develop strong antagonism to Germany throughout a large part of Russia.

This would not, in itself, reach Germany's gold supply, but through such a base there could be obtained information which might lead to the gold supply, and from it plans could be executed which might be most effective in that direction.

Germany's gold supply is accessible only through Siberia and Russia, so that if the United States is to be a party to the economic battle that will reach that supply the United States must co-operate with other Governments to that end. The two other Governments which can best participate and with which it will be necessary to co-operate, are those of Japan and China.

In order to maintain a political base in the neighborhood of the Ural Mountains it would be necessary to rely upon Japan (or Japan and China) to protect and hold the Trans-Siberian Railroad with a large military force.

The American Ambassador, having left Petrograd,[1] could be halted at a point in western Siberia and await the advancement to that point of the Japanese Military Expedition. He would be the first on the ground and would become the head of the whole undertaking. His diplomatic and economic staffs could be later augmented by appropriate specialists.

Russia and Siberia now offer a field for economic and industrial development. If left to Germany, without competition, it will be entirely filled by Germany. Japan and America have furnished much to Russia in the past and should fight Germany's effort to subjugate Russia economically. China, too, can import much to Russia and can join with America and Japan, not necessarily in military or diplomatic matters, but in an economic war.

This co-operation would be the proper subject of conferences between the United States, Japan and China. Tokyo would be the best place. A special Mission from this Government, composed of diplomatic, military, naval, manufacturing and financial specialists would be the most effective. It might be suggested to China to send a similar Mission to Tokyo. Such a conference between the three most interested powers, at the instigation of the United States, would enable this Government to take in the Orient the same leading and co-ordinating part it has taken in Europe, would extend over Asia a large influence and would increase the prestige of the United States.

This seems to be the psychological time for such a Mission. It would not only return the Japanese visit, which Japan expects and has several times inquired about, but it would permit us to assume the intellectual leadership in Asia.

The Mission could go so equipped as to permit certain members of it to go into Siberia as the Economic Staff of the American Ambassador who would be awaiting it near the Ural Mountains.

The tangible result of the visit to Tokyo would be the economic commission into Siberia, with which would co-operate similar bodies from Japan and China.

A possible result would be, through the agency of the economic commission and the American Ambassador, the drainage of gold from Germany.

A certain result of the visit would be the co-ordination of the three great countries geographically and commercially able to undertake such an enterprise.

Last, but far from least, Japan would be so identified with the aims, objects, spirit and work of the powers at war with Germany that she could not become estranged from the countries who are fighting Germany. She would be the military power in Siberia— but she would be inextricably identified with the United States. One of the great dangers, if not the greatest, incident to Japan's advance into Siberia is that acting independently of all restraint, above any influence, half way around the world, she will come in such contact with Germany through Siberia and Russia that she may determine her interests lie in the same direction as those of Germany.

The American Ambassador properly supported and equipped acting at the forefront of Japanese occupation and in conjunction with similar representatives of Japan and China, will prevent any possibility of intercourse between Japan and Germany.

T MS (WP, DLC).
¹ Francis (following the examples of the French and British ambassadors in Petrograd) had transferred his staff from Petrograd to Vologda, an important railroad junction on the Trans-Siberian Railway between Moscow and Archangel. The transfer of the staff occurred between February 24 and February 27; Francis arrived at Vologda on February 28.

Sir William Wiseman to Arthur James Balfour

[New York] March 4, 1918.

Following for Mr. Balfour from Col. House:

I have told the President that I am cabling you because I feel that the proposed Japanese action in Siberia may be the greatest misfortune that has yet befallen the Allies. This is said with the kindliest feelings for Japan and no desire to question her position in Far-Eastern affairs. The United States wishes in every way to assist, and in no way to obstruct the plans of the Allies for complete military victory, and is therefore unwilling to oppose this scheme, but it would be entirely unfair not to warn you of the dangers of the plan so far as public opinion in the United States is concerned.

Since the proposals have been made semi-public, I have sounded various shades of opinion here, and find them almost unanimous in their verdict; even so conservative a statesman as Root considers it would be a grave mistake. However altruistic the intentions of the Japanese may really be, they will be misrepresented by German propaganda everywhere. They will endeavor to show that the Allies, through the Japanese, are doing in Siberia exactly what the Germans are doing in the West; that the Siberian case is even worse because the Japanese have not been invited to come by any Russian body; that Japanese territory is not threatened as the Germans and Austrians claim theirs to be. The race question, in particular, will be sharply emphasized and an attempt made to show that we are using a yellow race to destroy a white one. This may result in the American press and public opinion getting out of hand, and adopting an attitude which will be resented in Japan and cause serious friction between the two peoples.

I feel this action will mean a serious lowering, if not actual loss, of our moral position in the eyes of our own peoples and of the whole world, and a dulling of the high enthusiasm of the American people for a righteous cause. Unless we maintain our moral position we must expect a very formidable anti-war party here, a general weakening of the war effort, and a breaking-up of that practically unanimous support upon which the Administration can now count.

The President has agreed to send a note to the Japanese Government associating himself with the notes of the Allies, but he would still like you to consider whether something cannot be done which will prevent part at any rate of the misrepresentations of the German propaganda from bearing fruit.

It will probably be suggested to the Allied ambassadors that the Japanese Government, when they receive their mandate, should be requested to make a public announcement to the effect that they are sending an armed force into Siberia only as an ally of Russia, and for the purpose of saving Siberia from the invasion and intrigues of Germany; that they will be willing to leave the settlement of all Siberian questions to the council of peace.[1]

T MS (WP, DLC).
[1] This was sent as W. Wiseman to A. J. Balfour, No. 70, March 4, 1918, T telegram (W. Wiseman Papers, CtY).

Sir William Wiseman to Sir Eric Drummond

[New York] March 4th 1918.

No. 71. *For your information only.* Following is the text of the note Enos [the President] proposes giving Japanese Ambassador: Begins: "The Government of the United States is made constantly aware at every turn of events that it is the desire of the people of the United States that, while cooperating with all its energies with its associates in the war in every direct enterprise of the war in which it is possible for it to take part, it should leave itself diplomatically free wherever it can do so without injustice to its associates. It is for this reason that the Government of the United States has not thought it wise to join the Governments of the Entente in asking the Japanese Government to act in Siberia. It has no objection to that request being made, and it wishes to assure the Japanese Government that it has the entire confidence that in putting an armed force into Siberia it is doing so as an ally of Russia, with no purpose but to save Siberia from the invasion of the armies and intrigues of Germany and with entire willingness to leave the determination of all questions that may affect the permanent fortunes of Siberia to the council of peace." Ends.

I think Tabriz [House] may exaggerate the effect Japanese action will have in the U. S. although there will be undoubtedly considerable opposition, particularly in the West, and it is this which Enos' note quoted above is intended to allay.

T telegram (W. Wiseman Papers, CtY).

From the Diary of Colonel House

March 4, 1918.

Today has been a stirring one. The President telephoned Gordon over Lansing's private wire and asked whether his memorandum which was to be sent to Japan had been submitted to me before I wrote my letter to him of yesterday which he had just received.

The State Department has started a courier service between the Department and me, using two of the Secret Service men for the purpose. This is done to avoid the danger of important despatches and papers becoming lost or stolen in the mails. It is a quicker and surer method.

The President was much disturbed over my letter and has stopped, for the moment, the memorandum or note which was to go to Japan. A copy of this first note, which really embodies what he and I agreed upon before I left Washington, is attached. I did not know he was going to act so quickly. The truth of the matter is I was not well while in Washington and was not able to give the matter as clear thought as its importance deserved. The President, too, was tired. I never realized before how important it is for both of us to keep in good physical condition and not over work. Neither of us, I think, was altogether fit last week to properly solve the problems which confronted us. There was never a more critical week in our history and the fact that it found us both at rather low ebb was unfortunate to say the least.

Upon my return to New York I quickly regained my equilibrium and on Sunday it was clear to me what should be done in the Far Eastern situation. I have sent the President, through Gordon (over the telephone) a memorandum which he transmitted.[1] A copy of this is attached. I am not at all satisfied with the situation as is [it] exists, neither is the President. My cable to Mr. Balfour is one of the important events of the day.

[1] Bullitt's memorandum printed at March 2, 1918.

From Benedict Crowell, with Enclosures[1]

PERSONAL AND CONFIDENTIAL.

The President: Washington, March 5, 1918.

Inclosed please find for your information the following:

Memorandum from Brigadier General W. V. Judson, National Army dated February 26th.

Memorandum from Brigadier General W. V. Judson, National Army, dated March 4th.

Memorandum from Lieutenant Colonel Sherman Miles dated March 4th, all regarding the Russian situation.

                          Respectfully,   Benedict Crowell

TLS (WP, DLC).
[1] Internal evidence strongly indicates that Crowell had his letter and its enclosures delivered to Wilson early in the morning of March 5, in response to a request from Wilson on March 4.

E N C L O S U R E   I

                    MEMORANDUM.[1]   Feb 26, '18.

From: Brig. General W. V. Judson, N.A.
To: Acting Chief of Staff.
Subject: Action in Russia. Urgent.

The wreck that has occurred of Russian military, political and economic functions appears to be so complete and so disheartening that the Allies seem to have abandoned themselves to expressions of resentment against Russia and to complete despair as to what may happen on the eastern front.

This seems to me to be very unfortunate and very dangerous. It is as though, after a severe defeat in battle, no effort were made to check the panic, rally the retreating forces and occupy a new line.

There is still an enormous margin in the Russian situation. For example, let us contemplate the worst, and then the best sequence of future events, viewed from our own standpoint, which it would be within the bounds of reason to anticipate.

The worst might involve the following: the speedy formation of independent (?) states, very friendly to the Central Powers, in the Ukraine, Poland, Roumania, Lithuania, the Baltic Provinces, Finland, and, possibly, in the Don Cossack region; the inhabitants of these "states" able and willing to protect themselves from internal disorders; to the eastward of these regions the complete absence of opposition to the Central Powers and possibly a growing desire to receive the order-compelling Germans; no good Central Power troops contained in Russia; a great readiness throughout Russia to furnish all kinds of supplies (food, fodder (forage), copper, manganese, guns, munitions, etc.); the release for active service of some 1,600,000 war prisoners held by the Russians; the retention by Germany of many former Russian war prisoners as laborers on a wage basis, and the employment of many additional Russians in the same manner; the addition to the fighting strength of the Cen-

[1] A handwritten note, dated March 1, 1918, which is attached to this memorandum, states that Newton D. Baker had discussed this memorandum with Wilson before he left for France.

tral Powers of great numbers of adventurous young men, recruited as volunteers from the newly created and friendly "buffer states"; at home, among the Central Powers, a feeling of exultation at enormous successes achieved; a growth in strength of the morale of the people, of the imperialistic instinct, and of the dominance of the military parties.

On the other hand, the *best* possible sequence of future events, from our standpoint, might be somewhat as follows: the military occupation by the Central Powers of the Russian territory lying along their borders, in the face of the continued hostility of a large part of the population, i.e., that part which is now radically socialistic or bolshevick; a hostile Russia to the east of the occupied territory; continued resistance, if not of an orthodox military character, along the eastern borders of what region the Central Powers may decide to occupy in force; no trade with Russia east of the occupied region; no systematic release of prisoners; compulsion placed upon the Central Powers to maintain large numbers of troops along the eastern border of the occupied territory; no important strategic relations possible between troops in Russia and troops on western front, due to distances involved and to consideration next stated; great deficiency of rolling stock in occupied territory, the gauges in Russia and in Germany being different and much of the Russian rolling stock having been destroyed or withdrawn to eastern Russia; greatly increased shortage of rolling stock in Germany due to requirements for same in Russia; waning strength of military party in Germany and Austria, due to disappointments and embarrassments created by Russian occupation; loss to the German military party of the Russian bogy, which has enabled it for twenty years to exact appropriations from the Reichstag for military preparations; relative weakness of Germany upon the western front, due to the detention of troops in Russia, out of strategic relations with the Western front; disappointment experienced by Central Powers in quantities of supplies obtained from southern Russia, west of the Dnieper, and from all that part of Russia lying west and north of a line joining Kiev with Moscow and Kostroma, these regions having been largely stripped of supplies before hostile occupation.

Instead of laying down our cards and "cussing" Russia, it seems to me we should consider quickly and deeply whether there are not some things we can do which will make the worst that can happen less probable and the best more so.

If there is reasonable hope that the Allies, and especially America, will come quickly to the rescue, there are many in western Russia who will not accept the German yoke but who will retire eastward before the German advance. A very careful but frank attitude of sympathy and friendliness to Russia and all anti-German Russians must accompany the inspiration of such hopes, and such sympathy and friendliness must not be withheld from any element, even because it is bolshevik and thus to many Americans anathema.

There is any quantity of food in Siberia and in eastern Russia and southern Russia east of the Dnieper. It could be made vastly easier to supply food to the troops deployed on the eastern borders of any Russian territory the Central Powers may soon occupy than it was formerly to supply the Russian Army in its old positions.

There are nearly 1,000,000 Siberians alone, trained in the use of arms, and far better soldiers than the average Russian. The governments lying to the east and southeast of Moscow are full of soldiers who have been returning from the front disgusted with war, but who are probably experiencing some reaction of feeling at the present time as their hopes depart for experiencing lives of luxurious ease as landed proprietors.

From those withdrawing before the German advance, and from those joining from Siberia and from southeast Russia, could be found the manpower for a great organized resistance along a line far more disadvantageously located, for the Central Powers, than was the line of 1917.

All of Russia is full of small-arms. Vladivostock has vast accumulations of all kinds of war materials. It would try the Germans sorely to be obliged to occupy Russia, against any kind of resistance, as far east as Vologda; so that the Archangel route could probably be kept open.

Doubtless much rolling stock will be moved eastward before the German advance. It should serve to make more plentiful than heretofore the rolling stock in eastern Russia and Siberia. We should, of course, have to resume shipments of rolling stock to the Trans-Siberian and we should have to actually manage and control all of the railways east of the region occupied by the Germans. It would be necessary to pay the Russian troops and to secure them by voluntary enlistment, at least at the beginning.

It would not be long under such conditions before some government stronger and better than the Bolshevick could establish itself, which would doubtless give us great satisfaction. Even a temporary military dictator would be acceptable.

To have a reasonable chance of success we should of course be sure in advance of a friendly reception. A week ago this might have been brought about by unofficial negotiations with the Bolshevicks. A week hence possibly some other element or elements must be looked to for an invitation. Besides administering the railways and paying and supplying troops, we would have to send over some American troops to show our good faith, to avoid the charge that we are merely employing Russians to be food for powder, and to secure a nucleus from which the well disposed Russians could gather moral support. The number of such troops should be at least 50,000. The knowledge that we were going to act as proposed would cause resistance to the enemy to form long before our assistance could become effective.

What is proposed is a big and expensive proposition. It is to a certain extent experimental, without absolute certainty of result. And its adoption would to a certain extent lessen our efforts on the western front.

In answer to these obvious strictures it must be noted that the debacle on the eastern front has changed the character of the war and made bigger and more expensive undertakings necessary, if the war is to be won. Furthermore, in the major operations of war there is usually absent certainty of result and nearly always present the experimental element. As to the lessening of our efforts upon the western front, the following observations are in order: 50,000 men placed upon the western front simply neutralize, it is fair to say, 50,000 enemy troops, while 50,000 men placed somewhere west of the Urals, inducing the active pressure of say 1,000,000 other men, might neutralize more than 1,000,000 enemy troops.

One thought is important in connection with any proposition to take troops to Russia via Vladivostock. Although the distance from Seattle to Vladivostock is greater than the distance from America to France, yet it is probable that the same vessel tonnage would transport more troops in a given time to Vladivostock than to France by reason of the fact that vessels would not have to wait for convoys and there would be no losses.

I would not expect any line formed in Russia to be of the character of the western front nor even of the character of the former Russian front, which was prepared for far less intensive fighting than is the front in France. The line proposed would be a line of slight resistance perhaps, but it would conform in position to the German front which would oppose it, retreating further into the depths of Russia if attacked in great strength, but taking the offensive, if the enemy anywhere should neglect to preserve his position in force.

The plan suggested would restore to Russia, perhaps, her historical role of conquering by the circumstance of her magnificent distances. The Kaiser might be overcome by the same weapon that destroyed the power of Napoleon and of Charles The Twelfth. There can be little doubt that the adoption of no other plan of action or of inaction would be so unwelcome to the Germans.

If we abandon Russia to the Germans, the people of the occupied regions, as the Ukraine, will think that Germany has become surely enough a super-nation, and may to a large extent make common cause with her. Nothing succeeds like success and nearby occurrences are naturally looked upon as affording the criteria of success or failure. And the undisputed occupancy of Russia would so fill the Austrian and German peoples with cupidity for empire that little hope could be entertained of detaching one from the other or the liberals of either from their respective governments. It would become very difficult to win the war.

I suggest the immediate issuance of a statement such as the following:

"If to the renewed attack of the imperialistic German Government upon free Russia it shall be determined by Russia to continue armed opposition, even if the final lines of resistance shall be far in the interior of Great Russia, and even if thus heroic sacrifices shall be demanded of the Russian people in the cause of liberty, the United States of America assures Russia that it will spare no effort in any direction to support her and to help defend her liberty. In this [thus] proferring assistance the United States makes no condition other than that of cooperation and seeks no end other than the satisfaction that follows its own efforts to promote international justice and to defend freedom."

On account of the immediate importance of the Russian situation, I hasten to submit this preliminary recommendation dealing with general policy.   W. V. Judson
                                                  Brig. Gen. Nat. Army.

ENCLOSURE   II

Memorandum   March 4, 1918.

From: Brigadier General W. V. Judson, N.A.
To: Acting Chief of Staff.
Subject: Action in Russia. Urgent.

On February 26, 1918, I submitted to the Acting Chief of Staff a memorandum on the subject "Action in Russia, Urgent." This memorandum was subsequently returned to me with notation by the Secretary of War that "The Secretary of State has charge of this." In the meantime the Secretary of State had requested from me a copy of the memorandum, which was furnished him on the morning of March 1.

The present memorandum is supplementary to that of February 26, 1918, and it is suggested that the original or a copy be immediately furnished the State Department.

Having been in Petrograd until January 23, 1918, and having

kept in close touch there with recent Russian opinions of all shades, I feel that I am quite sure of my facts in stating that the effect of Japanese intervention in Siberia would be as follows:

(1) The creation of a feeling almost universal in Russia, that the former allies of Russia, in rage at her defection, have adopted a policy of revenge and have decided upon punitive measures.

(2) Complete despair in Russia as it becomes evident that she lies prostrate between two military autocracies, each apparently free to work its will upon her. The democratic element will believe that similar elements among the former allies of Russia have rejected her through fear and displeasure at the forms adopted and the action taken by the Russian democracy or by the radicals who have been most recently in power. The moderate and the conservative elements will feel that Russia is completely isolated and that no action on their part can restore her to respectability among her former allies.

(3) Thinking that they have no other choice but between two imperialistic powers, each bent upon despoiling them, but feeling that the Germans have already done their worst, Russia will choose the white rather than the yellow peril. The Russian people as a whole will feel that no path lies open to them but to cultivate friendly relations with a power ready, by reason of its own needs, to appreciate such relations. Certainly if Japan intervenes on a large scale and if she intervenes alone, European Russia will fall into the lap of Germany. No number of enemy troops will be detained in Russia. The "buffer" states now in process of creation will be thoroughly pro-German. The remainder of European Russia will probably soon accept the control of a military dictator friendly to Germany and bent upon the restoration of monarchy. Russia will go to work raising food; mining coal, copper, platinum, iron and manganese ores, and manufacturing munitions, all for Germany. Many will seek service in the German Army.

Russia is the greatest reservoir in the world of supplies and manpower not today serving the interest of ourselves or our enemies. Nothing is more certain than that Japanese intervention in Siberia will place that reservoir at the disposal of Germany, and the Russians would not be merely passive in the matter, but would lend aid to Germany to almost the maximum of their ability.

Japan would find no friendly element in Siberia, welcoming her as a deliverer. We might hear of some individual Cossack commander with little if any following who would welcome the approach of the Japanese to relieve him of some present embarrassment, but this is unlikely and unimportant outside of press reports. The Siberians would destroy the railways to the greatest extent practicable before the Japanese advance and would make common cause with their fellow Russians west of the Urals. The Japanese would probably not get west of Lake Baikal. They would never get in touch with German or Austrian fighting men. They would never disturb German plans. In producing a pro-German feeling in European Russia they would in fact serve Germany's interests to the utmost. All that Germany needs can be secured, not only west of Lake Baikal but west even of the whole of Siberia.

In this connection, I would again recall certain revelations in the secret documents recently published by the Bolshevicks:

(1) The secret treaty between Japan and the old Russia Government evidently hostile to the United States.[1]

(2) The apprehension in Japan that differences may arise between Japan and the United States over interpretations that may be placed upon the terms of the recent United States-Japanese Entente.

(3) Indications that Japan is of the opinion that, with Russia out of the war, the outcome of the war may be entirely altered.

Japan does not go to war for reasons of sentiment. Her occupation of Siberia east of Lake Baikal would place that lake and the northerly projection of the Gobi desert between her and any military power to the westward, affording her a strong frontier for possessions in Manchuria, the Amur valley and the Ussuri region, the latter of enormous value by reason of its mineral resources.

Under all of the circumstances it seems worthy of consideration whether the proposed large-scale intervention by Japan in Siberia is dictated by a desire to serve any purpose of the Allies as a whole, or merely the purposes of Japan herself. And it is even to be considered whether the fact that such intervention would in a large degree serve the interest of Germany is not at that time present in the minds of Japan.

If Japan, having war ships present at Vladivostock, undertakes

---

[1] The Bolshevik newspaper, *Izvestia*, had published, on December 20, 1917 (under the heading "Secret Treaty Between Japan and Russia for Joint Armed Demonstration Against America and Great Britain in the Far East") what it described as the text of an agreement signed on July 3, 1916, by Sazonov and Motono at Petrograd. Article I stated that the two parties recognized that the "vital interests" of each required "the safeguarding of China from the political domination of any third Power whatsoever, having hostile designs against Russia or Japan," and that the two parties accordingly obligated themselves, when circumstances demanded, to consult on necessary measures to prevent such domination. American officials in Washington said on December 21, 1917, that they had no knowledge of the so-called secret treaty but that they considered the heading in *Izvestia* not to be borne out by the text of the published articles. *New York Times*, Dec. 22, 1917. A translation of the secret treaty from the New York *Evening Post* of March 2, 1918, is printed in John V. A. MacMurray, ed., *Treaties and Agreements with and concerning China, 1894-1919* (2 vols., New York, 1921), II, 1328. In a public treaty of the same date, Japan and Russia had each agreed not to take part in any arrangement or political combination directed against the other, and to consult if their recognized territorial rights or special interests were menaced. *Ibid.*, II, 1327.

merely the custody of the freight (nearly 700,000 tons) lying on and about the wharves at that place, if necessary landing marines as a part of this operation, it might possible [possibly] be made evident to the Russian people that Japan has no large and hostile ends in view.

If Japan does attempt to occupy large portions of Siberia, it is possible but not certain that participation in the movement by the United States would palliate the offence in the minds of the Russian people. If there were a joint occupation, the share and purposes of the United States would be emphasized as much as possible.

Intervention on a relatively small scale by the United States alone would do most to excite resistance to Germany on the part of the Russians themselves, and, after all, unless the Russians do themselves resist there can be no real obstacle to Germany in all of European Russia.

Even American intervention, as proposed, should not be undertaken unless and until it is made evident that it is acceptable generally to the Russian people.

Any allied forces operating west of Vladivostock must seem to be deliverers and not conquerers.

I submit this memorandum with a deep sense of the vast and immediate importance of the subject and of my duty, by reason of my recent presence in Russia, to make report upon it.

I enclose a memorandum by Lt. Col. Sherman Miles, General Staff, who recently served in Russia as Military Attache, upon the subject of the proposed Japanese intervention. I believe that his conclusions are thoroughly sound.   W. V. Judson

Brig. Gen. Nat. Army

E N C L O S U R E   I I I

MEMORANDUM FOR GENERAL JUDSON: 4th March, 1918

Subject: Japanese intervention in Siberia.

I. There is a vast difference between Japanese police patrol at Vladivostok (which would control the shipment of the 700,00[0] tons of military material stored there) and a Japanese occupation of Siberia up to Harbin or Irkutsk. The first would control, without serious friction with the Russians, the military stores which it is necessary to keep out of the hands of the enemy. The second would control very little else of military value besides the stores at Vladivostok, and this control would almost certainly lead to serious military conflict with the Russians. Vladivostok is situated at the extremity of a peninsula easily controlled from the sea. The railroad to the interior runs right along the shore. Harbin is 350 miles inland, and Irkutsk 1200 miles beyond Harbin. So far as the stores at Vladivostok are concerned (and they are practically the only material of immediate military value in Siberia) their control by means of a Japanese invasion of Eastern Siberia is as unnecessary as would be an invasion as far east as Denver to control stores at San Francisco.

II. With the possible exception of the stores at Vladivostok, there is no material, raw or manufactured, in all Siberia which the Germans now need, if they can work their will in European Russia. Since they can not touch Siberia without controlling the railroads and centers of European Russia, and since the control of the railroads and centers of European Russia would give them all the material they could use for the probable duration of this war, it is absurd to suppose that a Japanese invasion of Eastern Siberia would deprive them of any material now necessary to them. The idea of the danger of a German penetration as far as Eastern Siberia, during this war, is so far fetched as to suggest other and very different motives behind any movement nominally inspired by it. The great stores of food of all sorts in the Ukraine and the Don Cossack country, and the coal and minerals in European Russia are sufficient to satisfy the war needs of Germany, if she can get them, without the labor or the danger of a penetration into Siberia.

III. As entirely differentiated from the proposition of a Japanese police of Vladivostok, the following appear to be the dangers to be faced in the case of the much more ambitious proposition of a Japanese invasion of Eastern Siberia.

1. In the first place there can be no doubt that the movement will be regarded by the Russians as an invasion, and resisted as such. Racial antagonism between the Russians and the Japanese—between the white and the yellow people—is bound to lead to resistance, if only local and only in the form of destruction of bridges and tunnels on the railroad. The influence of the Germand [German] and Austrian prisoners in Siberia would lead to friction and resistance, even if no other influence existed. Once you get resistance to the Japanese, you get a break in the only line of communication between the Allies and Russia. It would be impossible to send any help, in any form, to any group in Russia. Revolutions are individualistic movements; and so complete an upheaval and reversal as the Russian Revolution has necessarilly led to all sorts of internal dissention which so far have precluded resistance to the external enemy. But now that the external enemy (the Central Powers) has come out into the open in its attempt to control and finally crush all factions of the

revolution, resistance in some form is almost inevitable. The peace signed by Lenine and Trotsky opens the way for German penetration and control into Russia. Since this influence is bound to be hostile to the revolution, it must crystalize both the centers of German influence and the centers of revolutionary influence. In spite of their violent factional dissentions, the great majority of the Russian people have, in the revolution, an ideal to fight for so near to their hearts and freshly won, that they are practically certain to resist the autocratic influences now striving to crush it. The crystalization of revolutionary and anti-autocratic groups in Russia may lead to a situation which will call for our help, in some form. It would appear necessary that we prevent the blocking, by the Japanese, of the only road by which we might send help if the opportunity offers.

2. Russia is honey-combed with German propagandists. As soon as the Japanese occupation of Siberia is resisted, these propagandists will spread the news of the "Japanese Invasion," and will start two lines of propaganda. The first will be the Yellow Peril (an idea to conjure with, even with a Russian peasant). The second, and by far the most dangerous, will be that resistance to pressure from both the east and the west by the most formidable armies in the world (and the only armies that the Russian knows and dreads) is impossible, and that if the Russian people are to escape being utterly crushed they must quic[k]ly choose between the Japanese and the Central Powers. The Russian will not know that the Japanese are coming no farther than Irkutsk. He will be told that a vast yellow horde is sweeping west. Caught between these two powerful military forces he is liable, in despair, to throw himself on the mercy of one of the two opposing forces, and as between the Japanese and the Central Powers he will not be long in choosing the latter—men of his own race and color. In other words, a Japanese occupation which can and will be construed into an invasion will be just the thing needed to counteract the Russian antagonism to the influence of the Central Powers, to crystalize the pro-German forces in Russia, and to throw the Russian people (not merely the Russian lands) into the hands of the Central Powers.

3. There is also another side to this matter of propaganda. The proletariat of England, France, Italy and the United States will be told by their more rabid leaders, and will very likely believe, that the invasion of Japan shows that the Allies, avowedly fighting for democracy and liberalism, are in reality so opposed to liberalism that when it rises in Russia they not only do nothing to prevent autocratic Germany from crushing it, but actually push

in autocratic Japan to make the crushing doubly sure. No matter
how preverted [perverted] liberalism has become in Russia, it is
still looked upon by the proletariat of the world as the greatest
inspiration which has come to them from this war. The result of
open conflict between liberalism in Russia and an autocratic power
like Japan, pushed on by the Allies, may therefore work in-
calcu[l]able harm among the protelatiat [proletariat] of the Allied
Powers. It begins to look as if the soldier alone would not win
this war. Probably it will be won by the producers—munitions,
food and ships. More probably still it will be won by the moral
collapse of one group or the other (the disaster in Italy was almost
entirely a moral breakdown.). The moral collapse of liberalism in
Russia, the abject surrender of the Russian people (not merely
the Bolsheviki group) to German autocracy through dispair of
resistance to pressure from the Central Powers and Japan at the
same time, would be a moral victory for the Central Powers which
might be a powerful factor leading to a collapse of Allied resistance and the loss of the war.

4. The Central Powers probably decided on an armed invasion
of Russia because they feared the effects of unchecked liberalism
there, and also because they want to get out of Russia three
things—(a) all of their military forces now occupied on the Eastern Front, (b) raw materials (food, oils, fats, minerals), (c) moral
prestige to the military party which will come from showing their
people at home that Russian liberalism itself acknowledges defeat
and the superiority of the militaristic system. To a certain extent
they have opened the way to all these things by the treaty of
peace with the Bolsheviki. But it is to be noted that the Central
Powers can not get these things, in anything like their full value,
in the face of resistance or antagonism on the part of the Russian
people, as differentiated from the Bolsheviki group, even if that
resistance is only in the nature of guerrilla warfare; but that they
can get the full measure of all of them if all factions in Russia
are driven into throwing themselves into the German arms. The
difference between getting out of Russia the military forces engaged there, the raw materials and the moral prestige, in the face
of resistance from an almost fanatical and extremely stubborn
people, and getting these things with the help of these same
people is an enormous difference. It is precisely the measure by
which we can hamper the enemy's designs if we can avoid the
inevitable conflict and propaganda which will result from a Japanese occupation of Eastern Siberia.

IV. The intervention of Japan in Siberia is, for the reasons given
above, to be avoided. The question immediately arrives, how can

this be done? It is suggested then the United States can bring pressure on England and France, through the great desire of these nations for our full support and our common fear of weakening the moral will to war of our laboring classes, to bring pressure on Japnan [Japan] to give up her project of the occupation of Eastern Siberia. We might well suggest to Japan, and thereby "save her face," that she can accomplish everything necessary, and avoid all dangers, merely by a police patrol of Vladivostok. In being instrumental in preventing an occupation of Russian territory by the Japanese, we would greatly increase our pre[s]tige and our ability to render aid in Russia, should it become possible to render such aid in the future.

Sherman Miles
Lt. Col., General Staff

TS MSS (WP, DLC).

A Memorandum

Department of State
Office of the Counselor [c. March 5, 1918]

Question of supplies and financial aid

Therefore (referring to all foregoing) since the U. S. regarded the very modest programme which she proposed as the only wise and practicable programme, the judgment of the Japanese government that that programme will not serve the purpose makes the U. S. gov't. reluctant to act at all.

14000

3500

2

400[1]

Perfectly understand Japanese position and motives. No desire to criticism or interfere with their independence of action.

But not our proposal—which had at its heart the impression which would be made on the *Russian* mind, which will receive the wrong impression unless the virtual equivalence of allies and Japanese were evident from the first. The actual limitation of the aggregate number equally necessary to the right impression.

WWhw MS (F. L. Polk Papers, CtY).
    [1] Japanese, American, British, and French troops, respectively.

Frank Lyon Polk to Roland Sletor Morris[1]

Message to Japan (*in re* Siberia)[2]
[Washington] March 5, 1918, 4 p.m. GREEN AND BLUE.

AMEMBASSY, TOKYO

(Green). At your earliest opportunity you will please read to the Japanese Government the following message but leave no copy unless they request you to do so. (Blue). Quote: The Government of the United States has been giving the most careful and anxious consideration to the conditions now prevailing in Siberia and their possible remedy. It realizes the extreme danger of anarchy to which the Siberian provinces are exposed and the imminent risk also of German invasion and domination. It shares with the governments of the Entente the view that, if intervention is deemed wise, the Government of Japan is in the best situation to undertake it and could accomplish it most efficiently. It has, moreover, the utmost confidence in the Japanese Government and would be entirely willing, so far as its own feelings towards that Government are concerned, to entrust the enterprise to it. But it is bound in frankness to say that the wisdom of intervention seems to it most questionable. If it were undertaken the Government of the United States assumes[3] that the most explicit assurances would be given that it was undertaken by Japan as an ally of Russia, in Russia's interest, and with the sole view of holding it safe against Germany and at the absolute disposal of the final peace conference. Otherwise the Central Powers could and would make it appear that Japan was doing in the East exactly what Germany is doing in the West and so seek to counter the condemnation which all the world must pronounce against Germany's invasion of Russia, which she attempts to justify on the pretext of restoring order. And it is the judgment of the Government of the United States, uttered with the utmost respect, that, even with such assurances given, they could in the same way be discredited by those whose interest it was to discredit them; that a hot resentment would be generated in Russia itself, and that the whole action might play into the hands of the enemies of Russia, and particularly of the enemies of the Russian Revolution, for which the Government of the United States entertains the greatest sympathy, in spite of all the unhappiness and misfortune which has for the time being sprung out of it. The Government of the United States begs once more to express to the Government of Japan its warmest friendship and confidence and once more begs it to accept these expressions of judgment as uttered only in the frankness of friendship. Unquote.   Polk,   Acting.[4]

T MS (WP, DLC).
[1] The text within the "Quote" and "Unquote" repeats the text of a WWT draft (SDR, RG 59, 861.00/1246, DNA) which was, as Polk wrote at the top of the document, "Handed to me by President March 5, 1918 to send to Tokio FLP."
[2] WWhw.
[3] Wilson's original draft reads: "the Government of the United States would deem it absolutely necessary that the most explicit assurances should be given. . . ." Wilson changed the text to read as printed below.
[4] This message was sent as FLP to R. S. Morris, March 5, 1915, T telegram (SDR, RG 59, 861.00/1246, DNA).

To Herbert Clark Hoover

My dear Mr. Hoover: The White House 5 March, 1918

I have your letter of March first and have considered the important matter it lays before me. I am returning the correspondence which you were kind enough to send with it.

I agree with you that Mr. Spreckels presents no sufficient reasons why he cannot join the other refiners in signing the contract with you and I therefore feel justified in issuing the instructions to which you refer. I am issuing them today.

Cordially and sincerely yours,   Woodrow Wilson

TLS (H. Hoover Papers, HPL).

To Edward Nash Hurley

My dear Mr. Chairman: [The White House] 5 March, 1918

I hereby authorize you to refuse all further transportation for the importation of sugar to the sugar refiner, Mr. C. A. Spreckels. I make this request because Mr. Spreckels has refused to sign the contract with the Food Administration which was necessary for the protection of the sugar supply and the sugar market, raising objections which were purely in the nature of quibbles, and because it is, therefore, necessary to control the market without Mr. Spreckels's cooperation.

Cordially and sincerely yours,   Woodrow Wilson[1]

TLS (Letterpress Books, WP, DLC).
[1] Wilson sent the same letter, *mutatis mutandis*, as WW to V. C. McCormick, March 5, 1918, TLS (Letterpress Books, WP, DLC).

To Benedict Crowell

My dear Mr. Secretary: [The White House] 5 March, 1918

Thank you for your letter of yesterday about that unfortunate sentence in the Manual of Instructions for Medical Advisory Boards.

I am heartily glad that justice has been done by the excision of the sentences and the substitution of other instructions.

Cordially and sincerely yours,   Woodrow Wilson

TLS (Letterpress Books, WP, DLC).

To William Kent

My dear Mr. Kent: The White House 5 March, 1918

I have, as you will observe from the enclosed, been trying to get the opinion of the Food Administrator and the Secretary of Agriculture about the memorial of the cattlemen presented by Mr. Heard and his associates. Will you not be kind enough, when you have time, to look over these letters and let me have your comment?

Cordially and sincerely yours,   Woodrow Wilson

TLS (W. Kent Papers, CtY).

From Frank Lyon Polk, with Enclosure

My dear Mr. President: Washington March 5, 1918.

I have read your telegram to Tokio on the subject of Siberia to the British and French Chargés, and will communicate with the Italian Ambassador tonight.

The telegram to Tokio has gone. Mr. Barclay, of the British Embassy, after I read him the despatch to Tokio, read me a telegram that had been sent by the British Foreign Office to Tokio on March fourth, and he was good enough to let me have a paraphrase of it, which I attach for your information. I called Mr. Barclay's attention to the last paragraph, which reads that the "United States Government has no objection" and reminded him that that was not the form of the memorandum I read him on Friday, as that memorandum merely stated that the United States Government had no objection to the British Government's making a suggestion. He promised to make the correction at once both in Tokio and London. I impressed on him the fact that the message the Department was sending today stated the present views of this Government, and the decision had been reached by you after further consideration of all the facts.

I found the French Secretary had discussed the matter with the French Ambassador, and the Ambassador had very clearly in mind your views as the result of his talk with you yesterday.

Yours faithfully,   Frank L. Polk

TLS (WP, DLC).

ENCLOSURE

(Dictated by Mr. Colville Barclay to
Mr. Howell,[1] March 5, 1918).

Telegram to Tokyo, March 4, 1918.

With the unconditional surrender of the Government at Petrograd to Germany, there now seems to be no barrier to prevent Germanic influences penetrating throughout Siberia. No Russian authority exists which can be trusted to guard the stores now lying at Vladivostok or to prevent foodstuffs in Siberia from being taken out by the Central Powers. Allied intervention seems, under these circumstances, to be practically inevitable, and as control of the Siberian railway probably as far as Chelyabinsk and, at any rate, as far as Omsk, is necessary to attain the objects desired, it is clear that the task must be undertaken by Japan for geographical reasons.

In order to make it quite clear that there is not the least similarity between the operations which the Japanese Government may be compelled to undertake in Siberia and those being carried on by Germany in European Russia, His Majesty's Government are of opinion that it is of utmost importance to Japan (acting as mandatory of her allies) to give the widest possible publicity to her aims and methods. Naturally it is not for the British Government to make any suggestions as to the form in which the proposed declaration should be drawn up but they think it of vital importance that it should be made quite clear that while Germany is bent on destruction of Russia, the allies aim and desire are to assist her, that while Germany has been warring not only upon Russia but upon particular forms of Government which [the] Russian people had established or may wish to establish, the Allies have neither the wish nor the intention to interfere in the internal affairs of Russia; that while Germany has taken advantage of Russia's temporary embarrassments and weakness to despoil her of large provinces, the allies pledge themselves to leave Russian territory intact, that while Germany's object is to exploit Russia economically after crushing her politically, the allies' desire is to see a strong and independent Russia.

I am to request you to approach the Japanese Government in the above sense. If they accept these views you should subsequently consult with French and Italian Ambassadors and upon their receiving instructions you should jointly invite Japanese Government, as mandatory of the allied powers to undertake the obligations outlined above.

We understand that the United States Government has no objection.

T MS (WP, DLC).
  [1] Humphrey Daniel Howell, a clerk in the office of the Counselor of the Department of State.

From Gordon Auchincloss

Dear Mr President: [Washington] March 5th [1918]

I've just finished transmitting to Mr House your memo. of telegram to be sent to Japan and he has asked me to tell you that he is happy beyond words at the absolutely perfect way you have handled this most worrying situation. I am

Faithfully yours   Gordon Auchincloss

ALS (WP, DLC).

From Theodore Marburg

Dear Mr President,   Wilmington, North Carolina. Mch 5, 18

If agreeable to you I should like to call to consult you about the matter referred to in the enclosed letter from Lord Bryce.[1] I shall be coming North next week and can come to Washington any time after 15th inst except 20th inst.

May I ask the favor of a reply at this address?

Sincerely,   Theodore Marburg

P.S The enclosed Draft Convention[2] is an attempt to deal with one of the problems Ld Bryce has in mind.

ALS (WP, DLC).
  [1] Bryce's letter (February 8, 1918) is missing in both WP, DLC, and in the J. Bryce Papers, Bodleian Library. In reply to it, however, Marburg sent two letters which indicate its contents. In the first, he sent Bryce a copy of WW to T. Marburg, March 8, 1918. In the second, on March 14, he wrote: "Your suggestion of a combined British and American group of experts to work out the details of a practical plan struck me as excellent. I am indeed sorry that President Wilson failed to approve of it." Theodore Marburg, *Development of the League of Nations Idea: Documents and Correspondence of Theodore Marburg*, John H. Latané, ed. (2 vols., New York, 1932), I, 418-20.
  [2] This document is missing in WP, DLC. However, it was a draft of a treaty by the executive committee of the League to Enforce Peace for a league of nations. The text as approved by the committee on April 11, 1918, is printed in Marburg, II, 791-94. The treaty provided for three classes of membership, with full, limited, and no responsibility to use economic and military power to enforce peace. It also established various organs to carry out the purposes of the league. For further details, see n. 6 to the memorandum by W. H. Taft printed at March 29, 1918.

From Bernard Mannes Baruch

Washington
My dear Mr. President   Saturday [c. March 5, 1918]

You know only too well how badly I express myself and I feel that handicap more than ever when I try to tell you how much I appreciate your photograph with its accompanying sentiment.

I wish I could relieve you of some of your great burdens. I am trying in my own field to show you my devotion and affection.

If I succeed however small I shall be happy.

Many thanks   Sincerely   Bernard M Baruch

ALS (WP, DLC).

From Emery T. Morris and Others

Boston, Mass., March 5, 1918.

Realizing extraordinary need of racial amity in presence of extraordinary world war, alarmed by extraordinary epidemic of mob murderings colored Americans, the National Equal Rights League, in home of Crispus Attucks who gave first life that country might be nation, on 148th anniversary his death in Boston massacre, in his name petition you publicly urge cessation lynching, and removal from American stage extraordinary attack upon racial peace, glorifier of lynch law, the "Birth of Nation," photo-play barred from Boston as act of patriotism by Mayor Boston,[1] doing away with creator of race hatred, while making world safe for democracy make us safe for colored protection from lynching mob lynching propaganda.

Emery T. Morris, William Brigham, William Trotter.

T telegram (WP, DLC).
   [1] See JPT to WW, April 24, 1915, Vol. 33.

Frank Lyon Polk to Robert Lansing

My dear Mr. Secretary: Washington March 5, 1918.

I enclose two letters addressed to you which Crane brought to me and which I took the liberty of opening as I thought they might require immediate action. I must apologize for having taken the liberty, which possibly I should not have done, but the letter from Francis I thought might require immediate attention.

The British, French, Italian and Japanese called on me and discussed the letter you wrote them just before you left. They all seemed to be quite satisfied with the way that matter is being handled by the President.

I sent for the British, French, and Italian and read them the telegram prepared on the subject of Siberia. They said they would communicate with their governments at once. The British and French I saw Friday and the Italian on Saturday. On Sunday the President sent for me to discuss the Siberian situation and was rather anxious that we should send the telegram to Japan on Monday. Monday morning he called me up and told me to wait until I heard from him again. Today he sent for me and gave me the enclosed message to be sent to Tokyo. He also asked me to communicate it to the British, French, and Italian. It is a change in our position, but I do not know that it will materially affect the situation. I argued the question with him a little, but he said he had been thinking it over and felt that the second message was absolutely necessary. On reading it you will probably see what influenced him, namely, the position of this Government in the eyes of the democratic people of the world. The message will be sent today and I shall make my rounds this afternoon.

I do not think the Japanese will be entirely pleased, but it is not a protest, so they may accept it as merely advice and go ahead and do what they want.

I hope you are having a good rest and not thinking about the office. I am sorry to even bother you with this, but I know you are naturally anxious to hear what is going on.

Please remember me to Mrs. Lansing.

With warmest regards,   Yours faithfully,   Frank L. Polk

TLS (SDR, RG 59, 861.00/1246, DNA).

Prince zu Fürstenberg to Count Ottokar Czernin von und zu Chudenitz

MOST SECRET   Madrid 5.3.18

HIS MAJESTY THE EMPEROR OF AUSTRIA, VIENNA.

I have received a reply from President WILSON as follows:

"I am gratified that my recent declaration of the principles to be observed in formulating the conditions of peace are so largely agreed to by His Majesty the Emperor of Austria and that His Majesty desires a closer comparison of the points of view of the two Governments. I should be heartily pleased if His Majesty were disposed to be more explicit concerning the *four* principles which I outlined in my message to the U. S. A. Congress on February 11th last. In that message I endeavored to specify with greater clearness than heretofore the principles which I had attempted to enunciate concretely in a message to Congress of January 8th. In that previous message I set forth in detail the manner in which the said principles ought to be put into practice. I presume that the Emperor of Austria is in possession of my message of January 8th and that he is acquainted with the terms of the programme which in my view should form the basis of a general peace. These terms were set forth in words so explicit and clear that a delegate sent to represent me in person could not have made them more precise. It would assist me materially in determining whether a more intimate and personal comparison of points of view were worth the trouble if I had before my eyes an equally explicit programme.

"The Emperor also says that he believes he has positive proof that certain proposals, which I made relative to the complicated Balkan situation, would be less acceptable to the peoples concerned and more likely to evoke new antagonisms than the adjustment proposed by Austria herself and that certain rearrangements desired by Italy, would not be acceptable to the peoples directly concerned, but he has not given me point by point what I ardently desire, the benefit of his positive programme.

"I can assure His Majesty of my willingness to take into consideration any solution he may have in mind. More especially should I like to know how His Majesty proposes to end the dispute in the Balkans and to satisfy the national aspirations of the Slav peoples who are so closely related to masses of his own subjects, and what solution he would suggest for the ADRIATIC coast? What definite concessions to Italy he would regard as just and what in his opinion is the best method of removing the rivalries and antagonisms of the Balkan States which have only been increased by the war, and who is to protect the non-Turkish peoples subject to Turkish rule?

"As I understand it the Emperor holds the same views about Belgium and Poland as myself.

"With such explanation and information I should be in a better position than at present to form an opinion with regard to the advisability of taking action. I assure His Majesty, if such assurances are necessary, that I seek no strategic advantage nor any advantage of a personal nature but a just settlement which will confer on the world a just and lasting peace."

The President received the Ambassador with the utmost cordiality. He told him that in order to maintain secrecy he had himself typed on the typewriter the message which he handed him. My Ambassador gave expression to his delight that the President had found in your message something that might form a basis for future

understanding and which might leave open the possibility of negotiation, a statement to which the President assented. At the same
time he remarked that in spite of his ✱ ✱ ✱ he was of opinion that
after direct conversations had taken place he would ✱ ✱ ✱ inform
his Allies.   (signed)   Fürstenberg.[1]

TC telegram (SDR, RG 59, 763.72119/8735, DNA).
   [1] This telegram was intercepted by British Intelligence, which gave this copy to Page.

From the Diary of Colonel House

March 5, 1918.

The President called for Polk this morning and handed him a
new note to Japan which was to be substituted for the one written
the other day and later held up. I agree with what the President
says in this last note. He told Polk he had written the new note and
held up the other under my advice and after receiving my letter.
Polk disagreed with him as to the advisability of his action, and
Polk and I had a long argument over the telephone about the matter
after he had seen the President. However unfortunate it may be
that the State Department had given the substance of the first
note to the Japanese and Allied Ambassadors, nevertheless, I believe
the President was wise in changing it and substituting the note
written yesterday. Copies of both notes are attached.

I had Gordon send him word that I approved entirely and thought
he had retrieved an awkward situation. I am sorry I did not suggest
his using the words "sending an expeditionary force into Siberia"
rather than using the word "invasion." Wiseman called my attention
to this when I showed him what the President had rewritten. He
did not like the last note as well as the one recalled, but in this
instance I wholly disagreed with him.

From the Diary of Josephus Daniels

March Tuesday 5 1918

Cabinet. W.W. Reminiscent of Princeton told story of Prof of
Chemistry.[1] "In my laboratory I am all mind; outside I am all soul."
Given to big words: "Why did I have to take out that anaemic,
dessicated —— female?" Like Disraeli said of Gladstone: "Inebri-
ated by his own verbosity[."]

Gregory: What shall I do with whiskey taken by marshals? No
authority to dispose of it. Much merriment. WW told of whiskey
put in buckets at Army canteen and a mule got its head in the

bucket and drank and drank and drank. Became so drunk it kicked over everything. But did not ["]kick the bucket." Burleson said it would be a sin to pour out good whiskey—it was getting too scarce & *high*. He suggested that it be given to hospitals

McAdoo: Hard to make people think Fed. Gov. should not pay everything. Secy. of stockgrowers in Minn. demanded more cars to carry stock to market. Cars were sent. Stock hurried in such quantities to market that price went down. They wrote McAdoo that the Gov. ought to pay loss of dif. in the price. WW thought this the limit. Everybody expecting the Fed Gov. to do everything.

[1] Henry Bedinger Cornwall, Professor of Analytical Chemisty and Mineralogy at Princeton, 1873-1910. Wilson persuaded him to retire in the latter year.

To Benedict Crowell

My dear Mr. Secretary: [The White House] 6 March, 1918
Thank you for your letter of yesterday with its enclosures, two memoranda from Brigadier General Judson and a memorandum from Lieutenant Colonel Sherman Miles. I have been very much interested in General Judson's view on the Russian situation, and am glad to have these statements from him and from Colonel Miles.
Cordially and sincerely yours,   Woodrow Wilson

TLS (Letterpress Books, WP, DLC).

From Frank Lyon Polk

My dear Mr. President: Washington March 6, 1918.
I have received a copy of the letter addressed to you February 27th by the Secretary of Commerce, on the subject of the supplies accumulated at Vladivostok,[1] and which you had referred to me.

The last reports from the Stevens Railway Commission indicate that the accumulation, which had reached seven or eight hundred thousand tons in the early part of 1917, had been reduced during the past summer to about four hundred thousand tons. Practically all of the supplies are understood to consist of materials purchased by the Russian Government from British credits. I have no information regarding any important supplies in the hands of private parties.

We have been in correspondence with Ambassador Francis and with the Embassies at London and Paris on this subject since last December. I find that Mr. Crosby and the representatives of the

Allies associated with him in London are also working on this question.

In this connection I may recall the recent arrangement you authorized, by which the American Military Attaché at Petrograd, like his French and British colleagues, has had put at his disposal ten million roubles. The plan is that the French, British and Americans together will cooperate in measures to safeguard by purchase or otherwise not only the supplies at Vladivostok and Archangel, but also such materials useful to the Germans as are available in the open market.

Regarding the supplies at Vladivostok, there is an initial difficulty of establishing a proper title. In the meanwhile it seems that they must be safeguarded. As I wrote you recently it was on this account that I was anxious to have Admiral Knight return to Vladivostok so that we might have the authority of his opinion on the subject. Admiral Knight arrived at Vladivostok March 1, and I am now informed that he has gone to Harbin by rail. He will report on the whole situation.

The value of these stores is very great as they consist of various kinds of munitions and explosives, motor cars and trucks, agricultural machinery, barbed wire and other miscellaneous supplies, including raw materials. A list of the supplies was mailed to the Department some time ago by our Consul at Vladivostok,[2] which should reach me very shortly.

Faithfully yours,   Frank L Polk

TLS (WP, DLC).
[1] W. C. Redfield to WW, Feb. 27, 1918, TLS (WP, DLC).
[2] John Kenneth Caldwell.

From Edward Mandell House, with Enclosure

Dear Governor: New York. March 6, 1918.

I am enclosing you a copy of a letter which has just come from Ackerman and which I think is full of interest.

I have seen both Jusserand and Reading today. Jusserand already thought largely as we do in regard to the Japanese excursion into Russia and I think I talked Reading out of his position and into ours. He tried to argue but could not maintain his position, and agreed to send a cable to his government this afternoon advising them to conform with your ideas in the matter.

Affectionately yours,   E. M. House

P.S. I suggested to Frank Polk that he tell the Japanese Charge, when he delivered your note, that the position you take is the same position their representatives took at the Inter-allied Conference in Paris, and with whom I cordially agreed.

E N C L O S U R E

Berne, Switzerland

My dear Colonel House: February Fourth [1918].

This letter is intended as a report on the political situation in Germany and the Central Powers. On January 28th. I asked the Legation to send you a long telegram on this subject but because the wires were "crowded" it could not be sent in the form I had written it and I do not know how it reached you.[1]

The address of the President, in which he stated the fourteen conditions of peace, has had the greatest effect upon the political situation within the enemy countries of any public address delivered since the United States has been a belligerent. It was successful in the following ways:

1. It separated absolutely, and I think permanently, the people and the Liberals from the Annexationists, the Military Leaders and the War Industrial magnates;

2. It forced the Austro-Hungarian Government to recognize the peace movement in that country and cemented the Dual Monarchy to the German Liberal party;

3. It gave more momentum to the revolutionary movement, which is under way in Germany, than the Russian revolution;

4. It increased the possibilities of success for the present confidential negotiations which are taking place with Bulgaria, and

5. It made a tremendous impression upon the small European neutrals.

I need not go into detail in regard to these points because you have undoubtedly received through the Department full information regarding the strikes, the fight over Count Hertling's reply and the dispute between Vienna and Berlin.

After Mr. Wilson's speech was printed in the Swiss papers, Dr. Louis Schulthess, a friend of mine, saw President Calonder,[2] of the Swiss Republic and the latter stated that "Now it is clear that the United States is fighting for an ideal; that the United States has nothing to gain by fighting except permanent peace."

At the same time President Calonder commissioned Dr. Schulthess, a former attache of the Swiss Legation in Washington, to study the question of a League of Nations and report on what part Switzerland could play in the formation of such an organization.

In my telegram of January 28th. I suggested that the President reply to Count Hertling and Count Czernin in order to force the issue of peace on our terms, which are essentially the terms of the German and Austrian people, or of war on Count Hertling's terms.

I believe that we should adopt a firm, determined and uncompromising attitude toward Count Hertling on the ground that he voiced the sentiments of the German War party, which wants to continue the war, and on the ground that he did not speak for the people.

I suggested that we assume a different attitude toward Vienna for the purpose of attempting to widen the gap between the two belligerents.

Since I made these suggestions I have concluded that it was fear of revolution more than anything else which prompted Count Czernin to aim his remarks at the President and say that Austria-Hungary considered the President's terms as possible basis for discussions. I believe our aims should be to strengthen the peace party in Vienna and Budapest so as to force Count Czernin to *ask* the United States, officially, to make peace between the Dual Monarchy and the Entente. Unless the Austrian government succeeds in getting food from Russia we may have an opportunity to talk separate peace with that country.

The situation within Germany and Austria-Hungary, to my mind, is the following:

If there is not peace, or a great military victory, there will be a revolution. Perhaps it is more accurate to say that there are three possible developments: 1. Peace; 2. Reformation; 3. Revolution, because I do not believe the German army and navy will be able to decisively defeat the United States and the Allies this year.

The war has reached the decisive period. To my mind, the problem facing the United States is this:

How far can the United States go in encouraging the peace movement and the reform forces within Central Europe without weakening the determination of the Allies to fight until a just peace can be concluded.

The solution is: War, relentless war with armies and speeches against the German War government but peace with the democratic, or reform, peace forces.

Very sincerely and respectfully,   Carl W. Ackerman

TLS (WP, DLC).
    1 It is printed in H. R. Wilson to RL, Jan. 30, 1918.
    2 Felix Ludwig Calonder.

From Benedict Crowell, with Enclosure

My dear Mr. President: Washington March 6, 1918.

Enclosed please find a very important cable just received from General Bliss.

The War Department concurs entirely in the recommendation submitted by General Bliss in Paragraph 4 of this communication.

Will you please instruct me what you wish done.

Very truly yours,   Benedict Crowell

TCL (WDR, RG 407, World War I Cable Section, DNA).

E   N   C   L   O   S   U   R   E

Received at the War Department
Washington—March 6, 1918. 7:10 A.M.

From: Versailles.

To: The Adjutant General, Washington.

Number 44 March 5th Very Confidential

For the Chief of Staff and Secretary of War.

Paragraph 1. Connect the following with paragraph five of my number twenty-one dated February 3d on the subject of Inter-Allied General Reserve.[1]

Paragraph 2. The special executive committee mentioned in paragraph five of my number 21 was charged with duty of determining the composition and strength of the General Reserve and the contribution of each nation thereto and so forth. The Committee began its work immediately and unanimously agreed upon the number of British, French and Italian divisions that should form the Reserve. After conference with each of them the French and Italian Commanders in Chief[2] concurred after certain minor modifications to which the committee agreed. Yesterday the British Commander Field Marshal General Sir Douglas Haig submitted a * * * (letter) in which for reasons given he declined to take part in the formation of the Inter Allied General Reserve. After very careful consideration the committee adopted the resolution which is quoted in following paragraph number three. Before communicating it to the respective governments the committee decided to wait 24 hours in order to enable General Rawlinson the British Military Representative to visit General Sir Douglas Haig's headquarters and discuss the matter with him. He has done so and has informed us that General Sir Douglas Haig declines to change the view taken in his letter. Our resolution follows:

Paragraph 3. "The Supreme War Council, at its session of February 2d, in the presence of the Commanders in Chief of the French and British armies and of the Italian Minister of War[3] decided upon the creation of an Inter Allied General Reserve and delegated to an executive war board its power in all that concerns the constitution, positions and use of this reserve.

"The executive war board, at its sitting of February 6th, drew up a joint letter to the Commanders in Chief, making certain proposals in regard to the constitution and positions of the General Reserve.

"By written and verbal communications General Foch and General Petain, an agreement with the French Commander in Chief was reached on February 19th.

"By written and verbal communications between General Giardino[4] and General Diaz the agreement with the Italian Commander in Chief was reached first March, as is shown by the minutes of the meeting of March 2d.

"In his letter of March 2nd, the Field Marshal, Commander in Chief of the British Armies, states that he is unable to comply with the request(s) contained in the first letter of the Executive War Board.

"Under these circumstances, the Executive War Board finds itself unable to continue its work and therefore unable to organize the Inter Allied General Reserve, as the Supreme War Council at its sitting of February 2d had instructed it to do; and the Executive War Board decides that each military representative shall so inform his own government and ask for instructions."

Paragraph 4. Field Marshal General Sir Douglas Haig and all military men present at the recent third session of the Supreme War Council end of January and beginning of February were unanimous in the belief that success of the Allied cause in approaching campaign(s) required the creation of an Inter Allied General Reserve. I suggest that this matter be taken up with the President at once and that with his approval acknowledgment of receipt by our Government of the resolution quoted in paragraph three above be cabled to the British Government. I further suggest that the American Government in its message to London, while admitting the possibility that the military situation on the British front may make it impracticable to assign British divisions to the Inter Allied General Reserve, nevertheless the principle of such a General Reserve should not be abandoned and that the other Allies who are able to contribute to it should promptly do so. My personal opinion is that there is danger that the Italian and French Commanders may hold aloof when they learn the attitude of the British Commander although they may not have the same reasons for doing so. If the entire lines from front of the North Sea to the Adriatic Sea were held by one homogeneous army its Commander in Chief would not hesitate to form his general reserve from his right and his center even although he could not use any troops on his left for that general reserve. That should be the view taken in this case. Wire me action taken.[5]

Bliss.

TC telegram (WDR, RG 407, World War I Cable Section, DNA).
[1] T. H. Bliss to H. P. McCain, Feb. 3, 1918, printed as an Enclosure with NDB to WW, Feb. 4, 1918.
[2] That is, Gen. Pétain and Gen. Armando Diaz. Diaz had succeeded Gen. Luigi Cadorna as commander in chief of the Italian army in November 1917.
[3] Vittorio Alfieri.
[4] Gen. Gaetano Ettore Giardino, Italy's representative on the Supreme War Council.
[5] See H. P. McCain to T. H. Bliss, March 12, 1918.

From Benedict Crowell

My dear Mr. President: Washington March 6, 1918.

Among the confidential papers brought from France by General March,[1] the most important is Joint Note No. 12.[2] I cannot emphasize too strongly the importance of this paper, and I beg that you will read it. The important points have been under-lined by me by pencil.   Very truly yours,   Benedict Crowell

TLS (WP, DLC).
[1] March had succeeded Biddle as Acting Chief of Staff, United States Army, on March 4, 1918.
[2] About which see T. H. Bliss to H. P. McCain, Feb. 4, 1918, and Peyton C. March, *The Nation at War* (Garden City, N.Y., 1932), pp. 24-27. Crowell's enclosure is missing.

From Thomas Watt Gregory

Dear Mr. President: Washington, D. C. March 6, 1918.

You wrote me on February 27th, enclosing a letter addressed to you by Mr. George Creel, asking me what I thought of the suggestion made by Mr. Creel with reference to about one hundred young Swedes at Rockford, Illinois, who were sentenced to the House of Correction for one year because of their failure to register.

Mr. Creel suggests that some prominent Swede talk with these prisoners and make recommendation as to pardons, based on a careful investigation of each individual case.

Just after your letter was received the Governor of Illinois[1] sent me a long wire, complaining of the situation in that State, in so far as disloyalty and kindred offenses are concerned.

Under the circumstances, I have thought that it was best to secure a general report from the District Attorney who prosecuted the parties referred to, and this was promptly called for. As soon as

I hear from him and from the Governor of Illinois in regard to the general situation, I will communicate with you further.[2]

Faithfully yours,   T. W. Gregory

TLS (WP, DLC).
[1] That is, Frank O. Lowden.
[2] See TWG to WW, March 24, 1918, printed as an Enclosure with WW to G. Creel, March 25, 1918.

From Joseph Hampton Moore

Dear Mr. President: Washington, D. C. March 6, 1918.

So far as I have observed, no Democrat has stated with authority that you approve the War Finance Corporation Bill as a war measure.

I do not know whether you would care to make a statement to me upon this subject, but I am frank to say I would not want to vote for the transference of such tremendous powers over securities and the business affected by them unless I knew that such a recourse was, in the judgment of the President, essential for war purposes.

If you feel justified in writing me upon this point, I will appreciate it. Or if this suggestion does not meet with your approval, will you not authorize someone to make a positive declaration as to the war urgency of this bill?

The Ways and Means Committee is now preparing to report the bill, but I have heard many Members of the House inquire as to the President's attitude thereon.

Very truly yours,   J Hampton Moore

TLS (WP, DLC).

Sir William Wiseman to Sir Eric Drummond

[New York] March 6th, 1918.

No. 73. Following for FALSTERBO [BALFOUR] from SUNDGAU [READING] (who is in New York until Saturday. Until then you can therefore reach him most quickly through me):

(Begins). Have discussed JAPANESE situation with BRUSSA [HOUSE], from which it is manifest that, after sounding opinion here, Administration, as cabled to you yesterday, has receded from position it first assumed and has reverted to view ADRAMYTI [WILSON] originally adopted at our last interview with him. I argued with BRUSSA that if France, Italy, and we ask Japan to act and America stands out, the position will be misrepresented by Germans as proving that our aims are not disinterested otherwise America would have joined. Thus the danger of Russians being driven into arms of Germany by seeking assistance against Japanese will be greater than ever. BRUSSA said that the Administration had already acted and had handed its note to Japanese representative this morning. BRUSSA wished me to cable the above conversation to you.

T telegram (W. Wiseman Papers, CtY).

To Benedict Crowell

Confidential.

My dear Mr. Secretary: [The White House] 7 March, 1918

Thank you for the confidential paper brought by General March from France.

I fully agree with you that it is a memorandum of the greatest importance, but, after all, is not the embarrassment about carrying out our part of the programme created rather by the conditions on the other side of the water than by the conditions on this side? We have been sending over more troops and more supplies than could be promptly landed and unloaded at the French ports assigned for our use, and faster than they could be got away from those ports after being landed and unloaded, and I am wondering if there is not some way of getting our friends on the other side of the water to realize that the dam our waters have to overflow lies in their neighborhood.   Sincerely yours,   [Woodrow Wilson]

CCL (WP, DLC).

To Joseph Hampton Moore

My dear Mr. Moore: [The White House] 7 March, 1918

I am very happy to answer the question contained in your letter of March sixth.

I am entirely in favor of the adoption of the War Finance Corporation Bill. I deem it in fact a necessary war measure.

Very sincerely yours,   Woodrow Wilson

TLS (Letterpress Books, WP, DLC).

To Julius Rosenwald

My dear Mr. Rosenwald: [The White House] 7 March, 1918

I consider your letter of yesterday[1] a very generous one, which does you real honor, and this is just a line to express my genuine appreciation.

I have realized that you must have felt recently that you and your associates were a bit thrown out of function, but I hope you realize that if that is true, it is largely because of the excellence of the work you did and the fact that it has come to a full fruitage.

I shall keep your generous suggestion in mind and hope that if you have any thoughts of your own in the matter, you will not hesitate to let me know what they are.

Cordially and sincerely yours, Woodrow Wilson

TLS (Letterpress Books, WP, DLC).
[1] It is missing.

To Charles Spalding Thomas

My dear Senator: [The White House] 7 March, 1918

I have been working on the lines of the memorandum you left with me last Saturday evening[1] and want you to know that I have followed each of the difficulties you mention up as far as I could. I think I can report that the difficulties and obstacles which disturbed you and your colleagues are being removed wherever it is possible to remove them, and I can assure you that I will keep in touch so as to hasten the processes of correction as much as possible.

When I went into the details I was not as much disturbed as I was when you left me. I may use this figure: The waters have not yet begun to run rapidly over the dam, because the dam has been unexpectedly high and the volume of the water slower than we expected in accumulating, but it will presently begin to run over faster and faster.

Cordially and sincerely yours, Woodrow Wilson

TLS (Letterpress Books, WP, DLC).
[1] It is missing. "Last Saturday" was March 2.

To John Sanford Cohen

My dear Mr. Cohen: [The White House] 7 March, 1918

Thank you very warmly for your note of March fourth[1] with the generous editorial enclosed.[2] I read such an editorial with deep gratitude and yet with very mixed feelings, because while I can conscientiously say that I have done my very best, it makes me very humble to be so commended, because I feel perhaps more keenly than others can the things that have been left undone and the things that might have been better done. None of this, however, robs me of the very deep pleasure of having such friends and supporters.   Cordially and sincerely yours,   Woodrow Wilson

TLS (Letterpress Books, WP, DLC).
    [1] J. S. Cohen to WW, March 4, 1918, TLS (WP, DLC). Cohen was editor of the *Atlanta Journal*.
    [2] "Five Years of Wilson," *Atlanta Journal*, March 4, 1918, which commemorated the fifth anniversary of Wilson's inauguration. The editorial recalled Wilson's prophetic remark in 1913, "Here muster not the forces of party, but the forces of humanity," and it noted that humanity had been "the guiding voice, the 'vision splendid' " of his entire administration. After five years of "all-searching test," the editorial concluded, Wilson stood "in the mind of America and of the world as a greater President, a more heroic figure" than his warmest admirers could have foreseen five years before.

To Josephus Daniels

Personal and Confidential.

My dear Daniels: The White House 7 March, 1918

    Representatives of the Norfolk Navy Yard Riggers called on me the other day,[1] and I must say made a very deep impression upon me to this effect (quite apart from what I may call the interior merits of the questions they raised), namely, that Constructor Watt[2] had probably better be relieved from his present duty at the Navy Yard in some way that will not in the least reflect upon him and someone put in charge who can better understand the temper and attitude of the men. I also got the impression that probably the man Lewis[3] referred to had also better be put elsewhere if he is to be retained at all. After all, the matters involved do not seem to be so much matters of policy as matters of personnel, and irritations have sprung up and been increased which it would surely be best to remove if possible.

    Of course, I formed this opinion without consultation with anybody in the department or at the Navy Yard and hold it subject to correction. I am merely stating it frankly to you for your consideration.   Cordially and faithfully yours,   Woodrow Wilson

TLS (J. Daniels Papers, DLC).
    [1] Wilson saw John N. Egense and James R. Christian, riggers at the Norfolk Navy Yard, on March 4.
    [2] Capt. Richard Morgan Watt, in charge of construction at the Norfolk Navy Yard.
    [3] "Master Laborer" of the riggers at the Norfolk Navy Yard.

From Herbert Clark Hoover

Dear Mr. President: Washington, D. C. 7 *March 1918*

I enclose herewith a letter which I addressed to Lord Reading and his reply thereto.[1] The situation with regard to wheat supplies in this country gets more and more difficult as time goes on and if we succeed in delivering to seaboard the amount of wheat products that have been allocated to the railways for transportation during the present month, we will apparently have a residue of about 130,000,000 bushels available to carry our people for a period of four months. And this assuming that we get every grain of wheat from the farmer except his seed. I do not presume that we can count on the last 30,000,000 bushels from the farmer and therefore we have now before us about 25,000,000 bushels a month against a normal consumption of 40,000,000 bushels. There is, in addition to this, a certain amount in transit and in retail stocks.

I have replied to Lord Reading that under these circumstances it seems to me it is a matter that requires your decision.

I remain   Your obedient servant,   Herbert Hoover

TLS (WP, DLC).
[1] Hoover had informed Reading that there was a temporary glut of beef and pork in the United States but a shortage of breadstuffs so serious that he did not see how the current level of exports could be maintained. On the theory that "food is food," Hoover suggested that the Allies take additional amounts of meat for the time being. H. C. Hoover to Lord Reading, March 1, 1918, CCL (WP, DLC). Reading replied that he had found Hoover's letter so important that he had immediately consulted with Tardieu and the Italian Ambassador. If satisfactory arrangements could be worked out, Reading went on, the Allies were willing to take more pork and beef, but these were not substitutes for bread. Hoover's statement about not being able to maintain the level of bread exports was "alarming," and the three Allied representatives were "anxious to ascertain" where their countries stood with regard to shipments of breadstuffs for April and May. Lord Reading to H. C. Hoover, March 4, 1918, TCL (WP, DLC).

From Joseph Patrick Tumulty

Dear Governor: [The White House] 7 March, 1918

Answering your inquiry, the results of the congressional elections in New York[1] of yesterday are most significant and carry a great deal of hope and promise. The New York Times, commenting on the result says:

"New York City can be counted on to stand by the President in the war. That much stands out from the returns of the Congressional elections held in four districts yesterday."

In another part of the editorial is found the following:

"The outlook for the Republicans in next fall's election is not particularly happy. This election is a straw and what is shown is that the wind is blowing strongly in the direction of a thorough-going, out and out support of the President that will innure to the advantage of the Democratic candidates. In every district a Democrat was elected in spite of the fact that one of the districts, the twenty-first, was counted as Republican."

Two of the districts had been recently gerrymandered by the New York Legislature, and the Democrats attempted to set this gerrymander aside by appealing to the courts, but were unsuccessful. In view of the results and the campaign recently carried on by Chairman Hays of the Republican National Committee[2] in his attempt to get together the various "shreds and patches" of the Republican party, I think the result is remarkable. Following in the wake of winter, with the results of the fuel order still fresh in the minds of the people, with the income tax burdening a great many of those who voted, and with the injection into the situation of woman suffrage, no Democrat can read these results without being able to prophesy with some degree of certainty as to the effect they will have on next fall's election.

For instance, in the Bronx district, which is by no means heavily Democratic, the Democrat[3] received 8,000 votes, the Socialist, 2600, and the Republican candidate 2,000. John Fitzgerald's district is by no means safely Democratic; in that district the Democrat[4] won by 5,000 majority. In this district there were a great many German and Socialist votes, particularly in Williamsburg.

With every political element against us that generally would work to our disadvantage, we triumphed. I think the significance of it will be found in the results in Wisconsin.[5] Every report I have from there indicates the election of Davies.

By the way, another straw which indicates the drift toward us is the election of Ole Hanson as Mayor in Seattle, Washington. You will recall that in the last campaign he played a prominent part in our behalf. He ran as Mayor with the record of your administration as a slogan and won by 4,000 votes.

I think what we ought to do is to encourage Mr. Hays and Mr. Roosevelt and Mr. Hughes and Mr. Wickersham to make their partisan attacks on us. We should remain silent and indifferent and attend to the business of war.   Faithfully,   Tumulty

TLS (WP, DLC).

[1] Democrats on March 5 had won special elections in four districts in New York City to replace members of the House of Representatives who had resigned.

[2] William Harrison Hays, a lawyer of Sullivan, Ind., and chairman of the Republican State Central Committee of Indiana, had been elected chairman of the Republican National Committee on February 13.

[3] Anthony Jerome Griffin.

[4] John Joseph Delaney.

[5] Joseph E. Davies, Democrat, and Representative Irvine L. Lenroot, Republican, were the two principal candidates to fill the unexpired term of the late Senator Husting. The election was to be held on April 2, 1918.

From Gordon Auchincloss, with Enclosure

Dear Mr Wilson: [Washington] March 7 [1918]

Mr House asked me to send you this

Faithfully yours   Gordon Auchincloss

ALS (WP, DLC).

E N C L O S U R E

A Memorandum by William Christian Bullitt

Department of State, March 6, 1918.

Memorandum for Mr. Polk and Colonel House.

Subject: The Political Situation in Germany and Austria-Hungary.

Substance: All Parties in Germany with the exception of the Minority Socialists are now supporting the Government's policy of creating a chain of vassal buffer states along the eastern border of Germany and Austria-Hungary. Even the Majority Socialists are tamely acquiescent. It is highly advisable that the President should not reply to Hertling until the present unity in Germany has again been disrupted.

Germany to-day is more unified in support of the policy of the Government than at any time since the first months of the war. This condition is surely temporary; nevertheless it predestines to failure any immediate attempt by the President to create differences between the Government and the people. Furthermore, Count Czernin has not yet spoken. And it seems imperative that the President should await Czernin's speech and a new swing of the pendulum in Germany before delivering another address directed at the Central Empires.

The addresses of Hertling and Payer on February 25[1] apparently created this new German unity, but its true cause lies much deeper in the joy of all classes in Germany at the signing of treaties of peace with the Ukraine and Russia.

The fact that the Government, although still professing to adhere to decent principles, has embarked upon an annexationist policy troubles only the Minority Socialists. *Vorwaerts* regrets the abandonment of its ideals but lets them slide. The German people are interested primarily in peace. If the Government insists on annexations with the peace—well, the peace has been achieved anyhow, and that is the important thing. Moreover, the Government is thoughtful enough to annex in the name of order and to subjugate in the name of liberation.

The policy of the German Government is now clear. England, France, Italy and Belgium will be offered something like the *status quo ante bellum*, provided they will allow the Central Powers to establish between themselves and Russia a line of dependent states! These states will stretch from the Black Sea to the Arctic Ocean. Finland will be wholly independent, but will be wholly within the German sphere of influence,—at least so long as the pro-German Bourgeoisie can be kept in power. Esthonia and Livonia, according to the Chancellor, will not be annexed; but will be kept in a condition of semi-dependence, by means of the pro-German upper classes who will be maintained by German bayonets. "In Courland and Lithuania our chief object is to create organs of self-determination and self-administration" says the Chancellor. The self-administration, one may safely assume, will be established beneath the guiding hand of a German general; and the self-determination will be managed in such a way that these countries either will be attached outright to the German Empire or will be brought within the Imperial Customs Union and will lapse into the position of Luxemburg.

Poland, apparently, is to suffer another partition. The Imperial Chancellor frankly admitted in his address of February 25 that Germany intended to annex portions of Russian Poland and attempted to show Germany's extreme humanity by saying, "Only what is indispensable on military grounds will be demanded on Germany's part." The German Government seems to have decided that it will be impossible to conciliate the Poles and to make them docile vassals. Lithuania and Ukrainia are, therefore, being favored with promises of territory which legitimately go to Poland; and Poland is to be made to[o] weak to offer resistance.

Ukrainia is to become a sort of Austro-German protectorate governed by a Bourgeois Rada relying wholly on the Central Powers for support. For only by Teuton bayonets can it be kept in power.

Hungary is to annex the mountain passes and sufficient additional Rumanian territory on the border of Transylvania to place the remainder of Rumania absolutely at the mercy of the Austro-Hungarian army. Bulgaria is to annex the whole of the Dobrudja as far as the mouths of the Danube and in addition is to seize portions of Serbian and Rumanian territory which lie between her and Hungary. There are, moreover, indications that the Central Powers will strive to bring Rumania altogether into their camp by dethroning the King, seating a German princelet in his place, and salving Rumania's wounds by the gift of Bessarabia.

The success of this scheme for the creation of a series of vassal buffer states on the eastern borders of Germany and Austria-Hungary depends wholly on the continuance of the military success of the Central Powers. For only by bayonets can the pro-German upper classes of these states be kept in power. Were it not for German interference all these states would be controlled by the revolutionary proletariat. They would be close to revolutionary Russia in spirit and would gravitate towards her rather than towards the Hapsburgs and the Hohenzollerns. All through this strip of Europe the nobles, the bourgeosie, the White Guards rely on Germany. The common people look for help to Russia. The Red Guards and the Poles are our only possible allies against Germany.

It is needless to quote at length from the comments of the press on the addresses of Hertling and Payer and on the ultimatum to Russia.[2] The Conservatives were deeply enraged that Payer coupled them with the Independent Socialists as enemies of the country. And the Conservatives also had little use for Hertling's lip-service to the President's principles. But they recognized that annexations were being made in Russia and therefore did not balk much at Hertling's words.

All other parties except the Independent Socialists were delighted with both Hertling and Payer, the latter earning particular applause for his insults to the Junkers.

The following excerpt from the *Berliner Tageblatt* of February 27 illustrates the strange state of mind of better Germany:

"The terms of the ultimatum to Russia will please even the most unrelenting advocates of violence. It would be interesting to hear Hertling, who accepted Wilson's second principle, that people are not to be bartered about from sovereign to sovereign, explain just what differences exist between the political methods of the past and those of to-day. One sees on examination that states are artificially created as in the case of the Rhenish federation and the Kingdom of Westfalia. Even in those days representatives of the people were able to press their wishes. It may be conceded that to-day the German Reichstag is informed of coming changes, but not until the matter has been settled without it. We all hope this policy will bring peace and prosperity, but we cannot conceal our anxiety at the birth of these new states."

It will not be long before the President can again appeal to the German Socialists and Liberals. But to-day a scathing indictment of German policy in the East would serve merely to unify the people behind the Government.

For the present, therefore, we had better fight and say nothing.

Respectfully submitted: William C. Bullitt.

TS MS (WP, DLC).

¹ About Hertling's speech, see also n. 1 to the draft of an address printed at March 1, 1918. Friedrich von Payer, the German Vice-Chancellor, had also addressed the Reichstag on February 25 about internal affairs and particularly about the wartime political truce, the *Burgfrieden*. He spoke of the need for unity at home and condemned the recent wave of strikes, which he said had had little practical effect but might encourage Germany's enemies and thus prolong the war. *New York Times*, Feb. 27, 1918. The text of Payer's speech is printed in *Schulthess' Europäischer Geschichtskalender*, LIX (1918), Part I, pp. 91-98.

² See n. 3 to Enclosure I printed with Lord Reading to WW, Feb. 27, 1918.

James Ripley Wellman Hitchcock to
Edward Mandell House

Dear Colonel House: New York March 7, 1918

May I express my very warm appreciation of your generous kindness in presenting to the President the various matters which we have discussed. I quite understand that the question of an association is one that could not have an affirmative reply at present; but I have hoped that our suggestion would be remembered and that when the proper time arrives it would be considered before any other arrangement were made.

May I refer again to the Limited Edition of the HISTORY OF THE AMERICAN PEOPLE which we are preparing in a Documentary Edition, increased to ten volumes by the addition of original papers and illustrations. There are to be four hundred (400) sets. Would it not be possible to make this edition of service to the Red Cross or some other form of War Relief, in addition to other considerations?

We venture to hope that the President may be willing to sign this edition on the understanding that we will pay a royalty of $3.00 on every set that is sold to whatever War charity the President may select. It would be stated of course that the edition has been signed in order that it might bring a contribution to War Relief. Of course the mechanical part would be arranged in the most convenient form. We feel that this would mean a great deal to readers and collectors of American History. We hope very earnestly that the President may consider the suggestion favorably, and that he may permit us to send the four hundred pages for signature. The War Relief royalty of $3.00 would be of course in addition to the author's royalty of five dollars a set.

Believe me, with deep appreciation of your courtesy,

Very faithfully yours,   Ripley Hitchcock

TLS (WP, DLC).

Sir William Conyngham Greene to the Foreign Office

PARAPHRASE OF A CABLE FROM H. M. AMBASSADOR IN TOKIO TO THE
FOREIGN OFFICE.

Tokio, March 7th. 1918.

In conversation today with the Minister for Foreign Affairs[1] I
spoke to him with regard to the probable attitude of his Government
if it was found that the United States did not approve of Japanese
intervention, without actually objecting to it. I said that I understood
that President Wilson feared that this measure would be misunderstood in Russia and would be turned to advantage by the enemies of the Revolution, with whose democratic aims he sympa-
thizes. His Excellency answered that if the attitude of the United
States made it impossible for Japan to obtain assistance from her
financially and in such materials as steel, it would be very difficult
for Japan to act on the invitation of the Allies, and, therefore, that
unless the Allies could count on the President's support it would
perhaps be better that action should be deferred. He seemed to
think that the situation in Russia was not so urgent as to make
such delay unwise, and that it would be a great misfortune to the
allied cause and a great assistance to the enemy if any disagreement
should occur or be represented as having occurred in allied ranks.
His Excellency's words are in agreement with the opinion which
I have lately heard expressed in responsible quarters, to the effect
that the former eagerness shown by the Minister for Foreign Affairs
for intervention had been reduced by the element in the Cabinet,
which includes the Prime Minister and the Minister of the Interior,[2]
who have doubts as to the endurance of the Allies and who consider
that intervention is impracticable without financial and material
assistance from the United States. If it is considered wiser to defer
action, I do not think that to do so will necessarily disappoint the
Cabinet who are satisfied with our action hitherto and who are
especially pleased with us for not insisting on our demand for the
participation of allied troops in intervention.

The General Staff continues to prepare to take action at short
notice, though this action would probably be influenced, particularly with regard to the extent of the advance into Russia, by the
desires of the Allies and by the financial and other assistance they
could give.

The above, of course, constitutes merely an appreciation of the
local aspect of the matter which does not take into consideration
the European situation of which I know nothing save that here it
is generally supposed that France is the most insistent of the Allies
in favour of intervention.

Sir Wm. gave me this for your information. He requests that it does not get beyond you. E.M.H.[3]

T MS (WP, DLC).
  [1] That is, Viscount Ichiro Motono.
  [2] That is, Count Masatake Terauchi and Baron Shimpei Gotō.
  [3] EMHhw.

To Theodore Marburg

My dear Mr. Marburg: The White House 8 March, 1918

Thank you very much for letting me see the letter from Lord Bryce which you were kind enough to enclose in your letter of March fifth and which I am herewith returning.

Frankly, I do not feel that it is wise to discuss now the formal constitution of a league to enforce peace. The principle is easy to adhere to, but the moment questions of organization are taken up all sorts of jealousies come to the front which ought not now to be added to other matters of delicacy. I am sure you will appreciate the force of these considerations.

In unavoidable haste, with much regard,
                    Sincerely yours,   Woodrow Wilson

TLS (WP, DLC).

To Herbert Clark Hoover

My dear Mr. Hoover: The White House 8 March, 1918

I have your letter of yesterday and realize the very great seriousness of the prospect you point out, namely, a probable shortage for our own people of 15,000,000[1] a month in the wheat supply, and you close your letter by saying, "It seems to me it is a matter which requires your decision."

I am not sure what it is you think I ought to decide. I suppose you mean that I ought to decide whether we are to continue our present scale of shipment of breadstuffs across the seas and so incur the shortage for our own people to which you refer. I am afraid there is no choice in the matter. The populations across the sea must be fed and have, as I understand it, no available substitutes for wheat, whereas our own people have at least substitutes and have them, I believe (have they not?) in adequate quantities. Personally, I feel confident that the spirit of our people would rise to the sacrifice and that, if there are adequate quantities of the available substitutes, they would be willing to use them. Is not that your own judgment?

Cordially and sincerely yours,   Woodrow Wilson

TLS (H. Hoover Papers, HPL).
  [1] Wilson dictated "bushels" at this point.

To Elizabeth Herndon Potter[1]

My dear Mrs. Potter: [The White House] 8 March, 1918

Through the courtesy of Senator Sheppard I have received your letter of March seventh.[2] I feel it a privilege to express my earnest hope that the Legislature of Texas may see its way to adopt a statute which will give women the right to vote in the primaries. The Democratic party is so clearly committed to the principle of woman suffrage that I feel it my duty as the leader of the party to urge this action by the Legislature, and it is also a privilege which I value to yield to my own personal convictions in this matter and urge such action on its merits. I sincerely hope that the measure may become law.   Cordially and sincerely yours,   Woodrow Wilson

TLS (Letterpress Books, WP, DLC).
  [1] Mrs. J. Edwin Potter, of Tyler, Tex., third vice-president of the Texas Equal Suffrage Association.
  [2] Elizabeth H. Potter to WW, March 7, 1918, TLS (WP, DLC), enclosed in M. Sheppard to WW, March 7, 1918, TLS (WP, DLC).

To Benedict Crowell

My dear Mr. Secretary: [The White House] 8 March, 1918

The enclosed telegram from the Governor of Arizona disturbs me very much.[1] The action of some of the local authorities in regard to the deportations from Arizona were very discreditable, grossly illegal, and I am a bit shocked to find that the Sheriff of Cochise County is now in the Reserve Corps. I wonder if there can be any mistake as to identity.

Cordially and sincerely yours,   Woodrow Wilson

TLS (Letterpress Books, WP, DLC).
  [1] This telegram from Governor Hunt of Arizona is missing, but, as subsequent documents reveal, it concerned the commissioning of Sheriff Harry C. Wheeler as a captain in the Reserve Corps of the Army Signal Corps.

From Frank Lyon Polk

My dear Mr. President: Washington March 8, 1918.

I thought you might be interested to know that I communicated on Tuesday this Government's position on the Siberian question to the Japanese Chargé.[1] He seemed to appreciate that the suggestion was made with a view to the best interests of the Allies. I reminded him of the fact that the Japanese Ambassadors from London and Paris at the Interallied Council had both unofficially and personally stated to Colonel House that they thought an intervention in Siberia by the Japanese would be undesirable. The Chargé admitted this, but said the situation had materially changed.

The British Embassy here informs me that the Japanese Ambassador in London[2] told Mr. Balfour some day this week that his Government would move cautiously as to any intervention in Siberia on the assumption that delay would not entail the loss of any important military advantages, and it might be a great utility from the standpoint of public opinion in Russia.

                                    Yours faithfully,   Frank L. Polk

TLS (WP, DLC).
  [1] Tokichi Tanaka, Counselor of the Japanese embassy in Washington.
  [2] Viscount Sutemi Chinda.

From Edward Mandell House, with Enclosures

Dear Governor: New York, March 8, 1918.

I am enclosing you one cable from Balfour in answer to the one I sent him about the Japanese exprditionary [expeditionary] venture into Siberia, and one concerning another proposed meeting between Austrian and British representatives. I cannot quite understand why Austria would want to continue conversations with England while they are having them with us. In the circumstances would it not be best to do nothing in the way of answering either Austria or Germany publicly. The longer the western offensive is put off, the better is it for the Entente for it gives us more time to get our men over and break them in.

I met Frank Munsey the other night and I gave him such a talk about you that he declared that in the future the Sun would support your foreign policy. I am doubtful of this, but the enclosed editorial is a good beginning.[1]

Root, Lowell and I think Taft have received letters from Lord Bryce urging that this Government should appoint a committee to meet with a committee which the English Government has already appointed with Bryce at its head, in order to formulate a plan for a league of nations.

Bryce says in his letter to Lowell that in the event our Government declines to name such a committee that one be self constituted. Root told me last Sunday when he was here that he wanted to discuss the matter with me and that he wished to conform with your views.

There is an editorial in the last Saturday Evening Post about this in which they urge such action. I am enclosing it.[2] I think they are wholly wrong in their view and I shall ask Blythe tomorrow to set Larimore[3] straight.

Lowell, too, has the wrong notion. He thinks the Allies should formulate a plan, institute a league at once, and permit other nations to come in if a majority or two thirds of the Entente sanction it. This would mean nothing more than an alliance of the Entente and a bid for whatever neutrals that could be persuaded to join. The Central Powers would undoubtedly form a similar league and you would have the great powers arrayed against one another, and each side bidding for neutral countries to join their particular group.

It seems to me that a committee might be formed over here, not with governmental sanction but with its tacit approval, to work out plans which might be used as suggestions at the peace conference. Further than this I do not think it would be wise to go, and yet public opinion is driving so hard in this direction, that I doubt if it would be wise to do less.

Will you not give me your views?

Affectionately yours,   E. M. House

TLS (WP, DLC).

[1] "The Acid Test," New York *Sun*, March 8, 1918. This editorial quoted part of the sixth 'point' of Wilson's address to Congress of January 8: "*The treatment accorded Russia by her sister nations in the months to come will be the acid test of their good will, of their comprehension of her needs as distinguished from their own interests, and of their intelligent and unselfish sympathy.*" The proposed intervention of the Allies in Siberia, the editorial continued, provided the acid test which Wilson had anticipated so strikingly in his speech. "Not since the war began," it concluded, "has anything illustrated in a more striking way the length of Mr. Wilson's vision and the accuracy of his insight than his omission to join offhand in the general approval by the Allies, for the sake of an obvious and important military advantage, of the proposed Siberian venture with its unmeasured possibilities of harm to Russia's future and to the cause of democracy throughout the world."

[2] "A Good Time to Start," *Saturday Evening Post*, CXC (March 9, 1918), 20. As the title and House's comment suggest, the editorial urged that an international conference be convened as soon as possible to outline a plan for a league of nations to maintain world peace.

[3] That is, Samuel George Blythe and George Horace Lorimer, editor in chief of the *Saturday Evening Post*.

ENCLOSURE   I

Sent. March 6th [1918].
Received. March 7. 12.30 P.M

Cable from Balfour to House.

I am grateful for your telegram of the 4th March, and much appreciate the frank exposition of your views which it contained.

Up to the moment when the Bolshivic Government decided to accept the German peace terms, I was opposed to Japanese intervention, as I hoped Bolshivic resistance to German aggression might continue.

When the Bolshivic surrendered unconditionally, it became of the utmost importance to prevent the rich supplies in Siberia from falling into German hands, and the only method by which this could be secured was by Japanese intervention on a considerable scale. Information reached us that Japanese Government were making preparations to take action in Eastern Siberia, while, owing to the public discussion of the question, it seemed likely that considerable resentment would be aroused in Japan if, the Japanese Government being willing to act on behalf of the Allies, a mandate were refused. The formidable pro-German party in Japan would have asserted that such a refusal was due to mistrust, and I fear that, however erroneous in fact, this sentiment would have predominated in Japanese opinion.

I need hardly emphasize the advantage to be gained by substituting for Japanese action alone and in her own interests action as mandatory of the Allied Powers. I am in full agreement with the proposals made in the last paragraph of your telegram, a telegram I sent to our Ambassador in duplicate on March 4th following these lines. This telegram was repeated to Lord Reading and I am telling him to send a copy to Sir William Wiseman immediately for your information.

Although reports have reached us that enemy prisoners in Siberia are being armed under Bolshevic instructions, yet the Bolshevic Government assert that they still intend to organize resistance to German aggression in spite of having signed a peace treaty. I have therefore telegraphed our agent to suggest to the Bolshevic Government that they should invite Japanese and Roumanian cooperation for this purpose. I fear, however, that there is little chance of the proposal being entertained, nor do I know how the Japanese and Roumanian Government would regard such an appeal.

I have done this so that we can put ourselves right with public opinion, if and when a statement is made on the whole subject.

I hope and believe that the action which has been taken and

which will, I feel sure, meet with the President's approval, will enable us to justify completely the intervention which we are asking Japan to undertake.

It will show that the Allies have been actuated by no selfish or mean motives, and if Japan consents to undertake the obligation on such terms, might not it contribute to allay the suspicion which exists in many quarters both here and in the United States.[1]

[1] Another copy of this telegram is A. J. Balfour to E. M. House, No. 62, March 6, 1917, T telegram (W. Wiseman Papers, CtY).

E N C L O S U R E I I

MOST SECRET. *Cable.* Despatched: March 7th [1918].
Received March 8th, 11 a.m

From Balfour to House.

You will remember that in my telegram of Jan. 2nd.[1] I informed you of conversations which were held in Switzerland between British and Austrian representatives and promised to let you know of any further developments. The respective representatives were General Smuts and Mensdorff and it was agreed when meeting ended that if Austria wished to approach us again with regard to peace possibilities she would make use of the same agent, who is an Austrian resident in Switzerland, as before.

We have recently had various telegrams from our Minister in Berne[2] containing statements made by this agent from which it appeared that Austria was desirious of making further communications to us on the subject.

In view of the past conversations and of great importance of keeping the door open, we think it very desirable that these approaches should not be ignored. The War Cabinet have therefore decided to send out an emissary[3] to see Austrian agent to explore the ground thoroughly and to report to them. He will not be empowered to negotiate nor to commit H.M.G. to any line of policy.

As soon as his report has been received the War Cabinet will consider matter further and I will not fail to keep you informed of results.

I do not think our action is in any way inconsistent with or can be harmful to interchange of messages which the President is conducting with the Emperor of Austria.

T MSS (WP, DLC).
[1] That is, R. H. Campbell to EMH, Jan. 2, 1918, Vol. 45.
[2] That is, Sir Horace George Montagu Rumbold.
[3] Philip Kerr. About this matter, see Sterling J. Kernek, *Distractions of Peace during War: The Lloyd George Government's Reactions to Woodrow Wilson, December, 1916-November, 1918* (Philadelphia, 1975), pp. 77-83.

From William Bauchop Wilson, with Enclosure

My dear Mr. President: Washington March 8, 1918.

With the hope of being able to devise some method of labor adjustment for the period of the war which would be acceptable to employers and employees, I have created a War Labor Conference Board composed of five men selected by the National Industrial Conference Board, an organization composed of about seventy thousand manufacturers, and five men selected by Mr. Gompers of the American Federation of Labor, each of these groups of five to select one additional member, making a body of twelve persons all told.

The representatives of the employers have selected Ex-President Taft as their additional member, and the representatives of labor have selected Frank P. Walsh as their additional representative. They will meet in this city Mondays, Tuesdays and Wednesdays of each week until they have either devised a plan or come to a final disagreement.

I am inclosing you a copy of my statement to the members of the Board at their first meeting, which sets forth the purpose of its creation and the hopes I have of beneficial results.[1]

Faithfully yours,   W B Wilson

TLS (WP, DLC).
[1] For the background, organization, and work of the War Labor Board, see Valerie Jean Conner, *The National War Labor Board: Stability, Social Justice, and the Voluntary State in World War I* (Chapel Hill, N.C., 1983).

E N C L O S U R E

FIRST SESSION.

The first meeting of the Commission was held at the office of the Secretary of Labor on Monday, February 25, 1918, and there were present Messrs. Hutcheson, Olander and Hayes, representing the employees,[1] and Messrs. Loree, Van Dervoort, Michael and Osborne, representing the employers.[2]

The Secretary of Labor gave a short talk, outlining the proposed task of the Commission, the substance of which is embodied in a letter since received from the Secretary of Labor, as follows:

GENTLEMEN of the WAR LABOR CONFERENCE BOARD:

I have asked you to undertake one of the most delicate and difficult tasks that has ever devolved upon any body of men in this country. I need not call to your attention all that is involved in the outcome of the war. We are not engaged in it solely out of sympathy with the countries of Europe that have been the victims of German militarism, although there would have been ample justification for our actions in the outrages perpetrated upon Belgium, Armenia, Serbia and the people of northern France. The sinking of our vessels on the high seas without warning, the destruction of the lives of our seamen, the blowing up of our manufacturing establishments, and the murder of our workmen employed in them, the attempt by intrigue to dismember our country and control the internal politics of the remainder, and the mandate of the German Imperial Government that we must only send one vessel a week to England, are conclusive evidence that the safety of our people and the continuity of our institutions are dependent upon the successful termination of the war.

We have been pioneers in blazing the way for democracy. We have established the most perfect government ever conceived in the mind of men. We have provided the means by which the masses of the people may work out their own destinies in their own way and at the same time protect the rights of minorities. We cannot afford to have these institutions menaced, let alone destroyed. It behooves us, then, to find some way of adjusting our own family quarrels at least until we have disposed of the common enemy without. It is for the accomplishment of that purpose that I have asked you to come together and utilize your combined intelligence and experience in devising a method of labor adjustment for the period of the war that will be mutually acceptable to labor and to capital.

Under the old methods of warfare it was frequently the case that an army could maintain itself upon the country through which it passed, using a comparatively small number of people at home to provide its munitions and equipment. That is now changed, and it has been variously estimated that it requires from four to ten workmen at home to maintain one soldier in the trenches. The vast amount of material needed requires the mobilization of labor in large numbers and the rapid transfer of many men from one line of industry to another. That means the training and retraining of men on a scale never before contemplated. One of the problems you will have to deal with will be the methods of providing for the retraining of men for the industries they are to follow to meet the dilution which must of necessity occur. I am not unmindful of the difficulties confronting you, but I am confident that you will find a way of solving them.

In the tour which I recently made across the country in connection with the work of the President's Mediation Commission I was thoroughly impressed with the absolute loyalty of the great mass of our people. The spirit of self-sacrifice was everywhere prevalent. There was no hesitancy on the part of either employers or employees to sacrifice all of their material possessions for the welfare of the country. The jarring notes that we found grew out of the fact that they were not willing to make sacrifices to each other. Nor were they willing to sacrifice the intangible things, like preconceived ideas and fixed prejudices about the relationship that should exist between employer and employee, which could not be computed in dollars and cents. I believe you will find these to be the greatest obstacles you will have to overcome, but I have an abiding faith that your practical common sense and profound patriotism will develop some just method by which we can maintain peace at home while we are fighting abroad.

When you have met and organized I will endeavor to provide such stenographic and clerical assistance as you may need.

CC MS (WP, DLC).
[1] William Levi Hutcheson; Victor A. Olander, vice-president of the International Seamen's Union of America and secretary-treasurer of the Illinois State Federation of Labor; and Frank J. Hayes, president of the United Mine Workers of America.
[2] Leonor Fresnel Loree, president of the Delaware and Hudson Co.; William Humphrey Van Dervoort, president and general manager of the Root & Van Dervoort Engineering Co. of East Moline, Ill.; Charles Edwin Michael, president of the Virginia Bridge & Iron Co.; and Loyall Allen Osborne, vice-president of the Westinghouse Electric & Manufacturing Co.

From Frank Lyon Polk

My dear Mr. President: Washington March 8, 1918.

The complete report of the conversation between Professor Lammash and Professor Herron has just been received from the Legation in Berne.[1] It is rather long but interesting, and I thought you might care to see it, particularly the last ten pages.

        Yours faithfully,   Frank L Polk

TLS (R. Lansing Papers, NjP).
[1] H. R. Wilson to the Secretary of State, Feb. 8, 1918, printed in FR-WWS 1918, 1, I, 82-105. The last ten pages reiterated Charles' desire for the reorganization of the Empire, said that the Vatican was deeply involved in the Emperor's peace overtures, and declared that only Wilson could bring things to a head in Vienna.

Pleasant Alexander Stovall to Robert Lansing

        Pontarlier (Berne), Mar. 8, 1918.

2811. Strictly confidential. My 2749.[1] Baron Jong has received a telegram dated February twenty-eight from Meinl which being interpreted reads as follows:

"Received your wire and cabled contents to chief[2] in Roumania at once. Hertling's speech very satisfactory and with Von Payer's pronouncement constitutes great progress. Please urge that President Wilson respond favorably which would contribute favorably towards peace in Germany."

Jong replied on his own initiative and without consultation that while progress was admitted, a favorable reply from the President might be greatly facilitated if Lammasch's suggestions were carried out as soon as possible in due form. He added that it would be important if assurances could be given that Eastern European problems would be reconsidered at general conference.

On March fourth Meinl replied to Jong having received telegram which in interpretation reads as follows:

"According to declaration of Lammasch Emperor is in favor of desired settlement. We hope Czernin also agrees. A change of cabinet officers is not favored. Reconsideration of Russian problems doubtful on account of Germany."   Stovall.

T telegram (R. Lansing Papers, NjP).
    [1] H. R. Wilson to RL, March 1, 1918, T telegram (R. Lansing Papers, NjP). Wilson here transmitted the text of a telegram from Lammasch to Baron Jong, written in Salzburg on February 18. Jong interpreted the covert language of the relevant portion of the telegram as follows: "Because of absence of Emperor the conversation was delayed several days. It took place on the fourteenth and I am very well satisfied with it. The Emperor accepts Herron's views concerning Austria's future and will soon announce this formally. I hope that the intrigues of Germany will do no harm. The proclamation of the Emperor (granting autonomy to racial units) which has been expected for so long will therefore soon appear."
    [2] That is, Count Czernin.

From the Diary of Josephus Daniels

1918 Friday 8 March

B. was pessimistic—predicted Constantine would be crowned King at Athens.[1] Germany would defeat the army at Salonica, & then go into Lombardy. Lane thought it would get help & provisions from Russia and other countries & could afford to wait before attacking on West front. "I am rather persuaded," said WW "that the friend who advised me to send members of cabinet out of Washington to learn what the country is thinking about is a good thing to do." Redfield thought Russia is liability instead of an asset. Lane disagreed. WW was grim, determined, & thought Japan should not go into Russia—it might throw Russia into protecting arms of Germany. He spoke of men in Wash. preaching pessimism, bitterly of dinner party gossip, and of others who lacked faith that history will repeat itself & that autocratic power must fall. It was glorious to hear his solemn & clear presentation of his faith & resolve—an antidote to selfish pessimism & it impressed all. McAdoo thought he ought to make a speech on April 6th. After discussing certain classes who were standing in way of victory &c., WW said "Now having proved that many of our fellow citizens are damn fools let us come to business.["]

Houston and nitrates. Hurley had, without consultation, taken boats for nitrates & put them to carrying nitrates to France. Crops need them. W.W. did not like taking them without consultation & McAdoo talked of loan & queer proposition[.] WW opposed class presentation whether of bankers or businessmen or labor men. WBW had said labor men had propaganda for labor man on Peace Commission

Henderson thinking of coming here. WBW feared his preaching socialism might divide labor. WW said it would be worse to make official protest

[1] That is, Burleson feared that the Germans would restore Constantine to the throne of Greece. See J. J. Jusserand to the French Foreign Ministry, Aug. 29, 1916 (second telegram of that date), n. 1, Vol. 38.

To William Bauchop Wilson

My dear Mr. Secretary: The White House 9 March, 1918

I have your letter of March eighth apprising me of the creation of the War Labor Conference Board and of the plans for its meeting three times a week. The plan is certainly a wise one and I hope that all you expect of it will come out of it.

Cordially and sincerely yours,   Woodrow Wilson

TLS (LDR, RG 174, DNA).

To James Henry Taylor

My dear Doctor Taylor: [The White House] 9 March, 1918

I am very much interested to hear of your plans for celebrating the fiftieth anniversary of the organization of the church,[1] and I wish most unaffectedly that I could say I would not only be present at one of the meetings, but would speak, but I am sure that you and the Session will realize that I am speaking the simple truth when I say that I every day use up all there is in my brain in performing the tasks from which I cannot in duty escape, and I have come to feel recently that I must save myself additional effort wherever it is possible to save it. I do not speak easily. It always costs me an effort, and I am never willing to speak unless I make some definite preparation. In view of these circumstances, I know that you will be generous enough to excuse me from speaking.

Cordially and sincerely yours,   Woodrow Wilson

TLS (Letterpress Books, WP, DLC).
[1] J. H. Taylor to WW, March 8, 1918, TCL (WP, DLC). Taylor was pastor of the Central Presbyterian Church of Washington, where Wilson usually worshiped.

To Emily Contee Lewis Stevens[1]

My dear Mrs. Stevens: [The White House] 9 March, 1918

May I not express to you the very deep distress with which I have heard of the death of your husband?[2] I always valued his friendship and it is with a distinct sense of personal loss that I hear of his departure. My heart goes out to you in profound sympathy.

Cordially and sincerely yours,   Woodrow Wilson

TLS (Letterpress Books, WP, DLC).
[1] Mrs. Edwin Augustus Stevens.
[2] Stevens had died on March 8 in Washington where he had been serving as a shipyard inspector.

To Maude Edwin Dunaway[1]

Personal and Confidential.

My dear Mr. Dunaway: [The White House] 9 March, 1918

Thank you for your interesting letter of March fifth with its enclosure, which I have read with great interest.[2]

I am afraid that you are under a misapprehension. The letter to Senator Robinson of which you speak[3] was written when I feared that the Senator might be contemplating withdrawing from public life, and was meant to express, as it did, my very great regret that he should entertain any such purpose and to express, also, the high value I have attached to his counsel and service to the Government; but I do not feel at liberty, Mr. Dunaway, to suggest who shall be candidates for Congress or who shall be preferred at the elections. I think that would be going beyond my prerogatives even as leader of the party. I have sometimes written letters to which some men in the public service seemed to me to be entitled, because all they asked of me was that I should state what their public services had been, but beyond that I do not think that it would be right for me to go.

You will understand that this letter is written with the most cordial appreciation of your own generous attitude toward me and toward the Administration.

Cordially and sincerely yours, Woodrow Wilson

TLS (Letterpress Books, WP, DLC).
¹ Lawyer of Little Rock, Ark.
² Dunaway's letter and its enclosure are missing.
³ WW to J. T. Robinson, Feb. 6, 1918.

From Benedict Crowell

My dear Mr. President: Washington, March 9, 1918

In response to your letter to me yesterday, in regard to the appointment to the Army of Harry C. Wheeler, of Tombstone, Arizona, a former sheriff about which matter Governor Hunt wired you on the 7th instant, I have the honor to enclose a report from the Adjutant General of the Army.¹ This shows that Mr. Wheeler was appointed to Captain in the Reserve Corps of the Signal Corps upon the recommendations indicated in this report. I beg you to note that two former governors of Arizona and two United States Senators from that state endorsed him, as well as officers of the Army and the Superior Judge. Upon the record as presented, it would appear that the Department's action in making this appointment, upon the recommendation of the Chief Signal Officer, was warranted. It will be noted that Captain Wheeler is under orders for service abroad.

I shall greatly appreciate any further expression of your views in the case. Very respectfully yours, Benedict Crowell

TLS (WP, DLC).
¹ H. P. McCain, "For the Assistant Secretary of War," March 9, 1918, TS MS (WP, DLC).

From Frank Lyon Polk, with Enclosure

My dear Mr. President: Washington March 9, 1918.

I enclose for your information and comment a note which was left at the Department by the Japanese Chargé.¹ As you will notice the Japanese Government are asking the views of this Government as to how the Allied Powers should regard Russia henceforth.

I take the liberty of suggesting that it might be well to tell the Japanese that conditions in Russia are so unsettled and change so from day to day that it would be unwise to announce any policy toward Russia for the present. The Chargé in leaving the paper with Mr. Long, whom he saw, said that even if this Government

were not prepared to state its views, his Government hoped the
United States would at least give some reply.

Yours faithfully,   Frank L Polk

TLS (R. Lansing Papers, NjP).
[1] Tokichi Tanaka.

E N C L O S U R E

Washington March 7, 1918.

If it is correctly reported that the Bolsheviki government of Russia
signed and proclaimed the peace treaty of Brest-Litovsk, the question naturally arises of how the allied powers should regard Russia
henceforth—whether they should now consider her as a neutral or
an enemy or they should take the stand that inasmuch as the said
treaty is an invalid act of the self-instituted government of extremists not recognized by any of the allies the relations between them
and Russia remain unaltered. The question is, in the opinion of the
Japanese Government, highly important not from a merely theo-
retical standpoint but from that of the line of policy to be followed
henceforward by the allies in regard to Russia. The Imperial Government is therefore desirous to be advised of the views of the
American Government in this respect.

T MS (R. Lansing Papers, NjP).

From Frank Lyon Polk, with Enclosures

My dear Mr. President: Washington March 9, 1918.

The French Ambassador called today and spoke to me of a declaration that he had mentioned to you yesterday, covering the attitude of the Allied Governments and this Government toward the
peace made between Germany and Russia. He told me that he had
left a copy of the proposed declaration with you.[1]

He also gave me the form of another proposed joint declaration
covering the treatment of Poland. I enclose for your information a
copy of his letter and the draft of the declaration, as you will probably
prefer to consider them together.

At the same time, I am enclosing, as more or less related, the
proposed statement to the Russian people, which was left with me
by Mr. Lamont.[2] As I told you on the telephone today, Mr. Lamont
discussed this matter with Mr. Brandeis, and it was Mr. Brandeis'
idea that he should submit it to the State Department at once as
it was worthy of serious consideration. Lamont did not intend that

this draft should be anything more than a very rough suggestion of the idea and repeated several times that he hoped that the State Department would not think that he had attempted to draft anything more than the outline of his plan.

Possibly some statement given out by Mr. Francis might be useful, but I can not make up my mind that it would be desirable to address the meeting of the Soviets which is to be held on the twelfth of March for the purpose of acting on the treaty of peace between Russia and Germany.   Yours faithfully,   Frank L. Polk

TLS (R. Lansing Papers, NjP).
¹ It is missing in the Wilson Papers, in the National Archives, in private collections, and in various French archives.
² This enclosure is missing. However the TWLhw draft in the T. W. Lamont Papers (MH-BA) reads as follows:
"The American nation desires to send this message to its friends the Russian people:
"We have watched, with the utmost sympathy, the efforts of Russia to free itself forever from the misfortunes of autocratic rule and, beginning with the first announcement of the Revolution a year ago, we have tried in every way to show our friendship for you and our belief in your high aspirations.
"We have realized the great longing for a just and permanent peace that has filled your hearts and we have, through our President's messages of Dec 4 and Jan 8 last, made manifest to the world that America will never accept a peace that fails to regard the principle of no forcible annexations; that principle that was plainly laid down months ago by the representatives of the Russian people.
"But we have of late witnessed with increasing concern the attempt by certain powerful parties in Russia to avoid the present issue and, by means of a so-called treaty with the Central Powers that can never be carried out, to bring down permanent calamity and even destruction upon the Russian nation. Without questioning the motives of those who have mistakenly advocated the acceptance from the autocrats of Germany of terms which if they could be fulfilled, would result in the dismemberment for all time of the ancient Russian provinces & peoples, we cannot but point out that the Central Empires are attempting to impose upon Russia not peace & a return to normal conditions, but rather the iron hand of a relentless military autocracy, far more subtle & cruel than any hitherto dreamed of by loyal generations of Russians of the past.
"Therefore we urge, with all our power, that the Soviets now assembling for the purpose of passing upon the proposed 'treaty,' will reject it in whole and will, in no uncertain tones, make known to the Central Empires that the great Russian nation will never consent to the dismemberment, the ignominy, and the oppression meted out for it in the shameful terms of the so-called peace haughtily laid down by the Imperial German Government.
"At this moment when all the democracies of the world have their eyes fixed upon Russia and when we are awaiting the decision of the Soviets that shall declare the fate of Russia, the American people send this message of greeting and of good cheer to Russia; declare that, as the traditional friend of Russia in the past, so America will continue as Russia's staunch & loyal friend for the future; will, side by side with Russia, never sheath its sword until Russian soil has been made free of the ruthless German hosts; will never, with Russia, consent to a peace until the enemies of both Russia and of America consent to terms that mean a just, an enduring peace for the nations of all the world; a peace under which the democratic peoples of Russia, of America and of all the liberty-loving peoples of the earth, can pursue, untrammeled, their ideals of humanity, of civilization & brotherly kindness."

ENCLOSURE I

Jean Jules Jusserand to Robert Lansing

Mr. Secretary of State: Washington, D. C. March 8, 1918.

My Government has just informed me that, in its opinion, the Allied Powers should not, without uttering a joint protest, witness the events which tend to culminate in another partition of Poland and to deliver up to Austro-German domination integrant parts of that ancient Kingdom.

Continued silence on this point would be contrary and harmful to the rights of the peoples which we have ceaselessly affirmed and to the fundamental requirements of a just and lasting peace. Again we should not turn a deaf ear to the appeals that come to us from the Polish patriots.

It is, to my Government's mind, the duty of the Allies to uphold the claims that have ever been formulated with respect to Poland and have been particularly so formulated with so much eloquence and accuracy by the President of the United States. It is likewise advisable in every respect to promote and encourage the resistance of a people whose role in the midst of our enemies may prove of the highest importance for the very outcome of the war.

In compliance with instructions received, I have the honor to inquire of Your Excellency whether the American Government would not be disposed to join in a declaration, a draft of which is herein enclosed. The text would of course be modified wherever it may be deemed advisable so to do. The early publication of such a document, however, is regarded as extremely desirable by my Government.

Be pleased to accept, Mr. Secretary of State, the assurances of my high consideration.   Jusserand.

TCL (R. Lansing Papers, NjP).

ENCLOSURE II

DRAFT OF DECLARATION.

The Government of * * * and of * * * continue to consider the Constitution of an independent Polish State as one of the prime conditions of the organization of a Europe constituted in accordance with the principle of nationalities and secure from the surprises of another war; they regard as null and void peace treaties imposed by force which ignoring the right of peoples to dispose of themselves assign to Ukraine or to the Central Empires territories that are unquestionably Polish from the ethnographic as well as from the historic standpoint.

They again proclaim their resolution to pursue the creation of an independent autonomous and free Poland capable of insuring its *independent* economic *and* political ⟨and military⟩ development, with access to the sea.[1]

CC MS (R. Lansing Papers, NjP).
   [1] Words in angle brackets deleted by Wilson; words in italics added by him. The Supreme War Council published this declaration in abbreviated form on June 6. See *FR-WWS 1918*, 1, I, 809-10.

From William Squire Kenyon

Dear Mr. President: Washington, D. C., March 9, 1918.

I have been out in the middle West and feel quite concerned about the agricultural situation. There is a great deal of unrest among the farmers. They are patriotic enough and there is no indictment can be drawn against them on that ground, but things are not going right with them, and it is especially affecting the cattle and hog situation. I talked with farmers in the middle West who have simply quit raising hogs because they claim the expense of raising them is more than they can get for them. We are going to have a great shrinkage also in cattle.

I suppose there is only one remedy for lack of efficient production and that is higher prices to the producer. That, of course, raises a question at once with the consumer and makes a mighty difficult question. With most of the farmers and stockmen there seems to be a deep-seated resentment against the packers. My own opinion is that the feeling is thoroughly justified, but, of course, I may be wrong about that.

Nothing would so tend to quiet the mind of the stock-raiser, in my judgment, as for the government to take over and operate the packing plants.

The farmers and stockmen feel they have been robbed by the packers, and the consumers have the same opinion. Governmental operation of these packing plants would restore confidence both to the producer and to the consumer. I would not bother you with this were the whole food question not so seriously on my mind, and a deep feeling that I cannot get rid of that the agricultural people of our country are becoming very restless over the situation. I believe if the present laws are not ample to grant this authority to the President, there would be no trouble in securing it from Congress.   Respectfully yours,   Wm S. Kenyon.

TLS (WP, DLC).

From Curtis Brown[1]

Sir,   London, W.C. 2. March 9th, 1918.

There have been many inquiries here and on the Continent as to whether an authorized biography of yourself is available for publication, and especially for translation on the Continent, where it would be of great service. The latest inquiry comes from Rome, and has been referred to us, as the European arrangements for the publication and translation of "THE NEW FREEDOM" were in our hands, in behalf of Messrs. Doubleday, Page & Co.

If, as I believe, no such biography is available, may I not ask, Sir, if in view of the real need of such a work and of its manifest usefulness here, you would now consent to the preparation of such a life providing the work were entrusted to some American man of letters of the first rank, to be approved by you? We are in a position to undertake all of the arrangements here and in the United States, but would not, of course, wish to take any steps in that direction until we can know that you would give consent to the preparation of this work, providing all the details were satisfactory to you.

Pray believe me, Sir, your most faithful servant,

Curtis Brown.

TLS (WP, DLC).
[1] A literary agent of London.

Pleasant Alexander Stovall to Robert Lansing

Pontarlier (Berne), Mar. 9, 1918.

2818. Strictly confidential. My 2811, March 8, 10 p.m. Jong has received telegram reading as follows:

"Your communication with Julius disturbed. Head of bookshop agrees. Head of printing establishment is in difficult position. Partner refuses revision of last sheets. Signed Lammasch."

Jong's interpretation follows:

"Your communication with Meinl disturbed. Emperor agrees with Herron's proposals but Czernin (or perhaps Seydler)[1] is making difficulties. Germany refuses revision of last treaties. Signed Lammasch."

Jong reports that special courier from Vienna informs him very bitter struggle is going on in Vienna now, that Germany is very hostile towards Austria and fearful that Austria might take such an initiative as would put lead of European affairs into her hands rather than in Germany's.

Swiss post has informed Jong that no further telegrams can be despatched unless he furnishes key to cipher. Communications will therefore be stopped.   Stovall.

T telegram (R. Lansing Papers, NjP).
¹ Ernst von Seidler, Prime Minister of Austria.

A Memorandum by Sir William Wiseman

March 9, 1918.

NOTES FOR A CABLE FROM THE AMBASSADOR TO THE FOREIGN OFFICE.

The question of Japanese intervention in Siberia has largely occupied my attention during the past week in New York, and I have had long conferences with House on the subject, and also had the opportunity of ascertaining the views of other prominent Americans.

It may therefore be of advantage to review the position and to inform you as fully as possible as to the mind of the President and Colonel House.

It was first suggested to Col. House at the Paris Conference in November that the Allies should send a force over the Trans-Siberian railroad to assist the Roumanian Army and Cossacks of the Don. House thinks that the scheme was put forward and particularly favored by General Foch and the French; that the British military authorities doubted its practicability; and that the Japanese representatives stated it was most unlikely that their Government would be able to employ any considerable force in such an enterprise. At that time the danger of misrepresentation as to the motives of the scheme do not seem to have been specially considered. On his return House reported to the President that the matter had been fully discussed and rejected as impracticable from a military point of view.

When the matter was re-opened, I discussed it very frankly with the President, and have reported his views, which may be summarized as a general opposition to the scheme on the ground that the loss of the Allies' moral position would not be compensated by the very doubtful military advantage to be gained. His attitude was strengthened later by a report from General Bliss, (whom he consulted at our suggestion) which we understand was to the effect that no military advantage would be likely to accrue from the scheme.¹

The President's position throughout has been that he is most anxious to cooperate in every way with the Allies, but he evidently fears that the proposed action will antagonize a large section of the public here and lessen American enthusiasm for the war generally. He thinks the Allies do not realise the resentment likely to be created in the Western part of America; though I must say that I have the impression that he is not sure American sentiment would be antagonistic to the scheme, but fears that it might be. The opposition would take the line that we are using a yellow-race to destroy a white one, and that, instead of helping Russian democracy, we should be dealing it another blow by invading Russian territory in opposition to the wishes of the Bolshevic authorities.

I consider, however, that it may yet be possible to secure the President's approval of the scheme, although he will never be enthusiastic about it. If this is to be done, definite assurances should be obtained from Japan, and the Allies should in some way guarantee the territorial integrity of Russia. It might be desirable to suggest that the United States themselves should become the guarantors of this integrity, as it could be pointed out that America would then be acting as a friend or trustee of Russian Democracy. Great stress should be laid on the importance of preventing Siberia from becoming a source of food-supply for Germany both immediately from existing stores, and next year when German activity would make the Siberian soil produce vast supplies. I do not think the President yet realises the danger that the war material furnished to Russia by the United States may yet be used against American troops by the Germans.

This cable is sent, of course, in ignorance of the Japanese attitude towards the matter but in the justifiable assumption that Japan awaits the arrival of BARON ISHII in Washington before discovering her stand. A satisfactory declaration from the new Ambassador would furnish a favorable opportunity for re-opening the whole question before the President, not only permitting us to bring pressure on him by further arguments, but it might also give him an opportunity of receding from his present standpoint.

After the above message was written I learned that BARON ISHII has not yet sailed from Japan. This modifies my last suggestion, but a declaration by the Japanese Government would still be a favorable opportunity for asking the President to reconsider his view.

Today's press despatches from London emphasize danger of German attack on INDIA. It would be most unfortunate if the idea prevailed here that we are encouraging Japanese occupation of Siberia in order to protect our own interests in India.

CC MS (W. Wiseman Papers, CtY).
[1] See T. H. Bliss to H. P. McCain, Feb. 19, 1918.

To Frank Lyon Polk, with Enclosures

My dear Mr. Secretary,   The White House 10 March, 1918

Will you not be kind enough to convey to the President of the Swiss Council, through the proper channels, an expression of my very sincere appreciation of this message. Please say that I not only understand his motive but deem it most honourable to him, and that he may rest assured that, should any opportunity offer itself upon which I could make use of his great kindness, it would afford me pleasure to do so.[1]   Faithfully Yours,   W.W.

WWTLI (SDR, RG 59, 763.72119/9138, DNA).
[1] Polk paraphrased Wilson's letter in FLP to Amlegation, Bern, March 14, 1918, T telegram (SDR, RG 59, 763.72119/9138, DNA).

ENCLOSURE   I

Pontarlier (Berne) March 3, 1918.

2766. Strictly Confidential. President of Republic summoned me last night and stated he desired in all confidence and frankness to ask my advice on a point of greatest importance and that he intended to open his heart and trusted I would be equally frank in response.

He continued that in Switzerland there is a great and growing desire for peace and he would not be doing his duty to his countrymen were he to fail in any way in his power to contribute thereto; not to a separate peace, that was well understood, but to a general and lasting peace.

Callonder stated that President Wilson is a man of extraordinary intelligence and foresight, has *marked for himself as that* of right and justice, also President Wilson is the man of greatest character and power on earth today. It was in no spirit of offering advice to the President that Callonder was speaking. Such action would be presumptuousness on his part as the President of a tiny country to the most powerful leader in the world. After careful reflection he had decided to speak to me because he had carefully studied, first the speech of Czernin, then that of President Wilson, then Hertling's. He thought he saw in them that the President had offered four principles which would be acceptable to Czernin as he interpreted it as well as a man who sincerely follows the path which he
* and had been accepted by Hertling though with reservations. He

* Apparent Omission

therefore felt that at least a certain atmosphere of peace had been created. He therefore desired to know whether, if he had interpreted the speeches correctly, there is any way in which President Wilson desired to make use of him to aid toward the great end we all desire. He put himself completely at the President's disposal, not in the spirit of advice or counsel but in the earnest desire to be of service if the President considered the moment opportune.

He then begged me to regard this matter as most confidential because peace was a thing so delicate that the fewer who knew this matter the better. He terminated by asking me whether I thought the President would be irritated by his proposal, how I considered he would regard it, and how I regarded it personally.

While he spoke as above I did not interrupt him. Pressing his questions I replied that he desired me to speak in all frankness but before doing so I must ask two questions: first, was he speaking on his own inspirations or after a conference with his Colleagues in the Federal Council. He replied that while the question had been discussed on broad lines he had been given full powers and could assure me that none of his Colleagues knew of his addressing me nor would he tell them unless President Wilson's reply called for it. He could however assure me that what he had done would meet with the hearty approval of them all. Second, I inquired if he already had made or intended to make the same proposal to any other Allied [or] enemy representatives here. To this he replied a flat negative, stating that the President was the man both from character and power who would have the making of the coming peace.

I then stated that of course he appreciated this was too important a matter for me to venture to hazard an opinion of my chief's ideas, that I would of course report his statement as nearly verbatim as possible to the President for his decision. I could only say, since he requested it, how it struck me, that President Wilson is a man who is actuated by great ideals only, a man who is too big to enter into the pettiness of bargaining; that he had made with all frankness a statement of what he, representing America, felt should be and would be accomplished. He had expected that the enemy leaders would in the same spirit of frankness answer his proposals. This Hertling had apparently failed to do, he has accepted the four principles but made reservations to each one of those principles in so far as they affected Germany, that if he was endeavoring to bargain he utterly misunderstood the President's character. Till this (?) principle and there is no compromise possible when right and justice are involved; and that, therefore, Hertling's speech had left me far from overconfident.

I then assured him that I would endeavor to reproduce to the President the spirit of frankness and respect to the President with which he spoke.

In this connection I venture to call the Department's attention to the fact that since Hoffmann's dismissal or resignation[1] the dominant influence in the Federal Council is Schulthess[2] a man whose attitude, in the opinion of the Allied representatives here is extremely doubtful. I believe Callonder spoke to me in absolute honesty and that if President Wilson desires to send any messages to him he can be trusted not to divulge it if his word of honor is requested.   Wilson.

T telegram (SDR, RG 59, 763.72119/1452, DNA).
    [1] About which, see T. N. Page to WW, June 27, 1917, Vol. 43.
    [2] That is, Edmund Schulthess.

ENCLOSURE II

Pontarlier (Berne) March 6, 1918.

2786. Legation's strictly confidential 2766, March 3, 12 noon. President of the Republic summoned Wilson again today and informed him that the atmosphere at present seemed more pessimistic and that therefore in order to relieve President Wilson of any embarrassment in answering his earlier message, Calonder desired to inform President Wilson not to answer the request unless he found it entirely convenient and to feel that he was always at the President's disposition in any steps that the latter might care at an opportune moment to make towards peace.

President Calonder during the conversation stated that the peace with Russia was a menace to the peace of the world and greatly to be regretted and that however horrible the fight on the west front may be there seemed at present no possibility of its being averted. President was careful to avoid blunt statements but intimated that the exorbitant dreams of the German annexation[is]ts were the only obstacles to peace.   Stovall.

T telegram (SDR, RG 59, 763.72119/8781, DNA).

Three Letters to Frank Lyon Polk

My dear Mr. Secretary,   The White House. 10 March, 1918.

I think that the Japanese Charge should be told that in the view of the Government of the United States recent events have in no way altered the relations and obligations of this Government towards Russia. It does not feel justified in regarding Russia either as a neutral or as an enemy, but continues to regard it as an ally. There is, in fact, no Russian government to deal with. The So-called Soviet government upon which Germany has just forced, or tried to force, peace was never recognized by the Government of the United States as even a government *de facto*. None of its acts, therefore, need be officially recognized by this Government; and I think that it is of the utmost importance, as affecting the whole public opinion of the world and giving proof of the utter good faith of all the governments associated against Germany, that we should continue to treat the Russians as in all respects our friends and allies against the common enemy.

Sincerely Yours,   Woodrow Wilson

WWTLS (R. Lansing Papers, NjP).

My dear Mr. Secretary,   The White House. 10 March, 1918.
    Thank you for letting me see this.[1] It is a very pregnant document.

Sincerely Yours,   W.W.

WWTLI (R. Lansing Papers, NjP).
    [1] Probably one of the documents referred to in FLP to WW, March 9, 1918 (second letter of that date).

My dear Mr. Secretary: The White House. 10 March, 1918.
    I am a good deal impressed by Mr. Reinsch's suggestion, here outlined.[1] I hope that you will be kind enough to sound the other Governments, through their representatives here or ours at their own capitals, whichever you think best, as to their opinions about it and as to its practicability, so far as they are concerned. A great deal of trouble and embarrassment will be avoided in the East, I am persuaded, if we can draw China into the best possible coop-eration and give her a more definite set of international connections in the common cause.   Sincerely Yours, W.W.

WWTLI (B. Long Papers, DLC).
    [1] See P. S. Reinsch to WW, Feb. 12, 1918.

To Benedict Crowell

My dear Mr. Secretary,   The White House. 10 March, 1918.
    I entirely concur in the recommendation which General Bliss makes in Paragraph Four of the enclosed and would be very much

obliged to you if you would be kind enough to take the matter up with the Department of State and ask them, for me, to send such a message as General Bliss outlines.[1]

Sincerely Yours,   Woodrow Wilson

WWTLS (WDR, RG 407, World War I Cable Section, DNA).
[1] See H. P. McCain to T. H. Bliss, March 12, 1918.

To Edith Gittings Reid

My very dear Friend,   The White House. 10 March, 1918.

I know that you will generously forgive a very busy man for not having written sooner (and this is my own handwriting, you know!) in reply to your very welcome letter of the fourth.[1] I did not delay a single twenty-four hours to send a line to the State Department about a passport for Doris[2] when she asks for it, and I hope she will have no difficulty there, but with regard to the part which concerned me personally I have taken the liberty of waiting until I could have a little Sunday leisure.

This little paper you have written about me has touched me very deeply. You give me credit for being very much finer than I am, and yet you have, with the insight of a true friend, seen all through these years what I was striving with all my heart to be, and it pleases and comforts me mightily that you should have seen it, that it should have *shown* through all the veils and imperfect expressions under which it lay.

Of course I am willing to have you publish it. Why should I not be? I would be proud to have you sign it; but, if you think that it would be better taste for you not to do so, or if for any other reason you prefer that it should appear without a signature, I consent without demur.[3] Only let me thank you from the bottom of my heart!

I have been greatly interested to learn that Henry van Dyke has gone into the service as a chaplain. Was that action on his part approved by those who love him best,[4] I wonder?

Give my love to Doris. I admire her very much, and my heart will follow all that she does and experiences in France.

My warmest regards to Mr. Reid.

With all my heart, Your Friend,   Woodrow Wilson

P.S. If there should happen to be any difficulty about the passport, please let me know at once, and I will straighten it out. W.W.

WWTLS (WC, NjP).
[1] Edith G. Reid to WW, March 4, 1918, ALS (WP, DLC).

² Mrs. Reid's daughter, Doris Fielding Reid, who was going to France to work with the Children's Bureau of the American Red Cross.
³ If the essay was published, it was done so anonymously.
⁴ Van Dyke's wife, Ellen Reid van Dyke, was a sister of Harry Fielding Reid.

From Edward Mandell House

Dear Governor: New York. March 10, 1918.

What would you think of sending a reassuring message to Russia when the Soviet meets at Moscow on the 12th?

Our proverbial friendship for Russia could be reaffirmed and you could declare our purpose to help in her efforts to weld herself into a democracy. She should be left free from any sinister or selfish influence which might interfere with such development.

My thought is not so much about Russia as it is to seize this opportunity to clear up the Far Eastern situation but without mentioning it or Japan in any way. What you would say about Russia and against Germany, could be made to apply to Japan or any other power seeking to do what we know Germany is attempting.

Affectionately yours,   E. M. House

TLS (WP, DLC).

From the Diary of Frank Lyon Polk

March 11, 1918.

PRESIDENT CALLED UP
and read me the statement to Russian people, in view of the approaching Soviet Congress to pass on peace terms. Suggested changing "revolution" to "struggle for freedom." Made change. Also suggested that communication be addressed to Russian people through Congress so that Congress could not consider it an official communication and treat it contemptuously.

PRESIDENT told me on the wire that he was not prepared to say anything about Russian-German peace, as suggested by French Ambassador, but was willing to make a declaration in regard to Poland. I sent over draft.

T MS (F. L. Polk Papers, CtY).

To the Fourth All-Russia Congress of Soviets[1]

[March 11, 1918]

May I not take advantage of the meeting of the Congress of the Soviet to express the sincere sympathy which the people of the United States feel for the Russian people at this moment when the German power has been thrust in to interrupt and turn back the whole ⟨process of revolution⟩ ⟨great⟩ *struggle for freedom*[2] and substitute the wishes of Germany for the purposes of the people of Russia. Although the Government of the United States is unhappily not now in a position to render the direct and effective aid it would wish to render, I beg to assure the *people of Russia through the*[3] Congress that it will avail itself of every opportunity that may offer to secure for Russia once more complete sovereignty and independence in her own affairs and full restoration to her great role in the life of Europe and the modern world. The whole heart of the people of the United States is with the people of Russia in the attempt to free themselves forever from autocratic government and become the masters of their own life.   Woodrow Wilson.[4]

WWT MS (R. Lansing Papers, NjP).
  [1] Scheduled to meet in Moscow on March 12 to ratify the Treaty of Brest-Litovsk. As it turned out, the meeting of the congress was delayed until March 14.
  [2] These changes, WWhw.
  [3] FLPhw.
  [4] There is a WWsh draft of this message in WP, DLC. The telegram was sent as F. L. Polk to M. Summers, March 11, 1918, *FR 1918, Russia*, I, 395-96.

To George Wylie Paul Hunt

Personal and Confidential.

My dear Governor Hunt: [The White House] 11 March, 1918

Your telegram[1] about Captain Harry Cornwall Wheeler as Captain in the Reserve Corps disturbed me not a little and I made immediate inquiry of the War Department. The Adjutant General reports as follows:

"On February twenty-sixth last an application from the Air Division of the Signal Corps, dated February twenty-first, was received for the appointment of Harry Cornwall Wheeler as a Captain in the Reserve Corps. The appointment was made on the date of the receipt of the application.

"The application was accompanied by recommendations from Governors Campbell and Kibbey[2] of Arizona and, United States Senators Ashurst and Smith of Arizona. It was also accompanied by other recommendations, including one from Colonel J. J. Hornbrook, United States Army, Captain John C. Walker, Jr.,

35th United States Infantry, and A. C. Lockwood, Judge of Superior Court.[3]

"It was stated in the application that Wheeler had attended a military school; that he had had five years and two months' service in the United States Cavalry as as a non-commissioned officer and was discharged with character 'Excellent'; that he had served two years in the Arizona Rangers as an officer; that he had had 'one year, mounted inspector, United States Customs Service, one year Deputy Marshal, United States Marshal's office, six years Sheriff, Cochise County, Arizona.' "

In view of these recommendations the appointment would seem to have been natural enough and fully justified. It had no connection whatever, of course, with any recent actions of Captain Wheeler in his office as Sheriff, actions concerning many of which I share your own judgment.

Have you any advice to give in the matter?

Cordially and sincerely yours,   Woodrow Wilson

TLS (Letterpress Books, WP, DLC).
  [1] About which, see WW to B. Crowell, March 8, 1918, n. 1.
  [2] Joseph Henry Kibbey, Governor of Arizona Territory, 1905-1909.
  [3] James Joseph Hornbrook, John Caffery Walker, Jr., and Alfred Collins Lockwood.

To Charles Spalding Thomas

My dear Senator: [The White House] 11 March, 1918

I will take up the matter of the prospective reduction of coal prices in Colorado at once with Doctor Garfield. I understood that the matter was to be discussed with coal representatives and I think it has been, but I will look into it again.

In haste

Cordially and sincerely yours,   Woodrow Wilson

TLS (Letterpress Books, WP, DLC).

To Harry Augustus Garfield, with Enclosure

My dear Garfield: The White House 11 March, 1918

I am going to have the pleasure of seeing you tomorrow, and I would be very much obliged if you would bring up the matter referred to in the enclosed letter from Senator Thomas. He is evidently very much concerned.

Cordially and sincerely yours,   Woodrow Wilson

TLS (H. A. Garfield Papers, DLC).

From Charles Spalding Thomas

My dear Mr. President: [Washington] March 9, 1918.

I am so much distressed over the order of the Fuel Administration of yesterday, reducing the prices of coal in Colorado, to become effective on March 11th, and so certain of its disastrous consequences, that I must again appeal to you regarding it, in the hope that it may be seriously modified, if not entirely withdrawn.

This order reduces the prices of November 1st last from 20¢ to $1.20 per ton and increases what is called the Mine Run by 5¢, and changes them subject to a further reduction from April to August of from 70¢ to 15¢, the latter being called Summer Reductions. The month of April in the high altitudes of the Rocky Mountains is fully as wintry and disagreeable as December or January, and the classification of that month, and indeed of the first half of May as Summer months, betrays a sad lack of familiarity with that region.

Mr. President, I am morally satisfied that this order will result in the suspension of 50% of the mines and a reduction of 25% of the out-put of coal in the State.

A summary of the reports filed by the operators with the Federal Trade Commission for August, September, October and November show net profits per ton ranging from 1.32¢ down to 3.7¢ averaging 29.5¢ per ton. This is true of 41 mines. The same reports show that 19 of the companies operated during the above period at a net loss ranging from 85¢ to 4¢ per ton. Among the latter, is the great C. F. & I. Company,[1] the principal producer in the State, which mined coal at a net loss of 10¢ per ton. The enormous business it is conducting at its steel plant, however, enables it to do this without serious injury. The others are not so fortunate.

The reductions made in the order of yesterday will wipe out the great majority of those operating at a profit during the period mentioned. The inevitable suspension of so many of these mines which the Government must take over if their out-put is to continue, will result in so serious a reduction of the out-put as to necessitate the importation of coal from other sections of the country into ours, where the greatest coal deposits in the country are situated. These operators increased the out-put last year by two millions of tons. They have accommodated themselves to the prices heretofore fixed and fully expected to double that increase for 1918.

Apart from the ruin which these operators now confront, is the equally unfortunate prospect of the extension of the C. F. & I.

monopoly, as it is called in the State. Its abundant capital will enable it easily to take over on its own terms the plants of its less fortunate competitors, and after the end of the war it will be in virtual control of the Colorado coal industry.

I beseech you, Mr. President, not to permit this order to go into effect. I am aware that Dr. Garfield, necessarily acting through subordinates, has done what seems to him to be right and proper under the circumstances, but I have every reason to know that the three engineers to whom the subject was originally referred, after a careful examination into the situation, would not recommend this reduction, and I am reliably informed that Mr. White of the Mine Workers of America, and a member of that Board, believes that the reduction of these prices will work disaster, and will be particularly injurious to the organization which he represents.

The discontent and bitterness which this order with its probably [probable] consequences must necessarily create, will be heightened by a sense of injustice, the results of which will, of course, be deplorable. The title of the so-called Food Conservation Act recites that its purpose is to *encourage the production*, conserve the supply and control the distribution of food products for fuel. This order, Mr. President, I feel sure will produce the opposite result. Regulations like this can, of course, be made effective, but they cannot compel the production of an article under conditions which involve the certainty of loss.

I must apologize for bringing the subject to your immediate attention, but its deplorable consequences seem so obvious, that I am compelled to do so as a last resort.

Awaiting an early reply, I am, Mr. President,
Your most obedient servant,   C S Thomas

TLS (H. A. Garfield Papers, DLC).
¹ The Colorado Fuel & Iron Co.

To Joseph Patrick Tumulty

Dear Tumulty: [The White House, c. March 11, 1918]

I don't want to answer this letter myself.¹ I wonder if you would be good enough to write to Mr. MacFarland and say that pressure of business prevents my writing in person, and that I have asked you to say to him, as I told him in my recent letter, I as a matter of fact knew nothing of this about which he writes; and that, as I think I had explained to him before, it seems to me a matter about which it would be very delicate for anyone officially connected with the Government to intervene. It is so distinctly a matter between the International News Service and the French and English Governments and ought not to be made a subject of diplomacy.

The President.

TL (WP, DLC).
    [1] G. S. Macfarland to WW, March 7, 1918, TLS (WP, DLC). Macfarland reported that, after much delay, the British and French cables had been reopened to representatives of the International News Service through the good offices of Colonel House. However, they had been closed again after only twenty-four hours. British diplomats indicated that the French were the source of the new difficulty. Macfarland requested that Ambassador Sharp be asked to make inquiries in Paris as to the nature of the problem.

From John Aldus McSparran

Dear Mr President   Furniss, Pa. Mar 11th 1918

I am enclosing you a resolution which represents the sentiment of the farmers of the State of Penna as it refers to the handling of the food proposition.[1] The retention by you of your present Secy of Agriculture who has the confidence and support of a very trifling percentage of the farmers of the country is going to cost the Democrats of which I am one hundreds of thousands of votes in the coming election. I hear the expressions of dissatisfaction as possibly you do not and I think that a republican victory now would be a calamity with such men as Lodge and Smoot and Cannon in the Harness. I hope that you will see your way clear to give real Farmers through their organizations a part in the affairs os [of] State that they have not enjoyed heretofore.

Sincerely Yours,   John A. McSparran

TLS (WP, DLC).
    [1] Granges of Centreport and Pomona, Pa., to J. A. McSparran, March 4, 1918, Hw MS (WP, DLC). This resolution declared that the farmers of the United States were not getting "a square deal" from the federal government, that the existing regulations and conditions were due more to ignorance than to antagonism on the part of governmental officials, and that the system of price fixing then in use tended to discourage the production of foodstuffs. The members of these granges respectfully requested governmental officials "to make more diligent inquiry, as to real farm conditions, and to consult more with the farmers themselves, and try to place men with real practical experience in charge of affairs in a crisis like this."

From Josephus Daniels

My dear Mr. President: Washington. 11 March, 1918.

I had a long talk last night with Mr. Baruch about the War Industries Board. I feel it is very important that direct representatives of the Army and Navy be placed upon the price fixing committee. If this is not done, when its recommendation of price comes down to each Department, in some instances they may feel the price is too high and it may be high, higher than would be the case had they been able to put before the committee all facts regarding munitions or commodities they have been purchasing. It is important that one representative from each Department should be on the Board, and that they should afterwards give the orders, or go before the Board as witnesses. Mr. Baruch was entirely agreeable to this but in your letter to him no member of the Army or Navy had been mentioned and suggested that it should be taken up with you.

If agreeable to you, I would be glad if you will request the Secretary of War and the Secretary of the Navy to name an officer in their respective Departments to serve on this Board. I am all the more earnest in this because in several instances when prices were fixed without consultation with us we have been able to give information that has resulted in reopening the question with benefit to the Government. If there is a representative of the Navy on the Board, I am in close touch with negotiations about price-fixing and through this office can give the benefit of our experience in the Navy; otherwise, they have no direct way of obtaining it.

Faithfully yours,   Josephus Daniels

TLS (WP, DLC).

From Robert Somers Brookings

My dear Mr. President: Washington March 11, 1918.

I beg to acknowledge receipt of your message through Mr Baruch to the effect that you would like me to assume the chairmanship of the new Price Committee. As I interpret the duties of the Chairman of this Committee, it will practically occupy all of my time, but, as Mr Baruch seems to feel that it would be a mistake to make any additional changes in the Board at present, we have concluded that I temporarily delegate the duties of the Finished Products Division to our Mr George M. Peek,[1] while I retain nominal control of that department.

I am of the opinion, Mr. President, that this price-fixing problem without additional legislation is likely to become more and more involved. However, I am willing to assume to the best of my ability any responsibility when sustained by your authority.

Sincerely yours,   Robt. S. Brookings

TLS (WP, DLC).
[1] That is, George Nelson Peek.

From Jefferson Bell[1]

Dear Mr Wilson: Miami, Florida March 11, 1918.

We are in the midst of a second agitation in Miami over German music and as you are quoted in an editorial in the afternoon paper in connection with the previous agitation[2] I am writing to ask if you are correctly quoted, or your position correctly stated in the editorial I have marked.

I had the honor to organize the protest against the Federation program referred to in November at Tampa[3] which was in charge of Miss Kreher, a German woman whose brother Paul Kreher, has recently been forced to withdraw from the shipbuilding plant in Tampa in response to a popular demand voiced in a mass meeting, he being an alien enemy and subject to exclusion under your proclamation.

The Metropolis is under censure for its pro-German sentiment and I feel sure it has given undue emphasis to your telegram.

Yours very truly,   Miss Jefferson Bell

TLS (WP, DLC).

[1] Reporter for the *Miami Herald*, which was leading the fight against the presentation of Handel's *The Messiah* in Miami. The *Herald*, March 10, 1918, said that Germany produced *The Messiah*, and "that everything German now savors of outrage, of brutal murder, of aggression on innocent people, with the killing of women and children and with chicanery, robbery, looting, broken promises, international bad faith and everything of which a government or a people can be guilty in the violation of the laws of man and of nations and of God." The editorial concluded that "all participants" would regret it if they carried out their "advertised intentions."

[2] The *Miami Metropolis*, March 10, 1918, reported that Wilson had earlier replied to an inquiry from Tampa to the effect "that he would indeed hate to see the war against Germany carried into a war against the beautiful things for which the Germans are responsible—their music, their philosophy and their science." About the concert involved, see the following note.

[3] The Florida Federation of Women's Clubs had met in Tampa from November 20 to November 23, 1917. Hulda Kreher, director of the Friday Morning Musicale Orchestra of Tampa, had announced that her orchestra would present a program which would include works by Beethoven, Haydn, Mendelssohn, and Weber. The program was indeed presented on November 20, following a "patriotic medley." *Tampa Morning Tribune,* Nov. 20 and 21, 1917; Mrs. W. S. Jennings to WW, Nov. 19, 1917, T telegram (WP, DLC). In reply to the latter, Wilson instructed Tumulty to say that he did not "regard the use of any good music as unpatriotic." JPT to Mrs. W. S. Jennings, Nov. 21, 1917, TCL (WP, DLC).

From John R. Mott

Mr. President: New York March 11, 1918

I am deeply grateful to you for the letters which you have so kindly sent me and your words of good wishes send me on my special mission with new courage.[1]

Your attitude toward the proposed intervention of Japan in Siberia to my mind is another illustration of your remarkable insight into the psychology of the Russian peoples and likewise enforces in the most impressive manner the guiding principles for our nation which you have enunciated with such clearness and quickening power.

With highest regard,

Very sincerely yours,   John R. Mott

TLS (WP, DLC).
  ¹ WW to J. R. Mott, March 8, 1918, TLS (J. R. Mott Coll., CtY-D); WW to diplomatic officers in Europe, March 7, 1918, and WW To Whom It May Concern, March 7, 1918, both TLS (Letterpress Books, WP, DLC). Mott was about to leave on a tour to inspect Y.M.C.A. facilities in Europe and to promote the welfare of prisoners of war.

From Ferris Greenslet[1]

Dear Mr. President,   Boston March 11, 1918.

We have been having, as we believe you know, some correspondence with Messrs. Harper & Brothers in regard to the taking over by them of your "Congressional Government" and "Mere Literature." In order that there may be no misunderstanding of our position in the matter, we are enclosing a copy of a letter which we have just written them.[2]

May we add that we have taken special pride in having these two very characteristic books upon our list and we should like very much to retain them there?

As we wrote you in December 1912, the result of the Presidential election of that year seemed to us to a peculiar degree the *revanche* of letters. This feeling has been heightened by the history of the past six years. For that reason, we are the more sorry to become disassociated completely from the publication of your work.

As we have written Messrs. Harper, we are prepared to accede to your wishes, but we have not liked to let the episode close without at least making this explicit statement of our own point of view.

Please believe us   Faithfully yours,   Ferris Greenslet

TLS (WP, DLC).
  ¹ Literary editor at Houghton Mifflin Co.
  ² Houghton Mifflin Co. to Harper & Brothers, March 11, 1918, TCL (WP, DLC).

Arthur James Balfour to Lord Reading

[London] 11th March [1918]

No. 1364 Your telegram No. 929 and Sir Wiseman's telegram No. 73.[1] I quite appreciate force of American objections and have given you reasons which appear to us on the whole to outweigh them. There is however one further consideration to which due weight should be attached. Collapse of Russia and Roumania and disastrous terms imposed upon them must produce throughout the world and more especially in East an impression of enemy might and invincibility very damaging to allied cause. It is essential that we should make some effective counter move to destroy this impression. Japanese intervention in Siberia especially if attended by allied operations elsewhere to bring help to Russia would provide imposing counter display of power and solidarity of allies which could not fail of its effect. I should be glad to know whether U.S.G. have any suggestions to offer for allied consideration and adoption with regard to any counter movement of which is likely to prove equally effective.

T telegram (W. Wiseman Papers, CtY).
    [1] W. Wiseman to E. Drummond, March 6, 1918. Reading's telegram No. 929 was Reading to A. J. Balfour, March 5, 1918, T telegram (FO 115/2445, p. 107, PRO). After reiterating that the Wilson administration had never favored Japanese intervention in Siberia, Reading gave a full paraphrase of WW to R. S. Morris, March 5, 1918.

To Robert Lansing

My dear Mr. Secretary: [The White House] 12 March, 1918
    I wish you would be kind enough to formulate a careful and conclusive memorandum for the use of the committee of the Senate with regard to the enclosed resolution.[1] I take it for granted that you feel as I do that this is no time to act as the resolution prescribes, and certainly when I pronounced for open diplomacy, I meant not that there should be no private discussions of delicate matters, but that no secret agreements of any sort should be entered into and that all international relations, when fixed, should be open, above-board, and explicit.

                 Cordially and sincerely yours,   Woodrow Wilson

TLS (Letterpress Books, WP, DLC).
    [1] Senator Borah, on January 9, had introduced the following resolution (S. Res. 178): "Resolved, That the Committee on Rules be, and the same is hereby, directed to prepare a revision of the rules of the Senate relating to the consideration of treaties so as to provide that all treaties hereafter shall be considered in the open executive sessions of the Senate, and, when such revision is so prepared, to report the same to the Senate for its consideration." Cong. Record, 65th Cong., 2d sess., p. 705. On January 11, Borah accepted, and the Senate adopted, an amended version of the resolution proposed by Senator Gallinger which read as follows: "Resolved, That the Committee on Rules be, and the same is hereby, directed to consider the advisability of preparing a revision of the rules of the Senate relating to the consideration of treaties, with a view to providing that all treaties hereafter shall be considered in the open executive sessions of the Senate, report to be made to the Senate at an early day." Ibid., p. 818. Lansing's memorandum is printed in FR-LP, II, 113-16. Senator Hitchcock read Wilson's letter to Lansing of March 12, 1918, to the Senate on June 11, 1918. Cong. Record, 65th Cong., 2d sess., p. 7653.

To Josephus Daniels

My dear Mr. Secretary: [The White House] 12 March, 1918

I have your letter of the eleventh about the advisability of adding representatives of the War and Navy Departments to the Price Fixing Committee. I think your argument is conclusive, and I am writing today to Mr. Baruch to authorize the arrangement.

In haste
                    Cordially and sincerely yours,   Woodrow Wilson

TLS (Letterpress Books, WP, DLC).

To Bernard Mannes Baruch

My dear Mr. Chairman: The White House 12 March, 1918

I have a letter from the Secretary of the Navy in which he recites to me the results of a conference he had with you on Sunday evening about the advisability of having representatives of the War and Navy Department on the Price Fixing Committee, and I understand from his letter that you were convinced by his argument, as I myself am. I write, therefore, to authorize such additions and hope that you will ask the two departments to name representatives.
                    Cordially and sincerely yours,   Woodrow Wilson

TLS (B. M. Baruch Papers, NjP).

To Robert Somers Brookings

My dear Mr. Brookings: [The White House] 12 March, 1918

I am gratified by your letter of March eleventh because I was anxious to have you undertake the important post of chairman of the Price Fixing Committee. I think that the arrangement you and Mr. Baruch have arrived at is a very sensible one indeed in retaining general oversight yourself of the finished products and assigning the active work to Mr. Peek.

We shall, of course, watch the whole development of the new programme very carefully and guide it at every point necessary.
                    Cordially and sincerely yours,   Woodrow Wilson

TLS (Letterpress Books, WP, DLC).

From Joseph Patrick Tumulty

Dear Governor: The White House. 12 March 1918.

There will be a vote on suffrage in a few days.[1] I am afraid of the effect on the Democratic party if the votes of a few Democrats prevent the passage of the amendment. Mrs. Catt and Mrs. Gardener have informed me that Senator Fletcher and Senator Trammel are inclined to favor it and would vote for it if you sent for them.   The Secretary

TL (WP, DLC).
    [1] Tumulty apparently referred to a movement by Republican senators to obtain a vote on the woman-suffrage amendment. As it turned out, the opponents of the amendment were able to delay a vote on it until October 1.

To Joseph Patrick Tumulty

Dear Tumulty: [The White House, c. March 12, 1918]

I would weaken my influence in a score of directions if I were to depart from the rule I have set myself and *send for* Senators, but I am eager to advise them to vote for the amendment if they will themselves give me an opportunity to do so. If you know of any way in which you could bring about a call from Senators Trammel and Fletcher that would not be a summons from me but which would lead them to ask my advice, I would be delighted.
                    The President.

TL (WP, DLC).

From Franklin Knight Lane

My dear Mr. President: Washington March 12, 1918.

At a recent meeting of the Cabinet the question was raised as to who should care for the re-education of the wounded men who come from France, and you said you would take the matter under consideration. It has seemed to me that there was a part that the Bureau of Education, as the Federal educational agency, could play in this work, perhaps more efficiently than any other bureau. After the Civil War a large number of veterans became teachers. This will undoubtedly be true after this war. Many more can be taught to be stenographers; some could be turned into translators; others can be made chemists, lawyers, doctors and draftsmen, as well as handicraftsmen of many kinds. I have asked Dr. Claxton to give me his views, and he sends me a full memorandum which I enclose,[1] which goes very extensively into the matter, even so far as outlining a possible personnel.

Faithfully and cordially yours,   Franklin K Lane

TLS (WP, DLC).

[1] It is missing.

From Joseph Edward Davies

My dear Mr. President: Washington March 12th 1918

Will you please accept herewith my resignation as a member of the Federal Trade Commission. It is with a deep regret that I feel impelled to take this course. As you know, this agency which you projected to preserve industrial democracy in our country has meant a great deal to me. I am happy in the belief that it has fulfilled, in a measure, your plan. Moreover, the war work that the Commission is now engaged upon, is of great importance.

I feel sure that you would know that no selfish reason could impel me to resign at this time.

My conviction is that I can render a greater service to my country, to my state, and to you by entering into the contest for the United States Senatorship in Wisconsin. The pride in and my affection for the state of my birth, have caused me to resent deeply the misrepresentations which has led many to believe that the state of Wisconsin was not as fully loyal to the country in this crisis as her sister commonwealths.

At the special election on April 2nd, Wisconsin will demonstrate that she stands with her sister states four-square in loyally supporting the President of the United States in the vigorous prosecution of this war.

Wisconsin is loyal and stands behind you. The issue will be clean-cut. I deem it a great and rare privilege to be permitted to engage in this fight for such a cause. Wisconsin will demonstrate at the special election on April 2nd that a united nation stands behind you.

In conclusion, will you let me say a personal word of appreciation for the privilege which you have afforded me of serving my country under your great leadership for five years last past, first as Commissioner of Corporations, and then as a member of the Federal Trade Commission. It will be an enduring satisfaction to know that even in a small way I have been associated with your administration which has rendered such noble service not only to the democracy of our own country, but to the cause of all humanity.

Faithfully yours,   Joseph E. Davies

TLS (WP, DLC).

From Charles Spalding Thomas

My dear Mr. President   Washington, D. C. 4[3]/12/18

Since my note of this morning[1] I have been handed the enclosed list of telegrams from mines which have quit or which must quit production.[2] Dr Garfields charts are carefully prepared, but the operators condition speaks for itself

With Greatest Respect   C S Thomas

ALS (WP, DLC).
[1] It is missing.
[2] The list is missing. However, Thomas enclosed fourteen telegrams from mine operators in Colorado, all addressed to one William H. Huff at the Powhatan Hotel in Washington. All protested against the prices for Colorado coal set by the Fuel Administrator and said that they would lose money if these prices were not changed. All stated either that they already had, or were about to, close their mines as a result of the government's action.

From Edward Nash Hurley

My dear Mr. President: Washington March 12, 1918.

Please let me thank you for your kindness in sending me a copy of your letter to Mr. Baruch. Quite frankly, I am enthusiastic over this reorganization of the War Industries Board and the centralization of its authority in the hands of Mr. Baruch. It gives us a single clearing house, easing the tremendous strain under which we have been laboring in the effort to locate and expedite the delivery of the materials which are essential to the shipbuilding program. I need hardly say that the War Industries Board, and Mr. Baruch personally, will have our entire cooperation.

In our plan for the elimination of any possibility of profiteering in the shipbuilding industry, we have reached a point where, if it is not burdening you too much, we would like you to suggest the name of some man of prominence, in whom you have complete faith, to direct this particular work.

I had an opportunity to talk over with Mr. Justice Brandeis the plan I have had in mind, and he suggested that the best way to put it into effect was to establish a definite and uniform cost accounting system in all the yards.

It is my feeling that the public should have full data and information regarding the cost of the ships that are being built. The result should be reassuring to labor. Some of the yards are making little, if any money, while others are making more than enough. We have asked the Atlantic Coast Shipbuilders' Association to appoint a committee made up of three of their leading cost accountants. We will ask the wooden shipbuilders to appoint a similar committee. These committees will merely aid us in working out a system that shall be uniform. The system of accounting thus established will enable us not merely to limit profits on existing contracts, but to determine prices at which future contracts should be let. At the head of this work in the Emergency Fleet Corporation, we should have a man of established reputation, someone in whom the country and the labor organizations as well will have complete confidence. I had thought of Doctor Albert Shaw, but you may have someone in mind, and I would appreciate any suggestion you may have in the matter.   Sincerely yours,   Edward N. Hurley

TLS (WP, DLC).

From Wharton Barker

My dear Mr. Wilson: Philadelphia March 12th 1918.

Your despatch to Russians, direct, vigorous, sent at a time when promise of support, moral and material, by the United States is vital, will, I believe, steady Russians and halt action by Great Britain and Japan in development of wrong policies.

Your action at this great crisis must have approval and support of all democrats—Americans, Europeans, Asiatics. I venture to write this letter because of knowledge of Russians, Chinese, Japanese and of Russian and Chinese democrats.

And now a word upon the political situation in Pennsylvania. If you can find time to do so, read a statement I published last Thursday; you will find it upon a sheet from The Philadelphia Inquirer I send you herewith.[1] Vance McCormick and A. Mitchell Palmer should confer at once with the Independents of Pennsylvania, who know of the campaigns of 1882 and 1890, when by coalition of Democrats and Independents, the Republican party of Pennsylvania, then representative of combinations inimical to common weal rights, was defeated. If the Democratic party of Pennsylvania plays the part in the campaign of this year, Republican party leaders would have it play and put aside a coalition with the Independents of Pennsylvania, they will blunder and fasten upon this Commonwealth the party of vested rights.

                    Yours very truly,   Wharton Barker

TLS (WP, DLC).
  [1] "Declare Principles, Is Barker's Appeal," *Philadelphia Inquirer*, March 8, 1918, clipping (WP, DLC). Barker proposed a "Declaration of Principles" for the coming campaign in Pennsylvania which covered a wide range of local, state, national, and international issues.

From Newton Diehl Baker

[Paris, received March 12, 1918]

It is most fortunate that my visit comes at this time. I am securing much important and helpful information and the efficiency of our cooperation will undoubtedly be greatly increased. I have spent two days in Paris and tonight I start a thorough inspection of the port terminal, transportation, supply and storage systems, all of which will include about ten days, including visits to British, French and Belgian military headquarters to gratify millions, then I shall visit the Italian headquarters and later on visit England for a few days. It is the belief here, from information obtained, that Germany is still massing fresh divisions on the western front (chiefly?) against the positions of the British so attacks may soon begin there in force. The German plan has occasioned much uncertainty and speculation with regard to the entire subject.

No definite news as yet as to the extent of damage occasioned by last night's air raid over Paris.   Baker

TC telegram (N. D. Baker Papers, DLC).

From John William Hamilton[1]

Washington, D. C.
My dear Mr. President: March Twelve, Nineteen-Eighteen.

You or your Secretary may recall that I wrote you about the time war was declared[2] I had every confidence that the rank and file of the German Methodists of this country would be loyal without question. I have presided at all the German Conferences from the Atlantic to the Pacific Oceans and am familiar with all the leaders of these Conferences and have had their confidence.

Soon after the arrest of an imprudent German Methodist preacher in Minnesota, who was noted more for his eccentricities than for his sanity,[3] a leading representative clergyman of all that territory and who is also a member of the National Committee on Foreign Missions desired to call upon you personally to represent the German Methodists in his territory. I discouraged his coming the long journey, for I knew that he could ill afford the expense and I did not think it was necessary for him to come on to see you, since the case was so exceptional.

But the Government has been made familiar with some imprudent utterances—I am quite sure they were nothing more—of the young President of Baldwin Wallace College at Berea, Ohio,[4] and to say the least, some very luke warm utterances of the Editor of the Apologete at Cincinnatti.[5] A council of Bishops, Preachers and Laymen was called and the young President of the German school was dismissed and the Editor of the German paper displaced, and the effect of this action leads a representative German Preacher to write me from Detroit saying "These unhappy experiences have both brought much calumny upon us and subjected us to gross injustice, as such matters are always exaggerated, especially in these critical times. Our people are loyal to their flag and toward the Government in carrying on the war and believe the splendid utterances of President Wilson really voices the true American spirit" He then states "A few days ago the District Superintendents of our German Conferences were in session in Chicago and their Resolutions I truly believe represent our people." He then asks me this question "Can you secure for two of us an audience of a few minutes with the President for the purpose of personally presenting him the adopted Resolutions, and to assure him of the German Methodists' loyal and unconditional patriotic support in winning the war on the basis of the lofty principles he has set before the world. Would this not be a good thing to do?"

Under these circumstances I bring this communication to you that you may advise me whether you would consent to receive these two representative men on this important errand. I am confident they represent the large constituency of German Methodists in this country—between 65,000 and 70,000 make up more than 200,000 population.

This is a matter for your decision not mine, but I will vouch for the representative character of the men. If you think best to have them come I will take occasion to present them when they do come.

If you think it is well for them to come and would indicate some day when you would be willing to receive them, I will communicate with them.[6]

I have written at length that I might acquaint you fully with the situation in which these loyal people are placed.

Yours sincerely and faithfully,   John W. Hamilton

P.S. The writer suggests that they could come on either Tuesday or Wednesday of next week. J.W.H.

TLS (WP, DLC).
[1] Bishop of the Methodist Episcopal Church; Chancellor of American University.
[2] The letter is missing.
[3] The Editors have been unable to find any information about this incident.
[4] The Rev. Arthur Louis Breslich.
[5] The Rev. Albert Julius Nast, editor of *Der Christliche Apologete.*
[6] The Head Usher's diary reveals that Wilson saw Hamilton and two unnamed persons on March 20 at 4:30 P.M. One of them was probably Fred William Mueller. See F. W. Mueller to WW, April 13, 1918.

From William Kent

Dear Mr. President: Washington March 12, 1918.

I shall soon have an answer in part to the comment of Mr. Hoover and Secretary Houston. There are in town at the present time Mr. Wallace, of Des Moines, Iowa, Editor of the Wallace Farmer, and my partner in the cattle business, Mr. E. L. Burke.[1] These men are intelligent, careful in their statements, and thoroughly understand the live stock business. Both of them are patriotic and devoted, and care more for the public welfare than for the prosperity of the live stock business in which they are interested, and which they believe to be intimately associated with the public welfare. I sincerely hope that you will find it possible to meet them to the end of obtaining more first hand information than I can give you as to the future of live stock as affected by the present or prospective procedure of the Food Administration and the Department of Agriculture.

Would it be possible for you to meet them prior to Friday, or even on Friday, if a previous date could not be made?[2]

Yours truly,   William Kent

TLS (WP, DLC).
[1] Henry Cantwell Wallace and Edward Lathrop Burke, respectively.
[2] Perhaps they were among the delegation of cattlemen led by Representative William W. Rucker which met with Wilson at the White House at 5:30 P.M. on March 13. There are no news reports of this meeting.

From the White House Staff

The White House.
Memorandum for the President: March 12, 1918

Mr. J. R. Hawkins,[1] (Franklin 4508) asks if a committee of seven of the leading Bishops of the Afro-American M. E. Church[2] may have a brief appointment to see the President tomorrow or Thursday, to present a memorial expressing appreciation of the President's attitude toward the negro race and thanking him for giving them an opportunity to participate in the war.[3]

T MS (WP, DLC).
[1] John Russell Hawkins, of Washington, Financial Secretary of the African Methodist Episcopal Church.
[2] Led by the "Rt. Rev." William David Chappelle, A.M., D.D., LL.D., of Columbia, S. C., presiding Bishop of the Seventh Episcopal District of the African Methodist Episcopal Church.
[3] Wilson saw the committee at 5 P.M. on March 14.

From Frank Lyon Polk, with Enclosures

My dear Mr. President: Washington March 12, 1918.

The Minister from the Netherlands is very anxious to see you, as he says he has a message from his Government to present to you. He told me it had nothing whatever to do with the difficulties between this country and Holland. Just as a guess, I think that the attached telegram may have something to do with his visit.

If you will be good enough to let me know when you can see him, I will communicate with him.[1]

With warm regards,   Yours faithfully,   Frank L. Polk

P.S. Since I wrote the above, the other telegram attached has come in, which seems to confirm my guess.

TLS (WP, DLC).
[1] See August Philips to Jonkheer John Loudon, March 24 and 25, 1918.

E N C L O S U R E   I

Pontarlier (Berne), Dated Mar. 9, 1918.

2816, Strictly confidential. George D. Herron reported to Wilson[1] that in conversation between himself and Baron Jong, the latter raised the question of whether it would be desirable Holland should call the bluff of Hertling by sending Germany a note, to the effect that Holland understood that Hertling accepted the four principles of President Wilson, and ask to be informed as to whether Holland was right in the assumption that all territorial questions and all previous separate peace treaties would be reopened and re-discussed on the basis of the four principles above mentioned.

Jong asked Herron whether he thought the President would be offended or pleased if Holland took such a step. Herron said that he could not answer such a question. Jong inquired whether President's views could be ascertained and Herron replied that he believed the Legation might submit the matter.

Jong was former Minister of Justice in Holland and claims to be in close relation with his Government. On his own responsibility, and without Herron's knowledge, he discussed the matter with the Dutch Minister here,[2] who declined to act believing such a note would be too great a peril for Holland. Jong thereupon telegraphed to the Minister for Foreign Affairs[3] in the Hague through the leader of the majority in Parliament.[4] The Foreign Minister immediately wired back asking for further information. The following note had been suggested by Jong to the Minister for Foreign Affairs, and was in the latter's possession when he asked for further information:

"The Dutch Government has learned with satisfaction that the German Chancellor declares his readiness to accept the four principles proclaimed by President Wilson, and to be willing to discuss peace on that basis.

The Dutch Government, assuming that also the other belligerents accept these principles, hopes to address itself to the belligerents, suggesting that they enter into a general peace discussion on that basis.

Before doing so, however, the Dutch Government feels obliged to try to make clear, beyond a shadow of a doubt, that it is also the conviction of the Central Powers that at those discussions, aiming at a general peace, all problems raised by this war ought to be a matter of consideration, including those concerning which the Central Powers have just concluded separate peace treaties. It seems evident that to bring about a real durable general peace, the last mentioned questions have to be reconsidered by the World Conference where all interests will be represented.

The Dutch Government therefore begs to ask the Governments of the Central Powers to be willing to affirm that this conception of the scope of a possible general conference on the basis of President Wilson's four principles, presumably agreed to by the Central Powers."

Jong maintains that the Dutch Government is thoroughly disposed to present this note to Germany providing they know that the President would not be displeased by such action, and Jong even suggests the advisability of the President insisting that the note be given out for publication at the time of its presentation. He also suggested that the Dutch Minister in Washington could be instructed to present the matter to the President.

After an exhaustive conversation between Herron and Wilson, it was decided that the former should inform Jong as follows: One. That he is absolutely without any official position or any official connection with the American Government. Two. That Herron should urge Jong to make it clear to the Dutch Government that Herron is an entirely unofficial person. Three. That the Legation will submit a comprehensive statement of the subject for the President's consideration. Four. That the Dutch Minister at Washington might well be informed by his Government that no initiative was to be expected on the part of the United States, and that he should ask for an interview and submit the entire proposal to the President. Five. That the Dutch Minister should submit for the President's consideration the note which they propose to present to Germany fully prepared. Six. That he should suggest the value of publication of the note coincident with its delivery, and seven, that no assurances of any sort could be given to the Dutch Government as to how the President would receive such a petition.

Jong maintains that the past month has seen a decided advance in sentiment toward the Entente in Holland, which has been precipitated by the Russian treaty. I believe that if the Dutch Government accomplishes such action as is premeditated, it will unquestionably have a tremendous effect in strengthening Entente sympathies among the neutrals, and should prove very serviceable in its effect upon the masses in Germany, when the German Government returns, as it doubtless will a negative answer to the proposal to submit all questions for discussion on the basis of the four principles.   Stovall.

[1] That is, Hugh R. Wilson.
[2] Jonkheer F. G. van Panhuys.
[3] Jonkheer John Loudon.
[4] It is difficult to identify this person. On March 9, 1918, the extraparliamentary (i.e., nonparty) cabinet of Cort van der Linden (1913-1918) was in its last months of office. This cabinet consisted entirely of progressives and drew its support from the left-wing, nondenominational parties. The three major liberal parties in the lower house of the Dutch parliament in early 1918 were the Liberale Unie, or Liberal Union, led by H. Goeman Borgesius; the Vrijzinnig Democratische Bond, or Progressive Democratic Union, whose leaders were H. P. Marchant, H. L. Drucker, and M. W. F. Treub; and the Vrij-Liberalen, or Free Liberals, led by A. P. C. van Karnebeek. B. D. Sasabone to A. S. Link, Aug. 17, 1982, TLS (WC, NjP).

E N C L O S U R E   I

Berne. March 11, 1918.

2827. Strictly confidential. My 2806 [2816]. Jong states he has received dispatch from Holland to the effect that Dutch Minister at Washington will today ask for interview with the President in order to submit to his consideration the proposed note quoted in my telegram above referred to.

Although this whole matter originated with Jong he is now extremely apprehensive as to the situation in which his country might find itself in relation to its great neighbor through such action.
                                                          Stovall.

T telegrams (WP, DLC).

From John St. Loe Strachey

Dear Mr. President,   London, W. C. Tuesday March 12th. 1918.

I hope I shall not be committing any unpardonable breach of ettiquette if I venture to write to you direct to thank you most sincerely for your great kindness in sending me, through Mr. Quincy,[1] the admirable photograph of yourself—a picture made memorable by your own hand. It will remain my most cherished heirloom. I was brought up with an intense devotion to, and pride in, America, and ever since I could think or write, my most earnest wish has been for a better understanding with America. All Stracheys are intensely proud that the first Secretary to Virginia was William Strachey, our direct ancestor. We can thus claim with pride, as a distinguished American once said to me, that we are "Founder's kin" of the United States.

But I must not weary you. May I, however, venture to ask whether I am not right in thinking that in your War Messages and Speeches you are moving, when you touch the subject of a League of Nations, on rather different lines from those generally current. As I read your words, they point to an International system based upon Treaty obligations (i.e. on contract) rather than on some scheme of Imperial or super-Imperial Federation, such as Alexander of Russia dreamed of when he set up the Holy Alliance. If nations could be made to respect their Treaties as men of business their bonds, a great deal would have been gained. It will be terribly difficult to get nations, comfortably at peace, to run the risks and perils of war in order to force a particular country to acknowledge that she is acting oppressively towards a weaker neighbour, or to adjudicate on the allegation that Nation "A" is fomenting civil strife in Nation "B," or again trying to alter a boundary declared to have been unjustly drawn in such and such a year. And even if Arbitration is enforced, how can we be sure that the whole world will agree to make good by the sword a decree which one party may declare is so flagrantly unjust that anything is better than submission? Suppose, however, that instead of aiming at a Universal Court of Arbitration, the essential point that the League of Nations agreed on was that Treaty Contracts between nations, as long as they existed, must be respected? If a nation felt a Treaty Contract was oppressive it might give a year's notice of determination. Till that year had expired, the resort to arms would be punished by a Universal Boycott—a non-intercourse Act being passed by every State in the League. Few nations would like to risk this. But the obligation to give a year's notice, even if it did not make a resort to arms impossible, would make it a very perilous business. No doubt the nations might still prove selfish, and indifferent as to putting on pressure during the notice year to stop the threatened war, or in applying the non-intercourse provision. But in any case they would be more likely to act in this limited field and on the simple issue "Obey your Treaty Contract," than to do something which involved, in the last resort, deciding whether a Boundary between say Finland

and Russia was just, or whether an Arbitration Court had not been "packed," or cajoled into deciding that Poland had fomented revolution in Courland! It would be curiously consistent with the spirit of her laws and institutions if America were to insist that the foundation stone of Internationalism should be "the sanctity of a Contract," and that no nation should be allowed to break its plighted word. There would, of course, be no injury done to the cause of Arbitration. If two nations agreed to arbitrate all their differences, then they must be forced as long as their Treaty remained undenounced to go to arbitration.

If I am right in thinking that your speeches show that your mind is moving cautiously in this direction of basing the new dispensation upon contract, I shall feel greatly encouraged in trying in the "Spectator" to get this view kept before the public mind.

With many sincere apologies and with a deep sense of your kindness in thinking of me,

Believe me, with all respect and gratitude,

Yours faithfully,   J. St. Loe Strachey

TLS (WP, DLC).
[1] Perhaps Josiah Quincy (1859-1919), former Mayor of Boston.

Henry Pinckney McCain to Tasker Howard Bliss

[Washington] March 12, 1918.

Number 33 Confidential. With reference to your 44[1] your recommendations on paragraph 4 were personally approved by President and cabled to Ambassador at London March 11th.[2] March.

McCain.

TC telegram (WDR, RG 407, World War I Cable Section, DNA).
[1] Printed as an Enclosure with B. Crowell to WW, March 6, 1918.
[2] FLP to WHP, March 11, 1918, FR-WWS 1918, I, I, 152.

Charles Richard Crane to Joseph Patrick Tumulty

Boston, Mass., March 12, 1918.

Please thank your friend for his latest message.[1] It was well directed and at the right moment and will have a fine carry. Warm greetings to you both.   Charles R. Crane.

T telegram (WP, DLC).
[1] That is, Wilson's message to the Fourth All-Russia Congress of Soviets printed at March 11, 1918.

Roland Sletor Morris to Robert Lansing

Tokio, March 12, 1918.

On March seventh, I read to the Minister for Foreign Affairs the contents of Department's telegram March 5, 4 p.m. and at his request left a copy with him. He expressed his deep appreciation of the frankness and friendly spirit of the communication. He assured me again that his government had made no formal request and had reached no decision in reference to the situation Eastern Siberia but had sought simply an exchange of views. On the evening of March ninth, the long postponed meeting of the Advisory Council of Foreign Affairs[1] was held. The deliberating lasted several hours, but no statement of the matters discussed has been issued.

Late yesterday afternoon in accordance with instructions received from his government, British Ambassador called upon the Minister for Foreign Affairs to suggest informally to him the advisability of Japan's intervention in Siberia. The plans as outlined by the British Ambassador contemplated military occupation as far as the Ural Mountains. If Japanese Government deemed special mission advisable at this time, formal request would be submitted by the government of Great Britain supported by France and Italy.

The Minister for Foreign Affairs expressed regret that this suggestion had not been offered earlier, when public sentiment in Japan was far more favorable than now to some form of intervention. Have repeated to Admiral Knight and Peking.   Morris.

T telegram (SDR, RG 59, 861.00/1271, DNA).
  [1] Established by the Emperor on June 5, 1917, to deliberate on important matters. Its members included representatives of the leading political parties, governmental departments, and the Privy Council. See James W. Morley, *The Japanese Thrust into Siberia, 1918* (New York, 1957), pp. 23-27.

From the Diary of Josephus Daniels

1918 Tuesday 12 March

Cabinet. Discussed R.R. bill.[1] McAdoo said States felt it would be OK now to impose heavier tax than when RRs were privately run and wished some check on it. Also some cities were withdrawing the police protection of RRs formerly given. Would see Secy. of War.

Redfield's man, clerk in Commerce, had lantern that revolves. Experimented at night when two secret service men demanded to be seen. Shows secret service men on their job.

Annapolis people wanted more time on dry order.[2] "Not a day" said WW "The city authorities had nothing to do with the order. They have therefore no responsibility." I so wrote Mayor.[3]

United Fruit Co. wanted to get concessions in San Salvador & State Dept. wanted us to give $25,000 for Telefunken plant & aid United F Co. Polk & Benson recommended. WW said No, he would not be party to getting concessions for private companies, besides radio service was not a part of work of fruit Co.

State Dept. wanted to allow Germans here to send messages to friends & relatives in Germany—"How is my father?" &c Burleson said it would be a method of getting news into Germany by making such simple messages into a code. Polk & Intelligence thought not. WW said he had three times decided no & would not permit it. Spain & Switzerland ministers had urged. "Spain is least neutral & Switzerland is the whispering gallery of Europe."

[1] That is, the bill (S. 3752) to deal with certain problems arising from federal control of the railroads and to provide just compensation to their owners. Earlier bills for the same purposes had been under discussion in both houses since early January. The Senate and the House passed differing versions of S. 3752 on February 22 and 28, respectively, and the bill then went to a conference committee. The committee added to the bill a section which provided that no state or subdivision thereof could levy on railroad property within its boundaries, while under federal control, any amount of taxes in excess of the ratio which such taxes had borne to the total taxes of the state or subdivision for the year previous to federal control of the railroads. On March 13, the full Senate voted that the committee, by adding the limitation on state and local taxation, had violated a recently adopted Senate rule which forbade a conference committee to add new matter to a bill under consideration. The offending provision was deleted by the conference committee, and the Senate accepted the revised conference report on the same day. The House agreed to the revised report on March 14, and Wilson signed the bill a week later as Public Law 107. *Cong. Record*, 65th Cong., 2d sess., pp. 2519, 2835-36, 3305-16, 3417-25, 3443, 3500, 3816.

[2] Daniels, on March 6, had issued a general order establishing "dry" zones within a radius of five miles surrounding the United States Naval Academy and seven other naval and marine training stations in the United States. Within these zones, alcoholic liquors, including beer, ale, and wine, were not to be "sold, given, served or knowingly delivered by one person to another," except within a private home or for medicinal purposes. No alcoholic beverages were to be transported into these zones. Even outside the zones, such beverages were not to be sold or served to officers and men of the naval forces, except for medicinal purposes. The saloon owners of Annapolis immediately appealed to Daniels for a month to six weeks in which to close out their businesses before the dry order went into effect. *New York Times*, March 7 and 8, 1918.

[3] James F. Strange.

INDEX

NOTE ON THE INDEX

THE alphabetically arranged analytical table of contents at the front of this volume eliminates duplication, in both contents and index, of references to certain documents, such as letters. Letters are listed in the contents alphabetically by name, and chronologically within each name by page. The subject matter of all letters is, of course, indexed. The Editorial Notes and Wilson's writings are listed in the contents chronologically by page. In addition, the subject matter of both categories is indexed. The index covers all references to books and articles mentioned in text or notes. Footnotes are indexed. Page references to footnotes which place a comma between the page number and "n" cite both text and footnote, thus: "418,n1." On the other hand, absence of the comma indicates reference to the footnote only, thus: "591n1"—the page number denoting where the footnote appears.

The index supplies the fullest known form of names and, for the Wilson family, relationships as far down as cousins. Persons referred to by nicknames or shortened forms of names can be identified by reference to entries for these forms of the names.

All entries consisting of page numbers only and which refer to concepts, issues, and opinions (such as democracy, the tariff, the money trust, leadership, and labor problems), are references to Wilson speeches and writings. Page references that follow the symbol Δ in such entries refer to the opinions and comments of others who are identified.

Two cumulative contents-index volumes are now in print: Volume 13, which covers Volumes 1-12, and Volume 26, which covers Volumes 14-25. Volume 39, covering Volumes 27-38, is in preparation.

INDEX